The Psychology of Law

The Psychology of Law

Integrations and Applications

Second Edition

Irwin A. Horowitz
Oregon State University

Thomas E. Willging
Federal Judicial Center

Kenneth S. Bordens
Indiana University/Purdue University at Fort Wayne

An imprint of Addison Wesley Longman, Inc.

New York • Reading, Massachusetts • Menlo Park, California • Harlow, England
Don Mills, Ontario • Sydney • Mexico City • Madrid • Amsterdam

Editor in Chief: Priscilla McGeehon
Executive Editor: Rebecca Dudley
Marketing Manager: Jay O'Callaghan
Supplements Editor: Cyndy Taylor
Design Adaptation: Joanne Del Ben
Cover Design/Photo Montage: Wendy Ann Fredericks
Cover Photo: © PhotoDisc
Art: Joanne Del Ben
Production Manager: Alexandra Odulak
Desktop Coordinator/Electronic Page Makeup: Joanne Del Ben
Manufacturing Manager: Hilda Koparanian
Printer and Binder: The Maple-Vail Book Manufacturing Group
Cover Printer: Phoenix Color Corp

Library of Congress Cataloging-in-Publication Data

Horowitz, Irwin A.
    The psychology of law : Integrations and applications / Irwin A.
  Horowitz, Thomas E. Willging. —2nd ed.
    Includes bibliographical references and index.
    ISBN 0-321-00600-3 (pbk.)
      1. Law—Psychological aspects.   2. Psychology, Forensic.
  3. Judicial process—United States.   I. Willging, Thomas E.
  II. Title.
  K487.P75H67   1997
  340'.01'9—dc21   97-37879
                                          CIP

Please visit our website at http://longman.awl.com

ISBN 0-321-00600-3

345678910—MA—0099

First, for Casey, as always. This book is also for some very special people with whom I have had the good fortune to work and teach. They, in turn, have taught me: Martin Bourgeois, Marc Feldman, Lynne ForsterLee, Keith Niedermeier, David Seguin, Kristin Sommer, and Liz Victor.

—I.A.H.

This book is for Judith and for my colleagues at the Federal Judicial Center's Research Division.

—T.E.W.

For Rikki.

—K.S.B.

CONTENTS

PREFACE

Thirteen years have passed since the publication of the first edition of this book. In 1984, the major research topic of interest was the behavior of eyewitnesses, followed by jury decision making. After selecting the eyewitness and the jury, we were confronted with deciding what else ought to be included in a book called *The Psychology of Law.* We had no such problem this time. The field has markedly changed since the early 1980s, moving in new directions and creating new areas of research and application. Therefore, this is an entirely new book, almost completely rewritten, as up-to-date and as comprehensive as possible.

The Psychology of Law: Integrations and Applications is the result of a collaboration that has drawn on our combined experiences as social psychologists (I.A.H. and K.S.B.) and as a lawyer and researcher (T.E.W.). We believe that our experience, gained in the classrooms of universities and law schools as well as in the courtroom and in a legal research center, has helped us write with a breadth of coverage and a legal sophistication not found in other texts available for psychology and law courses. This book offers a balanced, realistic view of the interconnections between the disciplines of law and psychology. The core of the text is focused on the trial, criminal and civil. We bring to that focus the very latest research and theory from social psychology, cognitive psychology, law, and forensic psychology. All three of us engage in research, and we are empiricists by nature; that approach is evident throughout the book.

Although the text is intended primarily for undergraduates, it will also offer law students ideas for improving their professional skills and will give graduate students in psychology a source of ideas for research. We hope that readers will find here insight into the sources and uses of knowledge in the legal system. We also hope that researchers find this book to be a valuable reference source.

In the first edition, we identified and encouraged new areas of research potential. Our major concern was integrating the disciplines of psychology and law in a meaningful way. The task of integration is somewhat easier now, as it has become clear that many issues facing the legal system are empirical. In the years since the first edition was published, studies of the legal system have become commonplace, and policymakers demand data before giving serious consideration to proposals for change. This book builds on its predecessor's concern for real-life applications and expands the scope of those applications into policy arenas that had much lower visibility earlier, such as judicial rule-making bodies.

In addition, the current text has other noteworthy aspects:

- We elucidate, compare, and critically analyze legal and scientific procedures and evidentiary rules and, with sensible illustrations, make them accessible to laypeople and students.
- We treat civil as well as criminal aspects of the legal process, including pretrial, trial, posttrial, and nontrial activities (negotiation and alternative resolution of disputes).
- We carefully analyze U.S. Supreme Court cases in which law and psychology have interacted, such as *McCleskey v. Kemp* and related cases in the death penalty arena.
- We have cut through jargon from both disciplines and have defined technical words and expressions in both text and glossary.

The organization of the book reflects our commitment to a collaborative, interdisciplinary effort. The initial chapters establish the major tensions between psychology and law. We explore the language, methodology, and education typical in law and psychology; we discuss the mystique of "thinking like a lawyer" and compare and contrast it with the thinking of the social scientist. Integrated with an overview of legal procedures are psychological insights into how these procedures can be understood on a behavioral level. We present a primer on evidence law and some of its psychological underpinnings. We then consider the major participants in the legal process: judges, jurors, lawyers, police officers, victims, and defendants.

In Chapter 5 the focus shifts to the trial, civil and criminal. The following chapters also cover such issues as the role of the psychologist as expert witness, eyewitness behavior, and the insanity defense. We also explore the role of scientific evidence in the court, particularly social science's place in the courtroom under the latest U.S. Supreme Court decisions.

The role of the jury is examined most closely in a chapter on jury decision making and its role in special circumstances, such as death penalty cases. We then discuss how and when juries and judges dispense justice.

The final chapter of the book demonstrates the legal system's use of psychological and social science evidence as well as implications for such use in the future.

This comprehensive, up-to-date view of the burgeoning, fast-changing field of the psychology of law should be valuable not only to students but also to practicing teachers, lawyers, and psychologists. Recognizing the importance of readability, we have interwoven fresh concepts, insights, and examples from the disciplines of law and psychology to maintain the reader's interest.

For this edition, we have prepared a combined instructor's manual and test bank featuring lecture outlines, essays and discussion points, multiple-choice questions, and background readings for each chapter.

ACKNOWLEDGMENTS

Many people made this a better book. Becky Dudley, our editor, took the project quickly in hand and moved it and us along at a pace faster than we were ready to go—but go we did. We thank Becky for her guidance and sound advice.

We would also like to thank Brian Cutler, Larry Heuer, Saul Kassin, Steven Penrod, and Alan Tomkins, who reviewed earlier versions of the manuscript and offered us helpful advice, direction, and compassionate criticism. And we would like to express our appreciation to Laird C. Kirkpatrick, who was kind enough to read several chapters and offer his advice and encouragement.

IRWIN A. HOROWITZ
THOMAS E. WILLGING
KENNETH S. BORDENS

PART ONE

Psychology and Law: Methods, Assumptions, and Procedures

CHAPTER

1

Introduction

THE LINKAGE: PSYCHOLOGICAL ASSUMPTIONS IN LAW

This book is about the application of psychological theory, research, and methods to legal issues and procedures. Both psychology and law make assumptions about the causes of behavior. Each is concerned with the prediction and regulation of human behavior.

Law, in its generic sense, is a body of rules of conduct prescribed by controlling authorities that has binding legal force. The law we refer to is American law and its English origins. When we refer to **psychology,** we mean primarily social psychology—the branch of scientific psychology concerned with the study of social behavior, or how individuals think about, interact with, and influence each other.

The focus of law on controlling human behavior supplies the fundamental linkage between psychology and law (Diamond, 1992). To control or condition behavior, however, one must know what mechanisms work to achieve this end. Law rests ultimately on assumptions about how people will behave. Social psychologists study legal issues by applying social psychological theory and methods to help clarify the assumptions undergirding law. Does capital punishment deter future homicides? Are eyewitnesses accurate? When are they accurate? How can we make eyewitness testimony more valid and reliable? Do the attitudes of jurors affect their perception of the evidence and therefore bias their verdicts? Does the size of the jury and the decision rules by which it operates affect the verdict it renders?

These are all empirical questions: They are testable by the application of scientific methods. Social psychologists can use these methods to clarify many of the assumptions the law routinely makes about human beings. They accomplish this by applying empirical methodology, theory, and research findings derived from the study of group behavior, attitudes, prejudice, and stereotyping as well as social perception.

One role social psychologists may play in the legal system is to inform the debate. They can add significant information that may be used by those who devise the laws—the legislators—and those who apply the laws—the police, judges, prosecutors, and juries. If, for example, an issue arises as to the fairness of procedures used to impose the death penalty, social psychologists can help to determine the impact of these procedures on the outcome of trials. Data from their research can be used by the courts to determine the fairness of the procedures (Ellsworth, 1991).

Beyond examining and clarifying the specific assumptions of law about human behavior, psychologists can further our understanding of the law simply by helping us recognize that the entire legal system operates in a social context (Haney, 1993). We can observe how important social and psychological contexts are throughout the system. An arrest by a police officer of a suspected criminal is a social act. The police officer responds to social cues. These cues include the suspect's dress, behavior, and language, and all these factors enter into the officer's determination of whether to make an arrest. The interactions and bargaining among attorneys, between attorneys and judges, and among jurors are all social-psychological exchanges.

Justice and the Legal System

The aim of the American legal system is to give our society fair and unprejudiced outcomes based on the application of a set of general rules and procedures. When we refer to the **legal system,** we mean all the institutions (such as courts and prisons) and officials (including police, judges, prosecutors, and defense lawyers) as well as the rules and procedures they use to resolve disputes and dispense justice at the state and federal levels of government. The purpose of the legal system, however, is not only to give fair and just outcomes. After all, the real truth sometimes cannot be known. Sometimes only the accused person really knows the truth about guilt or innocence. Therefore, perhaps a more critical function of the criminal justice system (that part of the legal system devoted to violations of criminal law) is to give the appearance of fairness. People must feel that the procedures used to determine justice give everyone a fair chance to have his or her case considered.

Here we have the basic dilemma of the legal system: We want just rules and procedures applied fairly by people often unaware that they are motivated by bias, faulty and inaccurate memories, and shifting notions of justice. In addition, we often do not want to have the laws applied strictly, for sometimes that might lead to unfair outcomes. It is probably not an overstatement to say that the perception that everyone is equal before the law is the main factor by which citizens determine whether that society is just. They must see the law applied impartially to feel confidence in their legal system.

The perception of fairness is at the core of the legal system, and this centrality explains why the system expends so much energy on issues of procedural justice. Many of us often believe that the criminal justice system spends too much time on concerns such as whether defendants were adequately advised of their rights (the Miranda warning, which requires arresting officers to inform the accused fully of their constitutional rights), or whether evidence was gathered in constitutionally prescribed ways. The important points are that the system cannot guarantee that the search for truth will be successful; it can only try to make that search fair.

What Citizens Want from the Legal System

Beyond providing courts and lawmakers with empirical data on important legal questions, psychology has made contributions to the legal system by providing **jurists** (judges, lawyers, and legal scholars) with a psychological perspective. Research by Tom Tyler and E. Allan Lind (1992) has revealed how ordinary citizens assess the legal system and how they determine whether an outcome is fair and just. Paul Robinson and John Darley (1995) examined the shared intuitive notions of justice held by ordinary citizens and related these to the American criminal codes. When they compared the community's view of insanity, sexual offenses, justifiable use of force, and other legal concepts with legal standards, they found significant differences. Research can give legal authorities a sense of how people view their world and what kinds of laws and punishments they consider just; it can enable lawmakers to understand the anguish of victims or the perspective of jurors dealing with highly complex evidence. In Haney's (1993) view, a psychological perspective can help challenge the conventional "judicial common sense" that reflects the prejudices of the legal system. This means that a psychological perspective can inform judges, legislators, and police officers about how citizens want to be treated and what procedures and outcomes they view as just.

Procedural fairness means getting a fair and open and noncoercive hearing. Outcome fairness, however, is often defined by citizens in the context of their commonsense views of which penalties are appropriate for which transgressions. As Tyler and Lind (1992) observed, many of the crucial social and legal conflicts of the 1990s are difficult to resolve because they involve competing definitions of legal rights. Abortion rights; gay rights; the rights of minorities; the use of the death penalty; the right to assisted suicide; and the competing rights of children and biological, adoptive, and divorced parents are among the conflicts that have no easy solutions. All these conflicts are contested at various levels of society, but eventually they are heard in court. It is crucial for the legal system to establish that it is a fair and impartial arbiter of these competing and conflicting rights. Furthermore, as Tyler and Degoey (1995, 1996) have shown, authorities are effective to the extent that they have social bonds with the members of the community. When people trust judges and other legal authorities and feel that these authorities are part of their community, citizens are more likely to have respect for the legal system and to obey the laws more willingly.

Tyler, Degoey, and Smith (1996) found that what matters most to participants in the legal system is fair procedures. Favorable outcomes are certainly important, but fair procedures matter because they communicate two symbolic messages about membership in the social system: whether participants can feel pride in the social system, and whether individuals are respected members of that system (Tyler et al., 1996). Tyler and Lind (1992) found that participants in the legal system want the playing field to be fair and level (neutrality), they want to trust the third parties—the judges and the police—to use their discretion benevolently and not mechanically, and they want people to be treated respectfully.

Participants in the legal system assessed the fairness of procedures and outcomes not only in terms of whether they obtained a favorable outcome but also with respect to the legal authorities' motivation and honesty. These participants placed importance on procedures that allow people enough opportunities to represent themselves as well as permit opportunities to correct errors and overcome the authorities' bias (Tyler, 1989). Of course, getting a favorable outcome certainly affects individuals' judgments about how fair legal procedures are (Vidmar, 1992).

PSYCHOLOGY AND LAW: A HISTORICAL PERSPECTIVE

Psychologists, and social scientists in general, have had a long and abiding interest in the law. One of the earliest effective uses of social science in the courtroom was the legal argument known as the **Brandeis brief,** a type of legal argument that used social science to buttress a legal position. Boston attorney Louis Brandeis, later to be an influential Supreme Court justice, often utilized the sociology and the economics of the early twentieth century in legal arguments about changes in the then-oppressive labor laws, particularly those afflicting women and children.

Psychologists were demonstrating an interest in legal issues at the start of the twentieth century. In a 1906 speech to Austrian judges, Freud suggested that psychology had some very practical applications for their field, emphasizing that judges might be influenced by their unconscious attitudes (Michelson, 1980). Perhaps the most visible attempt to bridge the two disciplines was exemplified by the work of the Harvard experimental psychologist, Hugo von Munsterberg, who published *On the Witness Stand* in 1908. Munsterberg questioned contemporary legal assertions about witness testimony and accuracy. As various legal critics trenchantly pointed out, however, psychology did not then have the experimental data needed to sustain Munsterberg's criticisms (Wigmore, 1909).

Psychologists were not the only professionals who predicted at the turn of the century that social science would play an important role in law. Justice Oliver Wendell Holmes, Jr., while on the Supreme Court of Massachusetts in 1897, suggested that statistics and economics would have a future role in law. Other prominent jurists, including Roscoe Pound, Benjamin Cardozo, and Felix Frankfurter, later echoed Justice Holmes's prediction (Michelson, 1980).

In 1935, Edward Robinson, a psychologist and law lecturer, published *Law and the Lawyers,* in which he championed the methodology and outlook of modern behavioral science. Robinson felt that every legal problem was fundamentally a psychological one. Nevertheless, when one examines the influence social science had on law between Munsterberg's 1908 book and 1954, the year the Supreme Court utilized social science in its landmark *Brown v. Board of Education* desegregation decision, the conclusion is that this influence was quite modest. Interest in applying psychological principles to law was sustained during this period, but apparently neither the courts nor the law schools paid much attention to these efforts. Psychologists demonstrated consistent interest in jurors and juries. The experimental psychologist Weld and his colleagues published several studies during the late 1930s and early 1940s on how evidence given in a trial was processed and evaluated by jurors (Weld & Danzig, 1940).

By the early 1950s, the U.S. Supreme Court was about to encounter a case that involved a direct challenge to the separate-but-equal doctrine, which permitted schools and other public facilities to maintain separate accommodations for white and black people. In an 1896 decision (*Plessy v. Ferguson*), the Court had decided that, as long as public facilities were "equal," segregated facilities could legally be maintained for the races. Almost 60 years after *Plessy* the U.S. Supreme Court in *Brown v. Board of Education* (1954) confronted the constitutionality of race-based segregated (separate-but-equal) school facilities, and psychology and social science would play an important role in the decision.

As future Supreme Court justice Thurgood Marshall—at that time an attorney for the National Association for the Advancement of Colored People (NAACP)—and other lawyers in *Brown* began to plan their strategy, they decided to explore what social science might offer them. They wanted to prove that prejudice, discrimination, and particularly segregated schools damaged minority children by promoting feelings of inferiority. These feelings, in turn, argued the *plaintiffs* (those who initiate a lawsuit), led to self-hatred and the child's rejection of his or her own racial group, lowering the child's academic performance.

When Marshall approached the more renowned social psychologists of the day, some were reluctant to testify to the negative impact of prejudice, saying the data were not clear enough (Kluger, 1975). Many others disagreed with that assessment, however. A survey conducted by the NAACP of social scientists showed that over 90 percent agreed that segregation, with or without equal facilities, harmed both the minority and the majority groups. These conclusions were cited in a social science appendix that was attached to the plaintiffs' brief in *Brown*. Chief Justice Earl Warren cited that appendix in the famous Footnote 11 of the Court's unanimous opinion that overturned *Plessy* and held that segregated facilities were unconstitutional. Scholars were left to argue how important the social science testimony had been with respect to the Court's decision.

From 1954 to the Present

In 1966, Harry Kalven, a lawyer, and Hans Zeisel, a sociologist, published *The American Jury*. This was the culmination of years of research at the University of Chicago, concentrating on the functioning of the jury. Kalven and Zeisel explored the similarities and differences between judges and jurors in evaluating trial evidence and in judging the defendant's guilt. The data were gathered by asking judges to convey their impressions of the trial, the defendant, the evidence, and the jurors. Judges and jurors appeared to have agreed on most cases. In the relatively few occasions when jurors disagreed with the judge's evaluation, the tendency was for jurors to be more lenient—that is, to find the defendant innocent. Even though the research methodology left much to be desired (it is impossible to know whether the relatively few judges who answered the authors' questionnaire were accurate in their perceptions), this research did provide a road map for future jury researchers (Hans & Vidmar, 1991).

One of the most visible events in psychology and the law during the 1970s was the presence of social psychologists and sociologists in the adversarial arena. Responding to a confluence of interests—political, adversarial, and scientific—social scientists began to act as advocates for defendants in the various antiwar conspiracy trials that resulted from America's involvement in Vietnam. Concerned that politically unpopular defendants would be unable to secure their Sixth Amendment rights to a fair and impartial jury, Jay Schulman and other social scientists (1973) pioneered a methodology for selecting jurors based on findings from psychology and sociology. This methodology, discussed later in the book, eventually led to jury consultants, who not only help those who can pay to choose jurors but also provide many other services to their clients (Stapp, 1996).

Within the last two decades, the psychology-law link began to take on a substantial structure of its own. New books and new journals have been devoted to studying the interaction between social science and law. In 1969, the American Psychology and Law Society (APLS) was formed and is now Division 41 of the American Psychological Association, with more than 4,000 members. The membership of the APLS reflects the many and varied interests and concerns in the field of psychology and law. Some members, perhaps 10 percent, consider themselves basic researchers. They have generally been trained in an empirical discipline. Many come from experimental psychology, usually social psychology. They bring the perspective of social science methods to the study of legal issues. The APLS publishes *Law and Human Behavior,* a journal dedicated to the interplay between law and the social sciences, including sociology, psychology, psychiatry, economics, anthropology, and other disciplines whose practitioners are interested in legal issues. Research in psychology and law was also helped immeasurably by the law and social science program of the National Science Foundation. This program provided grants to scholars to carry out research that otherwise would not have been done (Grisso, 1991; Ogloff, Tomkins, & Bersoff, 1996).

Other members of APLS are professionals trained in forensic psychology, who may interpret for the court the mental status of defendants in criminal trials. The American Board of Forensic Psychology exists to certify practitioners for courtroom testimony. Finally, there are other members who are active in formulating and changing policy and law so as to bring the latter more in line with the results of psychological studies (Grisso, 1991; Ogloff et al., 1996).

This hybrid field has now developed its own structure. The substantive investment in the field can be measured by the number of academic programs established to train this new breed of professional, who will receive both a law degree and a doctorate in psychology. These programs are designed to promote application of psychological knowledge to legal contexts. Although not attempting to equal the scope of the programs aimed at training individuals equally conversant in both disciplines, most psychology programs across the country have initiated courses dealing with the application of psychology to law.

A new journal, *Psychology, Public Policy, and Law,* has been on the scene since 1995 and focuses on the "actual and potential contributions of psychology to public policy and legal issues." In addition, psychologists are finding new and intriguing forums in which to use their theory and data (Loftus, 1991). For example, psychological testimony concerning the nature of stereotyping and gender prejudice have played a role in important cases concerned with sex discrimination in the workplace (Fiske, Bersoff, Borgida, Deaux, & Heilman, 1993).

METHODOLOGY

We have emphasized that psychology is an empirical science. A scientific explanation is based on objective and systematic observation, carried out under controlled circumstances. Let us examine how one might scientifically investigate a basic tactical issue that often occurs in a trial. Consider the notion of "stealing the other side's thunder." What do you do if, as an attorney, you are defending a client who has previously been convicted of a crime similar to the one of which he or she is now accused. For this to be known would clearly be damaging information. Should you reveal this information before your opponent does and thereby steal her or his thunder, or do you simply let the other side bring it up and hope you can counter the damage it does to your case?

Consider the answer given by a lawyer in a trial tactics book: "Where a weakness is apparent and known to the opponent, you should volunteer it. If you don't, your opponent will, with twice the impact" (Mauet, 1992, pp. 47–48).

The Experimental Method

Mauet relied on his considerable courtroom experience to reach this conclusion. That is a perfectly valid experiential basis for deciding whether volunteering damaging information before your opponent can is an effective tactic. In contrast, compare Mauet's experiential way of knowing with a scientific one. Kipling Williams, Martin Bourgeois, and Robert Croyle (1993) tested the effectiveness of similar situations—whether to reveal information before your opponent does—by asking participants to play the role of jurors in a criminal trial. Participants read one of three versions of a trial involving an assault and battery case. The negative information about the defendant was that he had previously been convicted of a similar assault. In one version of the trial, called the *thunder condition,* the prosecuting attorney introduced the fact that the defendant had previously been convicted of assault. In a second condition, called *stolen thunder,* the defense attorney told the jury (before the prosecutor did) that his client had previously been convicted of assault. The attorney also reminded the jury that the previous conviction in no way meant that the defendant was guilty of the current accusation. A final group of participants were assigned to a condition in which there was *no thunder;* that is, no information about the previous record of the defendant was brought up by either party.

Advantages of Experiments.   For those of you who are relatively unfamiliar with experimental research, a couple of things are worth noting. The first is that Williams and his colleagues (1993) had full control over the presentation of the evidence in each condition: The jurors in each of the conditions heard precisely the same trial with the exception of the thunder evidence. Therefore, any differences in verdicts had to be due to the thunder and nothing else.

Second, the researchers also had control over the assignment of jurors to their experimental conditions. Williams et al. (1993) randomly assigned the 257 mock jurors to one of the three experimental conditions. **Random assignment,** which means that each subject has an equal chance to be assigned to one of the conditions in the experiment, is important. As the apportionment of mock jurors to conditions was based on chance—or done at random—it was extremely unlikely that any systematic differences existed among the mock jurors in each of the three conditions that would have affected their responses to the thunder manipulation. In other words, any differences found among the three conditions in verdicts had to be attributed to chance, as that was how the jurors were selected.

To understand the importance of random assignment, consider the following scenario. We are spectators at a trial in which the prosecutor reveals an important piece of negative information about the defendant before the defense attorney can do so, and a guilty verdict results. However, based on a technicality, the verdict is overturned and a retrial ordered. This time, the defense attorney reveals the negative information before the prosecutor can do so, and the defendant is found not guilty. Can we conclude that the defense attorney's revelation—stealing thunder from the prosecutor—caused the not guilty verdict?

Reexamining the study by Williams et al. (1993), we see that they found early revelation of negative information by the defense, or stealing thunder, to be an effective strategy. Defendants have a better chance of being found not guilty if they present negative information about themselves than if they allow the other side to introduce it.

This result is essentially what we saw in our hypothetical courtroom examples. When the prosecution presented the negative evidence about the defendant, the verdict was guilty; when the defense presented the evidence, however, the verdict was not guilty. Even so, the courtroom scenario presents problems that make interpretation of the results (the verdicts) difficult. First, we really do not know whether the evidence was the same and was presented in exactly the same manner in the second trial as in the first. Perhaps one of the lawyers became more or less confident the second time around. Therefore, it may have been the lawyers' performance that really made the difference in verdicts. We have no such problem in the laboratory study.

A second issue relates to the random assignment of subjects (jurors) to conditions. In the study by Williams et al. (1993), we can assume, because of their random assignment, that jurors across conditions did not differ significantly on any factor or characteristic that could affect how they decided the case. For example, some people weigh negative information about someone much more heavily than anything that is positive. In the courtroom example, it is possible that more (or fewer) of these negative types were members of the first jury, by chance, than of the second jury. Thus, the result may not have been determined by which side presented the negative evidence. The result may have occurred because one jury weighed negative information more heavily than did the second jury. In the laboratory experiment, there was a better chance that all jury member characteristics were more evenly distributed across the three conditions—including the propensity of jurors to weigh negative information heavily or lightly.

Therefore, Williams and his co-workers could reasonably conclude that the condition in which the defense presented the negative information about the defendant led to fewer guilty verdicts than when the prosecutor introduced the information, or when it was mentioned by neither side.

Disadvantages of Experiments.   The experimental method has some drawbacks. In the Williams et al. study (1993), the participants merely *assumed* the role of jurors. Real jurors know that their decisions have real consequences. Furthermore, in the Williams study, jurors read a 13-page transcript of the trial. Real trials are moving, flesh-and-blood kaleidoscopes of faces, voices, emotions, and colors. Which side introduces a negative view of the defendant may be important in a 13-page transcript; it may be less so in a real trial. Among the criticisms of laboratory research are the following:

1. The laboratory situation is artificial and does not capture the full experience of the trial.
2. Often, experiments do not take into account legal realities (Vidmar, 1979). For example, in many of the early studies, individuals playing the role of jurors (mock jurors) simply read a short summary of a trial. Clearly, such a procedure does not capture the full complexity of a trial.
3. The variable the experimenter is manipulating, known as the independent variable, plays a bigger role in the experiment than it does in real life. Think about the "stealing thunder" experiment, for example. Being manipulated here was the variable involving negative information about the defendant—whether introduced by the defense attorney, the prosecutor, or neither. In a 13-page transcript, this incident may have resounded more sharply than it would have in a full-day trial. In 13 pages, a previous assault may assume great importance, a trial that lasts a day or two, the importance of that single piece of information *might* have less impact.
4. A number of commentators have suggested that laboratory research is not generalizable to the actual courtroom because only research done in the actual situation (**in situ research**) is relevant (Kerr & Bray, 1982). For example, in a real trial, an overworked judge may assign a sentence based solely on the recommendation of the district attorney. In a mock study of sentencing, the judge may take more time and render a more considered sentence. These are real and valid criticisms that researchers must take seriously. However, they are not particularly debilitating or overwhelming criticisms from our point of view.

Social psychologists often prefer to simulate the courtroom situation in the laboratory. In such cases, a researcher, interested in the dynamics of a trial, will try to develop a close correspondence between the elements of an actual trial and the simulated trial used in the laboratory. By doing so, the researcher hopes that the results of the experiment can be easily applied to the courtroom situation that is being simulated.

How may a simulation be best accomplished? First, we would draw individuals who are representative of real juries. Researchers may recruit individuals who are registered voters; many jury lists are made up of registered voters. We may also carry out the experiment in a room that architecturally represents a courtroom. Law schools usually have **moot courtrooms** where hypothetical cases are tried for the purpose of training law students. Psychologists can often use these moot courtrooms to conduct simulations rather than setting them in laboratories that bear no resemblance to an actual courtroom. The more realistic the trial and the trial setting, the more likely it is that mock jurors will be motivated to perform as actual jurors. The use of a videotaped trial provides a realistic presentation for mock jurors.

In a simulation, the researcher tries to re-create the real-world situation as nearly as possible. The trial used should approximate the complexity and diversity of an actual trial. Mock jurors should feel themselves as immersed in the experience as are actual jurors. Our experience with simulations suggests that mock jurors will respond and render a verdict that has real meaning to them.

A simulation is a specific type of experiment. It is a laboratory-based attempt to study a more complex social situation. There are, however, other equally practical social science methods.

Alternatives to Laboratory Research

Quasi-experimental designs are used when the researcher does not have full control over the important variables or over the social setting in which they occur (Cook & Campbell, 1979). In other words, the researcher cannot, as in the experiment, control and manipulate the **independent variable,** the factor that the researcher can change in an experiment.

A classic example of this approach is Donald Campbell's study of an attempt in Connecticut to reduce the frequency of highway fatalities. A well-publicized campaign was initiated in that state during which all speed ordinances and penalties were strictly enforced. After a period of time, state police reported that the campaign had resulted in a sharp decrease in highway fatalities (Ross & Campbell, 1978; Fisher, 1982).

Campbell and Ross (1968) studied these fatality statistics using a quasi-experimental design. They examined the number of highway deaths during the five years preceding the new campaign and compared them with the number of deaths in the four years after the campaign had begun. They observed that the number of fatalities varied sharply from one year to another, both before and after the initiation of the campaign. Some years showed a sharp increase in deaths whereas in other years, there was a decrease. In the year prior to passage of the law, there had been a sharp increase in the number of fatalities. In the year immediately after the crackdown started, highway deaths dropped. Soon after, however, a slow but steady increase in deaths became the norm.

The decline after the start of the campaign may very well have been part of the pattern of fluctuations observed in the five years before the crackdown.

Campbell and Ross concluded that the crackdown was probably not responsible for the decrease in highway deaths. The number of deaths was simply regressing toward the mean. That is, in time, the random fluctuations tended to converge on the average or mean number of highway deaths.

Konecni and Ebbesen (1975) argued that this type of research, conducted in real situations, is preferable to laboratory-based experiments. They do not believe that the models of the legal system derived from laboratory research adequately reflect the complex and subtle processes at work in the actual system. To demonstrate their belief, Konecni and Ebbesen investigated the process by which trial judges set bail. They presented judges with the case histories of convicted criminals and studied how they made bail decisions. Judges used a calculus that included the defendant's background, ties to the community, the recommendation of the district attorney, and other material relevant to the defendant's deportment. Later, the investigators sent trained observers into the courtroom where they observed the judges' real-life bail-setting decisions. The results indicated that in the actual situation, judges relied almost entirely on the district attorney's recommendation. Thus, the model observed in the laboratory did not reflect the actuality of the courtroom. Had Konecni and Ebbesen not tested their laboratory findings, we would have had a very neat but clearly inaccurate model of judicial decision making.

In addition to conducting experiments in real legal situations, researchers may use public records to answer important questions (**archival research**). Research on the decisions of parole boards is a good example of archival research (Carroll & Coates, 1980; Carroll & Payne, 1977). Archival research involves gathering evidence from public records. Carroll and his co-workers collected archival data about 1,000 cases from a number of parole boards to isolate the factors that were predictive of the boards' decisions. By providing the boards with a better understanding of the criteria they were actually using, the researchers helped these boards modify their procedures to better meet policy goals.

The Shifting Sands

One concern that lawyers often express about social science is that the results of research are impermanent. Researchers constantly report new findings, sometimes invalidating previous results. Occasionally, lawyers voice the opinion that keeping up with research results is a waste of time because the results keep changing. How do we respond to this not unreasonable criticism? What should lawyers know about how science functions?

First, legal scholars must recognize that psychology is quite good at making predictions about aggregates or groups of individuals. For example, we know that the very best predictor of a jury's verdict is the predeliberation choices of the jury members. Therefore, if you could poll the jury after they have heard the evidence but before they had deliberated, you would have a good indicator about how they would decide the case. The reason is **group polarization,** the intensification through group discussion of the initial tendencies of the group members.

Myers and Lamm (1976) found that, if a jury was leaning in the direction of innocence, group discussion led to a "shift to leniency." If, on the other hand, the jury was initially leaning in the direction of guilt, there was a "shift to severity." Group discussion amplified the members' initial tendencies, toward either innocence or guilt.

However, not all groups polarize and not all individuals conform to the group decision. We cannot predict with any reasonable certainty who will hold out and who will conform. We know that most groups in most situations will polarize. We cannot say this of all groups with absolute certainty, but science is not absolute. It is supposed to be tentative and skeptical and searching. Miracles and absolute truth are reserved for other realms of human endeavor.

Science gives an approximation of reality. That approximation will change over time. Phoebe Ellsworth (1991) reminded us that the search for knowledge in science is never complete. To keep silent about scientific issues because knowledge is not complete is to keep silent forever. What any science can give those who wish to use it is a consensus of what the scientific community thinks of the data in a particular area. For example, most scientists currently think that eyewitness accuracy is not very high—certainly not high enough for conviction solely on the basis of the report of an eyewitness. Not all studies show this lack of accuracy and not all researchers agree, but most studies indicate that even under the best of circumstances eyewitnesses can be wrong. There is a general, although not perfect, agreement on these conclusions (Kassin, Ellsworth, & Smith, 1989, 1994). This is the best we can do. Everyone in every scientific discipline knows that someday his or her work will be superseded by other and newer research.

Legal Research

Legal research is similar to, yet distinct from, social science research. We can best describe legal research by looking at a case as a research "project." Consider an example in which a bicycle rider has collided with an automobile at an intersection. The cause of the accident was (apparently) that the driver of the car failed to stop at a stop sign. The bicyclist was cruising along on a ten-speed bike, listening to music on a headset, and enjoying the scenery. Assume now that you are the lawyer for the bicyclist. How will you research this case?

The research task will involve two main features. One task is to research the facts; the other is to research the case law. Lawyers refer to the former as investigation, and to the latter (discovering how cases similar to the current one were decided) as legal (case) research.

Investigation.   At the start, you will attempt to categorize the case in ways that will aid in determining the facts of the case. Some initial categories will be immediately obvious even to the neophyte lawyer. The case involves damages resulting from noncriminal harm (personal injuries). The action of the defendant appeared to be negligent, not intentional. Your client reports that the auto driver failed to yield the right of way at a stop sign.

From these facts, you develop hypotheses about the case and test them against the evidence you will be able to present and the legal rules you will invoke. Your hypotheses are tentative, subject to change as you uncover more facts or find subtleties in your legal research. One hypothesis is that the driver was clearly negligent in failing to stop at a stop sign. Another is that the driver has a duty to look before crossing an intersection and failed to do so. Another hypothesis, derived from the lawyer's knowledge of tort law (which concerns noncriminal harm and personal injury cases), is that your client may be barred from obtaining damages if he or she was negligent and thereby contributed to the accident. You hypothesize that your client's listening to the headset radio and gazing at the flowers may have legal significance.

You will investigate by direct observation as much as possible. Visiting the scene of the accident, measuring the skid marks, plotting the angles of vision, photographing all the tangible items, and examining the wreckage of the bike and marks on the car all contribute in reconstructing the facts. You will also interview all eyewitnesses to the accident, starting with your client. Most trial lawyers will not question a witness in court without pretrial questioning of that witness. You might take a *deposition,* a procedure that involves either oral or written questions put to the witness under oath, usually done in the lawyer's office. You will want to *depose* the driver to discover any new information and to hear the driver's version, reducing the uncertainty of trial.

The focus of an investigation is the specific event. The foremost questions for the lawyer are (a) What happened? (b) How can we remedy it? The lawyer may also want to find general evidence to show that the reasonable and customary thing for the driver to have done would have been to look at the stop sign and stop, an action he did not take. Other such evidence could be essential in a medical malpractice case, for example, in which the deceased heart-attack victim's family claims that the doctor should have conducted a stress test before suggesting that the deceased ride a bicycle for exercise. Then, the customary practice (the standard of care) among other doctors will be highly relevant and indeed essential.

Case Research.   The next step will be legal (case) research and will entail a search for persuasive authority for the proposition that listening to a radio while riding a bike does not constitute **contributory negligence,** a condition that would mean your client did not exercise ordinary care and therefore was partly at fault. You would want authority from the highest court of your state. One common research strategy is to find cases as similar a possible to your own—for example, a trial involving a rider wearing ear muffs would be a good start.

The purpose of this type of research is to obtain **precedents,** previous legal decisions in similar cases, that will be persuasive to the court. The search is hierarchical and qualitative. The U.S. Supreme Court will be most persuasive on federal and constitutional issues. The highest court in your state will be the most authoritative on the state law issues in our negligence case. Your goal in this research is to find a recent decision from the highest court in a case that is indistinguishable ("on all fours" is the jargon) from your case. The more similarities there are in the cases, the better is the precedent. You will also do some research, formal or informal, in an effort to put a dollar value on the case. For example, you might try to determine how much a broken collarbone has yielded in recovered damages.

LAW AND PSYCHOLOGY: A COMPARISON OF FOUNDATIONS AND THEORIES

We have seen that psychology is empirical, relying on several research methods. Although many commentators have remarked on the differences between the law and psychology (see Marshall, 1966, for an early and thorough discussion of these differences), there are some important commonalities. A major common point, as John Monahan and Laurens Walker (1991b) noted, is that American courts have frankly acknowledged that empirical questions are fundamental to the law. Monahan and Walker illustrate the empirical nature of legal issues by pointing out that courts have dealt with the following questions: Does the death penalty deter murder? Does the design of a toy car confuse young consumers? (Someone might ask how is this a legal question? It is a legal question when a manufacturer makes a toy car that looks exactly like that of another, more popular toy maker.) Does one company's logo too closely resemble another's? These are all testable questions. As you can see, they range from the dramatic to the commonplace. Courts, legislatures, procedural rule-making committees, and other legal policymakers have increasingly turned to behavioral scientists to answer these kinds of questions.

Whereas empirical questions increasingly play a role in the legal system, judicial decisions are determined by law's basic theories and methodology. We examine these in the next section.

Legal Realism

In the nineteenth and into the twentieth century, jurists were influenced by the idea of **natural law,** the belief, derived from Roman jurists, that rules of conduct exist independently of the observer, or place, or situation. However, natural law, as the sovereign legal theory, has been supplanted in the last 50 years by the doctrine of **legal realism.** The legal realists profess that while there may be an innate sense of what is just and what is not, as invoked by natural law, in reality the law is constructed out of the more concrete concerns of everyday life. Therefore, realism suggests that laws are derived from experience and observation. For jurists, experience means mainly how previous cases have been decided. Judges pay a great deal of attention to previously decided cases, or precedents, because these precedents form the foundation for a rule of law.

The doctrine that judges' decisions must be guided by previous decisions in similar cases is known as **stare decisis.** This doctrine places constraints on judges.

They must conform to the sum and substance of what has occurred before. Judges ignore precedents at their own risk, for they stand the chance of being overruled by higher courts.

This is not to say that the law never changes. That is certainly not true. It can change with apparent rapidity as it did in *Brown v. Board of Education* (1954), in which 60 years of precedents were overthrown in one sweeping opinion. Of course, a closer look at the history of *Brown* would reveal that different courts in different parts of the country had been chipping away at the obvious inconsistencies prior to *Brown* for two decades before the Court's 1954 decision (Kluger, 1975). A court that cannot change is one that cannot acknowledge old mistakes or adjust to new insights.

While precedents regulate change in the legal system, they create a permeable barrier. When at least five judges on the U.S. Supreme Court decide a precedent no longer holds, it is gone. But such cases are quite rare. On the current Court, Justice Antonin Scalia is the most aggressive attacker of stare decisis. Dissenting in *South Carolina v. Gathers,* a 1989 decision that barred prosecutors in death penalty proceedings from introducing evidence about the importance and value of the murder victim's life and the grief of the survivors, Justice Scalia said that his oath of office bound him to interpret and apply the Constitution as he understood it, not as it may have been erroneously interpreted by justices in the past.

Few members of the Court have put the argument so bluntly, but even fewer have been unwilling to abandon precedents with which they disagreed (Greenhouse, 1991). Except for the discontinuity that occurs in the law when jurists realize that preceding decisions are now at variance with how people wish to live, the law does live by connection and fidelity to previous decisions. That is legal realism.

Law is derived from three primary sources. The first, is **common law,** derived from the law of England and the United States. Common law is in essence case law, the decisions of judges. Common law is not exactly a seamless thread of decisions, but it serves to bind a current case to a previous one. When courts are asked to make a decision on an individual case, they try to tie the decision to a general principle. This gives the law its continuity and also its credibility.

The second source is the new statutes written by federal and state legislators. Legislatures have the power to force the courts to overrule precedent (except when a constitution limits the legislative power).

The third and most powerful source of legal authority is a written **constitution,** the contract between the U.S. government, or a state, and its citizens. A constitution gives the courts a power they rarely use: authority to review a statute and declare it unconstitutional. The U.S. Constitution is the supreme law of the land, limiting the powers of the states and the federal government alike.

One of the fundamental purposes of the law is to maintain its own integrity. Law derives its power from the sanctions it may impose to regulate the behavior of citizens. The most important service the law can provide is to maintain its own standing in the public eye and produce results that the public willingly or even grudgingly accepts. The law is willing to tolerate a certain amount of error in the decisions it produces. After all, there is no certain way of proving that someone was guilty or was liable. However, as long as decisions appear to have been made in good faith and as long as it appears that the accused had a fair say, so be it.

Adversaries and Inquisitors

The principal methodological feature of the legal model in the United States is its *adversarial* nature, in contrast to the *inquisitorial* model used in much of continental Europe. In the adversarial model, the lawyer is expected to give undivided loyalty to the client and to present only material that promotes that client's position. The lawyer also anticipates and challenges the opponent's presentation to protect and promote her or his client.

Under the adversarial system, the decision maker (the judge or jury) does not have the burden of investigating and discovering the facts of the case. The assumption is that, in the give and take between both sides in the trial, all the relevant information that a decision maker needs to reach a fair verdict will be presented.

Note that the adversarial system has much in common with the economic assumptions promoted by a free enterprise economy. The adversarial system assumes that through the free play of competing presentations, the "market" (read judge or jury) will make the most rational decision.

The **inquisitorial system** requires the judge to take a very active role in the proceedings. Judges in this system examine witnesses and arrange the presentation of the evidence, functions that are carried out by lawyers in the adversarial system.

Laboratory research has generally supported the advantages of the adversarial system in deciding disputes. Such research involved mock jury studies in which people assume the role of juries and defendants in a trial. Work by Thibaut and Walker (1975) revealed that adversarial lawyers uncovered more facts for their clients (thereby increasing the total number of facts available for the decision maker) than did participants in the inquisitorial system. The judge in the inquisitorial system occasionally stopped searching for information when he or she thought the issue had been resolved and therefore sometimes neglected to uncover important facts. At least in the laboratory context of this research, adversarial lawyers who had a weak case tended to work very hard to present their client's case (Lind, 1982). Thibaut and Walker (1975) felt that a fair system of justice should favor the weaker party. Their research suggests that the adversarial system does that better than any other. Of course, adversaries are not equal. Many have access to resources that the poor and disadvantaged do not. Nevertheless, the participants in the Thibaut and Walker studies generally felt they had a better chance to state their case in the adversarial system than in the inquisitorial model.

Thibaut and Walker (1975) concluded that people involved in the legal system need to believe they have a reasonable amount of control over the procedures used to determine what will happen to them. Two kinds of control are available: process control and decision control. **Process control** defines the amount of control someone has over how the evidence is presented to the decision maker. What is important here is whether the disputants believe they had a chance to present their side fully.

Decision control concerns the influence the person has over the actual outcome of the trial or dispute. Neil Vidmar (1993) has given us a sense of why perception of control is important in determining the fairness of the system. In Vidmar's view, the prime motive is to obtain a good outcome. Therefore, it is important to have some decision control because such control obviously gives you a chance at least to reject an unfavorable outcome. A participant may be able to turn down an unfavorable offer in a civil suit because he or she has significant financial resources, or an individual might appeal an unfavorable verdict. Process control is important because it determines whether you can bring all your arguments and facts before the decision maker.

Truth as Seen by Scientific Psychology

Law accepts tolerable error. As long as the system appears to be fair, the public is relatively accepting of the legal system, if not necessarily of lawyers. Similarly, scientists do not believe they can get at the absolute truth. They will settle for verifiable, replicable data (Faigman, 1989).

"Truth" in social science can be considered a statistical concept. The usual and customary standard for defining a statistically significant event is that it may occur purely by chance 5 or fewer times out of 100. Hence, a finding is judged to be significant if the probability of occurrence by chance is .05 (written as $p < .05$; that is, the probability [p] that the finding will occur by chance is less than [<] 5 times in 100). Many psychological journals set a more stringent standard for statistical significance by defining it at a probability of .01. That is, a finding is accepted as significant if it could have occurred purely by chance less than one time out of a hundred. Keep in mind that a finding considered reliable will have been replicated a number of times and will have met that probability of less than .01 several times.

These kinds of conservative standards help protect researchers against their own biases. Although science may seem to be a value-free enterprise, it rarely is. Researchers' values affect the types of problems they choose to examine, the inferences they make about the research, and the forums they choose to publish the results. It is reasonable, however, to ask researchers to protect the business of science from their biases.

Theoretically, researchers face two potential problems. They may make a **Type I error;** that is, they may reject a null hypothesis when it is actually true. This means they conclude that a result had a significant effect when, in fact, it did not. The **null hypothesis** commonly, although not necessarily, states the assumption that there is no difference between the experimental conditions. The second error, the **Type II error,** occurs when researchers fail to reject the null hypothesis when it is actually false. That is, they conclude that a result is not significant when it is. By setting the level of significance (.05 or .01), researchers make a choice as to which error is deemed most damaging. If, for example, we set the level of significance at .01 as the basis for rejecting the null hypothesis, then we conduct an experiment that results in a finding that would have occurred by chance 2 percent of the time, we cannot reject the null hypothesis. Simply put, we must conclude that this finding, at $p = .02$, is not significant.

The lower the researcher sets the level of significance (at less than .01 compared to less than .05), the more the researcher is willing to err on the side of rejecting a result that might be significant, compared to accepting a finding that might not be true.

Level of significance, of course, is a tool meant to buffer the effects of the researcher's values, but it is not a cure. Both researcher and consumer ought to be aware that nothing is truly value-free. However, the setting of statistical standards, the use of appropriate methodology, peer review of a researcher's methodology and results, and the reliability (the replicability) of a result are all adequate if not perfect safeguards.

How the Law Should Use Social Science

The legal system has availed itself of scientific findings for most of the twentieth century. This use has evolved because, as we have noted above, many legal questions have an empirical component. The empirical approach favored by social psychology yields scientific findings that are improvements over opinion or intuition (Faigman, 1992). John Monahan and Laurens Walker (1991a) suggested that social science findings can be used by the legal system in several ways. First, courts could (and do) use social science findings as "social facts" (see below). In this use, social science can bring to bear its ability to apply empirical methods to an issue that a court has to decide.

Monahan and Walker (1994a) offer as examples cases involving questions about human perception and judgment. In a 1979 case (*The Squirt Company v. The Seven-Up Company*) the plaintiff (the party suing), the producer of the soft drink Squirt, argued that the Seven-Up Company had violated the Squirt trademark by marketing a product called Quirst. One need not be a champion anagram solver to note the similarity between the two trade names. Squirt is a grapefruit-flavored drink, Quirst had a lemonade flavor. How did Squirt go about proving its case against Seven-Up?

Squirt aimed to establish the (social) fact that customers would confuse Squirt and Quirst and might very well buy Quirst thinking it was Squirt. Researchers went into several stores and gave customers discount coupons toward the purchase of any *noncola* soft drink product. When the customers left the stores, they were asked whether they had used the coupon and if so, what they had purchased. Customers were also asked to show the interviewers which noncola product they had bought. Of the buyers who said they had purchased Squirt, 4.3 percent had in fact bought Quirst—and 4.3 percent of a multimillion dollar market adds up to an expensive bit of confusion. The district court relied on the findings of this survey to conclude that a trademark infringement had occurred. If a company believes someone has infringed on its trademark, it must, as a matter of recent court rulings, provide survey evidence of infringement (Monahan & Walker, 1991a, 1994a).

Therefore, what Monahan and Walker call social facts are in essence facts, empirically derived findings, that bear on a *particular case.* But what of the more general empirical findings of psychology or social science? We are referring to those findings that may not bear on a specific case but nevertheless may be important for decision makers in the courts and for legislators to know. Monahan and Walker (1994a) suggest that generally agreed on social science findings may be used as **social authority.** This is equivalent to legal authority.

Decisions have **legal authority** when they have been decided by the courts in previous cases and therefore have the power of precedent. Similarly, social science findings that have proved reliable (findings that have been replicated and have been published in recognized, peer-reviewed journals) and have been presented to previous courts and judged to be relevant would be considered as precedent. If the scientific community has generally agreed on the validity of the findings and the courts have used those findings, these scientific facts would have the same authority as previous legal decisions.

As an illustration of social science as social authority, Monahan and Walker (1994a) refer us to the case of *United States v. Leon* (1984) in which the Supreme Court reviewed the scientific research with respect to the "good faith" exception to the exclusionary rule. The **exclusionary rule** defines the admissibility of evidence in a criminal trial. If evidence is obtained illegally—for example, if a search warrant is required but is not properly obtained or executed—the confiscated evidence cannot be used in court. In *Leon,* the Supreme Court dealt with the issue of what to do with confiscated evidence when the police believed they were acting according to the law, in "good faith," but in fact were violating the law. Should the evidence gathered in good faith, but tainted by violation of the rules, be used?

An underlying question, essential to measuring the benefits of the exclusionary rule, is this: Does the exclusionary rule deter the police from engaging in illegal search and seizure? If so, then any weakening of the rule might encourage police misconduct. The Court, in its review of the social science literature, did not find any clear evidence that the exclusionary rule deterred illegal searches. Therefore, the Court "narrowed" the exclusionary rule by permitting good faith exceptions.

What really happened in *Leon* is that a review of the scientific literature revealed no direct, scientific tests of the effects of good faith exceptions to the exclusionary rule. The existing evidence, however, though anecdotal and impressionistic, suggested to the Court that the benefits of allowing a good faith exception outweighed the costs.

The Court was under no illusion that it had the ultimate truth of the matter. Justice Blackmun, a jurist with generally favorable views concerning the use of social science evidence, stated: "What must be stressed, however, is that any empirical judgment about the effect of the exclusionary rule in a particular class of cases is necessarily provisional. If it should emerge from experience that, contrary to our expectations, the good faith exception results in material change in police compliance, we shall have to reconsider what we have undertaken" (*Leon,* 468 U.S. at 928).

In other words, the Court used the best empirical facts available. If new evidence should emerge, the Court would have to reconsider its decision. Thus, if the social authority is available (that is, if there is a relevant, tested body of evidence), the courts will use it to inform their decisions. If not, they will use what is available and try to draw reasonable conclusions from that evidence as the Justices did in *Leon* (Monahan & Walker, 1991a; Monahan & Walker, 1994a).

One final thought about the use of scientific evidence in the legal system, a topic we explore later in the book: It is not easy for jurists to use the results of science. Judges, untrained in the ways of science, often do not know what to make of such evidence (*Daubert v. Merrell Dow Pharmaceuticals,* 1993). For example, in the *Daubert* case, which involved the morning sickness drug Benedectin, the issue was whether the drug caused birth defects in the offspring of the plaintiffs. The scientific evidence was complicated and unclear. Chief Justice Rehnquist exclaimed to a lawyer for the pharmaceutical company: "How are we supposed to know? . . . Here you are telling me that certain things are so in the scientific field. You may know, but I don't" (*Daubert v. Merrell Dow Pharmaceuticals,* 1993, p. 2799). Indeed, much of the time, that is how it is for judges and juries confronting scientific evidence. As we shall see, the Supreme Court is still struggling to define the rules that determine what scientific evidence is admissible in federal courts. Agencies like the Federal Judicial Center have turned their attention to the need to educate federal judges about basic issues of science, such as statistics, survey research, epidemiology, deoxyribonucleic acid (DNA) evidence, and other recurring issues.

SUMMARY

Psychological science began demonstrating an interest in legal issues at the start of the twentieth century. However, psychology did not become a force in the legal system until the major school desegregation case of the century, *Brown v. Board of Education* (1954), which relied to some extent on social psychological data to overturn the legal basis for segregated schools. New journals, books, and organizations soon followed as well as the flagship psychological organization, the American Psychology and Law Society, which has more than 4,000 members with expertise in a wide spectrum of topics and issues.

Psychologists use a number of research procedures to study legal issues. These include the laboratory-based experimental method, which often involves simulating events that occur in the courtroom or other legal settings. The advantage of this method is that it allows for causal analysis: We can say that *X* caused *Y* because we have controlled all other factors. Nonetheless, simulations are often criticized on the grounds that the method is too restrictive and artificial.

Other methods are available. In actual courtrooms or other legal settings, researchers can study real behavior, such as the decision making of parole boards. One concern that jurists frequently express about psychological research is that the findings are often impermanent. Research findings are rarely completely consistent; that is the nature of the scientific enterprise. What science can give those who wish to use it is a consensus of what the scientific community currently thinks of the data in a particular area. For example, most, although not all, scientists think that eyewitness accuracy is not very high under some circumstances and that there are specific ways to improve witnesses' reports about crimes or accidents.

Legal research differs from psychological research in both its methodology and its goals. A lawyer investigating a claim for a client will first investigate the facts of the case as well as develop hypotheses about how the incident occurred. After the facts have been ascertained, the lawyer conducts legal research, seeking similar cases to provide legal authority for the client's claims.

Although psychology and law have a number of attributes in common—for example, many legal questions require empirical answers—they have some significant differences. Lawyers are heirs to the philosophers of *natural law* who divided the world into categories that were good, bad, right, or wrong. These goods and rights were independent of time or place.

Natural law has been supplanted in the last 50 years by the notion of *legal realism.* The legal realists state that although there may be an innate sense of what is just and what is not, the law is constructed out of more concrete concerns of everyday life. The legal realists recognized that the law's prime function is to answer human concerns and to regulate conduct among people. Experience is important to the legal realists, and experience refers primarily to how previous cases have been decided. This principle, *stare decisis,* declares that decisions in previous cases, *precedents,* form the foundation for a rule of law.

The principal feature of the legal model in the United States is its *adversarial* nature, in contrast to the *inquisitorial* model used in much of continental Europe. In the adversarial model, the lawyer is expected to give undivided loyalty to the client and to present only material that promotes that client's position. The lawyer also anticipates and challenges the opponent's presentation to protect and promote the position of her or his client.

Under the adversarial system, the decision maker (the judge or jury) does not have the burden of investigating and discovering the facts of the case. The assumption is that, in the give and take between both sides in the trial, all the relevant information that a decision maker needs to reach a fair verdict will be presented.

The inquisitorial system requires the judge to be very involved in the proceedings. Judges take on an active role in the investigation of the facts of the case, examining witnesses and arranging the presentation of the evidence, functions that are carried out by lawyers in the adversarial system.

Research indicates that what participants want most in the justice system is fair procedures. Favorable outcomes are important, but fair procedures matter because they communicate two symbolic messages about membership in the social system: (a) whether participants can feel pride in the social system, and (b) whether individuals are respected members of that system. These results suggest that fairness of procedures and fair but flexible application of the rules by police and judges are highly valued.

CHAPTER
2

The Role of Procedure in the Legal System

THE ROLE OF PROCEDURAL RULES

Charles Rembar, a well-known trial lawyer, has noted that two halves make up the whole that is the law. One half is **substantive law,** which consists of the rules governing the substance or merits of a legal claim or defense. The other half is **procedural law,** the rules governing the steps to be taken in a civil or criminal case. If you die without providing a will, your spouse and children take your possessions. That is a rule of substantive law. If someone files a lawsuit against you, you will have a specific amount of time to answer that suit—say, 20 days. That is a rule of procedural law. The first (substantive law) is the right; the second (procedural law) is the path to a remedy (Rembar, 1980).

People tend to observe legal rights and the rules that govern those rights. Most people solve their problems without punching their adversaries in the nose, whatever powerful attraction that alternative offers. They stop at traffic lights, and by and large, they pay their taxes in a system that is to a surprising extent voluntary (Carroll, 1992). Of course, we all know people who run stoplights, cheat on their taxes, and break other laws. And there are over 20,000 murders in the United States each year. As Michael Saks (1992) noted, few psychological researchers have given much thought to how citizens decide what laws are good and worthy of obedience and which are bad and can be disobeyed.

This chapter presents an introduction to procedural law, the process by which (substantive) laws are applied. First, we emphasize the procedures used to apply criminal law. **Criminal law** has to do with the relations between the government and a citizen accused of violating the law. If you rob my store, you have violated a criminal law, and the government is the agent that finds you, tries you, and punishes you. That is why you hear intoned on lawyer shows on television the words as the trial begins, "Case number 97–7652, the People versus Smith," or "the United States versus Smith." The government, state or federal, has a direct and overriding interest in seeing that the public obeys the law. That is the fundamental glue of civilization.

There is, of course, another set of laws and procedures in the United States, and that is civil law. **Civil law** governs the relations among individuals (and entities as well, such as corporations). Civil law provides the rules and procedures used, for example, for rectifying breaches of contracts between individuals or for responding to claims for damages resulting from physical injuries. Criminal and civil law overlap each other in many situations. Later in this chapter, we examine a personal injury claim that can be pursued through criminal law or civil law or both.

In a manner of speaking, the government's role in civil law is that of a referee. The government provides the judges, the courts, and the procedural rules but does not initiate suit or penalty. If you buy a Handy Dandy lawn mower from your local Handy Dandy store, take it home, gas it up, and start it, and much to your chagrin, it explodes, injuring the family dog, breaking several nearby windows, and frightening you witless, it is up to you to seek redress. You do this as the **plaintiff,** the one who initiates the lawsuit. The redress you seek is monetary compensation from Handy Dandy, the **defendant,** the one whom the plaintiff sues. In this case, you would want money to pay for all the destruction caused by the defective lawnmower. That is, you would like to be compensated. You also might want to sue for **punitive damages,** which are designed to punish outrageous behavior. Punitive damages are sometimes called exemplary damages because they make an example of the defendant and are one way of telling Handy Dandy, and other lawn mower manufacturers, that they had better make their products more carefully.

By and large, the government presents a neutral face in civil disputes; in criminal law, however, it is an active participant. Criminal law sets the rules of behavior, specifies when those rules are violated, and provides the punishment for those violations. Civilization has spent centuries arriving at this system of maintaining law and order.

Procedural Law in Action

In 1989, the U.S. Supreme Court reviewed the case of *U.S. v. Sokolow.* The defendant, the accused in a criminal case, David Sokolow, went to Honolulu International Airport and bought a ticket to Miami, Florida. He doled out $2,100 in $20 bills and paid the ticket agent for the round trip. Sokolow appeared nervous and did not check any luggage. He spent less than 48 hours in Miami. On his return to Hawaii, agents of the U.S. Drug Enforcement Agency (DEA) searched Mr. Sokolow, discovered a substantial amount of cocaine in his meager luggage, and arrested him.

The law specifies that cocaine is a controlled substance, and Mr. Sokolow illegally possessed that substance. Clearly, David Sokolow violated what we have termed a *substantive law.* He brought back a souvenir of his Miami trip: cocaine. Why did the DEA agents search him? No secret there; he fit the profile of a drug smuggler: Sokolow paid for his ticket in cash, in small bills, and flashed a much larger roll of bills. He was nervous, did not check luggage, and spent less than 48 hours in Miami, a source city for cocaine (Cutler, 1989). Based on the fit between Sokolow's behavior and the profile of a typical drug smuggler, the DEA carried out its search of Sokolow.

The Fourth Amendment of the U.S. Constitution, however, prohibits unreasonable searches. Sokolow argued at trial that he had in fact been subjected to an unreasonable search; being nervous, paying for tickets in cash, and traveling light to Miami for a short period, he argued, does not justify a search and seizure of one's belongings.

Sokolow was convicted, but the court of appeals overturned the conviction. According to social psychologist Brian Cutler (1989), the appeals court in this case reasoned that Sokolow's suggestive behavior was relevant only if the DEA had evidence of ongoing criminal activity and in the absence of such evidence, the search was unreasonable and unconstitutional. Here is a clear application of procedural law. However, the story does not end there. The U.S. Supreme Court agreed to hear the federal government's appeal of the court of appeal's decision, ruled that the DEA conducted a justifiable search, and reinstated the original conviction. The majority opinion of the Supreme Court justices stated that the appellate court distinctions were too fine and that the report of the agents suggested that they indeed had had reason to suspect that Mr. Sokolow was engaged in criminal activity.

The Court's decision left several unanswered questions, some of which have psychological implications. For example, the reports of the DEA agents, written after the event, say they had reason to assume criminal activity by the suspect. How much of that reasoning was due to the effect of a *hindsight bias*—the effect of knowing the end of the story (the suspect did indeed possess cocaine) on the agents' reconstruction of the beginning and middle of the story (he acted in a suspicious manner)? The agents' knowledge that Sokolow was in fact smuggling cocaine led to a reconstruction of the events that would have been different had they not found any illegal substance. How is a judge to evaluate the reports of agents under these circumstances (Cutler, 1989)?

We can see that the issue was never whether Mr. Sokolow had violated a substantive law. He had: He possessed a controlled substance. The issue was whether the procedures used by the DEA agents had been constitutional. Why the concern over procedures? We consider this question next.

Procedural Rules and Criminal Law

"The history of liberty has largely been the history of observance of procedural safeguards" (*McNabb v. United States,* 1943, p. 339). In those words, Felix Frankfurter, a renowned lawyer, a Harvard Law School professor, and a justice of the U.S. Supreme Court from 1939 to 1962, captured the core of the legal system's concern for procedural protection of the rights of individuals. Lawyers, judges, and legislators, among others, tend to believe that procedural protections are necessary to protect personal liberty. In practice, the choice may mean protecting liberty at the expense of other values, even truth or social justice. We saw such a choice in the decision by the court of appeals to overturn Sokolow's guilty verdict despite his clear guilt. Although Sokolow seems a rather sorry figure on whom to hang the banner of liberty, what was important to the appellate court was that, in their view, fair procedure had been violated.

Many examples are available. The courts will exclude, as violating constitutional norms against self-incrimination, confessions produced by the involuntary injection of the "truth serum" sodium pentothal or by torture, no matter what their accuracy. In civil cases, if a party violates procedural rules governing pretrial discovery, which permits each side access to evidence the other side will present at trial, that evidence may be excluded from the trial to prevent unfair surprise.

This deep conviction that procedural fairness is critical to the maintenance of the justice system originates in great part in the attitudes of the public, as we noted in Chapter 1. The original research on the court resolution processes by John Thibaut and Laurens Walker (1975) showed that people were as much concerned about the fairness of the procedures as they were about the outcomes; Tyler and DeGoey (1996) have also demonstrated how critical procedural fairness is to the credibility of the legal system.

Constitutional Origins of Procedural Fairness

The **Bill of Rights,** the first ten amendments to the U.S. Constitution, is foremost a catalog of procedural protections, sometimes written in sweeping generalities, that have passed the test of time. In criminal cases, the procedural protections in the Bill of Rights are in some instances more explicit, reflecting concrete experiences with English oppression during the colonial era. For example, the Fourth Amendment says that "no warrants shall issue, but upon probable cause supported by oath or affirmation and particularly describing the place to be searched and the persons or things to be seized." Similarly, the Sixth Amendment says that "in all criminal prosecutions, the accused shall enjoy the right to a speedy trial, by an impartial jury." The Sixth Amendment also protects the right of an accused to confront unfavorable witnesses, to issue subpoenas to compel the testimony of witnesses, and to be represented by counsel.

The Fifth and Fourteenth Amendments each protect individuals against governmental actions that would deprive persons of "life, liberty, or property, without due process of law." There are two parts to the **due process** rights. The first is procedural: A person is guaranteed fair procedures. The second is substantive: A person is protected from repressive and unfair governmental interference. In its essence, due process means that, under the Constitution, we have the right to basic principles of fairness.

Incorporating the great principle over which the Civil War was fought, the Fourteenth Amendment guarantees "equal protection of the law." This means that every citizen, no matter his or her social standing, enjoys the same protection of the law as any other person. In civil cases, the Seventh Amendment preserves the right to trial by jury, but only in common law cases (that is, cases recognized by the law courts of England prior to the adoption of the U.S. Constitution in 1789—primarily cases involving money damages and not some other remedy such as a divorce) "where the value in controversy shall exceed twenty dollars." There are several exceptions to the right to a jury trial in civil cases, and this lack of specific procedural protections in the Constitution forces lawyers and judges to evaluate procedural issues in terms of whether the parties are afforded "due process of law." A constant danger is that procedural rules may snowball, creating such a web of complex rules and subrules that it becomes difficult to predict what judges expect.

We have seen the concern the lay citizen has about fair procedures. But what of the people inside the legal system—those who make the laws and devise the procedures. What are their assumptions when they devise the procedural steps applied in both civil and criminal law?

The Procedural Model

Three assumptions form the basis for the importance of procedure in the American legal system. The first is that, if rules and rights are clearly stated, justice will be served. A police officer who wishes to obtain permission to wiretap the telephone of a citizen based on some vague statement about suspicions concerning that citizen will not successfully convince a judge to issue such a warrant. The officer must present evidence to show "probable cause" to arrest or search an individual. Having evidence of **probable cause** to arrest means that the officer is aware of circumstances that would lead a prudent and reasonable person to assume that an individual has committed an offense. This system assumes a series of checks and balances. The prosecutor and magistrate control the police; the judge controls the prosecutor; the defense lawyer challenges police and prosecutor; the lawyers monitor the trial judge and the jury; and the appellate court regulates them all. The U.S. Supreme Court has the last word.

A second major assumption of the procedural model is that the participants need regulation, that without rules and enforcement procedures government officials will ignore the rights of those accused of crime or will not be accountable to citizens who apply for benefits.

A third assumption is that public exposure of the actions or inactions of government officials will lead to political accountability and changes in policies that will benefit all citizens. This assumption, in turn, presumes that most people do support the procedural protections embedded in the Bill of Rights. Legal scholar Laird Kirkpatrick (1995) observed that citizens may prefer—and may have greater satisfaction and trust in—a justice system (adversarial) that is perceived as fair because of procedural protections to one (inquisitorial) that promises more accurate verdicts.

The procedural model of justice is not the sole province of lawyers. Philosophers have theorized that procedural rules are at the heart of the rule of law. Philosopher John Rawls (1971) discussed procedural justice in terms of "justice as regularity" and concluded that departures from the fair and impartial administration of justice may raise "a serious question [about] whether a system of laws exists as opposed to a collection of particular orders designed to advance the interests of a dictator or the ideal of a benevolent despot" (p. 236).

In brief, Rawls asserted—and most lawyers would agree—that "the rule of law requires some form of due process" (p. 239). Central to this idea is that drafters of procedural rules should write the rules before the drafters become aware of how the rules will affect the outcome of any particular case. Rawls's notion is that rule makers should write as if they are in the "original position," in which they do not have knowledge of their own family or genetic fortunes and social circumstances—as though they are behind a "veil of ignorance." As we examine these procedural rules in operation, ask yourself whether the lawyers, judges, legislators, and policymakers who crafted the rules appear to have satisfied Rawls's test. Consider what rules you would write if you were in the "original position"—if you did not know whether you were rich or poor; black or white; Hindu, Jew, Christian, or nonbeliever; female or male; sighted or not; gifted or challenged. Do these rules operate even-handedly toward all, without regard to their position in society? Are changes in procedural rules justified by improvements in the social order that benefit all, not just a select few? Would you create these procedures without knowing your inherited position in the lottery of life? If not, what would you change? We ask these questions not simply to be provocative. These are the types of questions policymakers ask of themselves and of social science researchers. As we are social scientists, a major part of our role is to ask questions such as these: What data would clarify the policymakers' choices? Does a rule favor the prosecution or the defense? What is the impact on the defendant or on the victims of crime?

In the next section, we see how the law administers justice in both criminal and civil cases. Our introduction to the justice system starts with an examination of a case we describe as prototypical, a model case that can be used to show how both criminal and civil law operate. Our purpose is to identify and explain the main features of the system. We focus primarily on the law and its procedures, setting aside for the moment the contributions social science may make to the legal system. Social science has tested many of the assumptions that undergird legal procedures and we discuss the results of that research later in the book.

CIVIL AND CRIMINAL APPROACHES COMPARED

As you examine the legal system, observe whether or how well the procedures we describe stand up under Rawls's test of the neutrality of procedural rules: that they be written from behind a "veil of ignorance" in which the drafters are not aware of their own (original) position in society or of the advantages and disadvantages of the rules to people like themselves.

Facts

The following facts come directly from an appellate decision of the Maryland Court of Special Appeals in the 1988 case of *Rhodes v. Maryland.* Though this particular case involved a criminal charge of first-degree rape and battery, we use it to illustrate the pretrial and trial procedures in a criminal case and to compare them with the proceedings in civil cases. We chose a rape case because such cases illustrate the tensions between competing interests in procedural fairness and because such cases have both civil and criminal implications.

The **appellant,** the one appealing the case, was the defendant in the trial court who had been convicted. He and the **complaining witness,** the injured party who filed a complaint with the police, had become acquainted while attending a career institute in Silver Spring, Maryland. The appellant had given the victim rides home on at least three occasions. They had exchanged telephone numbers, and she had even given him a "friendship ring." On August 6, 1985, they had met at about 1:00 in the afternoon in the lunchroom. The victim accompanied the appellant outside, where an argument followed, and the appellant slapped the victim twice. Although the appellant was acting very aggressively, the victim testified that she thought she could handle the situation and did not break off the contact. In the appellant's car, they drove to the appellant's apartment. The victim voluntarily entered. The appellant directed someone else who was in the apartment to leave. In the court's words:

> The argument continued and Rhodes (the appellant) became increasingly more aggressive. At one point, he threatened to knock the victim out of the window. The appellant partially disrobed. He pulled out a handgun and threatened to blow the victim's "f . . . ing brains out." It was at that point that he ordered her to undress. She kicked him, whereupon he warned her that he would "break [her] f . . . ing leg" if she kicked him again.
>
> According to the victim's testimony, . . . [which is the version that the court must assume to be true in evaluating the sufficiency of the evidence to support a jury verdict of guilty], the appellant pushed her into the bedroom and laid the gun on the table. It was the appellant who removed the victim's shirt and brassiere, just before pushing her backward onto the bed. After ordering her to do various sexual acts, which she successfully refused, he ordered her to perform vaginal intercourse. When she refused to spread her legs, he pushed them apart and proceeded to rape her. When the two of them finally exited the appellant's apartment, he drove her to a 7-11 Store and ordered her out of the car. To several friends, whom she met shortly after that, she was obviously distraught but protested that nothing was wrong. She did, however, call home and report the rape to her cousin. (*Rhodes v. Maryland,* 1988, pp. 3–4)

Choice of Approach: Naming, Claiming, and Blaming

Ultimately, the victim—let's call her Kristin Kohl—reported the rape to the police. The police in turn notified the prosecuting attorney and a criminal proceeding began. A jury found Mark Rhodes guilty of rape and battery, the verdict leading to Rhodes's appeal (from which the above quote was taken). Kristin Kohl had other choices. Social psychologists describe the process of deciding to turn to the law for redress as involving stages of *naming, blaming,* and *claiming.*

The first step, naming, involves recognizing that a crime or a civil wrong occurred and giving the act a *name* like *rape* or *sexual assault* or, in lawyers' terms, *personal injury* or *intentional infliction of emotional distress.* Historically, of all violent crimes, rape has a very low reporting level (Estrich, 1987; Frazier, Candell, Arikain, & Tofteland, 1994). Based on telephone interviews with a sample of

4,000 women, all conducted by women, Kilpatrick, Edmunds, and Seymour (1992) concluded that 12.1 million women in America have been raped at some time in their lives.

The criminal process is often so onerous for the rape victim that a woman may decide to forgo reporting the crime rather than go through a public recounting of the ordeal. Sometimes, however, women, especially those attacked by acquaintances, may hesitate to attach the label *rape* to the encounter. The reluctance of prosecutors to prosecute or juries to convict defendants in non-stranger contexts is also likely to be a major factor. Documentation and social labeling of the phenomenon that we now call *date rape* may have freed women to name as a crime an event they previously labeled as a horrible twist in a personal relationship.

Naming the crime is necessary but not sufficient to initiate legal actions. The victim's *attribution of blame* may also be determinative. If the victim blames herself (or himself) for, say, poor judgment of character in an acquaintance rape, she may deem herself "guilty of the crime of trust" (Balos & Fellows, 1991) and decide not to step forward. Recent evidence reported by social psychologist Patricia Frazier (1990) suggests that although many rape victims engage in some self-blame, most victims appear to blame other factors more than they blame themselves. It appears that any reluctance rape victims may feel in reporting the crime is due less to self-blame than to a perception that the legal system may not treat them fairly.

The final step is *claiming*, that is, identifying a loss and asserting a claim against the one to blame for it. This step presumably involves balancing the benefits and costs of "going to law." A rape survivor always has to confront the very real costs of claiming rape. Psychological, economic, political, and social factors all come into the calculus of the decision. An individual facing the choice of whether to invoke one or more of the legal options might want to ask, "What do I want to accomplish? What outcome would I like to see?" Answers to these central questions may help to make sense of legal choices that range from pursuing civil or criminal redress to seeking counseling or other personal support.

Civil Versus Criminal Approaches to Redress

In the quoted case, Kristin Kohl could claim redress from the law in two distinct ways. She could proceed with a criminal case against Mark Rhodes for breaching state laws banning rape, sexual assault, simple assault, or physical battery. **Sexual assault** is an umbrella term that encompasses unwanted sexual touching, including intercourse. *Rape* is a more specific assault that is generally defined as sexual intercourse that results from the use of force or threat of death or serious bodily harm. Simple **assault** involves threatening another with bodily harm, and physical **battery** involves the forceful, harmful touching of another without consent. Another alternative would be for Kristin Kohl to proceed with a civil case against Rhodes, claiming that he intentionally caused personal injuries to her and perhaps also that he intentionally inflicted emotional distress on her. In this type of case, generally known as a *tort* or *personal injury* case, the plaintiff would typically ask for money damages. If the defendant continues to pose a threat of violence, she could ask the court to order him (to *enjoin,* that is, issue an **injunction** or *restraining order*) not to contact the plaintiff in any way. Violation of a restraining order amounts to a *contempt of court,* punishable by imprisonment without a jury trial.

Citizens unable to obtain what they consider justice from the criminal system are increasingly turning to the civil courts for satisfaction. The families of Nicole Brown Simpson and Ronald Goldman sued Orenthal James Simpson for civil damages while the state was presenting evidence in the criminal trial. Rodney King, who was beaten by Los Angeles police officers while they were arresting him, received a substantial settlement for his civil claim of a civil rights violation against the City and County of Los Angeles.

What do these cases have in common? Beyond being civil claims for compensation, both cases appear to involve defendants who may have so-called deep pockets and can compensate victims for the injuries that resulted from their crimes. Although some states have programs designed to help compensate victims of crime, funds are limited and are disbursed according to bureaucratic criteria. Needs for compensation may easily be brushed aside in the criminal context because of the dominant themes of punishing, deterring, and perhaps rehabilitating the defendant.

Civil suits may empower the victims by giving them, in the words of a victim's rights attorney, "control over something they had no control over when it occurred" (Copen, 1991, p. 35). Note that the victim of a crime does not have much control in a criminal case. In this situation, the prosecutor decides whether to go ahead with the case against the defendant and the state is the plaintiff. Kristin Kohl, as the victim, had little or no official standing in the trial of Mark Rhodes except as the complaining witness, the person who brought the complaint.

Bringing a civil case may satisfy two needs of the plaintiff: the need for compensation and the strong need for vindication, for an official determination that the defendant was wrong. The need for compensation is real: Someone needs to pay for the medical bills, the lost earnings, and the pain and suffering resulting from the physical and psychological injuries. Are compensation and vindication in fact what motivates many victims to pursue civil claims? That hypothesis seems plausible, worth testing in the laboratory and in the field.

The information in Table 2.1 can help us explore more deeply and systematically the differences between criminal and civil cases. Then we can examine the different legal procedures that apply to the two types of cases.

RULES OF PROCEDURE

Pretrial Procedure

Let's now look at the rules of procedure that govern civil and criminal proceedings. A few definitions may ease the reader's entry into the world of legal jargon.

TABLE 2.1 Differences Between Criminal and Civil Cases

	Criminal Case	Civil Case
Purpose	The purpose of a criminal case is to protect the *public* by deterring, punishing, or rehabilitating the defendant (or some combination of the above).	The purpose of a civil case is to resolve a dispute between two or more *private* (or governmental) parties; to render a final judgment about their rights and duties to each other, including compensation.
Parties and caption	The state prosecutes the case on behalf of the public. Kristin Kohl would be the *complaining witness*. Mark Rhodes would be the *defendant*. The caption would be *State* [or *Commonwealth*] v. *Rhodes* or *People v. Rhodes*.	Kristin Kohl files the case in her own name or asks the court to approve a pseudonym to preserve her privacy. She would be the *plaintiff*. Mark Rhodes would be the *defendant*. The caption would be *Kohl* [or *Jane Doe*] v. *Rhodes*.
Burden of proof	The prosecutor must prove all elements of the offense *beyond a reasonable doubt*.	The plaintiff must prove all elements of the tort by a *preponderance of the evidence*.
Elements to be proved	The prosecutor must prove that the defendant intentionally forced the complaining witness to engage in sexual intercourse by using physical force or the threat of bodily harm.	The plaintiff must prove that the defendant's negligent or intentional actions were a primary (*proximate*) cause of physical and mental injuries to the plaintiff.
Decision maker	The defendant has a Sixth Amendment "right to a speedy and public trial by an impartial jury" in the state and district where the crime was committed. The defendant could choose trial by judge if the defendant thinks that a judge would be more lenient than a jury. If the defendant chooses a jury trial, the judge has no power to decide that there are no factual issues for a jury to consider.	The plaintiff or defendant may assert a Seventh Amendment right to a jury trial to consider issues related to money damages, but not for orders to restrain further threats of violence. The plaintiff must show an issue of fact for the jury to resolve; the judge resolves purely legal issues by ruling on motions to dismiss or for summary judgment for the plaintiff or the defendant.
Decision	A jury *verdict* or a judge's decision would find the defendant *guilty, not guilty*, or (rarely) *not guilty by reason of insanity* or, in some states, *guilty but mentally ill*.	A judge or jury would find the defendant to be *liable* or *not liable* to the plaintiff, and the judge would enter a *judgment* to that effect.

Outcome	The judge sentences a defendant who is found guilty. The options are defined by the legislature and may range from fines to probation to alternatives to prison (halfway house, home confinement via electronic monitoring), prison, or the death penalty. In some states and in the federal system, judges must follow guidelines for sentencing.	The *judgment* may be an award of *damages* that the defendant must pay to the plaintiff, an *injunction* to forbid the defendant from continuing to interfere with the plaintiff's rights, or another remedy to restore the plaintiff's rights.
Lawyers	The state is represented by a publicly elected or appointed *prosecutor*. The complaining witness often has no lawyer. The defendant is represented by either a private (retained) lawyer or, if financially eligible, by a public defender or a court-appointed private lawyer.	The plaintiff generally hires a private attorney. If the prospect of collecting damages is high, a private attorney may accept the case on a *contingent fee* basis, that is, with payment of any fee contingent on the recovery of damages, in which case the lawyer would receive a share, typically one-third. The defendant would generally have to pay for a lawyer to defend.
Courts	States traditionally have authority to define the moral and legal code of conduct that takes place within their borders and does not affect those in other states. Most crimes, therefore, are prosecuted in state courts. Federal crimes—conduct violating laws written by the Congress—are generally limited to those with interstate implications (e.g., transporting illegal drugs over state lines) or crimes that directly affect the federal government, such as federal income tax fraud. *Maryland v. Rhodes* was filed in state court. Had Rhodes transported Kohl across the border into the District of Columbia or Virginia, a federal offense might also have been involved. In that event, Kohl could have filed a charge with either state or federal authorities and each prosecutor would have then decided whether to proceed.	States usually have a court of *general jurisdiction* that can hear any civil case. Federal courts are courts of *limited jurisdiction,* meaning they can hear only those cases that the Constitution and Congress have specified. The plaintiff in a civil case may have a choice of bringing the case in a federal or state court, although the basic claims arise from the tort (personal injury) law of the state. Where the plaintiff and defendant are citizens of different states, Congress has given the federal courts jurisdiction based on *diversity of citizenship.* In that case, the federal court applies the law of the state in which the injury occurred. If the defendant is a state or federal official, say a police officer, who acted under authority of office to deprive the plaintiff of his or her civil rights, the plaintiff generally has the option of bringing the case in federal or state court.

TABLE 2.2   Civil and Criminal Pretrial Procedures Compared

Stage of Case	Criminal Case	Civil Case
Initiation of case	Grand jury **indictment** or prosecutor's **information**	Plaintiff/attorney file a **complaint.**
Notice to defendant	**Arrest,** i.e., taking a defendant into police custody	Complaint is served with a **summons** calling for a written response.
Initial court appearance	**Arraignment,** setting of bail, entry of plea, possible preliminary hearing	No appearance is necessary. Defendant can file a written **answer** or motion to dismiss the complaint and can assert defendant's claims, called **counterclaims,** against plaintiff.
Discovery of evidence	Portion of procedure in which prosecutor must reveal exculpatory evidence on request; defendant can ask for discovery but must reciprocate	**Depositions** (sworn testimony taken before trial), **interrogatories** (written questions that must be answered in writing), exchange of documents, and physical examination of parties and evidence are all available and frequently used.

First, lawyers *plead* a lot. A **plea** of guilty or not guilty is a formal response to a *criminal charge*—an **indictment,** if issued by a grand jury, or an *information,* if issued by a prosecutor. The criminal charge is usually presented orally at an **arraignment** in court, a procedure during which charges against the accused are read and a plea is entered. A *pleading* is generally a written paper filed in court. Sometimes the term *pleading* refers to the initial papers in a civil case that set down the outlines of the case: The plaintiff's case is stated in a **complaint** and the defendant's in an **answer.** Another important aspect of the pretrial proceedings is **discovery,** a term referring to several procedures and tactics each side uses to learn what information the other side has about the case. Each side will know what witnesses the other side will call and what evidence it will present. The procedures include pretrial examination of the other side's witnesses, records, and physical evidence.

Lawyers also go through many motions—in the legal sense of the term. A **motion** is simply a formal way of bringing a matter to the court's attention. Motions may be presented orally, as in a motion for a recess during a trial; more commonly, motions are presented in writing. We refer in our discussion to motions that have become standard in civil and criminal procedural rules. A lawyer is not limited to traditional motions and may create a new form to meet the needs of a client in a case. For example, an attorney who speaks only English with a client who speaks only Spanish might ask that a translator be provided. An attorney for a destitute defendant might need to move for the appointment of an expert witness to examine the DNA evidence that the prosecution proposes to use.

Stage of Case	Criminal Case	Civil Case
Informal resolution	**Plea bargaining,** i.e., negotiations between prosecutor and defense attorney about entering a guilty plea to a less serious charge	Private negotiations, judge-hosted settlement conferences, **alternative dispute resolution (ADR),** such as **mediation, arbitration, summary jury trial** can be explored.
Pretrial (motions)	**Motion to dismiss** indictment; no equivalent to **summary judgment**	**Motion to dismiss** complaint; **motion for summary judgment** (no issue of fact for jury) can be entered.
Pretrial (publicity)	**Motion for change of venue** (request to move trial)	This is rarely an issue in civil cases.
Pretrial (evidence motions)	**Motion to suppress evidence** (e.g., products of an unreasonable search and seizure)	**Motion in limine** to exclude evidence may be entered.

Civil and criminal cases differ considerably in their terminology and content. Some differences are historical; some are designed to protect the constitutional rights of criminal defendants. The brief summary of the differences in terminology given in Table 2.2 may aid the student-researcher in designing comparative studies.

Trial Procedure

Once a case goes to trial, civil and criminal procedures become similar. The same **Federal Rules of Evidence,** uniform rules for all federal courts, govern the admissibility of evidence at trials in all federal courts. A number of states have also adopted these federal rules, which apply to both civil and criminal cases. Because of these similarities, we can look at trial procedures for both types of cases together.

Jury Selection. A cornerstone of the Anglo-American legal system is the principle that the jury's verdicts (and judges' decisions as well) are based solely on evidence presented by the parties in a trial. The underlying rationale is that the truth will emerge when opposing parties have an opportunity to challenge each other's evidence. This method, as you recall from Chapter 1, is the adversarial system. News reports, hallway conversations, insider gossip, and even jury experiences are no substitute for an open-minded, careful examination of facts.

This system is so embedded in our culture that we instinctively judge a teacher or parent to be unfair when he or she makes a hasty judgment and disciplines one participant in a fight without hearing both sides of the story. Most people recognize the absurdity of Fury's statement in *Alice in Wonderland,* before hearing any evidence: "'I'll be judge. I'll be jury. . . . I'll try the whole case and condemn you to death'." Jury selection is designed to avoid such prejudgments.

Both civil and criminal jury trials begin with jury selection. We discuss selection of jurors in more detail in Chapter 6, but here we can look at the basic procedures for recruiting jurors. To start the process, court officials draw together a master list, sometimes called a *master jury wheel,* of eligible citizens from the community. Potential jurors may be selected for placement in the pool from a variety of sources: voters' rolls, drivers' license records, the telephone directory, or similar lists. In the federal system, each district court must have a written plan for the random and nondiscriminatory selection of juries. A jury commissioner draws names randomly, mails juror qualification forms to those randomly picked, and determines eligibility from the information furnished on the forms. Congress has set the qualifications for federal jury service to include U.S. citizenship; age of at least 18 years; residence in the district for one year; ability to speak English; ability to read, write, and understand English "with a degree of proficiency sufficient to fill out satisfactorily the juror qualification form"; lack of physical or mental incapacity; and the absence of pending charges or a conviction of a felony (Jury Service and Selection Act of 1968, 28 U.S.C. Sec. 1865). Congress has forbidden discrimination in federal jury selection "on account of race, color, religion, sex, national origin, or economic status" (28 U.S.C. Sec. 1862). Challenges to selection procedures must be filed before the selection of jurors (**voir dire,** which is French for "look-speak" and known also as truth talk) begins in a given case. A panel of qualified jurors, called a **venire,** is then drawn from the master wheel. The number will depend on the needs of the cases scheduled for a given day or week. In criminal cases, the Sixth Amendment reference to a right to "an impartial jury" means that a panel should represent a "fair cross-section of the community," one that does not systematically exclude any distinctive community group. Distinctive groups are those based, for example, on a common race, gender, or national origin, but not groups based on common age, education, or socioeconomic status (Georgetown Law Journal Staff, 1991, pp. 989–990).

After a venire has been assembled, the judge and lawyers in a case conduct the voir dire. Either the lawyer, the judge, or both question the panel to uncover any biases or prejudgments among the potential jurors. Questions are generally addressed to the entire panel and individuals respond before their peers. For some types of questioning, prospective jurors are examined separately, perhaps even in the judge's chambers, to promote their honesty and to prevent their contaminating other jurors.

Questioning jurors during the voir dire brings up several social psychological questions. As a general rule, potential jurors are questioned individually but in an open court, in the presence of others. Should such examinations be conducted individually, outside the presence of other potential jurors? Are individuals likely to be more candid away from others? Are jurors more likely to be honest about their biases with lawyers or with judges? We discuss these issues in our chapters on the jury later in the book.

After the questioning, lawyers can move to **challenge** individual jurors **for cause**—that is, because they answered in a way that suggested they would be unable to make an unbiased judgment based solely on the evidence. Cause does not necessarily include having an opinion on the wisdom of the criminal law involved. For example, a juror in a drug trial who disapproves of drug use may be seated if she asserts that she can decide the case solely on the evidence (*United States v. Casey*, 1987). Lawyers may also exclude a juror by using one of a limited number of **peremptory challenges**—a procedure allowing the removal of a juror for no stated reason.

Opening Statements.   The prosecutor in a criminal trial or the plaintiff in a civil trial, because each has the burden of proof, presents the first *opening statement,* a preview of the evidence that side plans to present. The defendant may follow, may reserve the opening statement until immediately before presenting defense evidence, or may waive the opening statement altogether.

Opening statements are generally limited to previews of the evidence that the lawyer expects to have admitted. Arguments about what legal rules apply are improper during opening statements because they invade the province of the judge, who informs the jury about the law, usually at the end of the case. A lawyer's personal opinions on issues in the case—for example, attesting to the truthfulness of a witness—are also improper. Basically, such personal opinions are irrelevant and do not meet strict legal standards of the evidence that the jury may consider. Nevertheless, expressions of personal opinions are difficult to prevent or correct.

Because the prosecutors' role is to seek the truth through fair governmental procedures, their opening statement and conduct during the trial are more limited than those of lawyers for the defense. The prosecutor may cause a mistrial by commenting on the credibility of a witness, or by expressing a personal opinion about the defendant's guilt, or by making unsupported or inflammatory statements about the defendant or the defense counsel. To keep the balance fair, the courts allow prosecutors to respond to defense claims, applying a doctrine called invited reply. For example, an opening defense salvo against the prosecutor's integrity ("She's only prosecuting my client to further her political career") may open the door for a prosecutor to state a personal opinion about the defendant's guilt and to urge the jury to "do its job." Note the unexamined assumption that a lawyer's opinion about the guilt or innocence of the defendant will have an impact on the jury's decision making. For the psychologist, this is an empirical issue that can be tested experimentally. How would you design research to test the assumption that a lawyer's stated opinion about the defendant's guilt or innocence will sway the jury?

Presentation of Evidence.   The *order of proof* in a trial is that the plaintiff or prosecutor opens, the defendant follows, and the plaintiff has an opportunity to present rebuttal evidence. Rebuttal evidence can only respond to the other side's presentation, such as an attempt to disprove an alibi defense by showing that the defendant was not at the place asserted; it cannot be used to provide additional support for the plaintiff's case. Each party will have an opportunity to respond to the evidence presented by the other. This is a core concept of the adversarial system, which depends on the adversaries at trial to present evidence supporting their case and rebutting the opposing party's case.

Once the plaintiff or prosecutor finishes his or her case, the defendant often makes a motion for a **directed verdict** (a decision by the judge that there is not enough evidence of guilt to support a conviction) to test whether the plaintiff has proved all the elements of the case (including such technical facts as the location of the alleged acts within the jurisdiction of this court). If the judge denies the motion or postpones ruling on it until after the jury reaches a decision, presentation of evidence to the jury continues.

The defense need not present any evidence. In a criminal case, the Fifth Amendment privilege against self-incrimination frees the defendant from being called involuntarily as a witness for the prosecution. On the other hand, in a civil case, the opposing party can be subpoenaed and called to the witness stand as an *adverse witness.* The adverse witness, however, still retains any privileges against giving evidence, such as the self-incrimination privilege or an attorney-client or doctor-patient relationship. In the *Kohl v. Rhodes* case, Rhodes could refuse to answer questions about his activities on the grounds that his answers might be self-incriminating. Indeed, if he answered questions, those answers could be used in a criminal trial as voluntary admissions.

In a criminal trial, neither prosecutor nor judge may mention to the jury that the defendant failed to testify. One wonders whether the jury does not notice this omission or whether, contrary to the Fifth Amendment, they use the silence to influence their decision making. Empirical research on this issue shows that jurors often interpret a defendant's silence as suggesting that he or she has something to hide (Hendrick & Shaffer, 1975).

Each side has a right to confront and cross-examine the other's witnesses. In a criminal trial, a defendant's right "to be confronted with the witnesses against him" is embodied in the Sixth Amendment. The U.S. Supreme Court, however, has never held this right to be absolute, and in cases involving child sexual abuse, exceptions have been permitted in two contexts: one involving out-of-court statements and the other involving testimony in court. For example, in *Maryland v. Craig* (1990), a divided court ruled that a defendant's right to confront an accuser face-to-face might give way to a trial judge's finding that a child might suffer severe emotional distress if faced with the defendant. In that case, the court permitted a child to testify via closed-circuit television, with cross-examination. The court balanced the need for the limits with the safeguards against unreliable testimony and concluded that the safeguards (presence of the witness, testimony under oath, jury able to observe the witness, and witness subject to cross-examination) were adequate. The Court has also made it clear that a state may not presume that a child witness will always be severely traumatized by the experience; case-by-case assessments of the prospective impact on the child must be made (*Coy v. Iowa,* 1988).

Closing Arguments (Summation).   Closing arguments consist of the attorneys' attempts to summarize the evidence, organize it for the jury in persuasive form, and argue its practical implications. As with opening statements, the lawyers must leave the definitions and instructions about the law to the judge, but almost everything else is fair game. Stories, arguments from classical sources like the Bible or Shakespeare's works, down-home homilies, or any other form of persuasive communication can be, and is, used in closing arguments. As with the presentation of evidence, the plaintiff or prosecutor proceeds first, the defendant follows, and the plaintiff has an opportunity to rebut.

Jury Instructions.   Generally, not until after the final arguments and just before they begin their deliberations do the jurors hear from the judge about the legal rules that are to guide their decision making. The jury's role is to ascertain the facts and then apply to those facts the law as stated by the judge in formal instructions. Procedural rules governing federal criminal and civil trials permit the judge to instruct the jury either before or after the closing arguments, or at both times (*Federal Rules of Criminal Procedure,* 30, 1996; *Federal Rules of Civil Procedure,* 51, 1996).

Using standard definitions, usually read from a book of "pattern" instructions (Federal Judicial Center, 1987), perhaps supplemented by instructions proposed by the parties or tailored by the judge to fit the case, the judge reads the legal rules to the jurors. Although practices seem to be changing during the last decade, note taking by the jurors is generally not permitted, and a written copy of the instructions is generally not available in the jury room. Studies show that jurors typically do not understand the instructions when they are written in legal terminology. The findings suggest that jurors understand about half of what is presented (Diamond & Levi, 1996), and that the meaning of basic concepts such as burden of proof escape fully half the jurors (Strawn & Buchanan, 1976).

Jury Deliberations.   Judges make extensive efforts to insulate jurors from outside influences during a trial and deliberations on the verdict. The idea is to focus jurors' attention and deliberations on the evidence presented in the courtroom. Jurors are instructed not to discuss the case with anyone, even with each other, until they have heard all the evidence and have gone to the jury room. In cases of intense public interest, the jury is sometimes sequestered (i.e., the jury members are isolated from outside sources and reside in a hotel) during the entire trial to prevent contamination by the media or other outside influences. During sequestration, marshals screen newspapers before jurors read them and monitor their television viewing to eliminate references to the trial. Court personnel are also forbidden to discuss the case with the jurors (Levine, 1996).

The law draws a sharp distinction between outside efforts to influence the jury and internal factors that may affect jury deliberations. As to internal matters, *Federal Rules of Criminal Evidence* 606(b) (1996) forbids a juror from testifying "as to any matter or statement occurring during the course of the jury's deliberations or to the effect of anything" on any juror's mind, emotions or "concerning the juror's mental processes." In other words, jurors not be required to reveal what went on behind the closed jury room doors.

Application of this rule by the Supreme Court in a recent case illustrates the strength of the wall the law erects to protect jury deliberations. In *United States* (1987), the Court faced an allegation by a convicted defendant *v.* the jurors had been under the influence of drugs and alcohol during the deliberations. Statements of other jurors supported these allegations. The reasoned that these were internal factors, "no more an 'outside influence' t... virus, poorly prepared food, or a lack of sleep" (p. 122). The conviction of the fendant was upheld despite strong evidence that some jurors had been under th... influence of drugs and alcohol.

As to external threats, if someone slipped drugs in a juror's coffee, perhaps to distract attention from unfavorable evidence, that action would likely cause a mistrial. The difference in the second case is that the influence of the drugs comes from outside the individual juror.

In dealing with questions about deadlocks, judges face the delicate task of determining the seriousness of the stalemate without asking about the numerical split of the jury. Uncovering the actual vote, say 9–3, is considered a threat to the jury (to reach a verdict for the majority position) and therefore is automatic grounds for a new trial (*Brasfield v. United States*, 1926; Georgetown Law Journal Staff, 1991, pp. 1009–1010). This rule, of course, is consistent with the notion that the judge has no right to interfere with the jury's internal workings. After determining that a deadlock exists, the judge may instruct the jury, in a nonthreatening manner, to continue its deliberations.

The original instruction on this point is called the *Allen* charge (*Allen v. United States,* 1896), but defense lawyers also know it as the *dynamite charge.* The *Allen* charge emphasizes that the minority should reconsider its views; more modern versions emphasize that both minority and majority should reexamine their views (Georgetown Law Journal Staff, 1991, pp. 1010–1011).

Note that the emphasis in applying the *Allen* charge is that it be noncoercive. In the *Allen* charge, jurors are told that they should continue to deliberate even though they are deadlocked. Furthermore, dissenting jurors are encouraged by the charge to consider the correctness of their opinions. That is the dynamite in the charge—whether jurors in the minority will feel pressure to change their opinions because of the judge's *Allen* instructions.

Saul Kassin, Vicki Smith, and William Tulloch (1990) tested the notion that minority opinion jurors would feel more pressure in such a situation. All juries in this study heard the same trial but some were given the *Allen* charge when deadlocked and others were not. Kassin and his co-workers found that jurors in the minority were more likely than control group jurors—those who had not heard an *Allen* charge—to change to the majority opinion after hearing the *Allen* charge. Smith and Kassin (1993) speculated that juries may be more susceptible to the coercive power of the *Allen* charge when the trial involves community and moral standards such as abortion or euthanasia ("mercy killings") and similar value-laden issues. (We return in Chapter 11 to the issue of juries that must decide cases concerning moral issues.)

Posttrial Proceedings

After the jury's verdict of not guilty, the case ends. The Constitution prohibits **double jeopardy,** meaning that the Fifth Amendment protects the defendant against being prosecuted a second time for the same offense after acquittal or conviction. Jeopardy begins when a jury is impaneled and sworn or a judge begins to hear evidence. The underlying principle is that "jeopardy does not attach until the defendant faces the risk of a determination of guilt" (Georgetown Law Journal Staff, 1991, p. 912). Generally, the double jeopardy clause does not preclude a victim from pursuing a civil damages case based on the same conduct of which a defendant was acquitted in a criminal case.

Another interesting exception to the double jeopardy clause, one that troubles some legal scholars, is that an acquittal on charges by one sovereign government entity does not preclude another governmental body from trying the defendant for the same crime, if not on the same charges. Recall that the police officers who beat Rodney King in Los Angeles after he led them on a 100-mile-per-hour car chase down Santa Monica Boulevard were found not guilty in the original trial by jurors representing the State of California. Nevertheless, these officers were then tried by the federal government on charges of violating King's civil rights. Double jeopardy did not come into play because a second sovereign—that is, a government entity that has independent power—can and did try the officers for violation of a different federal law.

If the verdict is guilty, posttrial motions may follow, such as a motion for a new trial; this is a formal request for the court to order another trial because of errors in the first one. The trial judge decides the posttrial motions. In a *motion for a new trial,* the defendant will try to specify the *errors,* such as mistakes in instructing the jury or in admitting evidence, that the judge may have committed during the trial and seek to correct those without the need for an appeal. Generally, a second trial can be ordered, without violating the double jeopardy clause, if the defendant successfully challenges the fairness or legality of a trial that led to a conviction.

If a jury fails to reach a verdict (a condition commonly known as a hung jury), the judge may declare a *mistrial.* Generally, the judge can order a retrial under those circumstances.

Sentencing.   Since the first edition of this text, the federal law of sentencing as well as that of many states has undergone a significant change. Guideline sentencing and mandatory minimum sentencing for drug and weapons offenses have replaced the rehabilitative model that emphasized retraining and restoring the offender to a positive role in society. We discuss sentencing in detail in Chapter 11. Debate about sentencing reforms continues to swirl around us, and it is by no means clear that a comfortable consensus will appear during our lifetimes.

Spurred by powerful and clear social science findings of wide disparities among judges in sentencing for the same offenses, liberal and conservative political reformers found common ground during the early 1980s. "Liberals" sought equal treatment of similar offenders and basic fairness in the sentencing process. More "conservative" commentators and policymakers sought the certainty of punishment that would follow from an emphasis on equal treatment of similar conduct. After a number of controversial efforts to enact comprehensive criminal justice reforms, Congress passed the Sentencing Reform Act of 1984. That statute created the U.S. Sentencing Commission charged with achieving "certainty and fairness in sentencing and reducing unwarranted sentencing disparities." Multiple goals of sentencing recognized in the act are just punishment, deterrence, incapacitation (keeping dangerous criminals off the streets), and rehabilitation. Adoption of these goals reflected the Senate Judiciary Committee's conclusion that "coercive" rehabilitation had failed (Georgetown Law Journal Staff, 1991, p. 1231). The new sentencing guidelines emphasize the offense rather than the offender. Effectively, the guidelines serve to limit severely the judge's discretion in imposing sentence.

Appeal.   Appellate courts are society's answer to the age-old question "Who guards the guardians?" A party who is dissatisfied with the final outcome of a trial has the right to **appeal** the decision to a court of appeals—that is, to ask the higher court to review the trial court actions for legal errors. In some states, there is an opportunity to file two appeals; the second is allowed at the discretion of the court. In all cases, state and federal, the parties have the opportunity to apply for review by **certiorari** (Latin for "to make sure") to the U.S. Supreme Court, but fewer than 5 percent of these applications are granted.

The subject matter of appeals covers the range of decisions that a judge makes during the pretrial, trial, and posttrial stages. Appeals can challenge the legal substance of the decision or the procedure by which it was reached. Rulings on pretrial motions, the admission of evidence, rulings on motions during trial, instructions to the jury, and the final decision in the case (the sentence or award or denial of damages or other remedy) are all judicial decisions that may be appealed.

Generally, an appeal can be filed only after the case is over and a *final judgment* has been entered. Under some circumstances, an **interlocutory appeal**—an interim appeal filed before the final judgment—can be taken. For example, if the legal rule applicable to the case is unclear, efficiency may be served if the judge obtains a legal ruling on the disputed issue before conducting a lengthy trial. Federal law permits a trial judge to certify a case for such an early appeal.

Appeals of the content of jury decisions are more limited than appeals of judges' decisions. Because a jury need not state the grounds for its decision, the jury's reasoning process cannot be reviewed. As long as there is sufficient evidence from which a jury could have reached its decision, that decision is unassailable. And as we read earlier in the chapter, the deliberation process is immune from investigation. If a jury verdict is reversed on appeal, the reason is generally that the court of appeals found an action of the judge in the course of the trial or the judge's instructions to the jury to be below legal standards.

An independent panel of judges (usually three) decides an appeal. These should be judges who have had no involvement in the trial of the case and who have no personal stake in the outcome of the appeal. The case is decided on the *record*—the transcripts and pleadings—that was developed in the trial court. Usually the record consists of the written motions and decisions of the court, the transcript of evidence, and the documents introduced into evidence at trial. New evidence cannot be introduced on appeal.

Social science is involved in helping to define the record on appeal. One experiment, conducted by staff of the Federal Judicial Center, has shown that the transcript of a tape-recorded trial is superior to the transcript of a stenographically recorded trial in terms of accuracy and speed of transcription (Greenwood, Horney, Jacoubovitch, Lowensteine, & Wheeler, 1983). Some courts are experimenting with a new form of trial record: a videotaped version of the trial, with or without a written transcript. What difference would a review of this type of a record be likely to make in the nature and focus of appeals decisions? Is there any relevance to the use of videotaped transcripts in the findings of studies showing that videotaped depositions have a different impact on juries from that of live testimony? Where the choice of the medium is between videotape and a written transcript, what effects would you expect?

Arguments in appeals are both oral and written. Written arguments are generally referred to as **briefs,** but they are rarely short and their length may be inversely related to their merit. In the federal courts, oral argument is discretionary with the court. A panel of judges reviews the briefs and the record and decides whether oral argument should be heard. The practice varies from court to court;

the standard is that most appeals do not require oral argument. Indeed, many judges find that the vast majority of appeals are routine and that only a small percentage present a difficult issue.

In written briefs, lawyers frequently refer to social science findings and other empirical data from books, reports, and other public documents even though the contents and ideas were not presented as evidence during the trial. Recall that Louis Brandeis, who later became a renowned Supreme Court justice, pioneered this method of argument (known as a Brandeis brief) during the early twentieth century and, like many precedents, it has endured.

Appeals courts tend to look beyond the issues in dispute between the parties, to the implications of a written opinion for future cases. If the case simply involves resolving a dispute according to settled rules, the court may issue a perfunctory opinion, often not signed by an individual judge—a per curiam ("by the court") opinion. These opinions are frequently not published in the official reports, and some courts have rules against their use as precedents (Stienstra, 1985). If the case involves an element of lawmaking, the opinion is likely to be lengthy and signed by a judge. Sometimes the other judges will write individual opinions as well, carefully stating their reasons for joining or dissenting from the main opinion.

In this introduction to the field of psychology and law, we have laid out the basics of the legal system. In the next chapter we examine the legal process in criminal trials, discussing the roles of major players in the system: victims, defendants, and the judge.

SUMMARY

The legal system contains two complementary types of rules. One is substantive law, which is the rights we possess and the duties we must assume. The other is procedural law, which is how we enforce our substantive rights or defend ourselves from efforts to impose liabilities or punishments on us. Looked at from another angle, law is composed of criminal and civil law. Criminal law defines crimes and has to do with the relations between a citizen who violates such laws and the government. Civil law governs the relations among individuals, including corporations and other entities.

Judges, lawyers, and the general public have a deep conviction that procedural fairness is critical to the maintenance of the justice system. That conviction arises from the *adversarial system,* which depends on fair procedures to afford parties an even chance to present their side so the truth can emerge to yield an accurate decision. Legally, many procedural protections originate in the Bill of Rights, the first ten amendments to the U.S. Constitution.

Social psychologists describe the process of deciding to turn to the law for redress as involving the stages of *naming, blaming,* and *claiming.* Naming simply involves saying that a crime or a civil wrong has occurred and giving the act a *name* like *rape* or *sexual assault,* or *personal injury. Attributing blame* is also an essential element of invoking the law. Crime victims who blame themselves for getting into the situation may judge themselves guilty and may fail to blame the perpetrator. The final element is *claiming,* or identifying a loss and asserting a claim against the one to blame for it. This step involves balancing the benefits of using the legal system with the costs of doing so.

The criminal law focuses its attention on injuries to the public and on protecting the public from future harm at the hands of the defendant; the civil law concentrates on the injuries to the individual. A criminal case emphasizes retribution and punishment; a civil case focuses on restitution and compensation.

In a criminal case, the public prosecutor represents the state; the victim is only a witness, not a party. In a civil case, the plaintiff hires a private attorney whose professional duty is to advance the plaintiff's interests. If the defendant is found guilty in a criminal case, the judge generally imposes a sentence. If the defendant is found liable in a civil case, the jury generally specifies the amount of the damages that the plaintiff is entitled to recover.

Both civil and criminal jury trials begin with jury selection. A panel of qualified jurors, called a *venire,* is then drawn. The judge and lawyers in a case conduct what is called the *voir dire* by questioning the prospective jurors to uncover any biases or prejudgments among them. Lawyers can then move to exclude individual jurors for cause—that is, to excuse them from jury duty because they answered in a way that suggested they might not be able to make an unbiased judgment based solely on the evidence. Lawyers may also exclude a juror by using one of a limited number of peremptory challenges, which require no stated reason for dismissal.

The prosecutor in a criminal trial or the plaintiff in a civil trial, because each has the burden of proof, presents the first opening statement. In presenting evidence in a trial, the order is for the plaintiff or prosecutor to open, the defendant to follow, and the plaintiff to have an opportunity to present rebuttal evidence.

In closing arguments, the attorneys attempt to summarize the evidence, organize it for the jury in persuasive form, and argue the practical implications of the evidence. As with opening statements, the lawyers must leave the legal instructions to the judge.

The judge's instruction to the jury are generally not given until after the final arguments and just before the jury begins its deliberations; however, some courts now give preliminary and interim instructions. Instructions are designed to communicate the legal rules that are to guide jury decisions. The jury's role is to ascertain the facts and then to apply the law as stated by the judge to those facts.

After a jury verdict of not guilty, the case ends. Because of the constitutional prohibition against double jeopardy, an accused person cannot be tried twice for the same offense. If the verdict is guilty, posttrial motions, such as a motion for a new trial or a motion to appoint counsel for an appeal may be presented to the trial judge for rulings. If a jury fails to reach a verdict, a situation commonly known as a hung jury, the judge may declare a *mistrial.* Generally, the judge can order a retrial under those circumstances.

A plaintiff or defendant who is dissatisfied with the final outcome of a trial has the right to appeal the decision to a court of appeals. Generally, an appeal can be filed only after the case is over and a final judgment has been entered, but under some circumstances, an earlier appeal known as an interlocutory appeal can be filed. Appeals of jury decisions are more limited than appeals of judges' decisions. An independent panel of judges (usually three) decides an appeal by reviewing a *record* of the trial. By *independent*, we mean judges who have had no involvement in the trial of the case and who have no personal stake in the outcome of the appeal. On appeal, lawyers present their argument in written briefs that sometimes include social science materials. Appeals courts hear oral arguments as well. Courts of appeal generally decide their cases in written opinions that explain their reasons for their decision.

PART TWO

The Legal Process: Actors in the Legal System

CHAPTER
3

Victims, Defendants, and Judges

In Chapter 2 we examined the rules and structure of criminal procedure. We saw the form a criminal trial takes and the rules by which evidence is gathered, organized, presented, and analyzed before the bar. In this section, we take a closer look at the actors in the legal process: the victim and defendant, the judge, the lawyers and the police, witnesses and jurors. We will put some flesh on the skeleton introduced in Chapter 2.

We begin with crime victims and defendants. We also consider the role of the judge. These three actors in the legal process are our starting point for some obvious reasons. First, with few exceptions, the criminal justice process does not begin to move until a crime victim files a complaint. A complaint accuses someone of committing a crime, and that someone will be the defendant in a criminal case. Victims and defendants are linked in the criminal justice system.

The defendant's first contact with the formal courtroom procedures will occur when she or he is arraigned. This hearing before the judge is to determine whether sufficient evidence exists to hold the defendant. We begin by discussing the role of two private citizens, the victim and the defendant, both reluctant participants, and the judge, the neutral arbiter of the criminal justice system. In Chapter 4 we examine the part played by criminal justice professionals: the police and the lawyers.

THE VICTIM

The law acknowledges that criminal behavior harms the entire community. The state is therefore responsible for prosecuting criminal behavior and the victim is relieved of that responsibility. Because the state assumes the burden of prosecution, the victim is left with little power or role in the proceedings and becomes the forgotten actor in the criminal justice system. Nevertheless, victims are the gatekeepers of the criminal justice system because most investigations begin when they report crimes to the authorities.

Society has a surfeit of crime victims. Crime statistics from 1994 indicate that someone is murdered in the United States every 23 minutes; a woman is raped every 6 minutes; 1 household in every 20 had at least 1 member who was a victim of violent crime. We also know that homicide is the major cause of death among 15- to 24-year-olds (Frazier, Candell, Arikain, & Tofteland, 1994; Petersilia, 1994).

We can take some solace, however, in the most recent data from the Federal Bureau of Investigation (FBI), which indicate that serious crime declined in the United States for four consecutive years through 1995 (Federal Bureau of Investigation, 1996). Figure 3.1 shows the decline in incidence for five serious crimes over this period.

As Figure 3.1 reveals, homicide, the most carefully tracked category, had the sharpest drop of any of the five major crimes, continuing a decline in the homicide rate first observed in 1993. Criminologists are unsure about the cause of this essential element of invoking the law. Crime victims who blame themselves for getting into the situation may judge themselves guilty and may fail to blame the perpetrator. The final element is *claiming,* or identifying a loss and asserting a claim against the one to blame for it. This step involves balancing the benefits of using the legal system with the costs of doing so.

The criminal law focuses its attention on injuries to the public and on protecting the public from future harm at the hands of the defendant; the civil law concentrates on the injuries to the individual. A criminal case emphasizes retribution and punishment; a civil case focuses on restitution and compensation.

In a criminal case, the public prosecutor represents the state; the victim is only a witness, not a party. In a civil case, the plaintiff hires a private attorney whose professional duty is to advance the plaintiff's interests. If the defendant is found guilty in a criminal case, the judge generally imposes a sentence. If the defendant is found liable in a civil case, the jury generally specifies the amount of the damages that the plaintiff is entitled to recover.

Both civil and criminal jury trials begin with jury selection. A panel of qualified jurors, called a *venire,* is then drawn. The judge and lawyers in a case conduct what is called the *voir dire* by questioning the prospective jurors to uncover any biases or prejudgments among them. Lawyers can then move to exclude individual jurors for cause—that is, to excuse them from jury duty because they answered in a way that suggested they might not be able to make an unbiased judgment based solely on the evidence. Lawyers may also exclude a juror by using one of a limited number of peremptory challenges, which require no stated reason for dismissal.

The prosecutor in a criminal trial or the plaintiff in a civil trial, because each has the burden of proof, presents the first opening statement. In presenting evidence in a trial, the order is for the plaintiff or prosecutor to open, the defendant to follow, and the plaintiff to have an opportunity to present rebuttal evidence.

In closing arguments, the attorneys attempt to summarize the evidence, organize it for the jury in persuasive form, and argue the practical implications of the evidence. As with opening statements, the lawyers must leave the legal instructions to the judge.

The judge's instruction to the jury are generally not given until after the final arguments and just before the jury begins its deliberations; however, some courts now give preliminary and interim instructions. Instructions are designed to communicate the legal rules that are to guide jury decisions. The jury's role is to ascertain the facts and then to apply the law as stated by the judge to those facts.

After a jury verdict of not guilty, the case ends. Because of the constitutional prohibition against double jeopardy, an accused person cannot be tried twice for the same offense. If the verdict is guilty, posttrial motions, such as a motion for a new trial or a motion to appoint counsel for an appeal may be presented to the trial judge for rulings. If a jury fails to reach a verdict, a situation commonly known as a hung jury, the judge may declare a *mistrial.* Generally, the judge can order a retrial under those circumstances.

A plaintiff or defendant who is dissatisfied with the final outcome of a trial has the right to appeal the decision to a court of appeals. Generally, an appeal can be filed only after the case is over and a final judgment has been entered, but under some circumstances, an earlier appeal known as an interlocutory appeal can be filed. Appeals of jury decisions are more limited than appeals of judges' decisions. An independent panel of judges (usually three) decides an appeal by reviewing a *record* of the trial. By *independent*, we mean judges who have had no involvement in the trial of the case and who have no personal stake in the outcome of the appeal. On appeal, lawyers present their argument in written briefs that sometimes include social science materials. Appeals courts hear oral arguments as well. Courts of appeal generally decide their cases in written opinions that explain their reasons for their decision.

PART TWO

The Legal Process: Actors in the Legal System

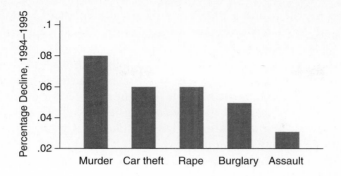

FIGURE 3.1 Decline in incidence of five serious crimes.

This figure shows the percentage decline in incidence of five major felonies for 1995 as compared to 1994.

Source: Adapted from data provided by Federal Bureau of Investigation.

decrease; they are equally unsure as to whether the decline represents a long-term trend or is simply a statistical fluctuation (Goleman, 1996). The reduction in crime rates occurred in most major cities and appeared to be unrelated to police strategies in those cities. These decreases are due primarily to a decline in crimes against adults; crimes involving individuals under the age of 25, however, have been increasing (Federal Bureau of Investigation, 1996; Goleman, 1996). Some observers suggest that the abatement in major crimes could be due to the tripling of the prison population. However, crime rates were much lower in the 1940s and 1950s than they are currently, and the prison population during those periods was proportionately lower than it is at present (Goleman, 1996).

A final note about the incidence of crime in the United States: We do not have very firm data about the amount of crime that actually occurs (Miller, Cohen, & Wiersma, 1996). Crime statistics are compiled from several sources, all of which may be incomplete. For example, the Federal Bureau of Investigation Uniform Crime Report is based on data gathered from police department crime reports. Because many crimes are not reported to the police, these records underestimate the frequency of crime. In addition, the Bureau of Justice Statistics conducts a continuous survey of American households concerning crime victimization but excludes certain categories of crimes, including crimes against children under 12, and crimes against the homeless (Miller et al., 1996). Consequently, crimes are both underreported and underestimated.

Reporting Crimes

The willingness of victims to report criminal acts is a significant indicator of the relationship between police and citizens, reflecting victims' perceptions of the effectiveness with which society fights crime. When society feels impotent about controlling crime, the result is a feeling of "learned helplessness." When this occurs, citizens are less likely to report crime and the police response to criminal activity may be less vigorous.

One 1992 study estimates that less than half of household and personal crimes are reported (Bastian, 1992). Whereas crimes against businesses and physical assaults with theft are most likely to be reported, physical assault without theft and larceny without injury to the victim are least likely to be reported (Cohen & Miller, 1995). The factors increasing the likelihood that crime will be reported include the amount of money or property lost and the use of a weapon, particularly when an injury occurs. In injury cases, of course, the victim's need for medical attention requires a report.

The reason most crimes were not reported to the police appears to be citizens' perception that nothing could be done or that the incident did not warrant the attention of the police (Federal Bureau of Investigation, 1996). Actually, those who do report crimes are no more optimistic that the crime will be solved than those who do not report. In fact, less than 50 percent of crimes are ever solved: The rate for burglary is 20 percent, for robbery 5 percent, and for forcible rape 50 percent (Bastien, 1992).

Experimental studies, simulated in the laboratory or in the field, confirm that the rate of reporting by bystanders is also quite low, ranging from zero to 40 percent, depending on the circumstances. Greenberg, Ruback, and Westcott (1982) conducted a study investigating the decision making of crime victims. These researchers used archival analyses of police records, simulation studies with college students as mock victims, and experimental studies of victims' behavior in a field situation. The last technique involved gathering a wide range of subjects from the community, bringing them to the "laboratory," and staging a crime.

Greenberg et al. demonstrated that situational factors in general and social influence forces in particular were responsible for the victims' decision to report the crime. These social influences were more important than any characteristic of the victim in predicting whether the crime would be reported. Specifically, if the victim was given definite advice ("Call the police") by a bystander who remained while the victim notified the police and who offered to be of help in the future, the likelihood of reporting was quite high.

The data gathered by Greenberg et al. cast some doubt on the notion that the motivation for reporting property crimes is related to potential reimbursement by insurance companies. Greenberg et al. found that in 65 percent of the cases, the victim in their studies did not qualify for reimbursement because the amount lost was lower than the deductible in the insurance policy, typically less than $100. Of course, it is possible that under the stress of the situation, victims may have had incomplete knowledge of their insurance coverage. Recent analysis suggests that crime victims' motivations for reporting the event have not changed in any significant manner since Greenberg et al. (1982) completed their studies (Goleman, 1996).

The Cost of Crime

Placing a monetary value on the suffering that results from violent crime may seem cold and uncaring (Cohen 1988, 1995; Miller, Cohen, & Wiersma, 1996). However, determining the cost of violent crime is useful for public policy purposes. Policymakers need to know the cost of crime in relation to the cost of programs aimed at preventing crime as well as the cost of building more prison space. Cohen (1995) showed that a criminal costs society about $1.2 million during a typical 5 to 15 year career. In comparison, the cost of a high school dropout is about $300,000. These monetary estimates include mental health care, police and fire services, victim services including placement of children of victims in foster homes, loss of productivity at work or at school. One example: Every homicide causes two individuals from the victim's family to require psychotherapy (Miller et al., 1996). The total monetary cost of criminal activity each year has been estimated to exceed $450 billion (Miller et al., 1996).

These monetary estimates provide a concrete sense of the scope of the crime problem. Table 3.1 shows the financial costs per victim for several nonlethal crimes. The costs calculated are primarily medical bills, property losses, and lost wages and productivity, and these are easily translated into dollars. The table cannot show intangible costs such as fear, pain, and a constrained quality of life

TABLE 3.1   Crime Severity Measured by Estimated Losses per Crime Victim (in 1994 Dollars)

Crime	Cost per Victim
Child abuse: sexual	$125,000
Rape and sexual assault (excluding child abuse)	77,000
Child abuse: physical	77,000
Arson	38,000
Child abuse: emotional	30,000
Drunk driving	18,000
Assault or attempt	12,000
Robbery or attempt	10,000
Motor vehicle theft	4,000
Burglary	1,600
Larceny	400

Note: Assault, robbery, motor vehicle theft, burglary, and larceny include "attempted" crimes that are never successfully carried out. Also, note that the monetary value was calculated on crimes that did not involve death or the risk of death.

Source: Table adapted from data provided by Miller, Cohen, & Wiersma, 1996.

TABLE 3.2 Costs and Consequences of Crime

Cost Category	Party Who Directly Bears Cost
I. Costs of Crime	
Direct property losses	
1. Losses not reimbursed by insurance	Victim
2. Losses reimbursed by insurance	Society
3. Administrative cost: insurance reimbursement	Society
4. Recovery by police	Society
Medical and mental health care	
1. Costs not reimbursed by victim's family	Victim/society
2. Costs reimbursed by insurance	Society
3. Administrative overhead of insurance coverage (2) above	Society
Lost workdays	
1. Lost wages for unpaid workdays	Victim
2. Lost productivity	Society/employer
Lost school days	
1. Forgone wages due to lack of education	Victim
2. Forgone nonmonetary benefits of education	Victim
3. Forgone social benefits due to lack of education	Society
Lost housework	Victim
Pain and suffering/quality of life	Victim
Loss of affection/enjoyment	Victim's family
Death	
1. Lost life	Victim
2. Loss of affection/enjoyment	Victim's family
3. Funeral and burial expenses	Victim's family
4. Psychological injury/treatment	Victim's family

(Miller et al., 1996) that are difficult to express monetarily. Researchers try to estimate the intangible costs of crime by extrapolating from jury awards for "pain and suffering." Juries in civil lawsuits may be asked to estimate the costs of a reduced quality of life, the victim's pain and suffering, or the loss of a spouse's companionship. Researchers assume that the awards reflect society's estimate of the financial value of these intangible losses.

Cost Category	Party Who Directly Bears Cost
Legal costs/wrongful death claims	Victim's family
"Second Generation" Costs	
1. Future victims committed by earlier victims	Future victims
2. Future social costs associated with point (1)	Society
II. Cost of Society's Response to Crime	
Precautionary expenditures/effort	Potential victim
Fear of crime	Potential victims
Criminal justice system	Society
1. Police and investigative costs	Society
2. Prosecutors	Society
3. Courts	Society
4. Legal fees	
a. Public defenders	Society
b. Private attorneys	Offenders/accused
5. Jail costs	Society
6. Nonjail sanctions (probation, etc.)	Society
7. Victim time	Victim
8. Jury and witness time	Jury/witness
Victim services	
1. Victim service organizations	Society
2. Victim compensation programs	Society
3. Victim time	Victim
Other noncriminal programs	
1. Hotlines and public service announcements	Society
2. Community treatment programs	Society
3. Private therapy/counseling	Society/offender
Incarcerated offender costs	
1. Lost wages	Offender/family
2. Lost tax revenue and productivity	Society
3. Value of lost freedom	Offender
4. Psychological cost to family	Offender's family

Source: Adapted from Cohen, Miller, & Rossman, 1994, Tables 1 & 2; and from Miller, Cohen, & Wiersma, 1996, Box 1.

Although victims bear the immediate costs of crime, tangible and intangible, society shoulders a major portion of the financial burden (see Table 3.2). Cohen and Miller (1995) estimated that in 1991 about 4 million people sought mental health counseling as a result of criminal victimization. This suggests that crime victims constituted close to 25 percent of the mental health caseload in 1991. Total mental health services for these victims were estimated at nearly $7 billion. The victims paid part of these fees; insurance companies paid the rest. Overall, insurance costs resulting from crime, including health, life, auto, fire, theft, and worker's compensation, totaled $45 billion in 1993 (Miller, Pindus, Douglas, & Rossman, 1995).

These figures may reflect the immediate costs produced by victimization, but they do not tell the whole story. Victims of violent crimes may sustain long-term mental and physical health problems. Mary Koss (1990) reported that physical and sexual victimization are linked to a lifetime of increased risk for mental disorders. Koss found that the more severe the crime, the more victims reported physical and emotional distress. Koss interviewed 316 crime victims and 64 nonvictims, all of whom were adult women. She analyzed the data gathered both from interviews with the women and from their medical records, and found that the severity of the crime was the single most important determinant of the amount and cost of later health care visits. Victimized women visited their physician 6.9 times per year, twice as much as nonvictims. Kilpatrick, Edmund, and Seymour (1992) reported that victimization was more important than family history in predicting substance abuse for female rape victims.

Victims and Syndrome Evidence

Koss (1993) reported that nearly a third of all survivors of rape suffered severe psychological stress after the rape (posttraumatic stress). That rate of severe stress reactions is roughly six times higher than for women who were never raped. Rape victims experienced depression three times more often than nonvictims. In addition, Burgess and Holmstrom (1974) noted that rape survivors often exhibited a number of related symptoms including extreme emotional responses, changes in lifestyle, and difficulty in day-to-day functioning. They called these interrelated symptoms **rape trauma syndrome.** This syndrome and battered spouse syndrome are the two categories of syndrome evidence that courts most frequently confront.

Rape Trauma Syndrome.   Burgess and Holmstrom (1974) defined rape trauma syndrome as acute behavioral, physical, and psychological reactions that occurred as a result of forcible rape or attempted forcible rape. Immediately after the rape, victims typically experienced an acute phase in which they had headaches, experienced difficulty sleeping, were afraid of any situation that reminded them of the assault, and tended to blame themselves for the rape. In essence, their lives fell apart (Frazier and Borgida, 1985).

A typical defense to rape is for the defendant's lawyer to try to "put the victim on trial." This means that the sexual history of the victim becomes an issue. As consent is the sovereign defense to a rape charge, any belief that the sex act might have been consensual aids the defendant. To give some protection to the victims, the legislators in many states have passed **rape shield laws,** aimed at limiting the questioning of the victim about her prior sexual history, except for relations with the defendant. Instituting these rules has sharply increased the percentage of convictions in rape trials. For example, the percentage of convictions in rape trials in Michigan before passage of a rape shield law was 30 percent; after passage, it was 80 percent (Borgida & White, 1978).

Despite the passage of rape shield laws, some states allow evidence of past sexual history of the victim when it is deemed to be in the interests of justice. Trial judges in these circumstances have broad discretion to determine what evidence should be allowed in a rape trial. In a 1993 trial in Glen Ridge, New Jersey, four young men charged with sexually assaulting a retarded 17-year-old girl were permitted to introduce evidence of the young woman's sexual history on the grounds that the evidence was needed in their defense.

Other rule changes, despite good intentions, may have also served to devalue the rape victim. Let us look briefly at these changes as documented by Giacopassi and Wilkinson (1985), and consider their social psychological impact.

The death penalty for rape was declared unconstitutional in 1977 (*Coker v. Georgia*). The Court reasoned that the death penalty was not proportional to the crime and sentences for rape have been lowered and graduated following *Coker*. The law now refers to "levels of rape," depending on the amount of intimidation used. In addition, rape is now a gender-neutral crime: It is now defined as "unlawful sexual penetration of another," recognizing the possibilities of male-female, male-male, female-female, and female-male rape. Finally, the crime is no longer called rape in many legal jurisdictions. It is "sexual battery" or "sexual assault" to emphasize its violent nature. Giacopassi and Wilkinson (1985) pointed out that these attempts to "normalize" the crime of rape by making it no different from other crimes have made it more likely that the crime will be viewed less seriously.

Battered Woman Syndrome. The woman in the following vignette shows some of the symptoms of **battered woman syndrome,** a pattern of perceptions and behaviors thought to be characteristic of women who have endured continuous physical abuse by their mates (Schuller & Vidmar, 1992). These relationships have a cyclical nature—first violent, then repentant—that traps the victim (Schuller & Vidmar, 1992).

> He always found something wrong with what I did, even if I did what he asked. No matter what it was. It was never the way he wanted it. I was either too fat, didn't cook the food right . . . I think he wanted to hurt me. To hurt me in the sense . . . to make me feel like I was a nothing. And that I did something wrong, when I didn't do anything wrong. . . . I can't talk to adults. I don't know how to talk to people because my opinion doesn't ever count. I feel like I never had an opinion on politics or on life. I don't know how to interact because he would always be going like this to me [mimicking abuser's gesture of drawing a line with his index finger]. . . . that was his big signal to make me shut up, or he'd be kicking me under the table to shut my mouth. (Fischer, Vidmar, & Ellis, 1993, p. 2117)

Lenore Walker (1984), after detailed interviews with several hundred women who were battered, described a cycle or culture of battering. The first stage (tension building) is characterized by a series of irritating and abusive incidents. The woman is surprised by the behavior because the suddenly and inexplicably abusive partner had been attentive and kind during the couple's courtship. The tension-building stage is eventually followed by an acute battering stage, in which the severity of the abuse increases and the woman is subjected to a violent battering incident. A contrition stage follows, consisting of a period of relative calm and remorse on the part of the abuser. The batterer's behavior in this final stage reinforces the woman's hopes that he will reform and influences her to remain in the relationship.

Fundamentally, the batterer comes to dominate the partner, physically, psychologically, sexually, financially, and emotionally, exerting systematic control and domination (Fischer et al., 1993). The battered woman feels that she is somehow at fault and tries to minimize or hide the abuse. It is common for abused women to wear sunglasses or other devices to mask obvious physical abuse.

Why Victims Stay with Their Batterers.   Battered women may bond to their abusers as a survival strategy. This adaptation of the so-called **Stockholm syndrome,** which involves bonding with one's tormentors, helps explain why battered women have difficulty leaving their abusers and why they may return if they leave. The Stockholm syndrome was identified in 1973, after four people held captive in a Stockholm bank vault for six days became attached to their captors (Graham & Rawlings, 1991). Police tend to be aware of this syndrome and will not disrupt it because it often helps the victims survive the ordeal. The basis of the syndrome is a cognitive distortion. The captive (or abused woman) sees herself and the world through the eyes of the abuser and she denies her own reality. This mind-set makes it very hard for her to leave the relationship. Her self-esteem is very low and she has little confidence that she can survive without her abuser. Paradoxically, the only person an abused women feels she can turn to is her abuser. Dee Graham and Edna Rawlings (1991) have argued that the Stockholm syndrome may be a universal response to inescapable violence.

Battered Women Who Kill.   Some victims strike back. Usually, when violence occurs in the home, it is the woman who suffers or is killed (Kasian, Spanos, Terrance, & Peebles, 1993). Some women, who can endure the abuse no longer, commit murder in self-protection (Ewing, 1987). However, self-defense is almost never a successful plea when an abused woman kills her abuser (Schuller, 1990, 1994). In the United States and Canada, evidence of battered woman syndrome is not a defense for murder. To plead self-defense successfully, the defendant must prove that she had sufficient reason to believe that her death was imminent or that grievous physical harm would occur and that the only reasonable way she could stop her own demise was to kill her tormentor (Crocker, 1985).

What is "reasonable" and what is "imminent?" A woman who shoots her partner in his sleep because he has abused her for years and has just threatened to "finish her off" in the morning, may determine that the threat is as imminent as a gun pointed at her head. However, juries do not often share this view. Of 100 cases Ewing (1987) examined that involved a battered woman who killed her husband, 83 used a self-defense plea, and only 27 of those 87 were acquitted. Those who were convicted typically received a long jail sentence. Research suggests that battered women who kill are more likely to be acquitted when they have the combination of having suffered severe abuse and having killed while in a "disassociated" state of mind (Kasian et al., 1993). That is, juries are more likely to forgive a woman who "loses her mind" and impulsively kills after continual and severe abuse than one who kills while consciously defending herself.

Victim Impact Statements

In all types of cases, the legal system has tried to find avenues for the victim to have a role in the justice system. Families of crime victims in some jurisdictions may address the court before the judge pronounces sentence. Some states have passed legislation called **victim impact laws** that permit explicit consideration in the sentencing process of the impact of the crime on the victim, the victim's family, and the community. Some argue that a victim who is more "important" in the community is worth more than one whose life is less than exemplary. Someone who deprives a family and a community of a valued citizen should receive a greater penalty because of the impact on the morale and sensibilities of the family and the wider community.

In *Booth v. Maryland* (1987), the U.S. Supreme Court held that evidence concerning the impact of the crime on the victim's family and on the community should not be used in determining the sentence of a murderer. The majority of the Court felt that such evidence could only inflame the jury and result in an emotional rather than a reasoned decision. The *Booth* decision struck down Maryland's victim impact law. Note that the Court said that such victim impact statements could not be used in death penalty cases. Such statements can be used in other trials. The Court also affirmed this ruling in *South Carolina v. Gathers* (1989).

However, in 1991, the U.S. Supreme Court reversed the decisions in *Booth* and *Gathers.* In *Payne v. Tennessee* (1991), a Court ruling upheld the use of victim impact statements in capital cases. The facts in *Payne* were as follows: On June 27, 1987, Payne's girlfriend, Charisse Christopher, resisted his sexual advances. Payne apparently left Mrs. Christopher's house after the rebuff and began drinking and using cocaine. Less than an hour later, police officer Sam Wilson found Mrs. Christopher, 28, and her 2-year-old daughter, Lacie Jo, on the kitchen floor slashed to death with a butcher knife. Nicholas, Mrs. Christopher's son, then 3, was also stabbed but survived. He no doubt saw his mother and sister horribly murdered.

In death penalty cases in many states, juries determine the sentence. Capital cases are the only crime in which juries are always permitted to impose sentence, although judges do have review power over the jury's sentence. In a 6-to-3 ruling, the *Payne* Court reversed the previous recent rulings and declared that juries choosing life or death for convicted murderers may consider the victim's character and the suffering of the victim's relatives.

Justice David H. Souter, who concurred with the majority opinion in *Payne,* argued that it was morally defensible to consider such evidence when sentencing a murderer. Souter noted that defendants can use mitigating (moderating) circumstances to argue for a more lenient sentence. Indeed, Payne did so. A psychologist testified that Payne had a low intelligence score and a pastor noted that Payne regularly attended church. In addition, Payne had no prior criminal record. Justice Souter said that any failure to take into account "victim impact" leads to an imbalanced process of justice.

What was the view of the minority of the Court in *Payne*? Justice John Paul Stevens was most eloquent. First, he was concerned that the Court too easily overruled past decisions, ignoring *stare decisis,* the legal standard that courts should rely on past decisions. Justice Stevens then argued that any decision, especially one that imposes the death penalty, should be based solely on evidence that informs the jury about the nature of the crime and the character of the defendant. He said that evidence that serves no other purpose than to appeal to the sympathies and emotions of the jurors had never before been permissible.

Currently, 41 states permit a victim impact statement. The 1994 federal crime bill gave victims the right to make a statement in federal cases involving violent crime or sexual abuse.

THE DEFENDANT

The most visible attribute of a defendant is her or his physical appearance. In the first trial of the brothers Menendez, charged with murdering their parents, the jury was unable to reach a verdict, compelling the state to retry the defendants. The appearance of the baby-faced Menendez brothers, with their "eagle scout," attractive, and vulnerable appearance (their lawyer had them dress in sweaters and button-down shirts) may have led some jurors to wonder how the defendants could have done the terrible deed. The brothers used an "extenuating" defense in the first trial: They killed their parents because their father had sexually abused them. This defense may very well have been enhanced by the appearance of vulnerability and all-American good looks. However, the judge in the second trial ruled that there was not enough evidence to use the extenuating (sexual abuse) defense, and the brothers were found guilty of murder in that trial.

The Attractiveness Bias

There is evidence that attractive individuals have an advantage over their less favorably endowed counterparts in every part of the criminal justice system. Deborah Davis (1991) noted that attractive individuals are less likely to get caught at illegal activities, and if caught, they are less likely to be reported, and if the case comes to trial, they are treated more leniently.

Research shows that good-looking customers who shoplift are less likely to be detected and when detected less likely to be reported than less attractive culprits (Davis, 1991). Davis surmised that people believe reporting an attractive shoplifter would cause more harm than reporting a homely culprit. This judgment is based on the cultural assumption that attractive individuals are more successful than less attractive people and therefore have more to lose if arrested.

Does attractiveness have an impact on the jury? Davis (1991) reported a study conducted in the Pennsylvania criminal courts in which researchers rated the physical attractiveness of 74 male defendants. A definite correlation was observed between attractiveness and sentencing. The study, controlling for the seriousness of the crime, found that the more attractive the defendant was, the lighter was the sentence. In fact, attractive male defendants, compared to less attractive males, were more likely to avoid serving any time at all. Similar effects occur in the civil arena, where judges in small claims courts have been found to make larger awards to attractive plaintiffs.

There are limits to the attractiveness bias, however, and these appear when individuals use their physical attributes as a weapon to carry out a crime. Con artists who use their undeniable physical allure to swindle a victim would face a harsh judgment from judges and jurors (Sigall & Ostrove, 1975). However, a juror would give an edge to an attractive bank robber over a less attractive one because, presumably, a robber cannot use his or her good looks to advantage when holding up the local bank (Sigall & Ostrove, 1975). In addition, jurors are also less likely to believe that attractive people have a need to commit certain "attractiveness-related" crimes. Jurors are particularly unlikely to believe, for example, that an attractive man would need to commit rape, although they are particularly likely to believe an attractive woman would be raped (Davis, 1991). Consider the role of the attractiveness of the accused and the accuser in 'Love and Murder in New Jersey" in the Courtroom Applications box on page 66.

Baby-faced Criminals.   Facial appearance has been shown to have a strong effect on our perceptions of a person's overall attractiveness through much of the life span (Berry, 1991). One facial attribute that seems to enhance attractiveness is a "baby-faced" appearance. For example, attractive people whose faces have a babyish look are perceived as warmer, more honest, and more sincere than individuals without that facial characteristic. A series of studies by Leslie Zebrowitz and her co-workers have shown that facial maturity is significantly related to judgments of personality (Zebrowitz, & McDonald, 1991; Zebrowitz, Olson, & Hoffman, 1993). Zebrowitz et al. found that a mature-looking defendant, compared to a baby-faced male defendant, was more likely to be convicted by jurors in a case involving negligence and less likely to be convicted in a case involving intent (Zebrowitz & McDonald, 1991). The rationale for these findings is that baby-faced individuals are viewed as naive and thus it is conceivable that they might neglect to carry out necessary precautions (negligence verdicts). However, these defendants are also more likely to be perceived as honest and therefore thought to be less likely to do something illegal (intent verdicts).

In civil cases, Zebrowitz and McDonald (1991) found that the less childlike defendants looked, the larger the awards they had to pay to plaintiffs—but only

COURTROOM APPLICATIONS

Love and Murder in New Jersey

Stephen J. Adler (1995) investigated the dynamics of the jury in several trials. Adler's technique was to follow the trials and then engage in long interviews with the jurors.

One case is especially relevant to the issue of attractiveness. Kevin Schneider, a good-looking, self-possessed Newark (New Jersey) narcotics police officer, was on trial for the murder of his estranged wife's lover. His wife, Marisol, reported that Kevin had burst into their home, found Fabio Hernandez nude in his wife's bed, beat him up, and then shot him with his (Kevin's) police revolver.

Kevin told a different story. He had gone to visit his wife, as he had in the past. He had been surprised by Fabio, who had sucker-punched him, and a fight had ensued. During the fight, a struggle for Kevin's weapon had occurred and Fabio was accidentally shot. There were some inconsistencies in both stories. For one thing, Kevin was a martial arts expert, and Fabio was an out-of-shape, obese man. Kevin should not have had much difficulty subduing Fabio.

Kevin's lawyer put Marisol's reputation on trial. He painted her as a woman who had been promiscuous since she was a teenager. That tactic worked. Adler (1995) quotes one juror as continually muttering that Marisol was "a shit, bitch, whore" (p. 188). But it was not only Marisol's moral defects that convinced the jury to acquit Kevin Schneider. Marisol was not very attractive. When Marisol Schneider took the witness stand, one male juror thought "Why would Kevin be so obsessed with her that he'd want to kill someone?" (p. 185). Adler describes Marisol as a mousy young woman with big teeth and kinky hair. The jurors were disappointed in her looks. They had expected a more bewitching figure in this drama about love and murder.

Kevin, on the other hand, was attractive. He was boyish looking, baby-faced; he was comfortable on the witness stand. He spoke easily, looked at the jurors, and appeared very sincere. Of course, Kevin was a narcotics officer and had testified before juries over 200 times previously as part of his job (Adler, 1995). The jury decided that Kevin had suffered enough in the year of turmoil before the trial. They decided that the homely Marisol had lied in the past and was lying now. A close examination of her account of the events would show that her story had fewer holes than Kevin's version; but to the jury, she was damaged goods and not credible.

if the plaintiffs were relatively baby-faced. Baby-faced plaintiffs seemed to be "protected" from defendants with a mature appearance by being awarded large amounts. These were simulated trials and could not show whether having a baby face is an attribute powerful enough to override other factors. However, there is enough evidence to suggest that jurors and judges are unconsciously affected by cultural stereotypes concerning appearance and that such factors play a role in the outcome of both civil and criminal trials.

Roots of the Attractiveness Bias.   One reason that physical attractiveness looms large in our judgments of individuals is the cultural stereotype that what is beautiful is good. We tend to believe that physically attractive individuals possess a wide range of desirable characteristics and that they are generally better people than unattractive individuals (Dion, Berscheid, & Walster, 1972). Bassili (1981) found evidence to support another attractiveness stereotype: What is beautiful is glamorous. We think that good-looking people have energy, competence, and good social skills (Eagly, Ashmore, Makhijani, & Longo, 1991).

However, not all researchers believe that attractiveness is a critical variable in the outcome of a trial. Attractiveness may very well play an important role in the early stages of the criminal justice process—such as the decision by a police officer to arrest a suspect—but in a trial, the attractiveness of the defendant and the victim becomes embedded in a network of law and evidence that may substantially reduce its initial impression on the jurors. In Kalven and Zeisel's (1966) American jury study, judges were asked to comment on factors other than the evidence that might have influenced the jury; they responded that certain defendant characteristics probably had an influence. Based on the judges' observations, Kalven and Zeisel's tongue-in-cheek advice to defendants was that he or she be disabled, elderly, or widowed; be in the military, or the clergy; have a pregnant wife; have children; be attractive; and be repentant. A defendant's personal attributes are especially important when the jury is uncertain about the evidence. Amid such ambivalence, personal attributes tend to be important. But in general, Kalven and Zeisel are inclined to believe that a defendant's attractiveness in itself is not a vital factor in trial outcomes. In a courtroom proceeding, the characteristics of the defendant will likely have less influence than more tangible factors, such as prior record, status and standing in the community, and credibility.

Defendant Status and Prior Record

Social psychologists have cataloged the advantages of higher status in both social and professional life (Bushman, 1988; Jemmott & Gonzalez, 1989; Skolnick & Shaw, 1994). In the legal arena, Rosoff (1989) reported that one high-status group, physicians, appeared to be shielded from punishment on minor offenses (insurance overbilling) but were judged more severely than lower-status individuals for serious offenses.

Shaw and Skolnick (1996) have clarified the manner in which status acts as a protective shield. These researchers found that individuals are willing to forgive physicians for minor legal offenses that are not professionally related; but when physicians transgress in professional activity, the higher their status, the more severe will be the condemnation. It appears that we are willing to forgive physicians (and probably other high-status individuals) for minor transgressions because we value them and need their services, but we will hold them to a higher standard in their professional realm. When physicians violate professional trust, we are more punitive in judging the high-status than the lower-status individuals.

In addition to the defendant's status, an offender's prior record may also be an issue. Information about a defendant's prior behavior may be admitted into evidence if the court finds that such information has a probative value (aids the decision maker) that outweighs the prejudice against the defendant. Not surprisingly, evidence about a prior criminal record makes conviction more probable (Borgida & Park, 1988).

Edith Greene and Mary Dodge (1995) investigated another aspect of the defendant's prior record. The U.S. Supreme Court in *Dowling v. United States* (1990) held that evidence of a *prior acquittal* does not prejudice the defendant. Dowling had previously been found *not guilty* of charges similar to the home break-in trial that was the focus of *Dowling v. United States* (1990). Dowling claimed that information about prior acquittal for a similar crime prejudiced his case. He argued his case on the grounds of double jeopardy and fundamental fairness (Greene & Dodge, 1995). The research evidence indicated that mock jurors *do not* convict a previously acquitted defendant at a higher rate than jurors who had no information about that prior acquittal. However, Greene and Dodge (1995) found that jurors' knowledge of a prior conviction does increase the probability of a guilty verdict in a subsequent trial.

We should note at this juncture that we have barely mentioned two apparently critical factors: the race and the sex of the defendant. We have scanty data derived from jury trials documenting racial prejudice among jurors; yet casual observation of jury selection in any case involving a black defendant suggests that lawyers, at least, believe racial attitudes are critical to the outcome of a trial. African Americans are often underrepresented on the jury rolls and may be excluded by challenges from actually serving when race could be an issue. While the U.S. Supreme Court has condemned the practice of using race or gender to exclude jurors, prejudice is difficult to document. Moreover, we are only beginning to understand the relationships between the characteristics of the defendant and those of the jurors (Kerr, Hymes, Anderson, & Weathers, 1995). We explore the issue of race in the justice system in later chapters.

The Psychology of Rapists

Researchers have focused on male sexual aggression because almost all reported rapes of adults, male and female, are committed by men. To get a close but still ethical look at sexual aggression in progress, Gordon N. Hall and Richard Hirschman (reported in Youngstrom, 1992) designed an experimental situation to serve as a metaphor for rape. The goal was to see whether men would "sexually aggress" against a woman by showing her pornographic slides, knowing that she would find the slides offensive (Youngstrom, 1992). Hall and Hirschman asked 250 male college students to distract a female confederate from a memory test by showing her slides. The men had a choice of slides to show: neutral, sexual, explicitly sexual, or deviantly sexual. The men were told that the female confederate "strongly disliked" pornography, and each man showed the slides while alone in a room with her.

The researchers ran this experiment five separate times, and on each occasion male subjects overwhelmingly (90 percent) showed either the explicit or deviant slides to the female confederate. One explanation may be simply that the male subjects did not care about the sensibilities of the woman and, in effect, symbolically raped her when given a chance to do so. It is also possible that since the assigned task was to distract the woman, they felt explicit slides would be more effective.

It appears that only a small minority of rapists are sexual outlaws driven by sadistic impulses. It seems that far more common are men with a normal sexual orientation who rape impulsively as the opportunity presents itself, often while on a date. In a 1987 survey of 3,187 college women, 15 percent said they had been raped. Eight out of ten said they had known the man who did it, and for 56 percent the rape occurred while on a date (Koss, Gidycz, & Wisniewski, 1987). These "date" rapists are opportunistic rapists and differ from the sadistic, compulsive rapist.

Malamuth (1986) conducted a study of the psychological characteristics of males who were prone to sexual violence against women. Malamuth investigated how six variables related to self-reported sexual aggression. The six predictor variables were dominance as a sexual motive (the degree to which feelings of dominance are important motives for sexual behavior), hostility toward women, attitudes of acceptance of sexual violence, antisocial characteristics/psychoticism, sexual experience, and physiological arousal to depictions of rape. The dependent variable was sexual aggression (assessed with a test that measured the use of pressure, coercion, force, and so on in a sexual relationship).

Malamuth found positive correlations between five of the six predictor variables and naturalistic sexual aggression against women (psychoticism was the only variable that did not correlate significantly with aggression). However, the presence of any one predictor alone was not likely to result in sexual aggression against women. For example, arousal to depictions of rape is not likely to translate into sexual aggression unless other variables are present. Therefore, because a male is aroused by depictions of rape does not mean that he will be sexually violent. There is no simple answer to the question of who will be likely to commit sexual violence against women. But the research does suggest that a not insignificant portion of the male population, perhaps 35 percent, possesses the requisite rape predictor variables.

THE JUDGE

When society elevates judges to a position on the bench, it expects them to bring wisdom and experience to bear on matters in dispute. Judges are attracted to the power of the bench because they are expected to establish and illuminate principles designed to guide people in their lives. This is what draws attorneys to leave lucrative law practices and become public servants. The founders of our country also recognized the importance of judicial power in framing the Constitution, giving judges a separate branch of government and providing individual federal judges with life tenure, subject to removal only by impeachment.

Judges as Decision Makers

An important constitutional objective is that judges be independent decision makers, that they rule on cases without personal gain from the outcome, and that they rule without fear of reprisal from a president or even a public that dislikes a decision. Chief Justice Warren Burger was appointed to the U.S. Supreme Court by President Richard Nixon, yet when Nixon tried blocking the release of incriminating tapes during the Watergate scandal, Chief Justice Burger wrote the opinion that sealed the fate of the Nixon presidency, leading to Nixon's resignation (*United States v. Nixon,* 1974).

To secure judges' freedom from outside threats and pressures, they have been made immune from suit for almost anything they do from the bench. For example, in *Mireles v. Waco,* (1991), the U.S. Supreme Court held that a judge was entitled to absolute immunity while on the bench. In this case, Judge Raymond Mireles of the Superior Court in Van Nuys, California, ordered police officers to seize Howard Waco, a public defender, who was in another courtroom about to represent a client before another judge. Mr. Waco was late for Judge Mireles's morning calendar call. Waco alleged that Judge Mireles ordered the police to use excessive force and that he, Mr. Waco, was dragged backward down the hall, cursed at by the police, and deposited in Judge Mireles's courtroom. Waco sued the judge for $350,000 in damages. He lost.

The Supreme Court stated in *Mireles* that "judicial immunity is not overcome by allegations of bad faith or malice." This doctrine of **judicial immunity** dates to the nineteenth century and has as its purpose the protection of judges' independence by making certain that judges will not be sued by angry or disappointed litigants. The doctrine does not make judges immune from criminal prosecution if they commit crimes. Nor does it protect them from suit in "nonjudicial actions." If, for example, a judge sexually harassed an employee, the affected employee could bring a suit against the judge. But the power of the judge to run an orderly courtroom is sweeping.

Aside from the Supreme Court, which issues decisions under the scrutiny of an eager press and public, other judges carry on their decision making away from the limelight. They preside over (bench) trials, write lengthy findings of fact and conclusions of law, publish opinions in the more important cases, and rule on the admissibility of evidence. Unlike jurors, who can walk away after a decision and never explain their verdicts, judges are compelled to state reasons for their decisions and to apply their reasoning to facts presented on the record.

Lest we paint too strong a picture of judicial independence, there are competing political, professional, personal, and social psychological pressures that restrain judges. True, federal judges are appointed for life and guaranteed by the Constitution not to have to take a pay cut (except through inflation), but judges are dependent on Congress for money to build their courthouses, pay their staffs, and buy their library books. Imagine a judge without a courthouse or a library or a law clerk and you have a picture of the reality of separation of powers in the federal government.

Federal judges also depend on Congress for their workload and can be controlled by congressional lawmaking. Congress can open the spigot and flood the federal courts with petty drug cases and fender-bender accidents. Congress can also set up the rules for deciding cases, taking away some of the discretion and ambiguity that can enhance judicial power. For example, in the sentencing area, Congress has done so through a combination of sentencing guidelines and mandatory minimum sentences for drug and gun violations.

Professionally, a judge takes a solemn oath to follow the law. When the law is general, as the Constitution necessarily is, the judge can decide what type of process is due, whether protection is equal, whether a search is reasonable. But when the law is clear (someone possessing more than 1.7 ounces of crack cocaine must go to jail for ten years), the judge has to follow the law.

Personally and professionally, judges are often isolated from the world they knew as lawyers. They see their former colleagues every day in the courthouse, but as judges have to keep their distance to avoid the appearance, or the reality, of favoring their friends. Often active in the political community before ascending to the bench, judges are expected to be neutral and to avoid membership in partisan organizations and clubs that practice discrimination. And judges work independently, perhaps with the help of law clerks and secretaries. They are expected not to consult with others in deciding the cases before them. They are to face that lonely task with the evidence and arguments presented by the parties, not the advice of others.

This is not to say that the lot of a judge is to be pitied. The respect and rewards given by society and the legal profession keep the line of candidates full. The purpose of highlighting the tensions in the job is to stimulate thought about the social psychology of judging. What motivates a successful lawyer to want to be a judge? What limits on judicial power are likely to control the excesses? What happens when we put a human being on a raised dais and ask all to rise when he or she enters the room? What feedback mechanisms are there to keep this person in touch with reality so that the wisdom applied is not too independent of everyday common sense?

Judging the Judges: Conduct on the Bench

Who judges the judges? In 1980, the Judicial Conduct and Disability Act was passed as a means of holding federal judges accountable and to guide the judicial branch of the federal government in regulating itself. Of course, the U.S. Congress has the power to impeach a federal judge, but that has been a rare event, occurring only a few times in U.S. history. Generally, self-regulation of federal judges falls to the chief judges of the federal circuit courts and to the judicial council, a body of judges representing other judges (Barr & Willging, 1993). While the 1980 act specifies formal procedures for the investigation and resolution of complaints, such as misconduct or a judge's inability to perform his or her duties, it appears that whenever possible, chief judges prefer informal methods of handling problems. They feel that if a judge has a physical or mental disability, the more humane approach is to handle it on a personal basis rather than make it public.

In even more sensitive cases, such as sexual harassment, there appear to be very few on-the-record complaints and there is some evidence that sexual misconduct might be the "untold story" of judicial impropriety (Barr & Willging, 1993). Generally, the chief judges of the federal circuits believe that the 1980 act has been a good thing. The act has given the public a chance to challenge judges' misconduct and it permits complaints to be evaluated by the judge's peers. On the other hand, chief judges complain that most of the complaints about judges lack merit (Barr & Willging, 1993).

In a recent incident, after many weeks of controversy, the case of Judge Loren Duckman was considered by the New York State Commission on Judicial Conduct charged with investigating cases of judicial misconduct. The commission, which has only one half-time investigator and usually takes a couple of years to resolve a case, operates in secrecy (Purnick, 1996).

The case of Judge Duckman was high profile. Judge Duckman had used racist and sexist language in court and had been insensitive to domestic violence, making negative remarks about the victims of such abuse. However, the most serious charge against the judge had been that he permitted a defendant to be released, despite strong evidence of the defendent's abusive and violent behavior against his girlfriend. Subsequent to that release, the defendant killed his girlfriend and himself (Purnick, 1996).

Clearly, the state commission could not adequately police the New York judicial system. Its lack of personnel and modest funding made it possible for the commission to deal with only the most outrageous cases of judicial misconduct. The Duckman incident was one of these cases. The judge was eventually reassigned to a less sensitive judicial post.

Judges and Gender Bias in the Court.   Although more women have recently entered the legal profession, numerous surveys about courtroom interactions indicate that subtle and not so subtle gender bias exists (Riger, Foster-Fishman, Nelson-Kuna, & Curran, 1995). Women lawyers generally perceive more gender bias than do male lawyers, who, in turn, are more aware of bias against women than are the judges. Judges, according to male attorneys, trust or respect other (male) lawyers with whom they have had informal contacts—interactions usually denied women attorneys (Riger et al., 1995).

Perhaps the most troublesome issue is what Riger and her colleagues call "instrumental bias," the use of disparaging gender-related comments as a trial tactic. One prominent female attorney recalled being referred to as "that young lady" during a well-publicized trial. A male judge suggested that in his experience, "female counsel are not above taking advantage of their gender . . . especially before a jury" (Riger et al., 1995, p. 471).

Research has shown that quite subtle events in the courtroom can detract from a woman's performance as counsel. Judges may call a woman attorney "dear" or "sweetheart," or the opposing attorney or other court employees might make negative comments about her appearance or weight or dress. These may be "courtroom tactics" and not gender bias, but it is up to the judge to maintain proper courtroom decorum (Riger et al., 1995).

The Role of the Judge

Under the common law system of England and the United States, judges are drawn from the legal profession. In England, judges are chosen from the ranks of the barristers, the 10 percent of the legal profession who are trial lawyers and are considered the elite of the profession.

In the United States, judges are practicing lawyers, legal academics, or researchers. They put on their judicial robes without any serious training in how to carry out their newly won roles. In France, in contrast, future judges are specifically trained for their roles and are part of the civil service establishment. A law student who wishes to become a judge in France will follow a different track from that of a law student who wishes to become an advocate. Roman law tradition influences the European continent. In that tradition, the judiciary is part of the administration of the country, which explains the different track for judges. Future French judges attend academies that train them for a judicial role as opposed to an advocate's role.

In the United States, the judge plays a dominant but neutral role in the proceedings—sometimes more active, sometimes less so. In the criminal justice system, the defendant must appear before the judge soon after arrest. The judge determines whether there is sufficient evidence to hold the defendant and makes a decision on the setting of bail to guarantee the defendant's future appearance in the courtroom. At about this time the defendant is arraigned before the judge and must enter a plea. If a guilty plea is entered, the judge will determine whether that plea was entered freely and not coerced by the police.

The defendant may decide to work out a plea bargain and enter a plea to a lesser charge. As only 5 or 10 percent of all criminal cases go to trial, the judge may be involved in ruling on any deal, or plea bargain, made between the defendant's lawyer and the prosecutor. Bargainers negotiate against the background of what the presiding judge will find acceptable, and the judge has the last word on the viability of the bargain. However, much of the time the judge is quite content to trust the prosecutor's judgment.

The role of the judge at trial is to be a neutral arbiter between the two sides. This is true in both civil and criminal trials. Judges rule on the admissibility of evidence both before and during the trial, interpret the law as it applies to the case, and instruct the jury on the law at the end of the trial.

Judges also instruct the jury in the law. Finally, and perhaps most important, judges impose penalties in criminal trials. These last two functions—instructing the jury and sentencing the defendant in criminal trials—are central to the judge's duties. However, a discussion of these functions properly belongs within the context of the basic drama of the justice system: the trial. We consider that in later chapters.

Setting bail, administering pretrial hearings, ruling on matters of law, instructing the jury, and sentencing the defendant are the tangible and visible functions of a judge in the trial. The judge is a respected figure in the courtroom and jurors often look to him or her for guidance in how to evaluate the evidence. Of course, the judge will not say to the jury, "This looks bad for the defendant. He's guilty," or "This plaintiff is trying to squeeze every dime she can." A judge may influence the jurors in much more subtle ways, however.

Allen Hart (1995) asked jurors waiting to serve in actual cases to view a videotape of a trial. All jurors saw the same trial but they were given different versions of the judge's reading of the same instructions. Judges in the videotapes gave subtle, nonverbal cues that suggested they thought the defendant was guilty or not guilty. Hart found that jurors generally followed the judge's nonverbal influence. That is, if the judge intimated that the defendant was guilty, jurors were more likely to vote guilty than if the judge leaned toward a not guilty finding. This effect was especially strong if the judge suggested guilt in both the preevidence instructions and the posttrial instructions.

These findings support previous research by Blanck (1993), who found that judges' nonverbal behavior while reading instructions to the jury conveyed their feelings about the case. Judges who expected a guilty verdict were perceived by observers to be less competent, less warm, and more anxious.

In a civil court, judges have much the same duties as their criminal trial counterparts but can be much more active in reaching resolutions. In civil courts, judges manage large staffs, schedule and process cases, oversee the probate system in which wills are adjudicated and administered, and encourage settlements (Menkel-Meadow, 1985; Wall & Rude, 1991). Unlike the criminal justice system in which judges do not usually take part in any pretrial settlement, the civil arena invites the judge's participation. In other words, the judge is encouraged to act as a referee to permit parties to settle their dispute without the expense of a trial. Federal courts encourage judicial mediation (*Federal Rules of Civil Procedure*, 1990). Most states also encourage judges to mediate in civil cases. Mediation essentially means resolution of the conflict without a trial and saves the cost of that trial.

Judges tend to mediate in cases in which they believe they can have an impact. In some cases, the parties are intransigent and no amount of mediation will lead to a pretrial resolution (Wall & Rude, 1991).

Judges as Policymakers

Federal judges make up the third branch of the United States government, the judicial branch. Alexander Bickel, a former Yale law professor and author, astutely labeled the judiciary "the least dangerous branch," a nickname that stuck. Courts have little power to enforce their orders, other than the moral force of law and an American civilization with some tradition of honoring the law (in tension with a tradition of flouting the law).

As a branch of government, the judiciary has some inherent powers of self-governance. In addition, Congress has explicitly given the judiciary the power to enact national rules of procedure for the federal courts. This includes the power to decide how many jurors will sit on a given type of case, how many cases can be consolidated into one large trial, or how many charges can be brought against a criminal defendant in one trial.

As policymakers, judges take a broad view. For example, when judges decide to admit or exclude evidence on the use of a new scientific test, they are making policy. When this happens, judges want to know more than their own collective experiences might tell them. One source of information is the social sciences. Judges are often not convinced of the usefulness of laboratory-based experiments because the research seems to be far removed from the courtroom; for them, systematic examination of court activity is the most persuasive evidence. Looking at a cross-section of cases rather than a select few gives judges a convincing picture of the backdrop against which they must legislate.

SUMMARY

Because the state assumes the burden of prosecution, the victim is left with little formal power or role in the proceedings and therefore is the forgotten actor in the criminal justice system. However, victims are the gatekeepers of the system because most investigations begin when victims notify the police of the crime.

Evidence indicates that violent crime has increased markedly in recent decades, although the rate of increase appears to have leveled off. In fact, the most recent data indicate that serious crime declined in the United States for four consecutive years through 1995. Criminologists are not sure why, and they are equally unsure about whether the decline represents a long-term trend or is simply a statistical fluctuation.

The willingness of victims to report criminal acts is one significant indicator of the relationship between police and citizens, reflecting victims' perceptions of the effectiveness with which society fights crime. Experimental studies of crimes, simulated in the laboratory or in the field, confirm that the rate of reporting by bystanders is also quite low, ranging from zero to 40 percent.

Determining the cost of violent crimes is useful for public policy purposes. These monetary estimates provide a concrete measure of the crime problem. Although victims bear the immediate costs of crime, society shoulders a major portion of the financial burden. Mental health costs for victims have been estimated at a minimum of $7 billion per year, and insurance costs reach a minimum of $45 billion. Total crime costs may be over $450 billion each year.

Victims of violent crimes sustain long-term mental and physical health problems. Research has revealed that physical and sexual victimization are linked to a lifetime of increased risk for mental disorders. The more severe the crime, the greater is the physical and emotional distress reported by victims.

Rape victims suffer particularly debilitating aftereffects of the violence. Rape survivors often exhibit a number of related symptoms including emotional responses, changes in lifestyle, and difficulty in day-to-day functioning. Immediately after the rape, victims typically experience an acute phase in which they have headaches, difficulty sleeping, fear of any situation that reminds them of the assault, and a tendency to blame themselves for the rape. This constellation of symptoms is known as rape trauma syndrome.

In the battered spouse syndrome, the batterer comes to dominate the partner, physically, psychologically, sexually, financially, and emotionally. This gives the batterer systematic control and domination. The abused spouse feels somehow at fault and tries to minimize or hide the abuse.

Some can endure the abuse no longer and commit murder in self-protection. However, self-defense is not usually a successful plea when an abused woman kills her abuser. Evidence suggests that battered women who kill are more likely to be acquitted when they had suffered severe abuse in combination with a "disassociated" state of mind. That is, juries are more likely to forgive a woman who "loses her mind" and kills impulsively after continual and severe abuse.

The legal system has tried to find avenues by which the victim can have a role in the justice system. In some jurisdictions, families of crime victims may address the court before the judge pronounces sentence. Some states have passed legislation, called victim impact laws, that explicitly considers in the sentencing process the impact of the crime on the victim, the victim's family, and the community.

There is evidence that people who are attractive have an advantage over their less favorably endowed counterparts at every stage of the criminal justice system. Attractive individuals are less likely to get caught at illegal activities; if caught, they are less likely to be reported; and if the case comes to trial, they are treated more leniently. There are limits to the attractiveness bias, however, and these emerge when individuals use their physical attributes as a weapon to carry out a crime.

Facial appearance has been shown to affect strongly our perceptions of a person's overall attractiveness through much of the life span. Defendants whose faces have a "babyish" appearance are perceived as warmer, more honest, and more sincere than individuals without that facial characteristic. There is enough evidence to suggest that jurors and judges are unconsciously affected by cultural stereotypes concerning appearance, such as a baby-faced look, so that attractive defendants are judged somewhat less harshly than less well-favored individuals in the outcome of both civil and criminal trials.

Judges in the adversarial system act as neutral umpires, ruling on the evidence but not taking a direct part in the trial. Judges tend to be relatively immune from sanction and most indiscretions by judges in the federal system are handled "in house." Judges may be decision makers when a jury is waived or in certain cases in which juries are not routinely used. They preside over trials, write lengthy findings of fact and conclusions of law, publish opinions in the more important cases, and rule on the admissibility of evidence. Unlike jurors, who can walk away after a decision and never explain their decision, judges must state their reasons and apply their reasoning to facts presented on the record, not to conjectures and personal experiences or expectations.

Judges, by their everyday decisions and in governing the judicial branch, also act as policymakers. Perhaps the most influential task of the judge occurs when he or she metes out punishment. In almost all criminal cases, it is the judge who imposes the sentence.

CHAPTER
4

Actors in the Criminal Justice System: Police and Lawyers

POLICE OFFICERS

An arrest is the most significant action police officers take. An **arrest** is an act by a legally appointed authority, the police officer, that deprives a citizen of freedom. Legally, an arrest can occur when police have a warrant or there is evidence of *probable cause* that a crime has occurred (or in some rare cases, that it is probably about to occur) and that the suspect can be linked directly to that crime.

Two elements define *probable cause:* a crime was committed, and the suspect was most probably the individual who committed that crime (*Georgetown,* 1980). One result of an arrest based on probable cause is that the police officer may search the defendant and the immediate area within the suspect's control (*Georgetown,* 1980). However, if a judge later finds that probable cause was not present, the evidence gathered by that search, no matter how incriminating, may be excluded from being used to show the suspect's guilt.

Whether an arrest has taken place may be a subject of occasional dispute. Police do not always use the magic words: "You are under arrest." In legal terms, an arrest takes place when "by means of physical force or a show of authority . . . freedom of movement [is] restrained" (*United States v. Mendenhall,* 1980, p. 553).

In a U.S. Supreme Court case (*Florida v. Royer,* 1983), the issue was whether a legal arrest had taken place before the officers searched the defendant—that is, was there probable cause to arrest the defendant? In *Royer,* the defendant was stopped by the police because he fit the profile of a drug courier. Royer had different names on his airline ticket and driver's license, paid cash for an expensive ticket, had little or no luggage, and was nervous and evasive. The federal agents "asked" Royer to accompany them to a mail room for questioning. There, Royer agreed to permit his luggage to be searched. Royer's suitcase was filled with marijuana. The Court held, in a 5–4 decision, that "as a practical matter, Royer was under arrest," and therefore his consent to the search was invalidated by his prior illegal arrest. Why was the arrest illegal? The Court indicated that the drug courier profile was not a sufficient basis for probable cause.

The officer on the street has broad discretion to decide whom to arrest. The police officer probably has more freedom to act than any of the other actors in the criminal justice system. An arrest is a social encounter and turns on extralegal factors—primarily, the suspect's behavior—as much as it does on probable cause and evidence. A suspect who is disrespectful is much more likely to be arrested than one who is courteous and compliant. Other social factors are probably critical as well in affecting the officer's judgment, but the empirical evidence is meager. Certainly, a suspect's dress, verbal ability, social class, and other less obvious factors play a role in the officer's decision to arrest.

However, police cannot arrest someone because that person uses language that is annoying, or even offensive, when the language does not involve physical interference with officers or contain "fighting words." This assertion comes from *City of Houston v. Hill* (1987). In this civil suit, Raymond Hill, a homosexual rights advocate, habitually confronted police officers whom he thought were acting improperly. Houston had an ordinance that made it a misdemeanor, punishable by a $200 fine, to "oppose or molest or . . . interrupt . . . a police officer in the performance of his duty" (perhaps Houston had no women officers). Hill had objected to the actions of two police officers who had stopped traffic for a friend of the officers. Hill, who had observed this action, proceeded to reprimand the officers, who then arrested Hill. Justice Brennan and the Court ruled that the freedom to oppose a police officer verbally without being arrested is a principal marker of a free nation.

An arrest will likely be made only when the complainant states a clear preference to press charges. Rarely—less than 10 per cent of the time—will an arrest be made if the complainant refuses to press charges (Scrivner, 1994). In many ways, arresting suspects is the most satisfying part, albeit the most dangerous, of a police officer's job. It is a clear act of law enforcement. Number of arrests is also a measure of an officer's effectiveness and productivity. Arresting a suspect gives the frontline police officer a sense of accomplishment. It is a crime fighting act.

On the other hand, police officers carry out a number of functions other than crime fighting. Officers provide community service in a variety of ways, and they maintain public order, such as traffic control. They also serve a kind of quasi-official judicial function, acting as a kind of roving court by settling family and neighborhood conflicts and other disputes that might otherwise end up in the justice system.

None of these functions have quite the satisfaction of arresting a suspect and at least temporarily removing a potentially dangerous individual from the streets. Resolving other kinds of conflict provides less of a psychological boost for the police officer because the officer rarely learns the ultimate resolution of the conflict and the results of the intervention.

With an increasing number of female police officers in frontline positions, there is some evidence that women officers are better than their male counterparts at helping defuse and resolving noncriminal confrontations, such as family or neighborhood disputes. Apparently the presence of a woman officer does not challenge an already overheated male. The intervention of a male officer in a supercharged situation often further enrages a male disputant (Brewer & Wilson, 1995).

Police Behavior in Special Circumstances

Police officers often have to deal with social issues as much as they fight crime. Police are often called to intervene in family conflicts and to handle the homeless and the mentally ill, duties that are sometimes difficult.

The Mentally Ill. We have noted that whether an arrest is made often turns on the comportment of the suspect. Linda Teplin (1983, 1984, 1990a, 1990b) has studied police officers' reactions to individuals who have exhibited behaviors that could be classified as typical of those who are mentally disordered. Among the symptoms that provoke an arrest are verbal abuse, belligerence, and disrespect (Teplin, 1984). The mentally ill often display such behavior.

Table 4.1 shows the impact of displaying signs of mental disorder on the probability that a person will be arrested. The numbers in the sample are not very large; nevertheless, we see that there is a tendency to criminalize mental disorder. Many individuals who should be hospitalized are arrested instead. Police officers may often be aware that this is the case, but they also know that the mental health facilities may not be able to accept these individuals because of lack of room and funds. The person must be removed from the streets, and so arrests are made. The criminal justice system thus becomes the repository of many mentally disturbed individuals even though it was never designed to handle these people (Teplin, 1990a, 1990b). Neither police officers nor judges are trained as sophisticated psychological diagnosticians (Teplin, 1985).

Police officers are often on the front line of social issues that society has been unable to resolve. One of these issues obviously is how to deal with the mentally ill, many of whom are homeless. Another such issue is domestic violence.

Domestic Violence. Arrests issuing from domestic violence situations are fairly rare. One study reported that the arrest rate for wife assault is 21.1 percent, even when police have clear-cut (prima facie) evidence that such an assault had in fact occurred (Dutton & McGregor, 1992). Two other investigators reported that in 24 major U.S. cities the average arrest rate for wife assault was 10 per cent (Worden & Pollitz, 1984). Worden and Pollitz (1984) studied the reaction of police officers to family violence incidents by having trained observers accompany the police. The observers noticed that officers paid less attention to the legal issues (that is, clear physical evidence that someone was assaulted) than to their

TABLE 4.1   Comparison of Arrest Rates for Mentally Disordered and Non–Mentally Disordered Suspects for Different Crime Types

| | Signs of Mental Disorder | |
| | No | Yes |
Nature of Incident	Percent Suspects Arrested	
Violent personal crimes	58.8 (17)	100 (3)
Interpersonal conflict	14.9 (148)	11.1 (9)
Major property crimes (felonies)	83.3 (12)	100 (1)
Minor property crimes (misdemeanors)	61.2 (49)	100 (1)
Public health, safety, or decency violations	60.9 (23)	100 (1)
Violations of public order	20.7 (227)	46.7 (15)
Total	27.9 (478)	46.7 (30)

Source: Adapted from Teplin, 1984, Table 2, p. 799. Parentheses indicate total number in each category.

own notions about what kinds of behavior constituted spousal abuse. The low arrest rate suggests that officers may think that such arguments are simply "family matters."

Arrest rates in child abuse cases are also low. Dutton and McGregor (1992) reported studies that suggested the arrest rate for child abuse is only 1 per cent. Other studies report arrest rates of about 17 percent, still extremely low. The rates are low whether the batterer is the parent and the victim is the child, or vice versa. The child-parent assault almost always involves elderly parents. However, like children, the elderly are particularly dependent on other family members and therefore are not likely to press a complaint. Recall that without a complainant, police are unlikely to make an arrest (Scrivner, 1994). Apparently, police will not arrest a perpetrator of assault within the context of a family situation unless the injury is relatively severe and/or a weapon is used. Of course, that rule of thumb may not be limited to family assault cases. We would have to see whether the probability and threshold for arrest are lower in similar assault cases before we could conclude with certainty that family assaults are handled differently from other such crimes.

The available evidence reviewed by Dutton (1989) suggests that given a report of an assault, police are as likely to respond to and make an arrest in a spousal abuse case as they are in any assault case. Furthermore, the likelihood of an arrested person's going to trial and being convicted for spousal abuse (52 percent) is equal to the likelihood for other assaults (53 percent). It appears, therefore, that the real obstacle to dealing with family violence is the tendency of victims not to report the assaults. Police can do little about that.

Does Arrest Matter?

We have all seen stories about drug dealers and others who are arrested and within hours are back on the streets. Police officers certainly experience that kind of frustration every day. They must question whether it does any good to arrest people for the garden-variety crimes they encounter. The evidence again is not abundant, but we can infer that arrest does matter. For one thing, the threat of arrest has a deterrent effect on both property theft and drug use in college students. Of course, most college students are concerned about their future and arrest may end their education and may also impose other social costs. The informal deterrent effect of potential arrest likely has little effect on career criminals. For them, arrest is simply an occupational hazard, a cost of doing business.

Arrest does seem to matter in spousal abuse cases, but not always in a positive way for the victim. Currently, 15 states and the District of Columbia have passed mandatory arrest laws in cases of domestic battery. Do these mandatory laws work and are they a good idea? For one view, see "Spousal Abuse" in the Courtroom Applications box.

Abused spouses are often fearful of calling the police because their partners may have threatened them with future beatings; but once an arrest occurs, the abused spouse has begun to alter the power relationship in the dyad. Dutton,

COURTROOM APPLICATIONS

Spousal Abuse

A U.S. Court of Appeals decision raises questions about the effectiveness of interventions for men who abuse their partners and about how public policy on domestic violence is informed by research (Brickman, 1995).

In *Ricketts v. City of Columbia, Mo.* (1994), the appellate court upheld a lower court decision in favor of the Columbia, Missouri, city police who had been sued for their failure to arrest a husband for harassment of his abused wife. The suit claimed that the police officers' failure to arrest the husband for prior harassment was a cause of his subsequent rape of his wife and murder of her mother. The appellate decision was based largely on assumptions about the psychological and behavioral impact such arrests may have had.

Kimberly Roth married Sonny Stephens in 1982 and was verbally and physically abused by him throughout their relationship. She received several protective orders aimed at keeping Sonny away from her. He violated those court orders. In April 1987, Stephens went to Roth's parents' house, killed her mother, then raped Kimberly Roth.

Roth and her father, Paul Ricketts, sued the city for compensation for the injuries caused by Stephens's continued harassment, sexual assault, and murder. The jury found for the plaintiffs on all three counts. However, the district court set aside the verdict. The plaintiffs appealed. The court of appeals, in deciding for the city, suggested that "to find that the injuries caused by Sonny's violent acts of sexual harassment would have been avoided had Sonny been arrested for prior harassment would be an exercise in pure speculation. Such speculation cannot establish causation because it is equally plausible that an arrest for the prior harassment might as easily have spawned retaliatory violence from Sonny" (p. 14).

As Ellen Brickman (1995) noted in her commentary on *Ricketts,* the courts did not cite any research on the effects of arrest on subsequent behavior of batterers, but the decision reflects the murky nature of the knowledge concerning the effects of arrest.

Hart, Kennedy, and Williams (1993) observed that men who had been arrested for spousal assault were more likely to tell others about the assault than individuals who had not been arrested. Arrest makes the couple's network of friends aware of the abuse and puts a damper on future assaults. The abuser may fear that arrest is the first step leading to divorce and the loss of the relationship.

Of course, all the above assumes that abusers are calculating rationally. This assumption is often false. Sometimes arrest leads to more spousal violence. A

1993 study by criminologist Lawrence W. Sherman (cited in Brickman, 1995) found that among men who were unemployed, arrest for spousal abuse preceded a 44 percent increase in violence after arrest. For employed men, however, there was a corresponding 16 percent drop in future violence after arrest. Although the difference between the two groups is significant, the numbers show that employed men are not entirely committed to family harmony. The actual rate was 750 repeat assaults per 1,000 unemployed men, and 503 assaults per 1,000 employed men (Brickman, 1995).

Perhaps employed men have a greater stake in the future or are better able to control themselves—or maybe they have less time on their hands. In neither group does the rate of recidivism (repeat offenses) suggest strongly that arrest tends to deter future assaults. But we should ask, "What is the baseline rate of recidivism?" How often do abusers repeat their offenses when no arrests are made?

In any event, the depressing inference that can be made from Sherman's study is that laws requiring mandatory arrests in domestic violence cases may lead to an increase in future violence. This inference is particularly striking in communities in which unemployment rates are high. Spousal violence by men is a major cause of death and injury for American women. In roughly one-third of the murders of women, the killer was a boyfriend or spouse (Goleman, 1991). The mandatory arrest laws may have to be reconsidered in light of these findings.

Police Culture

Police officers are members of a quasi-military force that has its own culture, enforced by a strict hierarchy not unlike that of the armed forces. To function effectively in such an organization, recruits must adopt its norms, its formal and informal standards of behavior. If they do not, they will quite likely leave police service (Touhy, Wrennal, McQueen, & Stradling, 1993).

What do we mean by the term *police culture?* Studies examining police forces in several countries, including the United States, Canada, and Great Britain, found a number of common elements (Touhy et al., 1993). These elements included a high level of masculinity, which means not only that male officers outnumber female officers by large numbers but, as we might reasonably expect, that masculine values reflecting toughness and aggressiveness are highly valued. In addition, police follow a code of honor, and they face strong social pressure to act in accordance with the powerful social norms of this military type organization. The pressure is both formal and informal. There is obviously no written code or handbook, but police recruits soon understand clearly what their peers expect from them.

Police officers often bond together and see themselves as an in-group with different attitudes from the "civilians" they protect. Touey et al. (1993) noted that police officers often adopt a "code of silence" that requires primary loyalty to the organization, reinforced by strong group pressure not to report violations of procedures or laws by other officers. Officers may feel compelled not to report police wrongdoing at the risk of losing their standing within the organization. Police officers, as do other professionals, draw much of their personal identity and self-esteem from their official duties.

Of course, the possibility exists that individuals who join police forces are different from other individuals to begin with and the "police culture" is a reflection of these initial differences. This assumption appears not to be true. Police recruits do not seem to have personalities that are particularly different from those of the general population. College-educated police are motivated and assertive, and Touhy et al. (1993) reported that many, if not most, recruits are quite idealistic to start with, but very quickly adopt the more pragmatic and sometimes cynical attitudes of the senior police officer. A study of prejudice toward Aborigines among Australian police suggests that officers become more prejudiced the longer they serve (Wortley & Homel, 1995). Again, this study indicates that police attributes develop as a function of the officers' experiences.

An interesting finding of some studies is that the more advanced officers are in service, the lower are their arrest rates (Sleek, 1993b). This phenomenon seems to reflect the experienced officers' more realistic view of the criminal justice system. They do not expect arrest necessarily to lead to punishment. Therefore, when the officer confronts a crime that does not seem to be "severe," or one that does not seem to be amenable to resolution by the system, the officer may simply not make an arrest.

Police and Stress

A police officer's job is not the kind that he or she leaves at the office. This is especially true for officers who do special assignments. An officer of our acquaintance spent 16 years as an undercover agent in a large city. He lived essentially a double life: one as a drug courier, which required that he adopt dress, attitudes, and a lifestyle that fit his occupation, and the other as a devoted family man. Our friend managed to do this successfully, even though he was often away from home for weeks at a time. Nevertheless, many officers cannot balance such a split existence, and the divorce rate among police officers is much higher than in the general population (Sleek, 1993a).

Not only may the police officer encounter fairly routine danger on the job, but the dangers have been increasing because of the easy availability of guns in the 1990s. Weapons are a constant threat to police officers because they make each confrontation on the street potentially lethal. The proliferation of guns is not the only factor that affects the way an officer does his or her job. Police are aware that criminals, particularly teenagers, and even younger children do not hesitate to shoot at them. Police, along with other authority figures, have lost some of the respect they once commanded (Seymour, cited in Sleek, 1993b). Therefore, life is much more volatile on the street, infused with the threat of sudden and deadly violence.

Police officers are also faced with the job stresses all workers encountered in the 1990s: financial instability, threat of job layoffs, unpredictable shift rotations, and unexpected overtime. In addition, the police faced an increasingly hostile community.

The very qualities that may make a good police officer often hinder the officer from dealing effectively with job stress. Police officers learn to keep their emotions in check and are quite unlikely to confide in anyone other than their working partners. In addition, the working hours make it difficult to maintain normal and regular family contacts with spouses and children. Yet support from the family is crucial to an officer's mental health. The problem is that when a police officer is involved in a shooting or other tragic event, other family members are so directly affected that they might not be able to render social support. In addition, police officers are involved in a higher-than-average incidence of family violence in their own homes. This may result from job stress as well as a tendency to respond to threats more physically than others might (Scrivner, 1994).

Constitutional Rights: Searches and Confessions

When individuals assert that they have "rights," they mean, among other things, access to fair and equal treatment (Haney, 1991). Fair and equal treatment before the law is most clearly represented in the Fourteenth Amendment. Two clauses of that amendment are crucial: the Due Process Clause and the Equal Protection Clause. *Due process* means, essentially, that an individual has the right to an orderly and fair hearing of his or her case and must be notified in a timely manner of charges in the case. Due process is fundamental fairness and substantial justice. **Equal protection** means that no person (or class of persons) can be denied the same protection of the law that other persons and classes enjoy.

The issue of fair treatment is raised not only in the Fourteenth Amendment but also in other amendments in the Bill of Rights. For example, the Fourth Amendment prohibits unreasonable searches and seizures. This directly affects the police and their daily confrontations with citizens suspected of criminal acts. The Fifth Amendment includes a clause protecting citizens from being compelled to incriminate themselves ("taking the Fifth"). Again, this protection has implications for police interrogation of subjects. Of special importance is the Fourth Amendment and its implication that citizens have a *reasonable expectation of privacy.*

Fourth Amendment and Police Searches. If a police officer decides there is not sufficient evidence to support a judgment that probable cause has occurred, that is not necessarily the end of the matter. The police officer may try to develop further evidence and in doing so may obtain a search warrant from a magistrate if "a reasonably prudent person, based on the facts and circumstances known to the officer, would be warranted in concluding that the items sought are connected with criminal activity and they will be found in the place to be searched" (*Georgetown*, 1991, p. 220). The warrant must identify the person or place to be searched and the evidence sought.

The Fourth Amendment, as we know, protects citizens against *unreasonable searches and seizures* by the government (*Bivens v. Six Unknown Named Agents*, 1971). However, the right of a citizen to privacy must be measured against the government's need to enforce the law. Evidence obtained in violation of the

Fourth Amendment may not be used in court to demonstrate the guilt of a defendant: The incriminating evidence cannot be used against the apparently guilty defendant.

Why do the courts exclude such evidence? The *exclusionary rule* is there to prevent, or at least to deter, police misconduct. Therefore, the police bear a heavy punishment for violating this protection against unreasonable searches. Of course, one might argue that another way to handle the problem of illegal search and seizure would be to admit the incriminating evidence and prosecute the police for their disregard of the law. The courts long ago decided that letting individuals go free when their rights had been violated was a better solution than punishing the police for their misconduct. For one thing, this is a solution within the courts' control whereas the decision about whether to file a lawsuit against the police lies with the person whose property was unreasonably searched or seized.

Warrantless Searches. Under certain circumstances, officers can conduct searches without executing a warrant. Warrantless searches can be conducted only under limited circumstances. The exceptions, though, are as important as the rule. If stolen property is in plain view, a warrant is not needed. For example, if a police officer sees stolen property visible through a car window, a warrant need not be obtained. Warrantless searches may also occur when there are *exigent circumstances.* These dangerous or critical circumstances can occur if the police go to the house of a suspect they reasonably believe committed a crime and find that she or he is about to destroy evidence. Assume, in another instance, there is a trail of blood from the suspect's vehicle leading to his or her house and the house lights are on, suggesting that the suspect is inside. Given these circumstances, the police can conduct a warrantless search.

In addition, a warrantless search can occur when the suspect does not have a reasonable expectation of privacy. What is a reasonable expectation of privacy seems like an empirical question, but generally judges have relied on their own experience and impressions to decide the issue. For example, in *Rakas v. Illinois* (1978), passengers in an automobile could not suppress evidence taken from the glove compartment and under the seats because, the *Rakas* Court concluded, they had no reasonable expectation of *privacy* in an automobile.

Consent to Warrantless Searches. Another condition under which a search can occur without a warrant is when the suspect consents to such a search. Recall in *Royer* the suspect apparently freely consented to a search, even though his luggage contained illicit drugs, not pajamas. In addition, a warrantless search can be conducted with the consent of a *third party.* This raises interesting and troublesome questions. What third party can consent to a search of your property? Under what circumstances and what property can be searched? Furthermore, how do the courts determine when there is a "reasonable expectation of privacy"?

In *United States v. Matlock* (1974), the Supreme Court permitted third party searches on the basis of a *common authority* test. By common authority, the court meant, for example, a living arrangement in which more than one person shared the premises. You share an apartment with a roommate and thereby you both have common authority, but only over shared areas. If you each have your own bedroom, you do not have the power to consent to a search of your friend's room. But you may consent to a search of the shared living or dining room (Kagehiro & Taylor, 1992). Does this meet your sense of fairness? Well, there are significant differences between the legal definitions of consent and voluntariness and the perceptions of many individuals.

Dorothy Kagehiro and her colleagues have looked at these issues empirically. Kagehiro, Taylor, Laufer, and Harland (1991) posed several warrantless search situations for individuals to evaluate. In one scenario, a police officer goes to a residence jointly owned by two people who have lived together for a year. In all the scenarios, the third party accedes to a search of the common space. In one of three situations presented to evaluators, the suspect or coresident was absent during the search; in a second vignette, the police waited for the suspect or coresident to leave; and finally, a third vignette was presented to other evaluators in which the suspect or coresident was present at the search and protested against it to the police officers. The police found incriminating evidence in half the incidents. Table 4.2 shows how the subjects assessed the fairness of the searches and seizures.

TABLE 4.2 Subjects Agreeing with Statements for Interactions Between Discovery of Evidence and Suspect Presence

---

Item: "Based on social expectations and understandings in our society, Resident B has the right to permit the police officer to enter the shared residence."

Suspect Presence	Discovery of Evidence	
	Not Found	Found
Absent	42%	92%
Present and protesting	83%	67%

Item: "Based on social expectations and understandings in our society, Resident B has the right to permit the police officer to search the coat closet in the living/dining area."

Suspect Presence	Discovery of Evidence	
	Not Found	Found
Absent	58%	83%
Present and protesting	92%	67%

Source: From Kagehiro et al., 1991, Table 1, p. 309.

Kagehiro and her co-workers discovered that if no incriminating evidence was found, the third party (the person who consented to the search) was judged to be justified in permitting the search. On the other hand, when incriminating evidence was found, people viewed matters somewhat differently. If the suspect was absent, the consenter was perceived as justified in allowing for a police search so as to establish his or her (the third party's) innocence. However, if the suspect was present and objected to the search, the warrantless search was seen as less fair.

Notice what is happening. When the suspect is away, the third party is seen as having independent power to allow a search of common areas. If incriminating evidence is found, then a search of common areas is judged to be more fair than if it was not found. This again seems to occur because the evidence clears the consenter. What we see is that the ordinary person's view of the fairness of warrantless searches is determined by a *hindsight bias* (see Table 4.2). That is, individuals judge the fairness of the procedures because they know the end of the story. They view the situation one way when things turn out bad (incriminating evidence is found) and another when no evidence is discovered.

Legal rules, however, cannot be based on a hindsight bias. The legal issue is whether the police acted in good faith based on what they knew when they decided to conduct the search (*United States v. Leon,* 1984). Otherwise there would be no judicial control over the legality of the searches. If no incriminating evidence was found, there would be nothing to challenge; if incriminating evidence was found, any challenges would be rejected because the incriminating evidence justified the consent. It appears that the beliefs of the research participants did not coincide with the legal standard, at least as written. Whether judges and juries follow that standard in deciding cases is an open question.

As Kagehiro and her colleagues note, the law focuses on the rights and interests of the suspect but has not taken into account the rights and interests of the third party. Note that once the third party consents to the search, the consenter takes the suspect along for the ride. The consenter has in essence waived, for both the suspect and himself or herself, the right to have the state prove there was reasonable justification for the police search in the first place (Kagehiro & Taylor, 1992; *Illinois v. Rodriguez, 1990*).

In addition, our view of such searches is colored by our general underestimation of the likelihood that bad things will happen to us. Shelley Taylor (1989) reported that many individuals react to threatening events by developing *positive illusions*—beliefs that include unrealistic optimism about their ability to handle threatening situations and obtain a positive outcome. Not only do we hope for and expect positive outcomes when faced with ill health and other threats, but we generally think that good things will happen to us. Therefore, because of this cognitive bias, we do not expect that our roommate will be a suspected drug dealer or that she might be hiding cocaine in the kitchen next to the Vermont maple syrup or the Oregon hazelnuts. We say, go ahead and search, no problem. The courts assume that individuals fairly estimate the risks involved in consenting to a warrantless search. However, social cognition argues that they do not.

We need to look more closely at how the courts and laypeople construe various crucial assumptions of both criminal and civil law.

These potential conflicts about what is considered fair and reasonable police behavior can also be examined when police execute a legal search warrant. The issue here is whether police officers must "knock and announce" when they are about to execute the warrant. Many states, but not all, do have a search and announce requirement. Federal law requires that a police officer give "notice of his authority and purpose" before a forcible entry to execute the warrant. Police officers feel that to knock and announce is to allow drug dealers the chance to get rid of the evidence.

In 1994, the issue of knock and announce was given wide publicity because of a case in which a 75-year-old retired minister in Boston (Massachusetts does not have a knock-and-announce requirement) died of a heart attack when police officers mistakenly broke into his apartment. The search warrant was intended for another apartment. The interpretation of unreasonable search and seizure, in an age of possible random drug testing and other potential intrusions, will no doubt be explored and redefined in the future.

A 1995 U.S. Supreme Court case overturned an Arkansas ruling in which police, executing a search warrant for narcotics based on an informant's tip, just walked in and searched the home of Sharlene Wilson in Malvern, Arkansas, on New Year's Eve, 1992 (*Wilson v. Arkansas*, 1994). The police had reason to believe that Wilson might be armed. Wilson's lawyer sought to exclude evidence (drugs and a gun) obtained in the search, partly on grounds that the police had failed to knock and announce themselves before entering her home. The court disagreed. Wilson was convicted of various drug offenses, sentenced to 31 years in prison, and fined $11,000.

On appeal, the Arkansas Supreme Court upheld the conviction, finding no legal authority for a knock-and-announce requirement in the Fourth Amendment. The U.S. Supreme Court reversed, concluding that American law traditionally incorporated the knock-and-announce principle, which can be traced to a thirteenth-century English legal doctrine that the King's men had to make a "solemn demand" before they could legally enter a citizen's "castle or fortress" to search for stolen goods (*Wilson v. Arkansas*, 1994).

In essence, before the police can knock down doors, they have to have some good reason for doing so. *Wilson* did not define what is a good reason ("reasonableness"). Empirical studies could help inform the courts when they deal with that problem.

Police and the Defendant.   The police function does not end with arrest. The arrest must be justified by evidence gathered by the police and presented to the courts. The next scene we all know from the TV cop shows: The suspect is in a windowless room, perhaps observed through a one-way mirror, while an interrogation takes place. Confession evidence is powerful. When the defendant implicates himself and seems to do so voluntarily, juries and judges, not unreasonably, are convinced as to the guilt of the confessor. A confession makes other evidence expendable.

However, the Fifth Amendment to the Bill of Rights has a clause that prohibits authorities from coercing an individual into self-incrimination. The question then is whether we can tell when a confession was voluntarily offered and when it was not. Also, can we tell what interrogation procedures are psychologically coercive?

In an early and path-breaking examination of police interrogation methods, social psychologist Philip Zimbardo (1967) examined manuals written for police interrogators. Zimbardo concluded that many of the tactics then employed by interrogators were psychologically coercive. The operative question is whether these methods increase the probability that an innocent person would confess to crimes that he or she did not commit.

Remember that on arrest a suspect must be informed of his or her Fifth Amendment rights that protect the individual against compulsory self-incrimination (*Miranda v. Arizona,* 1966). The *Miranda* decision required that suspects be advised that they have the right to remain silent, that any statement they make may be used against them at trial, that they have the right to an attorney, and that the court will appoint an attorney if they are unable to afford one (*Gideon v. Wainwright,* 1967).

Police may question suspects only if the suspects knowingly and voluntarily waive their rights. Courts may assess whether they understood their rights based on factors such as the suspects' intelligence, prior arrests, sobriety, and education. In other words, the court asks, given the state and the characteristics of the suspect, is it reasonable to assume that she or he understood these rights?

Not all suspects do understand their rights. Thomas Grisso (1981) found that more than 50 percent of 11-to-16-year-old suspects did not understand one or more of their *Miranda* rights. Grisso investigated one of the Court's assumptions—that repeat offenders would be aware of the rights because they are more "savvy" about the system—and found that this was not true. Predictably, IQ was positively related to comprehension.

An analysis of police interrogation techniques by Zimbardo (1967) revealed a very sophisticated use of psychological insights. Interrogators were instructed to pay careful attention to a number of factors, among which was the environment in which the interrogation takes place. This is to be structured so there are no distractions for the suspect, allowing the interrogating officer to bring the full weight of his or her personality and position directly on the suspect (Inbau, Reid, & Buckley, 1986).

Police interrogators may also be quite sensitive to social motives when questioning a suspect. For example, the well-known Mutt and Jeff technique falls into this category. Mutt is typically the cruel and relentless interrogator whereas Jeff is the kind-hearted family man—a sort of Mel Gibson–Danny Glover combination. The final scene in this play is when kindly Jeff asks Mutt to leave the room. Jeff then informs the suspect that Mutt is really a bad guy and likes to hurt people and there is not much that he, Jeff, can do about it. If the suspect will admit his crimes, however then everything will be all right. While this questioning is going on, trained interrogators, watching through one-way mirrors, are trying to "read" the suspect's body language and facial expressions to determine whether he or she is telling the truth.

Police were also trained in the semantics of interrogation, especially the effective phrasing of questions. The basic point was to phrase a question so it could not be answered with a "no." Social psychologists know that a public statement makes private attitudes much more difficult to change. Police interrogators were instructed not to permit a suspect to deny a crime directly.

Philip Zimbardo (1967), an investigator who has long studied how attitudes and behavior are modified, believes that these techniques can compel both innocent and guilty individuals to self-incrimination. Even if the defendant later claimed that the interrogation was coercive, this denial would probably not impress jurors. Attribution theory, which deals with how people decide the causes of behavior, tells us that we, as perceivers, have a bias for assuming that someone's behavior corresponds with that person's beliefs. Of course, if we observe that someone was beaten to coerce a confession, we will not assume that the confession corresponds to the person's deeds. One study showed that if a confession was clearly obtained by negative, coercive means, jurors rejected it. If the coercion was psychological, however, or if the coercion was positive, ("we'll get you a better deal if you confess"), jurors then accepted the confession at face value (Kassin & Wrightsman, 1981).

What of the *Miranda* warnings? How do they affect the likelihood of false or coerced confessions? Some observers have suggested that the *Miranda* rights do very little to protect the average suspect. Most individuals caught up in the criminal justice system harbor a distrust of lawyers. In addition, police officers may suggest to the suspect that all a lawyer does is get in the way if the suspect is not guilty. The suggestion may be offered that if you are not guilty, you do not need a lawyer or need to remain silent (Zimbardo, 1967).

Confessions are a valuable commodity. They take everybody else off the hook. That is, if the suspect confesses guilt, then the onus is entirely on the suspect, and the police do not have to work to obtain evidence.

In the years since Zimbardo's original analysis, police interrogation techniques have been modified to be less overtly coercive. Nevertheless, little else has changed. The current manuals emphasize the same categories of techniques that Zimbardo discovered: the importance of the interrogation room and the personality of the interrogator; the use of semantic distortion; and so on. Saul Kassin and Karlyn McNall (1991) analyzed the more subtle interrogation methods suggested by newer police manuals and found that they take one of two forms. The first approach Kassin and McNall call **maximization.** When interrogators use this technique, their goal is to intimidate the suspect into confessing by falsely claiming they have incriminating evidence or by exaggerating the seriousness of the crime. **Minimization,** the second approach, calls for the interrogator to use a "soft sell" to convince the suspect that the officers are sympathetic. An officer might try to minimize the seriousness of the crime or give the suspect a face-saving way out; he or she might even blame the victim, described as someone who deserved to be robbed, raped, or murdered. Note that these techniques are the same ones recommended in earlier police interrogation manuals.

In a series of studies using mock jurors, Kassin and McNall found that jurors will generally discount a confession known to have been gained by coercion, but they will place more credence in a confession obtained with the minimization technique. Even very bright college students underestimate the influence that subtle interrogation techniques may impose on suspects in a dangerous and anxiety-provoking situation. The Kassin and McNall (1991) analysis seems little different from Zimbardo's (1967) 30-year-old perspective. False confessions appear to fall into three categories:

1. *Voluntary,* involving no external pressure
2. *Coerced-compliant,* involving an innocent person who confesses to avoid a very negative situation or to get a promised reward
3. *Coerced-internalized,* involving an innocent person who comes to believe that she is truly guilty (Azar, 1995)

Kassin and Kiechel (1996) have shown that these subtle interrogation techniques can be very effective in obtaining confessions. They hypothesized that it would be possible to demonstrate experimentally that presenting false evidence to vulnerable individuals could induce them to confess. College students were induced to believe that they had committed a blunder in a laboratory experiment that led to the loss of important data. Kassin and Kiechel made some subjects feel vulnerable by reporting a false statement from another subject, saying that the subject had hit the wrong key on a computer keyboard and therefore was responsible for the data loss. Students were prodded to sign a statement (confession) that they were responsible for the data loss, and about two-thirds of them did so, although none of them were guilty. Comments by many subjects after the experiment showed that they actually felt guilty for a blunder they had not committed but for which they were induced to claim responsibility.

Improving Police Interviewing.   Ronald Fisher, who has studied the best ways to interview witnesses, has suggested several reforms that would yield more accurate results. Fisher (1995) noted that police take one side in the interview: They are adversaries working on the side of the prosecution. Police are reinforced for uncovering evidence that leads to the arrest and prosecution of criminals. They are not directly reinforced or rewarded for exonerating suspects (Fisher & McCauley, 1995). Therefore, Fisher observed, police are much more likely to search for and find incriminating evidence than exonerating data.

One possible solution is to limit the interrogator's knowledge of the crime and the suspect. Therefore, the interrogator would not be able to ask biased questions. The trade-off is, of course, that the officer would not have the special knowledge needed to ask questions that would elicit the most information (Fisher & Geiselman, 1992).

Fisher (1995) has also noted that in addition to the motivation of police interrogators, there are correctable problems that have to do with how police are trained and the nature of their career advancement. Police use an aggressive, controlling interview technique, making it unlikely that the interviewee will be able to volunteer unsolicited information. Police often ask a question that might take the following controlled format: "Was he wearing boots?" "Did she have jeans on?" The questions call for controlled answers and make it less likely that a witness's unique information will surface. Police training emphasizes that interviews are aimed at getting very specific information and are written up in a very concise form. This training carries over when officers are promoted and work as detectives who interview suspects. The research suggests a need for improved training for police and allocation of more resources for identifying and coaching better interviewers.

LAWYERS

The remaining actor in the criminal justice system that we will consider is the lawyer. Certainly judges are lawyers and some police officers may have law degrees. Practicing lawyers, however, occupy a special niche in the system. A recent survey suggests that although most people are satisfied with the legal services they have received, their resentment at the providers of those services, the lawyers, is high (Taylor, 1995). Newspapers, movies, television, and novels all support a widely held perception that the reputation of lawyers is, to say the least, tarnished. This perception seems most widely held among upper-income individuals, those most likely to have some contact with the legal profession (Taylor, 1995).

Lawyer-bashing jokes abound. "Why don't sharks attack lawyers? Professional courtesy." "Why does New Jersey have so many toxic waste dumps and California so many lawyers? New Jersey had first choice." "Why have some medical labs started using lawyers instead of white rats in experiments? There are more lawyers than white rats, lab technicians sometimes become attached to white rats, and there are some things a white rat simply will not do" (Taylor, 1995). An entire chapter or even a book could be filled with lawyer jokes. The jokes may be funny—lawyers tell them all the time—but they do the profession no good.

As with most professions, the reputation of lawyers has risen and fallen with the public mood. The first lawyer to enter the American colonies was imprisoned and then deported. Americans have been of two minds about lawyers. We have thought of them—and apparently think of them now—as being less than upright. Yet when our individual rights have been in danger, the virtuous lawyer has stood and defended us. It was John Adams who defended the British soldiers tried for murder in what history has called the Boston Massacre. A colonial jury returned a not guilty verdict in favor of the British troops. John Adams represents the positive image of the lawyer as protector of individual rights–one who stands with the individual against all odds and all pressures.

People tend to despise lawyers until they need them. We should remember that our country's most remarkable document, the Constitution of the United States, was penned, for the most part, by lawyers. Nevertheless, despite John Adams—and Perry Mason for that matter—lawyers continue to take it on the chin in the media. In the recent popular movie *The Firm,* Tom Cruise played a young lawyer suddenly enmeshed in a law firm that secretly represented the Mob and killed any of its lawyers who wanted to tell what was going on. It is interesting that *The Firm* replaced *Jurassic Park* as the top film in the summer of 1993. Lawyers apparently are more frightening than dinosaurs.

The *New York Times* ran a spoof by James Gorman who told of a man who had a vision: a theme park to surpass all theme parks. It would be the most frightening of them all. It would be filled not with dinosaurs or lions, but with something more terrifying: lawyers.

Ben, the hero of Gorman's story, paid barbers to give him hair from lawyers and with the help of scientists, extracted the DNA from the hair. He then deposited the DNA scrapings into hagfish egg cells. The hagfish, Gorman tells us, "is a pale, primitive snakelike creature that bores into the bodies of its victims and devours their innards. A perfect match" (Gorman, 1993, p. A13). The name of the theme park? Of course: "Juristic Park."

When asked, however, citizens report that they like and trust their own lawyer, but not others. Why is the public so upset with lawyers, but not with their own lawyer? These results are similar to findings that people are upset with Congress but not with their own representative or senator. Perhaps that analogy is not so far-fetched. Like Congress, lawyers represent the law and public faith in law is not strong. Citizens see criminals go unpunished, wealthy defendants buy their freedom by hiring slick lawyers, taxes evaded by rich individuals and corporations. At the other extreme, lawyers successfully sue large corporations, extract heavy damages to punish corporate profiteering from defective products like lung-invading asbestos, unstable all-terrain vehicles, infectious Dalkon shields, and leaking breast implants.

How Lawyers Think

Lawyers are trained in a special way of thinking. The primary goal of law school is to teach students how to "think like a lawyer." What does this mean? How is thinking like a lawyer different from, say, thinking like an experimental psychologist?

Law teachers employ the **Socratic case method.** This method relies on the written opinions of judges in important cases. In each particular case, students search for the general legal principles that the judge used to resolve the case. The technique is Socratic because the teacher will plumb the depths of the student's understanding of the issues in a one-on-one interaction with the student. "Does it matter that he was wearing a coat? That she was a widow? That he was ill?" Law professors, as represented in the old TV series *Paper Chase,* delight, it seems, in devising outrageous "hypotheticals" to test a student's understanding and wit: "Suppose the plaintiff had owned a red-breasted cuckoo carrying a stink bomb instead of a bluebird carrying a firecracker; would that have affected the court's ruling that obnoxious birds are fair game for a dart thrower?"

The object is to teach the student to decipher the core rationale of a case (*ratio decidendi* is the legal jargon), also know as the *holding* of the case. The holding is related to the concept of *stare decisis,* which we discussed earlier. Stare decisis directs a court, in most instances, to follow the holding of a similar previous case. Of course, if previous cases differ in some significant way from the case to be decided, the court need not follow the earlier holding. Whether cases differ significantly from each other is often an arguable point, providing a foothold for lawyers.

Earlier we noted that scientific findings may change. Science is an ongoing process. So, it turns out, is law. The law student learns that legal rules are much less certain than many may think. In an adversarial system, change is common. After all, each side hires its own lawyer who will take advantage of any uncertainties or loopholes in the law.

Lawyering in the Adversarial System

The popular view is that a lawyer will do anything to win the case. The renowned justice Oliver Wendell Holmes, Jr., once cut short a young lawyer's rhapsody to justice in the courtroom by noting, "This is a court of law, young man, not a court of justice" (Peter, 1977, p. 276).

Franklin Strier (1994) observed that the adversarial nature of the system places a premium on zealous promotion of the client's interests at the cost of other goals, such as truth. In fact, Strier suggested, anything less than promoting a client's interests may be grounds for a charge of legal malpractice. Strier argued that this adversarial posture belittles rationality and fairness and advances unfairness, animosity, and irrationality.

Valerie Hans and Krista Sweigert (1993) examined jurors' perceptions of lawyers in civil trials and concluded that the primary factors influencing jurors were the attorney's organization, credibility, and use of emotion. Jurors claimed they were most impressed with attorneys who were moderate in emotional appeals and were organized and professional. Moderate emotion means that their enthusiasm and arguments were calibrated to the severity of their client's injuries. As we see in Chapter 10, jurors seem naturally suspicious of individuals who sue because of relatively minor injuries. If the attorney adds too much emotion to that suspicion, jurors will, not unreasonably, conclude that they are being manipulated.

Like the rest of us, lawyers often misperceive the impression they make on others, especially significant others, such as jurors. Actually, lawyers believe the public opinion of them is worse than it is (Hans & Sweigert, 1993). Although people think attorneys are often greedy and tricky, the same public also believes they are not without redeeming or positive qualities. Hans and Sweigert (1993) hypothesized that lawyers may feel compelled to act in ways that fulfill the public's expectations, an unfortunate assumption for an attorney who has misread public opinion. That is, lawyers seem to think that what the public really wants is "Rambo" in the courtroom (Hans & Sweigert, 1993). Additional results show that more experienced attorneys rated themselves friendlier and less nervous than did the jurors they appeared before. Therefore, it seems that lawyers do not necessarily get better with age, just more confident. That is not a surprising finding. We know that individuals who are less sure of themselves, or are even depressed, are more accurate in their self-perceptions than are those who are confident and optimistic (Swann, Hixon, & de la Ronde, 1992). One can assume that many novice trial lawyers are not yet sure of their abilities.

Other evidence suggests that lawyers may not play as large a role in the minds of the jurors as you may think. Diamond, Casper, and Heiert (1994) recorded the deliberations and responses of jurors recruited from Cook County (Chicago) courts who had watched a videotape of one of several versions of either a death penalty case or a civil trial. Researchers examined the comments jurors made about attorneys to learn whether jurors focus primarily on lawyers' personal characteristics. They found that the comments about attorneys were primarily within the discussion of the evidence, and that jurors referred only 7 percent of the time to the lawyers' individual attributes.

Of course, it may be that jurors were affected by the lawyers' behaviors but simply did not refer to it in the deliberations. It is also possible that lawyers affect jurors in their opening statements to an extent not revealed by jurors' verbal comments (Diamond et al., 1994).

Tactics and Ethics in the Courtroom

We have noted that the prime attribute of our justice system is its adversarial intensity. Both sides want to win. It is probably not an overstatement to say that for trial lawyers, winning is the only thing that matters. Lawyers push the envelope of ethical behavior when they must to win. Lawyers who cannot live by those rules do not go into trial practice. It also should be noted that the lawyers' clients expect such zeal and would have it no other way. Casper, Tyler, and Fisher (1988) found that the attorney's intensity is one of the factors that determines whether convicted felons feel that they were treated fairly.

Winning at all costs does not mean, however, that the legal profession condones lying and cheating. The *Model Rules of Professional Conduct* identify as professional misconduct a lawyer's engaging in dishonesty or deceit, or any behavior prejudicial to the administration of justice.

Even so, philosopher Sissela Bok (1978) draws the analogy that for lawyers to lie in the service of their clients is not unlike bargaining in a bazaar. You are expected to exaggerate, lie, feign; it's all part of the game and nobody really thinks it is wrong. How far can lawyers go in the service of their clients? William Moran, a Miami defense lawyer who specialized in drug cases, had a client who wanted some information. Was it true, the client wanted to know, that a certain doctor from Colombia had been talking about him to federal investigators? Mr. Moran said yes, it was so. Shortly thereafter the doctor, Rafael Lombrano, was killed in front of a Miami restaurant.

Lawyer Moran asserted that he had done nothing wrong, but was merely fulfilling his duty of keeping a client informed on a source of potentially harmful information—all part of building a good legal defense (Treaster, 1995). But the U.S. Attorney for Southern Florida thought differently. It seems that Dr. Lombrano was a Drug Enforcement Administration (DEA) informant. Mr. Moran and two other attorneys were indicted and accused of practically working as members of the Cali (Colombia) drug cartel, which was the source of much of the world's cocaine traffic.

The lawyers entered a not guilty plea to charges of conspiracy, money laundering, and other crimes. Many of the charges indicated that the lawyers knew what their clients meant to do (murder the doctor, smuggle cocaine) and they knew that the money they had handled came from cocaine sales (Treaster, 1995). Some experts on legal ethics observed that all defense lawyers work very close to the line that defines ethical conduct, and that it was up to the attorney to recognize when that line was crossed (Treaster, 1995).

Of course, the behavior of these lawyers took place outside the courtroom and there the rules are different. In the courtroom, a lawyer may try to discredit a witness that he or she knows is truthful. That is part of the game. But if a lawyer gave a client technical advice on how to evade the law, then he or she might very well be an accessory to the crime (Gillers, cited in Treaster, 1995).

Let's look more closely at some of the tactics lawyers use before and during the trial to try to win. All these strategies are within the rules of the adversarial game.

Trial Tactics and Dirty Tricks

One of the most significant pretrial tools the law provides is known as *discovery* (see Chapter 2). This term means that one side can request of the opposition any piece of information deemed relevant to their case. There are some limits on these requests, and so certain documents may be protected by *privilege*. For example, you have no right to a working paper detailing the other side's trial tactics.

The discovery process eliminates the potential for trial-by-ambush. One side should not be able to introduce a surprise document or witness that the other side is not prepared to defend against. The types of evidence you can get through the discovery process are records, tests, documents, blood samples, or anything that is thought to be relevant (Strier, 1994).

In addition to eliminating a chance for a legal ambush, discovery also serves to prod parties to settle out of court. You may suddenly find that your case is not as strong as you thought, or that the other side is loaded for bear and you have a pop gun.

An important discovery technique is the *deposition,* during which you may question potential witnesses under oath, including those unable to appear at trial (Strier, 1994). As you may have guessed, discovery can be used to enhance the fairness of the trial, but lawyers can also use the procedure to delay, throw up smokescreens, irritate, and hide the truth (Schwarzer, 1991). Once the trial starts, the lawyers' concentration is on the examination of the witnesses. Legal scholars believe that cross-examination is the crucible from which truth is forged. Indeed, if the experiment is the mechanism by which experimental psychologists try to find truth, cross-examination is the mechanism by which attorneys uncover truth. In reality, cross-examination is the opportunity to weaken or destroy your opponent's case by discrediting that side's witnesses.

Kassin, Williams, and Saunders (1990) showed that juror perceptions of a witness can be biased by presumptuous cross-examination questions (the question presumes that the witness did something wrong, as in "When did you stop beating your wife?"). These authors referred to such tactics as "dirty tricks." To test the technique of cross-examining by innuendo, Kassin et al. (1990) designed a trial in which a lawyer asked an expert witness a question implying that the expert had a poor professional reputation. This technique, regardless of whether the expert denied, objected, or admitted the accusation, influenced the jurors to note the expert as less credible. In fact, as a result of the lawyer's implication, the expert appeared less competent, believable, and persuasive.

Experts on cross-examination suggest that no matter how truthful and competent the witness, there is always a way to make that witness look less competent (Keeton, 1973; Mauet, 1992). This might mean asking questions in a manner that forces the witness to say "I don't know" time after time; or to ask "did you know that . . . ?" so the lawyer can insert an unsupported statement of his own, as in "Did you know that Mr. Smith has always been an honest bookie?"

Sherri Ondrus (1994) noted that another dirty trick occurs when a lawyer holds a fake "statement" to frighten a witness into believing the lawyer has an incriminating document. However, this tactic, in addition to being unethical, may lead the jury to decide that the lawyer is tricky and to sympathize with the witness.

Lawyers may also try to distract the jury when the other side is presenting evidence, on the assumption that jurors will not process that information. An old story is that the great lawyer Clarence Darrow used to put a wire in his cigar so that the accumulating ash would not fall. This was when smoking was permitted in the courtroom. Jurors would be transfixed by the elongating ash and not pay attention to the opposing lawyer's arguments (Weinberg, 1975).

The evidence suggests that there is a danger in this distraction technique. If you distract the jurors when the other side is presenting what is weak evidence, you may be making a mistake. The effect of distraction is to keep the jurors from listening carefully and thereby figuring out what is wrong with the arguments. Distraction may make jurors uncritical and therefore they will be more vulnerable to your adversary's arguments (Rajecki, 1990).

Trial by Simulation.   Recently, high technology has made its way into the courtroom. Cameras, videotapes, graphics, and computer simulations have all entered the courtroom door. They can be used to clarify or confuse. A computer-generated hypothetical reenactment of the killings at issue in the O. J. Simpson trial was produced by a California company. This simulation highlights how this relatively new technology may, and has been, used in trials. Using what Foremski and Kehoe (1995) call "forensic animation" techniques, Failure Analysis Associates—FaAA—a California high-tech company that produces computer simulations for use in court—began by collecting data from the actual Simpson crime scene and from evidence presented in the pretrial hearings. These data were used to create a computer model of the crime scene. FaAA staff members then took the roles of assailant and victims in a reenactment of the crime, following directions from the company's biomechanics experts. Computer sensors attached to the actors' bodies recorded their every movement. Data from the sensors were used to create the simulation (Foremski & Kehoe, 1995).

The FaAA animation is not bloody and you cannot recognize facial features. Foremski and Kehoe (1995, p. 11) describe the three-and-a-half minute sequence as showing a simulated representation of "Nicole Brown Simpson walking down the steps outside her home to let Ronald Goldman into a fenced porch area. They stand on the steps talking, when suddenly a figure hiding behind a wall springs out, hitting the male figure on the head and throwing him to the ground, then quickly hitting the woman and knocking her unconscious. The assailant lifts the male figure, holding him from behind, and makes cutting and stabbing motions. He then turns his attention to the figure of the woman, lifts her in the same way and similarly stabs her with a knife" (Foremski & Kehoe, 1995).

Computer simulations have also been used in many civil trials in the United States over the past few years, including cases involving car and aircraft crashes, fires, explosions, and other disasters. The simulation company FaAA, for example, simulated the voyage of the Exxon Valdez, which ended in a huge oil spill in Alaska. However, forensic animation is rarely used in criminal trials, as few defendants can afford the tens or hundreds of thousands of dollars needed to produce a complex simulation (Foremski & Kehoe, 1995).

Computer simulations are admissible under federal rules of procedure. As with any computer-generated model, the result is totally dependent on the assumptions and data of the compilers and programmers. The simulation is their version of reality. However, the major concern is that reality may be compromised by such simulations (*Manual for Complex Litigation,* 1995). For example, a computer simulation of an accident that took place at night may show the roadway as better illuminated than it really was.

Graphics and Vividness.   In the technological age, lawyers are becoming aware of how much more powerful visual evidence is than written evidence. However, if jurors are uniquely receptive to visual demonstrative evidence, they may also be vulnerable to being deceived by it (Davis & Hastings, 1994).

Litigators' use of "designed" graphic evidence in the courtroom is increasing. Davis and Hastings define "designed" graphics as visual devices that have been designed and produced by artists, often with input from a trial consultant. The popularity of these types of graphics is based on a number of assumptions. These assumptions include the notion that jurors understand better, will retain more, and will be better persuaded by information that is presented visually rather than verbally; that the message of the graphics should be instantaneous and require little explanation; and that jurors have little or no ability to deal with complexity (Davis & Hastings, 1994).

The increased use of high-production graphics can be quite deceptive and may be used as a tool to either inflame the jury or distort the evidence. A simulation of a murder, gory or not, may have an emotional impact on the jury. In addition, evidence can be distorted. For example, scan parts a and b of Figure 4.1 (page 102). The two parts of the figure show two presentations of the same data. Note that the top example gives an accurate visualization; the bottom figure distorts the data. Experts in scaling can determine the accuracy of the visual representation, using this equation:

$$\frac{\text{Size of effect of graphic}}{\text{Size of effect of data}} = \text{Lie factor}$$

As you can see, the "lie factor" for part b in Figure 4.1 is 3.7. The part b representation suggests that the plaintiff's yearly income, using 1986 as a base, has increased by a factor of 3.7, whereas in reality it has increased from $60,000 to $108,500, a factor of only 1.

Videotapes have also been used extensively in recent years. Kassin and Garfield (1991) asked mock jurors to watch a "blood and guts" video of a violent crime scene showing a murder victim's body. Jurors who saw the videotape were more likely to convict a defendant by lowering their standard of proof for conviction than were those who viewed a videotape of an unrelated violent crime scene or no videotape at all. An interesting side effect is that jurors who saw the crime scene videotape subsequently gave a more serious rating to other crimes such as rape, arson, and assault.

Of course, lawyers may use vividness in language as well as graphics, and advocates have used vivid verbal depictions as a tool for a very long time. Loftus and Palmer (1974) demonstrated that a lawyer's phrasing of a question about an automobile accident (How fast was the car going when it "smashed/collided/bumped/hit/contacted" another car?) changed the witnesses' perceptions of the accident. The more extreme terms such as "smashed" caused people to estimate that the car traveled at higher speeds. A week later, when the same subjects were asked whether they had seen broken glass, more subjects who read the terms

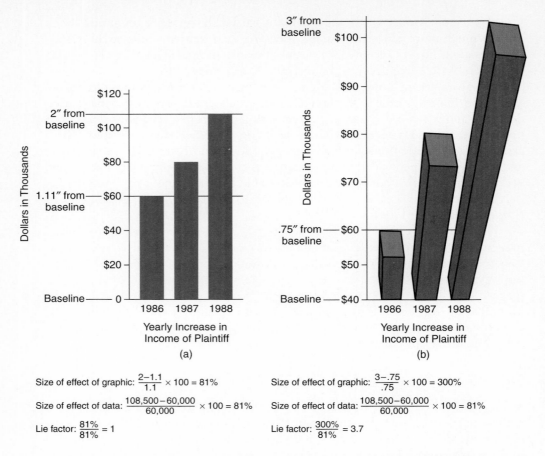

Size of effect of graphic: $\frac{2-1.1}{1.1} \times 100 = 81\%$

Size of effect of data: $\frac{108,500-60,000}{60,000} \times 100 = 81\%$

Lie factor: $\frac{81\%}{81\%} = 1$

Size of effect of graphic: $\frac{3-.75}{.75} \times 100 = 300\%$

Size of effect of data: $\frac{108,500-60,000}{60,000} \times 100 = 81\%$

Lie factor: $\frac{300\%}{81\%} = 3.7$

FIGURE 4.1   How to tell the truth with statistics but lie with graphics.

A close examination of parts (a) and (b) shows how graphics may be used to exaggerate one lawyer's arguments. Notice that graph (a) accurately presents the
yearly increase in a plaintiff's income both numerically and graphically. The critical change occurs between the initial $60,000 salary in 1986, which is presented
at 1.11 inches from the zero baseline and $108,500 which is presented at 2
inches from the baseline. Therefore, the increase both graphically (2 inches
minus 1.1 divided by $1.1 \times 100 = 81\%$) and statistically (the increase from 60,000
to 108,500 is also 81%) is precisely the same. But part (b) grossly increases the
graphic effect of the same data by increasing the distance from the baseline by
a factor of 3.7. A juror enthralled by the graph would conclude that the plaintiff's income would increase almost four times in two years.

Source: From "Litigators Should be Aware of the Uses of Deceptive Graphic Evidence," by D. S.
Davis and L. W. Hastings, 1994, *Inside Litigation, 8*(5), p. 28.

"smashed" said "yes" than those who read "hit," even though there was no broken glass. The researchers apparently planted false memories in the witnesses by altering the language of the questions (Loftus & Palmer, 1974).

One study examined the effects of vivid language in a trial (Wilson, Northcraft, & Neale, 1989). The mock trial concerned a dispute between a contractor and a subcontractor on a building project. People playing the role of jurors watched different videotapes of the trial. One version had vivid phrasing in the narration; the other used nonvivid language (p. 135):

1. There was a *spiderweb* of cracks through the slab. (vivid)
   There was a *network* of cracks through the slab. (nonvivid)
2. The slab was *jagged* and had to be sanded. (vivid)
   The slab was *rough* and had to be sanded. (nonvivid)

The "jurors" tended to award the plaintiff more money when they heard vivid phrases.

To this point, we have considered all the major players in the criminal justice system: victims and defendants, judges, police officers, and lawyers. Now we will see how the legal system resolves criminal and civil disputes. In the next chapter, we begin to explore how the legal system works.

SUMMARY

An arrest is an act by a legally appointed authority, the police officer, that deprives a citizen of freedom. Legally, arrest can occur when police have a warrant or there is evidence of probable cause that a crime has occurred and that the suspect can be linked directly to that crime. The officer on the street has broad discretion in deciding whom to arrest. An arrest in one sense is a social encounter and turns on extralegal factors, primarily the suspect's behavior, as much as it does on probable cause and evidence.

Police often confront special societal situations including family disputes, spousal abuse, and dealing with the mentally ill. There is a tendency to criminalize mental disorders. Many individuals who should be hospitalized are arrested instead. Police officers may often be aware that this is the case, but they also know that the mental health facilities may not be able to accept these individuals because of lack of space and funds.

The real obstacle to dealing with family violence is the tendency of victims not to report the assaults. Arrest does seem to matter in spousal abuse cases, but not always in a positive way for the victim. Currently, 15 states and the District of Columbia have mandatory arrest laws in cases of domestic battery. The most recent research suggests that arrest sometimes leads to more spousal violence, particularly when the abusers are unemployed.

The police function does not end with arrest. That arrest must be justified by evidence gathered by the police and presented to the courts. Obtaining confessions is a certain way of getting a conviction. Psychological research has shown that subtle techniques of interrogation make it possible not only to induce the guilty to confess but also to coerce the innocent into a confession as well.

Police have their own culture. Its elements include a high level of masculinity, which means not only that male officers outnumber female officers by large numbers but also that masculine values reflecting toughness and aggressiveness are highly valued. In addition, police follow a code of honor, and they face strong social pressure to act in accordance with the powerful social norms of this military-type organization.

Police officers face a great deal of stress on the job but often do not or cannot handle this stress. The very qualities that make a good police officer often hinder the officer from dealing effectively with job stress. Police officers learn to keep their emotions in check and are quite unlikely to confide in anyone other than their working partners about the extent of their distress.

Another professional in the justice system is the lawyer. Law school teaches students to "think like a lawyer," a process in which law students are taught to understand legal decisions and reasoning by making analogies to earlier cases. The fundamental fact of the legal system for lawyers is that it is an adversarial system in which the lawyer's highest calling is to present the client's case effectively. It is probably this aspect of the law that has led to the somewhat diminished reputation lawyers have acquired.

The adversarial nature of the system places a premium on zealous promotion of the client's interests at the cost of other goals, such as truth. In fact, anything less than promoting a client's interests may be grounds for an accusation of legal malpractice. The legal profession condemns lying, but the pressures of the adversarial system often push lawyers to the ethical brink. To gain a tactical advantage, trial lawyers may abuse the discovery process, throwing up smokescreens and using delaying tactics to keep information away from the other side. Cross-examination is used primarily to discredit the other side's witnesses, and a variety of dirty tricks may be used in the service of this goal.

Recently, high technology has made its way into the courtroom by way of cameras, videotapes, graphics, and computer simulations. They can be used to clarify or confuse. Computer simulations have been used in many civil trials in the United States over the past few years, including cases involving car and aircraft crashes, fires, explosions, and other disasters. As with any computer-generated model, the result is totally dependent on the assumptions and data of the compilers and programmers. The simulation is their version of reality. A major concern is that reality may be compromised by such simulations. For example, a computer simulation of an accident that took place at night may show the road as better illuminated than it really was.

Lawyers are also becoming aware of how much more powerful visual evidence is than written evidence with juries. However, if jurors are receptive to visual demonstrative evidence, they may also be vulnerable to deception by it. The popularity of graphic presentations is based on several assumptions, including the notion that jurors understand better, will retain more, and will be better persuaded by information that is presented visually rather than verbally; that the message of the graphics should be instantaneous and require little explanation; and that jurors have little or no ability to deal with complexity. High-production graphics can be quite deceptive and may be used as a tool either to inflame the jury or to distort the evidence. Vivid language used by witnesses also has the potential of engaging jurors' emotional rather than rational responses.

PART THREE

The Trial

CHAPTER
5

Pretrial Issues

ALTERNATIVE DISPUTE RESOLUTION

Most injuries or grievances do not result in litigation. Of those that do, most do not go to trial. The legal system has increasingly relied on out-of-court procedures to settle disputes. To learn about these, we first consider the origin of disputes and the outcome of cases that are not tried. We examine the procedures used to settle cases out of court. The formal name for these settlement procedures is *alternative dispute resolution* (ADR). Most of these procedures deal with disputes among private parties; that is to say, they are civil claims or cases.

In the criminal arena, many cases are resolved through pretrial negotiation also. This is referred to as **plea bargaining,** whereby the accused agrees to plead guilty in exchange for a lesser sentence. We examine the process of plea bargaining after discussing the origin and resolution of civil disputes.

The Origin of Disputes

Filing a lawsuit represents the end point of a process that begins with an injury or the perception of an injury. A cup of scalding coffee tips into the lap of a McDonald's customer causing second-degree burns in the groin area; a routine gall bladder operation turns into a nightmare of infection; a shiny new car turns out to be a bright yellow lemon. How often do such events occur in our daily lives and how do we decide which ones warrant further action? And what type of action should we take? A person usually does not start the process with a lawsuit, the legal and social equivalent of a declaration of war. So where do they start?

Researchers have identified at least four distinct stages that precede litigation (Miller & Sarat, 1981; Saks, 1992). The first, of course, is incurring some sort of *injury.* Step two is the perception that someone else caused that injury, thereby entitling one to make a claim for redress; in other words, *naming* the injury and defining it as a *grievance,* and pursuing that grievance by *claiming* a right to compensation or other amends from the party inflicting the injury. A *dispute* arises if the other party rejects that claim, and the dispute ripens into a *lawsuit* when the claimant goes to court, probably with the aid of a lawyer.

Contrary to popular conceptions that American society is especially eager to sue (*litigious* is the buzzword), few injuries lead to full-fledged legal disputes (Saks, 1992). Studies of medical malpractice injuries and claims illustrate the point. In a 1990 project, the Harvard Medical Practices Study, researchers documented, by reviewing medical files, that patients experienced injuries as a direct result of surgery or other treatment at a rate of 100 per 10,000 patients. Of those 100 who were injured, approximately 11 percent filed claims. In three separate studies of medical malpractice injuries, between 6 percent and 12 percent of such injuries led to the filing of lawsuits (Saks, 1992, pp. 1183–1184).

One might expect the extent of the injury to make a major difference in whether a lawsuit is filed, but even then, in a study of people with disabling injuries, 81 of every 100 did not even consider filing a claim. Of those who thought about it, two dealt with the injurer, four dealt with the insurer, and seven consulted a lawyer (four of whom hired the lawyer and two of whom filed suit) (Saks, 1992). In other words, 2 of 100 people with disabling injuries sued.

The statistics are similar in other types of litigation. Miller and Sarat (1981) surveyed members of the public about their grievances and claims. For every 1,000 grievances, 718 claims were presented to the other party; 449 of those claims were disputed; 103 of those claimants consulted a lawyer; and ultimately, 50 lawsuits were filed, representing 5 percent of the grievances (p. 544). Filing rates were lowest for discrimination claims (0.8 percent) and tort claims (a private or civil wrong or injury) (3.8 percent) and much higher for postdivorce matters (45 percent). Filing rates have not changed very much in the years since the Miller and Sarat study (Daniels & Martin, 1995).

One factor that stands out from the above data is the high rate of litigation for postdivorce matters, possibly explained because the legal system has a monopoly over such claims. Tort claims can be settled by private negotiation, often without the assistance of a lawyer. Of 857 tort claims per 1,000, all but 201 were resolved at the initial claiming stage without dispute. But divorce claims end up in a formal court order. This process limits the degree to which parties can settle their affairs without going to court.

These data lead us to our two next questions: What social psychological processes underlie the decision to make a claim, and what types of skills are used to persuade an opponent to honor a claim?

How Disputes Begin.   Before we look at ways of resolving disputes, we need to know why people decide to seek legal relief. Once we understand that, perhaps we can determine the best methods of settling these disputes.

Coates and Penrod (1981) made an intriguing use of models from social psychology to explain how disputes begin. We believe their approach was an important step in developing alternative techniques for resolving disputes. If we can understand what gave rise to a dispute, it is easier to determine an appropriate mode for resolving it. Among the models explored by Coates and Penrod is relative deprivation, the notion that people tend to compare their status and satisfaction with those of other people in similar circumstances. Disputes tend to occur, according to Coates and Penrod, in order to restore equity, the balance between one's inputs (hard work, educational level, training) and one's outcomes (pay, respect, other rewards). Individuals desire an equity balance, and lack of equity is often a potent factor in disputes. Unions, for example, may strike because they perceive an inequity in compensation and/or working conditions of their members and other workers. Teachers who have invested four or more years in college preparation may feel they should be paid more than sanitation workers, who have not made such an educational investment. Sanitation workers, of course, may feel that their jobs are dirtier than those of teachers, so they should be better compensated. As Coates and Penrod observed, equity has to do with people's perceptions of their entitlements.

Coates and Penrod (1981) have also explored the use of attribution theory to explain disputes and their resolution. This theory concerns the processes by which people explain the causes of their own and other people's behavior. These explanations, called attributions, have emotional and behavioral consequences.

Attributions can be assigned to external (environmental) or to internal (personal characteristics) causes. Furthermore, the causes can be perceived as stable or unstable, intentional or unintentional. If I buy a used car only to find the transmission on the garage floor 31 days later, after the warranty has expired, I can make a number of attributions, all of which will have different consequences. Table 5.1 illustrates the components and outcomes of attributions.

The kind of causal attribution made by the car buyer is likely to determine the occurrence and character of the dispute. Furthermore, inherent in the attribution is a solution with which the buyer will feel comfortable. If the buyer feels that the transmission failure was just unintentional bad luck, then any resolution that would make the car whole again would be acceptable. Perhaps a dispute would not even happen with this kind of causal attribution. If the buyer believes she or he has been the object of a con game, however, then simply repairing the car may not ensure satisfaction. He or she would probably wish to collect damages above and beyond the initial expenditure for the product or see the offender punished.

Informal Resolution of Disputes.   As shown, most disputes are resolved informally, without the intervention of attorneys, but simply by presenting a claim that the other party accepts. This type of resolution happens frequently in the personal injury (tort) context and much less frequently in the discrimination or postdivorce grievance contexts (Daniels & Martin, 1995; Miller & Sarat, 1981). The most recent data show that only 2.7 percent of all tort filings go to trial (Ostrom, Rottman, & Goerdt, 1996).

Of the disputes that are resolved through nonformal means, many are settled by the informal mediation of friends, neighbors, and relatives (Ostrom et al., 1996). In addition, various jurisdictions have established programs for nonjudicial mediation. Other communitywide dispute resolution activities have flourished in recent years. No-fault divorce and no-fault insurance laws arose from the concern that finding legal fault interfered with people's needs to resolve their disputes fairly and efficiently. Thus, in many states, a divorce or an automobile accident can be resolved without having to determine who was at fault. Also in

---

TABLE 5.1   The Effects of Attributions on Naming and Blaming

1. Intentional, internal, stable: "It's my fault, I'm always looking for bargains."
2. Intentional, internal, unstable: "I did not spend enough time shopping."
3. Intentional, external, stable: "It was a con game."
4. Unintentional, internal, stable: "I just didn't know enough to make a wise choice."
5. Unintentional, external, unstable: "I just got stuck with a lemon."

Source: Adapted from Coates & Penrod, 1981.

recent years, mediation programs attached to family court, based on similar principles, have grown, primarily to aid in resolving custody disputes (Bush, 1994).

Alternative Dispute Resolution Procedures

If somewhere between 2 percent and 3 percent of all grievances go to trial, what happens to the other 97 percent that do not have a trial? A sizable number, perhaps about 1 in 6, are resolved by judicial (judges') rulings on motions to dismiss or motions for summary judgment (Cecil & Douglas, 1987; Willging, 1989). Another group are dismissed voluntarily by the plaintiff—or simply not pursued—when the plaintiff discovers a missing element in the case or otherwise decides to drop the claim. The vast majority of civil cases settle with an agreement among the parties (Galanter & Cahill, 1994).

An important alternative to a trial is the expanded use of arbitration, mediation, and other forms of alternative dispute resolution (ADR). Use of such alternatives was stimulated primarily by two types of concerns. One grew out of increases in litigation and crowded court dockets as well as a desire to provide a less costly and more accessible means of resolving disputes (Meierhoefer, 1990). Another concern was for the quality of the resolution process. Proponents of ADR argue that high-quality dispute resolution occurs through the voluntary participation of those who can craft the solution that best suits their needs (Menkel-Meadow, 1991). Judicial (court-ordered) solutions, they maintain, necessarily have a rigid, all-or-nothing character that misses the optimum resolution for many cases. Consensual settlement engages fuller participation by those most affected, encourages direct communication, allows for more flexible procedures, avoids win/lose results, and addresses nonmonetary claims (Galanter & Cahill, 1994, p. 1359).

Empirical evidence that ADR programs in fact reduce costs and shorten delays is skimpy and inconclusive (Stienstra & Willging, 1995). By adding an extra layer to litigation, ADR can increase both costs and the time from filing to resolution (Stienstra & Willging, 1995). In reviewing the literature on ADR and judicial settlement activity, Galanter and Cahill (1994) found that "the studies provide little reason for confidence that judicial promotion of settlements produces more settlements or makes courts more productive" (p. 1366). Nevertheless, the myth of cost and delay reduction attributable to ADR persists in a form that legal scholar Carrie Menkel-Meadow (1991, p. 9) calls a " 'cultural' fact—believed by those who want to believe it even if belied by the empirical reality."

Alternative dispute resolution methods have three aims. One is the transformation of the dispute process so that it is less adversarial and lawlike. A second goal, according to Menkel-Meadow (1991), is to obtain faster resolutions that focus on the needs of the individuals rather than on the rituals of the adversarial process. The last goal is to relieve the courts; the court system does not have to expend energy and time on disputants handled outside the courtroom (Menkel-Meadow, 1991).

A number of types of alternative resolution procedures have evolved. We examine the most common of them in the next section.

Mediation.   Virtually any technique used by a neutral third party to promote negotiation can be regarded as mediation. However, **mediation** refers to the use of a neutral party who facilitates but does not decide the resolution of a dispute. Gifford (1985) suggests that most mediation techniques fulfill one or more of the following goals:

1. To improve communication between the negotiating parties
2. To improve the attitudes of the parties toward each other
3. To educate the parties or their attorneys about the negotiating process
4. To generate new proposals the parties have not themselves identified
5. To inject a dose of reality when one party is viewing his situation in an unrealistically favorable light
6. To protect a party from exploitation in the negotiation process by a more powerful or more sophisticated bargainer.

The goal of mediation is to provide an atmosphere in which both sides can engage in *cooperative* or *problem-solving* tactics. In other words, the mediator's goal is to create trust. Menkel-Meadow (1991), argues that a major goal of ADR and the mediation process—the method she prefers—is to transform the dispute process and allow parties to shape their own resolutions rather than be bound by the win/lose decisions of the law. This is frequently a difficult task, for often the parties in a lawsuit or other dispute are hostile and suspicious of each other.

The research generally shows that when a dispute is mediated, the parties are more positive about the outcome than if it was adjudicated (decided by the court) (McEwen & Maiman, 1986). There is also some evidence that mediation is less injurious to the long-term relationships between the parties than is adjudication (Kitzmann & Emery, 1993). The reduction of hostility would obviously be a very important benefit of mediation if the parties expect to be in a long-term relationship, as would be true in child custody cases, which can often take a venomous turn.

Katherine Kitzmann and Robert Emery (1993) examined the effectiveness of mediation as a mechanism for settling child custody cases in California, where legislation mandates mediation in all such cases. Lind and Tyler (1988) found that disputants' determination of the fairness of a procedure is affected by how much control they think they have over process and outcome, and how well they are treated by those making the decisions. Control is important, but so is being treated with respect and feeling that one can maintain a sense of dignity throughout the proceeding (Tyler & DeGoey, 1996).

Kitzmann and Emery (1993) found that the satisfaction reported by disputants in child custody cases was determined by both the outcome *and* the perception that the resolution procedures were fair. However, the relative importance of fairness and outcome was influenced by the level of conflict in the dispute and the characteristics of the disputants. People in low-conflict disputes were more concerned with outcome than fairness. That focus makes sense because fairness deals with the disputants' perception of whether they were treated with dignity and fairness. If two people in a child custody case are on good terms, the outcome rather than the process is what counts.

Kitzmann and Emery (1993) reported that those in high-conflict situations considered procedural issues to be most important. These disputants wanted to be sure their case got a fair hearing. In child custody cases, men were more concerned with procedural issues than were women; men had little power in most child custody cases and therefore were more concerned with a fair hearing. Kitzmann and Emery noted that not one father was given custody in the 71 disputes they studied.

The Kitzmann and Emery (1993) results, showing the generally positive effects of mediation, are important because the disputes they studied, unlike many other mediation situations, were required by law to have mediation. A great many mediation studies look at disputants who volunteer to accept the procedure. These cases, therefore, are self-selected. Disputants who seek mediation are probably eager, or at least ready, to settle on fair terms (MacCoun, Lind, & Tyler, 1992).

Arbitration.   **Arbitration** is a process in which the disputants agree to allow a neutral person, or sometimes a panel of neutral individuals, to hear arguments, consider evidence, and decide the outcome. In arbitration, unlike the mediation process, the resolution is in the hands of the arbitrator. Binding arbitration requires that the dispute be refereed by a third party, replacing adjudication by a court.

One variation of binding arbitration is called **final offer arbitration.** In this procedure, the parties submit their last, best negotiating offers to the arbitrator prior to the hearing. After hearing the evidence, the arbitrator is restricted to choosing one or the other of the final proposals. This is the procedure used by major league baseball. When a baseball player and team owner cannot agree on a player's salary, each submits his or her last, best proposal. The arbitrator chooses one or the other as the final outcome. Thus, if Spider Smith, possessor of an amazing fastball, wants $3.85 million in salary and his employer feels that Spider is worth a mere $3.2 million, the arbitrator must choose one of these two final offers. The idea is that final offer arbitration forces the parties to find their own agreement to avoid the cost and risk of arbitration. Gifford (1985) reported that final offer arbitration leads to more concessions and negotiated agreements than other forms of final arbitration.

Most of us encounter situations in which disputes will be resolved by binding arbitration. When we rent a car or buy stock through a stockbroker, the contract we sign will have a statement that any dispute will be submitted to binding arbitration. It is likely that most consumers are not aware of that clause in the contract.

Nonbinding Arbitration.   Binding arbitration produces a final resolution of claims. Nonbinding arbitration, on the other hand, is designed to boost the negotiation process by generating information about the value of a claim. The decision of a third party, although nonbinding, assists the lawyers and their clients in realistically valuing the case and thus provides a focus for settlement negotiations.

Nonbinding arbitration typically is "court-annexed" arbitration, as contrasted with arbitration voluntarily agreed to by the parties. In essence, this is another pretrial resolution technique. Instead of unstructured negotiation between the lawyers, a bargaining procedure is sanctioned by the court. Some courts provide the ADR service rather than sending the cases to a private ADR provider (Stienstra & Willging, 1995).

In court-annexed arbitration, statutes or local court rules authorize trial courts to require disputants in specified cases to engage in nonbinding arbitration before taking their cases to trial (Gifford, 1985). The cases stipulated for arbitration might be all cases in which the amount in controversy is less than $10,000 or all medical malpractice cases. The arbitration program is administered by the court. Hearings are informal, technical rules of evidence do not usually apply, and the parties present a shortened version of their case (MacCoun et al., 1992). If the arbitrator's award is accepted by both parties, it is entered as the judgment of the court. However, if no agreement is reached, then a trial can occur. Usually, however, if the party rejecting the arbitrator's award fails to do better in the trial than the arbitrator's award, it is forced to pay court costs, the other party's attorneys' fees, or some other specified penalty (MacCoun et al., 1992). Frequently, these penalties are minimal and do not stop the losing side from asking for a full trial, which increases the costs to both sides.

One useful outcome of nonbinding arbitration may be to give each side a realistic view of their case. Indeed, this is a major outcome of several ADR methods. One side's inflated expectations may be dimmed when confronted by the reality of an arbitrator's decision. The lowered expectations often lead that disputant to resolve the conflict.

In all, few arbitrated cases, perhaps 10 percent, go on to trial (MacCoun & Kerr, 1988; MacCoun et al., 1992). Sometimes, on hearing the arbitrator's decision, the losing party may demand a trial, but this is generally a tactical ploy to get a better deal through negotiation (Meierhoefer, 1990).

Lind et al. (1990) reported that most participants in arbitration think it is a fair procedure and preferable to adjudication in court. Winners, no surprise, like it better than losers.

MacCoun et al. (1992) think highly of arbitration, especially court-annexed arbitration. They think courts ought to view this ADR method as a way of providing increased access to "fair, impartial, adjudicative third-party hearings" without an increase in costs or number of trials. Research has supported this view and has shown that participants and attorneys are very satisfied with the arbitration process (Meierhoefer, 1990; Rauma & Krafka, 1994). But then litigants generally express satisfaction with most legal processes (Stienstra & Willging, 1995).

Early Neutral Evaluation.   Another creative variation of ADR is to ask a neutral expert to evaluate a case at an early stage, before expenses have been incurred to prepare a case for trial. The **early neutral evaluation** (ENE) program originated in northern California and has been used extensively in the federal district court there since 1985. This program is used for high-stakes cases, generally with more than $150,000 at issue. Within 150 days of case filing, the parties present their cases in summary fashion to a respected senior attorney who has expertise in the subject area of the dispute. The evaluator identifies the issues, assesses the strengths and weaknesses of each side, places a value on the case, and assists the parties in negotiating a settlement (Stienstra & Willging, 1995). Attorneys representing parties in cases that have gone through the process give it high marks, but a control group of attorneys whose cases did not go through early neutral evaluation were equally satisfied with the process and the results (Rosenberg & Folberg, 1994).

Summary Jury Trials. The **summary jury trial** (SJT), developed initially by retired federal district court judge Thomas Lambros, is another form of nonbinding adjudication designed to assist the parties in the negotiation process. It involves a summary presentation of evidence to a mock jury, which issues a nonbinding opinion. All elements of the trial are present, but in an abbreviated form, often without witnesses. The trial takes place when both parties are in fact ready actually to go to trial. The mock jury "verdict" now becomes the jumping off point for negotiation.

Judge Lambros has used the summary trial when he felt that the disputants were not able to settle through pretrial negotiations. The summary trial served to let both sides know what their case was worth, and thereby to speed settlement. Of course, as MacCoun et al. (1992) noted, one jury does not tell the whole story. Another jury on another day confronting the same evidence may give a different verdict. Nevertheless, the verdict of a jury in a summary trial can serve as a reminder of the risk of trial. An examination of the summary jury trial by Alfini (1989) found that most such cases settled several weeks after hearing the mock jury's verdict. As you might expect, the jury's verdicts tended to fall between the disputants' original negotiating positions.

One concern about the summary jury trial is the fear that it is used simply as another weapon in the lawyer's bag of adversarial tricks. The SJT may be a way of finding out what the other party's tactics will be, and once this is done, the adversaries may demand a trial (Menkel-Meadow, 1991). Many observers, such as Neil Vidmar (1996), believe that the summary jury trial does not work, in part because the court usually controls the procedure tightly and persuades often reluctant disputants to enter into the procedures.

Minitrials. **Minitrials** are voluntary and private proceedings in which both parties present evidence to assist them in reaching a negotiated agreement. The parties agree in advance about the rules and procedure for the conduct of the hearing. The participants include senior representatives of the parties who have the authority to reach a settlement and who actively participate in the *minitrial.*

Minitrials have been used primarily to resolve business disputes in which the parties have an ongoing relationship. The minitrial is much like a summary jury trial but is in essence a private affair. Negotiations may continue until an agreement is reached or the parties conclude that they cannot agree.

Rent-a-Judge Programs.   If you try to buy a judge, you could get into trouble. That's called bribery and usually carries a stiff sentence. But sometimes the parties to a dispute decide to pay a neutral third party, often a retired judge or an arbitrator, to hear their claims. The program began in 1976 in California and has spread to other states, usually under the authority of a state statute. Most states have such a system, but a majority rarely use it (Litkovitz, 1995). The advantage is that the disputants can schedule a trial at their convenience and control parts of the procedure. For example, they could decide to have a closed hearing and protect their secrets. Generally, they waive their right to a jury trial, and they can agree to be bound by the results. To ensure that the parties comply with the outcome, the private judge's ruling can be entered as a judgement of a state or local trial court. Unless the disputants agree to be bound by the judgment, it can be appealed.

The rent-a-judge program looks a lot like arbitration. The difference is that the courts have nothing to do with selecting the judge or controlling other features of the program. It is totally private until the "judge's" decision is entered in a court. The benefits seem to be speed and privacy, but the disputants also derive a sense of control and satisfaction from being able to select the decision maker and to decide on the procedures to be employed.

Alternative Dispute Resolution in Criminal Proceedings

The popularity of dispute resolution centers is increasing markedly even in criminal arenas. One of the oldest such programs was started at Brooklyn College of the City University of New York and was made possible by a New York state grant. It operates on the Brooklyn College campus and is staffed by university personnel. The Brooklyn Dispute Resolution Center (BDRC) deals with the relatively minor disputes that would clog the courts. These usually involve individuals who know one another and would normally consider filing charges in cases of harassment, larceny, criminal trespass, excessive noise, and uncontrolled pets.

The procedure at the BDRC involves mediation. Individuals are offered mediation rather than criminal prosecution. The complainant and the defendant meet face-to-face in the presence of a mediator. Most of these cases involve assaults, particularly domestic violence. These are cases that have the potential for repeat offenses. Furthermore, the parties are engaged in a long-term relationship, usually as neighbors, so these are instances that are peculiarly suitable for mediation. The mediation process does seem to have some positive effects because many complainants report an improved relationship, at least in the near term (MacCoun et al., 1992).

Current Status of Alternative Dispute Resolution

Most disputants prefer face-to-face (two-party) procedures for resolving conflicts over the use of a third party, as in mediation or arbitration. Some justice researchers have suggested that disputants prefer arbitration over other ADRs in competitive situations; others believe the preferences may be affected by the nature of the dispute. Heuer and Penrod (1994a) found that if a disputant believes there is room for concessions and it is a winner-take-all game, the preference is for mediation. If the situation is viewed as one in which each party can win some and lose some, however, face-to-face negotiation is preferred. The moral here is that for ADR to work most effectively, it must offer resolution methods that match the preferences and demands of the disputants.

One concern about using ADR is that individuals of different ethnic and racial backgrounds would differ in their perceptions of which procedures were fair. Lind, Huo, and Tyler (1994), in one of the few experimental studies on ADR, addressed this concern by offering individuals of different ethnic backgrounds access to various dispute resolution procedures. In a situation that involved a dispute with a close friend over money, the resolution procedures offered to the subjects included ignoring the situation or selecting from persuasion, negotiation, mediation, or arbitration. Subjects were asked to rate their willingness to use any of these procedures and to indicate their perception that the procedure was fair. Over 300 individuals representing four groups (Asian Americans, European Americans, Hispanic Americans, and African Americans) participated in this experiment.

Lind at al. (1994) provide data suggesting that the differences among the four groups represented in their study were minimal. As Figure 5.1 shows, all four ethnic groups gave relatively high ratings to persuasion and negotiation, somewhat lower ratings to social influence (face-to-face negotiation), and lowest ratings to mediation and arbitration. Recall, though, the dispute involved a close friend. Different procedures would likely be chosen in other dispute situations. The major point is the lack of substantial ethnic differences.

In personal injury cases, Lind et al. (1994) found that disputants preferred trial or arbitration over negotiations, believing that the first two procedures gave them a more respectful hearing. In a high-conflict situation, negotiating with someone who has caused you injury simply may not work. Trials, with their formalized procedures, tend to increase litigant perception of fairness, leading to the suggestion that if a case was not heard at trial, the litigant has not received the full respect the system owes him or her. Face-to-face (bilateral) negotiation may fail the test of fairness because one side competes with the other to show whose version of reality is better.

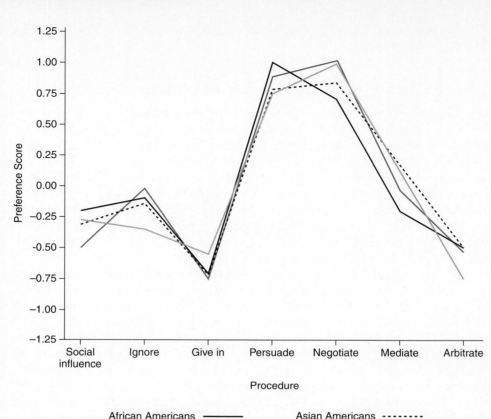

FIGURE 5.1   Preferences for dispute resolution procedures among four ethnic groups.

This figure shows that the four major population groups in the United States did not differ in significant ways in their preferences for dispute resolutions procedures.

Source: From ". . . And Justice for All: Ethnicity, Gender, and Preferences for Dispute Resolution Procedures," by E. A. Lind, Y. J. Huo, and T. R. Tyler, 1994, *Law and Human Behavior, 18*(3), p. 279.

Still to be addressed are the political implications of such alternative modes of resolution. How can we be sure that the alternatives will increase rather than limit access to justice? Alternatives might be a way for the courts not to have to deal with minor claims of less than perhaps $500 or $1,000. These claims, however, are hardly unimportant for the people involved. Of course, litigants always have the option of going to small claims court, where they can argue their case before a judge by themselves.

Has alternative dispute resolution actually lowered the courts' burden and quickened resolutions of disputes? Studies of the federal courts suggest that it may have, citing some possible cost savings and the perception of some judges that their caseload is less burdensome because of the availability of ADR (Meierhoefer, 1990). Recent research has shown that arbitrations can reduce the time required to process a case by as much as 30 percent to 60 percent. In many jurisdictions where ADR is used, the number of cases going to trial has gone down. The evidence is mixed, however, and often does not take into account the costs of the programs (Stienstra & Willging, 1995).

The record is less positive for mediation, at least in the small claims and child custody contexts. In one study of a small claims mediation program, no real difference was found in the time to mediate versus the time to adjudicate. In the case of California's mandatory mediation for child custody cases, there is some evidence indicating that mediation may actually slow the process rather than hasten it. Of course, convenience is not the only reason to engage in mediation. Improving the quality of the resolution and enhancing the long-term relationship between the disputants are probably as important as any other result. Lessening of hostility may mean fewer couples seek to return to court at some later point. On the other hand, recent studies of the use of mediation in federal courts show dramatic successes in reducing costs and delays (Stienstra & Willging, 1995).

Two final considerations should be noted. Alternative dispute resolution may be private or it may be public (i.e., rent-a-judge or court-annexed arbitration). When private parties pay private judges to help resolve disputes, what happens to the less affluent and to the poor? Do they have access to ADR? We may face the possibility of a two-tiered justice system in which the poor seek help in overcrowded and inferior courts while the affluent obtain access to a variety of effective alternative dispute forums.

A second concern is with the quality of the mediators and arbitrators. Who are they? Some are trained professionals, many of whom are lawyers and retired judges, who belong to the Society of Professionals in Dispute Resolution. The National Institute for Dispute Resolutions (NIDR) serves as a resource center for professional dispute professionals.

The dispute industry is beginning to set standards and decide on ethical guidelines. States such as Colorado, Florida, and Texas now regulate mediators (Bush, 1994). However, "buyer beware" remains the watchword ("Too Many Lawyers," 1992).

PLEA BARGAINING

Few alternative dispute resolution methods are available in the criminal arena. Clearly the difference between civil and criminal cases is the involvement in criminal cases of the prosecutorial arm of the state. The bulk of felony (serious crimes) cases, as we know, are resolved not by trial but by negotiation between attorneys or, in some jurisdictions, among attorneys and the judge. This *plea bargaining* occurs when the accused exchanges a guilty plea for a discounted sentence. Evidence from the states and the federal courts shows that 66 percent to 89 percent of the criminal cases are resolved by an agreement between the two sides.

Although negotiating skills are important here, plea bargaining has less flexibility than one would normally find in other negotiation situations. The courts view plea bargaining as advantageous to both defense and prosecution; evidence, however, suggests that the state has an overwhelming advantage in the negotiation (Gifford, 1983).

Legal Limits to Plea Bargaining

A plea bargain is in a sense a contract between the accused and the state. In return for a reduced sentence, the accused agrees to plead guilty, thereby absolving the court system of having to spend time and effort on the case. The accused may also offer information or other evidence that the prosecutor can use against other suspects.

The most important legal standard is the voluntariness of the defendant's guilty plea: Coercion should have no role in the bargaining. Of course, coercion is inherent when one of the participants is in all probability going to lose his or her liberty for a time. This bargained plea has been perceived by the U.S. Supreme Court as meeting the voluntariness standard so long as the defendant was represented by counsel and had the opportunity to compare the merits of a plea with those of a trial. The Court suggested that beyond the administrative advantages of a guilty plea, which makes an expensive trial unnecessary, a bargained plea serves a positive rehabilitative purpose. By admitting guilt, the defendant states that he or she broke the social contract and is willing to be rehabilitated (Gifford, 1983).

The accused often runs the risk of increased punishment, however, by refusing to plead guilty. Some critics of plea bargaining believe that offering this option compels individuals to incriminate themselves, violating rights secured by the Fifth Amendment (Tonry, 1995). In *Bordenkircher v. Hayes* (1978), an individual who had a prior record was charged with forging a check. The state offered this bargain: If the accused would plead guilty, the state would recommend a five-year prison sentence. The defendant rejected the offer. Apparently there was another side to the bargain. The prosecutor had informed the defendant that if the initial bargain was rejected, the state would seek a life sentence under Kentucky's Habitual Criminal Act (Alschuler, 1979). The case did indeed go to trial and a life sentence was imposed. The defendant appealed, arguing that the difference between pleading guilty to forging an $88 check or standing trial and being found guilty for the same offense was five years versus life imprisonment. The Supreme Court upheld the constitutionality of the sentence imposed upon the defendant.

The various court rulings taken together prohibit certain behaviors on the part of the prosecutor. The prosecutor cannot threaten to prosecute on a charge not justified by the evidence in the case. Also, if the defendant has indeed fulfilled his or her commitment, the prosecutor is proscribed from going back on a struck bargain, such as changing a recommendation from a lighter sentence to a more severe one once the plea bargain has been struck (*Santobello v. New York*, 1971). Once the bargain has been made, judges tend to follow the prosecutor's recommendations, though nothing requires them to do so. Of course, a prosecutor is unlikely to make a bargain that would not be accepted by a judge. To engage in such bargaining would undermine the prosecutor's credibility.

Plea Bargaining in Perspective

As Feeley (1979) suggested, plea bargaining, which he defines as "the explicit or implicit exchange of reduction in charge for a plea of guilty" (p. 199), must be understood as one part of the negotiation that pervades the entire system. The adversary system exists beyond the trial; its procedures penetrate the system from the moment an individual is funneled into the criminal or civil justice structure. Maynard (1988) has shown that both parties in a plea bargain try to devise a "story" so that both sides gain some advantage and, not so incidentally, that justice is roughly served.

The public belief is that plea bargaining occurs because of the crowded court docket, but there is evidence to the contrary (Tonry, 1995). It shows that plea bargaining has less to do with the current glut of criminal proceedings facing the courts than with the adversarial character of the legal system, in which issues are open to negotiation.

Pros and Cons of Plea Bargaining.   The most obvious philosophical difficulty with plea bargaining is that it denies the accused the opportunity to have his or her guilt proven beyond a reasonable doubt. For the issues not to be submitted to trial may be seen as subverting the individual's Sixth Amendment right to trial by an impartial jury. However, the accused is made to pay heavily for engaging his or her right to a criminal trial. Trial is a costly enterprise and plea bargaining is an efficient way of disposing of much of the load in the criminal justice system.

Early critics of plea bargaining believed that justice may not be served at all by the process (Hyman, 1979). Defenders of the system may accept this point in some cases but argue that if guilt seems relatively certain, plea bargaining is less offensive to standards of justice (Casper, 1979). Bordens (1984), and Bordens and Bassett (1985) found that sometimes even college students asked to play the role of an innocent suspect will plead guilty to cut their losses if they think they will be found guilty in a trial. More persuasively, in the Bordens and Bassett (1985) study, probationers from a county jail claimed that they had accepted guilty pleas in exchange for a sentence reduction when they were innocent. These were "savvy" veterans of the criminal justice system. Of course, their profession of innocence is hardly proof.

For a defendant, deciding whether to accept a plea bargain can be difficult. The Courtroom Application in the box below is a striking example of one pitfall of this type of resolution.

Among the most powerful arguments against the use of plea bargaining are those put forth by Kenneth Kipnis (1989), who believes that plea bargaining violates basic constitutional liberties, including the Fifth Amendment right not to incriminate oneself and the right to the most reasonable sentence compatible with the crime. Kipnis argues that plea bargaining offers defendants compelling reasons to incriminate themselves by pleading guilty. If the plea is not accepted, as we have seen in *Bordenkircher v. Hayes* (1978), the state is free to ask for a much more severe penalty at the trial level. Plea bargaining thus, in the critics'

COURTROOM APPLICATIONS

The Plea Bargain That Was No Bargain

Rather than take a chance on a jury verdict, Russell Barnes accepted a prosecutor's offer and pleaded guilty to one count of aggravated robbery in a mugging. In return, five other charges were dropped. Barnes, who was 19, was charged in an incident in which he and others allegedly beat several individuals and robbed them of $600.

The decision cost him at least three and a half years in prison. Barnes was on trial before a jury. He was scared. He thought the jury would find him guilty, despite his protestations of innocence. Barnes instructed his lawyer to ask the prosecutor to reconsider the plea bargain he had rejected earlier. His lawyer, a public defender, advised his client against the plea bargain. The defense lawyer apparently was confident in the jury's verdict. Defendant Barnes was not. The prosecutor was obviously in accord with the defense lawyer and must have thought Barnes had a good chance of being acquitted. The prosecutor and Barnes agreed to a deal. Then came the "O. Henry" twist.

The judge decided to let the jury read its verdict for the benefit of the attorneys who argued the case and to make a court record in case of appeal. The judge asked Barnes whether he wanted to hear the verdicts. He did.

Moments after Barnes agreed to the plea bargain, the jury had found him innocent of all charges. By then, the judge had accepted the guilty plea and it could not be withdrawn.

Source: "The Bargain That Was No Bargain," 1992, p. 9.

view, violates fundamental individual rights and results in sentencing procedures that are not reasonable.

Differences Between Plea Bargaining and Civil Negotiations.   In civil cases, the ultimate decision in the negotiation remains with the clients. True, clients very often accept the suggestions of their lawyers, but not until consultation between advocate and client takes place. Gifford (1983) reminded us that in plea bargaining there is no authority (judge) to ratify the prosecutor's decision. The prosecutor alone determines the public interest. Although a judge must agree to the outcome of negotiation, no one oversees the prosecutor's decision. The one party with a strong interest in plea bargaining, the victim, rarely has input into the decision.

Another difference between plea bargaining and civil negotiation is the adversaries' comprehension of the outcome. In civil cases, the outcome most often is expressed in money. If we settle now, we'll get $80,000. If we go to trial, we may get more, but there is the possibility in this kind of case that we might get only $40,000. Given the time, expense, and risk of a trial, the negotiated figure may seem a fair bargain. The options in this example are clear.

Gifford (1983) pointed out that in criminal plea bargaining cases the outcomes are not as clearly quantified for the defendant. The prosecutor's offer may appear to be reasonable compared with maximum possible sentences but may, in fact, be comparable to the *usual* sentences the court imposes in such cases. Also, defendants may not be informed of the parole possibilities. Gifford suggested that defendants often receive less in plea bargaining than they think they do. In Gifford's view, given the inequities of the plea-bargaining procedure, the defendant gives up a great many rights, including the Sixth Amendment right to trial, the right to have one's guilt demonstrated beyond a reasonable doubt, the right to confront witnesses as well as the Fifth Amendment right not to incriminate oneself.

After decades of relative acceptance for plea bargaining as a mode of administering criminal justice, very significant questions have been raised about its use. A number of changes have been proposed to increase the fairness in the procedure and lessen the possibility of coercion. Included in this proposal are clear written standards regulating the concessions a prosecutor can offer in bargaining. Gifford offers a rather precise formula. The prosecutor's recommendation would be determined by first recognizing the defendant's likely sentence if convicted by a jury. After determining this potential sentence, the recommendation would vary from that baseline according to four factors:

1. Whether the defendant pleaded guilty
2. The circumstances of the offense and the characteristics of the defendant
3. The likelihood of acquittal on the charges
4. Extent of the defendant's cooperation with authorities

Gifford's model would require the prosecutor to state in open court the reasoning behind any recommendation, showing how the guidelines were utilized in determining the sentence.

Some reformers believe that victims of crimes should be given a formal opportunity to participate in the bargaining. They should be able to provide additional information if such is available. Furthermore, victims should be able to express their view and feelings about negotiations and sentence recommendations (Gifford, 1983; Strier, 1994).

What happens if the accused does not enter a plea bargain and is held over for trial? The court has to be sure the defendant will show up in court and not leave town to avoid trial, so the judge may set bail.

Setting Bail

During the period between arrest and trial, a defendant may be allowed to remain free provided he or she posts **bail,** a sum of money set by the judge that the defendant must pay to remain free prior to trial. The defendant must post that amount as a guarantee that he or she will appear for trial. Bail allows the defendant to continue his or her normal activities (for example, going to work) and to contribute effectively to his or her defense.

Ebbesen and Konecni (1975) observed actual bail setting hearings of five judges. They found that a judge relies most heavily on the recommendations of the prosecuting and defense attorneys. None of the case-related variables (e.g., community ties, prior record, crime severity, etc.) had any *direct* effect on the judge's decision. However, these variables may have an *indirect* effect on the judge. Undoubtedly, the prosecuting and defense attorneys consider these factors when deciding what to recommend to the judge. Crime severity and community ties especially interact to determine the recommendations made by the attorneys (Ebbesen & Konecni, 1975).

Legally irrelevant variables may influence a judge's decision concerning how much bail to require. Generally, African Americans are less likely to be released on bail than are white individuals. Additionally, there may also be a sex bias in the bail-setting decision. Bernat (1984) studied court records of individuals arrested for prostitution or soliciting a prostitute. She found that only 12.9 percent of women arrested for prostitution were released prior to arraignment, whereas 73.6 percent of men soliciting prostitutes were released. It is interesting that this bias was reversed when male prostitution was considered. Male prostitutes were less likely than female prostitutes to be released prior to arraignment.

Although bail is generally available to most defendants, it may not be available to all. The Bail Reform Act of 1984 allows for the detention of an arrestee if it can be shown that there are no release conditions that could "reasonably assure" the safety of other persons and the community. For example, in *United States v. Salerno* (1987), the U.S. Supreme Court upheld the use of the Bail Reform Act to deny bail to a "lethally dangerous" Mafia leader. The Court reasoned that such a defendant would commit other crimes while out on bail and society's need for protection weighed more than the defendant's right to bail. Preventive detention has been applied to both adults and juveniles (Ewing, 1991).

PREJUDICIAL PRETRIAL PUBLICITY

When Aaron Burr, former vice president of the United States, was tried for treason in 1807, Chief Justice of the United States John Marshall, sitting as the trial judge, had to consider the issue of prejudicial pretrial publicity (PTP). The Burr trial was highly publicized in 1807. The former vice president was accused of forming his own army in order to carve out an empire in the southwest and Mexico. As you might imagine, interest in the trial was intense. The question was how to find 12 jurors who were competent enough to hear the Burr case but were not so prejudiced as to be unable to render a fair verdict.

Essentially, that is still a dilemma, especially in well-publicized trials. One of the most publicized trials in the twentieth century was the murder trial of celebrity O.J. Simpson. Publicity in this case was pervasive, ranging from TV news shows to sports reports to supermarket checkout tabloids to books by witnesses and interviews with jurors discharged during the case. Lawyers commented on the evidence on television and every breathless moment of the trial was televised. The wrongful death civil trial in which the families of the murder victims sued Mr. Simpson for damages was only somewhat less exploited by the media. Was there anyone in the country who did not have knowledge of the trial? And if the judge could have found acceptable jurors to serve who had not heard of the case, would we want such totally disconnected individuals to be on the jury?

Mark Twain's comments about juries in *Roughing It* (1871/1903) still captures the dilemma facing modern courts a century later. In describing a well-publicized trial, Twain noted that only the "fools and rascals" who were ignorant of the case were jurors. Twain lamented that men of intelligence and honesty were excluded.

> A minister, intelligent, esteemed, and greatly respected; a merchant of high character and known probity; a mining superintendent of intelligence and unblemished reputation; a quartz-mill owner of excellent standing, were all questioned in the same way, and all set aside. Each said the public talk and the newspaper reports had not so biased his mind but that sworn testimony would . . . enable him to render a verdict without prejudice and in accordance with the facts. But of course such men could not be trusted with the case. Ignoramuses alone could mete out unsullied justice. (p. 75)

In *Burr*, the basis for seating a juror was not ignorance. Chief Justice Marshall wanted men who could reasonably set aside their biases. Who did not have a bias in the *Burr* trial, a case involving the alleged treason of a famous and intriguing public man? With just a touch of skepticism, Marshall took most jurors at their word. If they said they could be unbiased, that was enough (most of the time). Marshall did exclude a close political ally of Burr's rival, President Thomas Jefferson. The excluded juror, a U.S. senator, took great offense at this and indicated with some vehemence that he could indeed separate his personal feelings from his civic duty as a juror. John Marshall stated that a potential juror who testifies that it was possible to set aside personal biases was, in most instances, acceptable as an impartial juror. That was generally the view the courts held for more than century. The following case changed that notion.

In *Rideau v. Louisiana* (1963), Wilbert Rideau robbed a bank, killed a bank employee, and kidnapped three others. Shortly after his capture, Rideau confessed to his crimes. The morning after his confession, in a filmed interview, he again admitted his guilt. The film was subsequently broadcast three times within the next two days.

Rideau was convicted by the trial court, and on appeal, the conviction was upheld by the Louisiana State Supreme Court. The subsequent appeal to the U.S. Supreme Court yielded a reversal on the grounds that Rideau was denied due process of law because the trial court did not grant a **change of venue motion,** a request that the trial be moved to another district to ensure a fair trial.

Of the twelve Rideau jurors, nine had not in fact seen the interview, whereas the three who had viewed the film testified that they could indeed lay aside their opinions and render a fair verdict. The majority of the U.S. Supreme Court assumed that simple exposure to the interview was enough to sustain a charge of juror prejudice. The Court simply examined the nature of the publicity, which clearly was prejudicial, and did not examine responses of the jurors. The modern approach clearly differs from Chief Justice John Marshall's approach in the trial of Aaron Burr, which involved trusting jurors to respond truthfully about whether they could be fair and impartial. One could argue, of course, that jurors' responses as to their prejudices in a public forum (the voir dire) should not be taken at face value. Few of us will admit publicly, or indeed sometimes privately, that we are unreconstructed bigots.

The constitutional issue is this: The defendant has a Sixth Amendment right to an impartial jury in a public trial and the press and the public have a First Amendment right to information of public interest. The First Amendment right may and can prejudice the defendant's Sixth Amendment right. How to balance the two is the question.

What do we need to know? Does pretrial publicity prejudice jurors? If so, under what conditions? What characteristics of PTP are more likely to prejudice jurors? What can be done about its biasing effects, if they exist?

The trials of William Kennedy Smith, Susan Smith, Mike Tyson, O. J. Simpson, and Rodney King are among the recent examples of trials that received massive pretrial publicity that was national in scope. There are also local trials that are covered quite extensively by the news media. By one estimate, about 12,000 trials every year involve some sort of pretrial publicity (Fresca, 1988). This is a relatively small proportion of the estimated 160,000 state and federal trials per year (Abramson, 1995), but aggregate statistics cannot define the right of an individual to a fair trial.

The impact of media coverage on the conduct of specific trials has been the subject of investigation and debate. For example, in Great Britain, concerns about a defendant's rights to a fair trial and an unbiased jury led to the passage of the Contempt of Court Act, which prohibits all but the most minimal reporting of matters pertaining to ongoing legal proceedings (Hans, 1990). However, in the United States, the media are generally free to publish whatever information they are able to obtain.

Simulation and Survey Studies

Researchers have been examining the effects of pretrial publicity on the attitudes of jurors for close to three decades now. The early research tended to be plagued by lack of realistic simulations and sometimes a lack of appropriate controls. These studies generally have shown that PTP does bias jurors' attitudes, but the researchers say nothing about jurors' verdicts (e.g., Tans & Chaffee, 1966).

Other studies have examined the effect of PTP on juror verdicts. Rita James Simon and colleagues (1966) carried out a simulation study in which a murder was written up in two ways: the first as it would be reported in the conservative style of the *New York Times;* the other as it would be reported in a sensational tabloid. In the sober account, headlines of modest size and moderate language were used, as in "New Evidence Revealed in Hyde Case." The more sensational tabloid style included the "ax-murder" approach to headline writing: "Woman Slashed to Death in Apartment"; "Knife Is Found in Murderer's Room." Simon concluded that the tabloid style, including the statement or implication that the murder weapon (the knife) was found in the home of the suspect, led to greater prejudice in pretrial publicity.

The Simon study used registered voters as subjects. Some were given the sober-sided story and others the more sensationally written account. These mock jurors were then asked their opinions as to the defendant's guilt or innocence. Almost twice as many subjects who had read the sensational account thought the accused was indeed guilty. In a subsequent study, Hoiberg and Stires (1973) found two factors that evoked and sustained prejudice in potential (mock) jurors. The first had to do with public statements about the crime made by people in positions of authority. A report by the chief of police that "We have the real culprits" was inimical to a fair trial. The second factor had to do with the heinousness of the crime. Crimes played up as brutal, with such affect-laden words as "bludgeoned" or "slashed" also tended to remain in the memory of potential jurors.

Simon took her study a step further: The mock jurors were asked to listen to a tape recording of the mock trial on the case they had read about in the newspaper. The trial included the usual admonition from the "trial judge" to lay aside all prejudice and biases about the issues in conflict. Jurors heard the trial, including the judge's instructions and the opening and closing statements made by the lawyers. As Simon (l975) reported, the most dramatic finding was that the majority of jurors now found the defendant not guilty. Of those who read the sensational story, the pretrial verdict of 67 percent was guilty. Only 25 percent of these same readers (jurors) found the defendant guilty after they heard the trial and all the evidence.

In a much more realistic simulation using a real murder case and jurors from actual jury rolls, Padawer-Singer and Barton (l975), showed that mock jurors exposed to a voir dire before their selection are less prejudiced than mock jurors not so exposed. That is, when attorneys, during the pretrial interrogation of the jurors (voir dire) advised them not to be influenced by pretrial publicity, the jurors appeared to set their preconceptions aside. This study did indicate, however, that pretrial publicity does color a potential juror's perception of the case.

More recent work by Hedy Dexter and her colleagues, however, suggests that although an extended (in-depth) voir dire does lessen some of the impact of pretrial publicity, the voir dire is not an effective means of reducing most of the effect of PTP (Dexter, Cutler, & Moran, 1992).

Furthermore, Moran and Cutler (1991), using two actual trials for which pretrial publicity had been significant, analyzed survey data gathered from potential jurors and found that the extent of jurors' pretrial knowledge of the case was significantly related to their perception that the defendants were guilty. Moreover, jurors influenced by PTP (that is, they believed the defendants were probably guilty) claimed they were impartial. So much for Justice John Marshall's trust. Moran and Cutler (1991) concluded from these surveys that modest amounts of pretrial publicity can prejudice potential jurors, and that jurors cannot be believed when they claim impartiality. This conclusion is supported by earlier research by Simon and Eimermann (1971), who surveyed potential jurors in a community in which a sensational murder trial was about to occur. They found that most people (almost 80 percent) had heard of the case and favored the prosecution. It is conceivable, of course, that a juror influenced by PTP could set aside those judgments and decide solely on the evidence expressed in the courtroom, but Moran and Cutler suggest that it is unlikely.

Effects of Different Types of Pretrial Publicity

Prejudicial pretrial publicity may target various aspects of a case. The media may report prejudicial information about a defendant's character or publish information about the alleged crime and the victim. The information might be reported sensationally or in a nonemotional, factual manner. Simon (1975) suggested that these various modes of pretrial publicity would have different effects.

Geoffrey Kramer, Norbert Kerr, and John Carroll (1990) varied the type of PTP jurors received. Factual publicity contained incriminating evidence about the defendant whereas emotional PTP did not explicitly provide incriminating evidence but did arouse a lot of negative emotion. Both factual and emotional publicity consisted of a number of television reports done in a very realistic way, with professional actors playing the roles of news reporters and interviewees.

In addition to the impact of the TV segments, Kramer et al. were interested in the effect of newspaper reports of the crime. The high-factual condition included an editorial noting that the defendant had a substantial criminal record for robbery, which was the crime alleged in the trial. In addition, potential jurors in the high-factual condition were informed of other incriminating evidence.

The high-emotional condition added several video clips of a seven-year-old girl who was hit by the automobile of the robber as he attempted his escape. Several episodes that were quite emotional and sympathetic to the child victim were added to the high-emotional condition. A baseline no-bias control condition was also used in the design of this research. The reports in the no-bias control condition gave few facts and conveyed little emotional content.

Unlike most other studies involving PTP, this one allowed the mock jurors to see the trial and then deliberate to a verdict. Jurors were asked for a preliminary response prior to their deliberation, and the results showed that PTP did not have a direct effect on their predeliberation judgments. There was, however, an important secondary effect of PTP: The predeliberation measures did not expose jurors' PTP-related biases, but the deliberations brought those biases to light. It seems that the pretrial publicity may have made the proconviction jurors more persuasive and reduced the resistance of the pro-acquittal forces.

Kramer et al. (1990) did not present direct evidence of these subtle effects, but their explanations seem reasonable in light of their data. Emotional PTP appears to have had a long-lasting effect compared to factual PTP and seems to have eroded the confidence of jurors who voted not guilty before deliberation. These less-confident jurors may simply not have been able to argue persuasively against conviction.

In another significant addition to our understanding of the impact of pretrial publicity, Amy Otto, Steven Penrod, and Hedy Dexter (1994) found that pretrial publicity does affect jurors' predeliberation judgments. Presentation of the evidence during the trial weakens the effects of PTP but does not eliminate it. Negative PTP seems to affect jurors' pretrial view of the defendant, and this in turn influences how jurors evaluate the evidence and make judgments about the defendant. Pretrial publicity about the defendant's criminal record influenced the jurors to believe the defendant had a criminal nature, and this in turn was related to their decisions after deliberating (Otto et al., 1994).

We know at this point that the influence of emotional pretrial publicity is long lasting and has an effect on the dynamics of jury deliberation. We also know that negative PTP about the defendant's character, in particular his or her past criminal record, also has an effect on both pre- and postdeliberation decisions.

In both the Kramer and the Otto studies, videotapes were used. Does the medium used to convey the pretrial publicity matter? Does television have a greater influence, as most of us believe, than a newspaper or magazine article? Would the beating of Rodney King have seemed so shocking had we simply read about it in our local newspaper or even if we had seen a news photo of it? James Ogloff and Neil Vidmar (1994) examined these questions with an actual case in Canada that received nationwide publicity. In this case, members of the Congregation of Christian Brothers of Ireland were charged with sexually and physically abusing young boys at an orphanage in St. Johns, Newfoundland. The videotapes of the "Mount Cashel Orphanage" case were taken from the Canadian Broadcasting Company's actual tapes. Newspaper accounts were garnered from a representative sample of news stories on the case.

Ogloff and Vidmar found, as they expected, that pretrial publicity information that was shown on television about sexual abuse had a significantly greater biasing impact than the same information in the print media. However, the combined effect of both television and the print media had the greatest biasing effect on their subjects. The materials that Ogloff and Vidmar (1994) used were very emotional. The materials depicted homosexual and child abuse by the lay priests at Mount Cashel. A comparison of the emotional content with that used by Kramer et al. (1990) suggests that the Mount Cashel materials are more vivid. Kramer et al. did not find an immediate effect of emotional PTP on jurors' pretrial attitudes but did find that emotional PTP influenced the jury deliberation. Sensational pretrial publicity presented graphically on television and in print has an immediate biasing effect on the recipients.

Given these most recent studies, we know that pretrial publicity can affect jurors' pretrial attitudes. We know that jurors may not readily admit these biases during the voir dire or may not be aware of how the biases can affect their verdicts. Furthermore, we now have some evidence that PTP influences the jury's deliberation in subtle ways. Perhaps most important, we know that certain types of information will have significant effects on the juror: Information about the defendant's character and criminal record has a biasing effect that influences decisions of the juror during jury deliberation. Finally, we have seen that emotional PTP presented on television, especially when combined with print media, has a powerful effect on jurors' attitudes and decisions. What if anything can be done to remedy the effects of pretrial publicity?

Potential Remedies for Pretrial Publicity

Kramer et al. (1990) carefully examined the possible remedies that might be used to eliminate or lessen the effects of pretrial publicity. Parenthetically, all the research we have reported has dealt with PTP that casts the defendant in a negative light. One may envision a scenario in which PTP is engineered by a charismatic defendant—or defense attorney—to bias the jury in favor of the defense. Imagine a famous and much admired celebrity on trial for some heinous crime. News reports recall the defendant's dynamic public image and previous worthwhile deeds—as a Marine or as mayor of a city. Defense attorneys call frequent press conferences discussing the defense's evidence. Researchers have not yet examined the effects of positive prejudicial publicity.

There are several methods by which a judge attempts to combat pretrial publicity:

1. Issuing judicial admonitions/instructions
2. Conducting extensive voir dire of prospective jurors and eliminating those who have read media accounts of the case
3. Issuing a continuance or delay of trial
4. Granting a change of venue
5. Imposing gag orders on the attorneys

The potential effectiveness of these remedies is examined in the next sections.

Judicial Instructions: Do Not Think of a White Bear.   The trial judge can tell the jurors to ignore all prejudicial pretrial information. Research suggests that these admonitions from the bench are not very effective in eliminating the effect of legally inadmissible evidence or prejudicial material. In fact, instructions designed to remove bias may strengthen it by calling attention to the proscribed material or arousing the jurors' reaction to it (Tanford, 1991b). This phenomenon was vividly demonstrated in an experiment in which subjects were told not to think of a white bear for five minutes (Wegner, 1989). Whenever the thought of a white bear popped into mind, subjects were to ring a bell. During the five-minute period, subjects rang the bell often. More interesting, however, was the discovery that once the five minutes were up, the white bears really took over, in a kind of a rebound effect. Subjects who had tried to suppress thoughts of white bears could think of little else after the five minutes expired. The study demonstrated that even if we successfully fend off an unwanted thought for a while, it may soon return to our minds with a vengeance.

Jury Selection.   Jury selection/voir dire is the most commonly used remedy for prejudicial pretrial publicity. Studies show that jurors who indicated that they could maintain impartiality in spite of their exposure to PTP are nevertheless influenced by it. Additionally, the voir dire has been found to increase conviction rates among those exposed to neutral PTP (Kramer et al., 1990). Last, elimination of all jurors who have heard about an important case produces a jury that is likely to be seriously deficient in its knowledge of current events (Hans, 1990). In any event, as we have noted earlier, recent research suggests that the voir dire may not effectively identify jurors contaminated by PTP (Moran & Cutler, 1991). It is especially noteworthy that Kramer et al. (1990) reported that biased jurors were as likely as nonbiased jurors to survive the voir dire interrogation.

Jury Deliberations: A Cure for Pretrial Publicity?   A fundamental finding of small group research indicates that group discussion tends to polarize individual sentiments (Myers & Lamm, 1976). One consequence is that a small publicity-induced bias at the individual level could be exacerbated by the group deliberation. Studies of jury deliberation suggest that PTP does have an effect on deliberation, in spite of admonitions.

Recall that Kramer et al. found that pretrial publicity that was either emotional or factual did not appear to affect predeliberation verdicts, ratings of likelihood of guilt, or length of sentence. However, jurors exposed to highly emotional publicity and who voted not guilty were significantly less confident than jurors exposed to publicity with a low emotional content and who voted not guilty.

This finding counters arguments that publicity has little effect on juror verdicts. Although the subjects seemed to disregard PTP, they were sensitive to it when recommending a sentence. An analysis of the deliberation process found that exposure to highly emotional pretrial publicity produced a significantly higher rate of comments based solely on the publicity. Exposure to prejudicial factual PTP also had a significant effect on the rate of comments based on specific features of the factual publicity. Postdeliberation results indicated that subjects exposed to emotionally biasing PTP were significantly more prone to convict than subjects not exposed to such publicity. Deliberation served to increase the impact of the emotional information.

Among the juries that Kramer et al. (1990) studied, those that had not been exposed to PTP did not render a single guilty verdict. The authors argued that PTP may erode the jurors' inclination to give a criminal defendant the "benefit of the [reasonable] doubt."

Use of a Continuance.   The use of continuance (postponement of the trial until the effects of the pretrial publicity can subside) does not substantially reduce the effects of emotional PTP. The passage of several days did not dilute the emotional reactions in subjects' memory (Kramer et al., 1990). The data on the results of a delay (a week to two months) indicate that a delay was effective in countering factually biasing publicity but not emotionally based PTP. Overall, PTP effects were stronger for juries than for jurors.

Gag Orders.   A trial judge can try to stop the media from publishing or broadcasting material deemed prejudicial. This is rarely attempted and even more rarely upheld (*Press-Enterprise Company v. Superior Court* (1984). Gag orders severely challenge the First Amendment; anyway, the critical information usually leaks out (Tanford, 1991b). The judge in the Simpson civil trial successfully placed a gag order on all participants and denied the use of cameras in the courtroom. Because the Simpson criminal trial had been perhaps the best publicized and reported trial ever, it is understandable that a competent and strong judge would impose restrictions on the civil trial.

Change of Venue.   Occasionally, residents in the community in which the crime occurred may be prejudiced against the defendant, and the bulk of the citizenry may have made a pretrial judgment on the guilt of the accused. Under these circumstances, a trial may be removed to a different location—*a change of venue.* For this to happen, certain conditions must exist. The first has to do with defendants who have accumulated such notoriety that most people have a negative attitude toward them and would be unable to evaluate the evidence fairly. Prejudice can take hold also when people have knowledge about the case to which a jury would not ordinarily be privy.

A change of venue may be obtained when the attorney requesting the change can document the prejudice and its effects. In recent years, courts have been more amenable to using public opinion polls to document the effects of prejudicial pretrial publicity on potential jurors. Deciding what level of prejudice requires a change of venue is a difficult call. What proportion of the population has to exhibit prejudice before a change may be ordered? It is difficult to get a criterion level a priori, but one can imagine some possibilities. For example, a court could address the issue as a mathematical-statistical problem. The court would change the venue only if the number of potential jurors in the venire would not be great enough for a trial after those biased by PTP had been excluded.

Other successful change of venue applications based on surveys often reveal similar data. McConahey, Mullin, and Frederick (1977) conducted a survey in a well-publicized case that involved the murder of a prison guard by the defendant Joan Little, a black woman. Little claimed that the deceased tried to rape her. She defended herself by plunging an ice pick into his body. The prosecutor argued that the jailer was lured into the cell by the defendant, who had planned to murder him.

McConahey et al. (1977) conducted a random telephone survey of the rural North Carolina county in which the incident took place and discovered that more than three-quarters of the community had had "a lot of exposure" to news of the case. Beyond this, the survey revealed a broad strain of racism and sexism in the county (Lind, 1982). This survey also included data from an adjacent county and a third county, more urban and distant from the other two. Such comparative baseline data are often lacking in survey investigations. The comparisons suggested that the rural county in which the crime occurred held twice as many people who were likely to convict Ms. Little and that they were twice as likely to hold sexist and racist views as those surveyed in a comparable rural county, as well as in the distant urban county. The survey data were complemented by presentation in court of analyses of newspapers and by expert witnesses, who testified about the effects of prejudicial pretrial publicity. Furthermore, these data were supplemented by 100 affidavits gathered from people in the community, documenting the hardening of community opinion against the defendant. The trial judge, clearly influenced by the survey data, granted the motion to change the venue.

In cases of massive nationwide publicity such as the Rodney King or O. J. Simpson trials, it is not at all clear that changing the site of the trial reduces the impact of pretrial bias. In fact, an argument can be made that change of venue in certain well-publicized cases is precisely the wrong thing to do. The old notion that the best juror is one who lives in the vicinity and understands the nature of life in that community may have validity.

In 1992, in the wake of massive publicity in the first Rodney King trial, the trial judge ordered the venue of the trial to be moved from Los Angeles County to Ventura County. Ventura was a neighbor in terms of physical proximity but a stranger in terms of race, income level, and other demographics of its residents. It was a haven for retired police officers and armed forces veterans. Observers argued that Ventura County jurors were not sufficiently aware of the climate in Los Angeles to understand the mind-set of the victim or the police. In this case, changing the venue may have blinded justice.

So where does this leave us? Is there no remedy for the effects of pretrial publicity? Selecting only ignorant jurors is no panacea unless we want to be ruled by the unknowing. The voir dire does not remedy PTP, although we suspect that an extended voir dire will weed out a fair number of fatally biased jurors. Judge's warnings (admonitions) do not work. The jury does not police itself during the deliberations as much as we would hope.

Change of venue can work in certain limited exposure trials, but perhaps not in trials that receive massive publicity. The behavioral science research does not point to a simple cure, but it is informative because it shows how vulnerable the jury system is to the impact of pretrial publicity.

SUMMARY

Most injuries or grievances do not end up in court. Filing a lawsuit represents a rare end point to a process that has at least four distinct stages: incurring an injury and perceiving it as such (naming), seeing the injury as being the fault of someone else (blaming), and claiming a right to compensation or other redress from the party inflicting the injury. Only when a dispute arises because the other party rejects that claim can a dispute ripen into a lawsuit—the fourth and final stage. Relatively few injuries, perhaps as few as 1 or 2 percent, lead to litigation. Even seriously injured people rarely consult a lawyer and file suit.

Causal attributions made by injured people are likely to determine the occurrence and character of a dispute. The nature of the attributions will also point toward the type of solution the disputant will want—for example, whether compensation will suffice or punishment will be sought.

Most disputes are resolved in some manner or other outside the formal legal system. Forms of alternative dispute resolution (ADR) have emerged in recent decades in the courts, in communitywide dispute resolution programs, and in the private sector.

Expanded use of arbitration, mediation and other forms of alternative dispute resolution was stimulated primarily by the expense of traditional litigation, by crowded court dockets, and by a concern for the quality of the process. There are several ADR methods. Mediation involves the use of a third party (mediator) to facilitate face-to-face discussions by the disputants and to help them assess each other's needs and come to a resolution that takes into account their needs and interests. Arbitration involves the use of a neutral party or sometimes a panel of neutral parties to hear arguments, consider evidence, and decide the outcome. Nonbinding arbitration is designed to boost the negotiation process by generating information about the value of a claim. Early neutral evaluation is used for high stakes cases. Soon after a case is filed, the parties present their cases in summary fashion to an experienced attorney who identifies the issues, assesses the strengths and weaknesses of each side, places a value on the case, and assists the parties in negotiating a settlement. The summary jury trial (SJT) is a nonbinding adjudicatory device. It involves a summary presentation of evidence to a mock jury that issues a nonbinding opinion; this opinion, if agreeable to both sides, becomes the beginning point for negotiations.

All the ADR processes have been researched to some degree, but much about them remains unknown. Policy questions are yet unresolved. When private parties create private programs to resolve disputes, less affluent citizens may be left with a lesser form of justice in overcrowded and underfunded public courts. Public attention also needs to be paid to the quality of the mediators and arbitrators and the standards of practice in those fields.

In the criminal area, pretrial negotiation is also a standard feature. The bulk of felony (serious crimes) cases, as we know, are resolved not by trial but by negotiation between attorneys or, in some jurisdictions, among attorneys and the judge. This *plea bargaining* occurs when the accused exchanges a guilty plea for a discounted sentence. In return for a reduced sentence, the accused agrees to plead guilty, thereby absolving the court system of having to spend time and effort on a trial.

The most obvious philosophical difficulty with plea bargaining is that the accused does not have the opportunity to have his or her guilt proven beyond a reasonable doubt. The fact that the issues are not submitted to trial may be seen as subverting the individual's Sixth Amendment right to trial by an impartial jury.

A final pretrial issue that the courts must deal with occurs when there is prejudicial pretrial publicity in the media. Under such conditions, the court must decide whether the defendant can receive a trial before an impartial jury. Research indicates that the most prejudicial pretrial publicity is the type that appeals to the emotions of the public. The primary affect of such PTP is seen in the jury's deliberations. Juries exposed to emotional PTP are more likely to use this information in their deliberations to the detriment of the defendant. There are no foolproof methods of counteracting pretrial publicity.

CHAPTER
6

The Trial: Selection of a Jury, Opening Acts, and Rules of Evidence

Faith in the jury system is an idiosyncrasy of English-speaking people, and even the English have excluded juries from many criminal and all civil cases. European jurists are dismayed by the common law practice of turning over responsibility for judging the guilt or innocence of a defendant to six or more lay people, untrained in the law. Nevertheless, whatever the drawbacks of the system, the criminal jury is viewed by many in the United States as a fundamental protection against potential governmental oppression (Abramson, 1995).

Yet as we will see, neither the public nor the judiciary has complete agreement about how juries should function and why faith in the jury is justified. In fact, our trust in the jury seems to wax and wan. One reason for this uncertainty is that the present form of the jury apparently represents an historical accident. The English jury began as a group of witnesses recruited from the accused person's own neighborhood, and about four centuries ago, it became a body of judgelike citizens seeking to render a verdict solely on the basis of the evidence presented at trial. How this happened and whether it happened for better or worse remains a point of debate even today (Fletcher, 1994).

BRIEF HISTORY OF THE JURY

The feature of the American legal system most clearly in the public consciousness is the adversarial trial by jury. The origins of trial by jury and its function are shrouded in myth and the veils of history. Jury trials were used in Greece five or six hundred years before the birth of Jesus. In the courts of Athens in 500 B.C., trials were played to juries alone, without judges (Abraham, 1980). The size of the jury varied in direct proportion to the importance of the case. Socrates imbibed the hemlock after being tried before 501 jurors, and Alcibiades' treason trial a hundred years earlier was played before 1,501 jurors. Greek tragedy played to a full house in Athens.

The trial closed in Athens, however, and moved to Rome some ten centuries later. Charles Rembar (1980) traces the modern jury to France and then to England with the arrival of the Norman conquerors. Thus, the law that we call Anglo-Saxon seems to be neither Anglo nor necessarily Saxon. The modern jury appears to have had its beginning during the reign of Henry II in the twelfth century. Henry, it seems, had a strong need for law and order. Prosecution of wrongdoers was a haphazard affair in the early part of his reign, although punishment was swift and sure. A crime might be observed, or imagined, and a "hue and cry" would be raised. All inhabitants of the locale would then give chase until the "criminal" was caught and punished.

Henry aimed at establishing one body of law for all of England and an orderly manner of initiating prosecution and distributing guilt. He made it clear that law would come from a single source: the king. Litigation, or trial by jury, would be part of this new arrangement of law and it would be a constant, available to the people for specified crimes. The procedure, according to Rembar, was that the king would send forth representatives, who would inquire about events among the local inhabitants. A number of "good and lawful" men were summoned to serve as jurors. This jury reported to the king's representative. Essentially, they handed down an indictment based on their personal knowledge of events, hearsay, and common knowledge of the case (Rembar, 1980).

If the accused went to trial, it was by "ordeal." He or she would be compelled to have hot coals or hot iron impressed on his or her body. If the wound healed properly, the defendant was declared innocent. If not, the verdict was guilty. In any event, innocent or not, the defendant would be compelled to leave the realm. In the middle half of the twelfth century, to be condemned to exile was a fearsome prospect.

The "good and lawful" men of the twelfth century may have been no less interested in discovering the truth of matters than their twentieth-century counterparts. The use of trial by ordeal may seem absurd from a modern point of view, but it was well within the worldview of Henry's times. The inhabitants of that world believed that unseen and unknowable forces controlled events. If someone was innocent, then the wounds inflicted during a trial by ordeal would allow these forces to aid the accused to prove his or her innocence (Fletcher, 1994).

The jury served a dual function. It determined whether the evidence was sufficient to justify a trial (a grand jury), and it also served as the trial jury, the modern petit (trial) jury. Thus, it served as both an accusing body and a body determining guilt or innocence. The two functions have, of course, been separated in the modern world (Abraham, 1980).

These dual functions help explain why the accused was banished even if he or she was found to be innocent. Just as the modern grand jury often serves the aims of the prosecutor, the jury served the aims of Henry II. It protected the crown by banishing troublemakers and even potential troublemakers. Banishment was the conservative, fail-safe decision; innocent or not, defendants were unlikely to cause much future trouble if they were banished.

The Jury in America

The right to a jury trial in colonial America was mandated in the charter granted to the Virginia Company by James I in 1606 (Hyman & Tarrant, 1975). The charter guaranteed to the settlers of Virginia all rights reserved for Englishmen, including the right to trial by jury. This right was not always given sanctity in the colonies. Certain classes such as African Americans and Native Americans were excluded from its protection.

Nevertheless, the institution of jury trials was an important part of the colonial legal system. Indeed, as friction between England and its colonists increased, colonial juries often refused to convict colonists accused by the king's representatives of violating laws deemed unfair and unjust. Most particularly, we recall the

1735 trial of the New York printer John Peter Zenger, accused of sedition for printing an anti-British tract without consulting the mayor, as English law required. Andrew Hamilton, a lawyer from Philadelphia, appealed to the jurors' conscience, their sense of what was fair and what was unjust, and Zenger was acquitted. The Constitutional Congress of 1787 enshrined the right to a jury trial, as did the Fifth, Sixth, and Seventh Amendments of the Bill of Rights.

The Fifth Amendment states that a person cannot be tried for a crime unless indicted by a grand jury, excepting people in military service during times of "War or public danger." The Sixth Amendment guarantees criminal defendants a speedy public trial by an impartial jury and a trial in the state in which the offense occurred. However, there is much debate as to what an "impartial" jury really means nowadays. The Seventh Amendment specifies a (civil) jury trial in all common law cases in which the issue exceeds $20.

The U.S. Supreme Court has ruled that the Fourth, Fifth, and Sixth Amendments are part of the core package of due process rights that limit the power of the state and therefore must be applied in a state criminal prosecution (*Duncan v. Louisiana,* 1968). The Court, however, has not recognized the Seventh Amendment's reference to civil jury trials to be as crucial to our personal freedom. Accordingly, the Court has ruled that the Seventh Amendment does not compel the states to provide jury trials in civil cases (*Minneapolis & St. Louis R. Co. v. Bombolis,* 1916). Nonetheless, most states do so, often as a right under the state's constitution. And the Seventh Amendment clearly calls for jury trials in civil cases brought in the federal courts.

The twentieth century has seen a diminution of the trial jury's importance. However, it is still the capstone experience of the American legal system. It is still a visible, living representation of democracy in action. Nevertheless, the institution has been attacked and considerably eroded within the last few decades.

Since 1933, courts in England and Wales have been allowed great latitude in deciding whether to resolve disputes with a jury trial. The perception that a judge may be better suited to deal with the issue of a case, civil or criminal; the laudable desire for a speedy trial; and the significant fact that litigants must pay the fees of the jurors, all militate against widespread use of the jury in England and Wales.

The United States has more than 80 percent of the jury trials in the world. Even here, most cases do not go to trial—in the federal system, fewer than 5 percent do—and the existence of that public trial option opens litigants' minds to other ways of resolving the conflict. The data show that about 65 percent or more of all criminal defendants plead guilty without going to trial (Abramson, 1995).

If nothing else, the jury system is the primary way in which citizens come in contact with their legal system. Abramson (1995) reports that in one state (Massachusetts) in 1988, individuals appearing for jury duty numbered 253,000, of whom 118,000 were actually sent to a courtroom; of those potential jurors, approximately 38,000 actually served on a jury. In the federal courts, a much higher proportion of potential jurors serve (about 30 percent, twice as many as in Massachusetts).

SELECTION OF JURORS

The Sixth Amendment to the United States Constitution requires that criminal defendants be tried before an impartial jury from the state and district in which the crime was committed. Defining and obtaining that impartial jury has proved to be a daunting task (Minow & Cate, 1991).

Jury selection is a two-step process. First, prospective jurors are drawn from an eligible population that, ideally, is representative of a district. The selection of a panel, or *venire* (which means "to come when called"), for a particular trial is usually made from local voter registration and other lists according to the Federal Jury Selection and Service Act of 1968. Some commentators have criticized the 1968 act, which required that voters' registration lists be used as the primary source for jury pool selection. Such lists may underrepresent certain segments of a jurisdiction—for example, people who are poor and/or African American and Hispanic. Kairys, Kadane, and Lehoczky (1977) were the first to suggest using several supplemental sources such as lists of licensed drivers and the unemployed. Kairys's advice has been taken in many jurisdictions, but even using such lists is no complete cure for underrepresentation. The principal problem is that individuals who are poor and who are unskilled laborers have much higher residential mobility than middle- and upper-class citizens. Because they move so much, attempts to contact them to serve on a jury are often fruitless. Even if the contact is made, they may not show up. Perhaps as many as 25 percent of those who are summoned for jury duty do not appear at the courthouse (Abramson, 1995). First, their serving may cost them a day's pay. Second, their investment in the justice system, manifested by a willingness to participate in it, may not be quite as profound as that of more affluent individuals (Fukurai, Butler, & Krooth 1993).

The second step in selecting the trial jury is the *voir dire* ("tell the truth"). This stage allows the judge, or the counsel for the prosecution and defense, or both the judge and counsel to question the panel of potential jurors. During the voir dire, prospective jurors who reveal biases and are unable to be open-minded are disqualified from jury duty. Thus, the primary theoretical function of the voir dire is to eliminate bias and ensure the right to a trial by an impartial jury as guaranteed in the Sixth Amendment. However, trial counsel may attempt to use the voir dire for other purposes—for example, to screen out potential jurors who will not be partial to their side. We begin our examination of the construction of the jury by seeing exactly how jurors are recruited from the community in which the crime occurred.

Juror Recruitment

In the Federal Jury Selection and Service Act of 1968 (which applies only to the federal courts), Congress interpreted the Sixth Amendment right to an impartial jury as meaning that the jury should be randomly selected from a "fair cross section" of the community. In *Taylor v. Louisiana* (1975), the U.S. Supreme Court made this requirement applicable to all the states. Therefore, the modern definition of an impartial jury is one chosen from a venire drawn from all parts of the community.

In fact, since 1975 the strategy of the courts has been to make sure that all segments of the population are represented. This means all ethnic and racial groups. In addition, fewer and fewer exemptions from jury duty have been allowed. Prior to 1975, for example, women, especially those with family responsibilities were usually excluded from jury duty. Curiously, in *Taylor,* the defendant appealed his rape conviction on the basis that women were routinely excluded from Louisiana juries. Courts have expanded the jury pool by using drivers' license lists, voter registration lists, and other lists such as city directories, tax rolls, utility lists, and telephone directories.

Figure 6.1 displays the various steps in the jury recruitment process as used by jury commissioners, those officials in charge of recruiting jurors. After the commissioners access their source lists, they then draw a random sample from those lists. All lists are updated and names that are duplicated are discarded. At this point a qualified jurors' file is constructed. Potential jurors are asked to complete a juror information questionnaire that asks for data about their qualifications. Some jurors are exempted or excused for reasons such as those under "Excuses" in Figure 6.1.

The names of the potential jurors that remain in the file now comprise the jury impanelment lists. These jurors again are randomly picked from the qualified jurors' file. They are then assigned to the various courts in the jurisdiction.

In the next step, potential jurors are called to serve on juries. As a potential juror, at this stage, you would receive a summons in a letter, certified or registered. In some jurisdictions, an officer of the court, a marshal, would personally serve the summons. Of course, individuals who are highly transient and whose work or home address tends to change will be much less likely to be called (Fukurai et al., 1993). Those who are summoned and who appear are again subject to the same tests and questionnaire completion required earlier. Why go through this again? It's simple. Americans believe in the jury system. If they had to go to trial, they would want to be judged by a jury. But they do not want to serve on a jury. Sixty percent of individuals who return the juror questionnaire indicate that they have a valid excuse to be exempted from service (Fukurai et al., 1993). Jury commissioners are in no position to decide the validity of all these excuses, so they sensibly call everybody and let the judge sort it out.

Do Jury Recruitment Procedures Work?   The ultimate aim of juror recruitment is to obtain an impartial jury. What precisely is an impartial jury? The current definition seems to be a jury that is drawn from a fair cross section of the community. This does not mean that the actual jury itself must consist of a fair cross section. In *Holland v. Illinois* (1990), the U.S. Supreme Court upheld a white man's conviction for rape, robbery, and kidnapping. The Court rejected

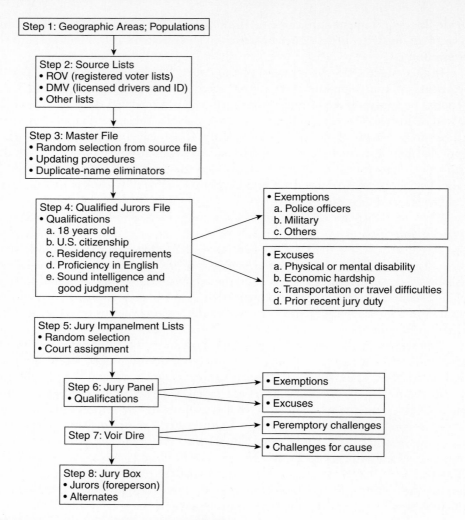

FIGURE 6.1   Jury selection procedures.

This figure illustrates the juror recruitment process, step by step.

Source: Adapted from *Race and the Jury,* by H. Fukurai, E. W. Butler, and R. Krooth, 1993, New York: Plenum Press, p. 41.

Daniel Holland's argument that his right to an impartial jury was violated by the removal of two potential jurors who were black. The majority of the Court concluded that the Sixth Amendment demands not a representative jury (a mirror of the community) but an impartial one. Although the pool of potential jurors obtained through the recruitment techniques must be representative, the jury itself may not be so, and this is acceptable.

One reason these elaborate recruitment techniques do not work as well as one might hope is because, as noted above, many citizens do not wish to be jurors. In New York City, only about half of all juror questionnaires are returned. In part, this is because the addresses are incorrect or the forms are tossed out by the recipients (Hoffman, 1993). Until recently, New York also had a large list of exemptions that are no longer allowed: Lawyers, firefighters, embalmers, podiatrists, clergy, police officers, and physical therapists were among the professional exemptions allowed.

The problem is not New York's alone. In Tennessee, a judge ordered the arrest of over 60 individuals who failed to show up for jury duty, and in Colorado, a judge sent deputies to the local shopping mall to press jurors into service (Hoffman, 1993). Not all the blame should fall on the jurors. Anyone who has served as a juror, particularly in a metropolitan area, can attest to the interminable waits, the less-than-opulent juror waiting rooms, the hard seats, and the unresponsive court personnel. People's reluctance to serve may be understandable.

Jurisdictions throughout the country have tried to lower the number of exemptions and to increase the proportion of African Americans and Hispanics who serve, as these two groups are woefully underrepresented on the venire (Fukurai et al., 1993). In New York City, juror deferments have become harder to get. In fact, the chief justice of the New York Supreme Court has served on a jury. In November 1996, jurors were surprised to see Mayor Giuliani in the courtroom as a potential juror (he was not chosen). In one vignette reported in the newspapers, an older woman with tubes running from her nostrils to a portable oxygen tank stepped up to the clerk to ask to be excused. The clerk, as only a New York City clerk can do, asked the woman if she had a doctor's note (Hoffman, 1993).

Race and Jury Service.   We have noted the underrepresentation of certain groups on the jury rolls—especially African Americans and Hispanics. To show that a jury's lack of representativeness is due to discrimination, however, three criteria must be met, as specified by the U.S. Supreme Court:

1. The jury recruitment techniques deliberately attempt to exclude jurors by race, gender, or ethnicity.
2. Statistical evidence is available showing the underrepresentation of particular groups.
3. Witnesses provide strong testimony that groups have been routinely excluded. (Fukurai et al., 1993)

In a variety of cases beginning in 1880, the U.S. Supreme Court steadily, if slowly, has ruled that certain "cognizable" (distinctive) groups in the community had unconstitutionally been excluded from jury service (*Duren v. Missouri*, 1979). Cognizable also means that this distinctive or uncommon group is subject to discrimination in the community and has a clear need for protection by the courts (*Hernandez v. Texas,* 1954). Cognizable groups can be based on race, gender, national origin, religion, and economic status. African Americans are a cognizable group; Chicago Cub baseball fans, however long-suffering, are not. In cases involving African Americans (*Strauder v. W. Virginia,* 1880), women (*Taylor v. Louisiana,* 1975), Hispanics (*Castenada v. Partida,* 1977; *Hernandez v. Texas,* 1954), and Native Americans (*United States v. Black Bear,* 1985), all these groups were found to be cognizable and to have been discriminated against in jury selection.

Those, however, were relatively easy cases, even for a Court whose view of racism was not always sensitive to the plight of "cognizable" groups. For example, in *Smith v. Texas,* a case decided by the Court in 1940, examination of the records showed that Harris County, Texas, discriminated against blacks in serving on grand juries. The Court found that in any year from 1931 to 1938 no more than two black citizens served on a grand jury. More than that, when the grand jury was selected for a roll of potential jurors, the black juror, if there was one, was always juror number 16. Chance? The Court thought not. Juror 16 was always excluded.

More recent cases present data that may not be as clear-cut as that in *Smith* or in *Strauder* (blacks had simply not served on West Virginia juries). Jeffrey Abramson (1995) noted that in the years since the cross-sectional requirement went into effect for federal courts, literally hundreds of litigants have challenged the validity of jury selection plans that rely exclusively on voter or registration lists and fail to supplement those with other lists. Of these, not one single decided federal case did the litigants win. For instance, in 1990, a federal jury selection plan survived challenge, despite clear evidence that Hispanics constituted only 1 percent of the master jury list in a district where they made up 15.7 percent of the adult population. In a North Dakota case, only 17 percent of eligible Native Americans who lived on reservations voted in the election; this led to only one Native American from the reservation being summoned out of 174 jurors that year, although Native Americans who lived on reservations constituted 2 percent of the population. The Court refused to find that the district was obligated to supplement the voter list with another source of names, such as tribal rolls (Abramson, 1995).

It seems that federal courts may not be supporting the cross-sectional principle. The states appear to be doing a better job. Many states have abandoned voter lists as an exclusive source for master jury lists. As we noted earlier, over 30 states now supplement the voter lists with names taken from drivers' license lists and other source lists (National Center for State Courts, 1995).

How can we determine whether the list used to obtain potential jurors is biased? In *Swain v. Alabama,* a 1965 case, the eligible black population was 26 percent. The actual representation of blacks on the jury venires (the panel from which juries are selected, not the actual juries) ranged from 10 percent to 15 percent. Was that evidence of (institutional) discrimination? The Court thought not. Justice White argued that "we cannot say that purposeful discrimination based on race alone is satisfactorily proved by showing that an identifiable group in a community is underrepresented by as much as 10 percent" (*Swain v. Alabama,* 1965, p. 209).

How did Justice White derive the 10 percent number? Well, he subtracted the 15 percent of the blacks on the venire from the 26 percent of blacks in the population and rounded off the result. But using the *absolute* disparity between the percentage of the population and the sample of that population found on the venire underestimates the actual damage done. Using the concept of *comparative disparity,* the absolute disparity divided by the proportion of the group in the population, we get a better sense of how that group is being harmed. In *Swain,* the comparative disparity falls between 42 percent (11 divided by 26) and 58 percent (15 divided by 26). The worst case would be that the venire from which actual juries are chosen underrepresented blacks by 58 percent. By 1972, however, the Court, using the comparative disparity index, found that a simple showing of a significant comparative disparity is **prima facie** (sufficient to prove the case but subject to rebuttal) evidence of discrimination, and therefore, the state had the burden of showing otherwise (*Alexander v. Louisiana,* 1972).

Economics and Jury Service. The Court has realized that discrimination might also be based on social class. Jury recruitment was historically particularly vulnerable to accusations of class discrimination because two of the most widely used methods were, in essence, aimed at excluding all but a select group of individuals. One traditional way of choosing a jury was the "key man" method. The key man, an important male member of the community, would ask like-minded men to serve on a jury. This method was very much like the "blue ribbon jury" in which specially qualified individuals, usually upper-class men, were called to jury service. So in *Thiel v. Southern Pacific,* a 1946 case decided by the Supreme Court, the clerk of the federal court in northern California was alleged to have deliberately excluded all workingmen from the jury. The Court found no fault with this, holding that it was reasonable to exclude workingmen because jury service would impose a particular hardship on them. It would not have been constitutional, according to the *Thiel* Court, to have excluded working people as a class, but it was justifiable to excuse an individual from service if the daily wage earner endured an economic hardship by serving. In other words, it was justifiable for wage earners to disenfranchise themselves. Workingmen could opt not to serve because it would cost them money (Fukurai et al., 1993).

The current impact of potential jurors' class and economic position on the probability of jury service is somewhat more subtle than that found in *Thiel.* One obvious reason that citizens view jury duty negatively is the financial hardship such service will impose. This is especially true when trials appear to be getting longer. The fees paid to jurors are nominal, ranging typically from $8 to $15 per day. Who will suffer? Certainly, we may assume that blue-collar workers in hourly pay jobs will bear a hardship by service. So will anyone in an insecure job and anyone whose employer will not continue to pay the individual's salary during jury service.

Fukurai et al. (1993) analyzed the effect of economics on jury service and found that company compensation significantly affects participation on a jury. If the juror's company will continue compensation during service, potential jurors generally will not try to avoid such duty. However, only about one-third of all employers will do so.

THE VOIR DIRE

The second stage of jury selection, the *voir dire,* involves the questioning of the potential jurors (the panel members) by the judge, or the prosecution and defense counsel, or by both counsel and judge, depending on the court. In federal courts, judges conduct the voir dire, although most permit lawyers to suggest various questions that the judge might ask jurors, and some federal judges permit lawyers to ask jurors direct questions.

Surprisingly, judges who permit lawyer participation report that voir dire does not take any longer than when lawyers are not allowed to question the potential jurors directly (Shapard & Johnson, 1995). Of course, it may be that judges who retain exclusive control over voir dire conduct a more thorough examination and that judges who delegate voir dire to lawyers place strict time limits on the process.

The original purpose of the voir dire was to reveal information from each potential juror that would help to determine whether that juror was fit to serve. In English courts, the voir dire served to show whether the potential jurors were acquainted with the lawyers involved in the case or whether they had been convicted of a crime or were otherwise incompetent to serve. The questioning of the jurors was also aimed at disclosing whether they were biased and had concluded that the defendant was guilty. If the jurors affirmed "indifference" to the outcome, their impartiality was assumed. Therefore, the original notion of the voir dire was to get just enough information to determine whether the juror should be disqualified from jury service.

A second purpose of the voir dire—less obvious and certainly less official—is to socialize the jurors. The courtroom experience is new to most jurors and the fundamental assumptions that the legal system adheres to with respect to judging a case may not be familiar to them. The voir dire process should make clear what it means to be a "good juror." Many potential jurors harbor notions that are contrary to important legal precepts (Strier, 1994). For example, many potential jurors do not know or believe that a defendant is presumed innocent until the evidence shows otherwise. Generally, the socialization function of the voir dire is overlooked and understudied (Johnson & Haney, 1994). For most trial lawyers, however, the primary purpose of the voir dire is to allow them to begin to present their case, to indoctrinate the jury, and to secure, if possible, jurors biased in their favor.

The attorneys and the court may challenge the acceptance of jurors for service. Challenges may be put for *cause* when a juror demonstrates clearly during the voir dire examination that he or she cannot render an impartial verdict. For example, a potential juror who says she cannot fairly judge someone who carries a firearm will be excused by the judge for cause in a case in which the defendant habitually kept a firearm in his automobile. A juror may also be challenged *peremptorily* when counsel suspects, for whatever reason or no reason at all, that the juror will not be impartial or will not favor the lawyer or her client. The number of peremptory challenges allowed an attorney is limited. Finally, a challenge may be put to the entire panel of prospective jurors, known as the *array,* a rare occurrence, when counsel feels that the entire panel may be biased.

From the lawyer's perspective, weeding out biased jurors and indoctrinating jurors are the two major tactical purposes of the voir dire. Clearly, lawyers see it as part of their duty to their client to attempt to exercise their challenges to secure a jury that will be favorable to their client. Furthermore, lawyers utilize the voir dire to implant their theory of the case and to stifle any developing prejudice toward their client that is not strong enough to warrant a challenge for cause.

Can lawyers and their consultants "pick juries"? If they can, how does this affect the notion of an impartial jury? And what of these challenges? Does the exercise of peremptory challenges strike at the idea of an impartial jury? Let's take a look at what is known as scientific jury selection.

Jury Selection: Science or Art?

The voir dire has been utilized to secure a favorable jury since the medieval period in England. To aid lawyers in this endeavor, an extensive legal literature and related folklore is available. Recently, scientific techniques have increasingly been used in the selection of jurors, apparently with some success (Covington, 1985). The use of social science methodology in the service of juror selection began in a number of publicized cases in the 1970s, including the trials of the Harrisburg Seven (a group of anti–Vietnam War protesters who were tried in the 1970s), Joan Little (a case noted in Chapter 5, involving a black, female North Carolina inmate claiming self-defense in killing a guard whom she claimed had attempted to rape her), and John Mitchell and Maurice Stans (two cabinet members in the Richard Nixon administration accused of conspiracy in the Watergate scandal). The introduction of social science methodology has raised a number of ethical (Etzioni, 1974) and constitutional questions (Moskitis, 1976).

Briefly, the social science technique involves both pretrial and voir dire courtroom procedures (Christie, 1976; Schulman, Shaver, Coleman, Emricle, & Christie, 1973). Research indicates that definable demographic and personal characteristics can be used to uncover biases and dispositions in a potential juror. Demographic and personal data can inform attorneys for one side about the probabilities of biases and thereby assist them in exercising peremptory challenges.

The first step typically involves surveying a sample of the population from which the jury will be chosen. The survey is an attempt to delineate the community attitudes relevant to the trial. The data obtained from this survey, and from telephone interviews, if time allows, are analyzed to find relationships between community attitudes and sentiments and various demographic characteristics (such as age, gender, race, religion, neighborhood, education, and occupation) in order to draw a profile of the "friendly juror." After the venire has been issued, a second survey may be carried out, unobtrusively, by interviewing friends and neighbors of the panel members so as to increase the probability of selecting friendly jurors. For example, in the trial of the Harrisburg Seven, the ideal defense juror was a female Democrat, sympathetic with the antiwar movement, who did not have a religious preference and held a skilled blue-collar job or a white-collar position (Schulman et al., 1973).

The voir dire procedure is based, in great part, on the friendly juror profile analysis. The voir dire examination is designed to elicit from potential jurors attitudes favorable or unfavorable toward the defendant. The techniques employed by social scientists in juror selection do not differ radically from those traditionally employed by lawyers. The social scientists, however, offer a comprehensive methodology in the service of selecting competent and friendly jurors.

Although constitutional and ethical questions about using social science methodology in selecting jurors abound, we may ask whether the empirical evidence supports the notion that these techniques are effective or indeed that they are any more effective than the methods and hunches traditionally employed by trial lawyers. The finding that various defendants have been acquitted when the defense availed itself of social science techniques obviously does not validate the efficacy of the procedures. A large defense fund buys not only social scientists but also expensive and skilled lawyers.

The effectiveness of the social science technique of juror selection has not been empirically demonstrated on a consistent basis. Its efficacy depends in part on the techniques themselves, and also on how effective the lawyers are if the techniques are not applied. We know something of the lawyer's performance in selecting jurors by conventional methods. Zeisel and Diamond (1976) reported an experiment carried out in the U.S. District Court for the Northern District of Illinois in which a series of cases were tried in the presence of three juries: the actual jury and two experimental juries. One of these experimental juries was made up of the potential jurors who were challenged peremptorily by either defense or prosecution; they did not know which side had excused them from serving. The second was the "English jury," chosen at random without being questioned by counsel or court. In England, jurors are rarely challenged, and the first 12 jurors who enter the courtroom constitute the jury, unless the defendant or lawyer is a relative. The evidence in this study indicated that prosecution and defense lawyers had some success in identifying jurors who were unfavorable. That is, jurors excluded by the defense showed a tendency to vote for the prosecution and the opposite held for jurors excluded by the prosecutor.

Research on the effectiveness of jury selection techniques has taken one of two approaches. The first method involves questioning actual jurors in real trials and then correlating their verdict with their age, sex, socioeconomic background, and other characteristics. The second approach is to use mock jurors and try to relate verdicts to jury attributes in the laboratory setting (Fulero & Penrod, 1990).

Generally, the research finds modest relationships between some juror attributes and their verdicts. For example, Mills and Bohannon (1980) found that jurors in criminal cases who were black, female, less educated, and older tended to vote for conviction. Generally, jurors attitudes about capital punishment seem to be predictive of their likelihood of voting guilty in a murder trial (Cowan, Thompson, & Ellsworth, 1984; Moran & Comfort, 1986).

Steven Penrod (1990), in a large-scale study in the Boston area, examined the attitudes and demographic attributes of 367 jurors. These jurors had participated in rape, murder, robbery, and negligence (civil trial) cases. Of all the factors that might account for the verdict (the evidence, the lawyers, the defendant, the jurors, etc.), Penrod found that juror attributes accounted for about 14 percent of the outcome in some trials but much less in others. Less of the variance was accounted for by individual juror attributes in the civil (negligence) and the robbery trials. Penrod did not find any series of related personality and demographic attributes that could be described as "conviction proneness." That is, he found no evidence that someone with a certain set of attributes will be likely to convict across a variety of different trials.

Penrod's (1990) findings conform to the general view of social psychologists that individual differences account for perhaps less than 10 percent of the total variance in any social situation. Mock jury trials find a somewhat higher correlation between juror attributes and verdicts than do field studies with real trials, but the differences are not marked. The differences may appear because mock jury studies tend to use cases that are unusual or complex and therefore may be more likely to tap important individual differences. Capital murder trials fall into this category. Individuals often have strong and emotional attitudes about such crimes, and these attitudes often relate to a person's fundamental beliefs. A juror's attitude about the death penalty appears to be more strongly related to his or her verdict in a capital case than in less emotional trials (Horowitz, 1980; Penrod, 1990). As Penrod (1990) noted, cases involving conspiracies, murder, Native Americans, and African Americans, and civil trials involving high damage awards may unearth biases not expressed in a garden variety gas station robbery trial.

A New Look at Jury Selection.   Some observers have argued that the voir dire can indeed reveal juror attitudes that may have a definite influence on how the jurors decide a case (Hastie, 1991). Jane Goodman-Delahunty and her co-workers (Goodman, Loftus, & Greene, 1990) report that in product liability cases, jurors' attitudes toward monetary awards and the tort system in general were indicators of their likelihood to vote for lesser or greater monetary awards.

Generally, jurors who were in favor of reforming the tort system (that is, they believe that awards are too high and many civil lawsuits are frivolous) are more likely to vote against monetary awards or to give smaller awards than jurors not in favor of reform. Other research also suggests that jurors' attitudes may be more predictive of their decisions than any other single factor (Moran, Cutler, & De Lisa, 1994; Moran, Cutler, & Loftus, 1990).

Moran and his colleagues argue strongly for an extended voir dire during which lawyers and the trial judge can fully explore the potential jurors' attitudes. Cutler, Moran, and Narby (1992) found that jurors' attitudes toward psychiatrists and the insanity defense were significant predictors of jurors' bias in cases in which defendants employed a defense of not guilty by reason of insanity. Jurors who did not favor psychiatrists were skeptical of the insanity defense. Moran et al. (1994) reported that jurors' verdicts significantly reflected their biases. It appears that the attitudes are specific to each case, however. As Penrod (1990) noted, there does not appear to be a specific set of "conviction proneness" juror attributes for most trials. What we do have, however, are attitudes specific to cases involving important social issues, such as drug abuse, tort reform, and the death penalty. In those trials, a juror's attitude seems to predict conviction proneness reliably (Cutler et al., 1992). Whether judges will allow lawyers to probe deeply enough to uncover those attitudes is unclear. Nevertheless, at this point, after rejecting the possibility of accurately identifying the relationships between juror attitudes and their verdicts, social scientists seem now to be taking a closer look at those relationships. In any event, selecting jurors during the voir dire is a very difficult judgment task because much of the time the true relationship between juror attributes and their verdict preferences are unknown, or at best ambiguous (Hastie, 1991).

Jury Consultants: Litigation Psychology.   The notion that one can "pick" a juror has attracted numbers of people who claim to be able to do this. Trial attorneys who hire Margaret Covington get someone who adds some psychological insight as well as a "gumshoe" (Couric, 1986). Ms. Covington looks at the potential juror's home to see whether the grass has been cut (a summer trial is helpful here) or if the windows need washing, and to see what bumper stickers are on the person's automobiles. Windows, grass, bumper stickers? Covington suggests that these factors reflect the personal philosophies of the potential jurors and a lawyer ignores them at his or her peril. According to Covington, people who post neighborhood crime watch stickers or who have burglar alarm systems are more conscious of crime and therefore are more disposed to convict (Couric, 1986).

The bumper sticker "Have you hugged your child today?" is a good predictor, according to Ms. Covington, of jurors who would be favorable in personal injury cases involving children. (What one does with the sticker proclaiming "Let's go, Mets" is unclear, however!)

The use of trial consultants is increasing. The American Society of Trial Consultants (ASTC), which was founded with 15 members in 1982, by 1996 had 350 active members. The field of trial consulting is not limited to scientific psychology. It includes consultants with backgrounds in clinical psychology, sociology, and anthropology as well as those trained in marketing, communications, even phrenology and astrology (Stapp, 1996).

In addition to helping lawyers pick juries during the voir dire, consultants also offer a range of other services (Shartel, 1994b). These services include witness preparation aimed at teaching witnesses to communicate in a manner that will make them more credible on the stand. Trial consultants also claim to help lawyers prepare effective opening and closing statements. In addition, they will advise lawyers on courtroom strategy. They will also test the litigants' theories and materials in front of mock juries in trial simulations. The mock jury's deliberations are videotaped and analyzed. Litigants may find that their approach to the case was likely to antagonize a jury and can restructure their case before trial begins (Stapp, 1996).

Often, in complex cases, litigants really do not know what their case is "worth." That is, they may not know whether a jury will consider a request for a $1 million award to be reasonable. Trial simulations can tell litigants what juries think the case is worth. One interesting consequence of pretrial simulations is that both sides may conclude the case has a specific worth and decide to settle rather than face the cost of a trial. In the long run, this may be the greatest impact trial consultants have on the judicial system.

Who uses trial consultants? The short answer is litigants with money. Defense lawyers more than plaintiffs or prosecutors are more likely to have access to insurance money and therefore may be willing to spend what is necessary. Are consultants worth their cost? The consultants certainly think so (Genevie & Sebolt, 1994). One predicts that in 10 to 15 years' time all courts will appoint trial consultants to help prepare litigants' presentations (Illig, 1995).

Empirically, we do not have a satisfactory answer about the worth of consultants. The research on jury selection suggests that at best, in some cases, the side using a scientific method of jury selection might get a 5 percent to 10 percent edge. That is not an inconsiderable advantage and could make the difference in winning and losing. But as we noted, these selection methods may work in a very limited range of cases.

Of all the services offered by consultants, trial simulations may offer the best value. The second most promising service is in the construction of opening statements. Jurors tend to form the trial evidence into a "story" and it is this story that guides their decisions (Pennington & Hastie, 1992). The purpose of a good opening statement is to give the jurors a plausible story that accounts for the evidence to be presented.

The effectiveness of pretrial simulations can be seen in a trial in which the communications company MCI sued AT&T for access to long-distance lines. In this antitrust case, prior to trial, MCI lawyers presented an abbreviated version of their case to a mock jury, selected by jury consultants to reflect the makeup of the jury pool for trial. Lawyers observed their deliberations. On the first presentation of their case to the mock jury, MCI found that jurors resisted forcing

AT&T to share its long-distance lines with competitors. Jurors thought this unfair. MCI then altered its strategy and in a second simulated jury trial, MCI focused on the duty to apply the law whether one agreed with it or not. This second jury followed the law.

MCI also presented their arguments for damage awards to the mock jury. On the first presentation, MCI said that the company had lost $100 million in profits from AT&T's monopolistic behavior. The jury awarded exactly $100 million. MCI then tried not specifying any dollar amount. The second mock jury deliberated and awarded $900 million. In the actual trial, MCI left the jury free to speculate about damages; the jury awarded $600 million. Because antitrust awards are trebled for punitive purposes, this entitled MCI to $1.8 billion in damages, the largest antitrust award ever given at the time (Abramson, 1995; Hans & Vidmar, 1986).

Who Should Conduct the Voir Dire?

Who should conduct the voir dire to best obtain a fair and impartial jury? In federal courts, the voir dire is generally conducted by the judge with input from the attorneys; most state court systems permit some combination of lawyer-conducted and judge-conducted questioning. What are the arguments and evidence for questioning by judges versus questioning by attorneys?

One argument is that the voir dire process is much shorter when potential jurors are questioned by the trial judge (Shapard & Johnson, 1995). Bermant (1985) reviewed several studies that measured the duration of the voir dire. One study found that the judge-conducted voir dire took one hour whereas, the attorney-conducted examination took two hours and twenty-five minutes. In another study, the voir dire conducted by trial counsel took less than 10 percent of the total trial time.

A second argument is that lawyers abuse the voir dire examination by pleading their case before the opening statement (Bermant, 1985). Reid Hastie (1991), in a review of the empirical research on voir dire, argued that attorneys can effectively identify jurors who may favor one side or the other and therefore attorney-conducted voir dire is a threat to the notion of an impartial jury.

Apparently, the legal system assumes that if both trial counsel reject those who are unfavorable to their position, their respective challenges will "balance out." However, this balance is highly unlikely given the fact that lawyers vary greatly in their perspective of jury selection. For example, some lawyers are simply not interested in jury selection because they think they can convince any jury to take their side. Furthermore, lawyers vary in their ability to select the kind of jury they want. Some commentators have argued that the jury should consist of the first 12 people who are picked at random from the venire (e.g., Van Dyke, 1970). After a review of all the arguments, Bermant (1985) has suggested that the extent of lawyers' participation should remain a matter of judicial discretion. More recently, Hastie (1991) agreed with Bermant's sentiment. Hastie would limit attorneys' participation in the voir dire to "modest levels." In 1995, the committee that writes procedural rules for the federal courts recommended that lawyers be afforded an opportunity to participate in voir dire subject to judges' limits on the time and manner of their involvement in any single case (Shapard & Johnson, 1995), but the judicial conference rejected that proposal.

The Impartial Juror and the Voir Dire

English common law defined an impartial juror as one who was capable of putting aside personal biases and interests and of deciding the case on its own merits. This impartial juror may have had an initial opinion on the case but was able to decide the case solely on the evidence presented in the courtroom (Abramson, 1995; Rembar, 1980). In Chapter 5 we briefly discussed the treason trial of Aaron Burr, a former vice president of the United States. Recall the allegation: Burr had devised a scheme to form a personal army and carve out an empire of his own by conquering Mexico and parts of what is now the southwest United States (Kammen, 1986). As you might imagine, this scheme and the response by the U.S. government and its president, Burr's rival, Thomas Jefferson, raised quite a storm. Could Burr get a fair trial? Where were the impartial jurors?

When Burr's trial began in Richmond, Virginia, in August 1807, almost all the potential jurors admitted they had read about the case and had some opinion about Burr's guilt. Chief Justice John Marshall, sitting as the trial judge (not an uncommon procedure then), essentially decided that if a potential juror had decided on guilt (or innocence), he was eliminated; but a juror could still have knowledge of the case and be an impartial juror as long as he had not prejudged the final outcome, guilt or innocence (*United States v. Burr,* 1807).

Chief Justice Marshall in *Burr* altered the old English version of an impartial juror. In English courts, it had been assumed that someone who resided near the defendant and therefore understood the defendant and his or her social situation would be the impartial juror. Marshall was skeptical that people could know and be exposed to all the rumors about a case and still remain totally fair. So Marshall questioned the potential *Burr* jurors and probed more deeply. He wanted to be sure they could "bracket" their biases—hold them aside and judge the case solely on the evidence. Still, a jury of one's peers meant anyone who could remain fair and impartial. It did not mean that the jury or the venire had to contain a proportionate number of individuals from various community groups.

In modern times, the defense and the prosection have different notions of what constitutes a fair jury. The notion of representativeness now leads to the interpretation that an impartial jury is one drawn from all cognizable groups of the community. That is to say, race, gender, class, and ethnicity are crucial elements that must be represented on the jury, or at least in the jury pool.

The defense interpretation of this requirement is that an impartial jury is composed of people who can understand the defendant's situation. This is based on the not unreasonable assumption that a juror who can empathize with the defendant will be more likely to attribute the defendant's actions to situational forces for which the person cannot be blamed. The prosecutor has a different agenda and would like a jury composed of individuals who will not be able to empathize with the defendant because they come from entirely different social backgrounds. The defense wants to challenge jurors who are not from the defendant's social background and the prosecutor wants to exclude those who are from that background.

Peremptory Challenges and the Impartial Jury.   The crucial decision in the voir dire centers on the use of challenges the lawyers can exercise without specifying a reason that the juror is to be eliminated. These are known as *peremptory challenges* (Chapter 2). These challenges go straight to the issue of what we consider to be an fair and impartial jury. The perceived importance of peremptory challenges is based on the following implicit assumptions:

1. Jurors are biased from the very start.
2. They cannot put aside these biases.
3. Therefore, the only way to obtain an impartial jury is to let all biased points of view be represented in the hope that they will cancel themselves out—through deliberate, structured discussion—and in the end justice will be served (Abramson, 1994; Fukurai et al., 1993).

In 1986 (*Batson v. Kentucky*), the U.S. Supreme Court ruled that prosecutors could not remove potential jurors on the basis of race. In *Batson,* the prosecutor challenged all potential jurors of the same race as the black defendant. This is not to say that individuals of different racial groups cannot be excluded. They simply cannot be excluded because of their race. In fact, lawyers now are often asked to tell the judge their reasons for excluding a prospective juror when suspicions are raised that something other than the juror's individual attributes are the basis for the peremptory challenge. However, the Court also affirmed a previous finding that the defendant does not have the right to a jury made up in whole or in part of members of his or her own race. In practice, lawyers can offer the flimsiest of excuses at times. One defense lawyer told the trial judge that he challenged a black juror because she reminded him of the defendant's white mother.

Currently, this peremptory challenge prohibition based on race, limited originally to criminal juries, has been expanded to apply to civil cases in state courts. In *Powers v. Palacios* (1995), postal worker Brenda Powers charged that she was injured by a pit bull while delivering mail at the house of Paul Palacios. During voir dire, Mr. Palacios's lawyer exercised a peremptory challenge against the only black person on the venire panel. Ms. Powers, who is black, objected. The trial court overruled the objection of Ms. Powers's lawyer, even though Mr. Palacios's lawyer admitted that race was a factor in his challenge. The high court held that such an exclusion violated the equal protection rights of the challenged juror.

In addition, in 1994, the Court, decrying "archaic and overbroad" stereotypes about men and women, stopped the practice of allowing the peremptory challenge of jurors on the basis of sex. Justice Blackmun wrote in *J.E.B. v. Ala. ex rel.* (1994) that gender, like race, is an unconstitutional limitation in the search for juror competence and impartiality. This decision further eroded the traditional use of peremptory challenges to remove jurors without explaining why. Ironically, the decision was a victory for a paternity lawsuit defendant who said his rights were violated when a women-only jury decided he fathered a boy born four years earlier.

Justice Blackmun indicated that discrimination in jury selection, whether based on race or on gender, causes harm to the litigants, the community, and the individual jurors who are excluded from participation in the legal process. Justice Blackmun also indicated that this decision does not eliminate all use of peremptory challenges. However, like race, gender may not serve as a surrogate for bias.

Justice Sandra Day O'Connor argued in a separate (concurring) opinion that the ruling should be limited to cases like the Alabama case, in which government lawyers use gender-based peremptory challenges. That is, she would limit the state's right, but not necessarily the defendant's right, to peremptory challenges based on a group bias. However, the majority opinion did limit the defendant's use of peremptories as well.

It is possible that the use of peremptory challenges may face increasing restrictions and perhaps elimination. There is a conflict between the call for a representative jury and the use of peremptory challenges. Certainly defendants will argue that eliminating peremptories hinders their ability to exclude prejudiced jurors. Hastie (1991) suggested that peremptory challenges be reduced or eliminated. As we noted earlier, some argue that the best bet is to return to the "English jury," which is the first 12 jurors randomly chosen from the venire (Colbert, 1990).

Content of the Voir Dire

For all the emphasis on jury selection, very little work has focused on precisely what happens during the voir dire. What do lawyers really ask? How do jurors feel about the questions asked of them? Recently, Cathy Johnson and Craig Haney (1994) explored the content of the voir dire in four separate felony trials. The first notable finding is that the seven attorneys involved in these four cases were reasonably effective in excluding jurors whose initial attitudes were unfavorable. That is, defense attorneys peremptorily excused potential jurors who were antidefendant while prosecutors were able to identify and exclude prodefense jurors. Recall the earlier similar findings of Zeisel and Diamond (1976) in their field study. However, the selection process was not foolproof. Both sides missed jurors who were quite unfavorable to their side. This was not because they had used up all their challenges. Quite the contrary; lawyers often had remaining challenges but simply did not identify the unfavorable potential jurors still in the jury box.

The voir dire was inefficient in that lawyers spent a fair amount of time gathering demographic data ("How long have you lived in the community?") that could have easily been gathered by questionnaire, as is sometimes done in the more complex and notorious trials, such as the O. J. Simpson trial. While attorneys have been accused of needlessly prolonging the voir dire, Johnson and

Haney (1994) observed that it was the judge who talked most of the time, even in this attorney-conducted voir dire. Of course, he may have talked a lot because he had to control the lawyers.

Earlier, we noted that one of the purposes of the voir dire is to instruct jurors on impartiality and fairness and what it means to be a "good juror." Johnson and Haney observed that jurors were questioned about their biases, but they were told little about what it meant to be a good juror and how to know whether they were fit to serve. As they noted (1994), little was done to socialize the jurors, and an effective socialization would be one of the easiest and cheapest methods of reducing jury bias. In fact, many jurors who survived the voir dire in these four felony trials held attitudes quite at variance with basic tenets of the judicial system. Several jurors who served did not believe in the presumption of innocence, for example. Although the evidence is not particularly extensive at this point, the voir dire does not seem to be effective in reducing juror bias. Furthermore, the voir dire did not effectively inculcate important legal values, such as presumption of innocence. Narby and Cutler (1994) have shown that the voir dire may not guard against more specific biases. They found that warning jurors about the limits of eyewitness accuracy did not prohibit jurors who displayed a general belief that eyewitnesses were accurate from placing great credence in such testimony when it was not warranted.

OPENING ACTS

Once the jury is chosen and seated, and the judge instructs the jury on their duties, both sides make opening statements. These statements are important because they tell the jurors the nature of the evidence each side will present. These statements lay out the opposing sides' "theory" of the case—what they hope to prove. In other words, the jurors hear the outlines of the "story" each side will tell.

Figure 6.2 presents a diagram of the stages of trial. This can serve as a guide to the remaining sections of this chapter as well as Chapters 7 through 10.

Opening Statements

The prosecution—or the plaintiff in a civil trial, because that side has the burden of proof—presents the first opening statement. The defendant may follow, may reserve the opening statement until immediately before presenting defense evidence, or may waive the opening statement altogether.

Opening statements are generally limited to previews of the evidence the lawyer expects to have admitted. Legal arguments are improper because they invade the province of the court (the judge), who informs the jury of the law at the end of the trial. Personal opinions on issues in the case are also improper (basically, as irrelevant to the issues) but they are difficult to stop.

Because the prosecutor's role is to pursue truth through fair governmental procedures, the prosecutor's opening statement and conduct during the trial are more limited than those of the defense counsel. The prosecutor may cause a mis-

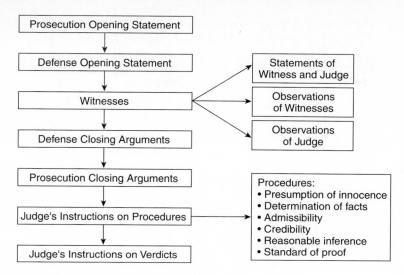

FIGURE 6.2   The flow of events in a criminal trial.

This is a graphic representation of the steps that occur in a criminal trial.

Source: Adapted from "Examining Death Qualification: Further Analysis of the Process Effect" by C. Haney, 1984b, *Law and Human Behavior, 8,* 133–151.

trial by commenting on the credibility of a witness or expressing a personal opinion about the defendant's guilt, or by making inflammatory statements, unless they are made in response to similar conduct of the defense counsel. Usually, however, such improprieties are thought to be cured by instructions from the judge to disregard the comment (*Georgetown,* 1991). For example, the statement that defense counsel was playing "fast and loose with the facts" was held "cured" by the judge's instructions to the jury to ignore the statement (*Georgetown,* 1991). Experimental research on the jury process questions whether the instructions can remove the prejudice from such remarks (Feldman, 1978).

There is experimental support for the notion that opening statements strongly influence the jurors' verdict. It has been shown that the promise of persuasive testimony proving the defendant's innocence made jurors more sympathetic to that defendant even though the promised testimony was never given in the trial (Pyszczynski, Greenberg, Mack, & Wrightsman, 1981). If the prosecutor, however, pointed out the discrepancy between the promises made and not kept, the power of the defense attorney's opening statement was reduced. Thus, even an unfulfilled promise can become part of the story woven by jurors and affect the outcome of the trial. Nevertheless, the research of Tom Pyszczynski (Pyszczynski et al., 1981; Pyszczynski & Wrightsman, 1981) shows that opening statements do tend to predispose jurors to favor one side or the other, and this predisposition tends to maintain itself throughout the trial. The opening statements may function as a cognitive framework that jurors use to process information heard subsequently during the trial.

Shari Diamond, Jonathan Casper, and Cami Heiert (1994) videotaped several versions of a death penalty case and tracked jurors' decisions at various points of the trial. For example, they stopped the tape after the opening statements and questioned the jurors. These researchers found that about two-thirds of the jurors reached a verdict after the prosecutor's opening statement (which included an accurate preview of the later evidence) that "remained constant for the rest of the trial." An additional 4 percent reached a verdict that never changed after the defense's opening statement. Therefore, 70 percent of the jurors did not change their verdicts during the trial. These data suggest the importance of opening statements. What we do not know is whether opening statements have a strong impact because they are persuasive or whether opening statements may accurately represent the evidence and jurors would have reached the same conclusions in any event, with or without those statements (Diamond et al., 1994).

When the defense chooses to present its opening statement may be important. The defense can present its opening statement immediately after the prosecution presents its, or the defense may wait until *after* the prosecution has presented its case. Gary Wells, Lawrence Wrightsman, and Peter Miene (1985) provide evidence suggesting that if the defense delays its opening statements, the defendant is more likely to be convicted than if the opening is presented immediately following the prosecutor's opening statement. They also found that delaying the defense opening statement reduces the influence of the defendant's testimony and the defense attorney's closing statement. Generally, it is better for the defense attorney to present his or her opening statement immediately after the prosecutor.

Order of Proof

In Chapter 2, we noted the order of proof in a trial: The plaintiff or prosecutor opens, the defendant follows, and the plaintiff or prosecutor has an opportunity to present rebuttal evidence. Once the prosecution finishes its case, the defendant may move for a directed verdict, a request for the judge to rule that the prosecution has not shown enough evidence of guilt to send the case to the jury. Asking for a directed verdict also tests whether plaintiff or prosecutor has proved all the legal elements of the case (see Chapter 2).

The defense need not present any testimony. In a criminal case, the Fifth Amendment privilege against self-incrimination frees the defendant from being called as a witness for the prosecution. In a civil case, the opposing party can be compelled to the witness stand as an adverse witness. The Fifth Amendment does not apply to civil matters. Neither prosecutor nor judge may call the jury's attention to the fact that the defendant in a criminal case has failed to testify.

One wonders whether this neglect means that the jury does not notice or, contrary to the Fifth Amendment, that they use the silence as part of their decision making. Experimental research by Hendrick and Shaffer (1975) has shown that a defendant who declines to answer on Fifth Amendment grounds is perceived as having something to hide and therefore may very well be thought guilty. This presumption of guilt may occur even when the judge informs the jury not to infer guilt when a defendant does not take the stand or invokes the Fifth Amendment (Tanford, 1991a).

Each side has the right to confront and cross-examine the other's witnesses. The defendant's right to confront and cross-examine is embodied in the Sixth Amendment. Direct examination of one's own witnesses permits each side to tell its story in an orderly way. All witnesses are likely to be cross-examined by the opposition. An advantage of cross-examination is that the questioner can control the responses by asking leading, and sometimes misleading, questions, as opposed to the open style of direct examination of a witness.

EVIDENCE LAW

Evidence law guides the presentation of proof at trial. The law has created a web of rules to select the fairest and most reliable evidence for use in a trial. Collectively, these are the *rules of evidence.* The rules are numerous and rather precise. They are set forth in the *Federal Rules of Evidence* (FRE) (1984). The FRE is a clearly written, brief statement of the rules governing the presentation of evidence. They are applicable, generally, in both civil and criminal cases, and they apply in all federal cases whether the *substantive law* (law that specifies the rights and duties of parties such as criminal law, law of contracts, etc.) is a federal or state law (Mueller & Kirkpatrick, 1995).

These rules serve several important purposes. Before we can examine how behavioral science can inform the presentation of evidence in court, it would serve us to look at the reasons such rules exist.

C. B. Mueller and Laird Kirkpatrick (1995), two outstanding legal scholars in the area of evidence law, have pointed out that the rules of evidence are aimed at controlling the jury. The legal system does not entirely trust the jury. For example, consider the **hearsay rule,** which refers to testimony given by a witness who tells not what she has observed or experienced but rather what someone told her or what she overheard. The issue here is that the jurors can perhaps determine the veracity of the sitting witness but have no way of judging the person who said the thing of interest to the sitting witness. Such testimony (with quite a few exceptions) is excluded. Hearsay is also excluded because courts feel that a lay jury is not capable of evaluating statements made outside its presence and might place too much weight on such statements.

A second reason for rules of evidence is to serve public policies that relate to the issues being litigated. For example, the legal system wants a conviction on a criminal charge to be based on a higher standard of proof than a judgment in civil court. Therefore, rules of evidence require the "burden of persuasion" to be defined differently for criminal as opposed to civil trials. In a criminal trial, conviction is based on the prosecution's meeting the standard of "reasonable doubt," sometimes defined as a doubt that would cause a reasonable person to hesitate to act. Compare that with the plaintiff's burden in a civil trial: the "preponderance of evidence" standard, usually defined as having 51 percent of the evidence on your side.

A third reason for rules of evidence, according to Mueller and Kirkpatrick (1995), is to influence positively or to protect noncourtroom behavior. For example, spouses cannot be forced to testify against their partners. This has the purpose of protecting marriage, a laudable noncourtroom policy.

Fourth, the law of evidence aims to ensure accurate fact finding. For example, there are rules that determine how a document entered into evidence is to be authenticated. Many of these rules have had to be adapted to the new electronic age of fax machines and electronic mail.

Finally, a fifth reason for evidence law is simply to control the scope and length of trials. Lawsuits ought not to drag on forever and a speedy trial for a criminal defendant is a constitutional guarantee. Federal Rule of Evidence (FRE) 403 allows the judge to eliminate evidence that is perfectly admissible but would take more time to present than the judge thinks it is worth. The same rule also applies if the judge thinks the evidence might be confusing to the jury. Rule 603 allows the judge to control the sequence of proof and the order of witnesses. So, in the recent Simpson case, the defense suggested that a potential alibi witness might flee and they wanted her testimony to be heard immediately even though the prosecution was in the midst of presenting its case. Instead, the trial judge took videotaped testimony from the witness in the absence of the jury; if the witness had not been available when the defense presented its case, the tape could have been used. Note that this action was entirely at the discretion of the trial judge.

Presentation of Evidence

Evidence given in a trial consists of oral or documentary presentations. Oral testimony is the spoken words of a witness sworn to tell the truth; documentary evidence pertains to written materials and physical things. The law of evidence determines who may be a witness and what that witness may or may not say, as well as which documents may be presented and in what form. Some witnesses and evidence are excluded: Witnesses too young or too sick may not be heard, and some documents, such as a marked copy when the original is retrievable, may not be acceptable.

Admissible Evidence.   Admissibility of evidence refers to whether the trier of fact (judge or jury) should hear and consider a particular item of evidence. Evidence may include testimony of a witness, photographs, computer printouts, charts, documents, objects, sounds, tapes, recordings, and virtually any other sense impression that can be communicated.

Judges and lawyers distinguish between admissibility and the weight of evidence, whether an item of evidence is worthy of belief. The laws of evidence state that for evidence to be admissible in court, its relevance must outweigh its potential for prejudice (Pickel, 1995).

The alibi testimony of a close friend or a mother's testimony about her child's good character goes to the weight of the evidence, not its admissibility. On the other hand, questions about the reliability of scientific experiments may be decided by the judge on the admissibility-inadmissibility basis. The effect is to prevent the jury from giving any weight to inadmissible testimony. However, there are quite a few data to suggest that jurors do often use inadmissible evidence in determining a verdict (Johnson, Whitestone, Jackson, & Gatto, 1995).

Jurors often make their own judgments about whether evidence ruled as inadmissible ought to be considered. Kerri Pickel (1995) found that jurors decide whether disregarding inadmissible evidence would result in a fair or unfair outcome. She reported that jurors tended not to disregard inadmissible evidence concerning a defendant's prior criminal record but did disregard inadmissible hearsay evidence because they felt that to consider hearsay was unfair.

At a minimum, to be admissible, evidence must be relevant. It must have a "tendency to make the existence of any fact that is of consequence to the determination of the action more probable or less probable than it would be without the evidence" (*Federal Rules of Evidence*, 1984, Rule 401).

The social scientist could be misled into thinking that scientific evidence will be automatically admitted. There is more to "relevance," however, than its surface meaning. In law, to be relevant, evidence must be related to a legal element of a claim or defense. In *People v. Collins* (1968), a trial involving a robbery committed by an interracial couple, the Supreme Court of California excluded as irrelevant mathematical testimony about the probabilities of these factors converging at one time and place: a partly yellow automobile, a man with a mustache, a girl with a ponytail, a girl with blond hair, a black man with a beard, and an interracial couple in a yellow car. A mathematician had testified at trial that the odds of such an occurrence were 1 in 12 million. The witness treated each of the factors as independent and then multiplied their probabilities of occurrence. The court treated relevance in this way:

> The prosecution's approach, however, could furnish the jury with absolutely no guidance on the crucial issue: Of the admittedly few such couples, which one, if any, was guilty of committing this robbery? Probability theory necessarily remains silent on that question, since no mathematical equation can prove beyond a reasonable doubt (1) that the guilty couple in fact possessed the characteristics described by the People's witnesses, or even (2) that only one couple possessing those distinctive characteristics could be found in the entire Los Angeles area. [*People v. Collins*, 1968, p. 438]

By narrowly defining relevance as limited to identifying the one couple who perpetrated the crime, the court excluded testimony that might aid the jury in interpreting the facts about the defendants' participation in the robbery. Legal relevance must be understood as defined by the purposes of law. Two main purposes are settlement of disputes and communication to the public of confidence in the resolution of disputes.

Admissible testimony must come from a competent witness. Historically, courts evaluated mental competence, age, and other factors, including prior conviction of crime, to make an independent decision about the capacity of a witness to testify accurately and truthfully. The modern trend, evidenced by FRE 601, is to provide that nearly everyone is competent to testify, except a judge or juror in the case. Interest, bias, or credibility are left to the jury because they apply to the weight that is to be accorded the testimony.

Except for expert testimony, a witness must have personal knowledge of facts based on personal sensory perceptions (FRE 602). The nonexpert witness should not state an opinion unless it is rationally based on his or her perceptions and is useful in helping the jury understand the behavior under examination (FRE 701). The witness should not say, "The driver stopped a safe distance behind the car," but "The driver stopped four feet behind the car." The witness should not say, "He acted like a crazy man." Instead, the witness should specify the behavior: "He mumbled about 'spirits,' held his hands over his head, and danced to music I could not hear." The theory is that the jury has the function of interpreting the facts according to legal criteria. Witnesses should not usurp that function by interpreting the facts or expressing opinions about them.

Inadmissible Evidence. Courts exclude evidence for the reasons stated above—namely, it is irrelevant, incompetent, inordinately prejudicial to one party, or unscientific opinion. Courts may also exclude evidence because it is not in a reliable form or in order to enforce legal policies relating to the method by which it was acquired. An example of inadmissibility due to form is the exclusion of hearsay evidence. To repeat, hearsay is any out-of-court statement or nonverbal assertion offered as proof of an assertion (FRE 801). Essentially, it is secondhand evidence. A letter written to complain about a defective toaster will be considered hearsay if it is used to verify the contents of the complaint (the toaster was defective). On the other hand, testimony that a letter was written and mailed as well as the letter itself may be admissible to show that a complaint (regardless of content) was made. Testimony in court about the content of the present complaint about the toaster would also not be hearsay because the statement is made in court and subject to the test of cross-examination.

The primary reason that the courts exclude hearsay is that it is not subject to cross-examination. The theory is that cross-examination will promote truthfulness and give the adversary a chance to probe the limits of the memory or perception of the speaker.

Many exceptions are made to the exclusion of hearsay evidence. They include statements of sensory impressions made during perception of an event; excited utterances; statements of then-existing mental, emotional, or physical condition; records of regularly conducted activities; public records; public reputation of a person's character; and various other public, family, and business records. Federal Rule of Evidence 803 lists 23 specific types of exceptions to the hearsay rule. An example of exclusion of evidence on the basis of public policy is the exclusionary rule applied to evidence seized by public officials in violation of the defendant's Fourth, Fifth, or Sixth Amendment rights. The courts have expressed two primary reasons for excluding such evidence regardless of its reliability. The first is subject to great empirical debate: whether the rule deters police misconduct. The second is more categorical: Courts reject such evidence to avoid the appearance of judicial support for police misconduct. If the police illegally seize evidence without a warrant, or if they pressure a defendant to confess despite the defendant's pleas for appointment of counsel, or if they trick a defendant into self-incrimination, the court may exclude such evidence, however relevant, probative, competent, and formally admissible it may be. On the other hand, a voluntary confession would be admissible into evidence if the defendant had been advised of his or her constitutional rights and chose to waive them.

Exclusion of confessions obtained from a defendant who is not assisted by counsel is based in part on the presumed unreliability of such statements (*Escobedo v. Illinois*, 1964). Critics argue that the exclusion of confessions deprives the judicial process of probative, reliable evidence (*California v. Minjares*, 1979).

As with many controversial areas, rules regarding admissibility of evidence deal with multiple factors that must be individually applied in each case. Because the factors are scattered along both sides of the admissibility line, lawyers have a basis for argument on behalf of their clients, and judges have a choice of rationales. Relevant evidence of some value can be excluded if the court finds "danger of unfair prejudice, confusion of the issues, or misleading the jury," or that the evidence is cumulative and will waste time (FRE 403). Faced with scientific evidence of the type used in *People v. Collins* above, a court could either admit or exclude the evidence.

SUMMARY

The feature of the American legal system the public is most aware of is the adversarial trial by jury. The history of the jury can be traced to ancient times, but its modern form had its origin in English law; the institution of the jury also played an important role in colonial America. The jury was enshrined in the U.S. Constitution in the Fifth, Sixth, and Seventh Amendments.

Selecting citizens for the jury is a two-step process. First, prospective jurors are drawn from an eligible population representative of a district. Second, eligible jurors who have been selected by some random technique undergo pretrial questioning in the courtroom, a process known as the voir dire; it is aimed, in part, at identifying possible juror biases. Lawyers see part of their duty to their client as attempting to exercise challenges to some potential jurors so as to secure a jury that will be favorable to their client. Furthermore, lawyers utilize the voir dire to implant their theory of the case. Jury consultants, trained in various disciplines, have been used to help select jurors. The evidence concerning the effectiveness of jury selection techniques is mixed.

The crucial decision in the voir dire centers on the use of the peremptory challenges lawyers can exercise without specifying why the jurors are to be eliminated. Recent decisions have begun to limit the use of peremptories, and some legal observers believe that the abolition of peremptories would aid in securing a more representative jury.

Once the jury is chosen and seated and the judge introduces the jury to their role, both sides make opening statements. These statements are important because they tell the triers-of-the facts, the jurors, the nature of the evidence each side will present. Opening statements are generally limited to previews of the evidence the lawyer expects to have admitted. Research evidence indicates that opening statements are quite important, and jurors may use those statements as a guide to organize the evidence they hear during the course of the trial. Indeed, in one study, the evidence suggested that only 30 percent of the jurors changed their minds about the verdict after they heard the opening statements. An effective opening statement can lead a juror to develop either a proprosecution or prodefense story. In essence, an effective opening statement can set the *theme* for a juror's view of the trial.

After opening statements are presented, the prosection or plaintiff in a civil trial carries the burden of proof and begins the presentation of evidence. The defense then presents its case and the prosecution (or plaintiff) has the right to rebut the defense. Evidence can be presented only if the court rules it to be admissible—that is, the evidence is deemed to be relevant and that relevance outweighs any potential prejudice. The rules of evidence are precise and codified and determine what can be presented, in what form, and who may or may not testify. This emphasis on procedure is the crucial component in protecting the rights of the accused. Several reasons drive the development of rules of evidence. These rules are aimed at controlling the jury because of the fear that juries will use the wrong kind of evidence. A second reason for rules of evidence is to serve public policies that relate to the issues being litigated. Therefore, the standard of proof for convicting a defendant in a criminal trial is higher than the standard for winning a civil case. A third reason for rules of evidence is to influence positively or to protect noncourtroom behavior. For example, spouses cannot be forced to testify against their partners, thereby presumably protecting marriage. Fourth, the law of evidence aims to ensure accurate fact finding. For example, there are rules that determine how a document entered into evidence is to be authenticated. A fifth reason for evidence law is simply to control the scope and length of trials. Trial judges have the power to move the trial along in a rapid manner.

Evidence given in a trial consists of oral or documentary presentations. Some witnesses and evidence are excluded: Witnesses too young or too sick may not be heard, and some documents, such as a marked copy when the original is retrievable, may not be acceptable. Admissibility of evidence refers to whether the trier-of-fact (judge or jury) should hear and consider a particular item of evidence.

Jurists distinguish between admissibility and the weight of evidence, whether an item of evidence is worthy of belief. The laws of evidence state that for evidence to be admissible in court, its relevance must outweigh its potential for prejudice. However, despite what the rules of evidence may specify, jurors often make their own judgments about whether evidence ruled as inadmissible ought to be considered. Researchers have found that jurors decide whether disregarding inadmissible evidence would result in a fair or unfair outcome. Often, there is not a sharp line between admissible and inadmissible evidence; therefore, it is up to the lawyers to argue for admission of favorable evidence.

CHAPTER
7

The Eyewitness

THE EYEWITNESS

The practice of taking oral testimony came into the trial system at the end of the sixteenth century. As the jury gained power late in the sixteenth and early in the seventeenth centuries, oral testimony was given more weight. With the central government in England gaining power at the expense of local lords, these lords became less able to intimidate witnesses. Judges were more willing to hear witnesses who, earlier, because of their vulnerability to intimidation, would not have presented credible testimony (Rembar, 1980).

Since the early 1600s, however, eyewitnesses to crimes have become more and more critical in the outcome of criminal trials. Such testimony often assumes primary importance. Without an eyewitness, evidence often may not be credible to a jury; with an eyewitness present, evidence often will convict. Loftus (1979) demonstrated that circumstantial evidence yielded an 18 percent conviction rate with no eyewitness, but the same evidence produced a 72 percent rate of conviction when an eyewitness testified. Even a discredited eyewitness will make a large difference in obtaining a conviction, if the discrediting was not powerful enough to undermine the testimony totally (Weinberg & Baron, 1982).

Of course, there are other types of witnesses who are not eyewitnesses. Recently, the expert witness has become an important part of the trial. The expert witness presents technical evidence concerning science, medicine, the state of mind of the defendant, or any issue that the trial judge agrees is not in the normal realm (purview) of the jurors' experience. Modern uses of scientific evidence often address the central issue of many trials—identification of the defendant as culprit. In this way fingerprints, fiber and hair analysis, and DNA evidence all serve purposes similar to eyewitness identification. The most familiar witness, however, remains the eyewitness, which we discuss first.

Famous Cases of Misidentification

Courts assume that human observers are much like an ideal perceptual machine: They observe stimuli and store them without interference from other events and memories; when called on, they can retrieve these memories with clarity and without prejudice. In other words, courts expect the eyewitness to react much like a human camcorder. This conception does not coincide with the modern psychological model of perception and memory (Cutler & Penrod, 1995).

Misidentification of individuals accounts for about half of all wrongful convictions (Penrod & Cutler, in press). Yarmey (1979) recounted a dramatic version of misidentification—the case of Adolf Beck. He was originally arrested in London in 1895 on the charge of illegally obtaining jewelry and money from women whose reputations were tainted by their occupation. Yarmey reports that ten of these "loose" women identified Adolf Beck with an accuracy and zeal that left no room for doubt. Some years later Beck proved that another man had committed the crimes and Beck was released from prison.

Making some unlucky choices, Beck again was in London in 1904. Again, a series of crimes occurred and these women too, with remarkable fervor, identified Beck as the culprit. Fortunately, however, the crimes continued after Beck's imprisonment. He was eventually cleared of all charges when another culprit was identified and convicted.

An interesting fact about witness testimony appears in Yarmey's recounting of the Beck case. He quotes a number of the eyewitnesses who identified Beck with statements full of sincerity and intensity. Truth clearly has a dual nature. A person may believe that he or she is telling the truth, although the reality is otherwise. Sincerity and accuracy are two sides of truth-telling, not one and the same. Indeed, strong evidence suggests that jurors tend to believe witnesses who appear to be sincere and confident, albeit inaccurate (Wells, Ferguson, & Lindsay, 1981). Loftus (1979) suggests that little evidence outside of a smoking gun has greater influence in obtaining a conviction than that of the eyewitness.

As we suggested, however, the most frequent factor in the conviction of innocent people derives from mistaken identification (Penrod & Cutler, in press). Rattner (1988) reported that of the approximately 8,500 known wrongful convictions annually, about one-half are due to faulty eyewitness identification. This means that over 4,000 individuals per year are misidentified by eyewitnesses and are convicted of crimes they did not commit. The importance of the eyewitness to the criminal justice system is made crystal clear by the finding that in one year (1987), 78,000 trials in the United States were decided primarily on the basis of eyewitness testimony (Rattner, 1988).

The problem of faulty eyewitness identification has fascinated psychologists for nearly a century. Hugo Munsterberg (1908) addressed the problem during the first decade of the twentieth century. Today, the fascination with the eyewitness continues. Researchers have devoted a great deal of time and effort to investigating various aspects of eyewitness identification and testimony.

Psychological scientists been drawn to the performance of the eyewitness for at least three reasons. First, eyewitness identification of a criminal involves psychological processes that have been central to the science of psychology. These include perception, attention, and memory. Second, research on eyewitness identification has strong applications beyond the laboratory: What we find out about the eyewitness may help the police and courts better handle eyewitnesses, perhaps increasing the accuracy of eyewitness identification and reducing wrongful convictions. Third, eyewitness testimony involves a dynamic interpersonal relationship between the witness and the police, and later the jury.

Factors Affecting Eyewitness Accuracy

Three factors are involved in the memory process: *encoding, storage,* and *retrieval.* The encoding process involves entering information into memory. It is analogous to placing information into your computer. When you encode information, for example, you select the information you wish to place into memory (just as you would if you were writing information into a spreadsheet). Unlike the computer, however, you encode information differently depending on its importance to the event. If you saw a person with a gun holding up a bank, you might encode information about the gun, the robber's clothing, height, weight, and so on. Other information (e.g., the color of the robber's shoes) may not be encoded. During the encoding process, the major psychological mechanism operating is selective attention. You attend to some important aspects of the event while ignoring others. Attention is the critical process in determining what information is encoded into memory.

Once you have encoded the information, it must be stored for later use. While in memory, as we shall see, the information may be altered by details about the event you encounter subsequently. In short, information stored in memory is not impervious to influence from outside sources.

Finally, retrieval involves recovering your memory for an event and reporting it. Unfortunately, your report may not be a one-to-one account of the event originally witnessed. At retrieval, we recover details stored with the event and reconstruct a report of that event. Memory is a reconstruction process, not unlike the procedure used by an archeologist who puts bit and pieces of relics together to present a picture of the past. This reconstructed report may not be an accurate representation of the original event.

Factors Affecting an Eyewitness's Perception of an Event

When an eyewitness views a crime, several variables will affect the accuracy of his or her perceptions. In some cases, an eyewitness may be confronted by an armed perpetrator. In others, the lawbreaker may use a disguise. To what does the witness pay attention? The gun? The perpetrator? Does the witness fearfully just stare at the floor? To say the least, the conditions under which the eyewitness operates are less than ideal. In the sections that follow we explore some of the major factors affecting the accuracy of eyewitness perception of a criminal event.

Weapon Focus.   Imagine you are a bank teller. You are taking care of customers, perhaps thinking about what you will do after work. The next person in line steps to your window and gives you a note saying, "This is a holdup. Put all your money into this bag. Do not shout or trip an alarm. I have a gun pointed at you." You look up and see the man holding a large caliber handgun under his jacket. You keep your eyes glued to the gun; as if in a dream, you begin filling the man's bag with the money from your drawer. Does the presence of a weapon affect the accuracy of an eyewitness's report? Generally the answer to this question is yes, because of a phenomenon called **weapon focus** (Loftus, 1979). Weapon focus occurs when a weapon draws our attention so that we pay less attention to other details.

We tend to select the features of a scene that stand out, that are salient details. Perceivers attend most to those details and remember them best later. Marshall, Marquis, and Oskamp (1971) demonstrated the importance of detail salience in an imaginative study. They showed subjects a two-minute-long movie depicting

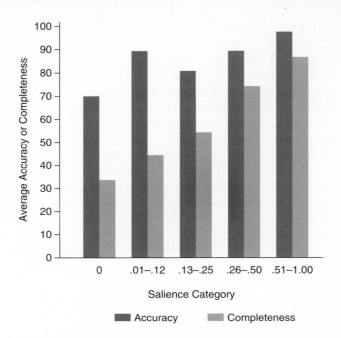

FIGURE 7.1 The importance of detail salience on eyewitness reports.

As shown here, salient details are more likely to be included in an eyewitness's report than less salient details. But even items of very low salience were recalled quite accurately (an accuracy score of near 70 out of 100). Detail salience is most important for the completeness of a witness's report.

Source: Adapted from "Effects of Kind of Question and Atmosphere of Interrogation on Accuracy and Completeness of Testimony," by J. Marshall, K. H. Marquis, and S. Oskamp, 1971, *Harvard Law Review, 84,* 1627–1628.

an automobile striking a pedestrian in a supermarket parking lot. Prior to the actual experiment, the film was pretested to determine the salience of the various details depicted. This was done by measuring the number of times each detail was mentioned by subjects who had viewed the film. After viewing the film, the actual subjects were interviewed concerning what they could recall about the film. Two measures were developed: the accuracy of the subjects' perceptions (proportion of details correctly reported) and the completeness of the subjects' perceptions (the proportion of details mentioned).

The results of this study are shown in Figure 7.1, which suggests that salient details are more likely to be included in an eyewitness's report than are less salient details. However, even items of very low salience were recalled quite accurately (an accuracy score of nearly 70 out of 100). Detail salience, as shown in Figure 7.1, is most critical for the completeness of a witness's report. In this case, the higher the item's salience, the more complete the report of that detail. Thus, details in a crime that are salient, such as a weapon, are most likely to be remembered and reported by an eyewitness.

Undoubtedly, a weapon is a salient detail. Research on the presence of a weapon parallel Marshall's findings. For example, Loftus, Loftus, and Messo (1987) found that when a weapon was present, fewer subjects were able to make a correct identification of a suspect in a lineup than if no weapon was present. Also, when a weapon was present, subjects tended to stare at it (measured by eye fixations on the weapon). While they are staring at the scene, particularly the weapon, observers are not looking at other details such as the suspect's face and clothing. Later, when witnesses are asked to identify a suspect, they are less able to do so accurately when a weapon was present than if no weapon was present (Maas & Kohnken, 1989).

The vast majority of studies have shown that the presence of a weapon does inhibit accurate eyewitness identification (Steblay, 1992). Steblay reported that the weapon focus effect is most pronounced in highly realistic simulated situations and that a delay between the witness's viewing the event and viewing a lineup enhances the effect. Generally, if a witness's attention is drawn to the weapon, his or her accuracy in later identification of the person committing the crime is reduced (Steblay, 1992).

Violence of the Crime. Another important variable that affects eyewitness accuracy is the presence of violence in the crime. Generally, when the crime is violent, eyewitnesses are less accurate than if the crime is nonviolent (Clifford & Scott, 1978).

The **Yerkes-Dodson Law,** illustrated in Figure 7.2, suggests that there is an inverted U-shaped function relating stress and performance. Under conditions of high stress, performance suffers. Under conditions of moderate stress, performance is enhanced. A violent crime is a highly stressful event that will impair perception. This effect probably occurs through the arousal of the autonomic

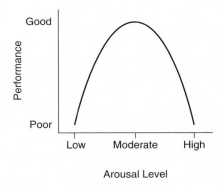

FIGURE 7.2 The Yerkes-Dodson law.

There is an inverted U-shaped function relating stress and performance. Under conditions of high stress, performance suffers. A violent crime is a very stressful event that impairs perception. This probably occurs through the arousal of the autonomic nervous system. When you are under stress, one of the events that occurs is that large amounts of adrenaline are pumped into your blood.

nervous system. When you are under stress, your body reacts by preparing for action, focusing on physical rather than cognitive responses.

A review of the literature by Sven-Ake Christianson (1992) concluded that in eyewitness memory situations, stress may interact with other variables—for example, the type of event (emotional or neutral) and the type of detail to be recalled (high or low salience). Eyewitness accuracy is a complex phenomenon involving memory processes that may be affected either positively or negatively by emotional arousal.

Cross-race Identifications.   Yet another variable affecting eyewitness accuracy is the racial similarity of witness and suspect. Generally, cross-race identifications are more difficult to make than same-race identifications (Lindsay, Jack, & Christian, 1991; Malpass & Kravitz, 1969). A white eyewitness will be less accurate identifying a black suspect than a white suspect (Brigham, 1986). Although some research suggests that "own race" bias is more prevalent among white than black subjects (Lindsay et al., 1991), most studies show that the bias exists in whites and blacks alike (Bothwell, Brigham, & Malpass, 1989). This effect probably occurs because we are more familiar with the facial characteristics of members of our own than another race. We may pay less attention to differences among faces of individuals outside our racial group.

Factors Affecting Eyewitness Memory

Human memory tends to be more frail and subject to greater outside influence than we are willing to admit. In our day-to-day lives we have memory failures all the time. We forget where we parked our cars, where we put our notebooks, and so on. These everyday failures amount to very little. Eventually we find our cars and notebooks. However, when the eyewitness fails to recall something accurately, the result may be that an innocent person goes to prison.

One view of human memory is that it works much like a camcorder. When we want to record something, we press record. When we want to remember something, we press rewind and play and out comes the information just as it went in. Basically, this is the view taken of human memory by the court system. Unfortunately, it is not the way human memory works. Our memories are stored in a dynamic way. We tend to store details of events and during recall we reconstruct the original event (Bartlett, 1932) through a process known as **reconstructive memory.** Several factors affect the dynamic nature of memory.

Exposure Time.   In decades of psychological research on human memory, scientists have found that a person's memory of an event is directly related to the amount of time he or she has to study a stimulus. Whether we are talking about words on a list, a paragraph of prose, or a person's face, the longer you can study a stimulus, the better your memory of it will be. Translated into the eyewitness situation, if you, as an eyewitness, have only a few seconds of exposure to a criminal, your memory for his or her face will be poorer than if you had more time. Unfortunately, crimes often occur quickly, with many features of the crime competing for your attention. Because of this, exposure to any one aspect of the crime may be brief and our memories for any one detail relatively poor.

The Misinformation Effect. The dynamic nature of human memory suggests that information in memory can be influenced by a variety of factors. For example, what we decide to put or encode into memory is affected by information already in memory. Also, information already in memory can be affected by new information that we encounter (Loftus, 1979). Imagine that you originally believe one of the suspects in the bank holdup was "short." However, the next day you read in the newspaper that another witness described the same suspect as "tall." Through a process of **compromise memory** (Loftus, 1979) you may blend the short with the tall and come to believe that the suspect was of "average" height. Loftus (1979) and others (Dodson & Reisberg, 1991; Lindsay & Johnson, 1989; McCloskey & Zaragoza, 1985; Tversky & Tuchin, 1989) have found, in a variety of studies, that postevent information in many forms can influence what eyewitnesses have in memory and their reports of crimes. This effect of biasing the memory of postevent information is known as the **misinformation effect** (Loftus, Schooler, & Wagenaar, 1985).

It is interesting that misleading information need not be encountered *after* one has witnessed an event for the misinformation effect to occur. D. Stephen Lindsay and Marcia Johnson exposed subjects to misleading information *before* exposure to a slide show. They found a misinformation effect, suggesting that the effect of misleading information is not limited to the disruption of preexisting memories. Misleading information may bias a witness by setting up an expectation that certain information will be encountered. Thus, memories from a variety of sources (based on information encountered either before or after a critical event is witnessed) can become integrated and serve as the basis for a report provided by an eyewitness (Lindsay & Johnson, 1989).

Misleading information need not even be specific to the event witnessed to produce a biasing effect. Gunter Kohnken and Claudia Brockman (1987) had subjects watch a film of an accident in which an automobile struck a motorcycle. One week after viewing the film, the subjects returned to the laboratory and were given a memory test. Before the test, however, some subjects were exposed to postevent information that was not a specific detail of what they had seen on the film. In one condition, subjects were told that the driver of the car left the scene of the accident without rendering aid to the motorcyclist (hit-and-run condition). In another condition, subjects were told that the motorist stopped and gave help to the cyclist and called for an ambulance (no-hit-and-run condition). Postevent information was also given for the motorcyclist. Some subjects were told that the motorcyclist was legally drunk at the time of the accident, whereas a second group was told that the motorcyclist was sober. Finally, subjects in a no-information control group did not receive postevent information.

The focus of this experiment was on the kinds of attributions of responsibility that were made to the driver of the car and the motorcyclist. Figure 7.3 shows the percentages of responsibility attributed to the automobile driver and demonstrates that the postevent information had an effect on attributions of responsibility. More responsibility was assigned to the car driver when the postevent information indicated that the accident was a hit-and-run than if it was not presented as a hit-and-run accident and the motorcyclist was sober. Attributions of responsibility to the car driver did not differ across hit-and-run conditions when the motorcyclist was said to have been drunk.

This experiment tells us that postevent information need not appear as a specific piece of incorrect information in a memory protocol. Postevent information can also affect the inferences witnesses make about the people involved in an event the witnesses observed.

Although the existence of the misinformation effect has been demonstrated quite frequently, some controversy exists over why this effect occurs. The debate over the locus of the misinformation effect has provoked controversies sur-

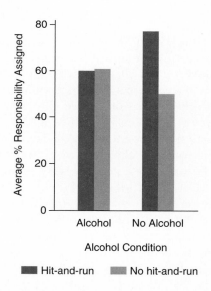

FIGURE 7.3   The effect of postevent information on assigning responsibility for an accident.

Figure 7.3 suggests that when witnesses were told, after viewing the film of an accident, that it was hit-and-run, they altered their attributions of responsibility, finding the driver more blameworthy when the driver was sober as compared to when alcohol was involved.

Source: Adapted from "The Effect of Postevent Information on Assigning Responsibility for an Accident," by G. Kohnken and C. Brockman, 1987, *Applied Cognitive Psychology, 1,* 197–207.

rounding the nature of human memory. In one view, Loftus (1980a,b) suggests that conflicting postevent information actually alters the initial memory trace that was created from the original information experienced by the eyewitness. This alteration makes the original memory trace unavailable to the eyewitness. In another view, McCloskey and Zaragoza (1985) dispute Loftus's idea of the altered memory trace on the basis of an experiment they conducted.

McCloskey and Zaragoza conducted a postevent information experiment under two conditions. Subjects viewed a slide show depicting a man holding a hammer (the critical item). Later, some subjects were exposed to a narrative description telling them that the man in the slide show had a screwdriver in his hand (misleading condition). Other subjects were not exposed to misleading information (control condition). The subjects were then given one of two memory tests. In the "original" test (used by Loftus in her research), subjects were asked to indicate whether the man was holding a hammer or a screwdriver. Notice that both items were part of the misleading condition. In a "modified" test, the subjects were asked whether the man had a hammer or a wrench (only one of the items is relevant to the slide show or narrative).

McCloskey and Zaragoza's results (collapsed over six replications) are shown in Figure 7.4. Notice that with the original method, the misinformation effect was replicated. However, it disappeared with the modified method. McCloskey and Zaragoza suggest that the original memory trace was retained and showed through in the modified test. Further, when a witness is asked what he or she has seen, elements of the original memory trace and/or postevent information can serve as a basis for answering questions.

It would appear, then, that the memory trace for the original information remained intact and was available to individuals, even if conflicting postevent information had been encountered. However, in the modified test, subjects in McCloskey and Zaragoza's experiment possibly were able to reject something they had never seen or heard about before, leaving them with only one option (Tversky & Tuchin, 1989). In yet another extension of Loftus's original misinformation paradigm, Tversky and Tuchin (1989) found evidence that postevent information does not affect memory on a global basis. Rather, postevent information may affect memory for specific pieces of information depending on what is seen or heard. From their experiment, Tversky and Tuchin concluded that the original memory trace laid down prior to exposure to misleading information *is* affected by such information. Further, they suggest that the original memory trace and a new trace based on the misleading information *coexist* and can be used when recalling an event. In fact, recent models of memory suggest that two memory traces may be superimposed on one another, forming a single blended entity (Metcalfe, 1990).

It is not possible to specify precisely the mechanism underlying the misinformation effect. We can safely conclude, however, that if a witness is exposed to misleading postevent information, the witness's *report* of what was experienced may be influenced in the direction of the misleading information. Regardless of

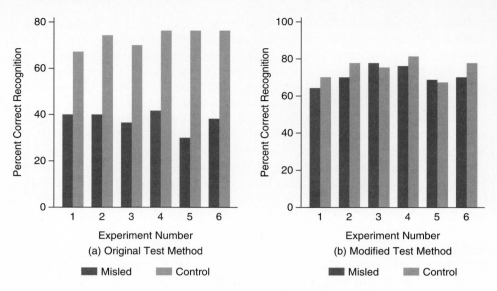

FIGURE 7.4   Remembrance of things past: Original memory traces are retained.

Note in Figure 7.4 that with the original method the misinformation effect was replicated. However, it disappeared with the modified method. McCloskey and Zaragoza suggest that the original memory trace was retained and showed through in the modified test.

Source: Adapted from "Misleading Postevent Information and Memory for Events: Arguments and Evidence Against the Memory Impairment Hypotheses," by M. McCloskey and M. Zaragoza, 1985, *Journal of Experimental Psychology, 114,* 3–18.

the reason for the distortion, what the witness reports may not be an accurate reflection of the original event he or she witnessed. Rather, it may contain elements of the original memory as well as new elements added after exposure to postevent information.

Unconscious Transference.   Researchers have long considered one threat to the accuracy of an eyewitness's memory to occur when the witness misidentifies a familiar but innocent person as the culprit (Ross, Read, & Toglia 1994). In one case, a ticket agent at a railway station was held up. At the police lineup, the agent picked out an innocent sailor as the culprit. It turned out that the sailor was simply a bystander who had bought a ticket from the agent. The agent had made an **unconscious transference** and confused the innocent but familiar sailor with the culprit. Unconscious transference means that the agent had misidentified the bystander as the culprit without consciously remembering exactly where he had seen the bystander.

In a series of experiments examining the concept of unconscious transference, David Ross and his co-workers (1994) have challenged the notion that the process of misidentifying a familiar but innocent bystander as the guilty party is an unconscious act. It may be inadvertent, but it is not unconscious. Ross's findings suggest that witnesses may misidentify a bystander as the culprit because they consciously infer that the person is the actual culprit. Often, witnesses can remember where they saw the bystander ("in the cafeteria"), but this knowledge simply reinforces the notion that they have seen this person in two different places—the crime scene and the cafeteria.

The precise theoretical underpinnings of the unconscious transference idea are in question at the moment. Nevertheless, the misidentification in lineups of faces that seem familiar is a continual problem. In the absence of a "true image" of the culprit, witnesses seem more likely to retrieve salient and accessible images.

Repressed Memories

In 1993, Chicago's Cardinal Joseph Bernardin was accused of sexually molesting Steven J. Cook, who alleged that Bernardin molested him while Cook was attending a program at a seminary in Cincinnati. Cook sought $10 million in damages. The molestation was alleged to have taken place between 1975 and 1977, when Cook was a teenager. Cook based his claim against Bernardin on memories revealed during years of psychotherapy. During his therapy session, Cook, with his therapist's guidance, claimed to have uncovered memories that had been repressed.

Repressed memories are remembrances of traumatic events that occurred a long time ago, typically in childhood, which the individual has buried so deeply that no hint of the event surfaced until the moment it was recovered. During all the years between the event and recovery, the individual has had no awareness that anything traumatic had happened. Keep in mind that most recovered memories seem to involve multiple traumatic events, usually sexual abuse or other violent incidents, that have occurred over a period of time. However, note that neither biological nor cognitive research indicate that one can totally bury memories, never having a hint that such memories exist (Loftus, 1995a).

The Bernardin case, although highly publicized, is not the only case involving an adult recovering repressed memories during therapy. Over the past few years, these cases have become more frequent, and occasionally more grotesque. In one case, Paul Ingram was accused by his two adult daughters of sexually abusing them as children. Ingram was the chief civil deputy in the Olympia, Washington, sheriff's department and the head of the local Republican party when the accusations were made. His daughters alleged various forms of abuse, which included physical abuse (being stabbed and burned), sexual abuse, and psychological abuse (one allegation was that Ingram dismembered his daughter's aborted fetus in front of her).

Initially, Ingram denied the charges. However, after developing his own method of recovering repressed memories, Ingram began to weave a story consistent with his daughters' accounts. On the basis of what he was discovering, Ingram confessed to the crimes and was sentenced to 20 years in prison. No physical evidence existed to corroborate Ingram's confessions. For example, there were no scars on Ingram's daughters that might be expected if they had been stabbed or burned. Also, there was no evidence that either of his daughters became pregnant at the time the abuse was alleged to have occurred. Because of the lack of evidence, charges against two of Ingram's codefendants were dropped. Ingram, having confessed, remains in prison (Loftus & Ketcham, 1994).

Are these repressed memories valid, or are they the product of suggestive therapy techniques used to "recover" such memories? It is important to note that the issue of recovered memories has a long cultural context. Sexual victimization of children historically has largely been ignored (Lindsay & Read, 1995). Only in recent years has child sexual victimization been given a fair hearing and been recognized as a serious and pervasive problem. The number of reported child sexual abuse cases has risen rapidly, and roughly 90 percent of the prosecutions are successful (keep in mind that only substantiated cases tend to be prosecuted) (Lindsay & Read, 1995). But recognition of the sad fact of child sexual abuse may be seen as independent of the question of whether recovered memories are veridical or illusory.

Sources of False Repressed Memories.   Elizabeth Loftus (1993) has reviewed the issue of validity of repressed memories. She suggests that several sources could contribute to an invalid repressed memory. For example, Loftus (1995a) suggested that books such as *The Courage to Heal* (Bass & Davis, 1988) could encourage a person to develop a false repressed memory. Bass and Davis claim that symptoms including low self-esteem, suicidal thoughts, sexual dysfunction, or depression can all be traced to early sexual abuse during childhood. The book suggests that the first hints that sexual abuse occurred during childhood may be a "vague feeling" and that this feeling is enough to presume the existence of abuse (Loftus & Ketcham, 1994).

A second source of invalid recovered memories may be the therapy process itself. Current controversy focuses on the issue of whether many clients truly do not remember the terrible events of abuse or whether "memory work," techniques used to reengage suspected lost memories, can provoke people who were not actually abused to think they were (Lindsay & Read, 1995). Many therapists assume that a patient entering therapy with any of a number of symptoms (e.g., anxiety, depression, low self-esteem, etc.) was the victim of childhood sexual abuse. Loftus (1993) reported that some therapists have expressed the need to consider child sexual abuse in just about every new patient they work with. There is, however, a large leap between considering the possibility of sexual abuse and setting out to confirm the existence of such abuse. Loftus (1995a) suggested that some therapists so firmly believe that sexual abuse and certain symptoms are related in a causal way that they sculpt the therapy to confirm that belief. The vulnerable patient, who believes that he or she cannot get better without facing and acknowledging the source of the problem, may be a willing participant in weaving a repressed memory of childhood sexual abuse to confirm the therapist's expectations and theories.

If the therapist is set on confirming the existence of abuse, there is a clear danger that a patient might fabricate a memory to please a persistent therapist. According to one source, in some cases patients come to question the validity of their memories after leaving therapy (Loftus & Ketcham, 1994). This happened in the case of Cardinal Bernardin. Eventually Cook dropped his case against Bernardin because he (Cook) became convinced that the memories recovered during therapy were false.

Poole, Lindsay, Memon, and Bull (1995), after a survey of therapists, concluded that perhaps 25 percent of all therapists engaged in behavior that might elicit false memory. If true, this is startling. However, the reported use of "risky" techniques and the concomitant report of recovered memories does not necessarily mean that the techniques caused the memories. For example, we would need to know how many patients recovered memories when therapists did not employ risky techniques as well as how many patients did not recover memories in the presence of risky techniques (Olio, in press; Pope, 1996). Finally, researchers really do not know what occurs in the actual therapy situation. Self-reports by therapists that they do or do not use procedures deemed to be risky may be of questionable use scientifically. Self-reports are not always reliable and there is no reason to assume that therapists are any better at reporting what they think they did than is anyone else (Olio, in press).

Can Repressed Memories Be Planted?   We have already seen how postevent information can influence the accuracy of an eyewitness's memory, but can a person be made to believe that something happened that never in fact occurred? Apparently, according to research by Loftus (1993) and her colleagues, the answer is yes.

Loftus (1993) reported research in which a 14-year-old boy (Chris) was convinced by his older brother that when he was 5 years old, he (Chris) became lost in a shopping mall. Over the next few days Chris started to remember more and more about the event that never occurred. First he remembered some of his emotions concerning being lost (he knew he was in trouble, he was afraid, etc.). Eventually he recalled details about the mall itself and the man who found him. Within a couple of weeks Chris's memory of the event became more elaborate. Thus, Loftus has demonstrated that it is possible to implant a memory in a person's mind that can become quite clear and well developed. Could the same thing occur in a patient who is motivated to get better and told by his therapist that his problems stem from being abused during childhood? Some researchers believe that the experimentally implanted memories reported by Loftus differ significantly from memories that are the result of acute or chronic acts of sexual abuse in childhood (Pope, 1996).

True and False Memory.   The validity of a memory is very hard to establish, as we have seen, but for the first time, psychological science may have found a way to study false memory in the making. In computer-enhanced images produced by a technique known as Positron Emission Tomography (PET) scanning, Daniel Schacter and fellow memory researchers have taken real-time photographs of the brain retrieving a memory, and pictures of the brain going amiss and producing a false memory (Schacter, 1996; Schacter et al., in press). In the images produced by these new brain scans, false memories can be clearly distinguished from those that are true (Hilts, 1996).

PET scans monitor the activation of brain cells by measuring blood flow to the cells. Cells working on making or retrieving a memory use more blood, so those brain areas show up as bright spots on the PET brain image (Hilts, 1996). In Schacter's experiment, participants were asked to remember words that were read to them. Next they heard a second set of words that contained only some of the words on the previous list. The subjects were then asked to identify the words they had heard on the first list. As they tried to retrieve their memory, the PET scans recorded their brain activity (Schacter et al., in press).

Another, similar study was done to test false memory, but in this test, some words on the second list were designed to be evocative of, but not the same as, the original list of words. For example, subjects were presented the words "candy," "cake," and "chocolate" in the first list, but they were later asked if the word "sweet" had been among the ones presented. It had not been, but it was similar enough to prompt many false memories (falsely recalling "sweet" as being on the original list) by the subjects (Schacter, 1996).

What did the PET scans show? There were commonalities in the scans of both true and false memories. Both activated the area of the brain that is involved in recall, adjacent to the left hippocampus. However, the scan of the true memory showed an additional sign of its validity. Recall that the experimenter had spoken the words to the subjects in the true memory study. That is, all subjects had actually heard all the words they were asked to recall. This was not so for the false memory subjects, who were asked to recall a word they had not actually heard (i.e., "sweet"). Therefore, true memory subjects should have an auditory representation of the word to be recalled whereas false memory participants do not. PET scans showed activation not only in the hippocampal area, but also in the left temporal parietal area where the brain interprets sound patterns and words. Therefore, a true memory called up both the word and some sensory detail from the moment when the learning had taken place. In other words, the sound of the voice speaking the words was recalled.

Whether this could be a diagnostic tool to sift false from true memories is unclear. Many questions remain about the limitations and potential of this technique (Hilts, 1996).

The Impact of Repressed Memory Testimony on the Jury.   There are civil cases on record in which juries, mainly on the strength of a person's recovered repressed memories, have awarded victims of alleged childhood sexual abuse large sums of money (Loftus, 1993). Research has only recently begun on the impact of repressed memories that have been recovered. Loftus, Weingardt, and Hoffman (1993) had subjects judge a case of a daughter (Roberta) who accused her father of raping her during childhood, a memory she had repressed for ten years. In the case, the jurors learned that Roberta had remembered the rape and abuse during therapy. Other subjects judged a case of a woman (Nancy) who did not repress her memory but told her therapist about it. Loftus et al. found that jurors were less inclined to believe Roberta (repressed memory) than Nancy (nonrepressed memory). Generally, males were more skeptical of Roberta's story than females. An interesting note is that even if subjects rejected the repressed memory claim, they were likely to attribute the false memory to an honest mistake and not to a deliberate lie. Loftus et al. report that overall a majority of subjects believed the claims of both Roberta and Nancy were true. Recent work by Holly Key, Amye Warren, and David Ross (1996) also found that jurors are generally skeptical of repressed memories, and that males are more skeptical than are females of testimony by female witnesses who report recovered memories.

Jonathan Golding and his co-workers showed that mock jurors demonstrate a degree of skepticism about an alleged victim's claim of recovered memory. For example, jurors put less credence in victims who claimed recovered memory than in a child sexual assault victim who testified without delay. (Key et al. found that an eight-year-old girl was a more credible witness than was an adult female with respect to recovered memories.) In the Golding et al. study, the victim alleging repressed memories had "delayed" for 20 years before recovering those memories. Delays in reporting alleged crimes led to fewer verdicts in favor of the alleged victims (Golding, Sego, Sanchez, & Hasemann, 1995). Golding et al. suggest that jurors understand the consistent findings of cognitive psychologists, who hold that memory is malleable over time and therefore is not totally trustworthy.

At this point, we are just beginning to explore jurors' reactions to recovered memories. It appears that jurors have some skepticism—not as much as cognitive psychologists but more than those who support the accuracy of recovered memories.

Repressed Memories: Summing Up.   With respect to past events, there are two kinds of truth. One is historic truth, what actually occurred. The other is narrative truth, the individual's memory of what may have happened. From the court's point of view, the aim is to determine historic truth. That truth may be unknowable. The therapist has to deal with narrative truth, the story we all tell ourselves to make sense of our memories (Loftus & Ketcham, 1994). Cognitive psychologists know that all memory is in one form or another narrative truth. There is valid reason for some individuals, who report memories that may not be valid, to feel so certain of their memories: Some of the same areas of the brain (occipital lobes) are activated when one is simply "imaging" an event as when one is retrieving a stored visual image. This physical reason may explain why events that people only imagined feel to them like events that actually happened (Schacter, 1996).

Clearly, distinguishing between real and imagined memories is a difficult issue for psychologists and for the courts. Experimental psychologists, given their knowledge of the ease with which memories can be modified and even created, are skeptical of recovered memories (Loftus, 1995b). Even the notion of repression, unconsciously burying unwanted memories, has little, if any, experimental support (Loftus & Pickrell, in press).

Case histories offered by competent clinicians suggest that there are individuals who are certain their recovered memories are true and give anecdotal, although not scientific, evidence to support the contention (Terr, 1994). However, Lindsay and Read (1995), in an exhaustive review of the literature, concluded that only a small minority of psychotherapy clients have hidden memories that are recoverable. Furthermore, they concluded that therapists actually are unable to differentiate between clients with real memories and those without, although they may think they can. Lindsay and Read (1995) stated that much therapeutic "memory work" is suggestive, perhaps highly so, and this provokes grave concern about the probability that many, although perhaps not all, memories recovered under these circumstances are false.

Despite what we know about human memory and the therapy process, the courts have been fairly lenient in allowing repressed memory evidence in court (Loftus & Rosenwald, 1993). They have relaxed the applicable "statute of limitations" (a law that specifies the number of years one has after a crime or other legal injury to bring criminal charges or file a civil lawsuit) to allow cases involving repressed memories of sexual abuse to be heard.

Washington is one of the states that has relaxed its statute of limitations to allow repressed memories to form the basis of a suit. Its state legislature permitted the application of what is known as the *discovery rule.* Typically used in medical malpractice cases, the discovery rule allows a plaintiff to file a suit a few (say three) years after the discovery of the injury. The statute of limitations period begins to run at the time of discovery, not at the time of injury. Therefore, if you discover ten years after surgery that the surgeon left an instrument in your stomach, you have three years to sue after you have discovered the injury. An individual who has recovered repressed memories about childhood sexual abuse has a few years to press a suit after that discovery (Loftus & Rosenwald, 1993).

The Michigan Supreme Court faced the question of whether to apply the discovery rule to repressed memory claims in *Lemmerman v. Fealk* (1995). Citing Ernsdorff and Loftus (1993), the court held that repressed memory claims were not "based on an evaluation of a factual, tangible consequence of action by the defendant, measured against an objective standard." Because of the lack of an objective measure, the court decided not to force a defendant to answer repressed memory claims years—or even decades—after the alleged events. The court, noting that psychological research has yet to determine the validity of repressed memories, decided to let the legislature resolve the issue of whether lawsuits can be brought on the basis of recovered memories.

It is clear that the courts would like to have science solve the issue of whether therapeutically recovered memories are valid. Charles Ewing (1996) has traced three very recent cases that dealt with this issue. In one case, the court found the theory of repressed memory to be validated and generally accepted by relevant scientists; but in the other two cases, the courts expressed serious reservations.

In *Shahzade v. Gregory* (1996), decided by the U.S. District Court for Massachusetts, a 68-year-old woman had sued her cousin for sexually abusing her when the two were teenagers. The woman claimed that she had repressed recollection of the abuse until undergoing psychotherapy nearly 50 years later. The defendant claimed the recovered memories evidence would not meet legal standards of reliability and should be inadmissable. In response, a psychiatrist called by the plaintiff testified that most psychiatrists did not believe recovered memory to be controversial and that its validity was accepted. The court denied the defendant's motion to prevent the introduction of "recovered memories" (Ewing, 1996).

In another case involving recovered memories the Texas Supreme Court (*SVR v. RVR*, 1996) cast doubt on the science underlying the validity of those memories. Finally, the U.S. Supreme Court let stand the ruling of the U.S. Court of Appeals for the Second Circuit in *Borowick v. Shay* (1995), which held that hypnosis used to unearth recovered memory did not provide enough "safeguards" to protect the defendant against the hypnotist shaping the hypnotic interview. Furthermore, there was no corroborative evidence to validate the plaintiff's claims of abuse (Ewing, 1996).

In sum, the issue of the validity of recovered memory is not entirely settled, psychologically or legally, and is awash in a strong emotional tide (Pope, 1996). Whereas the weight of science inclines us to question the validity of recovered memories, new approaches may qualify this conclusion (Freyd, 1996).

Hypnotically Refreshed Memory

A large body of research suggests that eyewitnesses often forget important details of a crime. In some cases, hypnosis has been used to refresh the memories of eyewitnesses. Perhaps the most famous case of hypnotically refreshed memory occurred after a school bus filled with children was kidnapped in Chowchilla, California. The bus driver escaped and under hypnosis provided police with all but one digit of the license number of a pickup truck involved in the incident. This led police to uncover more information and eventually solve the case.

In what is perhaps the most popular technique of "refreshing" memory, the witness is hypnotized and then taken back to the crime scene. The person is encouraged to form visual images of the scene, scan it, and report what he or she sees. In theory, an individual will be able to do this better while in a state of hypnosis. This is essentially the technique used in the Chowchilla kidnapping case.

The success of this technique in some cases has encouraged law enforcement officials about the use of hypnosis. However, many scientists doubt the validity of hypnotically refreshed memories.

Three major issues surround the use of hypnosis to refresh an eyewitness's memory. The first centers on whether hypnosis actually improves memory. Advocates claim that hypnosis can make a witness remember things he or she could not remember under nonhypnotic conditions (**hypermensia**). The second issue concerns the reliability of the memories produced under hypnosis. Hypnosis is widely considered to be an altered state of consciousness that makes an individual susceptible to suggestion. At issue is whether an individual becomes more susceptible to constructing false memories while in a state of hypnosis. The third issue deals with the jury's response to hypnotically refreshed testimony. Will the jury be more or less persuaded by hypnotically refreshed testimony, compared to nonrefreshed testimony? In the sections that follow we explore these three issues.

The Ability of Hypnosis to Improve Memory.   Many of us have heard about cases in which individuals have been hypnotized and can recall, with incredible detail, events that occurred many years earlier. This gives the impression that hypnosis can improve one's memory. However, are these "age regression" demonstrations proof that hypnosis improves memory for forgotten details?

Research on hypnosis and hypermensia has produced mixed results. Some studies have found that hypnosis significantly increases memory for an event (Sanders, Gansler, & Reisman, 1989) or a list of words (Barnier & McConkey, 1992), compared to a control condition in which no hypnosis is used (Sanders et al., 1989). However, more studies indicate that hypnosis does not significantly improve memory (e.g., Dinges, Whitehouse, Orne, Powell, & Orne, 1992). Individuals who are hypnotized do no better on a memory test than subjects who are told to relax for 15 minutes before answering questions.

Individuals differ in their susceptibility to hypnosis; some can be hypnotized more easily than others. Researchers looking at hypermensia, hypnosis, and susceptibility to hypnosis have found that hypnosis can be effective for some people under optimal conditions. For example, in one study subjects were asked to recall a prose passage under one of several conditions. Results showed that highly susceptible subjects who were hypnotized *and* were also highly motivated by the experimenters showed improvement in recall. However, hypnosis was not the critical factor. The motivating instructions given after the hypnosis were more important in successful recall (Dinges et al., 1992).

Hypnosis is not a panacea for the problem of vulnerable eyewitness memory. Only those witnesses who are susceptible to being hypnotized and are given highly motivating instructions may respond with enhanced memory. However, it is reasonably likely that these individuals might also be susceptible to the implantation of false memories (Schacter, 1996).

Hypnotically Refreshed Testimony and False Memories.   The second issue affecting the use of hypnosis is the possibility that under hypnosis witnesses, especially highly suggestible ones, will generate pseudomemories (Spanos, Gwynn, Comer, Baltruweit, & de Groh, 1989). Although some research suggests that the creation of false memories is not a significant problem (e.g., Spanos et al., 1989), several studies report higher rates of false memories among hypnotized subjects (Barnier & McConkey, 1992; Lynn, Rhue, Myers, & Weeks, 1994; Sheehan, Green, & Truesdale, 1992). Sheehan, Green, & Truesdale (1992) found that highly susceptible subjects who were hypnotized produced more false memories than nonhypnotized subjects. This was especially true when steps were taken to increase the rapport between the hypnotist and the subject; that is, when there was a warm relationship between the hypnotist and subject, the rate of false memories was high. Apparently, highly susceptible hypnotized individuals are motivated to please a hypnotist with whom he or she has good rapport. A motivated subject trying to please the hypnotist may have produced high quantities of information, some of which was false. Generally, reducing rapport between the hypnotist and subject *reduces* the rate of false memories (Sheehan et al., 1992). The use of hypnosis in a recent death penalty case is recounted in "Nonsense upon Stilts" in the following Courtroom Applications box.

COURTROOM APPLICATIONS

Nonsense upon Stilts

As Florida prepared in the late summer of 1995 to execute Joseph Spaziano, a man whose conviction rests on questionable testimony, Governor Lawton Chiles issued a temporary stay of the execution. Spaziano was convicted in 1976 of the murder of a young woman. The conviction was based on the hypnosis-induced testimony of a drug-using teenager who aspired to be a motorcycle gang member. The witness, Tony Dilisio, can barely recall the trial itself, much less his testimony against Spaziano. Dilisio said that he remembered, under hypnosis, that Spaziano had taken him to a dump, shown him the body of a woman, and bragged that murder was his "style." The judge allowed the jury to hear the testimony, though a later Florida Supreme Court decision, reflecting current scientific consensus, ruled that hypnotically induced evidence was inadmissible.

Richard Ofshe, a professor of sociology at Berkeley and an expert on the subject of false memories, reviewed Dilisio's testimony and concluded in a deposition that it was "nonsense on stilts." Dilisio's memories, he said, were not just enhanced but entirely created by the hypnosis. Even Dilisio expressed doubt about his story and called for a stay. Chiles granted it in June, 1995.

("Nonsense upon Stilts," *The New Republic*, June 15, 1995, p. 9; Schacter, 1996.)

What does the jury make of hypnotically refreshed testimony provided in court? Do they accept hypnotically refreshed evidence uncritically? An experiment by Edith Greene, Leanne Wilson, and Elizabeth Loftus (1989) showed that jurors are skeptical of such testimony. Hypnotically refreshed evidence was not given as much weight by jurors as evidence produced nonhypnotically. Also, hypnosis was found to *reduce* the credibility of the witness giving the hypnotically refreshed evidence (Greene et al., 1989). During deliberations, jurors who had heard from a hypnotically refreshed witness were more likely to make negative comments about the witness's credibility than were jurors who heard non-hypnotically refreshed testimony (Greene et al., 1989).

COURTROOM APPLICATIONS

Expert Testimony on Eyewitness Evidence

Do psychologists have a role to play in testifying about psychological research on eyewitness identifications? We consider this in more detail in the next chapter, but let's take a quick look at the issue here. One of the leading cases on the admissibility of expert evidence regarding the reliability of eyewitness identifications (*United States v. Downing*, 1985) was not your run-of-the-mill stress-packed violent crime. John W. Downing was accused of fraud that he allegedly carried out by posing as a clergyman of the Universal League of Clergy. In that pose, he allegedly falsified credit references, bought goods on credit from unsuspecting manufacturers, and (this is where he got into trouble) failed to pay for them. No fewer than 12 witnesses testified that Downing was the person who presented himself as "Reverend Claymore." They had had personal dealings with the clergyman for 5 to 45 minutes.

Downing contended that it was simply a case of mistaken identity, citing the short period of time they had to view the perpetrator, the innocuous circumstances of the meetings, and the substantial lapse of time between the meetings and the identifications. Downing offered to support his arguments with expert testimony from Robert Weisburg, a cognitive psychologist on the faculty of Temple University. The trial judge ruled that such testimony would be inadmissible because such testimony would "usurp the function of the jury." The jury convicted Downing and he appealed.

The United States Court of Appeals for the Third Circuit, in a lengthy and scholarly opinion by Judge Edward Becker, ruled in Downing's favor but was careful not to guarantee him a new trial. The court considered three issues to be salient:

Because of the problems associated with hypnotically refreshed testimony, it is not widely used. In fact, only 13 states allow the introduction of such testimony in court (Moen, 1994). In most of these states, hypnosis sessions must be videotaped so that the procedures used can be reviewed, and the hypnosis must be carried out by a professional who is not a police officer (Moen, 1994). These steps make it easier to evaluate the validity of the testimony produced. Expert witnesses often testify about the validity of hypnotically produced testimony, as shown in "Expert Testimony on Eyewitness Evidence" in the Courtroom Applications box below.

1. Was expert psychological testimony generally reliable? Factors to be considered include whether the knowledge comes from "established modes of scientific analysis," whether there is "a specialized literature" dealing with the subject, and whether the experts have the requisite professional qualifications. Judge Becker cited other cases in which judges found "the consistency of the results of [eyewitness] studies to be impressive" and referred to "the science of eyewitness perception" as being a "generally accepted explanatory theory."

2. Would expert testimony be helpful to the jury in resolving a factual dispute? Here the court noted that the research cast doubt on some everyday "common sense" and appears to have called into question popular assumptions about the reliability of eyewitness evidence. It might therefore help the jury reach an accurate decision.

3. How well does the research fit the facts of the case? On this issue, Judge Becker was most cautious. After all, it's hard to refute the testimony of enough eyewitnesses to fill a standard jury box. He sent the case back to the trial judge for a hearing to assess whether the proposed testimony "was sufficiently tied to the facts of the case." The key question concerns how well the research "fits" the facts of the case. The court noted that the encounters between the witnesses and Downing were not under conditions of stress and did not involve cross-racial identification. If you were the expert witness, what testimony, if any, would you present at such a hearing?

Source: Becker, 1980, pp. 1235–1236.

The Cognitive Interview

Hypnosis is not the only method used to enhance the memory of witnesses. Another method known as the **cognitive interview** (Geiselman & Fisher, 1989) is also used to aid the memory of adult and child eyewitnesses (see Chapter 8).

The cognitive interview has four memory enhancing elements: reconstructing circumstances, encouraging completeness, recalling events in different orders, and changing perspectives (Geiselman & Fisher, 1989). Reconstructing circumstances involves having a witness reconstruct the situation in which the witnessed crime took place. For example, a witness to an armed robbery might be asked to think about the environment in which the crime occurred, focusing on the people involved, objects in the room, and any sensory perceptions including smells, sounds, and so on (Geiselman & Fisher, 1989). This technique is based on the idea that if enough "retrieval cues" are uncovered, memory will be enhanced. Encouraging completeness involves having the witness report all information, even things that may seem unimportant (Geiselman & Fisher, 1989). Witnesses are also asked to report events in reverse order in addition to recalling events in their normal temporal order. The witness might additionally be asked to start with a detail that was most salient and work from there (Geiselman & Fisher, 1989). Finally, the witness is asked to recall the event from a different perspective—for example, the perspective of another witness to the crime (Geiselman & Fisher, 1989).

In addition to these four general memory strategies, Geiselman and Fisher (1989) use other specific mnemonic devices to help witnesses recall crucial elements. These include asking them whether the suspect reminded them of anyone they knew. Witnesses are encouraged to try recalling any unusual aspects of the suspect's physical appearance, reporting the first letter of any names mentioned that cannot be fully recalled, recalling numbers or letters or sequences of numbers or letters, identifying anything unusual about the speech characteristics of the suspect, and reporting their reactions to what was said during the crime and identifying any unusual phases that were used. Together with the four general memory strategies, the cognitive interview technique brings what psychologists know about how memory works to the problem of enhancing the recollections of witnesses to crimes (Fisher, 1995).

The Revised Cognitive Interview.   After a series of experiments, Geiselman and Fisher (1989) refined the cognitive interview technique to include five additional memory techniques to help witnesses recall events: (a) having the interviewer reestablish the context within which the crime took place (event-interview similarity), (b) encouraging the witness to focus his or her attention on the details of the crime (focused retrieval), (c) encouraging the witness to engage in as many recall attempts as possible (extensive retrieval), (d) tailoring questioning and question formats to individual witnesses (witness-compatible questioning), and (e) employing specific mnemonics. Generally, use of the revised cognitive interview increases the number of correct facts recalled while not decreasing the accuracy rate (McCauley & Fisher, 1995).

The Effectiveness of the Cognitive Interview. The cognitive interview seems to increase witness reliability. Geiselman and Fisher (1989, experiment 1) reported that, in their research, the cognitive interview technique elicited more correct facts than a standard interview procedure. Additionally, the cognitive interview produced slightly more correct facts than hypnosis. The increase in correct information was not accompanied by a concomitant increase in incorrect information produced. Geiselman and Fisher (1989, experiment 3) also reported that the cognitive interview does not make witnesses more susceptible to the effects of leading questions.

Other research has generally confirmed the power of the cognitive interview to improve eyewitness memory (Fisher, 1995; Fisher, Geiselman, & Amador, 1989). For example, Fisher et al. (1989) found that detectives trained in the cognitive interview technique elicited from witnesses 47 percent more information than before training and 63 percent more than untrained detectives. This increase in witness recall was not accompanied by a significant increase in the amount of incorrect information recalled.

Although the cognitive interview has been found to increase the amount of correct information recalled, there is some evidence that the cognitive interview technique may increase incorrect information as well (McCauley & Fisher, 1995). Additionally, there is evidence that the cognitive interview technique is most effective when free recall questions are used (i.e., when witnesses are asked a question and allowed to provide a report) than if detailed, specific questions are used (Aschermann, Mantwill, & Kohnken, 1991). Recent research also suggests that the cognitive interview enhances the ability of witnesses to aid police artists in constructing facial composites (Koehn, Fisher, & Cutler, in press).

Taken as a whole, the research on the cognitive interview technique suggests that it can be a highly effective method of increasing the amount of correct information a witness recalls, at the slight expense of more incorrect information being elicited. Given that the cognitive interview technique is easy to use and requires less training than hypnosis, it is a useful tool for police in eliciting information during the early stages of a criminal investigation (Fisher, Geiselman, & Amador, 1989).

LINEUP PROCEDURES

As a part of many criminal investigations, an eyewitness may be called to the police station to view a lineup with the aim of identifying a suspect. In some cases, the eyewitness may be asked to pick out a suspect from a live lineup that includes several individuals, one of whom may be the suspect. In other cases, the eyewitness may be asked to pick the suspect out of a photo array. In either case, the procedures used to conduct a lineup may influence the eyewitness's selection.

Constructing the Lineup

In a typical lineup, a suspect is included along with others who resemble him or her. These others are known as "foils" or "distractors." Their purpose is to make the recognition task more difficult for the eyewitness and reduce false recognitions.

Selection of Foils for a Lineup.   In most cases, police pick foils that resemble the suspect. However, this may not be the best practice. Elizabeth Luus and Gary Wells (1991) suggest that a better procedure may be to match the foils in the lineup to the eyewitness's description rather than to the characteristics of the suspect himself. For example, if the witness has described the criminal as a tall, middle-age white man with a beard, the foils should have those characteristics.

Is the match-to-witness description technique better than the match-to-suspect technique? One study suggests that it is (Wells, Rydell, & Seelau, 1993). In this experiment, a theft of a cashbox was staged in front of witnesses. A lineup was constructed for each witness. Each was exposed to one of three lineup types: match-to-witness description, match-to-suspect, or a mismatch condition (where the foils did not resemble the suspect). The results showed a greater percentage of accurate identifications with the match-to-witness description than with the match-to-suspect technique. There was no difference between these two lineup techniques for false identifications. However, a foil was more likely to be identified as the culprit in the match-to-suspect than match-to-witness description condition. Additionally, the match-to-witness technique was better (i.e., fewer false identifications) when the culprit was present in the lineup. If the culprit was absent, the two techniques did not differ. Overall, the match-to-witness description was as effective as the match-to-suspect technique in reducing false identifications. However, the match-to-witness description was superior in terms of accurate identifications.

Lineup Size.   How many foils are needed to ensure a "fair" lineup? To answer this question we must consider two aspects of size: nominal size and effective size. The *nominal size* of a lineup refers to the absolute number of individuals in a lineup. *Effective size* concerns the effectiveness of the foils included in a lineup (Malpass, 1981). An effective foil is one who would be expected to be chosen, at least at chance levels. A foil who would never be chosen (for example, because he does not resemble the suspect at all) would be an ineffective foil. Effective size, then, really is an index of how challenging a lineup is for a witness.

An extreme example can illustrate the distinction between nominal and effective size. Imagine that a suspect has been described as a black male. Imagine further that a black suspect is arrested and placed into a lineup with four white foils. The probability that one of the white foils would be selected by a witness is most likely zero. Increasing the nominal size of the lineup by adding two or three more white foils does not make the lineup any more challenging. So, simply increasing nominal size may not increase the effectiveness of a lineup in allowing suspects to be identified. We could increase the diagnosticity of the lineup by including four black men who resemble the suspect. In this case, we might expect each foil to have a one in five (20 percent) chance of being selected by a witness. Using foils who resemble the suspect increases the effective size of a lineup.

Target-present and Target-absent Lineups.   The traditional manner of constructing a lineup provides the witness with the opportunity to choose the actual culprit. However, the lineup has another purpose: It should allow the police to determine whether the witness is merely guessing about the identity of the suspect. One way to do this is to conduct a lineup in which the suspect is not included. This is known as a *target-absent lineup.* Cutler, Penrod, and Martens (1987) found that 71 percent of subjects falsely identified a foil in a target-absent lineup (only 29 percent of subjects correctly rejected the lineup). Compare this to a target-present lineup which produced a 27 percent rate of false identifications.

The type of instructions a witness is given prior to the lineup can affect a witness's performance in a target-absent lineup. Malpass and Devine (1981) staged an act of vandalism and later asked witnesses to identify a suspect. One-half the subjects were given information suggesting that the suspect was actually one of the individuals in the lineup (biased instructions); the other half were not given that information (no biased instructions). Subjects from each condition then viewed a lineup in which the suspect was or was not present. The results of this experiment are shown in Figure 7.5. In the most striking finding, when the suspect was not present but the witnesses were given biased instructions, they were much more likely to identify an innocent person than if they received no biased instructions. Overall, under biased conditions, subjects were more likely to select *someone* out of the lineup.

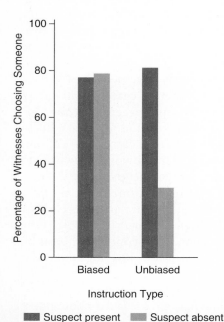

FIGURE 7.5   Making selections from target-present and target-absent lineups.

The important point to note in this figure is that when witnesses are given biased instructions they are more likely to choose an innocent person out of a lineup than when they are given unbiased instructions.

Source: Adapted from "Realism and Eyewitness Identification Research," by R. S. Malpass and P. G. Devine, 1980, *Law and Human Behavior, 4,* 347–358.

The Lineup Versus the Showup.   A lineup is not the only method used by police for suspect identification. In some instances the police will use a **showup** in which a single suspect is shown to the witness, often at the scene of the crime itself. This technique is used because it is very practical. The suspect can be shown to the witness a short time after the crime occurred and in the same place where the crime occurred (Gonzalez, Ellsworth, & Pembroke, 1993). Despite the fact that showups are controversial, the courts have generally upheld the validity of this technique (Gonzalez et al., 1993).

While the courts have lent support to the use of showups, some psychologists have expressed concern over the practice (Yarmey, Yarmey, & Yarmey, 1996). The major objection is the possibility that a witness will be more likely to misidentify an innocent individual in a showup than in a traditional lineup. Because the showup requires only a yes or no response from the witness (as opposed to a careful consideration of several individuals in a lineup), police cannot identify witnesses who are merely guessing at the identity of the suspect (Gonzalez et al., 1993). Presumably, the traditional lineup encourages witnesses to be more careful when making an identification because they must compare several similar-appearing individuals (Gonzalez et al., 1993). Does the showup, as critics suspect, lead to less accurate eyewitness identifications?

In a series of three studies, Gonzalez, Ellsworth, and Pembroke (1993) directly compared a showup and a lineup. In their first experiment, Gonzalez et al. staged a purse-snatching incident in a classroom. A black male, seated at the back of a classroom, walked to the front of the room and stole the instructor's purse, which was lying on a desk at the front of the room. The crime was staged so that all the witnesses got a good look at the perpetrator. Immediately after the crime, subjects were told that the crime had been staged and the subjects were asked to identify the perpetrator. Identification of the perpetrator was carried out as either a showup or as a lineup with five foils. Both the showups and lineups were conducted with the suspect either present or absent.

Gonzalez et al. found that subjects were more likely to respond "no" (that is, not identify the suspect) in the showup than in the lineup, regardless of whether the suspect was present. Therefore, showups and lineups engaged a definite "response bias": There is a tendency to say "no" to a showup and "yes" to a lineup. When the *accuracy* of the identifications was evaluated, Gonzalez et al. found that lineups resulted in more correct identifications than showups. However, the showups resulted in fewer false identifications than the lineups, perhaps due to the "no" response bias inherent in the showup technique (Gonzalez et al., 1993). In short, Gonzalez et al. reported that the response bias they observed leads to two different types of errors. In the showup, the response bias yields a high number of misses (failing to identify the suspect as the perpetrator) whereas the lineup response bias yields a high number of false alarms (identifying an innocent foil as the perpetrator).

In their second experiment, Gonzalez et al. replicated their findings using a different crime portrayed on videotape with a white perpetrator and a photographic showup or lineup. Additionally, in the second experiment, a lineup with a functional size of one (i.e., the foils did not resemble the suspect) was included. This latter manipulation allowed Gonzalez et al. to determine whether a showup was functionally equivalent to a poorly conducted lineup. When the suspect-present *showup* was compared to the suspect-present *lineup* with a functional size of one, the researchers reported the same response bias found in their first experiment— that is, whereas subjects rejected the suspect in the showup ("no" response bias), most subjects in the lineup condition made an identification. Therefore, suspect-present showups are not equivalent to poorly constructed suspect-present lineups.

Why do lineups and showups produce such different results? Gonzalez et al. suggest that the psychological processes inherent in the two techniques are different. In the traditional lineup, the witness must select an individual who *best matches* the perpetrator. Thus, in a lineup the witness makes a relative judgment. A suspect who provides a match that is "good enough" may elicit an identification (Gonzalez et al., 1993). In the showup, however, no such relative judgment is possible. The witness must identify the suspect on the basis of memory alone, making an absolute judgment, perhaps causing the witness to be more cautious. However, recent work by Yarmey et al. (1996) indicated that when witnesses were asked to identify a stranger with whom they had had only a very brief encounter, showups produced high false identification rates, especially when the target wore similar clothing to that worn by the encountered stranger.

Simultaneous and Sequential Lineups

In a typical lineup, the witness views a group of individuals all at once. Is this common practice the best way to do a lineup? Two studies reported by R. C. L. Lindsay (Lindsay & Wells, 1985; Lindsay, Lea, & Fulford, 1991) suggest that a sequential lineup procedure may be superior to the standard lineup. In a sequential lineup, the witness views suspects one at a time. Each time the witness indicates whether he or she recognizes anyone. Generally, the sequential lineup procedure produces fewer false recognitions (Lindsay & Wells, 1985; Lindsay et al., 1991) without reducing the number of correct identifications (Cutler & Penrod, 1988; Sporer, 1994). Sequential lineups are especially effective if the witness does not know how many suspects will be presented and is not given the opportunity to see remaining members of the lineup after a choice has been made (Lindsay et al., 1991).

All lineups can be made less vulnerable to error if several rules are followed. Wells and Seelau (1995) make the following suggestions.

- The person who conducts the lineup or shows the photospread should not know which member of the lineup or spread is the suspect.
- Eyewitnesses should be informed that the culprit may not be in the lineup and should therefore not feel compelled to chose someone.

- The suspect should not be different in any noticeable way from the distractors (the other members of the lineup or photospread) on the basis of the eyewitness's description.
- As soon as the witness makes an identification, a definitive statement concerning the witness's confidence about the identification should be obtained. This is done to make sure that the witness's confidence level is based solely on his or her immediate response to the chosen target and not on any postidentification information, such as information that others had made the same choice.

As we will see, the witness's confidence in the identification is a crucial factor in the jury's deliberations (Wells & Seelau, 1995).

THE EYEWITNESS AND THE JURY

We have seen how the memory of an eyewitness works and how the procedures used for making identifications can affect an eyewitness's accuracy. If a case involving an eyewitness goes to trial, that witness will be called on to tell his or her story to a jury. This brings us to another part of the eyewitness equation: How do jurors respond to the testimony of an eyewitness? What factors contribute to a jury's believing or disbelieving an eyewitness? What impact does the eyewitness have on the jury, relative to other evidence presented at a trial? In this section we explore these questions.

The Impact of Eyewitness Testimony on the Jury

Generally, the side that presents eyewitness testimony wins the trial, even if the other side has objective evidence to counterbalance the eyewitness testimony (Minshull & Sussman, 1979). Few events are as powerful as an eyewitness taking the stand, pointing to the defendant, and saying: "That's her, I'll never forget that face." Jurors are also more inclined to believe an eyewitness if the conditions under which a crime was witnessed were "good" (adequate lighting, time to see the event, etc.) rather than "poor" (poor lighting, events that occurred quickly, etc.) (Blonstein & Geiselman, 1990). Therefore, juries tend to believe eyewitnesses, even to the exclusion of conflicting objective evidence.

Confidence and Accuracy

The jury's belief in eyewitnesses is increased when the eyewitnesses appear confident while testifying, and they typically do. Confidence and accuracy are not two sides of the same coin, but rather different coins altogether. Accuracy is determined by factors affecting perception and memory. Confidence is a social issue; it has to do with belief, rehearsal, and anxiety. Jurors, however, often conflate confidence and accuracy.

Eyewitness confidence is strongly influenced by postidentification factors, including repeated interviews by the police and attorneys, knowledge of other witnesses' identification, and other social factors (Wells, Ferguson, & Lindsay, 1981). However, John Turtle and John Yuille (1994) have presented some opposing data. Turtle and Yuille asked witnesses to view a videotape and describe the event. The witnesses were then reinterviewed twice more. In the second and third interviews, witnesses were asked to recall the event from scratch, as if this were the first time they had been asked to report what they saw. Turtle and Yuille found an increase in the number of useful items recalled over the three interviews with no change in the witnesses' original confidence levels. The fact that new information was obtained without any change in the confidence levels suggests that if the interviews are conducted in a neutral, task-oriented manner, confidence levels might not be artificially inflated.

Witnesses are well rehearsed before they testify in court and they have told their story many times to the police, the lawyers, and their friends. We might expect that by the time the eyewitness is called to testify, he or she will make a confident presentation and show few signs of nervousness. Robert Bothwell and Mehri Jalil (1992) found that as the perceived nervousness of witnesses increased, jurors' ratings of the witnesses' identification accuracy, accuracy of testimony, and confidence decreased. However, the jurors' ratings of a witness's nervousness did not relate to the *actual* levels of witness accuracy (identification or testimonial) or confidence.

Reviews of the relationship between confidence and accuracy show a very modest relationship between witness confidence and accuracy (Sporer, Penrod, Read, & Cutler, 1995). Evidence suggests that very confident witnesses are only somewhat more likely to be accurate than witnesses who exhibit little confidence (Penrod & Cutler, 1995; Yarmey et al., 1996). Additionally, jurors are unable to discriminate between inaccurate and accurate eyewitnesses, convicting the defendant at about the same rate with accurate or inaccurate eyewitness testimony (Penrod & Cutler, 1995).

The courts inform jurors that one criterion they may use to evaluate eyewitness accuracy is the jurors' perceptions of the confidence of the witness (*Neil v. Biggers,* 1972). But, as we have noted, the relationship between confidence and accuracy is problematic. Confidence and accuracy are correlated when the event is viewed under highly favorable circumstances—if the lighting is good, stress levels are moderate, nobody has a gun pointed in your face, and you get a good long look. This is known as the optimality hypothesis (Deffenbacher, 1980). Optimality rarely occurs in an eyewitness situation. Most of the time the potential witness is unaware of the unfolding situation and is suddenly put in stressful circumstances under the least optimal conditions for accuracy.

Jurors are generally insensitive to the factors that may affect eyewitness accuracy, and even when they do possess knowledge of these factors, jurors tend not to use this information in deciding a case. This is even true when the judge informs the jury about the factors that might decrease eyewitness accuracy (Penrod & Cutler, 1995).

Earwitness Accuracy

In the mid-century trial of Bruno Hauptmann, accused and convicted of kidnaping and murdering the child of Charles Lindbergh, testimony was given by Lindbergh that he heard the kidnapper utter two distant words on the telephone ("Hi, Doc") and that he recognized Hauptmann's voice when he next heard it in the courtroom (Read & Craik, 1995). While earwitness identifications are certainly less common than are eyewitness identifications, they do occur. Are our ears any more reliable than our eyes?

Daniel Read and Fergus I. M. Craik (1995) did three experiments to determine the accuracy of earwitness testimony. They were concerned with the probability of accurate recognition when the content and tone of the voice differed from the original hearing. They asked how much of a voice fragment one needs to hear to increase recognition probabilities.

Read and Craik (1995) found that the odds of recognizing a voice weeks after first hearing, and when the tone and voice have changed, is at chance levels. In other words, someone who did not hear the initial utterance had just as much chance of "recognizing" the voice as did the earwitness. When the voice is similar in content and tone to the original hearing, the probability of correctly identifying the original speaker is higher. And, as you might expect, accuracy was highest when earwitnesses heard a recording of what they had heard originally.

What does this mean for voice identifications? The optimality hypothesis suggests that if the earwitness hears a good, long snippet of a voice and is prepared for a test to hear it again, and when heard again the voice is much the same as first hearing, then accuracy and confidence are high. However, that is not a realistic scenario. The second voice sample is not likely to be the same as the first, several weeks may transpire between first and second hearings, and the test may come unexpectedly (Hammersley & Read, 1995). Read and Craik (1995) reported accuracy rates for earwitnesses of about 30 percent.

Yarmey (1995) suggests many of the same recommendations noted by Wells and Seelau (1995) in the eyewitness realm for earwitnesses. For example, when presenting a witness with a voice lineup, the administrator of the lineup ought to be naive about the true culprit. The amount of hearing loss in earwitnesses needs to be examined, and police should be trained in the proper construction and administration of voice lineups.

Confronting an Eyewitness in Court

Discrediting an eyewitness, although not impossible, is difficult. An experiment reported by Loftus (1979) demonstrated this quite clearly. Simulated jurors were exposed to testimony from an eyewitness in which he identified the eyewitness as the person who committed the crime charged. In one condition (the *discredited eyewitness condition*), the jurors were told that the eyewitness was not wearing his glasses when he saw the crime committed and that his vision without his glasses was 20/400. In another condition (the *nondiscredited eyewitness condition*), the eyewitness was not discredited. Finally, in a *control condition,* no eyewitness was presented.

Loftus recorded the percentage of subjects convicting the defendant. Her results are shown in Figure 7.6. When no eyewitness was present, the conviction rate was very low: 18 percent. With an eyewitness, the conviction rate jumped markedly—to 72 percent. Notice, however, that discrediting the eyewitness did not significantly reduce conviction rates, which were 68 percent.

It does not take much to enhance the credibility of an eyewitness. If an eyewitness testifies that he or she remembers some trivial detail, unrelated to the crime itself, the witness's credibility and ability to persuade the jury are enhanced (Bell & Loftus, 1988, 1989).

One potential way to discredit an eyewitness is to try to show that the testimony is inconsistent over time. For example, a witness is usually interviewed several times about the crime, and inconsistencies may occur among those interviews. Pointing out inconsistencies raises two important questions about the eye-

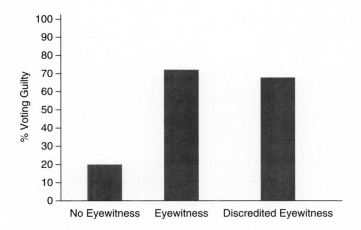

FIGURE 7.6   The effect of an eyewitness.

This graph shows that the presence of an eyewitness, even one who has been discredited, raises the conviction rate very significantly from the baseline (18% conviction rate) when no eyewitness is present.

Source: Adapted from *Eyewitness Testimony,* by E. F. Loftus, 1979, Cambridge, MA: Harvard University Press, p. 49.

witness. First, does the presence of these inconsistencies mean the witness is inaccurate? Second, how does the jury respond to information about inconsistencies?

Concerning the first question, the presence of inconsistencies does not necessarily mean that an eyewitness is inaccurate, according to work done by Peter Brock, Ronald Fisher, and Brian Cutler (1991). These researchers staged robberies, then interviewed witnesses twice after the event and had them pick the culprit from lineups in which the robber was either present or absent. In addition, in one of the studies, the witnesses had to identify the *victim* from lineups in which the victim was either present or absent.

Brock and his coresearchers measured consistency by scoring the two witness interviews on correct identification of items such as the culprit's hair and eye color, hair length, and other features. They found that those who were inconsistent in their description accurately identified the target 44 percent of the time whereas those who were completely consistent from interview to interview were accurate about 56 percent of the time.

Keep in mind that these differences were between the most consistent and most inconsistent. The differences between those in the middle were obviously smaller. Two points should be noted. One, a witness's accuracy should not be discredited solely on the basis of inconsistencies (Brock et al., 1991). As we have noted, the relationship between consistency and accuracy is quite complex and determined by a variety of factors. Two, even the most consistent witnesses were accurate only 56 percent of the time.

Does pointing out inconsistencies affect how jurors evaluate eyewitness testimony? Apparently it does. Evidence for this comes from an experiment by Berman, Narby, and Cutler (1995). In this study, testimony about central details (details important to the crime) and peripheral details (less important details) was either consistent or inconsistent. Simulated jurors viewed a videotape (showing direct examination and cross-examination) of an eyewitness who was robbed while working at a bank. The results showed significantly fewer guilty verdicts when testimony about *central details* was inconsistent. Further, the eyewitness was rated most positively when the testimony given across two interviews was consistent for both central and peripheral details. Conversely, if the witness was inconsistent on central and peripheral details, ratings were the most negative. Generally, inconsistency of any type decreased the credibility of the eyewitness.

The Accurate Eyewitness

Is it possible to distinguish accurate from inaccurate eyewitnesses? We know that a highly confident witness is very persuasive. A witness who says "I am certain that the defendant is the perpetrator of the crime" is most assuredly an influential witness. However, not only do we know that confidence and accuracy are only slightly related; we also know that the confidence of the eyewitness can change after he or she has made the original identification. What if, for example, the witness learns that another witness identified someone else. Not surprisingly, eyewitnesses lose confidence in their identification under such circumstances (Luus & Wells, 1994a).

There is evidence that accurate and inaccurate eyewitnesses do use different cognitive strategies (Dunning & Stern, 1994). In one study, mock witnesses viewed a videotaped (staged) crime and then had to identify the criminal from a series of photos. A definite marker of an accurate identification was the speed in which the identification was made. This supports previous findings (Sporer, 1994). Accurate eyewitnesses reported that the correct photo just "popped out" at them. Dunning and Stern (1994) concluded that this recognition was automatic.

In contrast, inaccurate eyewitnesses used a strategy of elimination. They compared the photos to each other until they narrowed their choice down to one most probable photo. In other words, inaccurate eyewitnesses analyzed their thought processes to match the target with their memory of the person. Accurate eyewitnesses made their identifications quickly and automatically. Therefore, it may be possible (if subsequent research supports these findings) to simply ask eyewitnesses to reveal the road they traveled to their identifications and get some sense of the accuracy of those identifications.

Why is speed of recognition a good marker of accuracy? Facial recognition appears to be an automatic process in which the witness makes an automatic comparison of the potential culprit's face with other images stored in memory. Research indicates that when witnesses fail to identify the face they are searching for in an array of photographs, they may then try to find an image that most closely matches their impression of the culprit (Wells, Rydell, & Seelau, 1993). This process of elimination is a different mental process from instant recognition and obviously takes much longer.

In sum, we know that accurate memory and confidence in that memory are two separate mental processes. Confidence can be increased or decreased by social factors as Luus and Wells (1994a) have shown. Corroboration or lack of it by other witnesses affects the witness's confidence level. Eyewitnesses are usually told by the police that other evidence exists that backs up their testimony. This, of course, increases the witness's confidence level. As Gary Wells (1995) stated, "False identifications are a double injustice. It is a nightmare for the innocent person, while the actual culprit remains at large (p. 731)."

SUMMARY

Several factors affect an eyewitness's ability to perceive a crime accurately. The presence of a weapon decreases that accuracy. Here the witness pays great attention to the weapon, thereby not attending to other important details. The violent nature of some crimes may also inhibit accurate perception. According to the Yerkes-Dodson law, if the eyewitness experiences too much arousal (associated with a violent crime), perception suffers. However, recent research suggests that the violence of the event interacts with other variables such as the type of event (emotional or neutral) and the type of detail to be recalled (high or low salience). Additionally, accurate perception is compromised if a cross-racial identification is necessary.

A number of factors can affect the accuracy of an eyewitness's memory as well. The amount of time the witness is exposed to the crime affects memory: The longer the witness has to encode information into memory, the better memory will be. An eyewitness's memory can be influenced by the introduction of postevent information. According to the misinformation effect, a new detail can be introduced into a witness's memory if the witness encounters information about the detail before or after witnessing a crime. In addition to biasing memory directly, postevent information can also influence the inferences a witness draws about the event.

A repressed memory is of an event that a witness experienced long ago but recalls recently. During all the time between the event and recovery, the individual has no awareness that anything traumatic has happened. Although courts have been rather lenient in allowing repressed memory evidence, the phenomenon has never received much scientific support. Some scholars claim that repressed memories are false in many cases, caused by the therapy process itself during which such memories are often uncovered. There is also evidence that false "repressed memories" can be planted in much the same way that postevent information affects an eyewitness. Research shows that hypnosis may make a witness more susceptible to false memories. Research also shows that jurors are skeptical of such testimony.

Another technique used to aid an eyewitness's memory is the cognitive interview which has four memory-enhancing elements: reconstructing circumstances, encouraging completeness, recalling events in different orders, and changing perspectives. In addition, several other mnemonic devices are used.

Eyewitnesses are usually called on to identify a suspect from a lineup. In a lineup, in which the suspect may or may not be present, foils (or distractors) are used to reduce the possibility that someone will be selected by chance. Usually, foils are selected who match the suspect. However, another technique is to match foils to the witness's description of the suspect. Another lineup issue is the size of the lineup. Generally, the absolute size (nominal size) of the lineup is less crucial than the "effective size" of the lineup, or how challenging the lineup is to the witness. Witnesses falsely identify a foil more often in a target-absent lineup than in a suspect-present lineup. In some instances, a witness is shown a single suspect in a "showup." Although concern has been expressed about this practice, research shows that witnesses are more likely to respond "no" (that is, not identifying the suspect) in the showup than in the lineup, regardless of whether the suspect was present.

Most lineups are conducted using a simultaneous format. That is, the suspect and foils are presented to witnesses at the same time. An alternative method is the sequential lineup, in which individuals are shown to the witness one at a time. Generally, the sequential lineup procedure produces fewer false recognitions without reducing the number of correct identifications and is most effective when the witness does not know how many individuals will be presented. Generally, the accuracy of a lineup can be increased if the person conducting the lineup does not know who the suspect is, whether the foils resemble the suspect closely, and whether the witness expressed confidence in the identification.

Juries are very receptive to eyewitness testimony. A confident eyewitness can be especially influential, even though the relationship between eyewitness confidence and accuracy is relatively low. Jurors tend to be poor at discriminating accurate from inaccurate eyewitnesses.

CHAPTER
8

The Child Witness and Expert Testimony

THE CHILD AS AN EYEWITNESS

With the recent explosion of sexual abuse cases, children are becoming an increasingly important source of eyewitness testimony in court. One way to deter abusive behavior has been to encourage young children to testify against their abusers (Woolard, Reppucci, & Redding, 1996). In some instances, however, the interrogation of abused children has been problematic. Consider, for example, the experiences of Kelly Michaels, a 26-year-old teacher at the Wee Care Nursery School. Michaels's problems began with the following offhand conversation between a three-year-old child and a doctor while the doctor was taking the child's temperature rectally (Shalit, 1993, p. 14):

> *Child:* "That's what my teacher does to me at school."
> *Doctor:* "What does your teacher do to you?"
> *Child:* "Her takes my temperature."

A nurse subsequently discussed the boy's statement with the mother. Eventually, the mother called the police who began an investigation. The names of other children were obtained, and these children were questioned. Soon after, the State of New Jersey launched a major investigation of the Wee Care Nursery School, and Kelly Michaels in particular. The child who made the comments to the doctor was interviewed using anatomically correct dolls (the use of anatomically correct dolls is discussed in detail later in this chapter). On one occasion he stuck his finger into the rectum of one of the dolls and said that other children had their temperature taken.

During interviews with children, therapists apparently questioned children in a highly suggestive way. Children were routinely berated for negative answers. Therapists threatened children who gave "no" answers until they changed their minds. What eventually emerged was a bizarre story involving allegations that Michaels forced children to eat feces, drink urine, and play nude games.

Despite the fact that there was no physical evidence to corroborate the allegations made by the children, Michaels was eventually indicted on 235 counts of child sexual abuse. She was placed on trial in New Jersey and was found guilty on 115 of those counts and sentenced to 47 years in prison. Michaels spent five years in prison before an appeals court overturned her convictions. The court criticized the prosecution, noting the irregularities in the procedures used to interview the children and obtain the indictments and convictions.

Kelly Michaels's case and similar cases (e.g., the McMartin Preschool case in Manhattan Beach, California), as well as nonabuse cases in which a child may be the principal witness, raise many questions concerning children as eyewitnesses to crimes. The two major concerns about child eyewitnesses are their competence and credibility as witnesses (Cashmore & Bussey, 1996). In this section we address the competence of the child eyewitness.

General Concerns About the Child Eyewitness

Generally, adults assume that younger children are less credible witnesses than older children and adults (Goodman, Golding, Helgeson, Haith, & Michelli, 1987), and in most jurisdictions, the competence of child witnesses must be established before the child will be allowed to testify.

The use of children as witnesses in court has a long, albeit uneven, history. Children were accorded almost mystical status during the infamous Salem witch trials during the sixteenth century. In those trials, children were the principal accusers of and witnesses against the "witches." Later, however, the courts began to look on testimony from children with skepticism. Until 1895 a child was assumed to be an incompetent (Haugaard, Reppucci, Laird, & Nauful, 1991). In 1895 (*Wheeler v. United States*), the U.S. Supreme Court ruled that children could not be deemed incompetent automatically. Instead, the competence of a child witness had to be determined on a case-by-case basis by the trial judge (Haugaard et al., 1991). Figuring largely in this determination is the perceptual process.

The Child's Perceptual Processes

Perception is the process through which we come to understand stimuli, and events, that occur in our world. Perception involves attention to a stimulus, processing that stimulus through the cognitive apparatus in the brain, and forming a final representation of that stimulus in the brain. This representation may ultimately become represented in the brain as a memory. If there are inadequacies or inaccuracies in the perception process, any resulting memory will be inaccurate as well.

The human perceptual system undergoes some important changes during childhood that will affect the ability of children at different ages to perceive events accurately. For example, one's ability to attend to a stimulus changes with age. Two aspects of attention have been investigated by developmental psychologists: scanning and selectivity. Scanning refers to one's ability to examine a stimulus visually. For example, in an eyewitness situation, we would want a witness to scan the perpetrator's face carefully, taking in the outstanding features. Selectivity refers to the ability to attend to important aspects of a stimulus while ignoring unimportant ones. We would like our eyewitness to look at facial features such as the nose, eyes, mouth, and any uncommon features (e.g., a scar). We would not want the witness looking at a nondescript forehead or cheek. Research evidence shows that a child's scanning abilities improve markedly with age (Day, 1975; Vurpillot, 1968). As children get older, their scanning becomes more efficient and accurate.

Children's selectivity also improves with age. Wright and Vlietstra (1975) report that children between the ages of 5 and 7 primarily use an unsystematic attention mechanism called an **exploration** whereas older children use a more systematic strategy called a **search.** Compared to a search, an exploration is more spontaneous and less systematic; it occurs in shorter sequences, is divergent, and is guided more by aspects of the external stimulus than by an internalized strategy (Wright & Vlietstra, 1975). Younger children are less likely to use attention to focus down or converge on important aspects of a stimulus. Additionally, they will be less systematic in their approach to selecting important information. In short, children's selectivity prior to age eight may contribute to incomplete perceptions of stimuli, such as a perpetrator's face.

Several important changes in attention occur with age (Gross & Hayne, 1996). A child develops greater control over attention with age; the older child will be better able to focus on relevant aspects of a stimulus and ignore irrelevant ones. Attention also becomes more adaptable with age, so that an older child can adjust his or her attention strategy according to the demands of the situation. A ten-year-old child can determine when to use the systematic search strategy, whereas a younger child is capable only of a less systematic exploration strategy (Wright & Vlietstra, 1975). Finally, younger children cannot focus attention for long periods of time and are more distracted by events that occur in the environment, even if those events are irrelevant to the task at hand. Older children, on the other hand, are better able to sustain attention over time and are less distractable.

Taken together, the findings on children's attention suggests that younger children (up to about age seven) will have a more difficult time attending to important aspects of a stimulus (e.g., a criminal's face or other important details of a crime) than will older children. The memories that result are less accurate and complete for younger children.

Children's Memory

When a child, or adult for that matter, views a crime, **episodic memory** (Tulving, 1981) comes into play. Episodic memory is the memory system involved in helping us encode, store, and recall events that happen to us (Schacter, 1996). An individual's memory for his or her ninth birthday party engages episodic memory. Because of the importance of episodic (event) memory in eyewitness identification, we need to explore how children form representations of events.

Event Representation.   An older view of a child's episodic memory suggested that children lacked sufficient cognitive sophistication to form accurate representations of events (e.g., Piaget). However, more recent research and theory suggest that a child's representations of events is much better than previously believed (Nelson, 1986).

According to Nelson (1986), children as young as three years of age are aware of the temporal nature of events: They understand that events are sequenced over time. Additionally, young children can produce accurate reports of events as long as those events are familiar to them (Nelson, 1986). Nelson (1986) also suggests that children's event representations are contiguous rather than fragmented, as previously believed. Finally, once a child develops a general event representation, that representation will support the perception and recall of events related to the representation. In other words, a child's memory for an event will be more accurate if there is a well-developed general event representation for it. Unfortunately, eyewitness situations are fairly uncommon. Therefore, young children, who tend to be more reliant on "scripted" information than older children or adults (Ceci & Bruck, 1993), may have more difficulty in spontaneous eyewitness situations than older children or adults.

Memory for Events. Generally speaking, a child's memory for events improves with age and is affected by how the child is questioned. Ornstein, Gordon, and Larus (1992) tested children's memories for a routine trip to a doctor. Ornstein et al. chose this situation because it has much in common with an abuse situation: bodily contact, some unpleasant events (e.g., an injection), and arousal of anxiety and stress.

During the office visit, the nurse or doctor filled out a checklist of what occurred during the visit. The children were then interviewed about their visit to the doctor. Half the subjects were interviewed immediately; the other half were interviewed either one week or three weeks after the visit. Additionally, two recall measures were used: a free recall measure (children were asked to tell, in their own words, about the office visit) or a structured yes-no measure (children were asked a series of questions that required a yes or no answer). The results of this experiment, shown in Figure 8.1, showed that older children (six-year-olds) had better recall for the office visit than younger children (three-year-olds).

Ornstein et al. also reported that the highly structured yes-no question format produced more accurate memories than the free recall format, especially for the three-year-olds. Dent (1991), however, found that free recall or "general" questions yielded greater accuracy than specific questions (Dent, 1991). This apparent conflict can be resolved by a close look at the phrasing of the questions in these two studies. Dent used specific questions that were open-ended (still requiring free recall). For example, a specific question in Dent's experiment was "What color was the man's hair?" Contrast this with the same question in a yes-no format used by Ornstein: "Was the man's hair blond?" The latter question taps into recognition memory, whereas the former draws on recall memory. Recognition is known to be a more sensitive measure of memory than free recall; people can often recognize things they cannot recall. Given these findings, it is probably advisable to question very young children with a highly structured question technique tapping into recognition memory. In addition, children are significantly less accurate in reporting an event when questioned with complex age-inappropriate questions rather than simple questions. Children are unlikely to voice their failure to understand complex questions (Carter, Bottoms, & Levine, 1996).

Ornstein's experiment, as well as other experiments (e.g., Carter et al., 1996; Dent, 1991), suggest that children can be quite accurate in recall for events, especially when the interviewers employ a highly structured interview that uses sim-

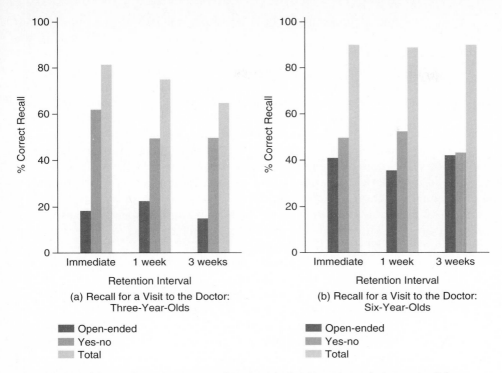

FIGURE 8.1   Recall for a visit to the doctor by three- and six-year-olds.

This figure shows that older children recall more events than do younger children and that older children seem to forget less over three weeks.

Source: Adapted from "Children's Memory for a Personally Experienced Event: Implications for Testimony," by P. A. Ornstein, B. N. Gordon, and D. M. Larus, 1992, *Applied Developmental Psychology, 6,* 49–60.

ple phraseology. However, will these results generalize to abuse situations in which children are often the only witnesses against the defendant?

The situation studied by Ornstein et al. (a visit to the doctor) is one in which children probably have a fairly good general representation of events, developed as a consequence of prior visits to the doctor. Even the youngest children in the study had visited the doctor several times. The high levels of memory shown by the children in Ornstein's experiment are most likely the result of the children's well-formed representations of the event. In an abuse situation, a child most likely has a poor representation of events in (episodic) memory. We might expect, then, that a child will be less able to recall events accurately for abuse situations.

Michael Leippe, Andrew Manion, and Ann Romanczyk (1992) investigated the accuracy of adults and of children of various ages (five to six and nine to ten) in recounting an actual incident that occurred to them. The results showed that five- and six-year-old children were less accurate in their narrative descriptions of the event than nine- and ten-year-olds or adults (the latter age groups did not differ). The younger children gave shorter, less complete descriptions than the older children or adults.

In another experiment on children's memory for events, Goodman and Reed (1986) investigated the relationship between a witness's age and his or her ability to perceive and recall an event correctly. Subjects (adults, six-year-olds, and three-year-olds) interacted with a same-race adult for five minutes. Five days later they came back and were given three tests: The subjects were asked to answer a series of questions about the situation, to identify the adult from a photo lineup, and to respond to a free recall test in which they were asked to tell what happened.

The results of this experiment showed that adults and six-year-olds performed equally well in selecting the person from a set of photos and in other measures of accuracy. The three-year-olds, as you might suspect, did worse than the other groups. Three-year-olds tended to spend less time than the adults or six-year-olds looking at the photographs.

More recent work by Julien Gross and Harlene Hayne (1996) qualifies the Goodman and Reed (1986) findings. When Gross and Hayne tested five- to six-year-old children with lineups in which the target (the person to be identified) was present, the children were very accurate in identifying individuals to whom they had had prolonged exposure. Furthermore, the children were also very accurate in identifying an individual to whom they had had brief exposure, if that individual did something unusual, such as slide down a pole. In contrast, when the target was absent from the lineup, children were very inaccurate and made many errors of commission: When the target was absent, children tended to "identify" a foil (Gross & Hayne, 1996). Again, we see that the methodology of interviewing and identification is critical for child eyewitnesses.

Furthermore, a child's memory for an event may not be as *enduring* as an adult's memory for the same event (Ornstein et al., 1992; Poole & White, 1992). Refer to Figure 8.1, which shows the results from Ornstein's research. Notice how memory for a trip to the doctor tends to decay over time for the younger subjects (three-year-olds). Deborah Poole and Lawrence White (1992) found that although children can be as accurate as adults in testifying about an event right after it happens, over a long period of time their memory for that event fades much more than the memories of adults. Poole and White reinterviewed the subjects in their experiment two years after the original incident. After two years, a young child's memory for central events tended to fade more than that of an adult. Over time, children appeared to embellish the original event with new information that was not part of the initial experience (Poole & White, 1993).

Suggestibility of Children's Memory.   Could the children in the Kelly Michaels and McMartin Preschool cases have fabricated information based on suggestive questions put to them by interviewers and therapists? This is another issue that researchers have investigated. **Suggestibility** refers to the lack of resistance of memory to outside information or pressure. We have already seen that an adult's memory can be influenced by the suggestion that an absent object was part of an event he or she had witnessed. Are children more susceptible than adults to having their memories influenced by suggestive, leading, or biased questions?

Based on common sense and the fact that children's memories are more limited than adults', it would appear obvious that the child, with a less mature view of the world, would be more suggestible. Let's see what the research on this issue indicates.

Some of the most recent research on children's suggestibility has been conducted by Steven Ceci, Maggie Bruck, and their colleagues. In one highly realistic experiment, children were examined by a pediatrician. Half the subjects were instructed to remove their clothing and underwear and to wear a hospital gown. During their examinations the doctor conducted an external genital exam (the doctor touched the child's external genitals) and an examination of the buttocks. The other half of the children kept their clothing on, were not touched on the genitals or buttocks, but were given a spinal exam for scoliosis. After the examination, the children were questioned about what occurred. Bruck et al. (1995) reported that 62 percent of the children whose genitals were touched reported the touching. However, 62 percent of the nontouched children also reported that their genitals were touched.

Bruck et al. (1995) assessed the influence of anatomically correct dolls on the accuracy of three-year-old children's reports of the pediatric exam. They found that use of the dolls increased *inaccurate* reporting. Children tended to falsely report that the doctor inserted a finger into the anal or vaginal cavity. While use of the dolls increased false reports, children who were asked to demonstrate using their own bodies inaccurately reported genital touching by the physician. In some cases, the children demonstrated events with the doll that never happened during the examination. For example, one subject showed that the doctor had tried to strangle her with a ribbon (during the exam the doctor measured the child's wrist with a similar object), demonstrated having had a ruler placed into her vagina (later being hammered in), and showed having had an anal exam with a scope. None of these events actually occurred (Bruck et al., 1995).

Based on this research, the researchers suggest that children (especially three- to four-year-olds; the suggestibility effect is less pronounced for five- to six-year-olds) can have their memories altered by suggestive questioning. The effect is increased by the use of dolls.

Other research has also verified that children are suggestible. For example, Goodman and Reed (1986), in the experiment described earlier, also examined the suggestibility of children's and adults' memories. After interacting with adults, the subjects were asked a series of questions about the situation, some of which were suggestive (i.e., relating to things that were not present or events that did not occur). Their results showed that suggestive questions fooled adults much less often than children. Three-year-olds were most susceptible to suggestive questions (Goodman & Reed, 1986).

Although children are generally more suggestible than adults, we should not overstate this difference. Recent evidence suggests that adults can also have false memories suggested or implanted (Ceci & Bruck, 1995). Several factors influence the amount of suggestibility children show. Children are especially suggestible when their memories are fuzzy to begin with or if the questioner is of high status (Goodman & Helgeson, 1988) and if the questioner is an adult rather than another child (Ceci, Ross, & Toglia, 1987). Children are also more suggestible if the event experienced is stressful (Ceci, 1994). However, children are not equally suggestible about all aspects of an event. For example, children are more suggestible about the appearance of objects (e.g., people or cars) than about the temporal sequencing of events witnessed or what people did during a witnessed event (Dent & Stephenson, 1979). Children will be less suggestible if they are forewarned that some of the questions might be confusing and that they should only give answers they feel confident with (Warren, Hulse-Trotter, & Tubas, 1991).

Another factor that seems to affect a child's suggestibility is whether the child is a bystander-witness to an event or an active participant-witness (Goodman & Clarke-Stewart, 1991; Rudy & Goodman, 1991). Lisle Rudy and Gail Goodman exposed children (four-year-olds or seven-year-olds) to a staged event. The subjects

COURTROOM APPLICATIONS

Witch Hunt

Magazine editor Ruth Shalit has reported on the Fells Acres Day School case, in which a family who owned various day care centers were convicted of abuse and sexual torture of numerous children. Three family members are currently serving 20 to 40 years in prison. All have professed innocence.

All the children involved were sent to a pediatric nurse who claimed expertise in recovered memory. She had also written on satanic conspiracies and "ritual abuse." Below we reproduce a transcript of one of these interviews. As Shalit (1995) observes, the transcripts of the children's interviews are truly astonishing. They show that the nurse, who was a graduate student in psychology, led the children into their accusations. A highly suggestive interviewing technique, designed for cases where abuse was already an established fact, was used even though no evidence of abuse existed (Shalit, 1995b). The nurse, using anatomically correct dolls with abnormally large genitalia, coaxed the children to incriminate their teachers:

> *Nurse:* Did anybody touch you on your bum?
> *Girl:* Nobody. Nobody didn't do it.
> *Nurse:* Oh, do you think anybody touched the children on their bum?
> *Girl:* No.
> *Nurse:* What should I do if they did touch the children?
> *Girl:* [No answer]
> *Nurse:* What should I do if they did?
> *Girl:* Nobody didn't do it!

were either active participants in the event or passive bystanders. Ten days later they were tested for their memory of the event. The results showed that the older subjects were more accurate than the younger subjects overall. Active participants were less suggestible than passive bystanders. On misleading questions, the active participants showed less influence of the suggestive questions than the bystanders. However, this effect was most pronounced for the *younger* subjects. Younger bystander-witnesses were more suggestible than older bystander-witnesses.

Finally, a child's suggestibility is affected by how the successive interview sessions are handled. In the celebrated child abuse cases (e.g., the Kelly Michaels case, the McMartin Preschool case), children were questioned on several occasions with an escalating pattern of misleading and suggestive questions. What effect will such questioning have on children? For another unusual example of interviews with children see "Witch Hunt" in the Courtroom Applications box below.

[Nurse persists, asking: "Don't you want to help me?" and "Ernie would be so happy if you tell me."]

Nurse: Did anybody ever touch that part on you?

Girl: No.

Nurse: No? Would you tell me if they did?

Girl: No. I don't want to.

Nurse: You don't want to tell me?

Girl: No.

Nurse: You can help me. Oh, come on, please tell Ernie. Please tell me, please tell me, so we can help you. Please? Mommy would be so happy if you would help us; so would Bert. Please tell me. Tell Bert. OK, you tell Ernie. You whisper it to Ernie. Susan's going to cover her face, and you whisper it to Ernie. All right. Who touched you there?

Girl: OK.

Nurse: OK?

Girl: My teacher.

Nurse: Your teacher? OK. Tell Ernie which teacher. While Susan's not looking, which teacher?

Girl: Tracy [a teacher who was never charged].

Nurse: And where did she touch you?

Girl: On my hands. (Shalit, 1995b, p.19).

The child would eventually answer yes to all the questions.

Gail Goodman and Allison Clarke-Stewart (1991) had children (five- and six-year-olds) witness an event: A janitor (actually a confederate of the experimenters) entered a room and either cleaned some dolls or played with them in a suggestive manner. One hour later, an interviewer interrogated the subjects in one of three ways. In one condition, the children were interviewed in a neutral (nonsuggestive) way. In a second condition (incriminating interview), children were interviewed in a manner that suggested that the janitor did something wrong. As the interview session progressed, the interviewer's questions became increasingly suggestive that the janitor had done something wrong. Finally, in a third condition (exculpatory interview), the interviewer becomes increasingly suggestive that the janitor did nothing wrong.

In all conditions, a first interview was followed up by a second one a week later. This second interview was either similar to the first interview (such as an incriminating interview followed by a second incriminating interview), or the opposite of the first interview (such as an incriminating interview followed by an exculpatory interview). Several types of questions were asked during the interview (free recall, factual questions, and interpretive questions).

When children were exposed to misleading questions, they tended to give limited but accurate answers (at both interviews). However, when the interview content conflicted with what the child saw (e.g., the janitor cleans the dolls but is questioned in a way that suggests he played with them in an inappropriate manner), even a mildly suggestive question resulted in 25 percent of the children giving inaccurate answers. The errors made were in the direction of the interrogator's suggestions. By the time the escalating, suggestive interview was over, 75 percent of the children were giving inaccurate answers. Misleading, suggestive interrogation had more effect on interpretive questions (e.g., "What do you really think? Was the janitor cleaning or kissing the doll?") than factual questions.

Comparisons were made across interview sessions, and Goodman and Clarke-Stewart found that when the second interview was consistent with the first, the suggestions made during the first interview carried over to the second. By the end of the second (consistent) interview, inaccurate reports were very frequent and in the direction of the suggestions made by the interviewer. When the second interview conflicted with the first, most of the children changed their stories so that they were consistent with the content of the second interview.

The preponderance of the research evidence leads to the conclusion that children are more suggestible than adults. However, one must also keep in mind that the difference between children and adults in terms of suggestibility is not very large (Rudy & Goodman, 1991). Generally, children are not *highly* suggestible (at least in the controlled laboratory environment) and show considerable resistance to being misled (Rudy & Goodman, 1991). Finally, there are individual differences in a child's suggestibility; some children accept the biasing influence of misleading questions more readily than others (Goodman & Clarke-Stewart, 1991).

The fact that children are more suggestible may not necessarily imply that they are less accurate in reporting the crucial events of an incident. William Cassel and David Bjorkland (1995) did a very realistic study of child eyewitnesses. These researchers had children view a videotaped event and then read a magazine for a while after the videotape. After this, they interviewed the child witnesses. The children either were asked to use free recall to remember the event ("What happened in the video?") or were interviewed using an unbiased, cued recall technique ("Tell me everything you can about the girl, . . .").

One week after the initial interview, the children were interviewed for a second time. Finally, one month later, another interview took place. Note that this is not unlike the process that an actual witness would experience. Table 8.1 shows the percentage of correct and incorrect free recall in each of the three interviews.

Clearly, overall recall increased with age. Note, however, that recall was reliable within each age group. Although younger witnesses, especially the six-year-olds, recalled less material than other groups, the core facts of the case, including an unauthorized taking of a bicycle, were recalled at high levels by all groups in almost an error-free manner (Cassel & Bjorkland, 1995).

In some of the interviews, Cassel and Bjorkland had interviewers ask leading questions to determine the witnesses' level of suggestibility. The results indicate that younger children are more susceptible to leading questions than older witnesses. Younger children tended to agree with positive leading questions about 80 percent of the time ("The bicycle frame was shiny chrome, wasn't it?" [True]), but responded incorrectly about 70 percent of the time to negative leading questions ("The bicycle was red, wasn't it?" [False]). Adults tended to reject leading questions about half the time whether they were negative (false) or positive (true). Therefore, when adults were asked leading questions, this rejection bias led to fewer correct responses.

The basic point of the Cassel and Bjorkland experiment is that although younger children provide fewer freely recalled items and may be more suggestible to negative leading questions, their ability to report fundamental facts accurately does not significantly differ from that of older children or adults.

TABLE 8.1	Percentage of Correct and Incorrect Free Recall in Three Interviews		
	6-year-olds	8-year-olds	Adults
Initial	7 (0)	13 (0)	20 (1)
One Week	9 (0)	12 (0)	31 (2)
One Month	7 (1)	11 (1)	28 (2)

Note: Numbers in parentheses refer to incorrect responses.

Source: Adapted from "Developmental Patterns of Eyewitness Memory and Suggestibility: An Ecologically Based Short-term Longitudinal Study," by W. S. Cassel and D. F. Bjorkland, *Law and Human Behavior, 19*(5), pp. 516, 518, Tables 1 and 3.

Should there be special procedures in the courtroom when children have to testify about sexual abuse? The next Courtroom Applications box reports a case we have considered in another context earlier in the book.

Using Props to Enhance Children's Memories.   A common tactic used when questioning young children about events such as sexual abuse is to provide them with props. These props could be miniature versions of the room in which an

COURTROOM APPLICATIONS

Special Procedures for Child Witnesses in Sexual Abuse Trials?

Should child witnesses be given special treatment to help avoid the trauma of facing an adult accused of abuse? What about the Sixth Amendment, which reads, "In all criminal prosecutions, the accused shall enjoy the right . . . to be confronted with the witnesses against him"?

Recall from Chapter 2 that Sandra Ann Craig was indicted in Howard County, Maryland, for child abuse, first- and second-degree sexual offenses, perverted sexual practices, assault, and battery. The named victim in each count was a six-year-old girl who had attended Ms. Craig's preschool. Before the trial, the prosecutor invoked a Maryland law that permitted a witness to testify via closed circuit television if the trial judge "determines that testimony by the child victim in the courtroom will result in the child suffering serious emotional distress such that the child cannot reasonably communicate." After hearing testimony from expert witnesses (e.g., one witness predicted that one of the children "would withdraw and curl up"), the judge found four child witnesses competent to testify but in danger of suffering severe emotional distress if they did so. The judge, therefore, permitted them to testify by using a one-way closed-circuit television arrangement.

The arrangements during the trial were to have the child witnesses testify in a separate room with only the prosecutor, defense attorney, video operators, and (unless the defendant had objected) a therapist. Meanwhile, the defendant and the judge observed the proceeding through one-way closed-circuit television in the courtroom. The defendant was able to communicate electronically and privately with counsel during the proceeding.

The jury convicted Ms. Craig on all counts, but the Maryland Court of Appeals reversed and ordered a new trial, ruling that the state had not made a sufficient showing of the necessity for the closed-circuit procedure because the judge had not observed the child witness in the presence of the defendant.

event occurred, or a **sexually anatomically correct doll** (or SAC doll). These props represent the secondary sexual characteristics of males and females in an anatomically correct way. The use of SAC dolls is quite common, with around 95 percent of child protection service personnel using them (Everson & Boat, 1990). Using props to help young children remember events has a strong empirical and theoretical basis (Goodman & Aman, 1990). Children, especially young (preschool-age) children, have language and memory limitations; therefore, using

Maryland petitioned the U.S. Supreme Court to hear the case and the Court agreed to do so.

The Supreme Court faced the question of whether the Sixth Amendment absolutely required a face-to-face confrontation in all instances. In a 5–4 decision, the Court concluded that the Sixth Amendment only imposes a preference, not an absolute right, to confront accusers face-to-face (*Maryland v. Craig*, 1990). The ultimate purpose of confrontation is to "ensur[e] that evidence admitted against an accused is reliable and subject to the rigorous adversarial testing that is the norm of Anglo-American criminal proceedings." In balancing the rights of the victim and the accused, the Court looked to psychological evidence, specifically the "growing body of academic literature documenting the psychological trauma suffered by child abuse victims who must testify in court," citing a brief filed by the American Psychological Association and also citing studies showing that face-to-face confrontation might undermine the truth-finding goal of the trial. The Court also cited an experimental study conducted by University of Michigan law students that found that children who testified in a small room gave more and better evidence than children testifying in a traditional courtroom setting.

The important result, however, was that Sandra Craig received a new trial. The Supreme Court sent the case back to Maryland to allow the court to determine the narrow question of whether a judge had to observe the child-witness in the presence of the accused before deciding whether to use the closed-circuit procedure. The Maryland Court of Appeals decided that the judge should personally observe and interview the child, on the record, either in or out of the courtroom. The judge would have discretion to permit the defendant to be present and to remove a defendant whose presence was having an adverse effect on the child.

a prop as a retrieval cue to help children correctly recall events is a sensible procedure (Goodman & Aman, 1990).

Despite the obvious advantages of using props and SAC dolls, some observers have expressed concern over such techniques (Bruck et al., 1995; Skinner & Berry, 1993). Linda Skinner and Kenneth Berry have pointed out that using SAC dolls raises concerns in several areas:

1. There is little standardization of the dolls used—that is, the dolls one person uses to assess children may differ from those used by another.
2. There is little standardization of procedures used when employing dolls to assess children.
3. There is little standardization of how children's behaviors with the dolls are scored.
4. Training for individuals who use SAC dolls has not been consistent.
5. Normative data are needed from nonabused children so that the behavior of allegedly abused children can be compared to some (known) standard.

These points raise several questions about the use of SAC dolls. How does the use of props or SAC dolls affect the accuracy of a child's memory? Can using an SAC doll lead a nonabused child to be incorrectly classified as abused? Do abused and nonabused children play with SAC dolls in similar ways? The available research suggests some answers to these questions.

Gemma O'Callaghan and Heather D'Arcy (1989) addressed the impact of props on the accuracy of children's memory. Subjects (male and female four-year-olds) watched a three-minute videotape; then their memories were tested under one of four conditions. One group of subjects was given a free recall task (to simply remember as much as possible). A second group of subjects also did a free recall task but were provided with props (a model and characters of what was on the tape). A third group was questioned with a series of 24 nonbiased short-answer questions. Finally, the fourth group were asked the same short-answer questions but were provided with props.

In this experiment, the short-answer format produced *more* information than the free recall format. Also, when the children used props, *more* information was produced than if no props were used. In terms of the accuracy of the information produced, the type of question and the use of props interacted. The relationship between these factors is shown in Figure 8.2. With short-answer questions, the use of props made no difference to the accuracy of recall. However, when free recall was used, props actually *reduced* the accuracy of the information recalled.

In a related study, Gail Goodman and Christine Aman (1990) compared children's recall of a real-life social event under four conditions. Goodman and Aman found no evidence that using SAC dolls adversely affected children's memory. For example, using an SAC doll did *not* increase a child's susceptibility to misleading questions. Nor did using an SAC doll lead nonabused children to make false reports of sexual abuse.

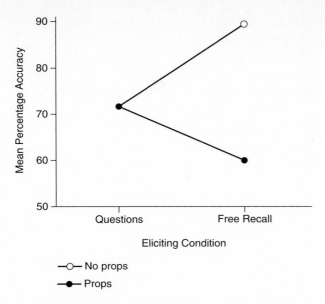

FIGURE 8.2 Accuracy of four-year-olds in an experiment.

This figure suggests that four-year-olds show more accurate recall when the questioners do not use props and allow the child to use free recall to report what happened.

Source: From "Use of Props in Questioning Preschool Witnesses," by G. O'Callaghan and H. D'Arcy, 1989, *Australian Journal of Psychology, 41,* p. 192, Figure 2.

Taken together, these two experiments suggest that using props or SAC dolls will not decrease the accuracy of what a child remembers. This is true, providing that children are interviewed with a specific questioning format rather than a free recall format. However, the age of the child is critical. Clearly, younger children are very susceptible to influence when using SACs.

As we noted above, Maggie Bruck and her co-workers have stated unequivo- cally that SAC dolls should *not* be used with very young children, specifically three-year-olds (Bruck et al., 1995). Recall that three-year-olds were given a med- ical exam and then asked to demonstrate on anatomically correct dolls and on their own bodies the events that took place during the exam. Under both condi- tions (dolls and own body) the three-year-olds were inaccurate in reporting touching of the genitals, and this was true no matter how they were questioned and regardless of whether they had actually received a genital examination. Chil- dren tended to report that the doctor had inserted his finger in the anus, particu- larly when the dolls were used. To summarize, the research on the use of anatom- ical dolls generally shows that, if used correctly, the dolls may aid in child sexual abuse cases (Everson & Boat, 1994), but they should not be used with very young children. Of course, dolls have an appeal for interviewers because young children have limited verbal skills.

JUROR PERCEPTIONS OF THE CHILD EYEWITNESS

Jurors' perceptions of witnesses play a crucial role in all trials. Having examined the competence of the child witness, we need to review the literature on jurors' perceptions of the credibility of the child eyewitness. We have seen that there are variables affecting the perceived credibility of an adult eyewitness (e.g., confidence, nervousness, witness identification conditions) (Cashmore & Bussey, 1996). How do jurors perceive the credibility of child eyewitnesses relative to adults?

In a survey of 101 actual jurors, Billie Croder and Reid Whiteside (1988) asked them several questions concerning the abilities of children as eyewitnesses in sexual abuse cases. They found that 70 percent of the jurors felt that child witnesses from age three and older could give accurate testimony about sexual abuse. Although 55 percent acknowledged that a child (age three to five) might lie about sexual abuse, 60 percent thought that older children were actually more inclined to lie, most likely out of loyalty to a parent, fear of being harmed, or pressure from an adult (Croder & Whiteside, 1988). The results from this survey seem to send a mixed message about the child eyewitness. On the one hand, a large majority of the jurors polled viewed the child as having the capacity to tell the truth in sexual abuse cases. On the other hand, a majority acknowledged that a child might lie, with older children being more inclined to do so.

In an experiment investigating the relationship between the age of an eyewitness and perceived credibility, Goodman et al. (1987) had subjects read a written transcript of a car-pedestrian accident that included an eyewitness. The age of the eyewitness was varied (6, 10, and 30 years old). Subjects rated the credibility of the witness and indicated the degree of guilt of the defendant. The results showed that the 6-year-old witness was perceived as the least credible and the 30-year-old the most credible witness. The degree of guilt assigned to the defendant, however, *did not* vary according to the age of the eyewitness.

Follow-up research by Goodman et al. found that testimony by a 30-year-old was persuasive enough to convince the jury, but when the witness was a 6-year-old, juries relied on other evidence to support the child's testimony. Unlike the adult witness, the child witness alone is not sufficient to convince jurors. Jurors, not unreasonably, want corroborative evidence.

Taken together, the survey study and the experiments suggest that adults are skeptical of children as witnesses. Whereas it appears that adults would like to believe children, they tend to believe them less than adults and require more than just the word of a child to convict a defendant. Why are children perceived to be less credible than adults? We evaluate this question next.

Sources of Reduced Credibility for Child Witnesses

Michael Leippe and Ann Romanczyk (1989) suggested three possible reasons for the child's relative lack of credibility:

1. Jurors may have negative stereotypes about children concerning their memory abilities and honesty.
2. Children may behave in ways on the witness stand that reduce perceptions of credibility—for example, children may appear more nervous and less confident than adult witnesses, and we have seen that lack of confidence reduces a witness's perceived credibility.
3. The age of a witness may influence how jurors examine and evaluate evidence from other witnesses.

There is evidence that all three factors are relevant. Leippe and Romanczyk (experiment 1) investigated the role of stereotyped expectations. Subjects read a description of an experiment in which witnesses of varying ages (between kindergarten and college age) viewed a live confrontation and then did a memory and face recognition task. The subjects were asked to estimate how well the witnesses performed in two areas: objective recall (e.g., How many questions about the event did the witnesses answer correctly?) and recognition (How many witnesses out of 100 made a correct identification in a photo lineup?). The subjects' estimates were then compared to actual results obtained from subjects who viewed the event. These results are shown in Figure 8.3. As you can see, subjects' estimates were well below the actual performance of witnesses. This finding was especially true for children in the age range of five to six and eight to nine. Thus, adults seem to doubt children's ability to recall correctly events that they see. As for the other two possible reasons, we know that nervousness reduces a witness's credibility, and when a child takes the stand, other witnesses are evaluated and used more for corroboration than if an adult takes the stand and gives the same testimony as a child (Cashmore & Bussey, 1996).

Child eyewitnesses generally violate jurors' expectancies about the demeanor of an accurate witness. We know that children typically deliver testimony less confidently and less consistently; they appear to be easily led by counsel. Goodman et al. (1987) concluded that when a juror encounters a child witness whose presentation contradicts the juror's negative expectation (about the child witness), the juror may not rely on his or her pretrial prototype. Leippe and Romanczyk (1989) argued that the inconsistent results found regarding a child's credibility as an eyewitness depend on the extent to which the child behaves consistently or inconsistently with the perceiver's expectations of the child's ability to perform competently. Indeed, Leippe and Romanczyck (1987, 1989) proposed that jurors' expectations about the child eyewitness operate as a kind of perceptual filter through which the child's testimony is evaluated. Recent research by Michael J. Markus showed that when a child eyewitness, even one as young as six years of age, testifies in a competent and assured manner, jurors find him or her

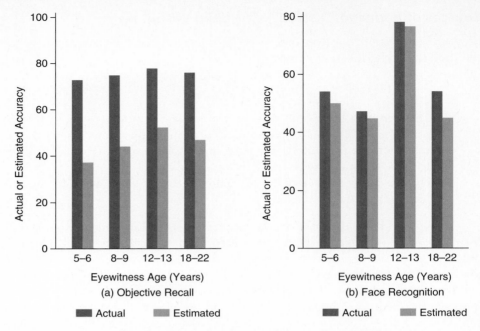

FIGURE 8.3   Actual and estimated eyewitness accuracy of children and young adults.

The figure shows that adults significantly underestimate the accuracy of child eyewitnesses.

Source: Adapted from "Reactions to Child (Versus Adult) Eyewitnesses: The Influence of Jurors' Pre-conceptions and Witness Behavior," by M. R. Leippe and A. Romanczyk, 1989, *Law and Human Behavior, 13,* 103–132.

credible (Markus and Horowitz, 1995). Luus, Wells, and Turtle (1995) reported that while jurors do have an age-based bias against child eyewitnesses, they tend to suspend that bias when they actually see the child testify. The child eyewitnesses in the Luus study were eight and twelve years old. However, in an actual courtroom children may appear extremely nervous (Luus et al., 1995), and although Markus and Horowitz found that jurors assess a confident six-year-old as a credible witness, there may be very few confident six-year-olds in the actual courtroom.

Given the difficulties we have cataloged concerning the testimony of not only the child eyewitness but the adult as well, is there any way the jury can be informed of these difficulties? One route is the presentation of evidence by experts who can describe to the court the general state of knowledge that exists in a particular specialty. Next we examine the use of expert witnesses in eyewitness cases and then explore the general issue of when and about what experts can testify in court.

THE EXPERT WITNESS

Jurors appear to be ignorant of the potential flaws of eyewitness identifications and testimony (Cutler, Penrod, & Stuve, 1988). As a result, some innocent defendants may be convicted based on faulty eyewitness testimony. About one-half of the wrongful convictions per year are estimated to be due to faulty eyewitness testimony (Rattner, 1988).

One solution to the problems surrounding eyewitness testimony, as suggested in the last chapter, is to have a psychologist provide *expert testimony* concerning the potential pitfalls of eyewitness identifications and testimony. The expert can "educate" or sensitize the jurors to eyewitness issues such as the accuracy of the content of the eyewitness's testimony (Kassin, Ellsworth, & Smith, 1994).

Whereas much of the emphasis is on what the expert can tell the jury about accurate and inaccurate eyewitness testimony, the expert in eyewitness research can inform the legal system in another way, by preventing or minimizing eyewitness errors from occurring (Wells, 1978). Gary Wells has convincingly argued that by concentrating on the procedures used to gather the reports of eyewitnesses, researchers can prevent errors in the first place and thereby avoid the need for experts to testify at trial (S. Seelau & Wells, 1995). Wells has referred to this view of eyewitness research as the system variable approach. **System variables** refer to the arrangements and methods used to debrief eyewitnesses. These system variables include a number of the lineup and interview procedures discussed in Chapter 7, such as the instructions given to eyewitnesses, target-absent lineups, and use of sequential procedures.

Sheila Seelau and Gary Wells (1995) argued that reliance on system variable research is the most productive route to increasing eyewitness accuracy and thereby effectively informing the legal system. Seelau and Wells contrasted research on system variables with experiments that focus on **estimator variables,** aspects of the crime situation (violence of the event, distance to the crime, presence of a weapon, etc.) or factors inherent in the witness (stress, health, prejudices, etc.). Estimator variables are often naturally intertwined or confounded in real events; therefore, laboratory experiments that aim at unambiguously manipulating variables may not fully capture the reality of the eyewitness situation. For example, in one study, researchers found that stress and accuracy were positively related (Yuille & Cutshall, 1986). This finding flies in the face of basic research that shows increasing stress to degrade accuracy. But in the naturally occurring situations these researchers studied, eyewitnesses who felt the most stress were closer to the event and therefore had greater opportunity to view the culprits.

In the following sections we discuss these and other aspects of the role of the expert witness in the trial. In an age when complex scientific and clinical topics become crucial issues in trials, the expert has assumed an increasingly important role.

Expert Testimony in Sexual Abuse Cases

The increase in sexual abuse cases involving children suggests that the testimony of experts may be required. Experts could be called to testify about the cognitive and perceptual abilities of children. Yet another type of expert who might be called in a sexual abuse case would provide "psychological" evidence concerning the symptoms and consequences of sexual abuse. In this section, we explore the ability of experts in these categories to influence the outcome of a sexual abuse case.

Expert Testimony and the Cognitive and Perceptual Abilities of Children. An experiment by Michael Crowley, M. Gemma O'Callaghan, and Peter Ball (1994) addressed the role of an expert who testifies about a child witness's cognitive and perceptual abilities. Jurors watched a videotape of a reenacted criminal case in which either a male or female child (the age of the child was varied: 6, 9, or 12 years old) was the principal witness against the defendant. Juries, which were gender balanced (three men and three women on each jury), completed predeliberation verdict measures, deliberated, and indicated a postdeliberation verdict. Subjects also completed several other assessments including measures of the child witness's credibility, the child's ability to distinguish fact from fancy, and so on.

Additionally, one-half the subjects were exposed to a version of the case including an expert witness whereas the other one-half viewed a version of the case that did not include an expert. The content of the expert's testimony included references to the major findings on children eyewitnesses such as susceptibility to suggestion, ability to distinguish fact from fantasy, and memory. The expert basically informed the jury about the current status of research on the mental abilities (cognitive and perceptual) of children.

The researchers found that jurors who heard expert testimony were more likely to have a positive view of the child witness's cognitive and perceptual abilities than were jurors who did not hear such testimony. However, the effect on verdicts was unclear. There was a tendency for expert testimony to increase guilty verdicts, but that trend was not statistically reliable.

Expert Testimony About the Psychological Consequences of Sexual Abuse. Margaret Bull Kovera and her colleagues have observed that prosecutors often present expert witnesses who testify to the psychological consequences of abuse in an attempt to enhance the credibility of the child witness (Kovera, Gresham, Borgida, Gray, & Regan, in press). An expert can enhance a child's sexual abuse case if that testimony is supportive of the child's case and meets certain conditions. For example, Gabora, Spanos, and Joab (1993) had subjects watch a videotaped sexual abuse trial in which the age of the child witness was varied (13 or 17 years old) along with the presence or absence of an expert witness for the prosecution. There were two versions of the expert testimony. One-third of the subjects received "general" testimony designed to dispel basic misinformation about victims of abuse and explain unusual symptoms to the jury. Another one-third of the subjects received "specific" testimony centered on the case being tried. The expert in this condition gave detailed descriptions of the victim's symptoms and told the jury that those symptoms were common among abuse victims. The remaining one-third of the subjects received no expert testimony.

The results of this experiment showed, first, that the defendant was more likely to be convicted when the victim was younger (13 years old) than older (17 years old). With respect to the effects of the expert testimony, jurors were more likely to convict after hearing the *specific* expert testimony as opposed to the *general* expert testimony or no expert testimony (the last two conditions did not differ significantly).

Kovera et al. (in press) qualified the Gabora et al. (1993) findings by reporting that testimony enhanced a child's credibility only if the child witness had behaved in a manner congruent with the expert's testimony, which had been repetitive, summarizing the facts a number of times. If the child behaved in a manner that contradicted the expert's description, jurors were less likely to believe the witness's testimony. The trap here is discrepancies between the child's behavior and the expert's testimony of what that behavior should be. Attorneys try very hard to prepare their child witnesses to appear confident on the witness stand. However, if the expert testifies that an abused child will have confused reactions, there is incongruence between the child's behavior and the expert's report. Kovera et al. (in press) suggest that lawyers may lose cases because they have not taken these incongruencies into account.

Expert Witnesses: Information or Influence

Although the use of experts in eyewitness cases is permitted, not all social psychologists agree with the practice (McCloskey & Egeth, 1983a). Two major issues arise in considering the role of expert witnesses: First, are jurors already aware of the problems associated with eyewitness testimony? Second, will an expert make jurors overly skeptical and inclined to reject too many eyewitnesses?

As you might expect, the controversy surrounding use of experts to educate jurors led to research on the impact of expert testimony on eyewitness identification. The research generally shows that an expert can make jurors more sensitive to the factors that affect eyewitness identification (Cutler, Penrod, & Dexter, 1989). For example, in the area of weapon focus, jurors are not generally aware of the degree to which the presence of a weapon degrades eyewitness performance (Cutler et al., 1989). An expert, giving descriptive testimony about the weapon focus effect, can increase juror knowledge in this area. Generally, an expert increases a juror's knowledge of the factors that can affect eyewitness identification, reduces the juror's reliance on the confidence of the eyewitness, and helps the juror make correct inferences about the credibility of an eyewitness (Cutler et al., 1989). There is also evidence that an expert who provides testimony specific to the elements of a case is more effective than an expert who provides general information about human perception and memory (Fox & Walters, 1986; Schuller, 1990).

The presence of a supportive expert witness (one who provides evidence suggesting that the eyewitness is accurate and credible) can enhance juror perceptions of an eyewitnesses's credibility (Blonstein & Geiselman, 1990). Conversely, the presence of an unsupportive expert decreases the perceived credibility of an eyewitness (Blonstein & Geiselman, 1990). This effect occurs regardless of whether the witnessing conditions were good or poor—that is, a supportive expert can enhance the credibility of an eyewitness who made his identification under poor witnessing conditions (Blonstein & Geiselman, 1990).

But what about making jurors overly skeptical of eyewitnesses? Will the presence of an expert lead jurors to "throw the baby out with the bathwater"? The answer is no. Brian Cutler and colleagues found that the impact of expert witnesses in eyewitness cases clearly is to raise jurors' knowledge and sensitivity without significantly increasing their skepticism (Cutler, Penrod, & Dexter, 1989, 1990). Overall, the benefits gained by having an expert present appear to outweigh any potential negative side effects. Recent work also suggests that experts do not prejudicially influence juror decision making (Kovera et al., in press).

The standards for admitting expert testimony have been a matter of controversy for a long time. The role of the psychological expert has at times been particularly problematic for the courts. Let's examine the current view of experts as seen by the U.S. Supreme Court.

DAUBERT AND EXPERT TESTIMONY

The U.S. Supreme Court in *Daubert v. Merrell Dow Pharmaceuticals, Inc.* (1993) put into place a new standard for the admissibility of expert testimony. The general standard had been the Frye test, after a 1923 case of the same name. The formulation in the Frye case was the "general acceptance" test, and this definition had been the dominant standard for determining the admissibility of scientific evidence at trial for over 70 years. This test required that the scientific principle on which an opinion was based must be sufficiently established to have gained general acceptance in the particular field in which it belongs (Tomkins, 1995).

In *Daubert,* the plaintiffs had alleged that their children's birth defects had been caused by the mother's prenatal ingestion of Bendectin, a prescription drug marketed by Merrell-Dow Pharmaceuticals. Merrell, the defendant, argued that the suit should be dismissed (summary judgment) on the basis of the trial judge's review of the published scientific literature, which, Merrell said, failed to show Bendectin as a risk factor in causing birth defects. The plaintiffs acknowledged that the published literature failed to support their claims but held that the testimony of eight "well-credentialed" experts, who based their opinions that Bendectin could cause birth defects on animal studies and unpublished materials, was sufficient to go to trial and preclude summary judgment. However, the trial court agreed with Merrell and granted summary judgment. The appellate court agreed and in doing so the court cited *Frye.*

The U.S. Supreme Court reversed the appellate decision and sent (remanded) it back to the lower courts. The Court held that the Frye test has been superseded by the adoption of the Federal Rules of Evidence (FRE). The Court held that Federal Rule 402 was the baseline for admissibility: "All relevant evidence is admissible, except as otherwise provided by the Constitution of the United States, by Act of Congress, by these rules, or by other rules prescribed by the Supreme Court pursuant to authority. Evidence which is not relevant is not admissible." FRE Rule 401 provides that relevant evidence is any evidence that tends to make the existence of any fact that is of consequence to the determination of the action more or less probable than it would be without the evidence. In other words, the testimony of the plaintiffs' experts was deemed to be relevant because hearing it would increase the jurors' understanding of the effects of Bendectin (Tomkins, 1995).

The *Daubert* Court did give some guidelines to lower courts with respect to determining what testimony would be considered relevant and reliable. They are as follows:

1. Whether the scientific technique can be and has been tested
2. Whether it has been subjected to peer review and publication
3. The known or potential rate of error
4. The existence and maintenance of standards controlling the technique's operation
5. Degree of acceptance for the technique in the scientific community

Note that none of these alone is determinative. The Court did not give a checklist but was content to provide some guidelines (Monahan & Walker, 1994b). The second of these concerns peer review, generally determined by whether the research has been submitted and accepted by reputable scientific journals that base acceptance of manuscripts on the favorable reviews of experts in the field. However, in *Daubert,* Justice Blackmun noted that nonpublished studies may be well done and innovative and because of that very innovation may not as yet have been published. Therefore, in Justice Blackmun's terms, published research may be relevant but not "dispositive." That is, it is not the only game in town. Nonpublished work may be considered relevant and reliable if it is well grounded.

Daubert also requires that judgment be made as to whether the scientific methodology used was valid, whether the research is applicable to the issue at trial, and whether other research supports the research of the expert (Penrod, Fulero, & Cutler, 1995). Therefore, the trial judge must perform a "gatekeeping" function to ensure that only trustworthy science is admitted. It is up to the judges now to keep bad science out and good science in (Tomkins, 1995).

Impact of Daubert on the Courts and Judges

The *Daubert* decision will likely have an impact on the use of relatively novel procedures in both civil and criminal trials. For example, newer evidence concerning the possible links between chemical emissions from industrial plants and various cancers may find its way into court. In the criminal courts, DNA fingerprinting, which we consider in the next chapter, and computerized ballistic tests are possible examples of less than consensually accepted procedures (Angier, 1993).

The minority opinion in *Daubert,* which was decided by a 7–2 vote, agreed that the Frye standard should be abandoned but did not agree that trial judges should be put in the position of evaluating scientific standards. Chief Justice Rehnquist, who wrote the minority opinion, did not want to put judges in the role of "amateur scientists." Few would argue that there is no wisdom in excluding innovative and well-grounded but unpublished research if it is relevant to the issue before the bar—but it may be unpublished for very good scientific reasons. Judges, untrained in scientific methodologies, do not seem to be the best gate-keepers. In truth, given the range of disciplines a judge might encounter—from molecular biology and vascular surgery to experimental psychology—it is unlikely that they could be trained to make reasonable decisions about the relevance and reliability of research from such disparate fields. *Daubert* does relax the standard for admissibility, but it is unlikely that judges will very much alter their own procedures for admitting expert testimony. Judges who object to certain areas of science will likely continue to do so and those who have a somewhat more flexible standard may indulge themselves a little more (Penrod & Cutler, 1995).

The Effect of Daubert on Expert Testimony in Eyewitness Cases. David Faigman (1995) has addressed the impact of *Daubert* on social science testimony in court. After all, *Daubert* says nothing about psychology or social science in general. The basic fact of *Daubert* is that judges will decide for themselves what is valid science and no longer have to defer to the relevant scientific community for its consensus on some scientific issue. How does the research concerning eyewitness identification track with the new *Daubert* standards?

There is general consensus on the maturity of the research that has been going on for 20 years, with agreement on a number of findings. These include the following areas: that the accuracy-confidence relationship is weak, that instructions to eyewitnesses can bias their lineup choices, that eyewitnesses have difficulty with cross-race identifications, and that stress levels affect performance (Kassin, Ellsworth, & Smith, 1994; Leippe, 1995; Penrod et al., 1995). The research on eyewitness reliability has been helped by the increase in **meta-analyses,** which are statistical integrations of the results of independent studies on the same issue (Johnson, Mullen, & Sagas, 1995). Nancy Steblay (1992) integrated the statistical findings from 19 studies, all dealing with "weapon focus," and found that the vast majority of studies show the presence of a weapon to inhibit accurate eyewitness identification. Keep in mind that the eyewitness research is grounded in the basic research and theory of experimental psychology. The relevant areas of memory, perception, cognitive development, and others have been investigated for a hundred years.

However, courts still have reservations about the use of experts in eyewitness cases as shown below:

1. Some judges do not believe the research on eyewitness identification has yet reached a level of scientific maturity to warrant automatic acceptance in court.
2. Other judges feel that cross-examination is the cure for inaccurate eye-witnesses. The legal system does have great faith in the curative powers of cross-examination to bring out the truth.
3. Those judges who do not put their faith in cross-examination may instead believe that instruction about eyewitness accuracy is a quicker and more efficient way than calling an expert to do the same.
4. Finally, some courts have felt that the expert witness may either confuse the jurors or that jurors may place too much weight on that testimony, (Penrod et al., 1995).

The consensus among experts refutes objection number one (Kassin et al., 1989; Leippe, 1995; Penrod et al., 1995). This is not to say there is unanimous agreement, but the standard in this objection is too high for any discipline to meet. Research further suggests that instructions and cross-examination are not curatives (Greene, 1988; Tanford, 1991a, 1991b). However, few of the mock jury studies include cross-examination of the expert. In one such study, Spanos, Dubreuil, and Gwynn (1991) manipulated whether the mock jurors heard a cross-examination of the expert witness. They found that when jurors heard the expert testify without being cross-examined they tended to bring in a verdict consistent with the expert's testimony, but the verdicts in the condition where no expert testified were not different from the verdicts in the condition where there was cross-examination of the expert. It appears that only an uncontested expert will be able to sway a jury to his or her point of view. However, enthusiasm for the curative powers of cross-examination should be checked by the observation that we are dealing with but one study.

For objection number four, jurors do not seem to accept without question the views of experts in the eyewitness area, as noted earlier (Kovera et al., in press; Penrod et al., 1995). Perhaps this is because jurors come to court with their own notions of the accuracy of eyewitnesses. Michael Leippe's (1995) review of the literature argues that expert witnesses are needed to counterpoise the consistent finding that jurors put undue belief in eyewitnesses. Expert witnesses do engage a modest amount of skepticism about eyewitnesses, but that skepticism is healthy (Leippe, 1995).

However, these findings do not suggest that experts are of no consequence. Data from both simulation studies (Brekke, Enko, Clavet, & Seelau, 1991) and studies of actual trials (Cecil & Willging, 1994) demonstrate that trial outcomes generally follow the testimony of the expert. In Nancy Brekke's study, she and her co-workers found that even if juries did not openly discuss the expert's testimony, their verdicts tended to follow the expert's line of reasoning. Kovera and her co-workers found that expert testimony significantly influenced jurors' decisions in child sexual abuse cases. Jurors who heard expert testimony, compared to jurors who did not, were more likely to convict the defendant and had better recall for the judge's instructions (Kovera, Levy, Borgida, & Penrod, 1994). It is likely that *Daubert* will increase the use of experts in the realm of eyewitness testimony. Faigman's (1995) view of the matter is that eyewitness identification research would hold up fairly well to the scientific validity factors enunciated by *Daubert*.

The Role of the Expert

Fundamental assumptions of the adversarial system are that each side may present its own evidence, that judges can sensibly rule as to whether that evidence is relevant and admissible, and that juries are able to comprehend that evidence and make reasoned decisions (Schwarzer, 1991). Reasoned decisions may be difficult, however, when new scientific evidence requires the ordinary jury to deal with complex and contradictory testimony. Scientific experts often present testimony that jurors have grave difficulties comprehending. Consider just this brief excerpt from the testimony of an economic expert in a complex civil trial dealing with unfair market practices:

> The outer boundaries of a product market are determined by the reasonable interchangeability of use or the cross-elasticity of supply and demand between the product itself and substitutes for it. The average variable cost test is a double inference test because if you find that Brown & Williamson priced below its reasonably anticipated average variable cost, you may infer that Brown & Williamson had predatory intent, and from predatory intent, you may infer that Brown & Williamson's conduct had a reasonable possibility of injuring competition in the cigarette market. . . . You may wish to reject an inference of predatory intent, if you find that a substantial motivation for Brown & Williamson's entry into black and white cigarettes was LIFO decrement avoidance tax benefits. (Adler, 1995, p. 131)

What are the jurors to make of this?

The legal process emphasizes the differences and inconsistencies in a body of data or literature. As Michael Saks (1992) has pointed out, a case often turns on those differences. There is general acceptance of the use of DNA in the courtroom, but trials that may hinge on the results of DNA tests ("genetic fingerprinting") focus not on the vast body of microbiological analyses of DNA but rather on the manner in which the tests were done and the meaning of those test results. In a sense, expert testimony presented by both sides suggests there is more disagreement about the discipline than actually exists.

The use of expert witnesses is a major pathway for introducing scientific evidence into trials. For example, psychological science has many roles in the courtroom. Clinical psychologists may testify to the state of mind of the defendant before or during the trial (competence to stand trial), while committing the offense (insanity pleas), and after the trial (prediction of future dangerousness as a criterion for the death penalty). Psychological experts may testify to the accuracy of both adult and child eyewitnesses, the impact of pretrial publicity, the presence of psychological trauma due to accidents or injuries, the use of hypnotically refreshed memory, the causes and effects of discrimination in the workplace, and the psychological issues raised in child custody cases.

In fact, almost any type of expertise (DNA testing, use of the polygraph, validity of opinion surveys) can be analyzed by psychological or applied statistical techniques (Saks, 1992). In one application, experimental psychologists have been asked to judge the validity of the polygraph test ("lie detector") and the expertise underlying that test because it is based on assumptions about human physiology and psychology. Psychologists may also testify concerning application of rules of evidence and procedure. In this use, psychological research has examined the effects on verdicts if a defendant is charged with multiple crimes (in one trial) or multiple issues are litigated in a civil trial.

Experts may assume any of three roles in the court. They may serve as conduits, as *educators* who inform the court about the state of the art of their science. The experts become representatives of their discipline and stand above the partisan fray (Saks, 1992). A second role experts may assume is that of *advocates* who present evidence favoring only their side (Hans, 1989). Unfavorable (to their side) evidence will have to be pried out of them by tough cross-examination. These experts usually have a cause they wish to promote. Finally, there are the *hired guns;* their testimony will be whatever the side that pays them wants them to say (Hans, 1989; Saks, 1992). In truth, almost every witness is paid by somebody. A witness paid by one of the two contesting parties will invariably be asked who paid the fee and how much it was. Discrediting the "hired gun" usually works by producing a small but reliable decrease in the jurors' acceptance of the expert's credibility (Honts & Devitt, 1992).

One other option judges have is to appoint their own experts. Federal Rule of Evidence 706 permits judges to find and appoint their own witnesses. Given the complexity of modern legal issues and the often confusing welter of claims for various scientific techniques, judges, under FRE 706, can enhance their ability to deal with such issues by hiring their own experts. In fact, however, judges rarely do so. Joe Cecil and Thomas Willging (1994) surveyed 331 federal judges and found that only 20 percent had ever used an expert to assist them. In the typical case, judges apparently saw little value in appointing an expert, although most of them thought an expert might be helpful in some circumstances. When judges did appoint an expert it was because the issue was unusual or one of the parties did not have an expert it should have had. This was especially true when the parties involved were children or other less powerful individuals.

Judges also felt that appointing their own expert would alter the adversarial system. Remember that judges see themselves as neutral arbiters, standing above the tumult of the trial, and many judges feel that to appoint their own expert would in essence mean they were entering the fray.

Cecil and Willging (1994) report that when courts did appoint their own experts, judges and juries tended to bring in verdicts that were consistent with the expert's testimony. This, however, does not concur with the finding of Brekke et al. (1991) that nonadversarial (court-appointed) expert testimony was accorded no more weight than adversarial expert testimony. However, Brekke's study was a mock jury experiment involving a rape case. It may be that nonadversarial testimony is weighed less in an arena in which jurors have some preconceptions, compared to trials in which they may not, such as a trial dealing with patent law. Furthermore, the Cecil and Willging (1994) data are derived from trials in which both sides generally presented their own expert witnesses and the court-appointed witness then sided with one of the two parties.

SUMMARY

Using children as witnesses in criminal cases raises three concerns: a child's ability to perceive and recall an event accurately, the suggestibility of children, and the impression child witnesses make on juries. The general assumption is that children will not be as accurate as adults in their perceptions and memories of a criminal event.

A child's memory for events improves with age and is affected by how he or she is questioned. A highly structured, concrete format leading to yes-or-no answers produces more accurate memories than the free recall format, especially for three-year-olds. Questions that tap into recognition memory in children produce the most accurate results. Finally, research on age differences in eyewitness memory suggests that memory may be a problem only among very young children (three-year-olds) but not among older children (six-year-olds).

One major area of concern is that children may be more suggestible and more likely to be influenced by leading questions. Research suggests, once again, that younger children (three- to four-year-olds) are more suggestible than older children (five- to six-year-olds). Additionally, the suggestibility effect is increased if anatomically correct dolls are used as part of the questioning protocol. Although children are generally more suggestible than adults, recent evidence suggests that adults can also have false memories suggested or implanted. However, children are more suggestible if the event is stressful, the interviewer is high status, the children were passive observers of the event, and they are asked about specific objects rather than the temporal sequence of events.

Because of the possibility that an individual may be falsely convicted of a crime on the basis of eyewitness identification, expert witnesses are sometimes used to "educate" the jury about the frailties of the eyewitness (attention, perception, and memory). Additionally, experts can also help the legal system reduce the number of erroneous identifications made by eyewitnesses during the investigative phase of a case. Experts can evaluate various system variables (e.g., questioning tactics, lineup procedures) and suggest procedures that will minimize errors. Research shows that, in some areas at least, experts do provide jurors with information they had not known earlier (e.g., the weapon focus effect). Research also shows that an expert makes jurors more critical of eyewitness testimony without making them overly skeptical. Overall, the benefits gained by having an expert present appear to outweigh any potential negative side effects.

Legal scholars and psychologists have debated the impact of the *Daubert* decision on the use of experts in eyewitness cases. This decision permitted the trial judge much more leeway than he or she previously enjoyed in deciding what scientific testimony to admit in court. A central question is whether there is sufficient scientific evidence on which to base firm conclusions about eyewitness identification. There is general agreement, based on over 20 years of eyewitness research, on a number of findings, including but not limited to the following areas: that the accuracy-confidence relationship is weak, that instructions to eyewitnesses can bias their lineup choices, that eyewitnesses have difficulty with cross-race identifications, and that stress levels affect performance. Jurors tend not to place undue belief in expert witnesses. This is most likely because jurors perceive that experts are brought in by one side or the other to make a point and that there is much disagreement among experts in various professions. Most jurors believe that each side can hire someone to support that point of view.

CHAPTER 9

The Presentation of Scientific Evidence

The legal system has had to deal with scientific evidence throughout the twentieth century. The advent of fingerprinting and ballistic sciences are past examples of the law's encounter with new scientific advances. After some initial resistance, these methods are now fully and unquestioningly accepted in the courtroom. However, as Saks and Koehler (1991) have noted, many other scientific tests were initially accepted and then discarded. Some twenty years ago, for instance, a small number of experts were able to introduce voiceprints into some courts as valid evidence. Later, the National Academy of Sciences found the technique to be unsupported scientifically and voiceprints are no longer admitted into evidence.

Several recent issues have been problematic for the courts. These include the use of DNA "fingerprinting," the role of the polygraph ("lie detector"), the use of probability statistics, and evidence concerning the state of mind of the defendant, all of which have both statistical and psychological underpinnings. We consider each of these issues in this chapter.

DNA ANALYSIS IN COURT

The techniques concerning DNA are relatively new to forensic science although not to molecular biology. The Federal Bureau of Investigation and numerous states are compiling DNA databases so that unknown DNA samples may be matched against the known samples of criminals. Illustrating the potential of DNA analysis, in a recent case in Oregon, a sample of skin taken from underneath the fingernails of a murder victim was sent to the state laboratory in Portland and a DNA match was found in a database, leading to the arrest of a suspect (Kirkpatrick, 1995).

DNA Testing

DNA analysis is based on fundamental biological principles of broad genetic variability among humans and the presumed uniqueness of each person's genetic makeup, identical twins excepted (McKenna, Cecil, & Coukos, 1994). The dominant procedure in isolating and analyzing DNA samples is RFLP, or restriction fragment length polymorphism, a technique of genetic fingerprinting or forensic DNA analysis. Briefly, the procedure operates along the following lines. In the first step, a known sample obtained from the suspect is matched against a DNA sample obtained from the crime scene. The aim is to compare the two samples of **DNA,** the long, coiled molecules that constitute the genes found in the nuclei of cells. The ultimate goal is either to support or refute the claim that the suspect's blood or hair samples or semen was present at the scene of the crime.

In step two, the DNA is extracted and cut into fragments with special "restriction enzymes." All individuals have different patterns of genetic (DNA) material, producing fragments of different sizes. In step three, the fragments of DNA are sorted by size. In a process called **electrophoresis,** in which an electric current is applied to the sample, the fragments are placed on a gel and pulled through it by an electric field. The smaller fragments move faster than larger fragments. In step four, special radioactive tags chemically bond to genetic sequences found within the segments. The actual genetic fingerprinting takes place when the now untwined and spread-out DNA samples are exposed to photographic film. When this is done, the processed DNA reveals a distinctive pattern of dark lines, the so-called genetic fingerprint. The spread-out DNA, when exposed to photographic film, produces patterns sometimes compared to a supermarket bar code. Again, the effectiveness of this technique depends on having a large enough sample (McKenna et al., 1994).

There is a second DNA test, a newer method known as the PCR test, for polymerase chain reaction. Its major advantage is that PCR can use as few as 50 cells, which could be found in a tiny sample of blood, and the blood cells can be somewhat degraded. This test can determine with certainty whether a defendant's blood is not in the sample, but it is less definitive than the RFLP test in identifying whose blood *is* in the sample. In criminal cases, therefore, PCR is often more definitive in excluding a suspect than in substantiating guilt (Kirkpatrick, 1995).

The PCR test examines several distinct genes with sequences that can vary slightly from person to person. Using an enzyme that copies each gene over and over, investigators can build up enough copies of the genes to determine their sequences accurately. If the gene sequences in the tissue samples from the crime scene do not match a defendant's sequences, the cells could not have come from the defendant. If they do match the defendant's gene sequences, there is a good chance they are the defendant's cells.

The RFLP test can make a positive match of two samples with the odds of an error ranging from one in tens of thousands to one in hundreds of thousands. When the PCR test indicates a match, however, the chance that the sample came from a different person is more like one in thousands (McKenna et al., 1994). This method amounts to a spot check of two samples to look for differences. Investigators typically examine predetermined DNA sites that they know are likely to differentiate between samples. If enough genes are cut into fragments and analyzed, eventually the differences between two people will become apparent in the RFLP patterns, and the odds against two people having the same DNA pattern are astronomical. That is, a properly executed and applied DNA test can yield probabilities of one to a trillion that a suspect's blood matches the sample collected at the crime scene (McKenna et al., 1994).

Status of DNA Testing

The DNA tests are not foolproof. Defense lawyers arguing against the validity of a match with their client's sample can question whether there was enough blood (or hair or semen) at the crime scene for an extensive comparison of the DNA taken from the defendant. Defendants with resources, such as O. J. Simpson, will run their own tests to look for a mismatch that the prosecutors missed. A mismatch totally exonerates the suspect. Defendants may try to sow doubt about the recordkeeping of the sample: Was the sample tested really taken from the murder scene? Questions also exist about the calculation of odds that the sample could only have come from the suspect. Furthermore, there is always the possibility of a laboratory error and contamination of the samples (McKenna et al., 1994).

Even if the tests were done perfectly, a faint possibility remains that another person exists with blood very similar to that of the suspect. However, if enough probes are made of the DNA, contingent on having a large enough sample, this possibility can be ruled out. The actual power of any DNA analysis then depends on how many sites the DNA samples were taken from (McKenna et al., 1994).

How does the introduction of DNA matching fare under the new *Daubert* standards? *Daubert* has several prongs relevant to the introduction of new scientific evidence: peer review, testing, rate of error, and general acceptance. In *United States v. Bond* (1994), the appellate judges concluded that the underlying principles and methodology used by the FBI (in this case) to declare matches of DNA and to estimate statistical probabilities was scientifically valid. The decision in this Oregon case tracks with a ruling by an Ohio district court, which agreed that the scientific community accepted the FBI's procedures for determining a match of the defendant's DNA fragments (*United States v. Yee*, 1991).

Daubert requires only that the evidence be scientifically valid to be admitted into court. Therefore, the standard for admission is quite flexible. Judges are to rely on cross-examination and presentation of opposing evidence as well as careful instructions to the jury as the best means to attack shaky evidence (*United States v. Bond*, 1994). The *Bond* court also noted that DNA testing stemmed from a sound scientific base founded in molecular biology and related fields.

The *Bond* judges also considered the possibility that the presentation of DNA evidence by an expert would simply overwhelm the jury. Federal Rule of Evidence (FRE) 403 states that the probative value of testimony should not be outweighed by the prejudicial value of that evidence. The defendant in *Bond*, whose semen was found at the crime scene and then was matched with his sample, argued that jurors would take the match as absolute proof of guilt. The trial court, and then the appellate court, reasoned that FRE 403 would apply to Bond only if the test (DNA) would lead to a decision on an improper basis. Because the courts concluded that DNA sampling was scientifically valid and all proper warnings were given to the jury, the defendant could not claim prejudice simply because the DNA analysis might prove guilt.

Since 1988, DNA evidence has been used in court. Much controversy existed over DNA evidence in its early applications, but these controversies with regard to technique have essentially been resolved. Over 400 scientific papers have been presented, 100 conferences have been held, and a major National Research Council (NRC) study has been conducted—all on DNA evidence. DNA has been used in numerous court cases as exculpatory evidence and as a marker of guilt (Lander & Baaed, 1994). Even so, arguments still exist about laboratory reliability and police techniques in gathering samples. In addition, a theoretical controversy continues about the impact of variations in DNA structure among different racial and ethnic subpopulations. This argument, however, may not have much practical implication in the mixed population that characterizes much of the United States (Lander & Baaed, 1994).

What is the current status of DNA evidence? Two leading exponents of the use of DNA in forensics argue that there is no scientific reason to doubt the accuracy of DNA typing results, *provided that the testing laboratory and the tests used are up to the current standards of the field* (Lander & Baaed, 1994; italics added). Indeed, DNA evidence is increasingly instrumental in obtaining convictions. Furthermore, we are beginning to see cases in which exoneration is also based on new DNA evidence. An example is the case of Terry Leon Chalmers. He was released in January of 1995 after serving eight years for a 1986 rape. The release came because his lawyer had swabs of evidence tested and the results of the DNA analysis exonerated Mr. Chalmers. He had been convicted after he was identified in a lineup and a photo array by the victim. Chalmers is one of a dozen recent cases in which DNA evidence freed convicted individuals (Goleman, 1995).

THE POLYGRAPH AND THE LAW

The use of physiological recordings to make inferences about the truth of an individual's statements is the basis of **polygraph** techniques, more popularly known as "lie detector" tests. The theory behind the polygraph is quite simple: The suspect answers a number of questions; some of these are "control" questions and others are related to the crime. Responses to control questions—such as "Have you ever stolen anything?"—give investigators a baseline response rate. This baseline is used to compare the suspect's reaction to questions about the crime: "Did you steal the Queen's jewels last Sunday?" The reactions to the questions are measured by data gathered from physiological changes in the suspect: blood pressure, skin conductance, respiration rate, and blood volume.

However, it is possible that the suspect could perceive a general question—a control item such as "Have you ever stolen anything?"—as a question about the Queen's jewels, and so the baseline would not differ from the guilt-relevant items. What we really have is a test that involves an attempt at an artful interpretation of a series of physiological measures to determine whether the person has reacted more strongly to guilt-relevant items, than to control items. The assumption is that a stronger physiological reaction indicates guilt. Therefore, the lie detection procedure embodied in the polygraph rests on a number of controversial assumptions about the physiological and psychological responses to lying and the ability of the examiner to detect deception from those responses.

Polygraph Techniques

An updated variation of the basic polygraph technique described above is now known as the **Control** (or **Comparison**) **Question Test** (CQT). The CQT makes the basic assumption that guilty suspects will exhibit physiological responses to crime-relevant questions. As we noted, innocent persons may also respond to these crime-relevant questions because they are emotionally laden items ("Did you steal the Queen's jewels?"). The CQT relies on comparison questions to protect against falsely classifying a suspect as guilty (**false positives**). A typical comparison question might be this: "Before this year, did you ever do anything illegal or dishonest?" The important aspect of the test is that the examiner, by subtle means, tries to maneuver the suspect into giving a *negative* answer (denying something that must be true) to the comparison question. The rationale is that guilty suspects will exhibit a greater physiological response to the relevant question than the lie told in response to the comparison question, whereas innocent individuals will respond more vigorously to the comparison than to the crime-relevant question (Honts & Quick, 1995).

Many critics of the traditional polygraph tests argue for the use of the **Guilty Knowledge Test** (GKT; also known as the Concealed Knowledge Test), which rests on the assumption that physiological (autonomic) arousal will be elicited in a guilty party by aspects of the crime that only a guilty person would know (Bashore & Rapp, 1993; Lykken, 1981). Lykken (1981) devised the GKT in response to the problems he saw in the traditional polygraph technique. Lykken believed that the function of the test was not to learn whether the suspect lied but to determine whether the suspect was guilty or innocent. Therefore, recognition of items known only to the guilty party would produce arousal. For example, in one well-known murder case, only someone who had been at the scene of the crime could have known that the drapes were drawn in one side of the crime scene and not the other. This information would serve as the basis of a guilty knowledge question.

A variation on the GKT is the **Guilty Action Test** (GAT). Someone might possibly have guilty knowledge but might not in fact have performed the guilty action. For example, you might know that your friend was the one who stole the math test from the professor's office. If you were asked a GKT question about the stolen test, your response might suggest that you were the culprit. The GAT avoids this problem by directly probing the suspect's actions (Bradley, MacLaren, & Carle, 1996; Honts & Quick, 1995). The GKT might pose the following question: "Do you know that the murder was committed in (the house, bank, store, hotel room, service station")? The GAT would rephrase that question in the following form: "You murdered the man in . . ." (Bradley et al., 1996).

In addition to the various versions of the GKT, researchers have suggested that event-related brain potentials (ERPS) might serve as neurocognitive markers that could be used in place of current polygraphic methods (Bashore & Rapp, 1993). However, neither the technology nor the theory for why ERPS would be accurate markers of guilt or innocence are well developed at this point. In time, perhaps techniques will be found to allow these neurocognitive markers to determine accurately whether the person in question has guilty knowledge or not.

Legal Status of the Polygraph

Although research indicates that rates for detecting guilty subjects with the polygraph have ranged from 68 percent to 100 percent in various studies (Bradley et al., 1996), there is a tendency for people telling the truth to be classified as deceptive. Recall that this error is known as a false positive. Although some researchers believe the polygraph is more effective than is commonly admitted, there is general agreement that innocent suspects are vulnerable to being classified as guilty because of their overreaction to guilt-relevant items. Recent evidence suggests that some versions of the polygraph may be less prone to false positives. Honts and Quick (1995) surveyed recent studies of the efficacy of various polygraph techniques and found that the CQT produced accuracy rates ranging from 69 percent to 88 percent. Innocent suspects were misclassified from 4 percent to 15 percent of the time. Studies using the GKT had accuracy rates ranging from 80 percent to 90 percent, whereas the false positive rate was very small—from 0 percent to 4 percent. The number of studies supporting the efficacy of the polygraph, however, is relatively small, and the scientific status of the test, particularly its theoretical foundation, is still in question.

Most states do not permit the introduction of polygraph evidence in court unless both the prosecution and the defense agree. The ambivalent status of the polygraph can be seen in the actions of a magistrate (a judicial officer) in *United States v. Fred Emerson Gilliard* (1996). Initially, the magistrate, who evaluated the pretrial evidence, was willing to admit polygraph evidence under the new *Daubert* guidelines. However, on reflection, the trial judge in *Gilliard* overruled the magistrate and decided not to admit the polygraph results despite defense objections (C. R. Honts, personal communication, September 15, 1996).

True, polygraphs are not generally accepted in courts, but that does not mean they play an insignificant role in the legal system. Polygraphs are widely used in law enforcement for interrogation purposes and are used extensively by private employers (Honts & Perry, 1992).

Defeating the Polygraph

Charles Honts, David Raskin, and John Kircher (1994) were interested in determining whether the traditional (control question test) polygraph could be defeated. Table 9.1 shows a typical question series used by these researchers. The authors note that these questions are not a very effective way of interrogating the witness.

Honts and his co-workers had some subjects enact a mock crime whereas other subjects did not. Some of these subjects were trained to defeat the polygraph by using a physical technique, such as biting their tongues or pressing their toes to the floor; others were trained to use a cognitive method, such as counting backward by sevens.

TABLE 9.1 Typical Question Series Used in the Polygraph Tests for a 35-Year-Old Subject

Type of Question	Question
Introductory	Do you understand that I will ask only the questions we have discussed? (yes)
Introductory	Regarding the theft of the rare coin, do you intend to answer all the questions truthfully? (yes)
Neutral	Do you live in the United States? (yes)
Control	During the first 34 years of your life, did you ever take something that did not belong to you? (no)
Relevant	Did you take the rare coin? (no)
Neutral	Is your first name [John]? (yes)
Control	Prior to 1984, did you ever deceive someone? (no)
Relevant	Did you take the rare coin from the desk? (no)
Countermeasure	Are you doing anything in an effort to defeat or distort this test? (no)
Neutral	Were you born in the month of September? (yes)
Control	Between the ages of 18 and 34, did you ever do something dishonest, illegal, or immoral? (no)
Relevant	Regarding the rare coin that was reported missing, did you take it? (no)

Note: Expected responses are given in parentheses after each question.

Source: From "Mental and Physical Countermeasures Reduce the Accuracy of Polygraph Tests," by C. R. Honts, D. C. Raskin, and J. C. Kircher, 1994, *Journal of Applied Psychology, 70*(2), p. 254, Table 1.

Both physical and cognitive countermeasures effectively defeated the polygraph. At least 50 percent of the guilty subjects were able to defeat the test. The countermeasure worked especially well with regard to measures of cardiovascular arousal—that is, heart rate and blood pressure changes were minimal. Furthermore, examiners were not able to detect the use of these countermeasures by the subjects. Clearly, someone given even cursory training has a chance at defeating the traditional polygraph examination. Honts, Devitt, Winbush, and Kircher (1996) have shown that both physical and mental countermeasures can also defeat the Guilty (Concealed) Knowledge Test (GKT).

At this point, the use of the polygraph is in transition, both in the legal and scientific realms. Questions about the training and ability of examiners, however, and potential for abuse by both the examined and the examiners generally continue to bar polygraph evidence from playing a major role in the courtroom.

STATISTICS IN COURT

Statistical evidence has been introduced into court with increasing frequency. Scientific evidence, presented in probabilistic terms, occurs when experts present such data as DNA analysis, blood types, and fiber and hair samples (Smith, Penrod, Otto, & Park, 1996). Jurors may be told that the probabilities of someone other than the defendant possessing the same DNA configuration as the defendant is one in ten million. A witness may testify that the defendant and perpetrator share a blood type found in 20 percent of the population. This is the first level of statistical presentation in court: a simple probabilistic statement (A & B share a blood type found in 20 percent of the population).

A second level of presentation of probabilistic data, according to Smith et al., occurs when a *combination of probabilities* is tendered to demonstrate co-occurrence. For example, the defendant may share a blood type with 10 percent of the population and an enzyme with 5 percent and the expert may wish to testify that this particular combination is found in only 2 percent of the population.

The Controversy

Some legal scholars question the wisdom of permitting probabilistic data to be admitted as evidence. Lawrence Tribe has been one of the earliest and most eloquent opponents of using mathematics in courtroom decision making. He believes that the cost of using these tools far outweighs whatever benefits might accrue (Tribe, 1971). Tribe has two broad objections: Using mathematics to quantify evidentiary factors would dehumanize the trial process; and statistical data on the base-rate probability of an event's occurrence are not applicable to the case-specific focus of the trial. He suggests that jurors, faced with statistical data that appear to be overwhelming, would undermine the tendency to decide the case in a "humanizing" manner. He further says that elements of "numeracy" were present in medieval law, which emphasized the mystical qualities of numbers. This suggested, at least by implication, that the use of modern statistics is likewise an unsatisfactory approach.

Opponents of statistical utilization worry about the weighing of psychological factors in the calculus of probability. How does one weigh "intent"? How does the juror weigh the interpretation of deliberately perjured evidence, and what if this evidence is taken at face value? Opponents believe that employing a statistical calculus might lead to an idealized model of decision making in an imperfect world; they simply are uncomfortable with justice dispensed by formula.

How Jurors View Naked Statistics

William Thompson (1989a) has argued that statistical evidence should not be considered strong enough evidence to support a legal argument by itself because, if it is strong enough, the litigant does not have to provide other evidence. In other words, some legal scholars believe that you should have to bolster your statistical argument with concrete proof. Thompson's point is not that statistical evidence is not relevant, only that it is not conclusive.

Gary Wells (1992) suggested that decision makers may very well have a reasonable intuitive understanding of some **naked statistics** (numbers without verbal descriptions) but they want something more tangible. He has investigated the relationship between decision makers' evaluation of the statistical probabilities that an event occurred and their willingness to accept those probabilities as the basis for rendering a verdict. Wells, in a series of five studies, compared the judgments of trial judges, business students, and psychology students. He found that the subjects' evaluations of statistical probabilities (their "subjective" probabilities) closely matched the true mathematical probabilities when there was a concrete statement that verbally described the statistic.

Wells reported an actual case in which an application for child support was denied despite a blood test that revealed a 99.8 percent probability that the man in question was the father of the child. The expert testifying about the blood test reported that "based on a blood test that is 99.8 percent accurate, there is a 99.8 percent probability that the defendant is the father." Wells persuasively demonstrated that a more effective strategy, and one the jurors will be more willing to accept, is a reframing of the blood test result in the following manner: "Based on a blood test, I conclude that the defendant is the father." Although the two statements are statistically equivalent, there is a psychological difference. The latter statement is a statement of *belief* based on evidence of a very high probability; the former is a statement of high probability.

It could be that both jurists and psychologists are too narrow in their view of what is rational thinking. Both a scientific information processing rule for making decisions and a legalistic decision rule are rational. Each set of rules, however, has different goals. Judges and jurors, in cases in which they disagree, may reflect not different standards of rationality but simply different criteria and rules for decision. Judges tend to make decisions that follow a legal pathway, aimed at determining guilt and punishment. Jurors may use other criteria, other rules, because they may perceive their task differently. They may feel that, as laymen, they represent the community and should reflect community values in their decisions. These include sympathy, a desire for equity, and other prejudices reflecting community wishes. The fact is that naked statistics are rarely, if ever, the sole evidence with which jurors have to contend. In the paternity case noted above, the man denied paternity and the woman testified that only the man in question could have fathered the child (Wells, 1991).

Although research has long shown that jurors tend to be insensitive to base-rate data and tend not to integrate incoming evidence according to its true weight (Hogarth, 1971; Saks & Kidd, 1986), recent evidence gives a somewhat more positive view. These newer findings indicate that jurors do reasonably well in handling a variety of probabilistic data. Smith et al. (1996) found this to be so. Smith's jurors embodied a great number of individual differences, but most of them slightly underused probabilistic data, which seems like a rational response. The jurors were sensitive to the statistics presented, and they varied their verdicts in a manner that reflected general appreciation of probabilistic evidence. Again, it is likely that they use probabilistic evidence in determining the defendant's motivations and potential for committing the alleged crime rather than plugging it into an algebraic or Bayesian formula. Human behavior does not appear to approximate these formulas (Zabel, 1993). Jurors did not become overwhelmed by combined probabilistic evidence, even if some jurors did overuse that evidence. Generally, Smith's study (Smith et al., 1996) is a much more positive appraisal of juror performance than many other juror studies.

Case Law and Statistical Evidence

In *People v. Collins* (1968), witnesses described two people who robbed a woman in a Los Angeles alley as a black man with a beard and mustache and a white woman with a blond ponytail riding in a yellow convertible. After a couple matching this description was apprehended and charged with the crime, the prosecutor assumed certain probabilities for each of the individual characteristics witnesses observed (e.g., man with mustache: 1 in 4; woman with ponytail: 1 in 10; interracial couple in car: 1 in 1,000; etc.), multiplied them together, and concluded that their joint probability was 1 in 12,000,000. A mathematics instructor testified that the joint probability of a series of *independent* events is equal to the product of their individual probabilities. The prosecutor argued further that because such traits were possessed by only 1 in 12 million couples, there was only 1 chance in 12 million that the defendants were innocent of this crime (Koehler, 1992). A jury was persuaded by the statistical analysis and convicted the Collinses.

In *Collins*, the Supreme Court of California excluded as irrelevant the mathematical testimony about the probabilities of certain descriptive factors converging at one time and one place. True, the court said, there may be few such couples (a black man with a beard and mustache and a blond woman with a pony tail, riding in a yellow open car) but that did not mean that the specific couple on trial had to be the couple who did the crime.

The court also noted that there was no empirical grounding for the assumptions made by the expert. Why, for example, did the prosecutor assume that the probability of a black man having a mustache is 1 in 4 as opposed to 1 in 3, or 1 in 6 (Koehler, 1992)? Why did the prosecutor assume that the events were independent? For example, someone who has a beard would also be likely to have a mustache; a woman riding in a convertible might be tempted to tie her hair back in a pony tail. If you assume the events are not independent, then probability theory requires that you *add* the probabilities, not *multiply* them. Furthermore, the prosecutor neglected to consider the possibility that the couple might be wearing disguises and that the witnesses were not perfectly accurate in their descriptions. In other words, the data set on which the probabilities were calculated might not have been reliable. One minor change—that the car was orange and not yellow, for example—would have exonerated the couple (Kaye, 1979; Kaye & Koehler, 1991).

Koehler (1992) notes that the courts have understood the importance of *Collins.* Courts are not willing to accept statistical testimony without some empirical or evidentiary basis. The assumptions have to be spelled out and the bases of those assumptions must have empirical support (*People v. Yorba,* 1989; *State v. Stukey,* 1987).

However, it is likely that under *Daubert* more probabilistic evidence will be admitted by trial judges. Even before *Daubert,* some state courts demonstrated willingness to admit probabilistic evidence. In *State v. Briggs* (1989), a Washington appeals court ruled that it was useful for the jury to hear a physician's testimony about the probability that a stutterer would not stutter in certain situations. Apparently, the defendant, a stutterer, was not heard to stutter when he committed an assault.

What seems clear is that the hard line drawn by *Collins* is easing and the courts are more willing to consider probabilistic data, but they are still unsure of how to use this evidence. Their reluctance is partly because of the courts' unfamiliarity with quantitative techniques and partly from a block against educating judges in statistical methods, although this is changing (Kaye & Freedman, 1994).

Koehler (1992) argued that jurors' understanding of probabilistic evidence and methods can be improved. This may be done by lectures that cover the statistical concepts the jurors might confront in the trial. Whether courts would do this and whether it would truly aid jurors is problematic. What we do know is that jurors, rather than being overwhelmed by probabilistic analysis, as a general rule tend to ignore it or underuse it (Kaye & Freedman, 1994; Kaye & Koehler, 1991; Thompson & Schumann, 1987).

THE CLINICIAN IN COURT

On March 30, 1981, John W. Hinckley, Jr., stood outside the Hilton Hotel in Washington, D.C., and waited in the rain for President Ronald Reagan to appear. As the president walked toward his waiting limousine, Hinckley began firing a pistol. The president was wounded, as were several bystanders, some grievously. This horror was recorded on videotape, and millions of viewers saw the tape.

In the early summer of 1982, the trial of John Hinckley, Jr., ended in a verdict of not guilty by reason of insanity. The verdict surprised most courtroom observers along with the general public. Hinckley's behavior had been bizarre and delusional, but he had been capable of stalking the president and shooting him. Nevertheless, the verdict galvanized legislators at both state and federal levels to redefine the insanity defense and thus fundamentally alter the legal definition of insanity.

Defendant Competence in Criminal Trials

Two separate determinations face the court when the defendant's mental competence is an issue. The first determination (**competence to stand trial**) concerns the defendant's state of mind at the commencement of the trial. The second centers on the defendant's mental capacities at the time the crime was committed (**criminal responsibility**).

With respect to competence to stand trial, defendants must be able to take part in their defense, which includes communication with counsel and ability to understand the charges and the trial procedures and consequences. If defendants are intellectually or psychologically disoriented, the court will rule that they are incompetent to stand trial.

What is the result of an incompetency ruling? In *Jackson v. Indiana* (1972), the U.S. Supreme Court ruled that an individual judged incompetent should be confined in a mental facility for a reasonable period to allow for determination of the person's future mental status. If this subsequent determination suggests no substantial chance that the person will regain competence, standard civil commitment procedures must be applied.

Because the American legal system is based on the adversarial model, defendants must be able to participate competently in their own defense. Competence is required in a variety of legal actions. For example, in civil law, issues may arise concerning an individual's competence to make a contract, draw up a will, marry, testify in court, or consent to medical treatment (Ogloff, Wallace, & Otto, 1992).

We are concerned here primarily with the competence of the defendant in the criminal arena. The integrity of the legal system and the individual defendant requires competence. The U.S. Supreme Court stated in *Drope v. Missouri* (1975) that the prohibition against trying an incompetent defendant is basic to the adversarial system. The Court indicated that to do so (convict an incompetent) violated due process. In essence, the definition of competence for the criminal defendant is whether the defendant has enough present ability to confer with his or her attorney with "a reasonable degree of rational understanding" and whether he or she understands the facts of the case and can relate to those facts in a rational manner (*Dusky v. United States*, 1960). A mental health professional may be called on to determine the defendant's competence to stand trial. There is some evidence that defendants with experience in the criminal justice system have learned how to modify their responses to standard interviews in order to be categorized as incompetent (Gothard, Rogers, & Sewell, 1995). Researchers are currently devising better methods to detect malingering in competency evaluations (Gothard, Viglione, Meloy, & Sherman, in press). However, as Ronald Roesch and his co-workers observed, there may not be a direct link between psycholegal concepts such as competence and clinical assessment procedures (Roesch, Hart, & Zapf, 1996).

Richard J. Bonnie (1993), in a careful examination of the concept of competence, notes that "competence" is an ambiguous standard. It depends on a number of interactive factors, including, but not limited to, the seriousness and complexity of the charges and facts as well as the skill and patience of the attorney. Bonnie (1993) discerned three independent reasons for barring an incompetent person from being tried. The first is a violation of the dignity of the system and the individual when defendants lack a rudimentary understanding of the case. A second reason is that a trial of an incompetent is a threat to the reliability of the system as we cannot be sure that the defendant could convey all the important facts, some of which may be exculpatory. In other words, the outcome would be untrustworthy.

TABLE 9.2   Aspects of Two Types of Competence in Criminal Defense

Competence to Assist Counsel
- Competence is a basic requirement.
- Incompetence prevents a trial.
- Competence maintains the dignity of the judicial process and the reliability of the verdict.

Decisional Competence
- This ability is independently significant only if defendant is competent to assist counsel.
- Competence is required only when decision must be made by defendant.
- Competence promotes interest in independent decision making by defendant.
- Abilities required depend on complexity of the decision-making context.
- Incompetence *does not preclude adjudication.*

Source: Adapted from "The Competence of Criminal Defendants: Beyond Dusky and Drope," by R. J. Bonnie, 1993, *University of Miami Law Review, 47*(3), p. 255.

Bonnie's (1993) third reason for considering competence essential derives from the legal rules mandating that defendants have "decisional competence" to determine the value of choices made on their behalf. For example, someone who pleads guilty must have some competence to understand what the plea means and the implications of such a plea. Table 9.2 details the two areas of competence in criminal trials: The first is competence to assist one's attorney; the other is the ability to make competent decisions.

Competence and the Ability to Consult with the Attorney.   How often do attorneys encounter clients whom they consider to be incompetent and what do the attorneys do about this state of affairs? Norman Poythress and his co-workers examined this issue in a public defender's office. In three studies, these researchers found that from 8 percent to 15 percent of the time, attorneys had expressed concern about the competence of their clients who faced serious charges (Poythress, Bonnie, Hoge, Monahan, & Oberlander, 1994). Generally, attorneys tended not to seek evaluation by a mental health professional. They may not want to undergo the effort of a formal hearing on competence or perhaps they believe it is difficult to obtain an evaluation that will confirm incompetence. In other words, proving incompetence may cost too much and take too much time and effort.

The fact is that most evaluations determine that the defendant is competent to stand trial (Nicholson & Kugler, 1991). Attorneys quite rationally try to get around their client's cognitive or emotional infirmities by getting the individual's family or friends to help in the defense. So the attorney prong of the competency issue may simply be determined by how tolerant the lawyer is concerning the eccentricities of the client.

Competence to Make Decisions.   Appelbaum and Grisso (1995) have specified the bases of decisional competence in criminal cases. They suggest that decisional competence includes the ability to do the following:

1. Communicate a choice (preference test)
2. Understand information (understanding test)
3. Appreciate the importance of that information with respect to one's own situation (appreciation test)
4. Be able to reason about that information (reasoning test)

One task is not necessarily more important than any other, nor does it preclude any other. For example, defendants might be able to reason about information but not fully appreciate what it implies for their defense.

In summary, when criminal defendants, because of mental illness or some other mental defect, are unable to comprehend the proceedings and cannot communicate with their counsel, they are ruled incompetent to stand trial. If this occurs, the proceedings are suspended until treatment can improve the defendants' condition so they may participate in their own defense (Winick, 1995).

Assuming that the court is convinced of the criminal defendant's competence, a second issue may arise as to the defendant's state of mind at the time the crime was committed (criminal responsibility). Criminal law requires that the defendant (generally) must have a blameworthy (culpable) state of mind when the act was committed. In other words, committing a prohibited act is not sufficient for criminal prosecution. The individual must have had some degree of awareness of the facts that make the conduct criminal (Robinson, 1993). The sanity of the defendant at the time of the criminal act is the determining factor in deciding criminal responsibility and the ultimate legal consequences of that act.

The Insanity Defense

A successful insanity defense will result in the defendant's being judged "insane" and not responsible for the criminal act. Treatment for the incapacitating mental state rather than punishment for the crime will be the consequence of such a determination.

The insanity defense exists in law because society is morally persuaded that it is unjust to punish someone unless he or she is responsible for the act in question. Society does not allow punishment where it cannot find the individual blameworthy. The history of society's recognition of these simple moral imperatives is long and unbroken. Certainly the Romans recognized that individuals at times did not have power over the workings of their mind. They suffered from **non compos mentis**—not having mastery of mind. As Robinson (1980) writes in his treatise on insanity and responsibility, synonymous with *non compos mentis* were the *fanaticus* and *furiosus*, all three descriptions suggesting a raving, raging beast. A responsible person was capable of having intended a course of action and of being cognizant of this connection. The *furiosus* is not responsible, for he or she does not have power over the mind, and lacking such power, cannot be held criminally responsible. That is, the *furiosus* lacks the essential condition for criminal responsibility, *mens rea,* the guilty mind (Robinson, 1993).

Modern Standards of Insanity. In 1800, James Hadfield was charged with high treason after he attempted to kill the English king, George III. Robinson (1980) calls *Hadfield* perhaps the most significant case in the modern history of the insanity plea. Hadfield had apparently been convinced by a friend that the Second Coming was indeed at hand and the current king was a disgrace. Given this revelation, Hadfield attempted to do away with the monarch. In Drury Lane, he took a shot at George III and missed.

Hadfield's counsel, Erskine, suggested to the jury that if Hadfield was impelled by a "morbid delusion," he was then "under the uncontrollable dominion of insanity" (cited in Robinson, 1980, p. 42). Erskine's adversary argued for the wild beast criterion (furiosus) and rejected the argument that any incompetence can allay responsibility. Hadfield's attorney pointed out that his client had served his king and in that service he had taken a gunshot wound to the head. Expert testimony was given to establish that such an injury could cause damage to the brain. Indeed, such a "medical model" of insanity was well accepted at the time (Robinson). The judge called a halt to the proceedings and directed that Hadfield be acquitted and sent to an institution.

If the Hadfield case initiated the revolution against the Roman concept of insanity, the *M'Naghten* case in 1843 was the major battle. *M'Naghten* once and for all established the primacy of the medical model. Daniel M'Naghten shot and killed Edward Drummond, the secretary of Prime Minister Robert Peel (he was aiming for Peel).

However, M'Naghten's acquittal by reason of insanity did not sit well with either the queen or the House of Lords. Their interest in the case, and the interrogatories the lords submitted to the judges in the case, give us a glimpse into the thinking behind the verdict. Lord Chief Justice Tindal, speaking for the court, held that to establish the defense of insanity, it must be proved that the individual, at the time of committing the crime, was acting under such a defect of reason, deriving from disease of the mind, as not to know "the nature and quality of the act he was doing," or, if that person did know, "that he did not know he was doing what was wrong" (cited in Dix, 1981).

Tindal's comments gave us the famous dictum that if the accused did not know right from wrong and was so morally impoverished because of disease, then that person was insane. Of course, there would be no way, a priori, to determine whether the individual was diseased prior to the act. Tindal could only infer from the crime, and the explanation of the accused, that disease was present. There was no obvious physically deformed structure (in the brain) for Tindal to examine.

It is clear, then, that the general standards used to determine insanity have been stated since at least the beginning of the nineteenth century. The

M'Naghten rule indicates that the defendant will be adjudged not responsible if the act was done while the individual was "labouring under such a defect of reason, from disease of the mind, as not to know the nature and quality of the act he was doing; or if he did know it, that he did not know he was doing what was wrong" (Dix, 1981, p. 7).

However, as understanding of human psychology increased, the M'Naghten standard came under fire. M'Naghten emphasizes the defendant's *cognitive* defects ("defect of reason . . ."). As early as 1887, according to legal scholar Paul Robinson (1993), the issue of *emotional* defects was brought up. Eventually a second standard arose against which the insanity defense may be adjudged, and that is the "irrestible impulse" formulation. In this conception of insanity, a person may have been aware of the moral and legal wrongfulness of the act but could not resist the impulse to commit it. The irresistible impulse formulation was used in conjunction with other standards of insanity and was never the sole basis for a successful insanity defense.

A third standard that has evolved into common usage in the last few decades is from the Model Penal Code of the American Law Institute (ALI) published first in 1956. In the ALI formulation used in federal courts, a defendant would be able to sustain a successful insanity defense if the evidence demonstrated a lack of "substantial capacity either to appreciate the criminality of his conduct or to conform his conduct to the requirements of the law due to mental incapacitation." Notice that this standard backs away from the absolute nature of the earlier criteria. That is, the ALI standard suggests that there are varying degrees of mental incapacitation. Under the ALI standard, the chances of a successful insanity defense increased (Golding, 1992).

The Public's View of the Insanity Defense.   The public view of the insanity defense is one of, at best, skepticism and, at worst, outright distrust. Hans and Slater (1983) and Hans (1986) surveyed Delaware residents before and after the Hinckley decision. They found that 73 percent of the sample would have found Hinckley guilty and thought the *not guilty by reason of insanity* (NGRI) verdict was unfair. Only 8.5 percent of the people felt the actual verdict was very fair.

The public believes that psychiatry is not very good at determining who is mentally ill. Only 12 percent of the sample that Hans and Slater surveyed had confidence in the abilities of psychiatrists. Two-thirds thought that "the insanity defense is a loophole that allows too many guilty people to go free." In fact, however, 71 percent of the sample could not give one element in the legal test for insanity, such as that the defendant "can't tell right from wrong" or "has a mental defect." The public does not appear to have a firm grasp of the details, but knows what it does not 1ike.

Michael Perlin (1990) observed that there are several assumptions and beliefs underlying the public's antipathy to the insanity defense. First, people believe that the defense is regularly used and juries are easily conned into accepting it. Second, mental illness is not observable and thus appears less objectively determined than physical illnesses. Third, if the criminal does not seem to be "crazy," then the public is not likely to give credence to an insanity plea. It may be that jurors follow their own intuition in such matters. They tend to follow the "fireplug rule": "Jurors think you're sane unless you think you're a fireplug or swinging from trees." Indeed, in the Hinckley trial the prosecutor often appealed to this "rule." The prosecutor suggested that since Hinckley had passed a number of college courses and was able to navigate his way from New York City to Washington, D.C., he was legally sane.

What is the truth of the matter? What type of individual mounts a successful insanity defense? Is this defense a refuge for scoundrels? The data show that those most likely to plead insanity are individuals who are poorly educated, have few personal resources, and have extreme psychiatric disorders (Nicholson, Norwood, & Enyart, 1991). One study indicated that most defendants found not guilty by reason of insanity (NGRI) have been admitted to the hospital at least once, often several times, before pleading NGRI at trial. They also have previous arrest records. Their psychiatric disorders are almost always diagnosed as some variant of schizophrenia (Nicholson et al., 1991; Steadman et al., 1994). In reality, it appears that most cases involving disordered defendants are settled informally among the judge and the parties.

What are the empirical findings with regard to the use and misuse of the insanity defense? The lay public overestimates the use and the success of the insanity plea and misunderstands the consequences of a successful plea (Silver, Cirincione, & Steadman, 1994). Eric Silver and his colleagues compared the public's notions of the insanity defense with data they had gathered from eight states and close to 9,000 defendants who were acquitted based on an insanity defense (NGRI). These researchers also checked over one million records of felony indictments in those eight states to determine the frequency of use of the insanity defense. Table 9.3 presents the major findings of this research.

Note the differences between the public's perception of the length of incarceration of insanity acquittees (21.8 months) and the actual state of affairs (32.5 months). Note as well that murderers spend considerably longer in a mental hospital than do other acquittees. It is possible that murderers are more disturbed than others or it may be that the severity of the crime, independent of the acquittee's mental status, determines the length of incarceration. Whatever the reasons, the primary determinant of the length of incarceration in a mental institution is clearly the seriousness of the offense for which the insanity acquittee was found not guilty (Silver, 1995).

Why do these differences exist between public perceptions and actual facts? Silver et al. (1994) suggest that the discrepancies are the fault of bad reporting by the media. The news reports generally link mental patients and violent crime, and therefore the frequency with which the two (violence and mental illness) are perceived to be related is higher than is actually the case. There does appear to be a small but definite relationship between mental illness and a tendency toward violent behavior (Silver et al., 1994). However, the relationship is less strong than the public thinks.

TABLE 9.3   Public Perceptions Compared with the Actual Use of the Insanity Defense

	Public Perception	Reality
A. *Use of the insanity defense*		
Percentage of felony defendants pleading insanity	37%	0.9%
Percentage of acquittals when using insanity plea	44%	26%
B. *Outcome for successful insanity defendants*		
Percentage of insanity acquittees sent to a mental hospital	50.6%	84.7%
Percentage of insanity acquittees set free	25.6%	15.3%
C. *Months in confinement for insanity acquittees*		
All crimes	21.8 months	32.5 months
Murder	————	76.4 months

Source: Adapted from "Demythologizing Inaccurate Perceptions of the Insanity Defense," by E. Silver, C. Cirincione, and H. J. Steadman, 1994, *Law and Human Behavior, 18,* p. 67.

In any event, the insanity defense does not seem to be a loophole for cunning defendants. Nor is it a loophole for the rich. It appears that most individuals who employ the insanity defense are poor and uneducated and unemployed (Nicholson et al., 1991). Finally, pleading insanity and being found guilty (i.e., an unsuccessful insanity defense) has some additional costs. The unsuccessful insanity defendant gets a 22 percent increase in confinement time compared to defendants who did not raise the insanity defense (Silver, 1995).

Contemporary Trends.   The force of contemporary (post-Hinckley) trends is to reduce the possibility that a successful insanity plea can be mounted. Some legal scholars believe that one of the most critical changes in the approach to the insanity plea in recent years pertains to the change in which side bears the burden of proof (Golding, 1992). Many states have shifted the burden. Prior to these changes, the rule was that once the defense has successfully initiated the insanity defense, the prosecution has the burden of showing that the defendant was sane at the time the criminal act. This held for federal courts and about half the state courts. In the remaining states, the burden for proving insanity rested with the defense. That is, the defendant must prove that she or he is insane. All the prosecution must do is provide sufficient evidence for a jury to discern a degree of "sanity" in the defendant's behavior. The suggestion here is that this shift in the burden of persuasion makes it more difficult to carry a successful insanity defense.

The change in the burden of proof is but one procedural alteration that reflects the underlying force motivating such changes. That force is the public's—and the lawmakers'—profound distrust of the insanity defense. Again, the public's consternation with the insanity defense can be traced directly to the Hinckley trial in 1982. Hinckley clearly shot the president. In a nation in which the political process has been subverted too often by assassination, the people deemed it important to make certain that the culprit did not "get off." And yet, it appeared that the defendant, backed by his family's considerable fortune and a number of highly credentialed expert witnesses, did "get off." (Note that as these lines were written, Mr. Hinckley was still a resident of St. Elizabeth's Mental Hospital in Washington, D.C.).

Guilty but Mentally Ill (GBMI).   Another far-reaching change in the evolution of the legal system's treatment of the insanity defense is the provision of a "guilty but mentally ill" plea. GBMI is an alternative verdict to NGRI. Steven Golding (1992) observes that the basic aim of the GBMI alternative is to make winning an NGRI acquittal more difficult. Again, this shift is in keeping with the contemporary trend to reduce the possibility of an NGRI verdict.

What is the GBMI alternative? Compare the State of Illinois's NGRI instructions with the same state's GBMI instruction presented in Table 9.4. The first thing to note about the GBMI instruction is that in reality it is simply a guilty verdict (Golding, 1992). GBMI means the jury believes that the defendant is mentally ill but not insane. It does not mean that the defendant will get special treatment because of his or her mental infirmity. It simply means that the defendant will go to jail. No state provides for special mental treatment nor have the courts ruled that such special treatment is required for such defendants (Golding & Roesch, 1987).

TABLE 9.4   Definitions from Illinois Statutes of Murder, Not Guilty by Reason of Insanity (NGRI), and Guilty but Mentally Ill (GBMI)

- *Murder:* A person commits murder if, in performing the acts which cause the death: 1) He either intends to kill or do great bodily harm to that individual or another; or 2) He knows that such acts create a strong probability of death or great bodily harm to that individual or another. (Illinois Revised Statutes, 1985, Chapter 38, Section 9.1)
- *NGRI instructions* (American Law Institute [1962] formulation and Illinois law): A person is insane and not criminally responsible for conduct if at the time of such conduct, as a result of mental disease or mental defect, he lacks substantial capacity either to appreciate the criminality [wrongfulness] of his conduct or to conform his conduct to the requirements of law. (Illinois Revised Statutes, 1985, Chapter 8, Section 6-2.[a])
- *The alternative GBMI instruction* (adding a GBMI clause to the traditional ALI instructions): A person who, at the time of the commission of a criminal offense, was not insane but was suffering from a mental illness, is not relieved of criminal responsibility for his conduct and may be found guilty but mentally ill. (Illinois Revised Statutes, 1985, Chapter 8, Section 6-2.[c])

Experimental research suggests that adding a GBMI alternative to the traditional "not guilty" and NGRI options makes obtaining an NGRI outcome more difficult. Caton Roberts, Erica Sargent, and Anthony Chan (1993) have reported that when the GBMI alternative is available, mock jurors are likely to choose the NGRI option only if they believe the defendant totally lacks moral/cognitive capacities. It is probable that the GBMI alternative is seen as a lessening of blame and responsibility attributed to the defendant. Roberts's data suggest that jurors did not wish to punish the GBMI defendant significantly—certainly not as much as if they returned a guilty verdict. It does seem that the true nature of the GBMI alternative is not fully conveyed by the judicial instruction to the jury.

Norman Finkel has shown that the jurors' own construals, their understanding and interpretations of the insanity categories, are prime determinants of their decisions (Finkel, 1991; Finkel & Handel, 1989). Finkel and Slobogin (1995) note that jurors' attributions of responsibility for the offense and for the defendant's mental instability play dominant roles in verdicts. Therefore, policymakers must be aware of how jurors construe insanity so they can provide jurors with comprehensible definitions of legal insanity (Finkel & Slogobin, 1995).

Abolishing the Insanity Defense

A final tactic in the attack on the insanity plea is to abolish the insanity defense entirely. In 1994, the U.S. Supreme Court let stand a Montana Supreme Court ruling that abolished the insanity plea in that state (*Cowan v. Montana*, 1994). In addition, Idaho and Utah have also abolished the insanity defense. Several other states are considering following the actions of those three. Many of these legislatures are considering a variant of the GBMI alternative called "insane, but guilty."

Several prominent psycholegal experts do not feel that this trend is a significant one but that it does reflect the public's continuing distrust of the insanity plea and of mental health experts (Monahan & Walker, 1994b). The controversy about the insanity defense is fueled by perceptions of increasing societal violence, crime, and lack of individual responsibility. Furthermore, the lack of full information concerning the insanity plea, and mental illness in general, makes the defense an easy target.

Civil Commitment and the Prediction of Dangerousness

We saw earlier that if a defendant is found not competent to stand trial, standard civil commitment procedures must be instituted. Emergency detention in a mental health facility usually occurs without resort to courtroom procedures. If, for example, a person has been in the habit of disturbing the peace of the neighborhood in the evenings by firing a weapon into the air while wearing nothing but his shorts and jogging shoes, it is quite probable that a police officer will take that individual for examination to the local mental health facility. The night jogger's relative, as an "aggrieved" person, may also institute a petition for civil commitment. It is true, however, as Linda Teplin has shown, that many severely disordered individuals are sent to jail rather than to mental facilities (Teplin, 1983; Teplin, 1990a, 1990b).

When the individual is sent to a mental facility, he or she will be examined by one or two medical doctors, depending on the requirements of the jurisdiction, and may be involuntarily detained for a specified time. Most states do not require judicial approval for emergency detention.

Following is a general description of what happens to the civil detainee although variations among states are rather expansive. Procedures may vary, but the detained individual is usually given a preliminary hearing within a specified time, ranging from 24 hours to 20 days. A demonstration of mental illness is not a sufficient reason for involuntary civil commitment. An individual must be shown to be mentally ill and to meet one other criterion before involuntary commitment can be imposed. Among the criteria used to determine the need for involuntary civil commitment are these:

1. The individual is deemed to be dangerous to himself and others and is likely to behave in a dangerous manner.
2. The individual is so incapacitated that he or she is unable to provide for basic personal needs.
3. The individual does not have sufficient capacity to decide whether to be hospitalized (Monahan & Shah, 1989).
4. The individual is in need of treatment in a hospital.

Thus, mental illness is a necessary but not a sufficient condition for involuntary hospitalization. At least one of these criteria must be additionally applied before involuntary civil commitment can be imposed. If, after a hearing, the court orders commitment, the individual has the right to a jury trial or a court review. If, after a hearing, the court decrees commitment, a similar demand for a jury trial or court review can be made by the individual, a relative, or a friend who instituted the original petition for commitment. Again, these are general procedures that vary from jurisdiction to jurisdiction.

An individual can voluntarily commit himself or herself to a hospital. Often, however, such "voluntary" commitment occurs because of pressure from relatives or police officers who may have previously threatened the individual with involuntary commitment (Monahan & Shah, 1989). Voluntary commitment does not usually mean that release is automatic when the patient decides to leave the institution. Generally, a voluntary patient must give prior notice of intent to leave and the institution may initiate involuntary commitment proceedings.

The Prediction of Future Dangerousness and the Death Penalty

Our brief review of involuntary civil commitment procedures indicates that the law requires an analysis—a prediction—of how the person is likely to behave in the future. The civil commitment procedure emphasizes not only the person's past behaviors but also future actions (Appelbaum, 1994).

Increasingly, with the application of modern psychiatry in the courts, psychiatrists and clinical psychologists have been asked, in both criminal and civil proceedings, to make assessments of the likelihood that the individual in question will commit violent acts in the future. In essence, the clinician is asked to predict the person's future dangerousness if that person should be released from custody.

Prediction of future dangerousness is the principal criterion in involuntary civil commitment procedures. Criminal cases involving prediction of future dangerousness, including death penalty cases in some states, are perhaps less numerous, but no less dramatic. The psychiatric establishment of a future likelihood to do harm would deprive the individual not only of liberty but of life itself. It is reasonable to ask, then, how good the predictions of the experts are in these matters.

Consider for a moment Dr. James Grigson, known by the chilling sobriquet "the killer shrink." Dr. Grigson was the examining (state-appointed) psychiatrist in *Estelle v. Smith* (1981). He interviewed defendant Ernest Smith before the trial to ascertain Smith's competence. Smith's attorney in fact never raised the issue of competence to stand trial, nor was the attorney informed of the psychiatric interview. In any event, Smith was not informed of his rights, specifically that his responses to Dr. Grigson's questions could be used against him at the trial.

In Texas, where Smith committed murder, as in many other states, capital cases require bifurcated proceedings: The first trial determines guilt or innocence; the second deals with the penalty. In *Estelle v. Smith* (1981), one of the issues in the penalty trial was the probability of Smith's future dangerousness. Grigson, on the basis of his 90-minute pretrial interview, testified that Smith constituted a continuing threat to society. The information was obtained from Smith when he was without benefit of counsel and did not suspect that his responses to a professional psychiatrist would lead to a decision that mandated the death penalty. Dr. Grigson was certain that Smith was not amenable to treatment and would "certainly" commit acts of violence in the future. The jury returned a verdict mandating capital punishment.

In the American Psychiatric Association's (APA) amicus curiae (friend of the court) brief in *Estelle v. Smith,* a dim view was taken of Dr. Grigson's actions. Furthermore, the APA suggested in its brief that "psychiatric testimony on the issue of future criminal behavior only distorts the fact finding process." The APA brief further suggests that if these are indeed important facts to be presented to a jury, then a lay witness ought to present this evidence to the court so that "the mantle of professional expertise" is removed. The data gathered by the APA revealing that predictions as to future violence and dangerousness of a particular individual are "fundamentally of a low reliability, primarily because such judgments are predictions of rare or infrequent events" (*Estelle v. Smith,* 1981, p. 455). True, if one knew that an individual had committed acts of violence in the past, a fair prediction would be that the person is likely to do so in the future. The APA brief indicates, however, that given such base-rate data, one need not be a professional to make such a prediction. Curiously, defendant Smith, prior to his murder conviction, had no history of violence. In essence, the brief stated that psychiatrists do not have the expertise to predict future dangerousness.

Dr. Grigson was subsequently removed from membership in the American Psychiatric Association because of his methods of predicting future dangerousness, "which went way beyond the bounds of what anyone could purport to know" (Appelbaum cited in Vincent, 1996, p. 9). Grigson had been the forensic expert of choice of prosecutors in Texas. By 1989, he had testified in fully one-third of all cases involving the future dangerousness of convicted murderers (Vincent, 1996). Grigson once ranked a defendant a "12" on a 1 to 10 scale of sociopathic tendencies (Vincent, 1996). It appears, however, that his popularity as witness in "future dangerousness" cases has diminished considerably. This is due in part to his controversial status but is also due to the new tactic of asking an assistant district attorney to convince the jury to impose a death sentence. Prosecutors, at least in Texas, would prefer to use prior convictions, testimony from neighbors, and similar evidence rather than call a psychiatrist and "get into that rat's nest" (Vincent, 1996, p. 10).

Defense lawyers have used research that demonstrates the inaccuracy of predictions of dangerousness to support the contention that these decisions are inherently arbitrary (Loftus & Monahan, 1980). Early research by Monahan (1978) showed that follow-up studies of one to five years after arrest, confinement, and release show that at least 66 percent of the predictions of dangerousness were incorrect. At times, the predictions were 90 percent incorrect. The errors were false positives—that is, individuals predicted to be violent were not.

Inaccurate Predictions and the Death Penalty. The courts and jurors seem more willing to overlook the apparent unreliability of predictions of future dangerousness in civil commitment procedures than in capital cases. In *United States ex rel Mathew v. Nelson* (1975), a case involving involuntary civil commitment, evidence that showed the lack of reliability and validity of future dangerousness predictions was dismissed by the three-judge panel. The judges ruled unanimously that commitment would be appropriate even if the mental health professionals who had committed Nelson did not know of a single past overt act of violence on which to base their predictions.

In contrast, Loftus and Monahan (1980) reported that in capital cases in which evidence on the lack of predictability of violent behavior was introduced, none of the defendants was sentenced to death. They recounted a case in which a jury convicted a defendant of premeditated murder, then was unable in the penalty phase to agree to the death penalty. The one juror who refused revealed that he was disturbed about the unreliability of predictions of future violence.

The issue of psychiatric testimony in death penalty cases has become important with increased use of the bifurcated trial, in which jurors, after deciding on a verdict, recommend punishment in a separate trial. The U.S. Supreme Court in *Burch v. Texas* (1976) stated that the death penalty may be based on predictions that certain classes of convicted murderers will persist in their violence if not executed. In *Estelle v. Smith* (1981), the Court refined the consideration of dangerousness in capital cases by requiring the defendant to be warned that material from a psychiatric interview could be used against him.

Evidence about the unreliability of psychiatric predictions seems to be very influential in capital cases for three reasons. First, civil commitment does not, or may not, have the finality one encounters in death penalty cases. If capital punishment is carried out, there is no redress. Those who are convicted of murder are unlikely to walk the streets for many years, even if the death penalty is not mandated. Jurors may therefore be more willing to entertain mitigating evidence in capital cases.

Second, the Supreme Court indicated in *Furman v. Georgia* (1972), in which capital punishment was held to be a cruel and unusual punishment because of its arbitrary imposition, that empirical data were needed on this issue. This decision may have made the courts more receptive to close scrutiny of such data in other kinds of cases.

Finally, standards of proof differ in civil commitment proceedings and criminal proceedings. The standard of proof in civil commitment is somewhat less rigorous than in criminal cases, and this less restrictive standard may permit some tolerance of ambiguity in the evidence. Besides, the only evidence available in civil commitment is often psychiatric.

Assessing Predictions: Latest Trends and Current Status

John Monahan, who is directing a large-scale study of the prediction of violence in the mentally ill, has suggested that clinicians are better than chance at predicting who will be violent, but that the field lacks standard procedures and the research base needed for careful assessment of clinicians' predictions (Monahan, 1984, 1988, 1993; Monahan & Steadman, 1994). Monahan (1984) called for new research—"second generation" studies that would employ better measures for the prediction of violence and more clearly defined definitions of violence. For example, in earlier studies, the "predictor" variables tended to be factors that dealt with the individual's diagnosis and demographics such as age and sex. These predictor variables often did not include the situational aspects of the individual's life, such as amount of social support, the degree of stress, and other factors that might inhibit or elicit violence. The measures of actual violence ("criterion variables") were also usually quite narrow and may have been limited to only one (the hospital) or two contexts of the individual's life (Petrilia, Otto, & Poythress, 1994).

Based on these second generation studies, how does risk assessment (prediction of dangerousness) fare now? Recent research suggests that accuracy stops at 40 percent—or optimistically, 50 percent. Menzies, Webster, McMain, Staley, and Scaglione (1994), using a wide variety of measures and criterion variables, reported about a 40 percent accuracy rate. Douglas Mossman (1994) reanalyzed

58 data sets derived from 44 studies of violence prediction and found that mental health professionals' predictions were "substantially" more accurate than chance. The predictions were as accurate for long-term (more than a year) as for short-term (less than seven days) predictions. Mossman concluded that past behavior (past violence) appears to be a better long-term predictor of future violence than does clinical judgment. Lidz and Mulvey (1995) reported that among 357 mentally disordered emergency room patients predicted by mental health professionals to be violent, 53 percent did commit a violent act in the following months. Of those individuals thought to be nonviolent, 36 percent were found to be violent in the subsequent few months. However, the acts of the "nonviolent" patients tended to be of a less serious nature.

Note that the prediction accuracy is higher in recent studies than in the older research. It appears that clinicians are better at predicting violence than previously thought but they are far from perfect (Lidz & Mulvey, 1995). Possibly in the future, statistical instruments might be used to screen those most likely to commit future violence (Monahan & Steadman, 1994). Gardner, Lidz, Mulvey, and Shaw (1996) note that actuarial methods, based on statistics gathered from large samples, are in fact much more accurate than clinical prediction but are rarely used because they either require a number of complex calculations or are too expensive to apply. Gardner et al. have devised a simplified version of actuarial prediction that seems to work well in predicting future violence.

In addition, further research is needed to clarify the nature of the "response scale" that clinicians use to make their risk assessment. Paul Slovic and John Monahan (1995) have discovered that the measuring device selected to predict dangerousness has a profound effect on the judgments both professionals and college students make concerning future violence. If, for example, the scale has finely differentiated probabilities (1, 2, 5, 10, 15 percent, etc., probability of future violence), much lower probabilities are chosen than if the differences among the choices are larger. This finding suggests that predictors do not hold a firm concept of "probability of harm or dangerousness," with the implication that the use of quantitative judgments of future violence may not be justified (Slovic & Monahan, 1995).

SUMMARY

Complex scientific evidence is increasingly being used in the courtroom. Concern has been raised as to how this evidence should be presented to the court so that it can effectively and fairly be used by jurors.

"Genetic fingerprinting," or DNA analysis, is the procedure in which a known sample obtained from the suspect is matched against a DNA sample obtained from the crime scene. The ultimate goal is to support or refute the claim that the suspect's blood or hair or semen was present at the scene of the crime.

The DNA evidence is presented in probabilistic terms—for example, "The odds of someone else having this DNA sequence are one in one million."

Polygraph assessment is based on the psychological observations that people tend to respond physiologically to stress, and that lying, for most of us, is stressful. The polygraph takes a baseline measure of a person's physiological reactions and compares that baseline with the person's responses to critical questions. One technique used is the Guilty Knowledge Test in which the individual is asked a question to which only the perpetrator would know the answer.

Generally, many people are classified as lying when in fact they are telling the truth (false positives). Innocent people are likely to overreact to guilt-related items. Most states do not permit the introduction of polygraph evidence in court unless both the prosecution and the defense agree. Recent evidence suggests that newer polygraph techniques are more effective at distinguishing guilty from innocent suspects.

Although research has long shown that jurors tend to be insensitive to base-rate data and tend not to integrate incoming evidence according to its true weight, recent findings give a somewhat more positive view. These newer findings indicate that jurors do reasonably well in handling a variety of probabilistic data. There is a great deal of individual difference among jurors, but most of those observed slightly underused probabilistic data. Jurors were sensitive to the statistics presented and varied their verdicts in a manner that reflected general appreciation of probabilistic evidence. It is likely that jurors use probabilistic evidence in determining the defendant's motivations and potential for committing the alleged crime rather than plugging it into an algebraic formula for deciding guilt.

Finally, we considered the role of the clinician in court. Primarily, the clinician is asked to describe the mental status of the defendant because criminal law requires that the defendant (generally) must have a blameworthy (culpable) state of mind when he or she committed the act. Two separate determinations face the court when the defendant's mental competence is an issue. The first determination (competence to stand trial) concerns the defendant's state of mind at the commencement of the trial. The second centers on the defendant's mental capacities at the the time the crime was committed (criminal responsibility). If criminal defendants, because of mental illness or some other mental defect, are unable to comprehend the proceedings and cannot communicate with their counsel, they are ruled incompetent to stand trial. When this occurs, the proceedings are suspended until treatment can improve the defendants' condition so they may participate in their defense.

The force of contemporary trends is to reduce the possibility that a successful insanity plea can be mounted. Two prongs of this attack on the insanity defense are the shifting of the burden of proof to the defendant and the institution of a guilty but mentally ill (GMBI) verdict option. GMBI means the jury believes that the defendant is mentally ill but not insane. It does not mean that the defendant will get special treatment because of the mental infirmity. In addition, a few states have abolished the insanity defense entirely. Although the standards on which the mental status of the defendant is judged have changed, evidence suggests that jurors tend to use their own notions of what constitutes insanity in reaching a verdict. The clinician is asked to make probabilistic statements about the potential future dangerousness of a defendant, primarily in death penalty cases. Techniques have recently been refined that appear to improve the odds of successful clinical prediction, although it appears that statistical (actuarial) methods are more effective at making accurate predictions of future dangerousness than are clinicians.

CHAPTER
10

The Jury's Decision

At this point in our journey through the trial, the jury has heard all the evidence. We now approach the endgame, during which two major events occur. The first event is that both sides present a summation of the evidence and its implications for the verdict. These are known as closing arguments. Following the closing arguments by each side, the second event occurs: The judge will instruct the jury on the law relevant to the evidence. After the instructions are given, the case is in the jury's hands. The decision is now theirs.

Closing arguments consist of the attorneys' attempts to summarize the evidence, organize it for the jury in persuasive form, and argue its practical implications. The lawyers must leave the legal instructions to the judge, but all else is fair game. Stories, arguments from classical sources such as the Bible or literature, down-home aphorisms, or any other type of persuasive communication can be, and are, used in closing arguments. If lawyers have any inclination to perform, this is the time they do it.

The plaintiff/prosecutor proceeds first, the defendant follows, and the prosecutor has an opportunity to rebut. This order apparently gives the advantage to the prosecution. This side has the advantage of primacy from the opening statement through the first presentation of evidence followed by the first presentation of the summation. Allowing the "last word" in the form of rebuttal closing arguments raises questions about the fairness of the ordering, because the advantage of both primacy and recency are with the same side (Lana, cited in Saks & Hastie, 1978).

JUDGE'S INSTRUCTIONS TO THE JURY

Traditionally, the judge instructs the jurors at the end of the trial about the law that must be applied to the evidence the jurors have heard. These instructions emphasize both procedural issues and instructions for the verdict. Procedural issues include definitions of the standard of proof, the presumption of the defendant's innocence, and the evidence that is admissible. Some procedural issues pertain to the specific trial. For example, the jury may be instructed in how to evaluate alibi evidence if an alibi was part of the defense. The judge will also instruct the jurors on the kinds of facts that must be used to determine the verdict.

Instructions are the court's attempt to ensure that the jurors are competent to decide the case on legally relevant grounds. Of course, you may have noticed a rather intriguing problem here: Jurors are instructed at the *end* of the trial about the laws they may use to judge the evidence they have already heard—as if the court believes jurors can withhold judgment of the evidence until they hear the judge's instructions.

There are different types of judicial instructions. First, judges read instructions to the jurors from a book of pattern instructions that has been prepared for them. These are known as charging instructions, and they inform the jurors of their role, which is to apply the law as given by the judge to the facts of the case. Next, jurors are instructed about procedure. They are informed that the state has the burden of proof and that defendants, presumed innocent until proven otherwise, do not have to prove their innocence. The burden lies exclusively with the state.

Reasonable Doubt: The Burden of Proof

An important concept in the charging instructions is the notion of *reasonable doubt.* This is the level of certainty jurors must have in the defendant's guilt before they can return a guilty verdict. Jurors are typically informed that "reasonable doubt is a doubt based on reason, a doubt for which you can give a reason. It is not a fanciful doubt, or a whimsical doubt, nor a doubt based on conjecture" (Tanford, 1991a, p. 78).

How important is the concept of reasonable doubt? Does it significantly influence the jurors' decision making? As the definition above suggests, the concept of reasonable doubt has an intuitive appeal until one tries to define it in a manner that is of use to the decision maker. The U.S. Constitution does not provide a definition of reasonable doubt. The Due Process Clause, however, requires that the state demonstrate a criminal defendant's guilt beyond a reasonable doubt and trial judges must refrain from characterizing reasonable doubt in a manner that allows conviction on less evidence than required by due process (*Victor v. Nebraska,* 1994).

In civil trials, the burden of proof is defined as the **preponderance of the evidence,** a lesser standard than obtains in criminal trials (reasonable doubt). Simon and Mahan (1971) found that judges quantified the civil burden at 61 percent certainty (interestingly, the most common definition of the civil burden is 51 percent) and the reasonable doubt standard at 89 percent certainty. However, jurors in the same study did not differentiate between the two standards, assigning a 77 percent score to preponderance of the evidence and 79 percent to reasonable doubt. This result does not seem surprising considering much of the research on the effects of judicial instructions. Most studies find that instructions do not significantly affect jury understanding of relevant legal concepts, nor do they prevent juries from employing legally antithetical or irrelevant notions (Diamond, 1993; Tanford, 1991b).

Kagehiro and Stanton (1985) conducted three experiments on juror's decision making. They compared verbal definitions of three standards of proof (preponderance of the evidence, "clear and convincing evidence," and reasonable doubt) and quantified definitions of the same standards to learn the effects of each on jurors' decisions. The researchers found that legal definitions of standard of proof had no effect on jury verdicts. That is, verdicts were not affected by changes in standards of proof. However, quantified definitions (51 percent, 71 percent, 91 percent of probability of truth) had their intended effect. The difficulty of obtaining a guilty verdict increased as the probabilities increased. These probability levels were presented as floors, below which the jurors had to decide the burden had not been met. Certainty could of course exceed those minimal levels.

In the absence of very specific quantifiable definitions of reasonable doubt, it seems that jurors may not properly incorporate the concept into their decisions. Indeed, recent data suggest that some instructions may lead to the perception that jurors may vote for conviction if their subjective reasonable doubt level is set at 65 percent certainty of guilt (Horowitz & Kirkpatrick, 1996). However, at this point the courts seem resistant to any major modification of the reasonable doubt definitions. Below, we present the currently acceptable definitions of the concept as reflected by several U.S. Supreme Court decisions.

Definitions of Reasonable Doubt That the U.S. Supreme Court Has Found Acceptable

Beyond a reasonable doubt (BRD) means you have an "abiding conviction as to the defendant's guilt" (*Sandoval v. California,* 114, S.Ct., 1239, 1994).

Reasonable doubt means doubt that would cause a reasonable person to "hesitate to act" (*Victor v. Nebraska,* 1994).

Proof BRD is proof that leaves you "firmly convinced" of the defendant's guilt; if you think there is a "real possibility" that the defendant is not guilty, you must give him the benefit of the doubt and find him not guilty (Federal Judicial Center instructions endorsed by Justice Ginsburg in *Victor,* but not approved by the majority of the Court).

"If having a conviction, it is one which is not stable but which wavers and vacillates, then the charge is not proved beyond every reasonable doubt and you must find the defendant not guilty because the doubt is reasonable" (*Cage v. Louisiana,* 490, 492, U.S. 39, 1990).

Reasonable doubt means "a real doubt based upon reason and common sense after a careful and impartial consideration of all the evidence in the case" (*United States v. Daniels,* 986 F.2d 451, 457, 11th Cir., 1993).

Cautionary and Other Instructions

To increase the jurors' competence, the next section of the charging instructions informs them about the relevant law. Jurors in a personal injury case may be informed that "proximate cause is a cause which, in a natural and continuous sequence, produces damage and without which the damage would not have occurred" (Federal Rules of Civil Procedure, 1996, p. 14). Jurors may also be given cautionary instructions that relate to potential problems in interpreting or evaluating the evidence. Eyewitness testimony, for example, usually calls for cautionary instructions. Jurors are cautioned to determine whether the witness had adequate opportunity to see the defendant, or if the identification was made solely on the witness's recollection and was not influenced by subsequent interviews about the offender by police and others.

The judge may also offer *admonitions,* cautioning jurors not to use potentially prejudicial information. If the results of a polygraph test were mentioned in violation of the rules of evidence, jurors would be warned to disregard that evidence. Obviously, one purpose of admonitions is to *limit* the use of certain kinds of evidence. In a trial in which a defendant is charged with several similar crimes, *limiting instructions* may take the form of telling the jurors that they may not use evidence about one crime to decide whether the defendant was guilty of a second or third crime (Bordens & Horowitz, 1985). Similarly, in a civil trial, if several individuals (plaintiffs) sue one or more defendants, limiting instructions may inform jurors to judge each plaintiff and each defendant separately on the merits of the individual's case.

Admonitions, however, may have a paradoxical effect. When judges tell jurors they must disregard something, that admonition seems to alert them to the possibility that the forbidden evidence is crucial in some way. Tanford (1991b) suggests doing away with admonitions entirely, for they motivate jurors to do precisely what the judge does not want them to do.

Elwork, Sales, and Alfini (1982) investigated jurors' understanding of the judge's instructions and reported that only 40 percent of the jurors correctly understood the judge's instructions. Furthermore, they misunderstood some of the most crucial aspects of the law as explained by the judge. These findings suggest that although pattern instructions are legally accurate, they appear to be incomprehensible to a majority of jurors. The next section explores what courts and researchers have done about this state of affairs since the Elwork studies were published.

Making the Incomprehensible Comprehensible. Charrow and Charrow (1979), a linguist and a lawyer, rewrote a series of jury instructions in simple language with the aim of clear expression. They found that jurors understood the new instructions much better than the old pattern instructions. Elwork and Sales (1985) rewrote Michigan pattern instructions within the context of a civil trial in which fault for an auto accident was at issue. These researchers found that, compared to the clearer, rewritten instructions, the earlier instructions led jurors to discuss legally inappropriate topics and to lose sight of the important legal issues in determining negligence.

As beneficial as rewriting instructions in plain English may be, it is not the complete answer to the confusion wrought by judicial instructions. For one thing, even modified instructions contain abstract terms that are difficult for laypeople to comprehend. Jurists assume that simple legal terms are instantly understood by jurors. Not so. Reifman, Gusick, and Ellsworth (1992) reported that jurors do gain a relatively decent understanding of procedural issues (say presumption of innocence). Judicial instructions, however, because of their cumbersome, legalistic phraseology, fail to convey the important substantive law jurors must comprehend to produce a fair verdict. Jurors do not appear to understand specific and substantive instructions defining, for example, assault or criminal sexual conduct (Reifman et al., 1992).

Helping the Jury

Given the courts' general reluctance to change, although many individual judges do employ simplified language in their courts, what else may be done to help the poor juror?

Written Instructions.   Some commentators have suggested that jurors ought to be given written instructions as well as the judge's oral presentation. If jurors have instructions in written form or hear them repeated several times, their comprehension should increase. However, most studies on the effects of repetition do not use materials as complex and as lengthy as judicial instructions.

Larry Heuer and Steven Penrod (1989) provided jurors with a written copy of the judicial instructions during the jury's deliberations. This procedure was used in real trial settings for both civil and criminal cases. There is some evidence from this study that written instructions may help. Jurors who had written instructions did not argue as much about legal issues during deliberations as jurors who only heard the instructions. But there was no support for assuming that jurors given written instructions would recall more of the judge's instructions (as a measure of jurors' comprehension), and the deliberation process was no shorter than for juries without written instructions. We have no comparison of verdicts in this study because different juries heard different trials.

Pre-evidence Instructions.   A number of judges and researchers have suggested that the judge's instructions should be given *before* the evidence is presented (Smith 1990, 1991b). Although judges do give jurors general instructions at the outset of the trial to orient and socialize them to the courtroom, jurors traditionally receive the applicable case-specific law at the close of the trial and are then required to integrate these legal principles with the trial evidence to render a verdict. Trial judges, however, have full discretion under the Federal Rules of Civil Procedure (Rule 51) to present substantive (related to case-specific law) preinstruction prior to the presentation of evidence for each trial issue. Criminal court judges may also permit instructions before jurors hear the evidence.

Given that jurors in many civil and criminal trials face a complex cognitive task, how would preinstruction enhance their competence? One hypothesis is that preinstruction would help the jurors recall legally appropriate (*probative*) evidence. The known effects of preinstruction on cognitive processing, especially evidence recall, are mixed. Several studies reported that placement of the instruction did not significantly affect the jurors' correct recall of the trial facts (Scott, 1989; Smith, 1991b). In a field study, Heuer and Penrod (1989) found no difference for evidence recall between pre- and postinstructed jurors.

Conversely, Elwork et al. (1982) found indirect support for the notion that preinstructed jurors have better recall for the trial evidence. Likewise, Kassin and

Wrightsman (1979) found that jurors had slightly better recall for trial material when they had been preinstructed. Evidence reported by ForsterLee, Horowitz, and Bourgeois (1993) indicated that preinstructed jurors were better able than postinstructed jurors to identify correctly items that were part of the trial. Furthermore, when jurors were shown items of evidence that could have plausibly been part of the trial but in fact were "lures" (false items made up by the experimenters), preinstructed jurors were more likely to reject the lures—correctly—than were postinstructed jurors.

Researchers have mixed opinions about the effectiveness of preinstruction in improving jurors' *recall* of relevant evidence; there is a much stronger agreement, however, for the efficacy of preinstruction in promoting legally appropriate *verdicts.* Vicki Smith (1991b) found that jurors pre- and postinstructed in a criminal trial were more likely to apply the law correctly and were less likely to decide the case before they heard all the evidence than were traditionally instructed jurors. Marc Feldman (1978) similarly demonstrated that pre-evidentiary instruction reduced the biasing effect of the defendant's characteristics. Kassin and Wrightsman (1979) reported that jurors who were preinstructed on procedural issues in criminal trials (standard of proof) returned significantly fewer guilty verdicts than did postinstructed jurors. Although Kassin and Wrightsman did not attempt to explain the cognitive processes underlying their finding, their results demonstrate clearly that jurors receiving instructions at the onset of the trial presumed innocence whereas those who were postinstructed presumed guilt. A reasonable conclusion is that jurors who hear evidence in a legal framework created by preinstruction would have enhanced cognition.

Lynne ForsterLee and her co-workers (1993) videotaped a complex civil trial in which four individuals (plaintiffs) sued a manufacturing company for injuries they suffered when that company carelessly disposed of chemicals. Jurors generally have difficulty distinguishing among the claims presented by several plaintiffs and tend to award each of the plaintiffs a similar sum despite differences in injuries (Selvin & Picus, 1987). ForsterLee et al. (1993) found that preinstructed jurors were able to devise an accurate legal model of the evidence. When jurors were probed about the kinds of evidence they used to decide the verdict, the results showed that preinstructed jurors recalled more probative (legally relevant) evidence and less nonprobative information than jurors who were postinstructed. Also, preinstructed jurors made appropriate distinctions among plaintiffs who had different degrees of injuries. These findings and other confirmatory results suggest that preinstructing jurors enhanced their ability to apply the law to the facts of the case (Horowitz, ForsterLee, & Brolly, 1996).

The research evidence suggests that preinstructing the jury may be a way of improving jury competence. This area has a number of as yet unanswered questions, however. Some observers worry that if jurors are told what to look for before they hear the evidence, the information search will be biased (Hastie, 1983;

Heuer & Penrod, 1989). The evidence on this point is still ambiguous, and further research will be required to resolve it (Bourgeois, Horowitz, ForsterLee, & Grahe, 1995; ForsterLee & Horowitz, 1997).

JUROR DECISION MAKING

When instructions have been completed, the jury retires to the jury room to deliberate until they reach a verdict. Thus far, jurors have operated as individual information processors. They have been told not to discuss the evidence with anyone else, especially their fellow jurors. First, we examine how individual jurors deal with the evidence; then we see how jurors combine their talents to agree on a verdict.

Juror Evidence Processing: Stories and Meters

The Story Model.   People seem to integrate information by "packaging" their reasons for believing something in a form that is most persuasive and reasonable to both themselves and others. According to the **story model,** we impose a structure on complex information by creating a coherent "story" and using it to connect facts and feelings about events (Pennington & Hastie, 1986, 1988, 1992). When individuals try to understand new events or information, they have a ready-made arsenal of tools to aid comprehension. One of these cognitive tools takes the form of a narrative, a story. We are all familiar with the narrative format. A story has a beginning, a middle, and an end. There are characters—good guys and bad guys—and there are motives and reasons for behavior. All these aspects of the story—motive, characters, and themes—are woven together into a narrative. A story is an elaborate schema constructed to make sense of different pieces of information. Often the sensory impressions and pieces of evidence we get from our social world are disjointed and confusing; stories help us make sense of them. For example, imagine that you are a juror on a complex murder trial. Over the course of a week, many witnesses testify. Each of these witnesses provides evidence about various aspects of the crime. Some evidence makes you think the defendant is guilty; other evidence makes you think otherwise. How do you make sense out of such diverse information?

Studies have shown that in a complex murder case, jurors spontaneously devise a story narrative that helps them explain the evidence (Pennington & Hastie, 1986, 1988, 1992). They start to form a story fairly early. They place this story in memory; it then guides their subsequent interpretation of the evidence. In other words, the juror actively searches for evidence that fits the preferred story. The story helps the juror understand and organize incoming information. Evidence that fits the story is remembered and incorporated; evidence that does not fit is forgotten. Where the story has gaps, the jurors fill those gaps with their own interpretations and beliefs to make it more plausible (ForsterLee et al., 1993).

Jurors may consider more than one story. There are probably individual differences in the ability to consider and weigh two or more competing stories. We examine these differences shortly.

The Meter Model.   Reid Hastie (1993) surmises that prosecutors may need to move jurors only a little way from an initial 50–50 split between the prosecution and the defendant to obtain a guilty verdict. Recall that jurists assume that the level of certainty needed to convict is at least 80 percent to 90 percent. Hastie observes that the presumption of innocence leads jurors to begin with an even-handed attitude toward the evidence. Hastie suggests that the amount of evidence needed to move jurors from that 50–50 point to a guilty rating is less than experts and jurors think. Rather than having to move jurors from zero on the scale to perhaps 90 percent certainty, all prosecutors need to do is move the needle on the scale from 50 to perhaps 65 percent certainty (Hastie, 1993; Horowitz & Kirk-patrick, 1996).

Note that the view of juror decision making inherent in this argument is analogous to the movement of a needle on a meter. The meter runs from 0 to 100 percent. It is probably set at 50 percent after jurors are instructed at the beginning of the trial (presumption of innocence). The meter moves as packets or bits of evidence are presented. At some point the meter may fall into the guilty range.

What determines the guilty zone? The juror will have some criterion for when the meter indicates guilt, affected by the severity of the crime and the harshness of the potential penalty. This point may be at 65 percent or it may be higher. Individual differences are important here. Jurors who are very much concerned about violent crime may set that guilty zone at a lower point on the meter than someone who is more concerned about giving defendants due process.

Lola Lopes (1993) considers a **meter model** to be based on the idea of decision makers holding one or more meters; these continuously track and read out a value that reflects the juror's current view of the evidence. Jurors may run multiple meters at the same time. A juror could possibly have one meter for the credibility of the witness, another for the state of mind of the defendant, and so on. Assuming that many jurors use more than one meter to assess various packets of evidence, the models do not specify precisely how these meters are combined into a final decision. Perhaps each meter is weighed for its value and then combined into one final meter that determines the verdict based on the decision criterion (i.e., the value on the meter that determines guilt).

The meter model assumes that jurors first determine the implications of the evidence for the defendant's guilt or innocence. A second decision-making stage then occurs in which the juror decides whether this quantity of evidence exceeds the decision criterion to reach a guilty or not guilty verdict (Kerr, 1993). Clearly, the decision criterion is critical. If Hastie's (1993) supposition is correct, when the meter hits 65 percent, a guilty verdict ensues. Note that this (65%) probability of guilt is a much lower level than courts generally believe jurors use. Of course, the decision level will be influenced by the type of case the juror is confronting. Research indicates that the more serious the charge, the higher will be the decision criterion. Finally, the confidence a juror has in his or her decision is directly tied to the value of the evidence in relation to the decision criterion: As the value of the evidence on the meter climbs past the decision criterion, a juror's confidence in his or her decision will increase (Kerr, 1993).

Which best captures the decision making of the individual juror—the meter or the story? We agree with Lopes's (1993) view that both reflect real psychological processes. If you ask jurors after they have heard the evidence to give a verdict and assign a confidence level to that verdict, they can do so readily. This ease in assigning confidence suggests that the meter model is a reasonable analog for individual decision making (Lopes, 1993).

The observation that decision makers accumulate evidence until they reach some decision criterion does not rule out the likelihood that they use an organizing structure, such as a story, to integrate all the information. In fact, when jurors are asked to explain their verdict, the result is almost always a narrative that approximates the story model (Bourgeois, Horowitz, & ForsterLee, 1993). The value of the meter is determined almost assuredly by some underlying organization of the evidence.

Individual Differences in Processing Evidence

We ought not to assume that each juror organizes and understands evidence in the same way. Jury researchers have tended to ignore this issue of individual differences among jurors, but Phoebe Ellsworth (1993) noted that in most trials, juries are unable to come to a verdict on the first ballot. This initial inability to agree certainly suggests that different jurors perceive the evidence in different ways.

What are these individual differences? Some evidence suggests that personality attributes matter, but general support for this notion is scanty. However, one such personality attribute, the authoritarianism of the juror, has received some support. Bray and Noble (1978) reported that jurors characterized as high authoritarians and juries composed of such individuals were more likely to return guilty verdicts than were low authoritarians.

What is authoritarianism? The study of the authoritarian personality has a long history in social psychology. Adorno, Frenkel-Brunswik, Levinson, and Sanford (1950) defined the **authoritarian** as an individual who has a strong belief in punishment for those who violate social values and laws. Authoritarians tend to think in rigid categories that generate simplistic answers and demonstrate an uncritical, positive attitude toward authority figures. They are traditional, rigid, and punitive toward those who do not obey social norms. Authoritarians are likely to be strongly influenced by a judge, but they may not be able to take into account a judge's instructions to ignore inadmissible evidence. In addition to favoring the prosecution, authoritarians are also more likely than nonauthoritarians to favor the death penalty (*Witherspoon v. Illinois*, 1968).

Douglas Narby, Brian Cutler, and Gary Moran (1993) have provided substantial support for the argument that a juror's level of authoritarianism is a valid predictor of the juror's verdict. Narby et al. (1993) measured a specific type of authoritarianism: legal authoritarianism. This measure deals with an individual's attitudes concerning the trial and the legal system. For example, agreement with the statement, "If the grand jury recommends that a person be brought to trial, then he probably committed the crime," would be scored high in legal authoritarianism. In other words, **legal authoritarianism** favors the prosecution over the defense.

Narby and his co-workers analyzed 20 studies dealing with a wide variety of trials in which authoritarianism of the jurors had been recorded. Their analysis showed that high scores on legal authoritarianism are associated with a tendency to convict, especially when the crime was a serious one such as a felony (e.g., armed robbery). Their data also suggest that this effect may be stronger in the courtroom with real jurors and live trials than in mock jury studies that use college students or even members of the community as participants.

How Well Do Jurors Perform?   Authoritarianism of individual jurors probably plays a role in certain trials that makes that trait especially important or salient, such as death penalty cases (Ellsworth, 1993); another important individual difference relates to how jurors devise the story that organizes their trial information and guides their decisions. Kaplan and Miller (1978) suggested that the pre-deliberation judgment of the jurors is produced by their integrating the trial evidence with their dispositional (personality) status and extralegal information, such as their personal experience.

Kuhn, Weinstock, and Flaton (1994) asked mock jurors to view a videotaped murder trial. Participants were then interviewed in depth concerning why and how they reached their verdict and what evidence they used to do so. Kuhn et al. found that the Pennington and Hastie story model well represented jurors' decision making; but they also found considerable variations in how jurors constructed their stories. Some jurors used a "black or white" mode of reasoning called *satisficing.* These **satisficers** based their conclusions on a minimal amount of evidence, and once they drew their conclusions, they simply stopped considering any other evidence, especially evidence that might contradict what they believed.

Furthermore, these satisficers tended to make more extreme judgments about guilt or innocence than did other jurors. In essence, satisficers wanted to decide the case quickly and focused on trying to convince other jurors to change their votes. These are individuals (about a third of all participants) who approach their task with closed minds and open mouths. Note that they are important individuals in that they likely will take an active, even vociferous, role in the deliberations.

In contrast, other jurors tended to consider at least two alternative explanations (stories) of the evidence and used evidence to argue for or against these alternative stories. This more effective type of reasoning, called the **theory evidence coordination mode,** requires the construction of two or more stories that are evaluated against the incoming evidence and against each other (Kuhn et al., 1994). Thus, we find that a distressing proportion of the jurors use a simple mode of reasoning that leads to premature decision making and unwarranted certainty.

JURY DYNAMICS

The jurors, who have thus far functioned as individuals, now must retire to the jury room, pool their knowledge and talents, deliberate, and come to a verdict. How do the individual opinions of jurors become forged into a jury decision? What social psychological variables affect the jury's decision? We explore the answers to these questions next.

Size of the Jury

The number of jurors used in Henry II's jury was at least 12. The number 12, Charles Rembar (1980) speculated, seems to have some magic about it. Twelve apostles, 12 tribes of Israel, 12 patriarchs, 12 officers at Solomon's court, 12 months in a year are among the credentials 12 has as a number of unusual potency. Even in the modern age, numerology lives with us, as anyone who has tried to find the thirteenth floor of a building can attest.

The 12 good and true jurors have had to arrive at a unanimous verdict from the earliest times of judicial history. Rembar suggests that this call for unanimity reflected the mind-set of the times: dogmatic, absolutist, unable to discern shadings and degrees. A person was either guilty or not; the judgment was absolute. In any event, things rational and things less rational seem to have fixed the jury at 12, at least until the latter half of the twentieth century.

In 1970, the U.S. Supreme Court in *Williams v. Florida* ruled that 6-person juries were constitutional. Juries of 6 (or 8 or 9) persons are now commonly used in almost all jurisdictions for certain types of trials (e.g., misdemeanors and minor felonies). The logic behind the 6-person jury is that it is less costly. Also, in the eyes of the Supreme Court, the quality of the decision made by the 6-person jury is the same as that made by a 12-person jury. In *Ballew v. Georgia* (1978), Justice Blackmun, using research on group dynamics, concluded that fewer than six jurors would be unconstitutional. A majority of the Court decided that a line had to be drawn somewhere for the minimally acceptable size of the jury, and *Ballew* drew that line at six. However, a fair reading of *Ballew* would suggest that 6-person juries were no less unconstitutional than 5-person juries.

Are 6-person juries fundamentally the same as 12-person juries? Yes and no. The actual size of the jury seems to affect the outcome of a trial less than social psychologists first anticipated. It now seems likely that there are no significant differences with respect to the verdicts between 6- and 12-person juries (Hastie, Penrod, & Pennington, 1983).

However, there appear to be important differences in the way smaller and larger juries function. Smaller juries on average give the same verdicts that larger juries do, but their verdicts are less likely to match the community's average verdict. Six-person juries seem more unpredictable. Their verdicts are more variable than those of 12-person juries (Saks, 1996). Six-person juries are less likely to come to a deadlock than larger juries, and smaller juries are also less likely to represent the community fully with respect to population and opinion distributions.

Also, 12-person juries will have substantially more cognitive resources than will 6-person juries (Saks, 1996).

Decision Rules

To complicate matters, at about the same time the Court changed the potential size of the jury, it also altered the decision rules that guide juries. In *Johnson v. Louisiana* (1972) and related cases, the Supreme Court allowed for nonunanimous rulings (9 out of 12, for example) in criminal cases.

A **decision rule** is a rule about how many members must agree before the group can reach a decision. Decision rules set the criteria for how individual choices will be blended into a group product or decision. Common decision rules are majority rule (the winning alternative must receive more than half the votes), and unanimity rule (consensus—all members must agree).

Question: If our jury of 12 needs only 9 people to reach a verdict, will an initial vote of 9 to 3 end the deliberations? Perhaps the three were right and the majority would be deprived of their wisdom. No, said the Court. A mythical "conscientious juror" will not let this occur. That juror will listen to all points of view, whether or not the decision rule has been met.

Some critics of the jury have noted how difficult it is for juries in controversial cases to reach a unanimous verdict, concluding that justice could be more effectively served if courts permitted a less than unanimous verdict (Abramson, 1995). Oregon voters in 1996 passed a ballot initiative providing for an 11 to 1 vote rather than a unanimous verdict in felony trials (the constitutionality of this measure is before the courts at this writing). In fact, most juries in criminal cases do reach consensus, and only about 6 percent cannot reach a verdict. Evidence suggests that most hung juries favor conviction; therefore, changing the decision rule to 11–1 or 10–2 would clearly favor the prosecution (Abramson, 1995).

A jury that does not have to reach a unanimous decision often can spend less time discussing the evidence than a jury required to reach consensus. Does this matter, if nonunanimous verdicts are the same as unanimous verdicts in similar cases? Most citizens would say yes, it matters very much. Citizens want juries to evaluate the evidence thoroughly and to put aside personal biases. They want the composition of the jury to reflect the community's population as a whole (Tyler & DeGoey, 1996). Both smaller juries and nonunanimous decision rules seem to violate these expectations.

Conformity Pressures

In almost any group situation, conformity pressures arise during discussion. Pressure is exerted on jurors who do not agree with the majority opinion to convince them to change their views. Because 6-person juries are less representative of the community than 12-person juries, minorities are less likely to be represented on a small jury (Saks, 1996). Minority refers not only to race, sex, and ethnic origin but also to individuals who hold different or dissenting opinions.

In *Williams v. Florida,* the Supreme Court reasoned that a 5 to 1 split was equivalent to a 10 to 2 split. The lone minority member should be able to hold out at least equally as well as the two-member minority in the larger jury. However, Asch's (1951) findings would refute that logic. Asch found that if you have a "true partner"—someone who firmly supports your opinion within a group— you are more likely to hold out against the majority than if you are alone. Therefore, in the 12-person jury, a 2-member minority is in a better position to withstand conformity pressure than the 1-member minority in the 6-person group. A dissenter will have a better chance of finding support in a 12-person jury than in a 6-person jury. Second, there is a nonlinear relationship between majority size and conformity. That is, conformity pressures maximize at about 4 or 5 to 1. Psychologically, a 5 to 1 divison brings maximal pressure on the outlier, the dissenter.

The Dynamics of Deliberations

The jury represents in microcosm the quintessential democratic ideal. Jurors, particularly those who have to reach a unanimous verdict, have to engage in face-to-face debate and must put their opinions at risk (Abramson, 1995). Jurors must consider the views of others, and if they change their position, they probably do so because they have been persuaded by the power of other people's argument and the collective wisdom of the group.

What really happens during the jurors' deliberation? Three kinds of events are most prominent. First, information on guilt or innocence is exchanged, and the evidence of the case is discussed. These statements about the case have been weighted for guilt or innocence. Evidence and points of view that might not have been considered by all the jurors prior to the deliberation are now exchanged. Note that there is a tendency for members of decision-making groups to withhold information or beliefs that are not brought out by other individuals (Gigone & Hastie, 1993). Unique points of view tend to be suppressed, perhaps because individuals think that if others have not introduced them, the views may not be relevant.

Second, persuasion also takes place. This stage involves attempts to alter the values some jurors have placed on particular pieces of evidence. Third, pressures for conformity are applied: Some jurors try to make others yield to their point of view. As we would expect, in most instances the majority puts pressure on the minority. Kaplan and Scherching (l980) indicate that all three of these processes probably occur simultaneously.

It appears that jurors' confidence in their decisions grows primarily from the information exchanged during deliberation (Stasser, Kerr, & Davis, 1989). Jurors change their opinions, however, only when faced with a combination of information and pressure from other members of the jury. The results of James Davis's research on social influence during deliberations suggest an essential asymmetry in the discussion about guilt or innocence. The influence applied tends to favor a not guilty verdict rather than a conviction (Davis, Kerr, Atkin, Holt, & Meek, 1975). Investigators have frequently noted this **leniency bias** in jury decision making. Robert MacCoun and Norbert Kerr (1988) found that in criminal trials in which there is the stringent reasonable doubt standard ("you must be almost certain of the defendant's guilt"), juries that are divided on the verdict at the outset of deliberations will tend to be lenient and vote to acquit. This asymmetry in verdict outcomes (a symmetrical pattern derived from an initial even split would lead to half guilty, half not guilty verdicts) is due to the high standard of proof specified by the use of the stringent reasonable doubt requirement. In comparison, juries given a standard of proof requiring a preponderance of the evidence (the weight of evidence must favor the prosecution for a guilty verdict) and who are split to begin with produce a symmetrical pattern of outcomes: half guilty, half not guilty. Because the preponderance of evidence criterion is used in civil trials, we should not expect a leniency bias in civil cases (MacCoun & Kerr, 1988). These results emphasize the importance of deliberations in accentuating the decision-making criteria, such as the standard of proof.

Generally, deliberation brings out the facts of a case and leads to agreement about the order in which the events under consideration occurred (Ellsworth, 1989). In other words, jurors discuss the account of the case and arrange the events in some temporal order. Juries, like most decision-making groups, seem able to recognize relevant facts, correct errors, and reject implausible events with some skill (Laughlin, VanderStoep, & Hollingshead, 1991). Although, as a *general rule*, deliberations do not seem to change many votes, a change in only one or two votes can alter the outcome of a trial. Ellsworth's (1989) research suggests that what will alter the jurors' votes are new interpretations of the law. Unfortunately, juries seem not to fully comprehend the judge's instructions and the relevant law.

Prediscussion ballots are indeed predictive of the final outcome, but they should not be thought of as conclusive. Sandys and Dillehay (1995) have reported that deliberations play a significant role in shaping the verdicts of actual juries. The deliberations influence and alter initial juror ballots. In some cases, deliberations may transform the initial juror tendencies. However, the evidence concerning the importance of deliberations in determining the verdict is still unclear, as the next section suggests.

Jurors Who Loaf.　　Imagine jurors listening to a trial and feeling bored, or overwhelmed by legal terminology, or just plain sleepy in the late afternoon. One might give in to the almost irresistible temptation to let one's attention wander and rely on other jurors to remember the relevant information. A well-known aspect of group dynamics called social loafing may apply in this situation. **Social loafing** refers to the tendency of individuals to exert less effort when working on a collective task (one in which all group members' inputs are pooled) than when working coactively (each individual's input is separate). Because the jury's task is seen as a collective one (each member's input is pooled with the others' to make a single group decision), individual jurors may exhibit social loafing. They may not carefully attend to the evidence, with the expectation that they can make up for any memory lapses during group discussion, with the information provided by other jurors (Karau & Williams, 1993; Latane, Williams, & Harkins, 1979).

Consider, for example, a riveting 1988 civil trial involving a former attorney general of the United States in Washington, D.C., District Court. It was late in the afternoon and the juror with the large gold earrings was nodding off, her earrings snapping with each nod of her head. Other jurors were at various levels of consciousness. The judge stopped the proceedings and had the jurors stand, waving their arms over their heads in a judicial seventh-inning stretch. Because jurors may feel that others will pick up the slack, they may be willing to lose consciousness when boredom or luncheon carbohydrates overwhelm their attention processes—and even a sensational criminal case may not keep jurors fully attentive.

Martin J. Bourgeois and his co-workers compared "nominal" jurors, who knew they would decide the case alone without deliberations, and "interactive" jurors, who knew they would deliberate with others to reach a verdict. The researchers wanted to test the prevalence of social loafing in juries (Bourgeois et al., 1995). Their results indicate that nominal jurors provided more accurate verdicts and remembered more relevant trial information than did interactive jurors. These findings suggest that, at least in this one study, deliberations do not always increase the amount of information jurors consider, nor do deliberations necessarily result in efficient and accurate consideration of the evidence.

Majorities and Minorities.   Using a model called the social decision scheme (SDS) perspective, James Davis (1973) suggested that predeliberation majorities win and predeliberation split juries tend toward acquittal (leniency bias). We have seen that the leniency bias has been supported by subsequent research (MacCoun & Kerr, 1988). Is this an accurate capsule summary of the power of majorities? Sarah Tanford and Steven Penrod (1986) carried out a thorough examination of the impact of predeliberation majorities on the outcome of the trial as well as the direction of the deliberations. Their results show that the initial vote of the jurors was a good predictor of the final outcome. Majorities tended to win.

In the classic film *Twelve Angry Men*, Henry Fonda portrayed a juror who was firmly convinced that a criminal defendant was not guilty. The only problem was that the other 11 jurors believed the defendant had committed the crime. As the jurors began to deliberate, Fonda held fast to his belief in the defendant's innocence. As the film progressed, Fonda convinced each of the other 11 jurors that the defendant was innocent. The jury finally returned a verdict of not guilty.

In this fictional portrayal of a group at work, a single unwavering individual was not only able to resist conformity pressure but also to convince the majority that they were wrong. Such an occurrence would be extremely rare in a real trial (Kalven & Zeisel, 1966). With an 11 to 1 split, the jury would almost always proceed in the direction of the majority (Isenberg, 1986; Kalven & Zeisel, 1966). The film does, however, raise an interesting question: Can a steadfast minority bring about change in the majority?

In the first published experiment on minority influence, subjects were led to believe they were taking part in a study on color perception (Moscovici, Lage, & Naffrechoux, 1969). Individuals were shown a series of slides and asked to say the color of the slide aloud. Unknown to the real subjects (four, making up the majority), two confederates (comprising the minority) had been instructed to make an error on certain trials—by calling a blue slide green, for example. Researchers found that 8.42 percent of the judgments made by the real subjects were in the direction of the minority, compared to only .025 percent of judgments in a control condition in which there was no incorrect minority. In fact, 32 percent of the subjects conformed to the incorrect minority. Thus, a minority can have a surprisingly powerful effect on the majority.

In this experiment, the minority were consistent in their judgments. Researchers theorized that consistency of behavior is a strong determinant of the social influence a minority can exert on a majority (Moscovici et al., 1969). An individual in a minority who expresses a deviant opinion consistently may be seen as having a high degree of confidence in his or her judgments. In the color perception experiment, majority subjects rated minority members as more confident in their judgments than the majority were in theirs. The consistent minority caused the majority to call into question the validity of their own judgments.

What is it about consistency that contributes to the power of a minority to influence a majority? A consistent minority is usually perceived as being more confident and less willing to compromise than an inconsistent minority. A consistent minority may also be perceived as having high levels of competence, especially if it is a relatively large minority (Nemeth, 1986). Generally, we assume that if a number of people share a point of view, it must be correct. As the size of the minority increases, so does perceived competence (Wood, Lundgen, Ouellette, Busceme, & Blackstone, 1994).

Wood and her colleagues showed that a consistent minority of individuals within a group has both a direct and an indirect effect on majority members. Those in the majority may not wish to offend other members of that majority but may incorporate the minority's ideas into their position (Wood et al., 1994). The minority's view is important because it ensures that other members do not simply dismiss an alternative opinion.

When the jury reaches its verdict, it has completed its task. Jurors need not explain their verdict or justify their reasons. They may go home and resume their lives. In most instances, they can do so. In other cases, jurors suffer an emotional aftermath of their jury service.

Stress and Jury Service

In the trial of mass murderer Jeffrey Dahmer, jurors heard of sexual torture and cannibalism as well as necrophilia. In the O. J. Simpson trial, jurors had to view horrifying photographs of the victims. Jurors may spend days or weeks dealing with frightful details, and this constant exposure takes its toll. How does viewing the horrors of a crime affect the jury and its verdict? What might the courts do about this grisly penalty jurors pay for their service?

Jurors exhibit a number of symptoms in very stressful trials, including depression, sleep disturbances, headaches, and sexual problems (DeAngelis, 1995). Costanzo and Costanzo (1992) have reported that jurors find **sequestration—**

being separated from home and family and residing in a hotel for the duration of the trial—and deliberations in gruesome trials to be anxiety provoking and stressful.

Sequestration likely increases group cohesiveness. Jurors who are separated from society except for occasional visits from family may take out their frustration and anger on the prosecutor or the defense, depending on whom they blame for their predicament. A recent study showed that sequestered juries convicted at a rate almost 20 percent higher than nonsequestered juries (DeAngelis, 1995). Jurors often resent being sequestered and may take out their anger on whoever they believe is responsible for their confinement (Levine, 1996). Of course, it may be that the nature of trials requiring sequestration elicits higher conviction rates, not the sequestration itself. Sequestration could make jurors decide to go along with the majority simply to go home; and lengthy confinements may lead to the formation of cliques within the jury that inhibit optimal decision making (Levine, 1996).

Graphic depictions of grisly murder scenes may accomplish what the prosecutors wish to accomplish: convicting the defendant. Saul Kassin and David Garfield (1991) found that exposing jurors to a "blood and guts" crime scene led jurors to use a lower standard of proof and brought out their biases for the prosecution.

Certainly capital trials will cause more stress than a garden-variety robbery case. S. Costanzo and M. Costanzo (1994) reported that most capital jurors they interviewed experienced stress. The symptoms included inability to sleep well, irritability, fatigue (not surprisingly), and a preoccupation with the trial. Some jurors reported having nightmares about the evidence presented in court. The weight of deciding a person's life or death combined with graphic crime scene details were the prime sources of the stress, as one might easily imagine (S. Costanzo & M. Costanzo, 1994).

Can the courts help jurors deal with stress? Some judges have hired counselors to debrief jurors. A major source of jurors' stress is their frustration and bewilderment in trying to make sense out of the unfathomable: How could the defendant have done the heinous act? This is especially true when the murder involves children (Monaghan, 1995). Many jurors feel betrayed by a system that requires them to decide life-and-death matters and then exposes them to prosecutors who show them terribly graphic exhibits to inflame them and defense attorneys who throw nothing but dust in the air to confuse them. This assessment is clearly not good news for our current system of justice (Monaghan, 1995).

Jury service on a death penalty case is surely an experience charged with emotional and moral issues. Next we examine how jurors perform these duties.

DELIBERATING DEATH

The jury's role in death penalty trials is unique. In *Spaziano v. Florida* (1984), the U.S. Supreme Court noted that juries were representative of the "conscience of the community." The Court saw the jury as bringing society's contemporary values about the death penalty to the sentencing process.

In all states that have capital punishment, juries either impose or recommend the death penalty. The judge has final oversight and in most instances she or he can decrease the severity of the penalty. However, the U.S. Supreme Court in *Harris v. Alabama* (1995) upheld the constitutionality of an Alabama law that permits the judge to impose a sentence of death even if the jury recommends life without parole. In addition to Alabama, the states of Florida, Delaware, and Indiana also permit the judge to order execution despite a contrary jury decision.

Legal Background

The availability of capital punishment in the United States was placed in serious constitutional doubt by a 5 to 4 decision of the Supreme Court in 1972. The Court held that such punishment, as then (statutorily) constituted, was administered in an "arbitrary and capricious" manner and violated the prohibition against "cruel and unusual" punishment found in the Eighth and Fourteenth Amendments (*Furman v. Georgia*). In 1976, the Court, ruling on a Georgia capital punishment statute enacted after *Furman,* altered course, and in a 7 to 2 decision upheld the use of capital punishment under specific and carefully defined conditions (*Gregg v. Georgia*).

The Court did not hold that capital punishment itself was unconstitutional. It held only that the manner in which the penalty had been imposed was unconstitutional in that it was arbitrary and capricious—that is, one could not reliably differentiate on legal grounds between murderers who were given the death penalty and those who were not. Death penalty recipients did not, for example, seem to commit more atrocious murders than those who received lesser sentences.

The states that had capital punishment statutes responded to the Court's ruling by trying to devise procedures that would guide the jury ("guided discretion") in a manner that would eliminate consideration of arbitrary factors. The guided discretion procedure would have to make sure the punishment fit the crime committed by the individual.

The Court in 1976 reviewed newly imposed capital sentencing procedures in Florida (*Profitt v. Florida*), Texas (*Jurek v. Texas*), North Carolina (*Woodson v. North Carolina*), and Louisiana (*Roberts v. Louisiana*), approving statutes that required "a structured exercise of discretion while guaranteeing individualized sentencing."

The Court approved the Georgia system under which determinations of guilt and punishment were separated into two different trials before the same jury. In this **bifurcated system,** capital juries first determine the defendant's guilt or innocence; if the defendant is found guilty, a second trial ensues, during which the same jury hears additional evidence and arguments concerning factors that are mitigating (anything the defendant believes would permit society to keep him alive) and aggravating (primarily a prediction that the defendant would continue to be a danger to society) (M. Costanzo & S. Costanzo, 1994). This bifurcated scheme emphasizes individualized sentencing (*Lockett v. Ohio*, 1978). With New York's (1995) adoption of the death penalty, 39 states now employ the bifurcated system.

These changes that the Court instituted can be subsumed under two constitutional headings. The first deals with the *rational orderliness* of the death penalty. This requirement is met if the state law defines aggravating and mitigating circumstances that may be used by the jury to determine the sentence (M. Costanzo & S. Costanzo, 1994). The second constitutional requirement is the *moral appropriateness* of the penalty (*Woodson v. North Carolina*, 1976). This means that the penalty should be imposed only if the jury has made an individualized decision concerning the defendant (*Lockett v. Ohio*, 1978).

The use of bifurcation was initiated because of a need to find a fair and equitable procedure to assign guilt and penalty for each individual defendant in a capital case. The unitary trial in which one jury assigned both guilt and penalty within the context of a single proceeding was deemed to be inherently unfair. A separate penalty proceeding was thought to be necessary for defendants found guilty in capital cases to ensure that the imposition of the death penalty was not done in an arbitrary and capricious manner.

Social scientists and jurists suspected that the bifurcated procedure may be inherently flawed (*Grigsby v. Mabry*, 1980; Horowitz & Seguin, 1986). In this procedure, the jury is required, if the evidence warrants, to commit itself to a guilty verdict. Jurors then know that such a verdict will require a second trial to address the penalty to be imposed.

Death-Qualified Jurors

The bifurcated trial is not the only unique feature of capital cases. Jurors in death penalty cases must be "death qualified" to sit on the jury. Death qualification (DQ) involves a methodology in which potential jurors are questioned about their opinions and likely course of action with respect to the death penalty. Potential jurors who state during the voir dire questioning that they are adamantly opposed to the death penalty or that they could not render a fair and impartial verdict because of their opposition to the death penalty are disqualified, excluded for cause, from serving on the jury (*Witherspoon v. Illinois*, 1968). **Scrupled jurors** are those who indicate that although they are opposed to the death penalty, their opposition is not total; they are very often excluded by peremptory prosecutorial challenge.

Prior to 1968, the prosecution could eliminate any juror with any degree of opposition to capital punishment. *Witherspoon v. Illinois* (1968) resulted in the implementation of Witherspoon excludables (WEs) in the selection of DQ juries. There are two types of WEs: (a) **guilt nullifiers,** whose opposition to the death penalty is so strong that it would interfere with their ability to render a fair verdict, even if convinced the defendant is guilty; and (b) **penalty nullifiers,** who refuse to vote for the death *penalty* in any case, regardless of the evidence. Thus, any potential juror who falls into one or both of the aforementioned categories would not be allowed to sit on a death penalty jury (Cox & Tanford, 1989).

The defendant in *Witherspoon v. Illinois* (1968) had argued that the absence of death penalty opponents from guilt determination increased the likelihood of a guilty verdict. The reasoning was that death-qualified jurors were more conviction prone and more prosecution prone than death-opponent jurors. The court was not persuaded by this argument in 1968 and noted that the evidence was thin and fragmentary, consisting of three unpublished studies. Currently, the evidence is overwhelming that jurors who are death qualifiable are more likely to convict a capital defendant than those jurors who are excludable (unwilling to impose death), and that these death-qualified jurors, when they are members of a jury made up of all death-qualified people, are less critical of witnesses, less able to remember evidence, and more satisfied with their jury than the excludables (Cowan, Thompson, & Ellsworth, 1984).

Moran and Comfort (1986), in a study of several hundred impaneled jurors, found that jurors who supported capital punishment were much more likely to favor conviction of a criminal defendant. Jurors who were more favorable to the death penalty were more likely to be white, married, well-off, Republican, male, conservative, and authoritarian.

Current Status of Death Qualification.   The state has an interest in having people on the jury who will obey the law. Weighed against this requirement is the defendant's right to a fair trial before an impartial jury. Does the death-qualification process alter the composition of the jury so that only jurors inclined toward prosecution survive the test of being death qualified?

In *Wainwright v. Witt* (1985) the Court decided to modify the Witherspoon standards, holding that jurors should be excluded only if it was absolutely clear that they would automatically vote against capital punishment no matter the evidence, or if the potential jurors stated clearly that they could not impartially evaluate the evidence because of their attitudes about the death penalty (Thompson, 1989a). *Witt* required only that potential jurors be excluded when the juror's attitudes on the death penalty would "substantially impair" the individual's ability to live up to the oath and instructions required by the trial court. This change, according to William Thompson's analysis, considerably enlarges the pool of potential jurors who can be excluded for cause from death penalty cases because of their opinions. However, recent data show that the relative size (perhaps about 20 percent of the public) of the excludable class has not changed from the Witherspoon standard (Haney, Hurtardo, & Vega, 1994).

The section of the public that is excludable clearly hold different attitudes from those who do not fall into the excludable pattern. Ellsworth and her colleagues have also demonstrated that the death-qualification process effectively limits the diversity of the jury, excluding at least 17 percent to 20 percent of the potential jurors. Particularly affected are a significant proportion of blacks and females, who are more likely than whites and males to vote against the death penalty (Fitzgerald & Ellsworth, 1984). Note that there is another excludable class: those who will automatically vote for the death penalty, no matter the evidence (*Hovey v. California,* 1980). This class may constitute about 2.5 percent of the potential capital jurors.

Ellsworth's research demonstrates that jurors' attitudes toward the death penalty are predictive of their likely verdict. Death-qualified jurors appear to hold a "lower threshold of conviction" than held by excludables (Thompson, Cowan, Ellsworth, & Harrington, 1984). The favorability of death-qualifiable jurors toward the prosecution is clear and has been recognized by various courts (*Hovey v. Superior Court,* 1980). In *Grigsby v. Mabry* (1980), the district court held that death-qualified juries were in fact unconstitutional. This decision was overturned by the U.S. Supreme Court. The district court specifically cited the empirical evidence showing that the Witherspoon excludables hold attitudes toward the criminal justice system (Fitzgerald & Ellsworth, 1984) that reliably distinguish them from death-qualified jurors. The district court judge noted that death-qualified jurors favor the prosecution, are antagonistic to the defense, and tend to be biased against minority groups. The judge also noted that death-qualified juries do not represent a fair cross-section of the population. Empirical research has shown that death-qualified juries are punitive—that is, they are more likely to convict and more likely to impose the death penalty than juries that include excludables (Horowitz & Seguin, 1986).

Haney (1984a, 1984b) has argued persuasively that the very process of death qualification biases the jury, whatever their dispositional characteristics, against the defendant. The process of death qualification contains the insinuation that the defendant is guilty. Why else would the court be interested in the jurors' attitudes about penalty prior to hearing the evidence? The process also desensitizes prospective jurors with respect to the death penalty, requires a public affirmation of the death penalty as a requirement of acceptance on the jury, and makes the death penalty more likely, as jurors, during the "rehabilitation" process, are often asked to imagine horrific crimes that would overcome any scruples they might have to the imposition of the ultimate penalty (Haney, Hurtado, & Vega, 1994). Haney et al. (1994) have shown the current attitudinal differences between excludable and death-qualified jurors (see Table 10.1)

Aside from the showing by Ellsworth and her colleagues that the death-qualification procedure impanels dispositionally biased individuals, direct empirical evidence that the process of death qualification is biasing is available in a study by Haney (1984b). This study demonstrated that those who simply observed the death-qualification process were more likely to favor the prosecution and were likely to be hostile to the rights of the defendant.

The death-qualification procedure, as currently constituted, is inextricably bound with the bifurcated trial. Jurors are questioned about their death penalty attitudes, in part because of the second trial, the penalty phase. Of course, a penalty trial will follow only if the defendant is found guilty. Jurors are so informed routinely by judge and counsel. Nevertheless, both procedurally and

TABLE 10.1   Effects of Modern Death Qualifications

	Excludables	Death Qualified
Person's beliefs about death penalty		
Death penalty deters murder	56.8%	76.2%*
Juror can focus only on crime, ignore background	45.3%	53.1%*
Too many innocent people are executed	35.8%	18.9%*
Death penalty is unfair to minorities	53.7%	38.%*
Juror accepts these mitigating factors		
Felony murder was not premeditated	54.7%	37.5%*
Convicted person is older than 30	33.7%	14.4%*
Convicted person is from background of poverty	32.6%	17.6%*
Convicted person has loving, supportive family and friends	35.8%	15.6%*
Convicted person never received treatment	48.4%	38%*
Juror accepts these aggravating factors		
Murder was especially brutal	67.4%	89.1%*
Crime involved more than one murder victim	58.9%	72.%*
Murder occurred during sexual assault	49.5%	69.2%*
Convicted person has prior violent felony	27.4%	35.5%*
Convicted person expressed no remorse	53.7%	72.5%*

Note: Asterisks mean that findings in a given row are significantly different. All rows here are significantly different.

Source: Adapted from " 'Modern' Death Qualification: New Data on Its Biasing Effects," by C. Haney, A. Hurtado, and L. Vega, 1994, *Law and Human Behavior, 18*(3), p. 629, Table 3.

semantically, to put forth questions about death penalty attitudes without the presumption of a penalty trial is difficult.

However, the U.S. Supreme Court in *Lockhart v. McCree* (1986) concluded that the social science data were "insufficient" and "flawed" and therefore held that death-qualification procedures were not unconstitutional. The court further said that no bias existed because none of the death-qualified jurors who tried Mr. McCree was proven to be prejudiced. The Court in *Lockhart* dismissed a coherent and consistent body of evidence demonstrating the biasing effects of death qualification.

Instructing the Capital Jury

As noted, the judge's instructions often confuse and bewilder the jurors. This is a serious issue in any criminal case, but it takes on deeper implications when the jury is deciding a life or death issue. If instructions do not guide jurors, the arbitrariness of decisions in capital cases is increased. Shari Diamond (1993) has suggested that there is simply a ceiling of consistency in capital cases that is a product of trying to decide rationally who lives and who dies. How can lay jurors or trained legal professionals make consistent and rational decisions on choosing which capital defendants should die from the pool of all those eligible for the death penalty (Diamond, 1993)?

It seems clear that a number of legal concepts in the capital instructions elude jurors' comprehension. Jurors spend 20 percent to 25 percent of their deliberations discussing the judge's instructions in capital cases (Diamond & Levi, 1996). Jurors are asked to sentence convicted murderers by weighing "aggravating" and "mitigating" circumstances. Both these words have common meanings, and so jurors have their own constructions of the terms. Often then commonsense notions conflict with the legal sense of the terms (Diamond, 1993).

Haney and Lynch (1994) examined juror understanding of California's penalty phase instructions. These instructions do not give jurors definitions of aggravating and mitigating circumstances nor do they indicate what factors might belong to which category. Generally, **mitigating factors** are those that would lead toward a verdict of life; they may include the defendant's mental capacity, age, motivation, prior felony record, or any other consideration of the defendant's character or record that can be used to argue for a lesser sentence than death. **Aggravating factors** are those that call for the death penalty and may include the brutality of the crime, the motivation of the defendant, or the likelihood that the defendant will continue to be a danger to others. Haney and Lynch (1994) had college students define the meaning of mitigating and aggravating factors and found that while 64 percent of the subjects were able to understand what was meant by "aggravating" circumstances, they were much less accurate in defining "mitigating " factors. Often jurors were confused enough to put a mitigating factor into the "aggravating" category. This shift occurred about 25 percent of the time. For example, some jurors classified "acting under the influence of mental or emotional disturbance" as an aggravating factor (it is presumed to be a mitigating one), and some participants thought that the defendant's prior criminal record was a mitigating factor.

Interviews with actual capital jurors confirm these findings (Bowers, 1996). Researchers have found that penalty phase jurors have turned what was used by the defense as a mitigating factor—"a good upbringing"—into an aggravating factor (Haney et al., 1994). Presumably, jurors thought that an individual with a better upbringing should be more responsible than someone who was less fortunate. It is clear that jurors have great difficulty comprehending the meaning of mitigating factors (Wiener, Pritchard, & Weston, 1995).

Bowers (1996) reported data from interviews with actual capital jurors showing that jurors misunderstand how death penalty sentencing is done, which factors can and cannot be used, what level of proof is required, and how mitigating and aggravating elements are weighed. Bowers (1996) also reported a provocative finding: Capital jurors disavow responsibility for the ultimate determination of the death penalty. Recall that the jury was given an enhanced role in death penalty cases so they could bring the "conscience of the community" into the sentencing decision. The U.S. Supreme Court had specifically stated that jurors must not believe the ultimate responsibility rests with others (*Caldwell v. Mississippi,* 1985). When jurors were asked who or what was most responsible for the death penalty verdict, only 6 percent chose the individual juror. It is not unreasonable to suggest that disclaiming responsibility makes it psychologically easier for a juror to vote for the death penalty.

Moreover, research on capital juries suggests that if jurors do not understand a concept, they are more likely to decide for the death penalty than for life imprisonment (M. Costanzo & S. Costanzo, 1994; Haney, Sontag, & Costanzo, 1994; Wiener et al., 1995). Generally, people tend to have a **negativity bias.** They give negative information more weight than they do positive information in decision making (Klein, 1991). Therefore, we should not be surprised to learn that death-qualified jurors are more persuaded by aggravating circumstances than by mitigating factors (Luginbuhl & Middendorf, 1988).

COURTROOM APPLICATIONS

Instructing the Menendez Juries

In the first trial of the Menendez brothers for the murder of their parents, the facts were not at issue. The defense admitted that the brothers had killed their parents. The issue the jurors had to decide was whether Erik and Lyle Menendez were guilty of a crime, and if so, what was the nature of the crime. The Menendez defenses ranged from self-defense against sexual abuse, and possibly the threat of murder by their father, to impaired mental capacity (Hacker, 1995).

Menendez juror Hazel Thornton's (1995) account of her experiences shows that the jurors had to struggle with legal constructions. Two juries sat in the courtroom, one for each brother. Each jury had to decide what type of crime their defendant had committed (Thornton, 1995). To further complicate matters, Andrew Hacker (1995) reports that the prosecution gave each jury the same set of choices. Each brother was charged with having committed all four of the following crimes against each of his parents: first-degree murder, which carries a mandatory death sentence in California; second-degree murder; voluntary manslaughter; involuntary manslaughter. And, as the defense stated, there was a fifth alternative: that they had committed no crime at all. As Hacker notes, "In law and in logic, the young men could not have committed all four or even any two of the offenses that had been entered against them. So the juries' job was to determine which offense, if any, took place when each defendant participated in each death" (Hacker, 1995, p. 47).

The two juries listened to testimony, as did the nation over the Court TV network, for almost half a year. The judge's instructions contained critical definitions of the crimes. From the juries' view, a legal construction such as

Why don't judges define mitigation and aggravation? Many judges refuse to give specific definitions because they fear being overruled by a higher court. Luginbuhl (1992) found that when jurors in North Carolina were given new instruction that offered clear definitions of mitigation and aggravation, they performed better—that is, they weighed the factors in a more rational manner—than did jurors who operated under an older instruction set that did not provide definitions.

Not surprisingly, jurors often look to sources other than legal authority to guide them in their decisions. Hoffman (1995) reported that many capital jurors look for divine guidance. This is probably not what the Court meant by "guided discretion" (Bowers, 1996).

The Courtroom Applications box below illustrates the difficulty jurors may have in following the judge's instructions. The example deals with the well-publicized first trial of the Menendez brothers.

"intent" to kill, which requires a clear aim to bring about death, was hard to distinguish from "premeditation," a preplanned design to kill. The distinction was important because both states (intent and premeditation) are necessary for a first-degree murder conviction. If premeditation was not present but intent was, a second-degree murder conviction was appropriate. Second-degree murder required "implied malice" (Hacker, 1995).

The manslaughter instructions were equally perplexing, turning on whether the brothers had been sexually abused and what psychological damage may have issued from that abuse (Hacker, 1995). A unanimous verdict was required.

The jury on which Hazel Thornton served continually asked the trial judge for clarification of the legal terms. The judge simply reread the arcane phrases the jury had already heard. Clarification was not forthcoming. Both juries were unable to reach a verdict after days of deliberation. News reports suggested racial or gender conflicts, but apparently those reports were false (Hacker, 1995; Thornton, 1995). Not one juror voted to acquit. The dividing line fell between those who wanted a murder conviction and those who wanted a manslaughter verdict.

In the second Menendez trial, completed in March of 1996, the trial judge prohibited a defense based on the abused child syndrome because the judge decided that the evidence would not support such a defense. Absent the "defendant as victim" strategy, and absent instructions concerning the abuse defense, the second trial resulted in first-degree murder convictions for both Erik and Lyle Menendez.

The Death Penalty in Action

In the last decade of the twentieth century, the use of the death penalty is neither swift nor cheap. Of the 50 states, Texas has carried out the most executions (92) since 1976. One of the last of these, a convict who was executed in February 1995, had spent 18 years on death row appealing his case. A recent study of the death penalty in North Carolina shows that to try, convict, and sentence a defendant to death costs twice as much as sentencing him and keeping him in jail for 20 years (Verhovek, 1995).

Most individuals sentenced to death since 1976 have not been executed. For those who die, the average wait between sentence and death is about eight years (Verhovek, 1995). Appeals are mandated in death penalty cases; imposition of the death penalty engages additional constitutional protection because "death is different" from other penalties.

Even within Texas, the likelihood that a convicted killer will die depends on the county in which the trial took place. The odds are several times higher that a defendant sentenced to death will be executed in Houston than in Dallas (Lewin, 1995). This disparity is one example that the court's concern about the arbitrariness of the death penalty has still not been resolved despite two decades of change since 1976.

The southern tier of states accounts for roughly 85 percent of all the executions since 1976 (Lewin, 1995). At least 12 of the states that have the death penalty on the books have not executed a single prisoner. Fifty-six convicted killers were executed in 1995, and 58 in 1996, the highest number since 1957. With 3,000 men and women on death row, the prospect for the future is a much higher total.

Death and Justice: Who Dies? Who dies depends primarily on the nature of the victim. Prosecutors will often bring capital charges when the victim is young, helpless, or female (Lewin, 1995). The death penalty is also more likely to be meted out to someone who kills a stranger as opposed to family members or lovers. David Baldus, a legal expert on the death penalty, notes that people identify more with the victim if he or she is a stranger because it suggests the randomness of murder and it evokes our greatest fears (cited in Lewin, 1995). Males commit most of the homicides; regardless, women are less likely to get the death penalty, probably because they tend to kill lovers or family members (Lewin, 1995).

In a number of cases since 1976, the U.S. Supreme Court has continually clarified the guidelines courts and juries must use in death penalty trials. For example, juries must be allowed to consider evidence of mental retardation (*Penry v. Lynaugh,* 1989). Juries must be told that there is an option of life imprisonment without parole. Sometimes juries may impose the death penalty because they fear that the defendant, if given a life sentence, could be released. If given the option of life without parole, juries may be less likely to vote for death (S. Costanzo & M. Costanzo, 1994). Also, the Court required consideration of aggravating and mitigating circumstances, including motivation, state of mind, remorse, and brutality of the murder (Lewin, 1995). There is another factor that relates to both the victim and the defendant: the issue of race.

Race and the Jury.   In *McCleskey v. Kemp* (1987), race as a factor in the death penalty was considered. Warren McCleskey killed a police officer in Atlanta during the commission of a holdup. In the seven-year period prior to McCleskey's trial, some 16 cases involving the murder of a police officer had occurred. McCleskey, who was black, was the only perpetrator to draw the death penalty.

McCleskey argued in his appeal that evidence provided by University of Iowa law professor David Baldus showed conclusively that black defendants who kill whites are more likely to be executed in Georgia than are killers of blacks (Baldus, Pulaski, & Woodworth, 1983; Baldus, Woodworth, & Pulaski, 1990). The statistical evidence showed that the death sentencing rate for "white victim" cases was 11 times that of "black victim" cases. Even taking into consideration that 230 other variables could have accounted for this result, such as the possibility that white victims may have been killed in a more vicious way than blacks, the Baldus data still showed that blacks who kill whites were four times more likely to receive the death penalty than any other class of murderers. The Court ruled in a 5–4 decision that although the statistical evidence was quite valid, such a discrepancy did not prove unconstitutional discrimination unless Mr. McCleskey could show that *he* received the death penalty because he was black.

Aside from the issue of the Court's skepticism about using clear social science data in its decision making as well as the dismissal of race as a factor in death sentencing, the case highlights the difficulty of applying general data to specific cases. The five majority justices wanted proof of discrimination in the specific case before them and statistical evidence gathered from 2,484 other cases in the Baldus study did not seem relevant to them.

Table 10.2 shows the probabilities of a defendant's receiving the death penalty based on the race of the defendant and the race of the victim. Note that the determining factor seems to be the race of the victim. Defendants convicted of killing whites get the death penalty 11 percent of the time (108 times out of 981 cases) whereas the death of a black victim elicits the death penalty only 1 percent of the time, or 20 out of 1503 trials (Abramson, 1995; Baldus et al., 1990).

TABLE 10.2   Effect of Racial Combinations on Death Sentence

Racial Combination	Death Sentence Rate
Black defendant/white victim	21%
White defendant/white victim	08%
Black defendant/black victim	01%
White defendant/black victim	03%

Source: Adapted from *Equal Justice: A Legal and Empirical Analysis,* by D. C. Baldus, G. Woodworth, and C. A. Pulaski, Jr., 1990, Boston: Northeastern University Press, p. 315.

TABLE 10.3   Factors Affecting the Death Sentence

Factors That Increase Death Penalty Probability	Factors That Decrease Death Penalty Probability
Victim was . . .	Victim was . . .
• Police officer	• Family member or lover
• Stranger	• In barroom fight
• Weak or frail	
• White	
• 12 years old or less	
Defendant . . .	Defendant . . .
• Committed murder for hire	• Was not the trigger person
• Killed two or more people	• Was under 17
• Tortured	• Was retired, student, or housewife
• Raped	
• Planned to collect insurance	

Source: Adapted from *Equal Justice: A Legal and Empirical Analysis,* by D. C. Baldus, G. Woodworth, and C. A. Pulaski, Jr., 1990, Boston: Northeastern University Press, p. 327.

Table 10.3 presents some of the factors that either increase or decrease the probability that a defendant will be sentenced to death, as noted by Baldus and his co-workers.

Although jurors no doubt reflect our society's racial attitudes, blame for sentencing differences in capital cases ought not to be laid solely on the jury (Gross & Mauro, 1989). Bias occurs at various, less visible points in the process. Bias arises from the initial decision of the prosecutor to ask for the death penalty or to allow the defendant to plead to a lesser charge. Prosecutors were more likely to accept a voluntary manslaughter plea in black victim cases in Georgia than in white victim cases (Baldus et al., 1990). The evidence also suggests that prosecutors discriminate more sharply between white and black victims than do juries (Baldus et al., 1990). This is not to say that the jury is less susceptible to racial bias than other aspects of the legal system. We suspect, though, that if deliberation works the way it should—a context in which individuals have to defend their opinions—the jury may do better than most legal institutions in putting aside at least some of the racial baggage we all carry. The more diverse the jury, the more likely this ideal is to be attained.

Norbert Kerr and his co-workers (1995) note that there is also a "black sheep" bias among jurors. This group provided empirical evidence that a defendant who is similar to the juror in race or religion but is especially unattractive or deviant is judged harshly by that (similar) juror because that "black sheep" (the disliked defendant) threatens the image of the group with which the juror identifies. Similarity in this case may lead to an extreme and harsh reaction. Kerr found that when evidence favoring conviction was weak, jurors were more likely to return a not guilty verdict for defendants of the same race or religion as their own than for other race/religion defendants. When the evidence clearly showed the defendant was guilty, however, and when jurors, black or white, knew that their racial group would be in the minority in the jury room, same-race defendants were perceived as more guilty than defendants of another race (Kerr, Hymes, Anderson, & Weathers, 1995).

Some commentators want to ensure that minority defendants always have juries containing members of ethnic, racial, or religious background similar to the defendant's (Kerr et al., 1995). Kerr and his colleagues have demonstrated that this approach may not always work to the advantage of the defendant, nor will it invariably serve to ensure a just outcome.

Again, the **black sheep effect**—treating a disagreeable same-race defendant harshly—holds only if the defendant's racial group is in the minority on the jury. The effect does not hold if they are in a majority. If the juror is surrounded by members of the same minority group, a negative same-race defendant is not seen as quite the threat to the esteem of the minority group (Kerr et al., 1995).

Some evidence also suggests that jurors are less likely to ignore inadmissible evidence when it involves a black defendant compared to a white defendant (Johnson, Whitestone, Jackson, & Gatto, 1995). In a trial involving information gained from an illegal wiretap, jurors were more likely to use the incriminating but inadmissible evidence when the defendant was black than white. Figure 10.1 shows these results.

The effects of race on sentencing is critical to the justice system. We consider the *McCleskey* decision fully in Chapter 12.

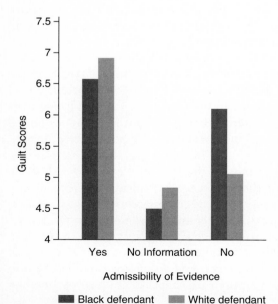

FIGURE 10.1   Jurors' verdicts as a function of race and evidence admissibility.

As the diagram shows, jurors are more likely to use inadmissible evidence when the defendant is an African American than when he or she is a white defendant. Higher scores indicate more guilt.

Source: Adapted from "Justice Is Still Not Colorblind: Differential Racial Effects of Exposure to Inadmissible Evidence," by J. D. Johnson, E. Whitestone, L. A. Jackson, and L. Gatto, 1995, *Personality and Social Psychology Bulletin, 21*(9), 893–899.

SUMMARY

Following closing arguments, the judge instructs the jury as to the law that must be applied to the facts (charging instructions). Instructions are the court's attempt to ensure that the jurors are competent to decide the case on legally relevant grounds. An important concept in the instructions is "reasonable doubt," which refers to the standard for certainty of guilt. A reasonable doubt level set at 85 percent suggests the juror is 85 percent certain of the defendant's culpability. Evidence suggests that jurors may not fully grasp the reasonable doubt instruction and may convict on a lesser standard.

Researchers have explored several potential jury aids to ease the confusion brought on by the often abstract and arcane legal language found in instructions to the jury. Among the procedures that have shown promise are providing written instructions to the jury and preinstructing jurors before the presentation of the evidence so they can apply the law to the evidence at the very start of the trial.

Jurors process information by "packaging" their reasons for believing something in a form that is most persuasive and reasonable to both themselves and others. According to the story model, we impose a structure on complex information by creating a coherent "story," and we use the story to understand and organize incoming information. Evidence that fits the story is remembered and incorporated, and evidence that does not fit the story is forgotten. Jurors may also use meters that range from 0 to 100 to evaluate evidence. As evidence is presented, the meter is constantly adjusted. The meter model is based on the idea of decision makers holding one or more meters that continuously track and read out a value reflecting their current view of the evidence.

We ought not to assume that each individual juror goes about the business of organizing and understanding the evidence the same way. Recent work has identified a type of juror known as a satificer who bases conclusions on a minimal amount of evidence without further consideration of other, contradictory evidence. A second manner of dealing with evidence has been identified as the theory evidence coordination mode, which requires the construction of two or more stories that are evaluated against the incoming evidence and against each other.

When we examined the way juries function to reach a verdict, we found that the size of the jury has less affect on the verdict and more on the dynamics of the jury. Smaller juries have fewer minority members and tend to be more unpredictable than larger juries.

Generally, deliberation works to bring out the facts of a case and to lead to agreement about the order in which the events under consideration occurred. Mock juries show greater ability to follow the judge's instructions and to ignore inadmissible evidence than actual jurors. Deliberation does not seem to change many votes, but what will alter the jurors' votes are interpretations of the law. Unfortunately, juries seem not to fully comprehend the judge's instructions and the relevant law. Jurors tend to base their verdicts and discussion on the facts, but as they consider more issues, jurors typically turn their attention to persuading nonmajority jurors to conform to the majority point of view. These findings—that initial discussion deals with information and later deliberation centers on conformity pressures—have been supported by several studies. Although the majority on the jury usually prevails, this is not always so. A consistent and rational minority can often influence the majority opinion, directly or indirectly.

In all states that have capital punishment, juries either impose or recommend the death penalty. The judge has final oversight. Jurors in death penalty cases must be "death qualified"— that is, they must either be in favor of or indifferent to the imposition of the death penalty. As a rule, death-qualified jurors are more conviction prone and more severe in their sentence recommendations than those who are excluded from service on a capital jury. The pace of executions of those on death row has increased and will continue to increase because most inmates have exhausted their legal bases of appeal.

CHAPTER
11

Judges, Juries, and Justice

The great jurist Oliver Wendell Holmes, Jr., observed that a fundamental requirement of a sound body of law is that it conform to the sentiment of the community (1881/1963). When law drifts too far from the aspirations and feelings of the public, it loses credibility. In this chapter, we examine the behavior and sentiments of judges and jurors and see how the system dispenses justice. We also consider some potential modifications of the justice system advocated by those who believe reform is long overdue.

JUDGES AND JUSTICE

Sentencing convicted criminals in a just and fair manner is at the core of ethical and legal practices in any society. It is probable that no other behavior of trial judges receives as much scrutiny as sentencing. For a long time, judges had great leeway in deciding the length of sentences. However, researchers found considerable disparities among sentences; an offender's sentence was often more dependent on the philosophy of the trial judge than on the actual criminal act (Diamond, 1981; Myers, 1988; Spohn, 1990). Because of these perceived disparities, the U.S. Congress passed a sentencing reform act that provided federal judges with specific guidelines.

Although the judicial system tries to isolate judges from societal pressures (federal judges have lifetime appointments), judges react to election returns and strong public opinion much like any other government official. Widespread contemporary opinion seems to be that sentencing is inadequate (Roberts & Edwards, 1989). In many public opinion polls, citizens respond that judges are too lenient in sentencing criminal defendants. As Loretta Stalans and Shari Diamond (1990) noted, this discontent leads people to lose confidence in the judicial system.

The public view of sentencing may be affected by a lack of information about the specifics of the cases that judges hear. Stalans and Diamond (1990) provided laypeople with examples of specific (and typical) cases and asked them to assign sentences. Curiously, the sentences proposed by laypeople were *less* than the minimum allowable sentences for residential burglary—the type of crime they were examining. It may be that when individuals think of a "typical" case, they remember the reports in the media about horrific crimes, not ordinary ones. Julian Roberts and Anthony Doob (1990) found that newspaper stories about criminal cases resulted in a negative attitude in readers about the judge, the sentence, the offender and the offense, and the judicial system in general. It is not surprising that citizens would demand harsher sentencing. However, when faced with an actual case and put in the role of the "judge," laypeople perceived the crime somewhat differently. Their responses were at least as "lenient" as those of the trial judge (Stalans & Diamond, 1990). Even so, public concern about the lack of strict sentencing has led to some rather significant changes in the way judges now sentence defendants.

The Impact of the Sentencing Reform Act of 1984

In 1984, the U.S. Congress established the United States Sentencing Commission and directed it to draft guidelines for judges in federal courts. The guidelines officially took effect in November 1987, but many judges considered the guidelines unconstitutional and did not immediately apply them. In 1990, however, the U.S. Supreme Court upheld the constitutionality of sentencing guidelines and they have been in effect since that date.

Sentencing guidelines have taken effect in a number of states as well. California, by ballot initiative, has passed a "three strikes, you're out" law, and 22 other states have similar statutes. The law requires prison sentences of at least 25 years to life if a person is convicted of a felony (the most serious category of crime) three times. Some judges in California, like their federal counterparts, have thought the guidelines unconstitutional. In fact, recent evidence suggests that except in California, both federal and state judges have "nullified" the "three strikes" law by not imposing mandatory life sentences (Gordon, 1996).

Sentencing guidelines are aimed at doing away with sentencing disparities among judges and jurisdictions. Before introduction of the guidelines, convicted felons might have received very different sentences with different judges in different locales. Proponents of the guidelines argue that such disparities are eliminated by the new regulations. Opponents of guidelines say they dispense "justice by the numbers" without taking into account the differences among defendants and the nature of the crimes. The Courtroom Applications box on the facing page provides such an example.

How the Guidelines Work.   Under the sentencing guidelines, all crimes are ranked on a scale from 1 to 43. The more heinous the crime, the higher the number. Murder is assigned 43, hijacking 38; robbery is worth 20 points; sexual abuse of a minor gets 15; blackmail merits a 9. These are base rates. These rates rise and fall like the stock market depending on a number of factors that either increase (aggravating factors) or decrease (mitigating factors) the individual's responsibility. These factors may include the individual's willingness to cooperate (that's good) or not (that's bad). Defiance is bad, contrition (it's never too late to say you're sorry) is good.

To see how the guidelines might work, assume we are dealing with a robbery. We check the guidelines and we find that this offense is worth 20 base points. We then note that if it involved a bank or a post office, we add 2 more base points, to reach 22. If a weapon was discharged, the base rises by an additional 7 points to 29. If the weapon, a gun, was only "used" (not discharged but pointed), we add only 6 points, to 28; but if our robber waved it around ("brandished" it), we add 5 points, for a total of 27. The base rate, and any additions to that base, correspond to the length of time the offender is to be incarcerated.

In a drug case, the contraband is weighed and additional points are added for increasing weights, a system that works against larger dealers. In one case, judges

COURTROOM APPLICATIONS

Sentence 'Em and Weep

Under the best of conditions, sentencing a convicted offender may be a judge's most difficult assignment. When Congress sets strict guidelines, the result may be a suppression of judicial ideas of justice and fairness. Consider a case that then federal district judge William W. Schwarzer faced. The defendant was a 48-year-old longshoreman with no criminal record. He brought the wrath of the law down on himself by driving a friend to a restaurant where the friend, while picking up lunch, carried out a drug deal with a federal undercover agent. The friend took off, but the longshoreman was arrested and convicted of conspiracy to sell drugs. Congress set the *minimum* penalty for this offense at ten years in prison.

Judge Schwarzer's role as a federal judge left him no room to maneuver. He imposed the ten-year sentence and wept as he did so. This is not a judge known as a "bleeding heart"; he is a no-nonsense jurist for whom the rule of law is a guiding passion. "We are required to follow the rule of law, but in this case the law does anything but serve justice," was the way Judge Schwarzer expressed his thoughts and feelings at the sentencing (Mydans, 1993b, p. A1). Later, Judge Schwarzer observed that "the [sentencing] Guidelines say you have to sentence the offense and not the offender. What bothers federal judges so much is that you can't sentence an offense. You have to sentence an offender" (Mydans, 1993b, p. A1).

Tears are powerful symbols. Grownups, especially federal judges, rarely cry, at least in public. What do Judge Schwarzer's tears symbolize? It seems to us that they represent a strong, disciplined commitment to what he calls the "rule of law," the central principle that legal rules, whether in the form of a congressional statute or a judicial precedent, govern a decision. A judge swears to put aside personal beliefs when faced with clear legal rules. The tears may also represent the disappointment of a skilled professional appointed to bring wisdom and experience to bear in pronouncing judgments but frustrated in trying to reach the ideal of doing justice. How frequently do these conflicts exist? What effects do they have on judicial morale? On the willingness of lawyers to aspire to the bench? Judge Schwarzer's tears raise these and other questions for students of the social psychology of judging. A survey of federal judges suggests that Judge Schwarzer's reaction was not unique. When asked whether they would support repeal of most or all mandatory minimum sentences, 79 percent of the federal district judges said they strongly or moderately support such a proposal; and 85 percent of those judges would change the rules to increase the leeway of a sentencing judge (Mydans, 1993b).

argued over whether the weight of the suitcase used to transport the drugs should count (Margolick, 1992). This is certainly an advertisement for soft-sided or even cardboard luggage!

The guidelines have become quite complex and essentially take discretion out of the sentencing process. In a sense, that's what they were meant to do. Many judges resent the constraints of the guidelines and have on occasion ignored them when they felt the sentence would be unfair (Margolick, 1992). Nevertheless, public support for guidelines seems to be strong. More people are spending more time in jail since the guidelines went into effect. The federal prison system is now at close to 200 percent capacity (Mydans, 1996).

Unintended Effects of the Guidelines.   Sometimes new laws have paradoxical effects—unintended effects that may frustrate the intent of the law. Again, consider the sentencing guidelines. California's new sentencing law, requiring a sentence of 25 years to life in prison for people convicted of a third felony, has led many convicted criminals in Orange County to be released early. The number of cases prosecuted under the new law, which went into effect in March 1993, is small, but courts are becoming crowded because many people facing charges are refusing to plead guilty out of fear of the sentencing guidelines, preferring to take a chance on a jury trial.

As the jails have filled up with people awaiting trial, there has been less room for convicted criminals, and they are being released early to free up space. From January 1995 to June 1996, early releases from county jails rose 122 percent. The number of guilty pleas in felony criminal cases has dropped 22 percent since the sentencing guidelines went into effect. The backlog of defendants awaiting jury trials increased to 700 in December 1995—up from 480 in January. The scenario is especially acute in bankrupt Orange County because that county is under a federal court order to limit crowding at the county's detention sites. As the prison population increases, inmates must be released early. The implementation of the three strikes law in California has led to the imprisonment of 15,000 offenders and will require an expenditure of about $5 billion for additional prison space (Gordon, 1996).

TABLE 11.1   A Comparison of Sentences for Robbery Before and After Institution of the Guidelines

Average months sentenced and served by offenders with no criminal record convicted of robbing one bank of less than $10,000.

	Robbed without a weapon		Used a weapon	
	Sentence	Time served	Sentence	Time served
Before guidelines	42.3	17.9	71.1	24.3
After guidelines	29.5	26.0	39.8	34.8

Source: Adapted from S. Miller, "At the Bar," *New York Times*, August 8, 1994, p. A16.

TABLE 11.2 **Sentencing by the New Guidelines**

Offenses

Aggravated assault	+15
Use of a dangerous weapon	4
Bodily injury	2
Civil rights violation	6
Subtotal	27

Sentence for 27 points: **70–87 months**

Deductions

Victim's conduct	−5
Notoriety, double jeopardy, loss of job, atypical case	−3
Total	19

Sentence for 19 points: **30–37 months**

Source: Adapted from data in the *New York Times,* August 6, 1993, p. B8.

Nevertheless, the sentencing guidelines generally have done what their proponents had hoped. Table 11.1 shows the average sentence and the average time served (for robbery) in months before and after institution of the guidelines. The point to notice is that the average actual time served in jail significantly increased after the guidelines were put in place.

Table 11.2 shows the impact the guidelines have had on one well-publicized crime: the beating of Rodney King in 1993. This table shows how the trial judge determined the sentences for police officers Lawrence M. Powell and Sgt. Stacey Koon, who were convicted of the beating. How did these sentences differ from the likely preguideline outcome? Experts guessed that the police officers would have received a five-year sentence before institution of the guidelines and would probably have served about half that time—roughly 30 months (Skolnick, 1993). Notice that the behavior of the victim of the assault, Mr. King, played a role in the sentencing. Mr. King had led the police on a 100-mile-per-hour chase down Santa Monica Boulevard and tried to resist arrest. Judge Davis also calculated that the humiliation of the defendants (the police officers) warranted a decrease in the sentence, including the fact that both had lost their jobs and neither was a danger to the community (Mydans, 1993a).

Psychology and the New Sentencing Guidelines. Paul J. Hofer, a researcher for the United States Sentencing Commission, has noted that the involvement of psychologists in sentencing has declined in recent years. The indeterminate, rehabilitation-oriented sentencing policies have been replaced by sentencing guidelines that seek to fit the punishment to the offense, not the offender. Under the old policies, psychologists were asked to evaluate the defendant and the likelihood that he or she could be rehabilitated. What role can psychology play in this new era in which the sentence is predetermined by numbers?

The new guidelines indicate that certain psychological circumstances permit a departure from the prescribed sentences (Hofer 1991, 1992b). These ordinarily would not include mental and emotional factors. For example, the Sentencing Commission's policy expressly states that defendants' "mental and emotional condition is not ordinarily relevant in sentencing" (Hofer, 1992b). However, as recent federal appellate court decisions have demonstrated, certain social or psychological characteristics of the defendant may justify departure from these constraints. These cases suggest a new role for psychologists and psychological research focusing on the defendant's responsibility for the crime. In one case, several members of a large drug ring were tried for drug trafficking. Three members used the defense of duress, claiming they had been coerced to work for the drug ring through physical violence and intimidation. Expert psychological testimony was presented on behalf of one of the defendants, indicating that she fit the profile of the battered woman syndrome. Psychologists testified that physical and emotional abuse can lead a woman to feel that she is helpless to escape from an intolerable situation.

The jury found all the defendants guilty. At sentencing, however, the defendant asked the judge to depart from the sentencing guidelines and allow for a lesser sentence. The appellate court found that psychological testimony with respect to the battered woman syndrome was relevant and could be used in the sentencing decisions (Hofer, 1992b).

Despite the apparent "give" in the system, many opponents of mandatory sentencing feel that permitting the crime rather than the offender to determine the sentence invites injustice. Michael Tonry (1995) concluded that mandatory sentencing shifts power away from judges to prosecutors and too often results in penalties that everyone involved considers too harsh and unjust (see the Courtroom Applications box on page 297).

JUSTICE AND THE JURY

The discussion of jury decision making in the last chapter shows that juries and jurors are not passive decision makers; they bring their own notions of what is right and wrong to the courtroom. Sometimes these notions outweigh the legal concepts given to them by the judge (Finkel, 1995). Indeed, throughout our history, Americans have been of two minds about the jury. One is that juries are fact finders who apply the law as stated by the judge to the case. This view is that jurors are prohibited from judging the merits of the law.

Although the jury is typically seen as fulfilling the role of fact finder (applying the law as explained by the judge to the evidence presented), it has also been described from time to time as serving a second function: A jury's decision should also reflect the morality of the community it is drawn from; the jury should act as the "conscience of the community" (Becker, 1980). One reason for this view is that juries have the power to ignore the law as given to them in the judge's instructions if they believe the application of the law would result in an injustice in a specific case. This power is known as **jury nullification** and has been described as a safeguard against government tyranny.

Note the tension, even the contradiction, with which we are dealing. On the one hand, the citizens who make up the jury are explicitly informed that law, and presumably justice, is defined by the judge. On the other hand, we expect the jury to go against the law if a miscarriage of justice might take place.

In 1994, 1995, and 1996, juries in Detroit acquitted Dr. Jack Kevorkian of violating a state law making it illegal to assist in a suicide. There was no question in each case that Dr. Kevorkian, the "suicide doctor," had taken an active role in an individual's death. In one instance he had placed a mask over the person's face and released carbon monoxide gas into the mask. Jurors interviewed after the trial suggested that Dr. Kevorkian acted only to relieve the person's suffering and did not intend to assist in suicide. Alleviating suffering is within the doctor's professional capacity. It seems obvious that the juries had selectively interpreted the evidence to render what they considered to be a just decision.

In 1990, a Washington, D.C., jury found Mayor Marion Barry guilty of one misdemeanor charge of cocaine possession. Barry was acquitted of several other, more serious narcotics charges. The jury had been shown a videotape of the mayor in a Washington, D.C., hotel room smoking cocaine with a woman, who turned out to be a police informant. Commentators speculated that the jury thought the African American mayor had been set up by the federal and police authorities, and although his behavior was not above reproach (hence the one guilty verdict), the jury was sending a message to the authorities not to attack elected African American officials (Abramson, 1995). In other words, in spite of the evidence and the law, the jury meted out its own version of justice. As we noted, the legal term for this type of verdict is *jury nullification.* One possible motivation for juries to nullify the law occurs when the criminal codes that specify the penalties for specific crimes call for outcomes the public thinks are either wrong or too harsh.

Juries and Criminal Codes

Paul H. Robinson (1994b) notes that a critical function of criminal law is to state publicly what conduct is prohibited and what conduct is required to conform to the law. This function of criminal law is central because citizens must know what the rules are if the law is to have an effect on their behavior. Furthermore, it is only fair that citizens know what is prohibited if they are to be punished for violating the law.

Robinson (1994a) raises the question of whether there is effective communication of what criminal law requires of the public. His sense is that the public's actual knowledge of the law is quite low. Robinson suggests that people have quite a different view of what the law commands than what is actually written in the criminal codes. If true, this inadequate knowledge would be a source of juror confusion in the court and could lead to jury decisions that do not conform to legal requirements.

A widespread lack of knowledge might explain, in part, why juries have so much difficulty understanding the judge's instructions. Not only is the language complex but the legal definitions of what makes an individual liable for a criminal offense and the degree of that liability do not ring true for the average juror. Does the public, at least in some instances, have a different notion from the law of what it means to commit a criminal offense, or the degree of seriousness of that offense? If so, what are the implications of the behavior and role of juries in meting out justice?

The Model Penal Code grades the seriousness of offenses and the degree of severity within offenses. Murder is graded more severely than is burglary. Within the category of murder, manslaughter is graded less seriously than is aggravated murder. Recall that the new sentencing guidelines discussed above essentially give judges quantitative gradings for types of offenses and seriousness within each offense.

The Model Penal Code is not published in our daily newspaper, so—not surprisingly—citizens are largely unaware of its contents; when they do become aware of it, they sometimes disagree with its assumptions. Legal scholar Paul Robinson and social psychologist John Darley (1995) collaborated on an extensive empirical study to learn the public's view of the requirements of law as set out in the Model Penal Code (MPC).

As noted, the MPC identifies various sexual offenses and also grades the seriousness within each offense. Forcible intercourse is adjudged more serious than consensual but unlawful intercourse. Therefore, forcible rape is graded as a more serious offense than is consensual intercourse with an underage partner. Within offenses, the law also makes distinctions. The MPC grades forcible intercourse as less serious when perpetrated on a voluntary social partner, or with someone with whom the defendant has had previous intercourse. Forcible intercourse is graded as simple assault (not rape) if the parties are married. Finally, forcible intercourse involving a gay couple living together is graded as less serious than rape (Robinson & Darley, 1995).

The procedure used by Robinson and Darley was to present various scenarios to the participants in their studies and ask them to assign liability—degree of guilt—for each offense. The researchers then compared these results to the outcomes mandated by the MPC. The scenarios given to the participants reflect the distinctions made by the MPC. For example, in one scenario, a woman was forcibly raped by a stranger with a weapon in a deserted parking lot. In a second scenario, a rape was perpetrated by a woman's "date" at her apartment. Other scenarios involved rape between cohabiting couples.

Citizens view important aspects of sexual offenses differently from the MPC. For example, the MPC views forcible intercourse in marriage, or with otherwise cohabiting couples, as misdemeanors, less serious crimes. How do private citizens assess sexual offenses?

Robinson and Darley suggest that the greatest difference between the MPC and the public's view involves forcible rape in which the aggressor and victim are a homosexual couple cohabiting. People saw this as of approximately the same seriousness as a similar situation involving a heterosexual married couple. The raters also considered as less serious than the MPC all forms of consensual sex, such as intercourse with a consenting minor, particularly if the minor initiated the contact. Clearly community sentiments on this issue differ in many respects from the decisions reflected in the MPC.

Sexual behavior resides on the boundary of public scrutiny and private behavior. It is not surprising that the public would view a private behavior, consensual sex, even if unlawful, as less punishable than coercive sex. The act of coercion puts the conduct in the public domain, whether the conduct concerns married or unmarried couples.

Justice and Private Behavior.   Norman J. Finkel (1995) has studied the impact of community sentiment on jury verdicts. He and his colleagues have examined other behaviors that cross the public/private boundary. Consider the issue of Dr. Kevorkian, the "suicide doctor." What is the community sentiment, as opposed to the dictates of the criminal code, with respect to a euthanasia case in which the patient asserts that he or she wishes to die? Finkel, Hurabiell, and Hughes (1993) had mock jurors give verdicts in trials in which a patient asks to be taken off life support, or in one case, asks to die and requests that her husband shoot her. He complies. In all the trials, the defendant is charged with first-degree murder and all the elements of that charge can be proved by the prosecution. The evidence supported a first-degree murder conviction.

Finkel et al. (1993) found that juries took several routes to express their disagreement with the requirements of the criminal code. First, about 25 percent of the jurors found the defendant not guilty. Finkel says these jurors simply nullified the law. Indeed, many jurors felt that death was a private matter and the law ought not to intrude. Nullifying jurors were careful as to which defendants they acquitted. A defendant who euthanized a patient who clearly expressed the wish to die, who was competent to do so, who had a living will, and who, along with the defendant, had tried (unsuccessfully) to get court approval for assisted suicide was not convicted. Another 39 percent of the jurors exhibited partial nullification—that is, they refused to find the defendant guilty of first-degree murder, but they did give a lesser, compromise verdict.

These findings suggest that when the law enters an area in which behavior falls into the "zone of privacy," many individuals are likely to conclude that the law does not have a place in regulating such behavior, or if it does have a place, the codes are out of touch with community sentiment (Finkel et al., 1993; Robinson & Darley, 1995). Also, we see here a tendency for juries to decide such cases on the basis of their own sense of justice rather than on the requirements of the law.

If the criminal codes and community sentiment differ, as they appear to do in a number of instances, what should be done? Should the law accommodate the sentiments of the public? Finkel (1990b) offers a conservative model. He says if there is a fundamental law at stake—such as the insanity defense in which a defendant lacking mens rea should not be found guilty of a crime—the law should not change according to community sentiment. As we learned earlier in this book, the public is quite suspicious of the insanity plea and some states have abolished it in theory, if not in fact. Finkel says that in this case, the law takes precedence over the sentiments of the public.

In fact, the public's view about what constitutes insanity does not seem to be significantly different from that expressed in law. Bailis and co-workers (1995) have shown agreement among ordinary citizens that both lack of ability to control one's behavior *and* serious impairment of one's cognitive functions constitute insanity; but citizens are more conservative in their judgment than the law. They want both dysfunctions to be present in a high degree before they will sustain an insanity defense (Bailis, Darley, Waxman, & Robinson, 1995).

If, however, a fundamental law is not at stake and the community's position is consistent with psychological and legal principles, but differs from the law on the books, then it would be profitable for the codes to be rewritten. An example is the views of juries and the requirements of the MPC on the seriousness of various sexual offenses. These viewpoints are quite different.

Juries, however, sometimes do not wait for the law to be rewritten; they act as mini-legislatures and rewrite the offending laws by refusing to convict defendants they believe are being treated unfairly by the law. This nullification is not limited to the public/private behavior boundary.

Research suggests that potential jurors have a somewhat different notion of the blameworthiness of some defendants in felony murder cases. Felony murder refers to killing that occurs in the course of a felony, such as robbing a bank. Criminal codes generally treat felony murders as more serious than murders that occur in nonfelonious circumstances (Robinson & Darley, 1995). Jurors tend to agree with this view, but as Finkel has shown, jurors assign less blame than do the codes to most accidental killings during a felony. The codes would punish with a murder conviction a defendant whose gun accidentally discharged during a robbery; jurors are more likely to return a lesser (manslaughter) verdict (Finkel and Duff, 1991; Robinson & Darley, 1995).

There are two types of law. There is "law on the books," commonly referred to as "black letter law." This is the law that legislators pass, the Constitution enumerates, and the judges declare in their common law decisions. But, as Finkel (1995) has observed, there is another "law" that he calls "commonsense justice," and it reflects what ordinary people think is just and fair. These are the lay representations jurors use to assess both the defendant and the law (Smith, 1991a). It is what ordinary people think the law ought to be (Sales, 1996, personal communication).

These commonsense notions are at once legal, moral, and psychological. They provide the citizen on the street and the juror in the jury box with a theory of why people think, feel, and behave as they do, and why the law should find some defendants guilty and punishable and others not. There is mounting and persuasive evidence that the "law on the books" may be at odds with common-sense justice in many areas (Finkel, 1995).

Jury Nullification as a Group Process

Juries have the implied power to acquit defendants despite evidence and judicial instructions to the contrary. Juries have this power because they may acquit without explanation or reprisal from the court. Those who favor the jury's right to nullify define that power as the right to return an acquittal when strict interpretation of the law would result in an injustice and violate the moral conscience of the community (Scheflin, 1988, personal communication; Scheflin & Van Dyke, 1991).

The most authoritative court decision concerning nullification is *United States v. Dougherty* (1972) in which the United States Court of Appeals for the Washington, D.C., Circuit debated the wisdom and historical basis of the nullification power, and the right of the jury to be informed of this power. *Dougherty* evolved out of the protests of the Vietnam war. The defense asked the trial judge to instruct the jury that they had the power to nullify unjust laws. The trial judge refused, and the D.C. Circuit upheld that ruling by a 2–1 margin.

Judge Leventhal, writing for the majority, argued that jurors knew full well through informal channels such as the news media that they could nullify without fear of reprisal. Judge Leventhal believed that juries would not abuse their nullification power if they had unofficial (anecdotal) knowledge of that power, but to tell the jury outright that they had nullification power was to loosen any restraints jurors might feel. The court recognized a curious situation: Juries can do what they wish but they cannot be explicitly told the true state of affairs. In Judge Leventhal's opinion, juries do not have the express right to nullify. They simply have the power to do so because the jury is free to return any verdict it wishes without explanation (Horowitz & Willging, 1991).

Horowitz (1985) investigated whether explicitly instructing jurors about their nullification power would increase acquittals as Judge Leventhal hypothesized. Juries who were explicitly informed of their nullification powers, as opposed to those who were simply "advised" of that power or who were given standard instructions, were less likely to find the defendant guilty in a euthanasia case and more likely to find the defendant guilty in a drunk driving case. The nullifying juries functioned differently from other juries in that they concentrated less on the evidence and more on their perception of the degree of fairness in the case.

A second experiment varied whether the defense attorney made an explicit nullification argument informing the jury that it may ignore the law if its application would lead to an unjust outcome. In addition, in each case the prosecutor either did or did not remind the jury of its responsibility to follow the law as explained in the judge's instructions (Horowitz, 1988). Generally, when instructed about the right to nullify the law, either by the judge's instructions or by the defense attorney's arguments, juries were more lenient than noninformed juries in a euthanasia trial and in a case of illegal possession of a weapon; defendants in both instances were very sympathetic. Conversely, juries rendered harsher decisions (more guilty verdicts) in a drunk driving case. The prosecutor's admonition to follow the law weakened the juries' nullification tendencies.

Juries, of course, may bring in a verdict contrary to legal guidelines without explicit nullification instructions. They may do so because of incompetence—that is, they may not understand the evidence or the law—or they may disobey the law when their preconceptions of the law conflict with the judicially provided definitions (Finkel, 1990a, 1990b, 1995). For example, Wiener, Habert, Shkodriani, and Staebler (1991) found that mock jurors' subjective views of the blameworthiness of defendants were the causal factors determining the verdict despite contrary judicial instructions. This occurred even when the juries clearly understood the instructions.

Not every jury decision that flies in the face of the law and the evidence is a nullifying verdict. We consider jury nullification an example of moral and/or political disobedience. A nullifying jury will decide that their role is not simply to follow the judge's interpretation of the law; rather, this jury assumes they have the explicit right to go beyond the judge's instructions.

We apply the term *jury nullification* to those situations in which juries understand the law and the facts and deliberately decide to ignore the evidence because to do otherwise would violate their sense of justice. These juries will objectively process the trial evidence and the judge's instructions but will make a moral decision to disobey the law. Nullifying juries will be driven by the perceived unfairness of the law. They may and often do consider the sympathy-arousing qualities of the defendant or plaintiff. The most important factor leading to nullification is the jurors' perception of legal injustice.

Nullifying juries differ from juries who follow the judge's instructions in that some aspect of the law provokes them to redefine their role as different from one that requires compliance with the judicial instructions. The new role places a higher value on the jurors' moral conscience, even if the dictates of that conscience do not conform with the requirements of the law. Levine (1983, 1984, 1992) has argued that juries are susceptible to changing political norms and has found evidence to support this thesis in the fluctuation of conviction rates in draft evasion, civil rights, and rape cases. When community sentiment changes on these issues, jury verdicts tend to reflect that change.

Of course, the law is understandably uncomfortable with the idea that juries can apply their own notions of justice regardless of the constraints of the legal codes. The nullifying power of the jury was welcomed by colonial America because colonial juries stood as bulwarks interposed between the citizenry and the English crown. Only at the turn of the twentieth century (*Sparf and Hansen v. United States,* 1895) did the courts curb the explicit power of juries to nullify.

However shadowy the jury's current nullification power, its existence provides a safety valve for those circumstances in which strict application of the law seems clearly unfair to members of the community. Nullification power places a check on the professional legal system, which can become too technical and insensitive to the needs of the citizens who use or are caught up in that system.

JUSTICE AND THE CIVIL JURY

Recall that in Chapter 2 we discussed the role of civil law in the United States. Civil law governs the legal relations among individuals and entities, such as corporations. Civil law provides the rules and procedures for repairing violations of agreements or duties between individuals. The government's role here is to be a referee. The government provides the law, the judges, the courts, and the rules of proceedings, but it does not initiate suit or penalty.

A Brief History of the American Civil Jury

The civil jury's role in the legal system derives from the Seventh Amendment to the United States Constitution, which guarantees civil litigants the right to a jury trial in federal court "in suits of common law, where the value in controversy shall exceed twenty dollars." The right to a civil jury trial (or criminal trial) was established primarily to secure the impartial resolution of facts and to guard against arbitrary action by the government. The civil jury was not in general use during colonial times and its inclusion in the Bill of Rights appeared to be a concession to those colonialists who owed money to the British and wanted to be sure that British claims would be heard before juries who were sympathetic (Kirst, 1982; Rutland, 1955).

　　The existence of the civil jury had everything to do with justice. Colonials rarely had a jury to protect them from foreclosures and other loss of property or liberty as a result of their failure to pay debts. Unlike the early juries in criminal trials, civil juries did not have unrestrained power. British judges effectively controlled juries by removing certain cases from them and reviewing or guiding their decisions (Kirst, 1982). Civil juries, for example, were excluded from cases involving divorce and certain complex business issues (equity courts) and shipping (admiralty courts) (Devlin, 1980). Indeed, one of the objections of the antifederalists (those who did not favor the new 1787 constitution) was the lack of a jury in such cases (Rakove, 1996).

　　When the British imposed trade laws that the colonists thought unfair, they evaded such laws by smuggling. If caught by the British, smugglers were set free by colonial juries who simply nullified what they considered to be unfair laws. Colonial juries not only nullified the enforcement of unpopular British trade laws by acquitting smugglers but they also punished the British naval officers involved by imposing civil liability, requiring the officers to pay damages to the smugglers. The British evaded this nullification tactic by simply trying smuggling cases in admiralty courts, before British judges and not colonial juries. Because of this history, the Seventh Amendment, as enacted, contains the seeds for evading a jury trial in cases deemed complex or otherwise inappropriate for the jury.

Modern Civil Law

Modern civil trials usually involve contracts, torts, or competitive or trade practices in business. Disputes arising out of contract law essentially involve the disappointed expectations of one of the parties to the contract. The existence of civil law relies on something other than the honor of the parties to live up to the contract. That "something" is that those who breach a contract and face a civil suit will be made to pay in coin of the realm for their infidelity. Indeed, the existence of civil law serves to keep people from shooting each other in the streets, something we do with some frequency. Even if a defendant wins a civil suit, the cost of defending may be punishment enough to satisfy the plaintiff.

Tort law, which dominates modern civil law, deals with noncriminal harm. **A tortious act,** an act that does harm, may be the basis of a lawsuit. The system of tort law serves several purposes, the first of which is to resolve the disputed claims of those who have been injured. Second, it also serves to compensate people for those injuries. Third, the system operates to deter others from engaging in negligent behavior. Finally, tort law may serve to set a standard so that individuals and companies are aware of what is considered acceptable and what is not. In other words, tort law has a moral or educative function (Wiener, 1990). Note that tort law may operate in the same way that criminal codes do in the criminal arena. It sets the standard for behavior in the civil arena and spells out what the consequences are for violating those standards.

One type of tort, negligence, has come to be the foremost basis for legal action in civil courts. Lawrence Friedman (1985) traces the explosive increase in tort law and especially negligence to the advent of the industrial revolution. The railroads, which dominated the life of the country after the civil war, caused accidents and injuries that were unforeseen in number and scope. The law, however, made it very difficult for the injured workers to receive compensation. In part, this was a cold-blooded decision to favor expanding industry over the injured. Railroads and factories would be hindered in their expansion if they were too concerned with safety. Commerce was favored over workers in the latter half of the nineteenth century (Friedman, 1985).

A plaintiff had to prove that he or she was entirely faultless in the event. If the plaintiff was even the least bit at fault, the defendant would prevail. Even if the plaintiffs passed that hurdle, they ran into the "fellow-servant rule." If the injury was caused by a fellow worker, say the railroad engineer, the injured worker could sue only the fellow worker, not the railroad itself.

Tort law began to change late in the nineteenth century. As Lawrence Friedman (1985) has shown, these changes came slowly but were forced on grudging lawmakers by a cascade of personal injuries. For example, in 1889, 1 out of every 35 railroad workmen sustained some form of serious injury. One out of 357 died on the job. Tort law, because of the fellow-servant rule, prohibited any compensation. Friedman reports that in 1876, 58 railroads doing business in Illinois paid out $119 million in damages for the death of cattle, but only $3,000 to injured workers. Tort law was ripe for change. The fellow servant rule disappeared into history.

In modern tort law, several legal rules may be applied. Most plaintiffs in product liability cases seek to be compensated under a **strict liability rule.** This means that if a manufacturer puts a product on the market and it is defective (unreasonably dangerous) and causes injuries to the user, the manufacturer is liable. Note that this rule says nothing about the behavior of the user. Negligence means that the producer of the product or drug is liable if it fails to take reasonable care to avoid harm to the user.

However, under a **contributory negligence rule,** the *defendant,* reacting to the plaintiff's complaint, tries to show that the *plaintiff* failed to exercise the care that a reasonable person would. The *defendants* argue, as a defense, that the plaintiffs acted in an unreasonable manner. Now, it is not up to the user to discover that the Handy Dandy lawn mower was defective or that a particular drug could cause birth defects. If you used the lawn mower in a particularly dangerous way, however, and you knew it was dangerous, then proof of this might bar you from recovering any damages at all under the contributory negligence rule.

Finally, under a third rule, the **comparative negligence rule,** the law attempts to divide liability between the plaintiff and the defendant in proportion to the percentage of fault each party bears. If the plaintiff is judged to be 30 percent at fault and the defendant 70 percent, the plaintiff is awarded 70 percent of what the full amount would have been if the plaintiff had been faultless.

That civil juries make judgments about the fairness of the rules under which they are asked to assign responsibility for a tort is not surprising. Central to a finding of negligence are attributions of blame and responsibility. Informing juries about the legal consequences of their decisions invites a judgment by the jury of the fairness of the law as well as the facts. Most courts do not inform juries of the consequences of these standards and when they have done so, appellate courts have overturned verdicts on that basis.

However, at least eight state legislatures have enacted laws permitting or mandating that the jury be told of the legal consequences of their decisions within the context of negligence cases. Several other states have reached the same result by judicial decision (Kotler, 1985). In the remaining states, juries are not told about the consequences of their decisions, but while they may be "blindfolded," they are not mute (Diamond, Casper, & Ostergren, 1989). When juries are asked to divide the responsibility attributed to the parties, we expect that they will be able to figure out why the court has asked for this judgment (Sommer, Bourgeois, & Horowitz, 1997).

The Power of the Jury and the Judge

We have previously traced the lessening of jury power and the increase of the controlling power of the judge. Civil juries are especially constrained and controlled by the judge. For example, judges have the power of **summary judgment** (the judge may issue a finding in the case without calling a jury) in civil cases in which the parties do not dispute the facts and only the interpretation of the law is at issue. For example, if plaintiff and defendant agree that they each signed a contract and that the defendant failed to pay his or her share, the judge will be able to decide whether the contract was legal and enforceable. This is an efficient and time-saving procedure. Therefore, juries are excluded from cases that have no significant factual dispute (*Anderson v. Liberty Lobby, Inc.,* 1986).

Judges in civil trials can also direct the jury to bring in a special verdict, one that answers questions in a controlled fashion. The judge may ask: Did the defendant manufacture the product? Did the product cause the plaintiff's injuries? What were the plaintiff's damages for medical care? Each question serves as a hurdle that must be answered before the next one can be considered.

The fact is that judges came to distrust the jury in civil cases. The professional judiciary simply did not think the jury was capable of dealing competently with modern complex civil cases (Kirst, 1982). The jury's power to speak as conscience of the community became muted, giving the judiciary more power to control the civil jury.

Although a judge may stop a case from going to the jury at a number of points for a variety of reasons, not every case can be pigeonholed. It is a rare tort case in which liability is decided not as a matter of fact (the jury's province) but as a matter of law (the judge's bailiwick). Some evidence suggests that judges' decisions on law tend to favor the defendants in tort cases (Ostrom, Rottman, & Goerdt, 1996), so a jury trial may give the plaintiff a better chance at winning. Keep in mind, however, that cases of which the judge takes control may differ significantly from those in which the judge permits a jury trial. Probably, the cases in which the judge finds the legal basis to be faulty will lead to a decision in favor of the defendant as opposed to the one who brought the case initially—the plaintiff. If the theory of the case, the law under which the case is brought, is wrong, then clearly the plaintiffs will suffer. Furthermore, as we will soon see, many jurors tend to be quite skeptical of plaintiffs and their claims for compensation (Hans & Lofquist, 1992).

Note that all this concern about the allocation of power to judges versus juries in civil trials is based on the assumption that judges have some special ability to control their emotions and that juries give free rein to their sympathies. Stephan Landsman and Richard Rakos (1994) have conducted one of the very few empirical investigations of this issue. These investigators compared the performances of actual judges and jurors in mock civil trials in which both were exposed to biasing information that was ruled admissible in some instances and inadmissible in others. Whether the information was ruled inadmissible or not, *both* judges and jurors were influenced by the information. This, of course, is but one study involving only 31 judges, but it suggests that judges are no less vulnerable than jurors to information that legally ought not to be considered.

Other research also suggests that judges may not be as hardheaded as supposed. Kevin Clermont and Theodore Eisenberg (1992) found that judges awarded almost twice as much money to plaintiffs who claimed injuries caused by medical negligence (medical malpractice) than did juries. However, judges and juries did not deal with the same cases, so there could have been something about the **bench trials** (trial before the judge) that may have involved more severe injuries. Still, one possibility is that judges were also more benevolent than juries (Vidmar, 1996).

Neil Vidmar and Jeffrey Rice (1993) compared jurors who were awaiting jury service in a mock medical malpractice trial with veteran lawyers who serve as arbitrators in cases not tried before a judge; some of the lawyers had actually been judges. The trial involved a scenario in which a surgeon had accidentally placed a very hot instrument on the plaintiff's knee. The action had caused severe pain to the plaintiff, and skin grafts were necessary to repair the injury. Table 11.3 shows that jurors and professional arbitrators gave roughly the same awards. The assumption that jurors are more generous than legal professionals (judges or arbitrators) is not supported in this or other empirical studies. Neither is the notion that juries are capricious in assigning awards for pain and suffering (Vidmar, 1996). If anything, compared to legal or medical professionals, juries gave less money than was warranted (Daniels & Martin, 1995). Michael Saks (1992) has made a strong case that juries undercompensate much of the time, especially for serious losses. Recent evidence presented by Stephen Daniels and Joanne Martin (1995) support Saks's findings.

Juries seem to be more variable in their awards than judges as Table 11.3 shows. Note the wider range of jury awards ($11,000 to $197,000) compared to arbitrators' awards ($22,000 to $82,000). Other research has also shown that juries tend to be more unpredictable than judges (Goodman, Greene, & Loftus, 1990; Horowitz & Bordens, 1988). This result is not really surprising because judges probably differ less on decision-making tactics than do juries, which comprise a much wider sample of the population than does the legal profession.

How Jurors Think About Torts

What we can conclude from the few empirical studies comparing judges and civil juries in awarding compensation is that by and large no significant differences

TABLE 11.3	Awards Made by Professional Arbitrators and Lay Jurors	
	Arbitrators	**Jurors**
Median	$57,000	$47,850
Mean	$50,433	$51,852
Range	$22,000–82,000	$11,000–197,000
Standard deviation	$16,730	$28,981

Source: From Vidmar and Rice, 1993, p. 901, Table 1.

exist and when we notice a difference, judges appear more generous than juries, although the latter finding is probably due to fact that judges deal with different cases than those assigned to juries. The causal observer of the scene might be surprised at these findings because the popular press portrays juries as out of control, giving outlandish awards for seemingly trivial injuries. One recent example inflamed jury critics. In the fall of 1994, 82-year-old Stella Liebeck bought a container of coffee from the drive-in window of a McDonald's in Albuquerque. She drove away and started to pry off the lid and in doing so spilled some coffee on her lap, resulting in third-degree burns and requiring skin grafts (Miller, 1995). She sued and received an award of $2.7 million. A judge subsequently reduced the punitive damages to $480,000. Judges have the power to reduce an excessive award (known as **remittitur**) or increase an inadequate award (**additur**).

Well, we all spill coffee, and sometimes it's painful, but $480,000 seems excessive. A closer look at the case however suggests some caution in drawing conclusions about "runaway juries." McDonald's had traditionally brewed its coffee at 180–190 degrees Fahrenheit and when coffee that hot spills in one's lap, it's very painful. Indeed, McDonald's had encountered 700 incidents over the years of customers being burned with its coffee. The 82-year-old plaintiff spent eight days in the hospital and underwent skin graft operations. She was willing to settle for medical costs. McDonald's refused (Miller, 1995). The jury considered the fact that McDonald's had ignored the 700 previous incidents and did not treat Liebeck's case seriously. The judge who reduced the award to $480,000 noted that McDonald's exhibited "callous conduct." The reality is that most lawsuits like this one would normally be settled out of court. Juries are considered unpredictable and insurance companies who pay the costs of suits against large companies such as McDonald's would rather settle than face what they feel is an unpredictable jury verdict.

Evidence shows that jurors do respond differently to individuals and business corporations, but there are many reasons for this difference. The role of the jury in civil litigation has been much debated and the notion that juries are unable to treat corporations fairly is one of the crucial points of the debate (Hans, 1996). The public perception is that the country is in a "litigation explosion," a phrase suggesting that the courts are overwhelmed with lawsuits and that many of the lawsuits are frivolous.

Another part of this perception is that the awards are outrageous (see the Liebeck verdict) and that lawyers actively seek these cases for greedy reasons. For example, this ad recently appeared in a newspaper: "Injured? Need legal help? We'll fight for you! No legal fees until you win!" ("Barring the Courthouse Door," 1995, p. B3). Is this an invitation to sue or not?

Implicit in this newspaper ad is one of the critical aspects of the American tort system: the contingency fee. With a contingency fee, lawyers will take a case without an up-front fee. If the plaintiff wins, the lawyer takes a large percentage of the award—perhaps 40 percent plus costs. If the plaintiff loses, he or she does not have to pay the attorney. Other legal systems, such as Great Britain's, do not have contingency fees. With the existence of contingency fees, people who could otherwise not sue have access to redress. Critics suggest that the downside is that people who ought not sue are given access to the courts.

Jurors' Views of Civil Justice: Business in the Dock.   Valerie Hans's research program has illuminated how ordinary jurors perceive the conflict between individuals and corporations. Hans and William Lofquist (1992) have found that the public's perception of a proliferation of lawsuits (litigation explosion) strongly affects their perception of justice. (Note that we have yet to address the issue of whether there really is an explosion of litigation.)

In any event, jurors think there are too many lawsuits. Hans and Lofquist (1994) interviewed 269 jurors who had participated in trials involving business over a two-year period. Most jurors believed that there are too many frivolous lawsuits, yet they feel that juries do a pretty good job in deciding cases and awarding appropriate damages.

What effects do these attitudes have on jury verdicts? Hans and Ermann (1989) conducted a mock jury study to learn whether jurors, when faced with precisely the same evidence, treated individual defendants and corporations differently. In this study, half the jurors were told that the defendant was a Mr. Jones; the remaining jurors were told that the defendant was Jones Corporation. Table 11.4 shows the differences in awards based on the identity of the defendant. Recall that the evidence was the same in both trials. Note that in every category (hospital bills, doctor bills, pain and suffering, and the total award) the Jones Corporation had to pay more than the Jones individual.

To understand the reasoning, look at Table 11.5. These data suggest that jurors thought the corporation was more legally and morally responsible for the injuries, and more reckless than the individual. These findings imply that jurors hold corporations to a higher standard of behavior than they do individuals. Jurors generally feel that corporations simply have more resources at their disposal and should behave more responsibly because of those resources—another instance in which the legal definitions do not match the views of the citizens. Do you think it is unfair to hold corporations to a higher standard?

TABLE 11.4   Awards as a Function of Individual or Corporate Wrongdoing

Category of Award	Against Mr. Jones	Against Jones Corporation	Statistically Significant
Hospital bills	$ 38,069	$ 40,000	Yes (F = 5.78)[*]
Doctor bills	$ 31,337	$ 36,910	Yes (F = 8.78)
Pain and suffering	$ 82,178	$170,700	Yes (F = 21.97)
Total award	$151,584	$248,610	Yes

Note: Asterisk means that $p < .01$.

Source: Adapted from "Responses to Corporate Versus Individual Wrongdoing," by V. P. Hans and M. Ermann, 1989, *Law and Human Behavior, 13,* p. 157, Table 1.

TABLE 11.5   Perceptions of Liability as a Function of Individual or
                       Corporate Wrongdoing

Item	Mr. Jones	Jones Corporation	Statistically Significant Difference
A. *Deep Pockets*			
Likelihood of having insurance	2.25	3.20	Yes[*]
Likelihood that award will cause bankruptcy	3.07	1.76	Yes[*]
Fairness of being sued	3.71	4.13	Yes[*]
Fairness of specific claims	2.77	3.35	Yes[*]
B. *Judgments of Wrongdoing*			
Knew of danger before suit	1.52	1.89	Yes[*]
Showed recklessness	2.50	3.08	Yes[*]
Behaved in a morally wrong way	2.28	2.78	Yes[*]
Deserves punishment	2.38	3.04	Yes[*]
C. *Consequences of Incident*			
Has regret over incident	3.96	3.60	Yes[*]

Note: With numbers, higher means more—more likely, more fair, more reckless, more
regretful. Asterisks mean that $p < .02$.

Source: Adapted from "Responses to Corporate Versus Individual Wrongdoing," by
V. P. Hans and M. Ermann, 1989, *Law and Human Behavior, 13,* p. 158, Table 2.

The differential treatment of corporations and individuals may change over
time. Hans and Lofquist (1992) interviewed jurors who had served in business-
related tort trials, and these jurors stated that their decisions were not influenced
by whether either party was corporate or individual. Keep in mind that judges
and lawyers (for the corporations) always admonish the jurors not to hold corporations to a different standard of conduct (Hans, 1996).

Are juries more inclined to side with the plaintiff? Apparently not. Ostrom
et al. (1996) reported that plaintiffs in medical malpractice trials win one out of
three times. Overall, judges rule half the time for plaintiffs; juries do so only 29
percent of the time. The trend is for corporations (defendants) to win an increasing percentage of trials. The plaintiff win rate depends on the type of case. Medical malpractice and product liability cases favor the defendants. Trials involving
toxic substances such as asbestos and automobile-related lawsuits favor the
plaintiffs (Ostrom et al., 1996). As Figure 11.1 shows, the dollar amount of
awards won by plaintiffs have stayed steady over the same period.

The public perception is also that when juries do favor the plaintiffs, the
awards are out of all proportion to the injury. Recall that in the Hans and Ermann (1989) study, mock jurors awarded the plaintiffs significantly more money

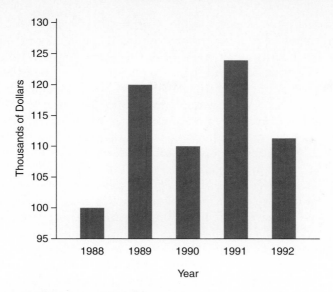

FIGURE 11.1   Median jury award by year.

This illustration suggests that despite the perception of sharply increasing jury awards, the actual amounts vary year to year; overall, however, they have not risen in recent years.

Source: Adapted from "Should Business Be Afraid of Juries?" by L. Himelstein, 1993, *Business Week,* November 8, p. 101.

when the defendant was a corporation rather than an individual. Let's take a closer look at this "deep pockets" effect.

Deep Pockets and Civil Juries.   As Hans (1996) notes, lawyers believe as an article of faith that juries award more money to plaintiffs if the defendant is a rich corporation. The assumption is that corporations have "deep pockets" filled with moneybags that can be used to improve the lives of those injured in tort cases. Juries are perceived by some to be modern-day Robin Hoods (Huber, 1991).

The evidence about the deep pockets tendency of juries is at best mixed and quite possibly leans toward the notion that juries do not excessively punish rich corporations. An early study by Chin and Peterson (1985) showed that corporations were assessed more damages than individual defendants but only when the injuries were severe. By severe, we mean injuries that affected the plaintiff's quality and length of life such as para- or quadriplegia.

In several experiments, Hans (1996) found that the *status* of the corporation makes a difference, not its "deep pockets." This means that the public holds a corporation to a higher level of responsibility than it does an individual defendant. More significant than the jurors' attitudes toward business was their belief that corporations must be responsible. Corporations may be held to a higher standard, and therefore required to pay out higher sums, not because they have more money but because they could have prevented the harmful (tortious) actions. Hans found little support for the deep pockets hypothesis. She gave mock jurors information about the financial status of the companies involved in her trial scenarios and jurors were certainly aware of their worth. But jurors did not take this financial information into account when assigning awards. Most jurors said that the assets of the corporation were not relevant to the assignment of awards (Hans, 1994). Lack of support for the deep pockets hypothesis has been supported by other studies as well (Vidmar, 1996).

The deep pockets hypothesis brings about controversy not only in the venue of corporate law but also in the medical malpractice arena. Again the public perception is that jurors have been giving huge awards and because insurance companies are always involved in these cases, jurors are willing to dip into the deep pockets of those organizations to recompense individual plaintiffs (Vidmar, 1996). Medical malpractice has a resonance with the public. Accidental removal of the wrong limb or brain damage caused by medical mistakes are devastating, and we all can identify or empathize with plaintiffs who have suffered from such errors. Often, as Neil Vidmar (1992) has shown, jurors will award very large sums in these instances.

However, what critics often choose to overlook is that the results of medical malpractice can be devastating both financially and physically. Vidmar (1992) recounts a case in which the parents of a baby who suffered severe brain damage at birth accepted a $750,000 settlement. The size of the settlement generally invites scrutiny from critics of the tort system, but as Vidmar noted, the parents immediately received a bill from the county health services for $650,000. Research shows that juries rationally award damages in line with the amount of economic loss suffered by the plaintiff (Daniels & Martin, 1995).

We should note here that although juries decide compensation in a rational manner (Vidmar, 1993), they are not immune to social influence techniques used by lawyers. Gretchen Chapman and Brian Bornstein (in press) found that the higher the compensatory damages requested by plaintiffs, the more likely the defendant was to be blamed for the plaintiffs' injuries. In addition, the plaintiffs' awards were related to the amount requested.

The **ad damnun** (the plaintiff's statement presented to the jury concerning the monetary loss suffered) serves as an anchor to help determine the worth of the injuries. An interesting finding is that jurors do not see high ad damnum requests as signaling a more severe injury and greater probability of defendant liability. Nonetheless, the amount requested provides a basis for estimates that the defendant caused the injuries, and the anchor directly affects the compensation awarded.

Deep Pockets and Punitive Damages.   When observers express concern about the size of the awards given plaintiffs, they are really referring to punitive damages, not compensatory awards. Compensatory awards are calculated on the basis of reasonably accessible numbers. In a medical malpractice case, testimony will provide estimates of how long the injured party will be expected to live and how much expense the family will incur in health care and other costs. Add pain and suffering of the family, and juries can do a rough rational calculation of how much will be required to compensate the parents, make them "whole" again.

Assessing punitive damages is an entirely different task. It is a kind of "black box" (MacCoun, 1989). Unlike awarding compensation, punitive damages permit juries to punish the defendant so as to deter such behavior in the future—in effect, to hit a defendant with a two-by-four to make sure he or she gets the message. Jury discussion about punitive damages centers on the jurors' values and sentiments (Kaplan & Miller, 1987). We really know very little of how punitive damages are decided or how juries calculate these damages (Saks, 1992). Statistical information about the tort system is quite limited, as Michael Saks (1992) has shown. What we do know is that only 4 percent of all verdicts won by plaintiffs include an award for punitive damages (Ostrom et al., 1996).

Vidmar (1993), however, in a well-designed study showed that there is no significant trend to award plaintiffs more when they sue a hospital (deep pockets) as opposed to an individual medical doctor. Other research suggests that when doctors are charged to pay higher damage awards, the reason is that jurors hold them to a high level of responsibility because of their training and position, not because medical doctors are more affluent than other defendants, as the deep pockets hypothesis holds (Bourgeois & Horowitz, cited in Vidmar, 1993). Saks (1992) reports that the median award for compensation (in product liability cases) during the years 1965 to 1990 was $510,000. The median punitive damage award was $625,000. Both these figures were reduced on appeal to $212,783 for compensatory and $135,000 for punitive damages.

Data derived from a study of the 75 largest counties in the United States found that in 1992, 762,000 civil suits (torts, contracts, disputes over property rights) were filed in these counties (Cohen & Miller, 1995). Only 364 cases involved punitive damages. In many ways, the jury is superfluous to the civil justice system. True, it represents the ultimate arbiter, but of the 762,000 cases only 12,000 went to trial. This shows clearly that 750,000 cases were settled or dismissed or withdrawn somewhere along the line. Among medical malpractice cases, 90 percent are settled without trial and most injuries caused by the health care system are not even reported (Daniels & Martin, 1995).

Who wins the jury trials? The plaintiffs lost 5,800 trials and won 6,200 trials. In 364 of those 6,200 trials, plaintiffs received punitive damages; in the remaining trials, only compensatory awards were given (Daniels & Martin, 1995).

The median award was $50,000, so half were below $50,000. The mean award was $750,000, an average figure that was inflated by a few large awards. Forty-two cases involved awards of $1 million or more and totaled (for all 42 trials) $267.8 million. Table 11.6 summarizes these and other findings.

And what of the "litigation explosion"? Are the courts clogged with an increasing number of civil lawsuits from a society whose citizens will sue at the

---

TABLE 11.6 Results of 762,000 Civil Suits in 1992

Total jury trials	12,000 (of 762,000)
Plaintiff wins	6,200
Plaintiff losses	5,800
Number punitive awards	364
Median award	$50,000
Mean award	$735,000
Number of million dollar awards	42
Sum of million dollar awards	$267.8 million
Product liability cases	360
Plaintiff wins	142
Number of punitive awards	3 (all less than $250,000)
Medical malpractice punitive damage awards	13 (of the 403 that the plaintiffs won; in 4 cases plaintiffs won more than $250,000 but not more than $1,000,000)

Source: Adapted from data provided by S. Daniels and J. Martin, *Civil Juries and the Politics of Reform*, Evanston, IL: Northwestern Press, 1995.

drop of a lawyer's contingency fee? The National Center for State Courts (1995) reported that product liability suits involve but 4 percent of all civil case filings. Furthermore, by one measure, product liability filings have been falling in federal courts since 1985 (Kuttner, 1995). The primary source of growth in civil cases comes not from torts but from domestic disputes, contracts, and real estate claims (Saks, 1992).

In conclusion, it would seem that the litigation explosion is more apparent than real. It is also clear that runaway juries, those who presumably give outlandish awards, have run so far away that we can hardly find them. They are few and far between. If anything, the evidence suggests that much of the time juries undercompensate victims. Even when juries do give large awards, judges tend to reduce them on appeal.

IMPROVING JUSTICE

On the surface, the case seemed fairly simple. A tobacco company, Liggett, losing money and noting that certain "generic" cigarettes were selling quite well at a lower price, decided to put out its own low-priced brand. Liggett marketed really cheap black-and-white packs and sold them at various discount stores in North Carolina. Sales skyrocketed.

Adler (1995), who has chronicled the jury's performance in the case we are considering (*Brown Group Ltd. v. Brown & Williamson Tobacco Corp.*, 1993), reported that Liggett's move was followed by competitor Brown & Williamson

(B&W). B&W put a low-priced brand on the same market and charged the wholesalers, those who distributed the cigarettes to the discount outlet stores, a much lower price than Liggett charged. Under the Robinson-Patman Act, companies could not charge some customers less than others if that strategy was aimed at undercutting a rival and interfering with the competitive market. B&W said no, that's not what we were doing; Liggett said, yes you were, and sued.

Of course, the trial turned out to be anything but simple. It was a complex commercial case dealing with accounting issues such as "average variable cost determinations" and the tax consequences of "last-in, first-out" accounting (Adler, 1995). The trial took five months and the jurors no doubt often experienced headaches listening to arcane arguments.

Furthermore, several jurors wondered what the argument was all about. Recall our previous discussion of community views of criminal and civil codes. What was wrong, some jurors wondered, with one company selling their product for less than a competitor? Wasn't that the name of the game—to capture as much of the market as possible? Certainly, the consumers of the product were not hurt by the lower prices.

The jury consisted of nine people, including a millworker, a school custodian, a receptionist, a furniture worker, a nurse's aide, and a housewife. The jury did not understand a great deal of the accounting verbiage but in the end they agreed that Liggett had violated the Robinson-Patman Act. Still some of the jurors thought that the law was wrong, but perhaps, they thought, they did not understand it.

In the end, the U.S. Supreme Court found that a "reasonable jury" could not have found B&W's actions illegal. As at least the jury's foreman had suspected all along, B&W had carried out some rough but legal competitive practices.

There is little question that in many complex trials the jury faces a formidable task. On a purely pragmatic level, it is not clear that the justice system, despite its many detractors, has a viable alternative to the jury. For example, none of the evidence we have reviewed suggests that judges would decide cases in a manner significantly different from juries.

Besides, juries have advantages. Jurors represent the community. Sometimes their combined wisdom may be more compelling than the law. George Barnard Shaw observed that all professions are a conspiracy against the public. Juries can function to keep the system more open and honest. However, none of this bars reform in the jury system. A number of changes might help the finders of the fact.

Proposed Reforms

Many critics of the justice system have suggested a variety of reforms (Brookings Institution, 1993; Strier, 1994). Proposed reforms appear to fall into two categories: empowering the jury, and reconstructing the justice system. For our purposes, the first category is more relevant. We consider the jury reforms in some detail and then briefly present the arguments of those who want not only to throw out the bath water but to trade in the baby as well. These critics want to alter the basic adversarial trial by jury.

Jury Reforms. According to a report prepared by the Brookings Institution (1993), there is nothing wrong with the jury that could not be cured by a little respect. The evidence we reviewed in this chapter suggests that, by and large, juries' decisions are not irrational or incompetent. Furthermore, juries take their responsibilities very seriously and try to reach fair and equitable verdicts (Brookings Institution, 1993).

The problem is that the justice system views the jury as a passive receptacle; it considers them nincompoops yet expects them to process the most arcane testimony and the most turgid instructions that can be written by unimaginative jurists (Margolick, 1993b). The Brookings Institution study summarized the results of a meeting during which practicing lawyers, judges, and law professors discussed and evaluated the jury. These scholars concluded the following:

1. Courts should permit more extensive use of visual exhibits, including videotapes of trial testimony and computer demonstrations or simulations.
2. The rules of evidence should be simplified, reflecting confidence in the ability of jurors to evaluate what they hear in court as intelligently as what they hear outside it.
3. Lawyers and judges should inform jurors more regularly and explicitly, through periodic instructions, statements, and summations, about the nature and direction of a trial.
4. Judges should spell out jury instructions in clear, plain English free of legal jargon and they should give juries printed copies of their instructions.
5. Juries of 12 members, rather than 6, should be used to assure greater predictability and a more representative jury.
6. Major improvements should be made in the conditions under which jurors perform their duties.
7. Jurors should be given certain rights to ensure that they are treated with the utmost respect by the system. This may be accomplished by instituting, among others, the following Brookings recommendations.

- The process of jury selection should be random so that it covers most of the eligible population and allows everyone to serve.
- The process of exclusion from the jury should be blind with respect to gender, race, religion, country of origin, or any other categorical criteria, and there should be no challenge of prospective jurors because of these criteria.*
- A potential juror should be called only in the strong likelihood that his or her service will be needed in voir dire or on a jury. The jurors must be treated with respect; they should have reasonable and comfortable sur-

---

*Some suggest that peremptory challenges be abolished and the jury be selected randomly from the venire. Eliminating this aspect of the trial would remove the perception that jurors are mere pawns to be manipulated by the attorneys. It would also make for a more representative jury (Strier, 1994).

roundings and should be excused as soon as their service is no longer required.

- Jurors should be reasonably free from coercion to answer questions from reporters and should be protected from threats or reprisals because of their verdicts (Brookings Institution, 1993).

Jury Aids. A number of commentators have suggested that juries should be better informed and given more tools to do their jobs. We have reviewed most of these potential aids, such as note taking and access to written transcripts, in earlier chapters. Some of the evidence on the effectiveness of these aids is mixed. The safe observation is that more research is needed, as indeed it is. Nevertheless, the following jury aids need to be seriously considered and evaluated.

Juries should be able to take notes, ask questions, obtain a transcript or videotape or a copy of any testimony or evidence, obtain a written copy or tape of instructions, and have the judge's instructions presented before and after hearing the evidence.

Finally, there is little evidence that "blindfolding" the jury does anything but make them suspicious of the system. Blindfolding means that the court hides certain evidence because it believes the jury will be unable to evaluate the evidence competently within the rules of evidence (Diamond et al., 1989). For example, in a medical malpractice case no mention is made of the liability insurance the defendant may have. Juries are often blind to the consequences of a contributory negligence standard. They may not know that if the plaintiff is even 1 percent at fault, no award will be made. As Diamond and her colleagues note, jurors probably go ahead and make their own assumptions anyway. If the jury is allowed to hear evidence concerning accounting practices such as variable cost accounting, they can be told about the defendant's insurance policy. At least, they will be operating with facts instead of fantasies.

Note that all these aids increase the jury's power and participation in the trial. Judges in civil trials have the power under Federal Rules of Evidence to institute many of these changes in their courtrooms. Federal judges currently use a surprising number of these proposed aids. Seventy percent of federal judges now allow jurors to take notes on a regular basis (ForsterLee & Horowitz, 1997). Some judges allow the jurors to ask oral or submit written questions. As a general rule, federal judges, who are appointed for life, tend to be a bit more innovative than judges in state courts. Traditions probably die harder in state courtrooms. An example of what might be done in a courtroom by an innovative judge is presented in the next Courtroom Applications box.

Data suggest that jurors and judges who experience innovations as described in this section are well pleased and believe they make for a more informed and enthusiastic jury (Dann & Logan, 1996). Generally, lawyers like the innovations least of all because they feel the changes cost them control of their presentation. Whether these innovations make for more informed decision making is still an open empirical question. Large-scale, well-controlled studies, especially in real courtroom settings, are needed.

COURTROOM APPLICATIONS

Increasing Jury Participation

One judge, U.S. District Judge Richard Bilby of Arizona, has experimented with a number of courtroom innovations. Judge Bilby allows his jurors to take notes and provides them with a "juror survival kit," which enhances their understanding of their duties. The kit, really several notebooks, includes preliminary instructions, blank note pages, and final instructions that are inserted after all the evidence has been presented. Additional items may be inserted, especially in complex cases—such as definitions of relevant scientific terms. Judge Bilby also allows jurors personally to inspect exhibits during the trial and deliberations (Dann & Logan, 1996).

In addition, he has borrowed a technique pioneered by a very imaginative trial manager, Judge Robert Parker, that requires attorneys to engage in what are termed "interim arguments," a short summary describing a particular exhibit or a witness's testimony. Attorneys are given an allotment of time for these arguments, say one hour, for the entire trial. They may use the time at any point they think doing so would be advantageous.

Judge Bilby does not allow oral questions because he thinks this practice may make jurors advocates rather than arbiters, but he will permit written questions to be submitted to the bench. Also, he allows what few other judges permit: In his courtroom, jurors may discuss testimony before all the evidence is heard as long as all the jurors are present. Current practice is to prohibit jurors from talking about the evidence before the trial is over. (The Brookings report argued against allowing juries to discuss materials before all the evidence is heard.) If jurors are having difficulty reaching a verdict, the judge permits them to ask that a particularly nettlesome issue or question be reargued briefly by the parties.

Recasting the Justice System

The reforms considered above are aimed at empowering the jury and increasing its participation. Many other proposed reforms in the jury system, however, are attempts to constrain, alter, or diminish the role of the jury in the justice system.

Special Juries.   We know that an argument swirls around the use of a civil jury in complex cases. Recall the concern about the roster of jurors in the Liggett trial discussed above. Some critics would like to remove complex trials from the domain of the usually constituted civil jury. This is known as the complexity exception to a jury trial.

The **complexity exception** proponents have two arguments. The first is historical and says that juries were excluded from complex trials when the Constitution was written (Devlin, 1980). Thus, there is historical precedent for excusing juries from complex trials. The second prong to the complexity exception argument is the defendant's Fifth Amendment right to due process, which in this case means the right to have the case heard by finders of fact who can produce a rational decision. The right to due process, according to this argument, overrides the Seventh Amendment right to a jury trial in civil matters (Wiggins & Breckler, 1987).

How can we help the jury handle complexity? One possibility is to enhance the quality of individuals who serve on juries. Many professionals are now excused. Courts have recognized that selected trials, such as complex antitrust and securities suits, are beyond the jury's capabilities. Juries in such cases have been dismissed and bench trials were held (Danzon, 1985)—but a judge may be no more qualified to deal with complex litigation than a lay jury. A more far-reaching notion is to construct juries of specially qualified individuals. Some observers have even suggested the creation of a "science court," a board of selected scientists who would have expertise in an area that is the focus of the trial.

Changing the Adversarial System

Certain commentators, such as law professor Franklin Strier (1994), advocate more radical changes in the justice system. Strier would change the roles of the players in the trial. The judge would become much more active, the lawyers and juries less so. All complex cases would be handled by (preferably) special juries. (Note that *complexity* is quite undefined by all except a very few empiricists [Heuer & Penrod, 1989, 1994c; MacCoun, 1989].)

Strier's model is the inquisitorial one. He acknowledges that the adversarial system is so strongly rooted in our culture and history and economic system (competing market forces determine the winners under a neutral authority) that we must keep some version of the adversarial system. He offers a hybrid. The jury, however attenuated, still exists, but the judge calls the shots. An activist judge can cure many ills. He or she can call witnesses, question them, search for new evidence, and call for expert testimony.

Strier argues that lawyers would be less likely to pull dirty tricks, that activist judges can help the downtrodden and underfinanced party, and more facts would emerge. To foster this new judicial role, Strier wants a merit-based judiciary, appointed for life, with requirements for continuous training and education.

Commentators who prefer that judges play a more active role also argue that bench trials are speedier than jury trials. However, a closer analysis by law professors Theodore Eisenberg and Kevin Clermont (1996) shows that bench trials are no faster than jury trials, and sometimes judges take longer to process a trial than do juries. One reason is that judges often have other duties or other cases that they must attend to and therefore their attention is divided.

Strier believes that the legal profession's monopoly over legal services should be abolished. This would give access to many people who cannot now avail themselves of legal services. For example, paralegals could be trained to do un-contested wills, divorces, and real estate searches, among other relatively simple but highly expensive services. Strier's reconstruction of the system requires that we come to believe that the adversarial system is only one, but perhaps not the best, mode of obtaining justice.

SUMMARY

This chapter has focused on the ability of judges and juries to deliver outcomes that the public perceives are just. The initial focus was on judges' sentencing of convicted criminals. The ability to pronounce sentences in a just and fair manner is at the core of ethical and legal practices in any society. On the federal level, and to some extent on the state level as well, the discretionary power of the judge to mete out sentences has been sharply curtailed. This is because of new federal sentencing guidelines passed by the Congress in 1984 that specify precisely what sentence may be given for each category of crime.

Sentencing guidelines are aimed at doing away with sentencing disparities among judges and jurisdictions. Before the guidelines, convicted felons might have gotten widely different sentences depending on who sentenced them and where they were sentenced. Opponents of guidelines call their use "justice by the numbers" that cannot consider the differences among defendants and the nature of the crimes.

The role of the jury in dispensing justice is controversial. The legally preferred mode of jury behavior is for juries simply to apply the law as enunciated by the judge to the facts of the trial. However, juries have always had the power, if not the explicit right, to act as the conscience of the community and to render verdicts that represent the sentiments of that community. The ability of juries to return verdicts that contravene both the facts and the law is known as jury nullification. Sometimes nullifying verdicts have served as beacons of freedom, and sometimes those verdicts have catered to the community's most vile and bigoted motives. Nevertheless, because juries can render any verdict they want without legal reprisal, the system has some "wiggle room."

If one of the purposes of the law is to guide behavior, then it makes sense that people ought to be aware of what is in the legal codes. In fact, few people are. With respect particularly to acts that fall into the zone of private behavior, such as sexual mores, research suggests fairly sharp disagreements between the codes and the public, with the public preferring less interference from the legal system in private behavior.

The existence of the civil jury had everything to do with justice, especially for colonials who rarely had a jury to protect them from foreclosures and other loss of property or liberty as a result of failure to pay debts. Tort law, which dominates modern civil law, deals with noncriminal harm. A tortious act, an act that does harm, may be the basis of a lawsuit. The system of tort law serves several purposes, the first of which is to resolve the disputed claims of those who have been injured. Second, it allows compensation of those people for their injuries. Third, the system operates to deter others from engaging in negligent behavior. Finally, tort law helps to set a standard so that individuals and companies are aware of what is considered acceptable and what is not. In other words, tort law has a moral or educative function.

In civil trials, the jury has less unrestricted power than in criminal trials. This is primarily because the judge has much more control over civil verdicts. One concern about civil juries is that they are perceived to be "runaway" juries, who award too much money for trivial harm. The data suggest otherwise. In fact, if anything, juries tend to undercompensate plaintiffs, especially those who are seriously harmed.

Commentators believe that the justice system is in need of reform. The proposed reforms range from conservative aids to improve jury performance to radical reconstruction of the entire system. Jury aids include permitting jurors to take notes, have access to trial transcripts, and ask questions. More radical reforms include using special juries of people with specific education or training to deal with paticularly complex and technical cases. Radical reformers would like to modify the adversarial system and give the judge greater power and discretion to run the trial.

PART FOUR

Use of Social Science in the Legal System

CHAPTER
12

A Case Study: Social Science and the Death Penalty

For the most part, law can be seen as a system of rules for the control of human behavior; therefore, law can be considered a branch of applied psychology. As we have seen, psychologists can generate relevant and reliable information about the workings of the legal system. In this chapter, we consider how social science enters the judicial system and how—and how well—that system, particularly the U.S. Supreme Court, uses or does not use psychological and social science data. We do this by focusing our attention on one case that used social science evidence in a critical death penalty trial.

A CASE STUDY: SOCIAL SCIENCE IN THE SUPREME COURT

To generate testable hypotheses about a subject, social scientists often use *case studies,* careful examinations of individual cases. By looking at completely documented illustrations of a phenomenon, we can tease out questions for further study—such as what factors seem to affect the outcome? How do they relate to each other? What is the direction of the observed effects? In the case study that follows, we might ask about the effects of the timing of social science research in relation to the events in question. How does the fashioning of specific studies with litigation in mind affect their impact? How well do the legal and social science issues fit with each other? How competent are judges, jurors, and lawyers in using social science findings? In reading the remainder of this chapter ask yourself, "What more would I like to know about the use of social science?" and "How can I test my theories about what's happening in the case?"

The following case was selected because of its historic importance, not because it is typical. This case does represent one approach to social science in the current era of Supreme Court jurisprudence. It is an unusual case, in part because it deals with the very controversial and emotional issue of the death penalty. The decision of the Supreme Court profoundly disappointed the social science community that was deeply involved and changed the community's expectations as to how much the court would rely on or fully understand social science. This is a case we briefly considered in Chapter 6.

McCleskey v. Kemp: Statistical Challenges That Create a Fear of Too Much Justice

The Players.   Warren McCleskey was a black man who was convicted on October 12, 1978, by a Fulton County (which includes Atlanta), Georgia, jury of killing Frank Schlatt, a white police officer, during an armed robbery of a furniture store. The evidence showed that the robbery had been planned by four men. All were armed and the robbery involved restraining a number of customers and employees. One of two bullets that struck the officer came from a gun like the one carried by McCleskey during the robbery. In the guilt determination phase of the trial, the jury found him guilty of murder. In the separate penalty phase that followed, the jury faced a choice between death or imprisonment for life. Under Georgia law, before it can impose the death penalty, a jury must find (a) beyond a reasonable doubt that at least one of ten statutory aggravating circumstances was present, and (b) that the aggravating circumstances outweigh any mitigating circumstances. In McCleskey's case, the jury found two aggravating circumstances: The murder was committed in the course of another felony, the armed robbery, and the victim was a peace officer. The defendant did not offer any mitigating evidence. The jury sentenced Warren McCleskey to death on the murder charge.

After exercising all appeals in the state courts, McCleskey filed a petition for a writ of habeas corpus in the federal district court for the Northern District of Georgia. (*Habeas corpus* involves the right of any prisoner to have the constitutionality of his or her conviction or sentence reviewed by a federal court.) The centerpiece of his claim was that the capital punishment process in Georgia, in the aggregate and as applied to his case, deprived him of the equal protection of the laws, contrary to the Fourteenth Amendment, and constituted cruel and unusual punishment, contrary to the Eighth Amendment. At the core of each of those claims was statistical evidence that the system operated in a racially discriminatory manner.

Professors David Baldus, Charles Pulaski, and George Woodworth (1990) conducted a major study of the capital punishment system in Georgia. Professors Baldus and Woodworth testified at a hearing on the habeas corpus case in the district court before U.S. District Judge J. Owen Forrester. At the time of the hearing, Baldus, a Yale-educated lawyer with an M.A. degree from Pittsburgh, was a professor of law at the University of Iowa, where he taught courses on scientific evidence, discrimination law, and capital punishment. He had also co-authored a book with statistician James Cole entitled *Statistical Proof of Discrimination* (1980). During 1975–1976, he directed the Law and Social Sciences Program at the National Sciences Foundation. Professor Woodworth was an associate professor of statistics at the University of Iowa and "qualified as an expert in the theory and application of statistics and statistical computation, especially with reference to analysis of discreet [sic] outcome data" (*McCleskey v. Zant,* 1984, p. 352).

Judge Forrester appeared to be no stranger to technical evidence and to mathematics and statistics. He had received a bachelor of science degree from the Georgia Institute of Technology and a law degree from Emory University in Atlanta. He was known as a tough, proprosecution judge.

Judge Forrester spent about two and a half weeks hearing evidence on the matter and issued a lengthy opinion. In this opinion, 36 pages were addressed to the claims of the Baldus study. Judge Forrester declined to grant a writ of habeas corpus on those grounds. In an interesting twist, the judge did grant habeas corpus relief to Mr. McCleskey's case on other grounds. So much for the claim by some lawyers that the judge was blindly proprosecution. It seems that the state had failed to disclose its promise to seek favorable treatment for a cellmate-witness for the state who faced a federal escape charge. The cellmate testified that McCleskey had confessed, in the privacy of their jail cell, to being the one who shot the officer. Judge Forrester thought that the state should have disclosed information about the promise to help this witness with his own legal troubles. He also thought that such information might have influenced the jury in its deliberation. This issue itself has empirical implications but was not the focus of the debate.

Addressing the capital punishment study, Judge Forrester noted that

> before he became involved in projects akin to that under analysis here, Professor Baldus apparently had little contact with the criminal justice system. In law school he took one course which focused heavily on the rationale of the law of homicide. During his short stint in private practice he handled some habeas corpus matters and had discussions with a friend who was an Assistant District Attorney concerning the kinds of factors which his friend utilized in deciding how to dispose of cases. (*McCleskey v. Zant*, 1984, p. 352)

Judge Forrester did not note that the third author of the study, Professor Charles A. Pulaski, Jr., taught criminal procedure at Arizona State University College of Law. Professor Pulaski did not testify.

The State of Georgia's experts consisted of Dr. Joseph Katz, an assistant professor at Georgia State University in the Department of Quantitative Methods and a recent graduate of Louisiana State University, and his mentor at LSU, Professor Roger L. Buford.

The Data as Seen by the Trial Judge.   In what seems like a grudging, limited endorsement, Judge Forrester summarized the qualifications of the experts in these words:

> The court was impressed with the learning of all the experts. Each preferred the findings and assumptions which supported his thesis, but it seemed to the court that no one of them was willing to disregard academic honesty to the extent of advancing a proposition for which there was absolutely no support. (*McCleskey v. Zant*, 1984, p. 353)

Translation: They may be biased, but they wouldn't lie outright.

The judge noted that Baldus et al. (1990) had conducted two studies of the administration of the death penalty in Georgia. The first, called the "Procedural Reform Study," found no "race of the defendant" effect and "a very unclear 'race of the victim' effect" (*McCleskey v. Zant*, p. 353). In other words, the study found a disparity in imposition of the death penalty based on the race of the victim but not the defendant. When the victim was white, the death penalty was imposed more frequently regardless of the race of the accused. On the basis of that study, however, "the [NAACP, the National Association for the Advancement of Colored People] Legal Defense Fund [which represented McCleskey in his habeas corpus cases] learned of Baldus's research and retained him to conduct the second study [called the 'Charging and Sentencing Study']" (*McCleskey v. Zant,* p. 353).

The "Charging and Sentencing Study" (Baldus et al., 1990) examined court records and other data for all death penalty cases imposed for crimes committed in Georgia under a new Georgia death penalty statute that went into effect on March 28, 1973. The accused had been arrested on June 30, 1978. Note that this new statute was in force during the trial of McCleskey and his cohorts. The study also included a random sample of 25 percent of all murder cases resulting in life sentences and 25 percent of all voluntary manslaughter cases. The final question-naire was 42 pages long and has 595 foils (blanks) for recording factors that might, in Baldus's opinion, affect the outcome of the case. Generally, the kind of information sought included the location of the offense, the details of all the charges brought against the offender, the outcome of the case, whether there was a plea bargain, characteristics of the defendant, prior record of the defendant, in-formation regarding contemporaneous offenses, details concerning every victim in the case, characteristics of the offense, statutory aggravating factors, a delin-eation of the defendant's role as related to the co-perpetrators', information on the outcome of co-perpetrators' cases, other aggravating circumstances such as the number of shots fired, miscellaneous mitigating circumstances relating to the defendant or the victim, the defendant's defenses at the guilt trial, and the strength of the evidence (p. 355).

Judge Forrester highlighted the limits of the data, emphasizing that "the questionnaire could not capture every nuance of every case" (p. 356). As an ex-ample, he cited that "on the variable 'Method of Killing,' only three foils were provided. . . . The effect of this would be to reduce the aggravation of a case that had multiple methods of inflicting death" (*McCleskey v. Zant,* p. 356) Another missed nuance was that the study "contains no information about what a prose-cutor felt about the credibility of any witnesses" (p. 357). Notice that in criticiz-ing the study for not being able to "capture every nuance of every case," the judge appears to hold the statistical data to a standard not imposed on other evi-dence. Does even a full trial transcript "capture every nuance" of a case? How of-ten is reliable evidence available concerning the prosecutor's feelings about the credibility of a witness? One cannot help wondering how realistic the judge's ex-pectations were for this study.

The judge also examined closely the methods for determining whether a fac-tor was present, absent, or unknown, noting that ambiguities were to be resolved in favor of supporting the finding of the judge or jury and the legitimacy of the sentence. He then looked at a prosecution witness's testimony that compared the consistency of the coding in the earlier study to the coding of the same variables in the later study. In what seems like a fair critique of the studies, the judge sum-marized the rate of coding discrepancies between the two studies. Some of the more objective factors and their discrepancy rate were "Number of Prior Felonies (33%) . . . Execution Style Murder (18%) . . . Bloody (28%) . . . Defen-dant Drug History (25%) . . . Two or More Victims in All (80%) . . . Victim is a

Stranger (12%)" (p. 357). Judge Forrester also scrutinized the treatment of unknown data in the study and concluded that omitting the observations coded as unknown—as opposed to treating them as not supporting the hypothesized effect—exaggerated the effects. For example, in 62 of the 1,084 cases, the race of the victim was coded as unknown. These cases were dropped from the analysis. The researchers could have presumed that the victims with missing data were minorities whose assailants did not receive the death penalty. Such an assumption would guard against the possibility that the unknown data included a higher proportion of minorities and in that way helped produce the race of the victim effect. Judge Forrester noted that Professor Woodward did run a "worst case analysis" on five small models of the data and concluded that this analysis had the effect of depressing the coefficients of racial disparity "by as much as 25%" (p. 359).

Concluding his scrutiny of the data, Judge Forrester expressed his opinion that "the data base has substantial flaws and . . . petitioner has failed to establish by a preponderance of the evidence that it is essentially trustworthy" (p. 360).

The Statistical Models.   The judge then shifted his attention to the accuracy of the multiple regression models—the statistical analyses examining a number of predictor variables; here, the independent variable used were the circumstances of the crime, regressed on the single dependent variable: imposition of the death penalty. Forrester used Baldus's testimony to establish the proposition that "if a particularly important background variable is not controlled for" or if a study "does not focus on the individual stages in the process," it does not present the "whole picture" and "is limited in its power to support an inference of discrimination" (p. 360). He also noted that the lack of a measure of the "strength of the evidence" was a weakness of the first study that Professor Baldus and his colleagues hoped to correct in the second study. Having set the stage, the judge proceeded to examine microscopically all the multiple regression models used to analyze subsets of the 230-variable data set. Anything short of full analysis of all 230 variables would be suspect under his "whole picture" criteria. Even that test might not be sufficient because it was based on the flawed assumption that the decision makers knew all that could be known by hindsight about the data (p. 361).

Concentrating on the 230-variable model, the judge looked at the adjusted r^2, which he defined as "a method for measuring what portion of the variance in the dependent variable (here death sentencing rate) is accounted for by the independent variables included in the model." The r^2 here is between .46 and .48, which "does not predict the outcome in half the cases" and therefore cannot support an inference of discrimination.

In case the above might not be enough to convince the reader, or the court of appeals, Judge Forrester relied on Georgia's expert, Dr. Katz, who testified that having a statistical significance of .02 was insufficient because the addition of variables tended to decrease the statistical significance. Thus, if 20 variables were added to the 230 and if analysis of appellate decisions were included, the statistical significance might drop to .04 or .05. Based on these criteria the court concluded that "none of the models utilized by the petitioner's experts are sufficiently predictive to support an inference of discrimination" (p. 362).

The judge also found that the data exhibited multicollinearity—that is, a high correlation among two or more variables. Judge Forrester found that a higher proportion of white victim cases had a higher number of aggravating circumstances than the black victim cases. At the same time, a higher proportion of black victim cases had a higher number of mitigating circumstances than the white victim cases. Both effects, however, would lead one to expect a higher proportion of death sentences in white victim cases. But, on that point, the judge concluded that "multi-collinearity substantially diminishes the weight to be accorded to the circumstantial statistical evidence of racial disparity" (p. 364).

Statistics and the Individual Case.   In what may represent a fundamental tension between law and social science, Judge Forrester addressed the extent to which these statistics shed light on what happened to Warren McCleskey. The primary issues in the case are whether the imposition of the death penalty on Mr. McCleskey discriminated against him or imposed cruel and unusual punishment on him. Statewide data about the administration of capital punishment in Georgia may attempt to prove too much and too little. The data suggest that racial considerations have an effect in all cases and that racial considerations did not have a clear and definitive effect in Warren McCleskey's case. The statewide data may show that generally the race of the victim has a significant effect on the punishment imposed throughout the state. They do not, however, purport to show that the race of the victim determined the outcome in any particular case. Using aggregate data has a built-in limit that way. Using a batting average or a test score does not determine how an individual will do in the next at-bat or test—or, for that matter, in the last at-bat or test. Social science data, like most statistical data, help guide decisions in terms of probabilities, not absolutes in a single case.

In a similar fashion, the Baldus study did not show that the race of the victim had a conclusive effect in all cases. The propositions about which social science can provide conclusive data are generally simple propositions, like "Do people tend to want to avoid the electric chair?" Less clear issues tend to produce probabilistic data. This is a core difficulty in using statistical evidence in legal proceedings. The legal issues are these: "Is the death penalty applied in a discriminatory manner in this case?" "Is the death penalty's application in this case cruel and unusual punishment?" The legal questions call for "yes" or "no" answers. Social science answers are, at best, "probably yes" or "probably no." Sometimes they are "maybe, depending on which of 230 factors are present" or "possibly, but check back later when we've had a chance to replicate our data."

Professor Baldus did not overstate his data in this regard. Judge Forrester quotes him as testifying that capital punishment cases are part of "a system that is highly discretionary, highly complex, many factors are at work in influencing choice, and no one factor dominates the system" (p. 366). The judge also under-scored Baldus's testimony that

> the central message that comes through is [that] the race effects are concen-trated in categories of cases in which there is an elevated risk of a death sen-tence. There's no suggestion in this research that there is a uniform, institu-tional bias that adversely affects defendants in white victim cases in all circumstances, or a black defendant in all cases. There's nothing to support that conclusion. It's a very complicated system. (p. 366)

The judge then hoists the researcher on his own testimony and "agrees that any racial variable is not determinant of who is going to receive the death penalty and . . . there is no support for a proposition that race has any effect in any given case" (p. 366).

One could attempt to fit research data more closely to McCleskey's case in two ways: Look at the factors involved in the case at hand and look at subsets of the data that might focus on the decisions made in that case. Judge Forrester's opinion suggests that the lawyers and social scientists attempted both methods. They tried to place McCleskey within the subgroup of defendants who had a rel-atively higher number of aggravating circumstances in their cases and who were more likely to have racial factors applied to them. They also attempted to look more closely at the data from Fulton County, where the trial took place, which would be more relevant to the prosecutors, juries, and judges who decided Mr. McCleskey's fate.

Recall the facts in McCleskey's case. The murder was committed in the course of a felony, the victim was a police officer, and the shooting was commit-ted to avoid arrest. These three factors are the aggravating factors that the study showed were most likely to lead to the death penalty. Baldus and Woodworth, however, found that even if these three factors are given, a defendant convicted of murdering a white victim has an increased probability of between .18 and .23 of receiving the death penalty. Baldus and Woodworth made this determination by looking at a 39-factor model. Judge Forrester probed further, however, and found that other aggravating factors were present in the McCleskey case that might also be likely to lead to the death penalty. Those factors were the defen-dant's lack of remorse and his bragging about the crime while in jail (p. 375). Based on a police officer's testimony that McCleskey had exhibited these factors, Judge Forrester found that including them would have eliminated the finding of disparity based on the race of the victim. In other words, the discrepancy could have been accounted for by the defendant's lack of remorse or his braggadocio. The point seems well taken. At the same time, the judge's point dramatizes the researcher's burden: Failure to account for a particular variable or two may un-dercut an otherwise sophisticated and persuasive study. The result is that the fo-cus on the individual case deflects the court from considering data about discrim-ination that infects the entire system to a tangible degree.

Finally, the players examined the Fulton County (Atlanta) data in an effort to show a more particularized discriminatory effect against Warren McCleskey.

According to Judge Forrester, who had the last word at this level, the data did not support the theory. Baldus used a *stepwise regression,* a form of multiple regression selected to identify the variables most likely to account for the differences in outcomes in Fulton County cases. Race of victim and race of defendant effects were included for decisions by the prosecutor regarding plea bargains and regarding advancing the case to a penalty phase. There was not, however, any evidence of disparity of outcomes. Indeed, there was a slightly higher death penalty rate for white defendant cases and for black victim cases as well, but this rate was not statistically significant (p. 377). Later proceedings, however, reveal that the Fulton County data show a disparity in a small number of cases. There were 17 cases in which the defendant was charged with murdering a police officer in Fulton County. In only two of these cases did the prosecution seek the death penalty. In the other case, involving the murder of a black officer, the jury imposed life. McCleskey was the only one of the 17 to receive the death penalty.

The advocates and the court then shifted from statistical analysis to case-by-case examination. Using the database and personal judgment, Baldus selected 32 cases that he felt were similar to McCleskey's and then looked at the aggravating factors in those cases. The judge found nonracial differences in the cases and disagreed with Professor Baldus's conclusion that these cases showed discrimination.

In the end, Judge Forrester rejected the claims of racial discrimination in administering the death penalty. He granted the writ of habeas corpus on the grounds that the state had failed to disclose information about inducements it gave a prisoner to testify against McCleskey.

Neither side was happy. The state won the war, but lost the skirmish. McCleskey's lawyers won his potential freedom, but not the principle that would end the death penalty for the state of Georgia and perhaps the nation. Not surprisingly, both sides appealed to the court of appeals. And everyone knew that, regardless of the outcome there, the court of appeals was simply a stopping place on the way to the U.S. Supreme Court.

On Appeal.   The court of appeals also knew the stakes. They decided to hear the case *en banc,* meaning that all 12 of the judges would participate instead of the typical three-judge panel. This unusual procedure is reserved for the most troublesome cases. Systemwide challenges to the death penalty are always difficult. Throw in some multiple regression models and a few tests of statistical significance and a judge wants all possible help.

The judge to whom the majority opinion was assigned was Paul Roney, second in seniority on the court, a Nixon appointee who had impressive judicial credentials and was not a stranger to social science evidence. Paul Roney was known as a professional and fair-minded judge. Also on the court were two judges known as leaders in the desegregation of the Deep South after *Brown v. Board of Education:* Judges Frank Johnson and John Godbold, both of Montgomery, Alabama, and both mentioned prominently in the book *Unlikely Heroes,* a paean to the judges from the South who took great personal risks to enforce *Brown v. Board of Education* in a hostile environment (Bass, 1981). In short, this is not a court with either a history or a reputation of hostility to civil rights. We could expect the Baldus study to get a fair-minded reception by intelligent users of social science data here.

Baldus's data did fare better here, but McCleskey lost both ends of this battle. The majority (8–4) held that the state's failure to disclose its inducements to the inmate-witness was a "harmless error"—that is, one that would not have affected the jury's decision. Note that the majority is saying, in effect, that facts that persuaded one district judge and four court of appeals judges to rule in favor of a convicted murderer would have had no impact on the jury. This seems intuitively unsound; one cannot help wondering how mock jurors in a laboratory context might react to the situation.

On the racial discrimination issues, the court voted 9–3 to affirm at least some of Judge Forrester's conclusions about the issues. In some ways, this vote tells more about judicial use of social science data than the later Supreme Court opinion. Unlike the Supreme Court, the court of appeals did not dance around the issue. They faced the question squarely in these words:

> As to whether the system can survive constitutional attack, statistical studies are at most probative of how much disparity is present, but it is a legal question as to how much disparity is required before a federal court will accept it as evidence of the constitutional flaws of the system. (*McCleskey v. Kemp*, 753 F. 2d, p. 893)*

The court of appeals intentionally bypassed the controversy about whether the Baldus study was valid in the sense of measuring what it purported to measure. The court assumed the validity of the study and determined that it was not sufficient to show a constitutional defect.

How do the legal-constitutional issues interact with the statistical issues and findings? The legal definition of a constitutional violation requires proof, by a preponderance of the evidence, that the state intentionally discriminated against Warren McCleskey because of either his own race or the race of his victim. The Baldus data do not show that McCleskey himself was the direct target of intentional racial discrimination. When one looks at the number of cases in Fulton County alone, the number is too small to permit any statistical finding that racial discrimination infected those decisions. Even if the number were larger and the evidence of racial discrimination more pervasive, it would still require a leap of logic, an inference, to conclude that the prosecutor, judge, or jury intended to sentence Warren McCleskey to death because of his race or the race of his victim.

This is not to say that Judge Roney or the court looked at the statistical evidence only from the narrow lens of the Warren McCleskey facts. The court also treated the evidence as a systemic attack on the administration of the death penalty. Certainly if racial considerations permeate the system, it would be said

---

*The name of the case changed from *McCleskey v. Zant* to *McCleskey v. Kemp* because the defendant—the prison warden—changed.

to operate in an "arbitrary and capricious" manner, a legal conclusion that would bring into question the death penalty's constitutional validity across the board. A number of Supreme Court justices used similar reasoning in *Furman v. Georgia* (1972), a case discussed in Chapter 10 that invalidated an earlier version of the Georgia death penalty and set the criteria for judging modern death penalty statutes. If the discrimination was pervasive enough, a court would presume it affected *McCleskey.* But what is pervasive enough? Judge Roney's characterization of the statistical evidence and its limits indicated that the Baldus study

> only shows that in a group involving blacks and whites, all of whose cases are virtually the same, there would be more blacks receiving the death penalty than whites and more murderers of whites receiving the death penalty than murderers of blacks. The statisticians' "best guess" is that race was a factor in those cases. . . . An analysis must be made as to how much disparity is actually shown by the research. (*McCleskey v. Kemp,* 753 F. 2d, p. 895)

Applying that analysis, Judge Roney found that "Baldus' most conclusive model, on which *McCleskey* primarily relies, showed an effect of .06, signifying that on average a white victim crime is 6 percent more likely to result in the [death] sentence than a comparable black victim crime" (*McCleskey v. Kemp,* 753 F. 2d, p. 896). The court concluded that a 6 percent disparity "is not sufficient to overcome the presumption that the statute is operating in a constitutional manner" (p. 897). The court reasoned that

> in any discretionary system, some imprecision must be tolerated, and the Baldus study is simply insufficient to support a ruling, in the context of a statute that is operating much as intended, that racial factors are playing a role in the outcome sufficient to render the system as a whole arbitrary and capricious. (p. 897)

Unfortunately, the court does not explain this 6 percent figure. Is it a difference between rates of imposition of the death penalty, of .06 compared to .12? If it is, a 6 percent difference in the rate would represent a 100 percent difference in the proportions of imposition. If the 6 percent simply represents a difference in the ratios of white victim to black victim cases, it would mean that black victim cases represent 47 percent of the total and white victims 53 percent. One might expect that the latter is true because the dissenting judges did not trumpet the difference in rates. It appears, however, that the 6 percent figure represents six percentage points in the rate of imposition of the death penalty. Given that the rate of imposition of the death penalty in all cases in the Baldus study was only 5 percent (*McCleskey v. Kemp,* 753 F. 2d, p. 847), a difference of 6 percent indicates more than a 100 percent difference in rates based on the race of the victim. This difference appeared to be lost on the court of appeals judges, majority and dissent alike. The apparent confusion permitted the majority to call the race-of-victim effect a "marginal disparity" without challenge from the dissent on the mathematics of the effect. As we will see, McCleskey's attorneys did not miss the point in their arguments to the Supreme Court.

In the court of appeals, the attorneys argued, using Baldus's data, that one should focus on the "close cases," those in which the evidence of aggravating and mitigating circumstances was unclear. The theory is that only in those cases can juries feel free—"liberated"—to reach their own conclusions, perhaps based on their own biases. In all other cases, juries follow the evidence that is so clear that only one outcome is possible. In the McCleskey case, focusing on the subset of close cases seems to be another point at which social scientist and judges part ways. Looking only at the close cases, the court observed, would mean that murderers of white victims were 20 percent more likely to receive the death penalty than equally aggravated black victim murderers. Note that as discussed in the last paragraph, a 20 percent increase in the rate means an increase from 5 percent to 25 percent or a fivefold increase in the absolute numbers. The probability estimate, as Judge Roney saw it, is "a composite of all cases" and "an aggregate containing cases in which the race of the victim is a discernible factor and those in which it is not" (p. 896).

The court refused to look solely at the close cases. Judge Roney reasoned that because the evidence amounts to a challenge to the entire system, one cannot focus simply on ill-defined, indeed undefinable, "close cases." He concluded that it is "simply not satisfactory to say that the racial effect operates in 'close cases' and therefore that the death penalty will be set aside in 'close cases.'"

The other side of the "close cases" coin is that there is little disparity in the not-so-close or "clear cases." Cases in which there was clear evidence of aggravating circumstances tended to receive the death penalty without any racial distinction. Cases without any aggravating circumstances tended to receive a lesser sentence, again without any racial effect.

Looking at the system as a whole, the court asserted that the "Baldus study revealed an essentially rational system, in which high aggravation cases were more likely to result in the death penalty than low aggravation cases" (p. 896). Racial effects are only in the mid-range of close cases, an area where "some imprecision must be tolerated" (p. 896).

In Dissent.   The dissent did not see it quite the same way. Judge Frank Johnson, one of the "unlikely heroes" of the federal bench during the civil rights movement, pressed the statistical argument. He focused on different figures, starting with "a single unexplained fact: killers of white victims in Georgia over the last decade have received the death penalty eleven times more often than killers of black victims" (p. 911). This led to the Baldus study, which produced regression figures showing that defendants convicted of killing white victims were 6 percent more likely to receive the death penalty than defendants convicted of killing black victims. Regression analysis controlled for other factors and showed that "the race of the victim remained one of the strongest influences" in producing the 11 to 1 disparity noted above.

In a separate dissent, Judge Thomas Clark searched for a way to bridge the gap between the multiple regression analysis and the legal context of capital punishment. Judge Clark, a University of Georgia–educated former county solicitor of Decatur County, Georgia, highlighted the role that the race of the victim played in explaining the 11 to 1 disparity. In his words,

> race influences the verdict just as much as any one of the aggravating circumstances listed in Georgia's death penalty statute. Therefore, . . . race of the defendant and of the victim, when it is black/white, functions as if it were an aggravating circumstance in a discernible number of cases." (p. 925)

If the Georgia legislature were to write race into the statute as an aggravating factor, that law would clearly be unconstitutional. The Baldus study shows an equivalent effect.

Judges Johnson and Clark each searched for the legal analogies to establish some baseline to which to compare the racial disparities in capital sentencing. They focused on the jury selection cases. Judge Clark looked at the mathematics and showed that "the mathematical disparities that have been accepted by the Court as adequate to establish a prima facie case of purposeful discrimination range approximately from 14 percent to 40 percent" (p. 923). Tying those figures into the Baldus study, however, requires focusing on the mid-range cases in which the 20 percent disparity was shown. The only basis for defining the mid-range, however, comes from the Baldus study, and the majority rejected that approach because it leaves no room for salvaging the portion of the death penalty that Baldus documented to be operating in a racially neutral manner—cases with a large number of aggravating factors.

Judge Joseph Hatchett, a former Florida Supreme Court justice, joined the two dissenters and asserted in clear, unmistakable terms the central features of the Baldus study and his conclusion that "race should not be allowed to take a significant role in the decision to impose the death penalty" (p. 919).

A common feature of the three dissents is that none asserted that there had been proof of McCleskey's having been sentenced to death because of race. Judge Johnson faced the probabilistic nature of the evidence and asserted that "the statistics in this case show that a certain number of death penalties were probably imposed because of race." He accused the majority of ignoring "the fact that McCleskey has shown discriminatory intent at work in the sentencing system even though he has not pointed to any specific act or actor responsible for discrimination against him in particular" (p. 911).

Finally, Judge Johnson's dissent addressed Judge Forrester's challenges to the validity of the Baldus data. His was the only opinion to do so and, if needed, it could have provided a basis for the Supreme Court to uphold the validity of Baldus's methods. He concluded that the coding discrepancies between the first two studies were intentional improvements and that the overall error rate in the data was less than 1 percent, a "scientifically negligible" amount (p. 915). He concluded that removing cells with unknown data from the study properly followed procedures recommended by the National Academy of Sciences. Judge Johnson also corrected Judge Forrester's "misinterpretation of the r^2 measurement" (pp. 916–917). Judge Johnson noted that the r^2 measurement "represents the influence of random factors unique to each case that could not be captured by the addition of another independent variable" and concludes that an r^2 of .48 was not "too low" in an area with as many random variables as death penalty decision making. Finally, he asserted that multicollinearity dampened rather than enhanced the race-of-victim variables. Thus, Baldus had understated rather than overstated the race-of-victim effects.

In the Supreme Court. To no one's surprise, Warren McCleskey petitioned the Supreme Court to review his case. The Court granted review, continuing a tradition of reviewing major challenges to capital punishment statutes and major challenges to racial injustice. The media portrayed the McCleskey case as the last frontal assault on capital punishment, the last across-the-board attack on systemic practices that might be considered arbitrary, discriminatory, and unconstitutional. The Court's review focused entirely on the claims related to the Baldus study.

The arguments paralleled those of the lower courts, but the vote was much closer than in the court of appeals. As the supreme voice in U.S. constitutional interpretation, justices of the Court may feel more power and freedom to invalidate governmental programs that infringe on individual liberties. The Court came one vote from invalidating the Georgia system and sending state legislatures there and elsewhere back to the drawing boards.

Justice Powell wrote the majority opinion that captured four votes: Justices Byron ("Whizzer") White, Sandra Day O'Connor, Antonin Scalia, and Chief Justice William Rehnquist. The majority confronted the Baldus study head-on, starting with the raw figures that defendants charged with killing white victims received the death penalty in 11 percent of the cases compared to defendants charged with killing black victims, who received the death penalty in 1 percent of the cases. The majority clouded up this data, however, by noting that a "reverse racial disparity" was shown by the figures that a higher percentage of white defendants (7 percent) received the death penalty than did black defendants (4 percent) (*McCleskey v. Kemp,* 481 U.S., 286–287). Rather than a reverse twist, though, these data simply illustrate the race-of-victim effect. Black defendants are more frequently involved in the killing of blacks than are white defendants. If the race of the victim is a major factor, this means fewer death penalties for black defendants—a fact that vividly demonstrates the discounting of black life, not leniency toward black defendants.

The majority also presented data on prosecutorial discretion. Baldus found that prosecutors sought the death penalty in 70 percent of the cases involving black defendants and white victims; 32 percent of the cases involving white defendants and white victims; 19 percent of the cases involving white defendants and black victims; and 15 percent of the cases involving black defendants and black victims. Overall, defendants convicted of killing white victims were 4.3 times as likely to receive a death sentence as defendants convicted of killing blacks. Black defendants, like McCleskey, have the greatest likelihood of receiving the death penalty.

The Court called attention to the controversy in the district court about the validity of the Baldus data but did not feel the need to resolve the issue. The Court simply observed that the court of appeals assumed the validity of the data and found that the data were not sufficient to prove a constitutional violation.

Like the lower courts, the Supreme Court emphasized that McCleskey had to "prove that the decision makers in *his* case acted with discriminatory purpose," that he "offers no evidence specific to his own case that would support an inference that racial considerations played a part in his sentence. Instead, he relies solely on the Baldus study" (pp. 292–293, emphasis in original).

Despite the data that documented the prosecutorial discretion to seek the death penalty, the majority emphasized that "each particular decision to impose the death penalty is made by a [petit] jury from a properly constituted [that is, representing a cross-section of the community] venire." Cases dealing with discrimination in employment or in the selection of a venire were not really comparable because fewer decision makers and fewer variables are involved in those decisions.

As to prosecutorial discretion, the Court underscored the "wide discretion" that prosecutors enjoy and their reluctance to call them to explain decisions. The Court ruled that it is enough that the state's law permitted the death penalty in cases like McCleskey's, ignoring the question of how the prosecution justified *not* seeking the death penalty in cases involving black victims. In a statement that must ring hollow with families of black victims, the Court justified its hands-off approach by looking at "the context of his challenge," namely, "decisions at the heart of the State's criminal justice system" that involve "'one of society's most basic tasks . . . that of protecting the lives of its citizens . . . through criminal laws against murder.'" (*McCleskey v. Kemp,* p. 297).

Although the majority restated the data concerning the race of the victim, one cannot help wondering whether the justices understand the context beyond this single case. The thrust of the story told by the Baldus data is that society has failed to perform this "basic task" of "protecting the lives of its citizens" who happen to be black. Maybe the McCleskey story tells more about the lack of a voice for victims in the criminal process than it does about the application of the data in a case involving a white victim.

The core data are undisputed; the difficulty is that McCleskey, a convicted murder of a white victim, may not be the best person to tell the story of discrimination against murder victims in the black community. The Court swept his challenge aside, saying "McCleskey cannot prove a constitutional violation by demonstrating that other defendants who may be similarly situated did *not* receive the death penalty" (pp. 306–307). Can anyone then challenge the lack of protection of life in the black community?

That glitch in the majority's reasoning perhaps reveals more about their thinking. They seemed to see McCleskey's challenge as implicating the power of states to impose the death penalty at all. Like the court of appeals, the majority seemed to despair, implicitly at least, of finding a way to ensure equal treatment for all in capital sentencing.

The majority's opinion then moved more in the direction of evaluating policies and procedures designed to safeguard the administration of the death penalty from arbitrary or discriminatory administration. For example, the state has a system of separating the guilt determination phase of the trial from the penalty determination phase, of specifying aggravating and mitigating factors, and of requiring appellate court review of the sentencing decision. The implicit question is "What more can a state do?"

If these implications were not enough, the majority converted McCleskey's challenge into a challenge of jury decision making and of all sentencing decision making in the criminal justice system. Ironically, the Court cited Kalven and Zeisel's classic study *The American Jury* (1966) for the claim that "it is the jury's function to make the difficult and uniquely human judgments that defy codification and that 'buil[d] discretion, equity, and flexibility into a legal system.'" (p. 311). The majority then observed that "discretion in the criminal justice system offers substantial benefits to criminal defendants." Again, the implication is that the challenge goes too far, that juries may be responsible for the discrimination, and that challenges may end up hurting criminal defendants. In case the reader missed the point, the court stated it more bluntly: "Of course, 'the power to be lenient [also] is the power to discriminate'" (p. 312).

And if those implications were not enough, the court asserted that McCleskey's claim, "taken to its logical conclusion, throws into serious question the principles that underlie our entire criminal justice system" (p. 314). Similar

> claims could apply with equally logical force to statistical disparities that correlate with the race or sex of other actors in the criminal justice system, such as defense attorneys or judges. Indeed, such a claim could—at least in theory—be based on any arbitrary variable, such as the defendant's facial characteristics, or the physical attractiveness of the defendant or the victim that some statistical study indicates may be influential in jury decisionmaking. As these examples illustrate, there is no limiting principle to the type of challenge brought by McCleskey. (p. 318)

Finally, the Court asserted that "legislatures also are better qualified to weigh and 'evaluate the results of statistical studies in terms of their own local conditions and with a flexibility of approach that is not available in the courts'" (p. 319). In brief, the Court declined McCleskey's invitation to be the vehicle for dismantling capital punishment, the jury system, prosecutorial discretion, sentencing, and the criminal justice system as we have known it. With all due humility, they said, that is a legislative task.

The Four Dissents: "A Fear of Too Much Justice."

The dissents were not so shy or so bold. Justice Brennan opened the attack by honing in on the majority's "fear that recognition of McCleskey's claim would open the door to widespread challenges to all aspects of criminal sentencing. Taken on its face, such a statement seems to suggest a fear of too much justice" (p. 339).

Justice Brennan spent little time discussing the Baldus study. He summed up the study as indicating that "after taking into account some 230 nonracial factors that might legitimately influence a sentencer, the jury *more likely than not* would have spared McCleskey's life had his victim been black" (p. 325, emphasis in original). Like Judge Clark in the court of appeals, Justice Brennan emphasized that the race-of-victim variable is as powerful an explanation of disparity in capital sentencing as "nonracial aggravating factors such as a prior murder conviction or acting as the principal planner of the homicide."

The important points to Brennan were the policy reasons that the majority gave for countering the force of the statistical data and upholding McCleskey's death sentence. He saw in the majority's approach

> four factors on the scales opposite McCleskey's evidence: the desire to encourage sentencing discretion, the existence of "statutory safeguards" in the Georgia scheme, the fear of encouraging widespread challenges to other sentencing decisions, and the limits of the judicial role. (*McClesky v. Kemp*, p. 322)

Justice Brennan did not discount the role of discretion in the administration of the criminal justice system. No one who is familiar with the courts can argue that prosecutors should have no discretion. All cases cannot be prosecuted to the fullest extent permitted by law. We all would have to be full-time jurors, judges, prosecutors, and defense attorneys to handle all the trials. Nonetheless, the "presumption that actors in the criminal justice system exercise their discretion in responsible fashion . . . is rebuttable" (p. 337). He then asserted that the majority "rejects evidence drawn from the most sophisticated capital sentencing analysis ever performed, that reveals that race more likely than not infects capital sentencing decisions" (p. 337).

As for the safeguards in the Georgia statute and procedure, Brennan asserted that the "challenge to the Georgia system is not speculative or theoretical; it is empirical." For that reason, "the Court cannot rely on the statutory safeguards that such evidence calls into question" (p. 338).

The majority's fear of future challenges to sentences on factors other than race "fails to recognize the uniquely sophisticated nature of the Baldus study," in Justice Brennan's view. He argued that "acceptance of [McCleskey's] evidence would therefore establish a remarkably stringent standard of statistical evidence unlikely to be satisfied with any frequency" (pp. 341–342).

Finally, Justice Brennan flatly disagreed with the majority's assertion that the legislature should be heard and followed. Here, he became a poetic and passionate advocate:

> Those whom we would banish from society or from the human community itself often speak with too faint a voice to be heard above society's demand for punishment. It is the particular role of courts to hear these voices, for the Constitution declares that the majoritarian chorus may not alone dictate the conditions of social life. (p. 343)

Justices Stevens and Blackmun were not so absolute in their condemnation of the death penalty as Justices Brennan and Marshall generally have been. Both argued that the Baldus data could enable the state to identify aggravating circumstances that judges, jurors, and prosecutors seem to agree deserve the death penalty. According to Justice Stephens, one of the lessons of the Baldus study

> is that there exist certain categories of extremely serious crimes for which prosecutors consistently seek, and juries consistently impose, the death penalty without regard to the race of the victim or the race of the offender. If Georgia were to narrow the class of death-eligible defendants to those categories, the dangers of arbitrary and discriminatory imposition of the death penalty would be significantly decreased, if not eradicated. (*McCleskey v. Kemp*, p. 367)

That voice of compromise, of acting on the data and only the clear data, was not heeded.

Almost 13 years after the murder of officer Frank Schlatt, in the last week in September, 1991, Warren McCleskey, age 44, was electrocuted in Georgia's electric chair when a volunteer Georgia state employee pressed a button to start the electrical flow. According to one report, there was "no shortage of volunteers" (Montreal *Gazette*, 1991).

POSTMORTEM OF IMPACT, COMPETENCE, AND GOODNESS OF FIT

What should one make of this dramatic saga of social science evidence in the courts? Are there lessons to be learned, problem areas to be identified, theories to be tested?

Social Science Impact

The first question to be asked in assessing the process is this: "Did social science have an impact on the reasoning and opinions of the courts?" A second question follows closely from the first: "Were the social science data used well?" Note that we do not ask "Did social science determine the outcome?" This simple question obscures the differences between the roles of judges and social scientists. Just as scholars who study procedural justice from the perspective of litigants focus on the fairness of the process rather than the outcome, it seems reasonable to expect that social scientists would focus on the process in which their data are received and used.

In many ways, the impact of the Baldus study is apparent and central. The data defined the issues to be addressed. Without the data, legal claims of discriminatory treatment, cruel and unusual punishment, and arbitrary and capricious decision making would have been empty rhetoric. Because Warren McCleskey had no evidence of discrimination by prosecutor, judge, or jury in his case, legal claims made without Baldus's data would have been totally unfounded. One can safely predict they would have been dismissed out of hand.

Judicial Competence in Applying the Data

The data were used. "Were they used well?" is a more difficult question, one that seems central to modern debates about use of social science in legal decision making as well as general policymaking. This question forces one to face squarely questions about the competence of generalist judges to interpret and apply scientific evidence. As with jury decision making, one should also ask, "How can the competence of judges to apply social science data be enhanced?"

McCleskey was not a case in which generalist judges blindly followed the blandishments of the experts. Judge Forrester picked apart the study from all angles. Two or three problems, however, seem apparent. Judge Forrester held the evidence to a standard beyond science or law: absolute certitude. Because the models used could not "capture every nuance," they could be discarded. In approaching the evidence this way, Judge Forrester failed to look for and apply legal bridges relating to the standard of proof, such as whether the preponderance of the evidence showed that discriminatory treatment was more probable than not in McCleskey's case. Such traditional legal standards allow judges and juries to come to conclusions that appear definitive for the individual case without imposing paralyzing demands for certainty of evidence.

By demanding certainty and even rejecting evidence that met the demanding scientific standard of a 95 percent probability of not having occurred by chance, Judge Forrester ignored the baseline level of information that courts ordinarily use in addressing similar issues (Tversky & Kahneman, 1986). In doing so he exhibited a common error committed by generalists who are not used to asking a core methodological question: "Compared to what?" Judges and juries frequently rely on testimony that falls far short of scientific standards. Eyewitness evidence does not "capture every nuance" or even come close to scientific standards. Comparing baseline evidentiary standards for ordinary witnesses to those for scientific experts seems a more realistic test of whether science can assist a judge or jury.

On the other hand, Judge Forrester displayed a hard-nosed approach to coding of the data, focusing on what appeared to be serious questions of interrater reliability between the first and second studies. His observations about multicollinearity, level of variance, and coding discrepancies warranted a response. They were equivalent to the types of questions a peer reviewer might ask about an article submitted for publication. Judge Johnson's treatment of these issues in his dissent seemed to respond by applying appropriate scientific concepts in a plausible manner.

Judge Roney similarly showed a willingness and facility for confronting the data and facing squarely the relationships of the data to the legal issues. Unfortunately, none of the court of appeals judges appeared to understand the significance of the 6 percent discrepancy in rate, dismissing it as a minor variation rather than as representing a doubling of the rate of death sentences. Although it is somewhat encouraging that this error was corrected at the Supreme Court level, presumably with the help of the briefs of McCleskey's attorneys, most cases do not reach that level.

At the court of appeals and Supreme Court levels, the majority presumed the validity of the data, avoiding the difficult questions that Judge Forrester raised. Had the vote in the Supreme Court tilted to 5–4 the other way, the courts would have to face those troublesome issues. The fact that Judge Johnson had tackled them competently is encouraging. As is typical with methodological issues, it is by no means clear that there is a right answer or that generalist judges would have adequately appraised the methodological issues.

In all, some of the judges appeared very competent to address the issues raised by the Baldus data. Apparently, they relied on the adversary system to feed them information and analysis. Both sides were represented by experienced litigators and had the resources to present well-credentialed expert witnesses. The hearings at the district court level established a record that would inform the appellate courts. The data were both empirically tested, peer reviewed, and *adversarially tested* (that is, subjected to cross-examination by the prosecutor) by the time the case reached the reviewing courts. Apparently, enough information was available as long as the court, with assistance from counsel, could evaluate its validity and significance.

One wonders, in a case of this magnitude in which conflicting experts may tend to complicate the data and confuse the decision makers, whether the courts could use special resources such as court-appointed experts or technical advisers to help them sift through the conflicting claims. Cecil and Willging (1993) found that judges who faced complex issues that required reasoned decisions (not jury trials) sometimes saw the need for neutral guidance. Judges who found and appointed neutral experts were almost unanimously pleased with the results, but appointment of such experts remains a rare event. Judges tend to rely on the adversarial system and their own wits.

In the end, the Supreme Court deferred to the state (and presumably federal) legislatures. Was this a matter of competence or of political ideology and conception of the role of the courts? One suspects the latter. Legislators, like judges, tend to be generalists with no special expertise in social science and with staff who tend also to be generalists. It's difficult to imagine a legislative hearing that would examine discrimination in the administration of the death penalty as deeply as Judge Forrester did in this case. However, one substantial difference stands out. Unlike the courts, legislators have an explicit mandate to examine all social implications of a given problem and are not limited to reviewing a single case at a time. Let's look a little more closely at the issues each body addressed.

Goodness of Fit

A central issue remains: Are judges and social scientists asking the same questions in cases like *McCleskey*? Social scientists essentially ask empirical questions like "What is the level of racial disparity in capital cases? What variables are associated with it? What amount of variance do these variables explain?"

Judges face similar issues under the terms "Is the death penalty being administered in a racially discriminatory manner?" "Was the defendant a victim of discrimination?" and "What can be done to remedy any deficiencies in the process?" Yet, as *McCleskey* shows, the focus on a single case skews the thinking of judges away from the aggregate issues. When we look for the victims of the discrimination that Baldus demonstrates, the primary victims seem to be the deceased black homicide victims whose lives were not valued as highly as the white victims' lives. Indeed, in one view, black defendants more often benefit from this discrimination because their victims are more often black than white. No doubt McCleskey is affected in some way. His victim was white and he would not have been facing execution had his victim been black. But the narrow legal issue is whether McCleskey has been discriminated against because of his race, and the evidence does not support the conclusion that he has been the direct victim of discrimination.

In contrast, black homicide victims can be directly represented in the legislative process. The question is no longer "Should this defendant be executed?" Instead, the legislature, representing all constituents, is called on to make a social judgment about the fairness of the process to all—victims, survivors, defendants, prosecutors, judges, and jurors. Legislatures can also draw new lines, define new aggravating or mitigating circumstances, or even establish clear standards for racial fairness in administering a law. Social science data about the fairness of the system in handling clear cases can be used to salvage what is working and discard what is not.

The legislature can ask the question more broadly: "Is the system of capital punishment in Georgia being administered in a racially discriminatory or arbitrary manner?" To a certain extent the courts *did* address those issues, but the response from the data was that there is strong evidence of discrimination in the close cases but not so much in the clear cases. Overall, the amount of discrimination was about 6 percent, a doubling of the rate of capital punishment if the victim was white. In close cases, the rate is 20 percent; in clear cases, the rate must be negligible.

The ultimate issue is "How much of a disparity will be tolerated as the unavoidable consequence of a system that needs to vest discretion in public officials?" Here is the line-drawing question, the bottom line. This is a normative issue, one that allows judges to draw on precedent, perceptions of the judicial role, perhaps even personal, constitutional, and political values. Social science can tell us what values are involved in an issue, what public opinion says, what norms others have applied, and the like. Ultimately, though, the norms to govern the case at hand depend on the wisdom and honesty of the judge hearing the case.

CONCLUSIONS AND QUESTIONS

What do we know and what do we want to know about the use of social science in the legal system, and why? Generalizing from our in-depth look at *McCleskey* and from other cases in which social science has played an important role, we can tease out seven relatively clear hypotheses about the use of social science in the legal system.

1. *Social scientists studying the legal system have produced valuable insights into the administration of justice that have only occasionally been understood and applied by judges deciding individual cases.*

Social scientists bring systematically collected, relevant data about significant and controversial elements of the legal system. For example, we have seen in Chapters 7, 8, 9, 10, and 11 that social psychologists have amassed relevant findings about the operations of the jury system and about the accuracy of eyewitness testimony; yet these findings frequently fail to make their way into the legal system. Sometimes this research attacks fundamental elements of the status quo, such as the use of eyewitness evidence or the fairness of the administration of the death penalty.

The enormous policy consequences of applying social science findings in these individual cases may cause judges to shy away from such applications. *Brown v. Board of Education* may well be the exceptional case in which a court used social science in the course of undertaking a major change. The linking of the social science findings with the moral and legal absolutes seems a key factor in those cases.

2. *Legal issues involved in an individual case frequently do not match up well with empirical issues that frame social science findings. Legal issues relating to equality tend to fit better with social science findings than do other legal issues because the concept of equality conveys quantitative and comparative elements.*

Even in areas of equality, as the Brown and McCleskey cases show, legal concepts of equality do not line up exactly with mathematical concepts of equality. Justice is not quite so simple. Opportunities or punishments do not have to be exactly equal. How much tolerance to allow is generally a policy question, but one that can be informed by social science. For example, social scientists may be able to measure whether deviations from the norm are likely to be random.

Other legal concepts, such as fairness, do not match well with scientific measures. Social science can measure opinions or attitudes about fairness, but ultimately the judgment about whether an individual action is fair is one that society has assigned to judges. Social science can contribute, however, to testing various objective elements of fairness, such as the likelihood of having dissenting viewpoints on a jury of a particular size. Again, applying these findings in a single case is problematic because aggregate social science data do not usually point to a clear resolution of an individual case.

3. *Judges, even justices of the U.S. Supreme Court, differ widely in their ability to comprehend and apply social science data.*

Indeed, Supreme Court justices may be less able to apply social science data competently because their legal skills and judgments may inhibit their looking at quantitative data until it's too late. Lawyers are trained to make judgments on behalf of individual clients and to gather evidence to support those judgments. Faced with a conflict between a legal principle and social science evidence, most judges are comfortable with the former and not the latter. Changes have occurred over time and the proliferation of data and the growth of social science and law have stimulated judges to adjust to the times.

4. *An element of the inability or unwillingness of judges to apply social science findings is a belief in the absoluteness of legal principles and the related absence of a habit of looking for baseline information about the status quo.*

As we saw in the McCleskey (death penalty) case and to a degree in the Ballew (jury size, Chapter 10) case, judges tend to look at the status quo as at least adequate, if not perfect. In examining a competing way of examining an issue, there is a tendency to look for perfection as opposed to asking whether the innovation is an improvement over the current system. A study that does not "capture every nuance" of the system may be discarded by that logic.

5. *Judges charged with deciding individual cases are likely to find it difficult to bridge the gap between aggregate data and the facts needed to decide the case at hand.*

For all the sophistication of the Baldus study, it did not answer directly the question of whether there had been any element of racial discrimination involved in Warren McCleskey's case. Basically, the social science data addressed policy questions at the aggregate level (and could not clearly resolve the policy issues, either).

6. *Social science evidence that is presented at the trial level by expert witnesses is more likely to capture the attention of appellate courts than is social science evidence that lawyers present in a brief or that another judge discovers from personal study.*

Here, *Brown v. Board of Education* and *McCleskey* show the power that presenting scientific evidence through testimony at trial has on the case. It forces judges at all levels to confront the evidence, if not to agree with it. On the other hand, Justice Blackmun's uncovering of social science evidence through his own research regarding jury size in *Ballew* does not force other judges to confront that evidence. Judicial colleagues may be skeptical of such evidence because it has not been *adversarially tested*. The parties have not had an opportunity to challenge it. Such evidence can be seen to be outside the record in the case and therefore outside the legitimate purview of the judge.

7. *Policymakers in general, including judges, legislators, and administrators, are more likely to use social science competently than are judges in individual cases, perhaps because the social science findings are likely to fit the policy issues more clearly than they do a single case.*

Social science data generally examine the full range of behavior and produce an aggregate overview of the system. It is precisely this quality that renders it difficult to apply to individual cases. Judges cannot find where the individual fits. This quality makes social science data all the more inviting for the policymaker. Policymakers need to see the full range of behavior, to account for all the behavior in a general rule that does not unduly focus on a single case. For this reason, social scientists should generally target their data to the policymaker. As Tanford (1991) found, even in an area as central to the judicial system as the effectiveness of jury instructions, policymaking bodies, including legislatures and rule-making bodies, are more likely to get the social science right than are judges faced with individual cases.

SUMMARY

We started the *McCleskey* case study with some questions and conclude with some tentative answers or hypotheses. Our questions included these: What, if any, effects flowed from the timing of the social science research in relation to the legal events in question? More specifically, how did the fashioning of specific studies with litigation in mind affect their reception in the courts? How well do the legal and social science issues fit with each other? How competent are judges, jurors, and lawyers in using social science findings?

The data concerning death penalty cases indicated that racial considerations have some effect in all cases and that racial considerations did not have a clear and definitive effect in Warren McCleskey's case. The statewide data showed that generally the race of the victim had a significant effect on the punishment imposed throughout the state. The data did not, however, purport to show that the race of the victim determined the outcome in any particular case. This application of aggregate data illustrates a built-in limit of such information. Social science data, like most statistical data, offer guidance in terms of probabilities, not absolutes. The result is that the law's focus on the individual case deflects the court from considering data about discrimination that infects the entire system to a tangible degree.

Generalizing from our in-depth look at *McCleskey* and from other cases in which social science has played an important role, we identified seven relatively clear hypotheses about use of social science data in the legal system.

1. Social scientists have contributed to the administration of justice in individual cases and might contribute more if judges deciding those cases were trained to understand and use social science data.

2. Legal issues in individual cases often do not fit the issues that social scientists are able to study quantitatively because legal issues rarely include quantitative and comparative elements.

3. Judges differ widely in their ability to comprehend and apply social science data.

4. One conceptual weakness of judges in considering social science findings is their tendency to believe that legal principles are generally based on reality (for example, that eyewitness evidence is accurate). Accordingly, judges often fail to look for probabilistic baseline information about the status quo (for example, about the probability of erroneous eyewitnesses) and discard social science evidence about eyewitness fallibility.

5. Judges are likely to find it difficult to apply aggregate data, focusing on broad policy issues, to an individual's case.

6. Social science evidence that is presented at the trial level by expert witnesses and subject to cross-examination by the opposing party is more persuasive to judges than social science evidence presented in an appellate brief or discovered by another judge on appeal.

7. Policymakers are more likely to use social science competently in fashioning general rules than are judges in individual cases, probably because the social science findings usually fit broad policy issues more clearly than they fit a specific case.

In short, it appears that psychological findings are likely to have their greatest impact in the policy arenas. The process of decision making in individual cases seems to be less hospitable to social science than decision making about broad policies and principles.

GLOSSARY

ad damnun: The plaintiff's statement presented to the jury concerning the monetary loss suffered.

additur: A judge's action that increases a jury's award the judge considers to be inadequate.

adversarial system: The legal model used in Anglo-American law that assumes just results will emerge when each side presents its own case to neutral fact finders, judges, or juries.

aggravating factors: Those that call for the death penalty and include the brutality of the crime, the motivation of the defendant, and the likelihood that the defendant will continue to be a danger to others.

Allen charge: Instructions given to a deadlocked jury to encourage reconsideration of the evidence to bring forth a verdict. Also known as the "dynamite charge."

alternative dispute resolution (ADR): Procedures other than formal trials that are used to evaluate civil cases and facilitate settlement without a full trial. Examples include arbitration, mediation, and summary jury trials.

amicus curiae: A term meaning friend of the court. A person or group, not a party to the legal action, may ask the court for permission to present views in support of one of the parties.

answer: A formal statement containing the defendant's response to the plaintiff's complaint in a civil case.

appeal: A formal procedure asking a higher court to review the actions of a trial court to decide whether legal errors were committed in the trial or judgment. Generally, litigants have a right to at least one appeal.

appellant: One who appeals the decision of a lower court case.

arbitration: A process in which the parties to a dispute agree to submit to a neutral party, who will hear arguments, consider evidence, and decide the outcome.

archival research: Researchers' use of public records to answer research questions.

arraignment: A proceeding in a criminal case in which the defendant is advised of his or her legal rights and called on to enter a plea of guilty, not guilty, or otherwise to the charges.

arrest: An act by a legally appointed authority, the police officer, that deprives a citizen of freedom.

assault: Threatening another with bodily harm.

authoritarian: A personality type characterized by a strong belief in punishment for those who violate social values and laws.

bail: A sum of money set by the judge that the defendant must pay to remain free prior to the trial. The defendant must post that amount as a guarantee that he or she will appear for the trial.

battered woman syndrome: A pattern of perceptions and behaviors thought to be characteristic of women who have endured continuous physical abuse by their mates.

battery: The forceful, harmful touching of another without consent.

bench trial: A trial in which the judge is sole fact finder and decision maker.

bifurcated system: System used in death penalty trials in which capital juries first determine the defendant's guilt or innocence; if the defendant is found guilty, a second trial follows to set the person's penalty.

Bill of Rights: The first ten amendments to the U.S. Constitution. These amendments guarantee personal freedoms, including freedom from unreasonable search and seizure, the right to trial by jury, and the protections of due process of law. Many of the procedural safeguards in criminal proceedings originate in the Bill of Rights.

black sheep effect: Result of jurors' tendency to judge a disagreeable same race defendant harshly, if the defendant's racial group is in the minority on the jury.

Brandeis brief: Type of brief named for lawyer and Supreme Court justice Louis Brandeis, who initiated the use of social science to buttress legal positions.

brief: A written statement of one side's legal view of a case submitted to the judge or judges hearing the case. Typically, a brief contains a table of relevant cases, a statement of the facts, the issues, and at least one legal argument for each issue.

burden of proof: The obligation of the prosecutor in a criminal case or the plaintiff in a civil case to establish by evidence a legally determined degree of belief in the mind of the juror as to the truth of the evidence. Specifically, in a criminal trial the prosecution must prove all the elements of the crime beyond a reasonable doubt. *See also* plaintiff, preponderance of evidence, reasonable doubt.

certiorari: An action or writ removing a case from an inferior court to a superior court for review. This is the main path for review of a case by the U.S. Supreme Court. A litigant petitions the Court to grant a writ of certiorari, which the Court grants or denies, at its discretion, usually without stating reasons. (Literal translation is "to make sure.")

challenge for cause: A claim that a juror is not fit to serve because his or her answers to voir dire questions show an inability to decide the case without bias. *See also* voir dire.

change of venue motion: A request to the court that a trial be moved to another district to ensure fairness.

civil law: The body of law concerned with the private relationships among individuals and other entities, including corporations. Civil cases are brought to enforce private rights, often to seek damages from another individual or entity. *See also* criminal law.

closing arguments: In a trial, the attorneys' attempts to summarize the evidence, organize it for the jury in persuasive form, and argue its practical implications.

cognitive interview: A technique employing various memory-enhancing strategies that is used to question eyewitnesses.

common law: Law derived from judges' decisions in courtroom cases; judicial as opposed to legislative law.

comparative negligence rule: A rule that attempts to divide liability between the plaintiff and the defendant in proportion to the percentage of fault each party bears.

competence to stand trial: Ability of the defendant at the commencement of the trial to understand the proceedings and to assist in his or her defense.

complaining witness: The injured party who filed a complaint with the police.

complaint: A charge that an offense has been committed by the person named or described. In a civil case, a pleading that is filed to begin the case. A complaint should contain a concise statement of the facts and legal theory on which the plaintiff relies.

complexity exception: The assumption that history and the threat to the defendant's right to a trial before a fair and impartial jury permit judges to exclude juries from complex (civil) cases.

compromise memory: The memory phenomenon of "averaging" disparate pieces of information in memory.

constitution: The contract between the U.S. government, or a state, and its citizens.

contributory negligence rule: A rule under which the defendant tries to show that the plaintiffs failed to exercise the care a reasonable person would use and thereby contributed to the (plaintiff's) injuries. This rule applies to civil negligence cases, and proof of contributory negligence on the part of the plaintiff may prohibit the awarding of damages.

Control (or Comparison) Question Test (CQT): A polygraph technique using the assumption that guilty suspects will exhibit physiological responses to crime-relevant questions compared to control questions.

criminal law: The body of law concerned with the relationship between a person or other entity and government. Criminal cases are brought to enforce public standards of conduct. *See also* civil law.

criminal responsibility: The blameworthiness of the defendant at the time the crime was committed; to be criminally responsible, the defendant must have been aware of what he or she was doing in committing the crime.

decision control: The influence the defendant and/or plaintiff has over the actual outcome of the trial or dispute.

decision rule: A rule setting the number of members who must agree before the group is considered to have reached a decision.

defendant: The individual or party against whom relief or recovery of damages is sought, or the accused in a criminal trial.

deposition: A procedure in which oral or written questions are answered by the witness under oath; usually done in the lawyer's office.

directed verdict: A ruling by a trial judge that a dispute has too little factual basis to warrant a jury decision in the case; sometimes known in a civil case as "judgment as a matter of law."

discovery: The procedure by which a litigant is compelled to disclose facts relevant to the case, including documents within the litigant's possession or control. The purpose of discovery is to make the trial fair and to allow each party to know beforehand the information to be used at trial.

DNA (deoxyribonucleic acid): The long, coiled molecules that constitute the genes found in the nuclei of cells.

DNA analysis: Text based on fundamental biological principles of broad genetic variability among humans and the presumed uniqueness of each person's genetic makeup, identical twins excepted.

double jeopardy: A rule, based on the Fifth Amendment of the Bill of Rights, that an accused person cannot be tried twice for the same offense. Jeopardy begins when a jury is impaneled and sworn or a judge begins to hear evidence.

due process: An individual has the right to an orderly and fair hearing of his or her case and to be notified in a timely manner of charges in the case.

early neutral evaluation: Consideration by a neutral observer of the merits of the case early in the proceedings in the hope of reaching a settlement.

electrophoresis: A step in the analysis of DNA in which an electric current is applied to the sample and the fragments are placed on a gel and pulled through it by an electric field.

episodic memory: The (memory) system that helps us encode, store, and recall events.

equal protection (of the law): Provision that no person (or class of persons) can be denied the same protection of the law that other persons and classes enjoy. Every citizen, whatever his or her social standing, enjoys the same protection of the law as any other person.

estimator variables: Aspects of the crime situation (violence of the event, distance to the crime, presence of a weapon, etc.) that may affect the performance of an eyewitness.

exclusionary rule: Rule that excludes from a criminal trial evidence that is gathered illegally by the police unless the prosecution can show that the police acted in good faith.

exploration (visual): The unsystematic visual scanning mechanism used by children between the ages of five and seven.

false positive: Generally, the result when one believes something is true when it is not. Specifically, the result of falsely classifying a suspect as guilty on the basis of a polygraph reading.

Federal Rules of Evidence: Uniform rules that govern the admissibility of evidence at trials in federal courts.

final offer arbitration: A procedure in which the parties submit their last, best negotiating offers to the arbitrator prior to the hearing. The arbitrator chooses one of the offers.

group polarization: The intensification through group discussion of the initial tendencies of the group members.

guilt nullifier: A belief—such as opposition to the death penalty—that is so strong it would interfere with a juror's ability to render a fair verdict (guilty or not), even if the juror was convinced that the defendant was guilty.

Guilty Action Test (GAT): A polygraph variation of the GKT used because of the possibility that someone might have guilty knowledge without actually having performed the guilty action. The GAT probes the suspect's actions.

guilty but mentally ill (GMBI): A verdict option in many states when the insanity defense is raised. It means that the jury believes the defendant is mentally ill but not insane. It does not mean that the defendant will get special treatment because of mental infirmity.

Guilty Knowledge Test (GKT): Test resting on the assumption that physiological (autonomic) arousal will be elicited in a guilty person if he or she hears about aspects of the crime that only a guilty person would know. Also known as the "Concealed Knowledge Test."

hearsay rule: Any testimony given by a witness who relates not what he or she knows personally, but what others have told the witness. Generally, such evidence is not admissible, but numerous exceptions exist, such as one for learned treatises that an expert used to develop an opinion.

hypermensia: The hypothesis that hypnosis can make a witness remember things he or she could not recall under nonhypnotic conditions.

independent variable: The variable manipulated by the researcher in an experiment to cause change in the dependent variable.

indictment: A formal accusation of a crime, issued by a grand jury at the request of a prosecutor. *See also* prosecutor.

information: A formal accusation of a crime, issued by a prosecutor acting without a grand jury.

injunction: A judge's order that a person perform or refrain from performing a specific act.

inquisitorial system: The legal model used in continental Europe that assumes just results emerge when the judge takes an active role in determining guilt or innocence and the court appoints the lawyers rather than permitting each side to hire their own.

in situ research: Research done in the actual situation, say the courtroom, as opposed to laboratory research.

interlocutory appeal: An appeal taken before the final judgment in a case. Usually, a court will hear such an appeal only under special circumstances because it disrupts the case in the trial court.

interrogatories: Written questions related to the issues in a civil case, typically addressed to one of the parties and requiring a written response under oath.

judicial immunity: A policy dating to the nineteenth century that protects judges' independence by ensuring that they will not be sued by angry or disappointed litigants.

jurists: Judges, lawyers, and legal scholars.

jury nullification: The act of a jury that understands the law and the facts and deliberately decides to ignore the evidence because to do otherwise would violate the jurors' sense of justice.

law: The body of rules and principles that govern our behavior.

legal authoritarianism: Characteristic of individuals who generally favor the prosecution over the defense.

legal authority: The authority that previous decisions have in the courts.

legal realism: The belief that the law is constructed out of concrete concerns of everyday life.

legal system: All the institutions (such as courts and prisons), the officials (including police, judges, prosecutors, and defense lawyers), and the rules and procedures they use to resolve disputes and dispense justice at the state and federal levels of government.

leniency bias: The assumption that social influence applied in jury deliberation tends to favor an acquittal rather than a conviction.

lineup: A procedure for suspect identification in which a witness views several individuals (live or photographed) and attempts to identify one of the individuals, who may or may not be present, as the suspect.

maximization: A technique in which the goal of interrogators is to intimidate the suspect into confessing by falsely claiming they have incriminating evidence or by exaggerating the seriousness of the crime.

mediation: Intervention of a neutral party who facilitates but does not decide the resolution of a dispute.

mens rea: Guilty mind or criminal intent; a requirement for criminal responsibility.

meta-analyses: Statistical integrations of the results of independent studies on the same issue.

meter model: A model of juror information processing based on the idea that decision makers hold one or more meters that continuously track and read out a value reflecting the juror's current view of the evidence.

minimization: A technique in which the interrogators use a "soft sell" to try to convince the suspect that the officers are sympathetic.

minitrials: Privately organized trials used by business to settle disputes.

misinformation effect: The effect of postevent information that biases eyewitness memory.

mitigating factors: Those that would lead toward a verdict of life (in a murder trial) and may include the defendant's mental capacity, age, motivation, prior felony record, and any other factor of the defendant's character or record that may be used to argue for a sentence less than death.

moot courtrooms: Courtrooms in law schools where hypothetical cases are tried for the purpose of training law students.

motion: An application for a ruling or order, made either orally or in writing to a court or judge.

motion for change of venue: A request that a judge move a trial from one location to another, often because of the amount of unfavorable pretrial publicity in the first locale.

motion for summary judgment: A request in a civil case that the judge rule in favor of the party requesting the judgment because there are no genuine issues of fact for the jury to decide and the undisputed facts show that the requesting party should win the case.

motion in limine: A request filed "at the threshold" of a civil or criminal trial asking the judge to determine the admissibility of specified evidence and other ground rules for the trial.

motion to suppress evidence: A request that the judge order specified evidence to be inadmissible; generally used in a criminal trial to deal with evidence obtained in violation of a defendant's constitutional rights.

naked statistics: Numbers without verbal descriptions or explanations.

natural law: The belief, derived from Roman jurists, that rules of conduct exist independently of the observer, place, or situation.

negativity bias: The tendency to weigh negative information more heavily than positive information in decision making.

non compos mentis: Not of sound mind.

null hypothesis: The negative form of a hypothesis used for testing; the statement that an observation is due to chance rather than to a systematic cause.

penalty nullifiers: Jurors who refuse to vote for the death penalty in any case, regardless of the evidence.

peremptory challenges: Challenges to potential jurors that lawyers can exercise in the voir dire without specifying why the juror is to be eliminated. Lawyers are usually allowed only a small number of challenges.

plaintiffs: Those who initiate a lawsuit and who have the burden of proof in civil cases.

plea: The defendant's response to an indictment or information. The choices are "guilty," "not guilty," "not guilty by reason of insanity," or "no contest" (i.e., that the defendant chooses not to dispute the charges; the equivalent of a guilty plea but not a formal admission of guilt).

plea bargaining: Exchange by the accused of a guilty plea for a discounted sentence.

polygraph: A machine that makes physiological recordings as a person answers questions. The purpose is to detect deception, using the physiological readings to make inferences about the truth of the person's statements.

positive illusions: Unrealistically optimistic beliefs about one's ability to handle threatening situations and obtain a positive outcome.

precedents: Previous legal decisions in similar cases.

preponderance of the evidence: The standard of proof required for a verdict in civil trials, usually defined at 51 percent of the evidence, which is a lesser standard than that in criminal trials (reasonable doubt).

prima facie: Evidence that makes a clear case sufficient for proof but subject to rebuttal.

probable cause: A basis for legal action showing that a crime was committed and that the suspect was most probably the individual who committed that crime.

procedural law: Rules governing the steps to be taken in a civil or criminal case. Procedural rules affect the timing and form of legal arguments, discovery of facts, selection of a jury, and the like. *See also* substantive law.

process control: The amount of control a party to a legal proceeding has over how the evidence is presented to the decision maker.

prosecutor: The public officer appointed or elected to carry out criminal prosecutions on behalf of the state or the people.

psychology: The scientific study of behavior.

punitive damages: Damages awarded to the plaintiff over and above monies allotted to compensate for actual losses. The aim of punitive damages is to set an example to deter malicious or outrageous conduct when the wrong done to the plaintiff was an aggravated wrong; also know as "exemplary damages."

quasi-experimental: Descriptive of designs used when the researcher does not have full control over the important variables or over the social setting in which they occur.

random assignment: Selection of participants for conditions in an experiment in such a way that all participants have an equal chance of being assigned to any one of the conditions, making it extremely unlikely that there would be any systematic differences among the participants in each condition.

rape shield laws: Laws that limit the questioning of the victim about her prior sexual history, except with the defendant.

rape trauma syndrome: Symptoms often exhibited by rape survivors, including emotional responses, changes in lifestyle, and difficulty in day-to-day functioning.

reasonable doubt: The level of uncertainty of the defendant's guilt a juror must feel to fail to return a verdict of guilty in a criminal trial.

reconstructive memory: The theory of memory suggesting that we tend to store details of events, and that during recall we reconstruct the original event.

recovered memories: Memories brought to consciousness in the "spontaneous" recovery of memories of traumatic events, usually involving child sexual abuse, that occurred a long time ago and which the individual buried so deeply that no hint of the event surfaced until the day the memory was recovered.

remittitur: Action by a judge to decrease an excessive jury award.

rules of evidence: Rules for selecting the fairest and most reliable evidence for use in a trial.

satisficers: Jurors whose individual information processing is based on a minimal amount of evidence and an avoidance of evidence that might contradict what they believe.

scrupled jurors: Individuals who indicate they are opposed to the death penalty.

search: An information-seeking strategy used by older children and adults that is planned, sustained over time, systematic, convergent, and directed internally. *See also* exploration.

sequestration: Practice used in special trials to separate juries from home and family, having them live in a hotel for the duration of the trial.

sexual assault: An umbrella term that encompasses unwanted sexual touching, including intercourse.

sexually anatomically correct doll (SAC doll): A doll on which the secondary sexual characteristics of males and females are presented in an anatomically correct way.

showup: A method of suspect identification in which a single suspect is shown to the witness, often at the scene of the crime itself.

simple assault: The act of threatening another with bodily harm.

social authority: Generally agreed-on social science findings.

social facts: Empirically derived findings that bear on a particular case.

social loafing: The tendency of individuals to exert less effort when working on a collective task (one in which all group members' inputs are pooled) than when working coactively (each individual's inputs are separated from the others).

Socratic case method: A method of law school teaching that relies on the written opinions of judges in important cases. In each particular case, students respond to hypotheticals and search for the general legal principles the judge used to resolve the case.

stare decisis: The doctrine that judges' decisions must be guided by previous decisions in similar cases.

Stockholm syndrome: "Bonding" by hostages with their tormentors; may be a universal response to inescapable violence.

story model: Device for organizing and explaining trial evidence in which jurors create a narrative that takes the form of a story.

strict liability rule: Rule that holds a manufacturer liable if that manufacturer puts a product on the market that is defective and causes injuries to the user.

substantive law: Rules that specify the rights and duties of parties, governing the substance or merit of legal claims or defenses, such as criminal law or the law of contracts.

suggestibility: The lack of resistance of memory to outside information or pressure.

summary judgment: A finding that a judge may issue in the case without calling a jury if there is no dispute about the facts—only about the law.

summary jury trial: A summary presentation of evidence to a mock jury, which issues a nonbinding opinion.

summons: A formal paper served at the outset of a civil case advising the defendant about the steps to be taken to respond to the attached complaint.

system variables: The arrangements and methods used to debrief eyewitnesses; they include a number of lineup and interview procedures.

theory evidence coordination mode: An individual evidence processing mode requiring the construction of two or more stories that are evaluated against the incoming evidence and against each other.

tort law: Area of law that deals with noncriminal harm (personal injury cases).

tortious act: An act that does harm and may be the basis of a lawsuit.

Type I error: Rejection of the null hypothesis when it is actually true; concluding that a result had a significant effect when, in fact, it did not.

Type II error: Failure to reject the null hypothesis when it is actually false. The researcher concludes that a result is not significant when it is.

unconscious transference: A threat to eyewitness accuracy that occurs when the witness misidentifies a familiar but innocent person as the culprit.

venire: The panel or group of citizens for a particular trial, usually selected from local voter registration and other lists.

victim impact laws: Laws that introduce in the sentencing process the impact of the crime on the victim, the victim's family, and the community.

voir dire: The stage of jury selection during which the judge and/or counsel question the panel of potential jurors to determine their biases and suitability for service in the trial.

weapon focus: The phenomenon in which a witness's attention is so drawn to a weapon being used in a crime that he or she pays less attention to other details of an event.

Yerkes-Dodson law: The law relating performance to the amount of arousal experienced. The inverted U-shaped function suggests that at very low and very high levels of arousal, performance is poor, whereas at moderate levels of arousal, performance is optimal.

REFERENCES AND SUGGESTED READINGS

Abraham, H. J. (1994). *The judicial process* (4th ed.). New York: Oxford University Press.

Abramson, J. (1994). *We, the jury.* New York: Basic Books.

Adler, S. J. (1989, December 21). Can juries do justice to complex suits? *Wall Street Journal,* p. B1.

Adler, S. J. (1995). *The jury: Trial and error in the American Courtroom.* New York: Times Books.

Adorno, T. W., Frenkel-Brunswik, E., Levison, D. J., & Sanford, R. N. (1950). *The authoritarian personality.* New York: Harper & Row.

Alfini, J. J. (1989). Summary jury trials in state and federal courts: A comparative analysis of the perceptions of participating lawyers. *Ohio State University Journal of Dispute Resolution, 4,* 213–234.

Alschuler, A. W. (1979). Plea bargaining and its history. *Law and Society Review, 13,* 211–245.

American Bar Foundation. (1993). *Commemorating forty years of research.* Chicago: Author.

American Law Institute. (1962/1985). *Model Penal Code and commentaries.* Philadelphia.

Angier, N. (1993). Court ruling on scientific evidence: A just burden. *New York Times,* June 30, p. A8.

Appelbaum P. S. (1994). Civil commitment from a systems perspective. *Law and Human Behavior, 15*(1) 61–74.

Appelbaum, P. S., & Grisso, T. (1995). The MacArthur treatment competence study. I: Mental illness and the competence to consent to treatment. *Law and Human Behavior, 19*(2), 105–126.

Aronson, E., & Carlsmith, J. M. (1968). Experiments in social psychology. In G. Lindzey & E. Aronson (Eds.), *The handbook of social psychology* (Vol. 1, 2nd ed.). Reading, MA: Addison-Wesley.

Asch, S. E. (1951). Effects of group pressure on the modification and distortion of judgments. In H. Guetzkow (Ed.), *Groups, leadership, and men.* Pittsburgh: Carnegie Press.

Aschermann, E., Mantwill, M., & Kohnken, G. (1991). An independent replication of the effectiveness of the cognitive interview. *Applied Cognitive Psychology, 5,* 489–495.

Azar, B. (1995, October). Police tactics may border on coercion. *APA Monitor,* p. 27.

Bagby, R. M., Parker, J. D., Rector, N. A., & Kalemba, V. (1994). Racial prejudice in the Canadian legal system: Juror decisions in a simulated rape trial. *Law and Human Behavior, 18*(3), 339–350.

Bailis, D. S., Darley, J. M., Waxman, T. L., & Robinson, P. H. (1995). Community standards of criminal liability and the insanity defense. *Law and Human Behavior, 19*(5), 425–446.

Bailis, D. S., & MacCoun, R. J. (1996). Estimating liability risks with the media as your guide: A content analysis of media coverage of tort litigation. *Law and Human Behavior, 20*(4), 419–430.

Baldus, D., & Cole, J. (1980). *Statistical proof of discrimination.* New York: McGraw-Hill.

Baldus, D. C., Pulaski, C., & Woodworth, G. (1983). Comparative review of death sentences: The Georgia experience. *The Journal of Criminal Law and Criminology, 74*(3), 661–753.

Baldus, D., Woodworth, G., & Pulaski, C. (1985). Monitoring and evaluating contemporary death sentencing systems: Lessons from Georgia. *UC Davis Law Review, 18,* 1375–1396.

Baldus, D. C., Woodworth, G., & Pulaski, C. A., Jr. (1990). *Equal justice: A legal and empirical analysis.* Boston: Northeastern University Press.

Balos, B., & Fellows, M. L. (1991). Guilty of the crime of trust: Nonstranger rape. *Minnesota Law Review, 75,* 599–618.

The bargain that was no bargain. (1992, September 10). *Toledo Blade,* p. 9.

Barnier, A. J., & McConkey, K. M. (1992). Reports of real and false memories: The relevance of hypnosis, hypnotizability, and context of memory test. *Journal of Abnormal Psychology, 101,* 521–527.

Barr, J. N., & Willging, T. E. (1993). Decentralized self regulation, accountability, and judicial independence under the federal Judicial Conduct and Disability Act of 1980. *University of Pennsylvania Law Review, 142*(1), 25–207.

Barring the courthouse door. (1995, February 19). *Oregonian,* p. B3.

Bartlett, F. (1932). *Remembering: A study in experimental and social psychology.* Cambridge, England: Cambridge University Press.

Bashore, T. R., & Rapp, P. E. (1993). Are there alternatives to traditional polygraph procedures? *Psychological Bulletin, 113*(1), 2–22.

Bass, E., & Davis, L. (1988). *The courage to heal: A guide for women survivors of child sexual abuse.* New York: Harper & Row.

Bass, J. (1981). *Unlikely heroes.* New York: Simon & Schuster.

Bassili, J. N. (1981). The attractiveness stereotype: Goodness or glamour? *Basic and Applied Social Psychology, 2,* 235–252.

Bastian, L. D. (1992). *Criminal victimization 1991: Bureau of Justice Statistics Bulletin* (NCJ-136947). Washington, DC: U.S. Department of Justice.

Becker, B. C. (1980, October). Jury nullification: Can a jury be trusted? *Trial,* pp. 41–45.

Bell, B. E., & Loftus, E. F. (1988). Degree of detail of eyewitness testimony and mock juror judgments. *Journal of Applied Social Psychology, 18,* 1171–1192.

Bell, B. E., & Loftus, E. F. (1989). Trivial persuasion in the courtroom: The power of (a few) minor details. *Journal of Personality and Social Psychology, 56,* 669–679.

Berman, G. L., Narby, D. J., & Cutler, B. L. (1995). Effects of inconsistent eyewitness statements on mock jurors' evaluations of the eyewitness, perceptions of defendant, culpability and verdicts. *Law and Human Behavior, 19,* 79–88.

Bermant, G. (1985). Issues in trial management: Conducting the voir dire examinations. In S. M. Kassin & L. S. Wrightsman (Eds.), *The psychology of evidence and trial procedure* (pp. 298–322). Beverly Hills, CA: Sage.

Bernat, M. (1984). Race and gender as factors in setting bail. *Criminology, 24,* 221–230.

Berry, D. (1991). Attractive faces are not all created equal: Joint effects of facial babyishness and attractiveness on social perception. *Personality and Social Psychology Bulletin, 17,* 523–528.

Bersoff, D. (1987). Social science data and the Supreme Court: Lockhart as a case in point. *American Psychologist, 42,* 52–58.

Blanck, P. D. (1993). Calibrating the scales of justice: Studying judges' behavior in bench trials. *Indiana Law Journal, 68,* 1220–1234,

Blonstein, R., & Geiselman, E. (1990). Effects of witnessing conditions and expert witness on testimony on credibility of an eyewitness. *American Journal of Forensic Psychology, 8,* 11–19.

Boat, B. W., & Everson, M. D. (1988). Use of anatomical dolls among professionals in sexual abuse evaluations. *Child Abuse and Neglect, 12,* 171–179.

Bohm, R. M. (1994). Capital punishment in two judicial circuits in Georgia: A description of the key actors and the decision-making process. *Law and Human Behavior, 18*(3), 319–338.

Bok, S. (1978). *Lying: Moral choice in public and private life.* New York: Pantheon Books.

Bonnie, R. J. (1993). The competence of criminal defendants: Beyond Dusky and Drope. *University of Miami Law Review, 47*(3), 539–601.

Bordens, K. S. (1984). The effects of likelihood of conviction, threatened punishment, and assumed role on mock plea bargain decisions. *Basic and Applied Social Psychology, 5,* 59–74.

Bordens, K. S., & Abbott, B. B. (1996). *Research design and methods: A process approach* (3rd ed.). Mountain View, CA: Mayfield.

Bordens, K. S., & Bassett, J. (1985). The plea bargaining process from the defendant's perspective: A field investigation. *Basic and Applied Social Psychology, 6,* 93–110.

Bordens, K. S., & Horowitz, I. A. (1985). Joinder of criminal cases: A review of legal and psycho-

logical literature. *Law & Human Behavior,*
9(4), 339–353.

Bordens, K.S., & Horowitz, I. A. (1989, June–July).
Mass tort civil litigation: The impact of procedural changes on jury decisions. *Judicature,*
23–32.

Borgida, E., DeBono, K. G., & Buchman, L. E.
(1990). Cameras in the courtroom. *Law and
Human Behavior, 14,* 489–509.

Borgida, E., & Park, R. (1988). The entrapment defense: Juror comprehension and decision making. *Law and Human Behavior, 12,* 19–40.

Borgida, E., & White, P. (1978). Social perception of
rape victims: The impact of legal reform. *Law
and Human Behavior, 2,* 339–351.

Bothwell, R. K., Brigham, J. C., & Malpass, R. S.
(1989). Cross-racial identification. *Personality
and Social Psychology Bulletin, 15,* 19–25.

Bothwell, R. K., & Jalil, M. (1992). The credibility
of the nervous witness. *Journal of Social Behavior and Personality, 7,* 581–586.

Bottoms, B. L., Shaver, P. R., & Goodman, G. S.
(1996). An analysis of ritualistic and religion-
related child abuse allegations. *Law and Human Behavior, 20,* 1–34,

Bourgeois, M. J., Horowitz, I. A., & ForsterLee, L.
(1993). The effects of technicality and access to
trial transcripts on information processing in a
civil trial. *Personality and Social Psychology
Bulletin, 19*(2), 220–227.

Bourgeois, M., Horowitz, I. A., ForsterLee, L., &
Grahe, J. (1995). The performance of nominal
versus interactive jurors in complex trials. *Journal of Applied Psychology, 80*(1), 67–98.

Bowers, W. J. (1996). The capital jury: Is it tilted toward death? *Judicature, 79*(5), 220–229.

Bradley, M. T., MacLaren, V. V., & Carle, S. B.
(1996). Deception and nondeception in guilty
knowledge and guilty action polygraph tests.
Journal of Applied Psychology, 81(2), 153–160.

Braff, J., Arvintas, T., & Steadman, H. J. (1983).
Detention patterns of successful and unsuccessful insanity defendants. *Criminology, 21,*
439–448.

Bray, R. M., & Noble, A. (1978). Authoritarianism
and decisions of mock juries: Evidence of jury
bias and group polarization. *Journal of Personality and Social Psychology, 36,* 1424–1430.

Brekke, N., & Borgida, E. (1988). Expert psychological testimony in rape trials: A social-cogni-

tive analysis. *Journal of Personality and Social
Psychology, 55*(3), 372–386.

Brekke, N. J., Enko, P. J., Clavet, G., & Seelau, E.
(1991). Of juries and court-appointed experts:
The impact of nonadversarial expert testimony.
Law and Human Behavior, 15(5), 451–477.

Brewer, N., & Wilson, C. (1995). *Psychology and
policing.* Hillsdale, NJ: Erlbaum.

Brickman, E. (1995, April). Public policy and domestic violence. *APA Monitor,* p. 14.

Brigham, J. C. (1986). Race and eyewitness identifications. In S. Worchel & W. G. Austin (Eds.),
Psychology of intergroup relations (pp.
260–282). Chicago: Nelson Hall.

Brigham, J. C., & Bothwell, R. K. (1983). The ability of prospective jurors to estimate the accuracy of eyewitness identifications. *Law and
Human Behavior, 7,* 19–30.

Brigham, J. C., Maass, A., Snyder, L. D., & Spauld-
ing, K. (1982). Accuracy of eyewitness identifications in a field setting. *Journal of Personality
and Social Psychology, 42,* 673–680.

Brigham, J. C., & Wolfskiel, M. P. (1983). Opinions
of attorneys and law enforcement personnel on
the accuracy of eyewitness identification. *Law
and Human Behavior, 7,* 337–349.

Brock, P., & Fisher, R. P. (1994, March). *Effectiveness of the cognitive interview in a multiple-
testing situation.* Paper presented at the bian-
nual meeting of the American Psychology–Law
Society, Santa Fe, NM.

Brock, P., Fisher, R. P., & Cutler, B. L. (1991,
March). Consistency of eyewitness reports as a
predictor of eyewitness identification accuracy.
In B. L. Cutler (Chair), *Theoretical and practical issues in the assessment of eyewitness testimony.* Symposium presented at a meeting of
the Southeastern Psychological Association,
New Orleans.

Broeder, D. W. (1965). Voir dire examination: An
empirical study. *Southern California Law Review, 38,* 503–528.

Brookings Institution. (1993). *Charting a future
for the civil justice system.* Washington, DC:
Author.

Brown, R. (1986). *Social psychology* (2nd ed.). New
York: Free Press.

Brubaker, B. (1992, March 25). Prison wouldn't
shelter Tyson from legal storm. *Washington
Post,* pp. D1, D6.

Bruck, M., Ceci, S. J., Francouer, E., & Renick, A. (1995). Anatomically detailed dolls do not facilitate preschoolers' reports of a pediatric examination involving genital touching. *Journal of Experimental Psychology: Applied, 2,* 95–131.

Buckhout, R. (1974). Eyewitness Testimony. *Scientific American, 231,* 23–31.

Bureau of Justice Statistics, U.S. Department of Justice. (1984). *Review of criminal case dispositions: 1980–1981.* Washington, DC: Government Printing Office.

Bureau of Justice Statistics, U.S. Department of Justice. (1995/1994/1993). *Prisons and prisoners in the United States.* Washington, DC: Government Printing Office.

Burgess, A., & Holmstrom, L. (1974). Rape trauma syndrome. *American Journal of Psychiatry, 131,* 980–986.

Bush, Robert A. (1994). The dilemmas of mediation practice: A study of ethical dilemmas and policy implications. *Journal of Dispute Resolution, 1,* 1–55.

Bushman, B. J. (1988). The effects of apparel on compliance: A field experiment with a female authority figure. *Personality and Social Psychology Bulletin, 14,* 459–467.

Campbell, D. T., & Ross, H. L. (1968). The Connecticut crackdown on speeding: Time-series analysis in quasi-experimental designs. *Law and Society Review, 3,* 33–53.

Caplan, L. (1992, March 20). Not so nutty. *The New Republic,* pp. 18–21.

Carlsen, W. (1994, August 23). Lab tests a blow—but not conclusive. *San Francisco Chronicle,* p. 1.

Carroll, J. S. (1992). Taxation: Compliance with federal personal income tax laws. In D. S. Kagehiro & W. S. Laufer (Eds.), *Handbook of psychology and law.* New York: Springer-Verlag.

Carroll, J. S., & Coates, D. (1980). Parole decisions: Social psychological research in applied settings. In L. Bickman, (Ed.), *Applied social psychology annual* (Vol. 1). Beverly Hills, CA: Sage.

Carroll, J. S., Kerr, N. L., Alfini, J. J., Weaver, F. M., MacCoun, R. J., & Feldman, V. (1986). Free press and fair trial: The role of behavioral research. *Law and Human Behavior, 10,* 187–201.

Carroll, L. (1865/1988). *Alice's adventures in wonderland.* Exeter, UK: Justin Knowles Publishing Group.

Carter, C. A., Bottoms, B. L., & Levine, M. (1996). Linguistic and socioemotional influences on the accuracy of children's reports. *Law and Human Behavior, 20*(3), 335–358.

Cashmore, J., & Bussey, K. (1996). Judicial perceptions of child witness competence. *Law and Human Behavior, 20*(3), 313–334.

Casper, J. D. (1979). Reformers v. abolitionists: Some notes for further research on plea bargaining. *Law and Society Review, 13,* 567–572.

Casper, J. D., & Benedict, K. (1987, June). *Juror decision making, attitudes, and the hindsight bias.* Paper presented at the Law and Society Association Meeting, Washington, DC.

Casper, J. D., Tyler, T. R., & Fisher, B. (1988). Procedural justice in felony cases. *Law and Society Review, 22*(3), 483–507.

Cassel, W. S., & Bjorklund, D. F. (1995). Developmental patterns of eyewitness memory and suggestibility: An ecologically based short-term longitudinal study. *Law and Human Behavior, 19*(5), 507–532.

Cavaliere, F. (1995, August). Psychology and law field well positioned for growth. *APA Monitor,* p. 43.

Ceci, S. J. (1994, May 5–7). *Children's testimony: How reliable is it?* Invited address, Midwestern Psychological Association, Chicago.

Ceci, S. J., & Bruck, M. (1993). The suggestibility of the child eyewitness: A historical review and synthesis. *Psychological Bulletin, 113,* 403–439.

Ceci, S. J., & Bruck, M. (1995). *Jeopardy in the courtroom: A scientific analysis of children's testimony.* Washington, DC: American Psychological Association.

Ceci, S. J., Ross, D. F., & Toglia, M. P. (1987). Suggestibility of children's memory: Psycholegal implications. *Journal of Experimental Psychology: General, 116,* 38–49.

Cecil, J. S., & Douglas, C. R. (1987). *Summary judgment practice in three district courts.* Washington, DC: Federal Judicial Center.

Cecil, J. S., Hans, V. P., & Wiggins, E. C. (1991). Citizen comprehension of difficult issues: Lessons from civil jury trials *American University Law Review, 40,* 727–774.

Cecil, J. S., & Willging, T. E. (1992, August). Defining a role for court appointed experts. *Federal Judicial Center Directions,* p. 4.

Cecil, J. S., & Willging, T. E. (1993). *Court-appointed experts: Defining the role of experts appointed under Federal Rule of Evidence 706.* Washington, DC: Federal Judicial Center.

Cecil, J. S., & Willging, T. E. (1994). Court appointed experts. *Reference manual on scientific evidence.* Washington, DC: Federal Judicial Center.

Chapman, G. B., & Bornstein, B. H. (in press). The more you ask for the more you get: Anchoring in personal injury cases. *Applied Cognitive Psychology.*

Charrow, B., & Charrow, F. (1979). Making legal language understandable: A psycholinguistic study of juror instructions. *Columbia Law Review, 79,* 1306–1374.

Chin, A., & Peterson, M. (1985). *Deep pockets, empty pockets: Who wins in Cook County?* Santa Monica, CA: Rand.

Christianson, S. A. (1992). Emotional stress and eyewitness memory: A critical review. *Psychological Bulletin, 112,* 284–309.

Christie, R. (1976). Probability versus precedence: The social psychology of jury selection. In G. Bermant, C. Nemeth, & N. Vidmar (Eds.), *Psychology and law.* New York: Lexington Books.

Church, T. W., Jr. (1979). In defense of bargain justice. *Law and Society Review, 13,* 509–526.

Clermont, K., & Eisenberg, T. (1992). Trial by jury or judge: Transcending empiricism. *Cornell Law Review, 77,* 1125.

Clifford, B. R., & Scott, J. (1978). Individual and situational factors in eyewitness testimony. *Journal of Applied Psychology, 63,* 352–359.

Coates, D., & Penrod, S. (1981). Social psychology and the emergence of disputes. *Law and Society Review, 15,* 655–680.

Cohen, M. A. (1988). Pain, suffering, and jury awards: A study of the costs of crime to victims. *Law and Society Review, 22,* 537–556.

Cohen, M. A. (1995, November). *Report to NLT on the monetary value of saving a high risk youth.* Owen Graduate School of Management Working Paper. Nashville, TN: Vanderbilt University.

Cohen, M., & Miller, T. R. (1995, December). The cost of mental health care for victims of crime.

National Institute of Justice Research Report. Washington, DC: National Institute of Justice.

Cohen, M. A., Miller, T. R., Rossman, S. B. (1994). The costs and consequences of violent behavior in the United States. In A. J. Reiss, Jr., & J. A. Roth (Eds.), *Consequences and control of understanding and preventing violence* (pp. 67–166). National Research Council. Washington, DC: National Academy Press.

Cohn, A., & Udolf, R. (1979). *The criminal justice system and its psychology.* New York: Van Nostrand Reinhold.

Cohn, D. S. (1991). Anatomical doll play of preschoolers referred for sexual abuse and those not referred. *Child Abuse & Neglect, 15,* 455–466.

Colbert, D. L. (1990). Challenging the challenge: The Thirteenth Amendment as a prohibition against the racial use of peremptory challenges. *Cornell Law Review, 76,* 1–128.

Cook, T. D., & Campbell, D. T. (1979). *Quasi-experimentation: Design and analysis issues for field settings.* Chicago: Rand McNally.

Cook, S. W. (1975). Social science and school desegregation: Did we mislead the Supreme Court? *Personality and Social Psychology Bulletin, 5,* 420–436.

Coon, L. (1994, November). *DNA analysis.* Presentation at the University of Oregon School of Law, Eugene.

Cooper, C. (1991, June 9). Picking a jury: Science or art? *San Francisco Examiner,* p. B5.

Cooper, J., Bennett, E. A., & Sukel, H. L. (1996). Complex scientific evidence: How do jurors make decisions? *Law and Human Behavior, 20*(4), 379–394.

Copen, J. (1991, December). Rape victims sue over safety. *American Bar Association Journal,* 34–35.

Costantini, E., & King, J. (1980/81). The partial juror: Correlates and causes of prejudgment. *Law and Society Review, 15,* 9–40.

Costanzo, M., & Costanzo, S. (1992). Jury decision making in the capital penalty phase: Legal assumptions, empirical findings, and a research agenda. *Law and Human Behavior, 16*(2), 185–202.

Costanzo, M., & Costanzo, S. (1994). The death penalty: Public opinions, legal decisions, and juror perspectives. In M. Costanzo & S. Oscamp (Eds.), *Violence and the law.* Thousand Oaks, CA: Sage.

Costanzo, S., & Costanzo, M. (1994). Life or death decisions: An analysis of capital jury decision making under the special issues sentencing framework. *Law and Human Behavior, 18*(2), 151–170.

Couric, E. (1986). Jury sleuths: In search of a perfect panel. *The National Law Journal, 8*(45), 1.

Covington, M. (1985). Jury selection: Innovative approaches to both civil and criminal litigation. *St. Mary's University Law Journal, 16,* 575–579.

Cowan, C. L., Thompson, W. C., & Ellsworth, P. C. (1984). The effects of death qualification on jurors' predispositions to convict and on the quality of deliberation. *Law and Human Behavior, 8,* 53–79.

Cox, M., & Tanford, S. (1989). Effects of evidence and instructions in civil trials: An experimental investigation of the rules of admissibility. *Social Behavior, 4,* 31–55.

Crocker, P. C. (1985). The meaning of equality for battered women who kill men in self-defense. *Harvard Women's Law Journal, 8,* 121–153.

Croder, B. F., & Whiteside, R. (1988). A survey of jurors' perceptions of issues related to sexual abuse. *American Journal of Forensic Psychology, 3,* 37–43.

Crowley, M. J., O'Callaghan, M. G., & Ball, P. J. (1994). The juridial impact of psychological expert testimony in a simulated child sexual abuse trial. *Law and Human Behavior, 18*(1), 89–105.

Cutler, B. (1989, June). Reasonable suspicion and investigative detention. *APA Monitor,* p. 28.

Cutler, B. L. (1990). The status of scientific jury selection in psychology and law. *Forensic Reports, 3*(3), 227–232.

Cutler, B. L., Moran, G., & Narby, D. J. (1992). Jury selection in insanity cases. *Journal of Research in Personality, 26,* 165–182.

Cutler, B. L., & Penrod, S. D. (1988). Improving the reliability of eyewitness identification: Lineup construction and presentation. *Journal of Applied Psychology, 73,* 281–290.

Cutler, B. L., & Penrod, S. D. (1989). Moderators of the confidence-accuracy relationship in face recognition: The roles of information processing and base-rates. *Applied Cognitive Psychology, 3,* 95–107.

Cutler, B. L., & Penrod, S. D. (1995). *Mistaken identification: Eyewitnesses, psychology and the law.* New York: Cambridge University Press.

Cutler, B. L., Penrod, S. D., & Dexter, H. R. (1989). The eyewitness, the expert psychologist, and the jury. *Law and Human Behavior, 13,* 311–332.

Cutler, B. L., Penrod, S. D., & Dexter, H. R. (1990). Juror sensitivity to eyewitness identification evidence. *Law and Human Behavior, 14,* 185–191.

Cutler, B. L., Penrod, S. D., & Martens, T. K. (1987). The reliability of eyewitness identification: The role of system and estimator variables. *Law and Human Behavior, 11,* 233–258.

Cutler, B. L., Penrod, S. D., & Stuve, T. E. (1988). Juror decision making in eyewitness identification cases. *Law and Human Behavior, 12,* 41–55.

Dane, F. C. (1985). In search of reasonable doubt: A systematic evaluation of selected quantification approaches. *Law and Human Behavior, 9,* 141–158.

Daniels, S., & Martin, J. (1995). *Civil juries and the politics of reform.* Evanston, IL: Northwestern University Press.

Dann, B.M., & Logan, G., III. (1996). Jury reform: The Arizona experience. *Judicature, 79*(5), 280–288.

Danzon, P. (1985). *Medical malpractice: Theory, evidence and public policy.* Evanston, IL: Northwestern University Press.

Davis, D. (1991, Spring). Standards of proof: Do jurors distinguish? *The Mind's Eye, 1,* 1.

Davis, D. S., & Hastings, L. W. (1994). Litigators should be aware of the uses of deceptive graphic evidence. *Inside Litigation, 8*(5), 27–30.

Davis, J. H. (1973). Group decision and social interaction: A theory of social decision schemes. *Psychological Review, 16,* 97–125.

Davis, J. H. (1980). Group decision and procedural justice. In M. Fishbein (Ed.), *Progress in social psychology* (Vol. 1, pp. 234–278). Hillsdale, NJ: Erlbaum.

Davis, J. H., Kerr, N. L., Atkin, R. S., Holt, R., & Meek, D. (1975). The decision processes of 6- and 12-person mock juries assigned unanimous and two-thirds majority rules. *Journal of Personality and Social Psychology, 32,* 1–14.

Day, M. C. (1975). Developmental trends in visual scanning. In H. W. Reese (Ed.), *Advances in child development and behavior* (Vol. 10, pp. 123–167). New York: Academic Press.

DeAngelis, T. (1990, May). Blackmun: Psychology belongs in legal issues. *APA Monitor,* p. 35.

DeAngelis, T. (1991, July). Police stress takes its toll on family life. *APA Monitor,* p. 38.

DeAngelis, T. (1995, January). Psychologists work with police to curb use of excessive force. *APA Monitor,* p. 40.

Deffenbacher, K. A. (1980). Eyewitness accuracy and confidence: Can we infer anything about their relationship? *Law and Human Behavior, 4,* 243–260.

Deffenbacher, K. A., & Loftus, E. F. (1982). Do jurors share a common understanding concerning eyewitness behavior? *Law and Human Behavior, 6,* 15–30.

Dent, H. R. (1991). Experimental studies of interviewing child witnesses. In J. Doris (Ed.), *The suggestibility of children's recollections.* Washington, DC: American Psychological Association.

Dent, H. R., & Stephenson, G. M. (1979). An experimental study of the effectiveness of different techniques of questioning child eyewitnesses. *British Journal of Social and Clinical Psychology, 18,* 41–51.

Devlin, L. (1980). Jury trial of complex cases: English practice the time of the Seventh Amendment. *Columbia Law Review, 80,* 43–105.

Dexter, H. R., Cutler, B. L., & Moran, G. (1992). A test of voir dire as a remedy for the prejudicial effects of pretrial publicity. *Journal of Applied Social Psychology, 22,* 819–832.

Diamond, S. S. (1981). Exploring sources of sentence disparity. In B. Sales (Ed.), *The trial process.* New York: Plenum Press.

Diamond, S. S. (1992). Foreword. In D. K. Kagehiro & W. S. Laufer (Eds.), *Handbook of psychology and law.* New York: Springer-Verlag.

Diamond, S. S. (1993). Instructing on death: Psychologists, juries, and judges. *American Psychologist, 48,* 423–434.

Diamond, S. S., & Casper, J. D. (1992). Blindfolding the jury to verdict consequences: Damages, experts, and the civil jury. *Law and Society Review, 26,* 513–563.

Diamond, S. S., Casper, J. D., & Heiert, C. L. (1994, June). *Reactions to attorneys at trial.* Annual meeting of Law and Society Association, Phoenix.

Diamond, S. S., Casper, J. D., & Ostergren, L. (1989). Blindfolding the jury. *Law and Contemporary Problems, 52*(4), 247–268.

Diamond, S. S., & Levi, J. N. (1996). Improving decisions on death by revising and testing jury instructions. *Judicature, 79*(5), 224–232.

Dinges, D. F., Whitehouse, W. G., Orne, E. C., Powell, J. W., Orne, M. T., & Erdelyi, M. H. (1992). Evaluating hypnotic memory enhancement (hypermnesia and reminiscence) using multitrial forced recall. *Journal of Experimental Psychology: Learning, Memory, and Cognition, 18,* 1139–1147.

Dion, K. K., Berscheid, E., & Walster, E. (1972). What is beautiful is good. *Journal of Personality and Social Psychology, 24,* 285–290.

Dix, G. E. (1981). Mental health professionals in the legal process. *Law and Psychology Review, 6,* 1–20.

Dodson, C., & Reisberg, D. (1991). Indirect testing of eyewitness memory: The (non)effect of misinformation. *Bulletin of the Psychonomic Society, 29,* 333–336.

Drazen, D. (1989). The case for special juries in toxic tort litigation. *Judicature, 72,* 292.

Dunning, D., & Stern, L. B. (1994). Distinguishing accurate from inaccurate eyewitness identifications: Inquiries about decision processes. *Journal of Personality and Social Psychology, 67,* 818–825.

Dutton, D. G. (1989). The victimhood of battered women: Psychological and criminal justice perspectives. In E. Fattah (Ed.), *The plight of crime victims in modern society* (pp. 161–176). London: Macmillan.

Dutton, D. G. (1994). *The domestic assault of women: Psychological and criminal justice perspectives.* Vancouver: University of British Columbia Press.

Dutton, D. G. Hart, S. D., Kennedy, L. W., & Williams, K. R. (1993). Arrest and the reduction of repeat wife assault. In E. Buzawa (Ed.), *Domestic violence: The criminal justice response.* Dover, MA: Auburn House.

Dutton, D. G., & McGregor, B. M. S. (1992). Psychological and legal dimensions of family violence. In D. S. Kagehiro & W. F. Laufer (Eds.), *Handbook of psychology and law.* New York: Springer-Verlag.

Eagly, A. H., Ashmore, R. D., Makhijani, M. G., & Longo, L. C. (1991). What is beautiful is good, but . . . : A meta-analytic review of research on the physical attractiveness stereotype. *Psychological Bulletin, 110,* 109–128.

Ebbesen, E. B., & Konecni, V. J. (1975). Decision making and information integration in the courts: The setting of bail. *Journal of Personality and Social Psychology, 32,* 805–821.

Eisenberg, T., & Clermont, K. M. (1996). Trial by jury or judge: Which is speedier? *Judicature, 79*(4), 176–199.

Eitzen, D. S., & Timmer, D. A. (1985). *Criminology: Crime and criminal justice.* New York: Wiley.

Ellsworth, P. C. (1988). Unpleasant facts: The Supreme Court's response to empirical research on capital punishment. In K. C. Haas & J. Inciardi (Eds.), *Adjudicating death: Moral and legal perspectives on capital punishment* (pp. 177–211). Beverly Hills, CA: Sage.

Ellsworth, P. (1989). Are twelve heads better than one? *Law and Contemporary Problems, 52,* 705–745.

Ellsworth, P. C. (1991). To tell what we know or to wait for Godot? *Law and Human Behavior, 15,* 77–90.

Ellsworth, P. C. (1993). Some steps between attitudes and verdicts. In R. Hastie (Ed.), *Inside the juror* (pp. 42–63). New York: Cambridge University Press.

Elwork, A., & Sales, B. D. (1985). Jury instructions. In S. Kassin & L. Wrightsman (Eds.), *The psychology of evidence and trial procedure* (pp. 280–297). Beverly Hills, CA: Sage.

Elwork, A., Sales, B. D., & Alfini, J. J. (1977). Juridic decisions: In ignorance of the law or in light of it? *Law and Human Behavior, 1,* 163–178.

Elwork, A., Sales, B. D., & Alfini, J. J. (1982). *Making jury instructions understandable.* Charlottesville, VA: Michie.

Ernsdorff, G. N., & Loftus, E. F. (1993). Let sleeping memories lie? Words of caution about tolling the statute of limitations in a case of memory repression. *Journal of Criminal Law and Criminology, 84,* 129–174.

Esser, J. K., & Marriott, R. G. (1995). A comparison of the effectiveness of substantive and contextual mediation tactics. *Journal of Applied Social Psychology, 25*(15), 1340–1360.

Estrich, S. (1987). *Real rape.* Cambridge, MA: Harvard University Press.

Etzioni, A. (1974). Creating an imbalance. *Trial, 10,* 28–30.

Evans, S., & O'Hara, R. (1992, March 15). Young victims of sexual abuse go unheard. *Washington Post,* pp. B1, B5.

Everson, M. D., & Boat, B. W. (1990). Sexualized doll play among young children: Implications for the use of anatomical dolls in sexual abuse evaluations. *Journal of the American Academy of Child and Adolescent Psychiatry, 29,* 736–742.

Everson, M. D., & Boat, B. W. (1994). Putting the anatomical doll controversy in perspective: An examination of the major uses and criticisms of the dolls in child sexual abuse evaluations. *Child Abuse and Neglect, 18,* 113–129.

Ewing, C. P. (1987). *Battered women who kill: Psychological self defense as legal justification.* Lexington, MA: Heath.

Ewing, C. P. (1990). Psychological self-defense: A proposed justification for battered women who kill. *Law and Human Behavior, 14,* 579–594.

Ewing, C. P. (1991). Preventive detention and execution: The constitutionality of punishing future crimes. *Law and Human Behavior, 15*(2), 139–164.

Ewing, C. P. (1994, July). Judicial notebook. *APA Monitor,* p. 22.

Ewing, C. P. (1996, July). Judicial notebook: Courts consider repressed memory. *APA Monitor,* p. 14.

Faigman, D. (1986). The battered woman syndrome and self-defense. *Virginia Law Review, 72,* 619–647.

Faigman, D. L. (1989). To have and have not: Assessing the value of social science to law as science and policy. *Emory Law Review, 38*(4), 1006–1095.

Faigman, D. L. (1992). Struggling to stop the flood of unreliable expert testimony. *Minnesota Law Review, 76,* 877–889.

Faigman, D. L. (1995). The evidentiary status of social science under Daubert: Is it "scientific," "technical," or "other" knowledge? *Psychology, Public Policy, and Law, 1*(4), 960–979.

Farrell, R. A. (1971). Class linkages of legal treatment of homosexuals. *Criminology, 9,* 49–68.

Federal Bureau of Investigation, U.S. Department of Justice. (1996/1995/1994). *Uniform crime reports.* Washington, DC: U.S. Government Printing Office.

Federal Judicial Center. (1987). *Pattern criminal jury instructions.* Washington, DC: Author.

Federal Rules of Civil Procedure. (1996/1990). St. Paul, MN: West.

Federal Rules of Criminal Procedure. (1996). St. Paul, MN: West.

Federal Rules of Evidence. (1984). St. Paul, MN: West.

Feeley, M. M. (1979). Perspectives on plea bargaining. *Law and Society Review, 13,* 149–210.

Feldman, M. (1978). *Juror competence through judicial instructions.* Unpublished doctoral dissertation, University of Toledo.

Fidel, N. (1991). Preeminently a political institution: The right of Arizona juries to nullify the law of criminal negligence. *Arizona State Law Journal, 23,* 1–60.

Finkel, N. J. (1990a). Capital felony-murder, objective indicia, and community sentiment. *Arizona Law Review, 32,* 819–913.

Finkel, N. J. (1990b). De facto departures from insanity instructions: Toward the remaking of common law. *Law and Human Behavior, 14,* 105–122.

Finkel, N. J. (1991). The insanity defense: A comparison of verdict schemas. *Law and Human Behavior, 15*(5), 533–556.

Finkel, N. J. (1995). *Commonsense justice.* Cambridge, MA: Harvard University Press.

Finkel, N. J., & Duff, K. B. (1991). Felony-murder and community sentiment: Testing the Supreme Court's assertions. *Law and Human Behavior, 15,* 405–429.

Finkel, N. J., & Handel, S. F. (1988). How jurors construe "insanity." *Law and Human Behavior, 13,* 41–59.

Finkel, N. J., Hurabiell, M. L., & Hughes, K. C. (1993). Right to die, euthanasia, and community sentiment: Crossing the public/private boundary. *Law and Human Behavior, 17*(5), 487–506.

Finkel, N. J., Maloney, S. T., Valbuena, M. Z., & Groscup, J. L. (1995). Lay perspectives on legal conundrums: Impossible and mistaken act cases. *Law and Human Behavior, 19*(6), 593–608.

Finkel, N. J., & Slobogin, C. (1995). Insanity, justification, and culpability toward a unifying schema. *Law and Human Behavior, 19*(5), 447–464.

Finkel, N. J., & Smith, S. E. (1993). Principals and accessories in capital felony-murder: The proportionality principle reigns supreme. *Law and Society Review, 27,* 129–156.

Finkelstein, L. (1966). The application of statistical decision theory to the jury discrimination cases. *Harvard Law Review, 79,* 338–367.

Fischer, K., Vidmar, N., & Ellis, R. (1993). The culture of battering and the role of mediation in domestic violence cases. *SMU Law Review, 46*(5), 2117–2174.

Fisher, R. J. (1982). *Social psychology: An applied approach.* New York: St. Martin's Press.

Fisher, R. P. (1995). Interviewing victims and witnesses of crime. *Psychology, Law, & Public Policy, 1*(4), 732–764.

Fisher, R. P., & Cutler, B. L. (1996). The relation between consistency and accuracy of eyewitness testimony. In G. M. Davies, S. Lloyd-Bostock, M. McMurran, & C. Wilson (Eds.), *Psychology and law: Advances in research* (pp. 21–28). Berlin: De Gruyter.

Fisher, R. P., & Geiselman, R. E. (1992). *Memory-enhancing techniques for investigative interviewing: The cognitive interview.* Springfield, IL: Charles C. Thomas.

Fisher, R. P., Geiselman, R. E., & Amador, M. (1989). Field test of the cognitive interview technique: Enhancing the recollection of actual victims and witnesses to crimes. *Journal of Applied Psychology, 74,* 722–727.

Fisher, R. P., & McCauley, M. R. (1995). Information retrieval: Interviewing witnesses. In N. Brewer & C. Wilson (Eds.), *Psychology and policing* (pp. 81–99). Hillsdale, NJ: Erlbaum.

Fiske, S. T., Bersoff, D. N., Borgida, E., Deaux, K., Heilman, M. E. (1993). What constitutes a scientific review?: A majority retort to Barrett and Morris. *Law and Human Behavior, 17*(2), 217–234.

Fitzgerald, R., & Ellsworth, P. C. (1984). Due process vs. crime control: Death qualification and jury attitudes. *Law and Human Behavior, 8,* 31–52.

Fletcher, G. P. (1994, December 11). We, the jury. *New York Times,* p. 14.

Foremski, J., & Kehoe, M. (1995, July 8). Forensic animation techniques. *Financial Times,* p. 11.

ForsterLee, L., & Horowitz, I. A. (in press). Enhancing juror competence. *Applied Social Cognition.*

ForsterLee, L., Horowitz, I. A., & Bourgeois, M. J. (1993). Juror competence in civil trials: The effects of preinstruction and evidence technicality. *Journal of Applied Psychology, 78,* 14–21.

ForsterLee, L., Horowitz, I. A., & Bourgeois, M. (1994). Effects of notetaking on verdicts and evidence processing in a civil trial. *Law and Human Behavior, 18,* 567–578.

Fox, S. G., & Walters, H. A. (1986). The impact of general versus specific expert testimony and eyewitness confidence upon mock juror judgment. *Law and Human Behavior, 10,* 215–228.

Frank, J. (1949). *Courts on trial: Myth and reality of American justice.* Princeton, NJ: Princeton University Press.

Frazier. P. (1990). Victim attributions and postrape trauma. *Journal of Social and Clinical Psychology, 59,* 298–304.

Frazier, P., & Borgida, E. (1985). Rape trauma syndrome in court. *American Psychologist, 40*(9), 984–993.

Frazier, P. A., & Borgida, E. (1988). Juror common understanding and the admissibility of rape trauma syndrome evidence in court. *Law and Human Behavior, 12*(2), 101–122.

Frazier, P. A. & Borgida, E. G (1992). Rape trauma syndrome: A review of case law and psychological research. *Law and Human Behavior, 16,* 293–312.

Frazier, P. A., Candell, S., Arikain, N., & Tofteland, A. (1994). Rape survivors and the legal system. In M. Costanzo & S. Oscamp (Eds.), *Violence and the law.* Thousand Oaks, CA: Sage.

Freiberg, P. (1990, November). APA testifies: Rape estimates far too low. *APA Monitor,* p. 25.

Fresca, R. (1988). Estimating the occurrence of trials prejudiced by press coverage. *Judicature, 72,* 162–169.

Freyd, J. J. (1996). *Betrayal trauma theory: The logic of forgetting abuse.* Cambridge, MA: Harvard University Press.

Friedman, L. M. (1979). Plea bargaining in historical perspective. *Law and Society Review, 13,* 247–260.

Friedman, L. M. (1985). *History of American law* (2nd ed.) New York: Simon & Schuster.

Fukurai, H., Butler, E. W., & Krooth, R. (1993). *Race and the jury.* New York: Plenum Press.

Fulero, S. M., & Penrod, S. D. (1990). Attorney jury selection folklore: What do they think and how can psychologists help? *Forensics Reports, 3,* 233–260.

Fullin, J. L., Jr., & Myse, G. (1987, October). We can improve the quality of jury deliberations. *Inside Litigation, 1,* 12.

Gabora, N. J., Spanos, N. P., & Joab, A. (1993). The effects of complainant age and expert psychological testimony in a simulated child sexual abuse trial. *Law and Human Behavior, 17,* 103–119.

Galanter, M. (1993). The regulatory function of the civil jury. In R. Litan (Ed.), *Verdict: Assessing the civil jury system.* Washington, DC: Brookings Institution.

Galanter, M., & Cahill, M. (1994). "Most cases settle": Judicial promotion and regulation of settlements. *Stanford Law Review, 46*(6), 1339–1391.

Gardner, W., Lidz, C. W., Mulvey, E. P., & Shaw, E. C. (1996). A comparison of actuarial methods for identifying repetitively violent patients with mental illnesses. *Law and Human Behavior, 20*(1), 35–48.

Geiselman, R. E., & Fisher, R. P. (1989). The cognitive interview technique for victims and witnesses of crime. In D. C. Raskin (Ed.), *Psychological methods in criminal investigation and evidence* (pp. 191–215). New York: Springer.

Genevie, L., & Sebolt, S. (1994, August). Jury consulting assists defense counsel in assisted suicide trial. *Inside Litigation, 8,* 19–22.

Georgetown Law Journal Staff. (1980). Project: Tenth annual review of criminal review of criminal procedure: United States Supreme Court and Court of Appeals, 1979–80. *Georgetown Law Journal, 69,* 211–689.

Georgetown Law Journal Staff. (1991). Project: Twentieth annual review of criminal procedure: United States Supreme Court and Courts of Appeal, 1989–90. *Georgetown Law Journal, 79,* 591–1295.

Giacopassi, D. J., & Wilkinson, K. R. (1985). Rape and the devalued victim. *Law and Human Behavior, 9,* 367–385.

Gibson, J. (1983). From simplicity to complexity: The development of theory in the study of judicial behavior. *Political Behavior, 5,* 7–45.

Gifford, D. G. (1983). Meaningful reform of plea bargaining: The control of prosecutorial discretion. *University of Illinois Law Review, 52,* 37–98.

Gifford, D. G. (1985). A context based theory of strategy selection in legal negotiation. *Ohio State Law Journal, 46*(1), 41–94.

Gigone, D., & Hastie, R. (1993). The common knowledge effect: Information sharing and group judgment. *Journal of Personality and Social Psychology, 65,* 959–974.

Golding, J. M, Sego, S. A., Sanchez, R. B., Hasemann, D. (1995). The believability of repressed memories. *Law and Human Behavior, 19*(6), 569–592.

Golding, S. L. (1992). The adjudication of criminal responsibility: A review of theory and research. In D. S. Kagehiro & W. S. Laufer (Eds.), *Handbook of psychology and law.* New York: Springer-Verlag.

Golding, S. L., & Roesch, R. (1987). The assessment of criminal responsibility. In I. B. Weiner & A. K. Hess (Eds.), *Handbook of forensic psychology,* (pp. 396–436). New York: Wiley.

Goleman, D. (1991, December 9). Do arrests increase domestic violence? *New York Times,* p. B9.

Goleman, D. (1993, November 13). The mind of the rapist. *New York Times,* p. B7.

Goleman, D. (1995, January 15). Studies point to flaws in lineups of suspects. *New York Times,* pp. A13, B7.

Goleman, D. (1996, May 6). Major crimes fell in 1995. *New York Times,* pp. A1, A12.

Gonzalez, R., Davis, J., & Ellsworth, P. B. (1995). Who should stand next to the suspect? Problems in the assessment of lineup fairness. *Journal of Applied Psychology, 80*(4) 525–531.

Gonzalez, R., Ellsworth, P., & Pembroke, M. (1993). Response biases in lineups and showups. *Journal of Personality and Social Psychology, 64,* 525–537.

Goodman, G. S., & Aman, C. (1990). Children's use of anatomically detailed dolls to recount an event. *Child Development, 61,* 1859–1871.

Goodman, G. S., & Clarke-Stewart, A. (1991). Suggestibility in children's testimony: Implications for child sexual abuse investigations. In J. L.

Doris (Ed.), *The suggestibility of children's recollections* (pp. 92–105). Washington, DC: American Psychological Association.

Goodman, G. S., Golding, J. M., Helgeson, V., Haith, M. M., & Michelli, J. (1987). When a child takes the stand: Jurors' perceptions of children's eyewitness testimony. *Law and Human Behavior, 11,* 27–40.

Goodman, G. S., & Helgeson, V. (1988). Children as witnesses: What do they remember? In L. E. A. Walker (Ed.), *Handbook on sexual abuse of children* (pp. 109–136). New York: Springer.

Goodman, G. S., & Reed, R. S. (1986). Age differences in eyewitness testimony. *Law and Human Behavior, 10,* 317–332.

Goodman, G. S., & Tobey, A. E. (1994). Memory development within the context of child sexual abuse allegations. In C. B. Fisher & R. M. Lerner (Eds.), *Applied developmental psychology.* New York: McGraw-Hill.

Goodman, J. (1992). Jurors' comprehension and assessment of probabilistic evidence. *American Journal of Trial Advocacy, 16,* 361–389.

Goodman, J., Greene, E., & Loftus, E. (1989). Runaway verdicts or reasoned determinations: Mock juror strategies in awarding damages. *Jurimetrics Journal, 29,* 285–309.

Goodman, J., Loftus, E. F., & Greene, E. (1990). Matters of money: Voir dire in civil cases. *Forensic Reports, 3,* 303–329.

Goodman-Delahunty, J,. & Foote, W. E. (1995). Compensation for pain, suffering and other psychological injuries: The impact of Daubert on employment discrimination claims. *Behavioral Sciences and the Law, 13*(2), 183–206.

Gordon, M. (1996, September 10). Three strikes law affects few felons. *The Oregonian,* p. A5.

Gorman, J. (1993, July 12). Juristic park. *New York Times,* p. A13.

Gothard, S., Rogers, R., & Sewell, K. W. (1996). Feigning incompetency to stand trial: An investigation of the Georgia Court Competency Test. *Law and Human Behavior, 19*(4), 363–374.

Gothard, S., Viglione, D. J., Jr., Meloy, J. R., & Sherman, M. (in press). Detecting malingering in competency to stand trial evaluations. *Law and Human Behavior.*

Graham, D., & Rawlings, E. (1991, August). *Battered women and the Stockholm syn-*

drome. Paper presented at the annual meeting of the American Psychological Association, San Francisco.

Greenberg, M. S., & Ruback, R. B. (1982). *Social psychology of the criminal justice system.* Monterey, CA: Brooks/Cole.

Greenberg, M. S., Ruback, R. B., & Westcott, D. R. (1982). Decision making by victims: A multi-method approach. *Law and Society Review, 17,* 85–104.

Greene, E. (1988). Judge's instruction on eyewitness testimony: Evaluation and revision. *Journal of Applied Social Psychology, 18,* 252–276.

Greene, E., & Dodge, M. (1995). The influence of prior record evidence on juror decision making. *Law and Human Behavior, 19*(1), 67–78.

Greene, E., & Loftus, E. (1985). When crimes are joined at trial. *Law and Human Behavior, 2,* 193–207.

Greene, E., Wilson, L., & Loftus, E. F. (1989). Impact of hypnotic testimony on the jury. *Law and Human Behavior, 13,* 61–78.

Greenhouse, L. (1991, July 21). A long time precedent for disregarding precedent. *New York Times,* p. 4.

Greenhouse, L. (1995a, November 5). Court weighs issue of judicial autonomy. *New York Times,* p. A15.

Greenhouse, L. (1995b, February 23). Judges may override juries. *New York Times,* p. A10.

Greenwood, J. M., Horney, J., Jacoubovitch, M. D., Lowensteine, F. B., & Wheeler, R. W. (1983). *A comparative evaluation of stenographic and audiotape methods for United States district court reporting.* Washington, DC: Federal Judicial Center.

Gregory, W. L., Mower, J. C., & Linder, D. E. (1978). Social psychology and plea bargaining: Applications, methodology, and theory. *Journal of Personality and Social Psychology, 36,* 1521–1530.

Grisso, T. (1980). Juveniles' capacity to waive Miranda rights: An empirical analysis. *California Law Review, 68,* 1134–1166.

Grisso, T. (1981). *Juveniles' waiver of rights.* New York: Plenum Press.

Grisso, T. (1991). A developmental history of the American Psychology-Law Society. *Law and Human Behavior, 15*(3), 213–232.

Gross, J. (1994, July 22). Suit asks, does memory therapy heal or harm? *New York Times,* p. B16.

Gross, J., & Hayne, H. (1996). Eyewitness identification by 5 to 6 year old children. *Law and Human Behavior, 20*(3), 359–376.

Gross, S. R. (1984). Determining the neutrality of death-qualified juries: Judicial appraisal of empirical data. *Law and Human Behavior, 8,* 7–30.

Gross, S. R., & Mauro, R. (1984). Patterns of death: An analysis of racial discrepancies in capital sentencing and homicide victimization. *Stanford Law Review, 37,* 27–110.

Gross, S. R., & Mauro, R. (1989). *Death and discrimination.* Boston: Northeastern University Press.

Hacker, A. (1995, September 21). Twelve angry persons. *The New York Review of Books,* pp. 44–50.

Hammersley, R., & Read, J. D. (1995). Voice identification in humans and computers. In S. L. Sporer, R. S. Malpass, & G. Kohnken (Eds.), *Psychological issues in eyewitness identification.* Hillsdale, NJ: Erlbaum.

Haney, C. (1984a). On the selection of capital juries: The biasing effects of the death-qualification process. *Law and Human Behavior, 8,* 121–132.

Haney, C. (1984b). Examining death qualification: Further analysis of the process effect. *Law and Human Behavior, 8,* 133–151.

Haney, C. (1991). The fourteenth amendment and symbolic legality: Let them eat due process. *Law and Human Behavior, 15,* 183–204.

Haney, C. (1993). Psychology and legal change: The impact of a decade. *Law and Human Behavior, 17,* 1–19.

Haney, C., Hurtado, A., & Vega, L. (1994). "Modern" death qualification: New data on its biasing effects. *Law and Human Behavior, 18*(3), 619–634.

Haney, C., & Lynch, M. (1994). Comprehending life and death matters: A preliminary study of California's capital penalty instructions. *Law and Human Behavior, 18*(4), 411–436.

Haney, C., Sontag, L., & Costanzo, S. (1994). Deciding to take a life: Capital juries, sentencing instructions, and the jurisprudence of death. *Journal of Social Issues, 50*(2), 149–176.

Hans, V. P. (1989). The jury's response to corporate wrongdoing. *Law and Contemporary Problems, 52*(4), 177–204.

Hans, V. P. (1990). Law and the media: An overview and introduction. *Law and Human Behavior, 14*(5), 390–394.

Hans, V. P. (1994, June 6). Robin Hood myth may be challenged. *National Law Journal,* p. C1.

Hans, V. P. (1995). *Lay judgments of corporate defendants.* Unpublished manuscript. University of Delaware.

Hans, V. P. (1996). The contested role of the civil jury in business litigation. *Judicature, 79*(5), 242–248.

Hans, V. P., & Elmann, M. (1989). Responses to corporate versus individual wrongdoing. *Law and Human Behavior, 13,* 151–166.

Hans, V. P., & Ivkovich, S. K. (1994). How jurors evaluate experts. *Texas Trial Lawyers Forum, 27*(2), 5–11.

Hans, V. P., & Lofquist, W. (1992). Jurors' judgments of business liability in tort cases: Implications for the litigation explosion debate. *Law and Society Review, 26,* 85–115.

Hans, V. P., & Slater, D. (1983, June). *Public views of the insanity defense.* Paper presented at the annual meeting of the Law and Society Association, Denver.

Hans, V. P., & Sweigart, K. (1993). Jurors' views of civil lawyers: Implications for courtroom communication. *Indiana Law Journal, 68*(4), 1310–1326.

Hans, V. P., & Vidmar, N. (1986). *Judging the jury.* New York: Plenum Press.

Hans, V. P., & Vidmar, N. (1991). The American jury after twenty-five years. *Journal of the American Bar Foundation, 16*(2), 323–351.

Hart, A. J. (1995). Naturally occurring expectation effects. *Journal of Personality and Social Psychology, 68*(1), 109–115.

Harvard Medical Practice Study. (1990). *Patients, doctors, and lawyers: Medical injury, malpractice litigation, and patient compensation in New York.* Report of the Harvard Medical Practice Study to the State of New York.

Hassett, J. M. (1980). A jury's pretrial knowledge in historical perspective. *Law and Contemporary Problems, 43,* 155–168.

Hastie, R. (1983). *Final report to the National Institute for Law Enforcement and Criminal Justice.* Unpublished manuscript, Northwestern University.

Hastie, R. (1991). Is attorney-conducted voir dire an effective procedure for the selection of impartial juries? *American University Law Review, 40,* 703–726

Hastie, R. (1993a). Algebraic models of juror decision processes. In R. Hastie (Ed.), *Inside the juror* (pp. 81–115). New York: Cambridge University Press.

Hastie, R. (1993b). *Inside the juror.* New York: Cambridge University Press.

Hastie, R., Penrod, S., & Pennington, N. (1983). *Inside the jury.* Cambridge, MA: Harvard University Press.

Haugaard, J. J., Reppucci, N. D., Laird, J., & Nauful, T. (1991). Children's definitions of the truth and their competency as witnesses in legal proceedings. *Law and Human Behavior, 15,* 253–272.

Hendrick, C., & Shaffer, D. R. (1975). Effect of pleading the fifth amendment on perception of guilt and morality. *Bulletin of the Psychonomic Science Society, 6,* 449–452.

Heuer, L., & Penrod, S. D. (1989). Instructing jurors: A field experiment with written and preliminary instructions. *Law and Human Behavior, 13,* 409–430.

Heuer, L., & Penrod, S. D. (1994a). Predicting the outcomes of disputes: Consequences for disputant reactions to procedures and outcomes. *Journal of Applied Social Psychology, 24*(14), 750–775.

Heuer, L., & Penrod, S. (1994b). Trial complexity: A field investigation of its meaning and its effect. *Law and Human Behavior, 18,* 29–52.

Heuer, L., & Penrod, S. (1994c). Juror notetaking and question asking during trials: A national field experiment. *Law and Human Behavior, 18*(2), 121–150.

Heumann, M. (1975). A note on plea bargaining and case pressure. *Law and Society Review, 9,* 515–520.

Hilts, P. J. (1996, July 2). In research scans, telltale signs sort false memories from true. *New York Times,* p. B10.

Hindelang, M. J. (1976). *An analysis of victimization survey research results from eight cities.* Albany, NY: Criminal Justice Research Center.

Hofer, P. J. (1991, November). Psychology in a new era of sentencing. *APA Monitor,* p. 36.

Hofer, P. J. (1992a, May). Battered woman's syndrome as a sentencing consideration. *APA Monitor,* p. 12.

Hofer, P. J. (1992b). Plea agreements, judicial discretion, and sentencing goals. *FJC Directions, 3,* 1–12.

Hoffman, J. (1993, September 25). New York casts for solutions to gaping holes in juror net. *New York Times,* p. 1.

Hoffman, J. (1995). Where's the buck—Juror misperception of sentencing responsibility in death penalty cases. *Indiana Law Journal, 70,* 1137.

Hogarth, J. (1971). *Sentencing as a human process.* Toronto: University of Toronto Press.

Hoiberg, B. C., & Stires, L. K. (1973). The effect of several types of pretrial publicity on guilt attributions of simulated juries. *Journal of Applied Social Psychology, 3,* 267–271.

Holmes, O. W. (1963). *The common law.* Cambridge, MA: Harvard University Press. (Original work published 1881)

Honts, C. R., & Devitt, M. K. (1992, March 2). *The hired gun cross-examination tactic.* Paper presented at the American Psychology and Law meeting, San Diego.

Honts, C. R., Devitt, M., Winbush, M., & Kircher, M. (1996). Mental and physical countermeasures reduce the accuracy of the concealed knowledge test. *Psychophysiology 33,* 84–92.

Honts, C. R., & Perry, M. V. (1992). Polygraph admissibility: Changes and challenges. *Law and Human Behavior, 16*(3), 357–377.

Honts, C. R., & Quick, B. D. (1995). The polygraph in 1995: Progress in science and the law. *North Dakota Law Review, 71*(4), 989–1020.

Honts, C. R., Raskin, D. C., & Kircher, J. C. (1994). Mental and physical countermeasures reduce the accuracy of polygraph tests. *Journal of Applied Psychology, 70*(2), 245–259.

Horowitz, I. A. (1980). Juror selection: A comparison of two methods in several criminal cases. *Journal of Applied Social Psychology, 10,* 86–99.

Horowitz, I. A. (1985). The effect of jury nullification instructions on verdicts and jury functioning in criminal trials. *Law and Human Behavior, 9,* 25–36.

Horowitz, I. A. (1988). Jury nullification: The impact of judicial instructions, arguments, and challenges on jury decision making. *Law and Human Behavior, 12,* 439–454.

Horowitz, I. A., and Bordens, K. S. (1988). The effects of outlier presence, plaintiff population size, and aggregation of plaintiffs on simulated civil jury decisions. *Law and Human Behavior, 12*(3), 209–229.

Horowitz, I. A., & Bordens, K. S. (1990). An experimental investigation of procedural issues in toxic tort trials. *Law and Human Behavior, 14*(3), 269–285.

Horowitz, I. A., Bordens, K. S., & Feldman, M. (1980). A comparison of verdicts obtained in severed and joined criminal trials. *Journal of Applied Social Psychology, 10,* 444–460.

Horowitz, I. A., ForsterLee, L., & Brolly, I. (1996). The effects of trial complexity on decision making. *Journal of Applied Psychology, 81*(6), 757–769.

Horowitz, I. A., & Kirkpatrick, L. C. (1996). A concept in search of a definition: The effects of reasonable doubt instructions on certainty of guilt standards and jury verdicts. *Law and Human Behavior, 20*(5), 655–670.

Horowitz, I. A., & Seguin, D. G. (1986). The effects of bifurcation and death qualification on assignment of penalty in capital crimes. *Journal of Applied Social Psychology, 16,* 165–185.

Horowitz, I. A., & Willging, T. E. (1991). Changing views of jury power. *Law and Human Behavior, 15*(2), 165–182.

Houlden, D., LaTour, S., Walker, L., & Thibaut, J. (1978). Preference for modes of dispute resolution as a function of process and decision control. *Journal of Experimental Psychology, 14,* 13–22.

Houlden, P. (1981). Impact of procedural modifications on evaluations of plea bargaining. *Law and Society Review, 15,* 267–292.

Huber, P. (1991). *Galileo's revenge: Junk science in the courtroom.* New York: Basic Books.

Hyman, H. H., & Tarrant, C. M. (1975). Aspects of American trial jury history. In R. J. Simon (Ed.), *The jury system in America.* Beverly Hills, CA: Sage.

Hyman, J. M. (1979). Philosophical implications of plea bargaining. *Law and Society Review, 13,* 565–566.

Illig, D. (1995, Spring). *Trial and courtroom strategy.* Presentation at University of Oregon School of Law.

Illinois Revised Statutes. (1983). Chapter 38, Sections 6–2, 115–1 to 115–4.

Inbau, F. E., Reid, J. E., & Buckley, J. P. (1986). *Criminal interrogation and confessions* (3rd ed.). Baltimore: Williams & Wilkins.

Isenberg, D. J. (1986). Group polarization: A critical review and meta-analysis. *Journal of Personality and Social Psychology, 50,* 1141–1151.

Jemmott, J. B., & Gonzalez, E. (1989). Social status, the status distribution, and performance in small groups. *Journal of Applied Social Psychology, 19,* 584–598.

Johnson, B. R., Mullen, B., & Salas, E. (1995). Comparison of three major meta-analytic approaches. *Journal of Applied Psychology, 80*(1), 94–107.

Johnson, C., & Haney, C. (1994). Felony voir dire: An exploratory study of its content and effect. *Law and Human Behavior, 18,* 487–506.

Johnson, J. D., Whitestone, E., Jackson, L. A., & Gatto, L. (1995). Justice is still not colorblind: Differential racial effects of exposure to inadmissible evidence. *Personality and Social Psychology Bulletin, 21*(9), 893–899.

Johnson, M. T., & Krafka, C. (1994). *Electronic media coverage of federal civil proceedings.* Washington, DC: Federal Judicial Center.

Jury Service and Selection Act of 1968. Public Law 90-274, 82 *Statutes-at-Large* 54, codified at 28 *U.S. Code* Sections 1861–1878.

Kadane, J. B. (1984). After Hovey: A note on taking account of the automatic death penalty jurors. *Law and Human Behavior, 8,* 115–120.

Kadish, M. R., & Kadish, S. H. (1973). *Discretion to disobey.* Stanford, CA: Stanford University Press.

Kagehiro, D. K., & Stanton, W. C. (1985). Legal vs. quantified definitions of standards of proof. *Law and Human Behavior, 9,* 159–178.

Kagehiro, D. K., & Taylor, R. B. (1992). Exploring the fourth amendment: Searches based on consent. In D. S. Kagehiro & W. S. Laufer (Eds.), *Handbook of psychology and law.* New York: Springer-Verlag.

Kagehiro, D. K., Taylor, R. B., Soufer, & W. S., Harland, A. T. (1991). Reasonable expectation of privacy and third-party consent searches. *Law and Human Behavior, 14,* 125–138.

Kairys, D., Kadane, J. B., & Lehoczky, J. (1977). Jury representativeness: A mandate for multiple source lists. *California Law Review, 65,* 776–827.

Kairys, D. J., Schulman, J., & Harring, S. (1975). *The jury system: New methods for reducing prejudice.* Philadelphia: National Jury Project and National Lawyers Guild.

Kalven, H., & Zeisel, H. (1966). *The American jury.* Boston: Little, Brown.

Kammen, M. (1986). *A machine that would go of itself.* New York: Knopf.

Kaplan, M. F. (1982). Cognitive processes in the individual juror. In N. L. Kerr & R. M. Bray (Eds.), *The psychology of the courtroom* (pp. 197–220). New York: Academic. Press.

Kaplan, M. F., & Kemmerick, G. D. (1974). Juror judgments as information integration: Combining evidential and nonevidential information. *Journal of Personality and Social Psychology, 30,* 493–499.

Kaplan, M. F., & Miller, C. (1983). Group discussion and judgment. In P. Paulus (Ed.), *Basic group processes* (pp. 65–94). New York: Springer-Verlag.

Kaplan, M. F., & Miller, C. E. (1987). Group decision making and normative and informational social influence: Effects of type of issue and assigned decision rule. *Journal of Personality and Social Psychology, 53,* 306–313.

Kaplan, M. F., & Miller, L. E. (1978). Reducing the effects of juror bias. *Journal of Personality and Social Psychology, 36,* 1443–1455.

Kaplan, M. F., & Schersching, C. (1980). Reducing juror bias: An experimental approach. In P. Lipsitt & B. D. Sales (Eds.), *New directions in psycholegal research.* New York: Van Nostrand Reinhold.

Karau, S. J., & Williams, K. D. (1993). Social loafing: A meta-analytic review and theoretical integration. *Journal of Personality and Social Psychology, 65,* 681–706.

Karlovac, M., & Darley, J. M. (1988). Attribution of responsibility for accidents: A negligence analogy. *Social Cognition, 6*(4), 287–318.

Kasian, M., Spanos, N. P., Terrance, C. A., & Peebles, S. (1993). Battered women who kill: Jury simulation and legal defenses. *Law and Human Behavior, 17,* 289–312.

Kassin, S. M. (1984). TV cameras, public self-consciousness, and mock jury performance. *Journal of Experimental Social Psychology, 20,* 336–349.

Kassin, S. M., Ellsworth, P. C., & Smith, V. L. (1989). The "general acceptance" of psychological research on eyewitness testimony: A survey of the experts. *American Psychologist, 44,* 1089–1098.

Kassin, S. M., Ellsworth, P. C., & Smith, V. L. (1994). Déjà vu all over again: Elliot's critique of eyewitness experts. *Law and Human Behavior, 18*(2), 203–210.

Kassin, S. M., & Garfield, D. A. (1991). Blood and guts: General and trial-specific effects of videotaped crime scenes on mock jurors. *Journal of Applied Social Psychology, 21*(18), 1459–1472.

Kassin, S. M., & Kiechel, C. L. (1996). The social psychology of criminal confessions: Compliance, internalization, and confabulation. *Psychological Science, 7*(1), 125–128.

Kassin, S. M., & McNall, K. (1991). Police interrogations and confessions: Communicating promises and threats by pragmatic implication. *Law and Human Behavior, 15*, 233–252.

Kassin, S. M., Smith, V. L., & Tulloch, W. F. (1990). The dynamite charge: Effects on the perceptions and deliberation behavior of mock jurors. *Law and Human Behavior, 14*(6), 537–550.

Kassin, S. M., & Sukel, H. (1997). Coerced confessions and the jury: An experimental test of the "harmless error" rule. *Law and Human Behavior, 21*(3), 27–46.

Kassin, S. M., Williams, L. N., & Saunders, C. L. (1990). Dirty tricks of cross-examination: The influence of conjectural evidence on the jury. *Law and Human Behavior, 14*(4), 373–384.

Kassin, S. M., & Wrightsman, L. S. (1979). On the requirements of proof: The timing of judicial instructions and mock juror verdicts. *Journal of Personality and Social Psychology, 37*, 1877–1887.

Kassin, S. M., & Wrightsman, L. (1981). Coerced confessions, judicial instruction, and mock juror verdicts. *Journal of Applied Social Psychology, 11*, 489–506.

Kaye, D. H. (1979). The laws of probability and the law of the land. *University of Chicago Law Review, 47*, 34–56.

Kaye, D. H., & Freedman, D. A. (1994). *Reference guide on statistics.* Washington, DC: Federal Judicial Center.

Kaye, D. H., & Koehler, J. J. (1991). Can jurors understand probabilistic evidence? *Journal of the Royal Statistical Society,* Series A, 154, part 1, 75–81.

Keeton, R. E. (1973). *Trial tactics and methods* (2nd ed.). Boston: Little, Brown.

Kerr, N. L. (1978a). Beautiful and blameless: Effects of victim attractiveness and responsibility on mock jurors' verdicts. *Personality and Social Psychology Bulletin, 4*, 479–482.

Kerr, N. L. (1978b). Severity of prescribed penalty and mock jurors' verdicts. *Journal of Personality and Social Psychology, 36*, 1422–1431.

Kerr, N. L. (1981). Effects of prior juror experience on juror behavior. *Basic and Applied Social Psychology, 2*, 175–193.

Kerr, N. L. (1993). Stochastic models of juror decision making. In R. Hastie (Ed.), *Inside the juror* (pp. 116–135). New York: Cambridge University Press.

Kerr, N. L. (1994). Behavioral research on the effects of pretrial publicity. *From the Mind's Eye, 1,* 3.

Kerr, N. L., Atkin, R. S., Stasser, G., Meek, D., Holt, R. W., & Davis, J. H. (1976). Guilty beyond a reasonable doubt: Effects of concept definition and assigned decision rule on the judgments of mock jurors. *Journal of Personality and Social Psychology, 6*, 282–294.

Kerr, N. L., & Bray, R. M. (Eds.). (1982). *The psychology of the courtroom.* New York: Academic Press.

Kerr, N. L., Hymes, R. W., Anderson, A. B., & Weathers, J. E. (1995). Defendant-juror similarity and mock juror judgments. *Law and Human Behavior, 19*(6), 545–568.

Kerr, N. L., Kramer, G., Carroll, J., & Alfini, J. (1991). On the effectiveness of voir dire in criminal cases with prejudicial pretrial publicity: An empirical study. *American University Law Review, 40*, 665–701.

Kerwin, J., & Shaffer, D. R. (1991). The effects of jury dogmatism on reactions to jury nullification instructions. *Personality and Social Psychology Bulletin, 17*, 140–146.

Key, H. G., Warren, A. R., & Ross, D. F. (1996). Perceptions of repressed memory: A reappraisal. *Law and Human Behavior, 20*(5), 555–564.

Kilpatrick, D. (1990, August 21–25). *PTSD and crime victims.* Paper presented at the annual meeting of the American Psychological Association, Boston.

Kilpatrick, D., Edmunds, C. N., & Seymour, A. (1992). *Rape in America.* Arlington, VA: National Victim Center.

Kilpatrick, D. G., Resnick, H. S., Saunders, B. E., & Best, C. L. (1994). *Survey research on violence against women: Measuring violence assaults against women.* Paper presented at the 46th annual meeting of the American Society of Criminology, Miami.

Kipnis, K. (1989). Plea bargaining: A critic's rejoinder. *Law and Society Review, 13*, 555–564.

Kirkpatrick, L.C. (1995). *Behavioral science seminar.* University of Oregon College of Law, Eugene.

Kirst, R. W. (1982). The jury's historic domain in complex cases. *Washington Law Review, 58,* 1–38.

Kitzmann, K. M., & Emery, R. E. (1993). Procedural justice and parents' satisfaction in a field study of child custody dispute resolution. *Law and Human Behavior, 17*(6), 553–568.

Klein, J. G. (1991). Negativity effects in impression formation: A test in the political arena. *Personality and Social Psychology Bulletin, 17,* 412–418.

Kleinmuntz, B., & Szucko, J. J. (1984). Lie detection in ancient and modern times: A call for contemporary scientific study. *American Psychologist, 39,* 766–776.

Kluger, R. (1975). *Simple justice.* New York: Knopf.

Koehler, J. J. (1992). Probabilities in the courtroom: An evaluation of the objections and policies. In D. K. Kagehiro & W. S. Laufer (Eds.), *Handbook of psychology and law.* New York: Springer-Verlag.

Koehler, J. J., Chia, A., & Lindsey, S. (1994, March). *DNA evidence and statistics: Normative considerations, descriptive studies, and policy recommendations.* Paper presented at the biennial conference of the American Psychology-Law Society, Santa Fe, NM.

Koehn, C. E., Fisher, R. P., & Cutler., B. L. (in press). Using cognitive interviewing to construct facial composites. In D. Cantor (Ed.). *Psychology and criminal detection* (Vol. 2). Aldershoot: Dartmouth.

Kohnken, G., & Brockman, C. (1987). Unspecific postevent information, attribution of responsibility and eyewitness performance. *Applied Cognitive Psychology, 1,* 197–207.

Konecni, V., & Ebbesen, E. (1981). A critique of theory and method in social psychological approaches to legal issues. In B. S. Sales (Ed.), *The trial process* (pp. 481–499). New York: Plenum Press.

Konecni, V., & Ebbesen, E. (1984). The mythology of legal decision-making. *International Journal of Law and Psychiatry, 7,* 5–18.

Koss, M. P. (1990). The women's mental health research agenda: Violence against women. *American Psychologist, 45,* 374–380.

Koss, M. P. (1993). Detecting the scope of rape: A review of prevalence research methods. *Journal of Interpersonal Violence, 8,* 198–222.

Koss, M. R., Gidycz, C. A., & Wisniewski, N. (1987). The scope of rape: Incidence and prevalence of sexual aggression and victimization in a national sample of higher education students. *Journal of Consulting and Clinical Psychology, 55,* 162–170.

Kotler, M. A. (1985). Reappraising the jury's role as finder of fact. *Georgia Law Review, 20,* 123–171.

Kovera, M. B., Gresham, A. W., Borgida, E., Gray, E., & Regan, P. C. (in press). Does expert psychological testimony inform or influence juror decision-making? *Journal of Applied Psychology.*

Kovera, M. B., Park, R. C., & Penrod, S. D. (1992). Jurors' perceptions of eyewitness and hearsay evidence. *Minnesota Law Review, 76,* 703–722.

Kramer, G. P., Kerr, N. L., & Carroll, J. S. (1990). Pretrial publicity, judicial remedies, and jury bias. *Law and Human Behavior, 14,* 409–438.

Kuhn, D., Weinstock, M., & Flaton, R. (1994). How well do jurors reason? Competence dimensions of individual variation in a juror reasoning task. *Psychological Science, 5,* 289–296.

Kuttner, R. (1995, March 20). The trumped up charge against damage awards. *Business Week,* p. 22.

Lander, E. S., & Baaed, B. (1994). DNA fingerprinting dispute laid to rest. *Nature, 371,* 735–738.

Landsman, S., & Rakos. R. (1994). A preliminary inquiry into the effect of potentially biasing information on judges and jurors in civil litigation. *Behavioral Sciences and the Law, 12,* 113.

Landy, D., & Aronson, E. (1969). The influence of character of the criminal and his victim on the decisions of simulated jurors. *Journal of Experimental Social Psychology, 5,* 141–152.

Langbein, J. H. (1979). Torture and plea bargaining. *University of Chicago Law Review, 46,* 12–13.

Latané, B., Williams, K. D., & Harkins, S. G. (1979). Many hands make light the work: The causes and consequences of social loafing. *Journal of Personality and Social Psychology, 37,* 822–832.

Laughlin, P. R., VanderStoep, S. W., & Hollingshead, A. D. (1991). Collective versus individual induction: Recognition of truth, rejection of error, and collective information processing.

Journal of Personality and Social Psychology, 61, 50–67.

LeDoux, J. C., & Hazelwood, R. R. (1985). Police attitudes and beliefs toward rape. *Journal of Police Science and Administration, 13,* 211–220.

Leippe, M. (1995). The case for expert testimony about eyewitness memory. *Psychology, Law, & Public Policy, 1*(4), 909–959.

Leippe, M. R., Manion, A. P., & Romanczyk, A. (1992). Eyewitness persuasion: How and how well do fact finders judge the accuracy of adults' and children's memory reports? *Journal of Personality and Social Psychology, 63,* 181–197.

Leippe, M. R., & Romanczyk, A. (1987). Children on the witness stand: A communication/persuasion analysis of jurors' reactions to child witnesses. In S. J. Ceci, M. P. Toglia, & D. F. Ross (Eds.), *Children's eyewitness memory* (pp. 155–177). New York: Springer-Verlag.

Leippe, M. R., & Romanczyk, A. (1989). Reactions to child (versus adult) eyewitnesses: The influence of jurors' preconceptions and witness behavior. *Law and Human Behavior, 13,* 103–132.

Lempert, R. O. (1981). Dessert and deterrence: An assessment of the moral bases of the case for capital punishment. *Michigan Law Review, 79,* 1177–1231.

Lerner, M. J. (1980). *The belief in a just world: A fundamental delusion.* New York: Plenum Press.

Lerner, M. J., & Simmons, C. H. (1966). Observers' reactions to the "innocent victim": Compassion or rejection? *Journal of Personality and Social Psychology, 4,* 203–210.

Levine, J. P. (1983). Jury toughness: The impact of conservatism on criminal court verdicts. *Crime and Delinquency, 35,* 71–87.

Levine, J. P. (1984). The legislative role of juries. *American Bar Foundation Research Journal, 34,* 605–634.

Levine, J. P. (1992). *Juries and politics.* Pacific Grove, CA: Brooks/Cole.

Levine, J. P. (1996). The impact of sequestration on juries. *Judicature, 79*(5), 266–272.

Lewicki, R. J., Litterer, J. A., Minton, J. W., & Saunders, D. M. (1994). *Negotiation.* Burr Ridge, IL: Irwin.

Lewin, T. (1993, February 12). Rape and accuser: A debate still rages on citing sexual past. *New York Times,* p. B12.

Lewin, T. (1995, February 23). Who decides who will die? *New York Times,* p. A1.

Lidz, C. W., & Mulvey, E. P. (1995). Dangerousness: From legal definition to theoretical research. *Law and Human Behavior, 19*(1), 41–48.

Lind, E. A. (1982). The psychology of courtroom procedure. In N. L. Kerr & R. M. Bray (Eds.), *The psychology of the courtroom* (pp. 13–34). New York: Academic Press.

Lind, E. A., Huo, Y. J., & Tyler, T. R. (1994). . . . And justice for all: Ethnicity, gender, and preferences for dispute resolution procedures. *Law and Human Behavior, 18*(3), 269–290.

Lind, E. A., MacCoun, R. J., Ebener, P. A., Felstiner, W. L. F., Hensler, D. R., Resnick, J., & Tyler, T. R. (1990). In the eye of the beholder: Tort litigants' evaluations of their experiences in the civil justice system. *Law and Society Review, 24*(4), 953–996.

Lind, E. A., & Tyler, T. R. (1988). *The social psychology of procedural justice.* New York: Plenum Press.

Lindley, D. A. (1977). Probability and the law. *The Statistician, 26,* 203–220.

Lindsay, D. S. (1994). Memory source monitoring and eyewitness testimony. In D. F. Ross, J. D. Read, & M. P. Toglia (Eds.), *Adult eyewitness testimony: Current trends and developments* (pp. 27–55). New York: Cambridge University Press.

Lindsay, D. S., Jack, P. C., & Christian, M. A. (1991). Other race face perception. *Journal of Applied Psychology, 76,* 587–589.

Lindsay, D. S., & Johnson, M. K. (1989). The reversed eyewitness suggestibility effect. *Bulletin of the Psychonomic Society, 27,* 111–113.

Lindsay, D. S., Lea, J. A., & Fulford, J. A. (1991). Sequential lineup presentation: Technique matters. *Journal of Applied Psychology, 76,* 741–745.

Lindsay, D. S., & Read, J. D. (1994). Psychotherapy and memories of childhood sexual abuse: A cognitive perspective. *Applied Cognitive Psychology, 8,* 281–338.

Lindsay, D. S., & Read, J. D. (1995). "Memory work" and recovered memories of childhood sexual abuse: Scientific evidence and public, professional, and personal issues. *Psychology, Law, & Public Policy, 1*(4), 846–908.

Lindsay, R. C. L., & Wells, G. (1985). Improving eyewitness identifications from lineups: Simultaneous versus sequential lineup procedures. *Journal of Applied Psychology, 76,* 741–745.

Lindsay, R. C. L., Wells, G. L., & O'Connor, F. J. (1989). Mock juror belief of accurate and inaccurate eyewitnesses: A replication and extension. *Law and Human Behavior, 13,* 333–339.

Lindsay, R. C. L., Wells, G. L., & Rumpel, C. M. (1981). Can people detect eyewitness identification accuracy within and across situations? *Journal of Applied Psychology, 66,* 79–89.

Litkovitz, A. L. (1995). The advantages of using a "rent-a-judge" system in Ohio. *Ohio State Journal Dispute Resolution, 10*(2), 491–506.

Loftus, E. F. (1979). *Eyewitness testimony.* Cambridge, MA: Harvard University Press.

Loftus, E. F. (1980a). Impact of expert psychological testimony on the unreliability of eyewitness identification. *Journal of Applied Psychology, 65,* 9–15.

Loftus, E. F. (1980b). The eyewitness on trial. *Trial, 16,* 29–35.

Loftus, E. F. (1991). Resolving legal questions with psychological data. *American Psychologist 46*(10), 1046–1048.

Loftus, E. F. (1993). The reality of repressed memories. *American Psychologist, 48,* 518–537.

Loftus, E. F. (1995a, May). *Recovered memories.* Invited speech presented at the annual meeting of the Midwestern Psychological Association, Chicago.

Loftus, E. F. (1995b). Memory malleability: Constructivist and fuzzy trace explanations. *Learning and Individual Differences, 7,* 133–137.

Loftus, E. F., Garry, M., & Feldman, J. (1994). Forgetting sexual trauma: What does it mean when 38% forget? *Journal of Consulting and Clinical Psychology, 62,* 1177–1181.

Loftus, E. F., & Ketcham, K. (1994). *The myth of repressed memory.* New York: St. Martin's Press.

Loftus, E. F., Loftus, G. R., & Messo, J. (1987). Some facts about "weapon focus." *Law and Human Behavior, 11,* 55–62.

Loftus, E. F., & Monahan, J. (1980). Trial by data: Psychological research as legal evidence. *American Psychologist, 35,* 270–283.

Loftus, E. F., & Palmer, J. C. (1974). Reconstruction of automobile destruction. *Journal of Verbal Learning and Verbal Behavior, 13,* 585–589.

Loftus, E. F., & Pickrell, J. E. (in press). The formation of false memories. *Psychiatric Annals.*

Loftus, E. F., & Rosenwald, L. A. (1993, November). Buried memories, shattered lives. *ABA Journal,* 70–73.

Loftus, E. F., Schooler, J. W., & Wagenaar, W. A. (1985). The fate of memory: Comment on McCloskey and Zaragoza. *Journal of Experimental Psychology: General, 114,* 375–380.

Loftus, E. F., Weingardt, K. R., & Hoffman, H. G. (1993). Sleeping memories on trial: Reactions to memories that were previously repressed. *The International Digest of Human Behaviour Science and Law, 2,* 51–59.

Lopes, L. L. (1993). Two conceptions of the juror. In R. Hastie (Ed.), *Inside the juror.* New York: Cambridge University Press.

Luginbuhl, J. (1992). Comprehension of judges' instructions in the penalty phase of a capital trial: Focus on mitigating circumstances. *Law and Human Behavior, 16,* 203–218.

Luginbuhl, J., Kadane, J. B., & Powers, T. (1990). *Death scrupled jurors: They are not always more lenient.* Technical Report #465. Pittsburgh: Carnegie Mellon University, Department of Statistics.

Luginbuhl, J., & Middendorf, K. (1988). Death penalty beliefs and jurors' responses to aggravating and mitigating circumstances in capital trials. *Law and Human Behavior, 12,* 263–281.

Luus, C. A., & Wells, G. L. (1991). Eyewitness identification and the selection of distractors for lineups. *Law and Human Behavior, 15,* 43–57.

Luus, C. A. E., & Wells, G. L. (1994a). The malleability of eyewitness confidence: Co-witness and perseverance effects. *Journal of Applied Psychology, 79,* 714–723.

Luus, C. A., & Wells, G. L. (1994b). Determinants of eyewitness confidence. In D. E. Ross, J. D. Read, & M. R. Toglia (Eds.), *Adult eyewitness testimony: Current developments.* New York: Cambridge University Press.

Luus, C. A., Wells, G. L., & Turtle, J. W. (1995). Child eyewitness: Seeing is believing. *Journal of Applied Psychology, 80*(2), 317–326.

Lykken, D. T. (1981). *Tremor in the blood: Uses and abuses of the lie detector.* New York: McGraw-Hill.

Lynn, S. J., Rhue, J. W., Myers, B. P., & Weeks, J. R. (1994). Pseudomemory in hypnotized and simulating subjects. *International Journal of Clinical and Experimental Hypnosis, 42,* 118–129.

Maass, A., Brigham, J. C., & West, S. G. (1985). Testifying on eyewitness reliability: Expert advice is not always persuasive. *Journal of Applied Social Psychology, 15,* 207–229.

Maass, A., & Kohnken, G. (1989). Eyewitness identification: Simulating the "weapon effect." *Law and Human Behavior, 13,* 397–408.

MacCoun, R. J. (1989). Experimental research on jury decision-making. *Science, 244,* 1046–1049.

MacCoun, R. J. (1993). Inside the black box: What empirical research tells us about decision making by civil juries. In R. Litan (Ed.), *Verdict. Assessing the civil jury system.* Washington, DC: Brookings Institution.

MacCoun, R. J., & Kerr, N. L. (1988). Asymmetric influence in mock jury deliberations: Jurors' bias for leniency. *Journal of Personality and Social Psychology, 54*(1), 21–33.

MacCoun, R. J., Lind, E. A., & Tyler, T. R. (1992). Alternative dispute resolution in trial and appellate courts. In D. S. Kagehiro & W. S. Laufer (Eds.), *Handbook of psychology and law* (pp. 95–114). New York: Springer-Verlag.

Malamuth, N. (1986). Predictors of naturalistic sexual aggression. *Journal of Personality and Social Psychology, 50,* 953–962.

Malamuth, N., & Check, J. V. P. (1985). The effects of aggressive pornography on beliefs in rape myths: Individual differences. *Journal of Research in Personality, 19,* 299–320.

Malpass, R. S. (1981). Effective size and defendant bias in eyewitness identification lineups. *Law and Human Behavior, 5,* 299–309.

Malpass, R. S., & Devine, P. G. (1980). Realism and eyewitness identification research. *Law and Human Behavior, 4,* 347–358.

Malpass, R. S., & Devine, P. G. (1981). Eyewitness identification: Lineup instructions and the absence of the offender. *Journal of Applied Psychology, 66,* 482–489.

Malpass, R. S., & Devine, P. G. (1983). Measuring the fairness of eyewitness identification lineups. In S. M. A. Lloyd-Bostock & B. R. Clifford (Eds.), *Evaluating witness evidence* (pp. 81–102). London: Wiley.

Malpass, R. S., & Devine, P. G. (1984). Research on suggestion in lineups and photospreads. In G. L. Wells & E. E Loftus (Eds.), *Eyewitness testimony: Psychological perspectives* (pp. 64–91). New York: Cambridge University Press.

Malpass, R. S., & Kravitz, D. A. (1969). Recognition for faces of own and other race. *Journal of Personality and Social Psychology, 13,* 330–334.

Mantwill, M., Kohnken, G., & Aschermann, E. (1995). Effects of the cognitive interview on recall of familiar and unfamiliar events. *Journal of Applied Psychology, 80,* 68–78.

Manual for Complex Litigation (MCL) (3rd ed.). (1995). Washington, DC: Federal Judicial Center.

Manuet, T. A. (1980). *Fundamentals of trial techniques.* Boston: Little, Brown.

Margolick, D. (1992, April 11). Chorus of judicial critics assail sentencing guides. *New York Times,* p. 1/20.

Margolick, D. (1993a, April 13). At the bar. *New York Times,* p. B9.

Margolick, D. (1993b, January 1). Call for jurors to take bigger roles in trials. *New York Times,* p. B7.

Margolick, D. (1994, May 3). Jurors acquit Dr. Kevorkian. *New York Times,* p. A1.

Markus, M. J., & Horowitz, I. A. (1995). *The child eyewitness: The effects of confirmation or disconfirmation of expectancies on jurors and juries.* Unpublished manuscript, University of Toledo.

Markus, R. L. (1995). Confronting the consolidation conundrum. *Brigham Young Law Review, 43,* 879–924.

Marshall, I. (1966). *Law and psychology in conflict.* Indianapolis: Bobbs-Merrill.

Marshall, J., Marquis, K. H., & Oskamp, S. (1971). Effects of kind of question and atmosphere of interrogation on accuracy and completeness of testimony. *Harvard Law Review, 84,* 1620–1643.

Mauet, T. A. (1992). *Fundamentals of trial techniques* (3rd ed.). Boston: Little, Brown.

Maynard, D. W. (1988). Narratives and narrative structure in plea bargaining. *Law and Society Review, 22,* 449–482.

McCarthy, K. (1990, November). Victims of crimes incur rise in health problems. *APA Monitor,* p. 44.

McCauley, M. R., & Fisher, R. P. (1995). Facilitating children's eyewitness recall with the revised cognitive interview. *Journal of Applied Psychology, 80,* 510–516.

McCloskey, M., & Egeth, H. E. (1983a). Eyewitness identification: What can a psychologist tell a jury? *American Psychologist, 38,* 550–563.

McCloskey, M., & Egeth, H. E. (1983b). A time to speak, or a time to keep silence? *American Psychologist, 38,* 573–575.

McCloskey, M., Egeth, H., & McKenna, J. (1986). The experimental psychologist in court: The ethics of expert testimony. *Law and Human Behavior, 10,* 1–13.

McCloskey, M., & Zaragoza, M. (1985). Misleading postevent information and memory for events: Arguments and evidence against the memory impairment hypotheses. *Journal of Experimental Psychology, 114,* 3–18.

McConahey, J., Mullin, C., & Frederick, J. (1977). The uses of social science in trials with political and racial overtones: The trial of Joan Little. *Law and Contemporary Problems, 41,* 205–229.

McEwen, C. A., & Maiman, R. J. (1986). The relative significance of disputing forum and dispute characteristics for outcome and compliance. *Law and Society Review, 20,* 439–447.

McFatter, R. M. (1978). Sentences, strategies, and justice. *Journal of Personality and Social Psychology, 36,* 1490–1500.

McGillis, D., & Mullen, J. (1977). *Neighborhood justice centers.* Washington, DC: U.S. Government Printing Office.

McKenna, J. A., Cecil, J. S., & Coukos, P. (1994). Reference guide on forensic DNA evidence. *Reference manual on scientific evidence.* Washington, DC: Federal Judicial Center.

Meierhoefer, B. S. (1990). *Court annexed arbitration in ten district courts.* Washington, DC: Federal Judicial Center.

Melton, G. (1994). Expert witnesses and questions of scientific validity. In B. D. Sales & G. R. VandenBos (Eds.), *Psychology in litigation and legislation* (pp. 59–99). Washington, DC: American Psychological Association.

Melton, G. B. (1991a). Psychology in the law: Why we do what we do. *Law and Human Behavior, 14,* 315–332.

Melton, G. B. (1991b). President's column. *American Psychology/Law Society News, 11*(2), 1.

Melton, G., & Wilcox, B. (1989). Changes in family law and family life. *American Psychologist, 44*(9), 1213–1216.

Menkel-Meadow, C. (1984). Toward another view of legal negotiation: The structure of problem solving. *UCLA Law Review, 31,* 54–98.

Menkel-Meadow, C. (1985). Judges and settlements. *Trial,* 24–29.

Menkel-Meadow, C. (1991). Pursuing settlement in adversary culture: A tale of innovation co-opted or "The law of ADR." *Florida State University Law Review, 19*(1), 6–13.

Menzies, R., Webster, C., McMain, S., Staley, S., & Scaglione, R. (1994). The dimensions of dangerousness revisited: Assessing forensic predictions about violence. *Law and Human Behavior, 18*(1), 1–28.

Metcalfe, J. (1990). Composite holographic associative recall model (CHARM) and blended memory in eyewitness testimony. *Journal of Experimental Psychology: General, 119,* 145–160.

Michelson, S. (1980, June). *Reception of social science by legal institutions.* Paper presented at the annual meeting of the Law and Society Association, Madison, WI.

Miene, P., Borgida, E., & Park, R. (1993). The evaluation of hearsay evidence: A social psychological approach. In N. J. Castellan (Ed.), *Individual and group decision making: Current issues* (pp. 151–166). Hillsdale, NJ: Erlbaum.

Milgram, S. (1974). *Obedience to authority.* New York: Harper Colophon Books.

Miller, B. (1995, March 12). Hey waiter! Now there's a lawyer in my soup. *New York Times,* p. 16.

Miller, R. E., & Sarat, A. (1981). Grievances, claims, and disputes. *Law and Society Review, 15,* 525–565.

Miller, S. (1994, August 8). At the bar. *New York Times,* p. A16.

Miller, T. R., Cohen, M. A., & Wiersma, N. B. (1996, February). *Victim costs and consequences: A new look.* NCJ-155282. Washington, DC: National Institute of Justice Technical Report.

Miller, T. R., Pindus, N. M., Douglass, J. B., & Rossman, S. B. (1995). *Nonfatal injury incidence, costs, and consequences: A data book.* New York: Urban Institute Press.

Mills, C. J., & Bohannon, W. E. (1980). Juror characteristics: To what extent are they related to juror verdict? *Judicature, 64,* 23–31.

Minow, N. N., & Cate, F. H. (1991). Who is an impartial juror in an age of mass media? *American University Law Review, 40,* 631–664.

Minshull, M., & Sussman, M. (1979, August 17–23). *Strength of eyewitness testimony vs. strength of objective evidence in influencing jury decisions.* Paper presented at the annual meeting of the Midwestern Psychological Association, Chicago.

Moen, S. P. (1994). The use of expert witnesses in the defense of repressed memory claims. *Shepard's Expert and Scientific Evidence Quarterly, 2,* 417–425.

Monaghan, P. (1995, April 14). The stress of jury duty. *Chronicle of Higher Education,* pp. A12–A15.

Monahan, J. (1978). The prediction of violent criminal behavior: A methodological critique and prospectus. In A. Blumstein (Ed.), *Deterrence and incapacitation: Estimating the effects of criminal sanctions on crime rates.* Washington, DC: National Academy of Sciences.

Monahan, J. (1981). *The clinical prediction of violent behavior.* Washington, DC: U.S. Government Printing Office.

Monahan, J. (1984). The prediction of violent behavior: Toward a second generation of theory and policy. *American Journal of Psychiatry, 141,* 10–18.

Monahan, J. (1988). Risk assessment of violence among the mentally disordered: Generating useful knowledge. *International Journal of Law and Psychiatry, 11,* 249–257.

Monahan, J. (1993). Limiting exposure to Tarasoff liability: Guidelines for risk containment. *American Psychologist, 48,* 242–250.

Monahan, J., & Shah, S. (1989). Dangerousness and the commitment of the mentally disordered in the United States. *Schizophrenia Bulletin, 15,* 541–553.

Monahan, J., & Steadman, H. J. (Eds.) (1994). *Violence and mental disorder: Developments in risk assessment.* Chicago: University of Chicago Press.

Monahan, J., & Walker, L. (1986). Social authority: Obtaining, evaluating, and establishing social science in law. *University of Pennsylvania Law Review, 134,* 477–520.

Monahan, J., & Walker, L. (1991a). Judicial use of social science research. *Law and Human Behavior, 15,* 571–584.

Monahan, J., & Walker, L. (1991b). Empirical questions without empirical answers. *Wisconsin Law Review, 4,* 569–594.

Monahan, J., & Walker, L. (1994a). *Social science in law: Cases and materials.* Westbury, NY: Foundation Press.

Monahan, J., & Walker, L. (1994b). Judicial use of social science research after Daubert. *Shepard's Expert and Scientific Quarterly, 2,* 327–342.

Moran, G., & Comfort, J. G. (1982). Scientific juror selection: Sex as a moderator of demographic and personality predictors of impaneled felony juror behavior. *Journal of Personality and Social Psychology, 43*(5), 99–121.

Moran, G., & Comfort, J. G. (1986). Neither "tentative" nor "fragmentary": Verdict preference of impaneled felony jurors as a function of attitude toward capital punishment. *Journal of Applied Psychology, 71,* 146–155.

Moran, G., & Cutler, B. L. (1991). The prejudicial impact of pretrial publicity. *Journal of Applied Social Psychology, 21*(5), 345–367.

Moran, G., Cutler, B. L., & De Lisa, A. (1994). Attitudes toward tort reform, scientific jury selection, and juror bias: Verdict inclination in criminal and civil trials. *Law and Psychology Review, 18,* 309–328.

Moran, G., Cutler, B. L., & Loftus, E. F. (1990). Jury selection in major controlled substance trials: The need for an extended voir dire. *Forensic Reports, 3*(3), 331–348.

Moscovici, S. (1985). Social influence and conformity. In G. Lindzey & E. Aronson (Eds.), *Handbook of social psychology* (3rd ed., pp. 347–412). Hillsdale, NJ: Erlbaum.

Moscovici, S., & Lage, E. (1976). Studies in social influence III: Majority versus minority influence in a group. *European Journal of Social Psychology, 6,* 149–174.

Moscovici, S., Lage, E., & Naffrechoux, M. (1969). Influence of a consistent minority on the responses of a majority in a color perception task. *Sociometry, 32,* 365–369.

Moscovici, S., & Zavalloni, M. (1969). The group as a polarizer of attitudes. *Journal of Personality and Social Psychology, 12,* 124–135.

Moskitis, R. L. (1976). The constitutional need for discovery of pre-voir dire juror studies. *Southern California Law Review, 49,* 597–633.

Mossman, D. (1994). Assessing predictions of violence: Being accurate about accuracy. *Journal of Clinical and Consulting Psychology, 62*(4), 783–792.

Mueller, C. B., & Kirkpatrick, L. C. (1995). *Evidence.* Boston: Little, Brown.

Mugny, G. (1975). Negotiations, image of the other and minority influence. *European Journal of Social Psychology, 5,* 209–228.

Munsterberg, H. (1908). *On the witness stand.* New York: Doubleday.

Murray, D. M., & Wells, G. L. (1982). Does knowledge that a crime was staged affect eyewitness accuracy? *Journal of Applied Social Psychology, 12,* 42–53.

Mydans, S. (1993a, October 19). Jury acquits. *New York Times,* p. A1.

Mydans, S. (1993b, August 6). Behind beating sentence: Guidelines and sympathy. *New York Times,* p. B8.

Mydans, S. (1996, August 12). Federal prison system close to capacity. *New York Times,* pp. A2, C18.

Myers, D. G., & Lamm, H. (1976). The group polarization phenomenon. *Psychological Bulletin, 83,* 602–627.

Myers, M. A. (1988). Social background and the sentencing behavior of judges. *Criminology, 26*(4), 649–675.

Nagao, D., & Davis, J. H. (1981). The effects of prior experience on complex social decisions: An illustration with mock jurors. *Quarterly Journal of Social Psychology, 43,* 190–199.

Narby, D. J. & Cutler, B. L. (1994). Effectiveness of voir dire as a safeguard in eyewitness cases. *Journal of Applied Psychology, 79*(5), 724–729.

Narby, D. J., Cutler, B. L., & Moran, G. (1993). A meta-analysis of the association between authoritarians and jurors' perceptions of defendant culpability. *Journal of Applied Psychology, 78*(1), 34–42.

National Center for State Courts. (1995). *State court organization.* Williamsburg VA: National Center for State Courts.

Nelson, K. (1986). *Event knowledge: Structure and function in development.* Hillsdale, NJ: Erlbaum.

Nicholson, R. A., & Kugler, K. E. (1991). Competent and incompetent criminal defendants: A quantitative review of comparative research. *Psychological Bulletin, 109,* 355–370.

Nicholson, R. A., Norwood, S., & Enyart, C. (1991). Characteristics of insanity acquittees in Oklahoma. *Behavioral Sciences and the Law, 9,* 487–500.

Nietzel, M., & Hartung, C. (1993). Psychological research on the police: An introduction to a special section on the psychology of law enforcement. *Law and Human Behavior, 17,* 151–155.

Nieves, E. (1993, May 2). Jail sentences for sex crimes are rarely very harsh. *New York Times,* p. E3.

Nightingale, N. N. (1993). Juror reactions to child eyewitnesses. *Law and Human Behavior, 17*(6), 679–694.

Nonsense upon stilts. (1995, June 15). *New Republic,* p. 9.

Norris, F. H., & Kaniasty, K. (1991). The psychological experience of crime: A test of the mediating role of beliefs in explaining the distress of victims. *Journal of Social and Clinical Psychology, 10,* 239–261.

O'Callaghan, G., & D'Arcy, H. (1989). Use of props in questioning preschool witnesses. *Australian Journal of Psychology, 41,* 187–195.

Ogloff, J., Tomkins, A., & Bersoff, D. (in press). Education and training in psychology and law/criminal justice. *Criminal Justice and Behavior.*

Ogloff, J. P., & Vidmar, N. (1994). The impact of pretrial publicity on jurors: A study to compare the relative effects of television and print media in a child sex abuse case. *Law and Human Behavior, 18*(5), 507–526.

Ogloff, J. P., Wallace, D. H., & Otto, R. (1992). Competencies in the criminal process. In D. K. Kagehiro & W. S. Laufer (Eds.), *Handbook of psychology and law.* New York: Springer-Verlag.

Olio, K. (in press). Are 25 percent of clinicians using potentially risky therapeutic practices? *Journal of Psychiatry and the Law.*

Ondrus, S. (1994). *Lawyer tactics.* Unpublished manuscript. University of Toledo, Ohio.

Orne, M. T., Soskes, D. A., Dinges, D. F., & Orne, E. C. (1984). Hypnotically induced testimony. In G. Wells & E. Loftus (Eds.), *Eyewitness testimony: Psychological perspectives* (pp. 171–213). New York: Cambridge University Press.

Ornstein, P. A., Gordon, B. N., & Larus, D. M. (1992). Children's memory for a personally experienced event: Implications for testimony. *Applied Developmental Psychology, 6,* 49–60.

Ostrom, B. J., Rottman, D. B., & Goerdt, J. A. (1996). A step above anecdote: A profile of the civil jury in the 1990's. *Judicature, 79*(5), 233–241.

Otto, A. L., Penrod, S. D., & Dexter, H. R. (1994). The biasing effects of pretrial publicity on juror judgments. *Law and Human Behavior, 18,* 453–470.

Padawer-Singer, A., & Barton, A. H. (1975). Free press, fair trial. In R. J. Simon (Ed.)., *The jury system: A critical analysis.* Beverly Hills, CA: Sage.

Paternoster, R. (1991). *Capital punishment in America.* New York: Lexington.

Pattern Jury Instructions, Criminal Cases. (1985). Jury Instruction Committee of the Eleventh Circuit, Atlanta.

Payne, D. G. (1987). Hypermnesia and reminiscence in recall: A historical and empirical review. *Psychological Bulletin, 101,* 5–27.

Payne, J. W., Braunstein, M. L., & Carroll, J. S. (1978). Exploring pre-decisional behavior: An alternative approach to decision making. *Organizational Behavior and Human Behavior, 22,* 17–44.

Pennington, N., & Hastie, R. (1986). Evidence evaluation in complex decision making. *Journal of Personality and Social Psychology, 51,* 242–258.

Pennington, N., & Hastie, R. (1988). Explanation-based decision making: The effects of memory structure on judgment. *Journal of Experimental Psychology: Learning, Memory, and Cognition, 14,* 521–533.

Pennington, N., & Hastie, R. (1990). Practical implications of psychological research on juror and jury decision making. *Personality and Social Psychology Bulletin, 16,* 90–105

Pennington, N., & Hastie, R. (1992). Explaining evidence: Tests of the story model for juror decision making. *Journal of Personality and Social Psychology, 62,* 189–206.

Penrod, S. D. (1990). Predictors of jury decision making in criminal and civil trials: A field experiment. *Forensic Reports, 3*(3), 261–278.

Penrod, S. D., & Cutler, B. (1995). Witness confidence and witness accuracy: Assessing their forensic relation. *Psychology, Law, & Public Policy, 1*(4), 817–845.

Penrod, S. D., & Cutler, B. L. (in press). The case against traditional safeguards: Preventing mistaken convictions in eyewitness identification trials. In R. Roesch & S. D. Hart (Eds.), *Psychology and law: The state of the discipline.* New York: Plenum Press.

Penrod, S. D., Fulero, S. M., & Cutler, B. L. (1995). Expert psychological testimony on eyewitness reliability before and after Daubert: The state of the law and the science. *Behavioral Sciences and the Law, 13*(2), 229–260.

Perlin, M. L. (1990). Psychodynamics and the insanity defense: Ordinary commonsense and heuristic reasoning. *Nebraska Law Review, 60,* 3–45.

Peter, L. J. (1977). *Peter's quotations* (p. 276) New York: Morrow.

Petersilia, J. (1994). Violent crime and violent criminals: The response of the justice system. In M. Costanzo & S. Oscamp (Eds.), *Violence and the law.* Thousand Oaks, CA: Sage.

Petrila, J., Otto, R. K., & Poythress, N. G. (1994). Violence, mental disorder, and the law. In M. Costanzo & S. Oscamp (Eds.), *Violence and the law.* Thousand Oaks, CA: Sage.

Pfeiffer, J. E. (1990). Reviewing the empirical evidence on jury racism. *Nebraska Law Review, 69,* 230–250.

Pickel, K. L. (1993). Evaluation and integration of eyewitness reports. *Law and Human Behavior, 17*(5), 569–595.

Pickel, K. L. (1995). Inducing jurors to disregard inadmissible evidence: A legal explanation does not help. *Law and Human Behavior, 19,* 407–426.

Poole, D., Lindsay, D., Memon, A., & Bull, R. (1995). Psychotherapy and the recovery of memories of childhood sexual abuse: U.S. and British practitioners' opinions, practices, and experiences. *Journal of Consulting and Clinical Psychology, 63,* 426–437.

Poole, D. A., & White, L. T. (1991). Effects of question repetition on the eyewitness testimony of children and adults. *Developmental Psychology, 27,* 975–986.

Poole, D. A., & White, L. T. (1992, April 30). *It happened two years ago: Question repetition and the eyewitness testimony of children and adults.* Paper presented at the annual meeting of the Midwestern Psychological Association, Chicago.

Poole, D. A., & White, L. T. (1993). Two years later: Effects of question repetition and retention interval on the eyewitness testimony of children and adults. *Developmental Psychology, 29,* 844–853.

Pope, K. S. (1996). Memory, abuse, & science. Questioning claims about the false memory syndrome epidemic. *American Psychologist, 51*(9), 957–974.

Poythress, N. G., Bonnie, R. J., Hoge, S. K., Monahan, J., & Oberlander, L. (1994). Client abilities to assist counsel and make decisions in criminal cases: Findings from three studies. *Law and Human Behavior, 18*(4), 437–452.

Prettyman, E. B. (1960). Jury instructions—first or last? *American Bar Association Journal, 46,* 1066.

Priest, G. (1993). Justifying the civil jury. In R. Litan (Ed.), *Verdict: Assessing the civil jury system.* Washington, DC: Brookings Institution.

Pruitt, D. G., & Carnevale, P. J. (1993). *Negotiation in social conflict.* Pacific Grove, CA: Brooks/Cole.

Purnick, J. (1996, March 7). Low priority for judging of the judges. *New York Times,* p. A20.

Pyszczynski, T., Greenberg, J., Mack, D., & Wrightsman L. S. (1981). Opening statements in a jury trial: The effect of promising more than the evidence can show. *Journal of Applied Social Psychology, 11,* 434–444.

Pyszczynski, T., & Wrightsman, L. S. (1981). The effects of opening statements on mock jurors' verdicts in a simulated criminal trial. *Journal of Applied Social Psychology, 11,* 301–313.

Quote . . . unquote. (1991, October 6). *Montreal Gazette,* p. B2.

Raitz, A., Greene, E., Goodman, J., & Loftus, E. F. (1990). Determining damages: The influence of expert testimony on jurors' decision making. *Law and Human Behavior, 14*(5), 385–396.

Rajecki, D. W. (1990). *Attitudes* (2nd ed.). Sunderland, MA: Sinauer.

Rakove, J. N. (1996). *Original meanings.* New York: Knopf.

Rattner, A. (1988). Convicted but innocent: Wrongful conviction and the criminal justice system. *Law and Human Behavior, 12,* 283–293.

Rauma, D., & Krafka, C. (1994). *Voluntary arbitration in eight federal district courts: An evaluation.* Washington, DC: Federal Judicial Center.

Rawls, J. (1971). *A theory of justice.* Cambridge, MA: Harvard University Press.

Read, D., & Craik, F. (1995). Earwitness identification: Some influences on voice recognition. *Journal of Experimental Psychology: Applied, 1,* 6–33.

Realmuto, G. M., & Wesco, S. (1992). Agreement among professionals about child's sexual abuse status: Interviews with sexually anatomically correct dolls as indicators of abuse. *Child Abuse and Neglect, 16,* 719–725.

Reifman, A., Gusick, S. M., & Ellsworth, P. C. (1992). Real jurors' understanding of the law in real cases. *Law and Human Behavior, 16,* 539–554.

Rembar, C. (1980). *The law of the land.* New York: Simon & Schuster.

Reynolds, D., & Sanders, M. (1975, April). *The effects of defendant attractiveness, age, and injury on severity of sentence given by simulated jurors.* Paper presented at the meetings of the Western Psychological Association, Anaheim, CA.

Riger, S., Foster-Fishman, P., Nelson-Kuna, J., & Curran, B. (1995). Gender bias in courtroom dynamics. *Law and Human Behavior, 19*(5), 465–480.

Riggs, D., Kilpatrick, D., & Resnick, H. (1992). Long term psychological distress associated with rape and aggravated assault. *Journal of Family Violence, 7*(4), 283–329.

Roberts, C. F., Sargent, E. L., & Chan, A. S. (1993). Verdict selection processes in insanity cases: Juror construals and the effects of guilty but mentally ill instructions. *Law and Human Behavior, 17*(3), 261–276.

Roberts, J. V., & Doob, A. (1990). News media influences on public views of sentencing. *Law and Human Behavior, 14,* 451–468.

Roberts, J. V., & Edwards, D. (1989). Contextual effects in judgments of crimes, criminals, and the purposes of sentencing. *Journal of Applied Social Psychology, 19,* 902–917.

Roberts, J. V., &. Gebotys, R. J. (1992). Reforming rape laws: Effects of legislative change in Canada. *Law and Human Behavior, 16,* 555–576.

Robinson, D. N. (1980). *Psychology and law.* New York: Oxford University Press.

Robinson, E. (1935). *Law and the lawyers.* New York: Macmillan.

Robinson, P. H. (1990). Rules of conduct and criminal adjudication. *University of Chicago Law Review, 57,* 729–771.

Robinson, P. H. (1993). The criminal-civil distinction and the dangerous blameless offenders. *Journal of Criminal Law and Criminology, 83*(4), 693–717.

Robinson, P. H. (1994a). Are criminal codes irrelevant? *Southern California Law Review, 68*(1), 159–202.

Robinson, P. H. (1994b). A functional analysis of criminal law. *Northwestern University Law Review, 88,* 857–913.

Robinson, P. H., & Darley, J. M. (1995). *Justice, liability, and blame.* San Francisco: Westview Press.

Robinson, R. J. (1993). What does "unwilling" to impose the death penalty mean anyway? Another look at excludable jurors. *Law and Human Behavior, 17*(4), 471–478.

Roesch, R., Hart, S. D., & Zepf, P. A. (1996). Conceptualizing and assessing competency to stand trial: Implications and applications of the MacArthur Treatment Competence Model. *Psychology, Public Policy, and Law, 2*(1), 96–136.

Rosenberg, J. D., & Folberg, H. J. (1994). Alternative dispute resolution: An empirical analysis. *Stanford Law Review, 46,* 1487–1520.

Rosenhan, D. L., Eisner, S. L., & Robinson, R. J. (1994). Notetaking can aid juror recall. *Law and Human Behavior, 18*(1), 53–62.

Rosoff, S. M. (1989). Physicians as criminal defendants: Specialty, sanctions, and status liability. *Law and Human Behavior, 13,* 231–236.

Ross, D. F., Hopkins, S., Hanson, E., Lindsay, R. C. L., Hazen, K., & Eslinger, T. (1994). The impact of protective shields and videotape testimony on conviction rates in a simulated trial of child sexual abuse. *Law and Human Behavior, 18*(5), 553–566.

Ross, D. F., Read, J. D., & Toglia, M. P. (Eds.). (1994). *Adult eyewitness testimony: Current trends and developments* (pp. 223–244). New York: Cambridge University Press.

Ross, H. C., & Campbell, D. T. (1978). The Connecticut speed crackdown: A study of the effects of legal change. In H. L. Ross (Ed.), *Perspectives on the social order: Readings in sociology.* New York: McGraw-Hill.

Ruback, R. B., Greenberg, M. S., & Westcott, D. R. (1984). Social influence and crime-victim decision making. *Journal of Social Issues, 40*(1), 51–76.

Rubin, J. G. (1974). Police identity and police role. In J. G. Goldsmith & S. S. Goldsmith (Eds.), *The police community.* Pacific Palisades, CA: Palisades Publishers.

Rudy, L., & Goodman, G. S. (1991). Effects of participation on children's reports: Implications for children's testimony. *Developmental Psychology, 27,* 527–538.

Russell, D. E. H. (1984). *Sexual exploitation.* Beverly Hills, CA: Sage.

Rutland, R. A. (1955). *The birth of the Bill of Rights, 1776–1791.* Boston: Little, Brown.

Safian, J. (1991, May). Murder. *The American Lawyer,* pp. 73–76.

Saks, M. (1976, January). Social scientists can't rig juries. *Psychology Today,* 48–57.

Saks, M. (1992). Do we really know anything about the behavior of the tort litigation system—and why not? *University of Pennsylvania Law Review, 140*(4), 1147–1292.

Saks, M. (1993). Judicial nullification. *Indiana Law Journal, 68*(4), 1281–1295.

Saks, M. J. (1996). The smaller the jury, the greater the unpredictability. *Judicature, 79*(5), 263–266.

Saks, M., & Baron, C. (1980). *The uses/nonuse/misuse of applied social research in the courts.* Cambridge, MA: Abt Books.

Saks, M., & Blanck, P. D. (1992). Justice improved: The unrecognized benefits of aggregation and sampling in the trial of mass torts. *Stanford Law Review, 44,* 815–851.

Saks, M., & Hastie, R. (1978). *Social psychology in the courtroom.* New York: Van Nostrand Reinhold.

Saks, M., & Kidd, R. (1986). Human information processing and adjudication: Trial by heuristics. In H. Arkes & K. Hammond (Eds.), *Judgment and decisionmaking.* Cambridge, England: Cambridge University Press.

Saks, M., & Koehler, J. L. (1991). What DNA fingerprinting can teach the law about the rest of forensic science. *Cardozo Law Review, 13,* 361–370.

Sales, B. D. (Ed.). (1977). *Psychology in the legal process.* New York: Spectrum.

Sanders, G. S., Gansler, D. A., & Reisman, S. (1989). The effects of hypnosis on eyewitness testimony and reactions to cross-examination. *American Journal of Forensic Psychology, 7,* 33–60.

Sandys, M., & Dillehay, R. C. (1995). First-ballot votes, predeliberations dispositions, and final verdicts in jury trials. *Law and Human Behavior, 19*(2), 175–196.

Saywitz, K. J., Geiselman, R. E., & Bornstein, G. K. (1992). Effects of cognitive interviewing and practice on children's performance. *Journal of Applied Psychology, 77,* 744–756.

Saywitz, K. J., & Snyder, L. (1993). Improving children's testimony with preparation. In G. Goodman & B. Bottoms (Eds.), *Child victims, child witnesses* (pp. 117–146). New York: Guilford Press.

Schacter, D. (1996). *Searching for memory.* New York: Basic Books.

Schacter, D., Bandy, D., Curran, T., McDermott, K., Reimen, E., Roedinger, R., & Shen Yung, L. (in press). PET scans of true and false memories. *Nature.*

Scheflin, A., & Van Dyke, J. (1980). "Jury nullification": The contours of a controversy. *Law and Contemporary Problems, 43,* 52–115.

Scheflin, A. W., & Van Dyke, J. (1991). Merciful juries: The resilience of jury nullification. *Washington and Lee Law Review, 48,* 165–183.

Scheppele, K. L. (1987). The revision of rape law. *University of Chicago Law Review, 54,* 1095–1115.

Schuller, R. A. (1990). The impact of battered woman syndrome testimony on jury decision making: *Lavallee v. R.* considered. *Windsor Yearbook of Access to Justice, 10,* 105–126.

Schuller, R. A. (1994). Applications of battered woman syndrome evidence in the courtroom. In M. Costanzo & S. Oscamp (Eds.), *Violence and the law.* Thousand Oak, CA: Sage.

Schuller, R. A., & Vidmar, N. (1992). Battered woman syndrome evidence in the courtroom: A review of the literature. *Law and Human Behavior, 16,* 273–292.

Schulman, J., Shaver, P., Colman, R., Emricle, B., & Christie, R. (1973). Recipe for a jury. *Psychology Today,* 37–44, 77, 79–84.

Schwartz, B. (1974). *The law in America.* New York: McGraw-Hill.

Schwarzer, W. W. (1991). Reforming jury trials. *Federal Rules Decisions, 132,* 575–596.

Schwarzer, W. W., Hirsch, A., & Barrans, D. J. (1991). *The analysis and decision of summary judgment motions.* Washington, DC: Federal Judicial Center.

Scott, L. A. (1989). *An application of the elaboration likelihood model to jurors' decision making in a complex lawsuit.* Unpublished master's thesis, Loyola University of Chicago.

Scott, P. B. (1989). Jury nullification: An historical perspective on a modern debate. *West Virginia Law Review, 91,* 389–419.

Scrivner, E. (1994). Police brutality. In M. Costanzo & S. Oscamp (Eds.), *Violence and the law.* Thousand Oaks, CA: Sage.

Seelau, S. M., & Wells, G. L. (1995). Applied eyewitness research: The other mission. *Law and Human Behavior, 19*(3), 319–324.

Selvin, M., & Picus, L. (1987). *The debate over jury performance.* Santa Monica, CA: The Rand Corporation.

Severance, L. J., Greene, E., & Loftus, E. F. (1984). Toward criminal jury instructions that jurors can understand. *Journal of Criminal Law and Criminology, 75,* 198–233.

Shalit, R. (1995a, June 19). *Michaels v. New Jersey. The New Republic,* p. 14.

Shalit, R. (1995b, July 29). Witch hunt. *The New Republic,* p. 16.

Shartel, J. S. (1993). Computer animation often provides winning edge for litigators. *Inside Litigation, 7*(5), 17–27.

Shartel, J. S. (1994a). Federal judges employ wide variety of jury procedures. *Inside Litigation, 8*(1), 15–20.

Shartel, J. S. (1994b). Litigators describe key factors in use of jury consultant. *Inside Litigation, 8*(7), 1–23.

Shaw, J. I., & Skolnick, P. (1996). When is defendant status a shield or a liability? Clarification and extension. *Law and Human Behavior, 20*(4), 431–442.

Sheehan, P. W., Green, V., & Truesdale, P. (1992). Influence of rapport on hypnotically induced pseudomemory. *Journal of Abnormal Psychology, 101,* 690–700.

Sheehan, P. W., & Statham, D. (1989). Hypnosis, the timing of its introduction, and acceptance of misleading information. *Journal of Abnormal Psychology, 93,* 170–176.

Sheehan, P. W., Statham, D., Jamieson, G. A., & Ferguson, S. (1991). Ambiguity in suggestion and the occurence or pseudomemory in the hypnotic interview. *Australian Journal of Clinical and Experimental Hypnosis, 19,* 1–18.

Shepard, J., & Johnson, M. T. (1995). *Voir dire survey.* Unpublished memorandum to the Advisory Committees on Civil and Criminal Rules. Washington, DC: Federal Judicial Center.

Short, E. H. (1981). *Evaluation of California's experiment with extended media coverage.* Sacramento: Ernest H. Short.

Sigall, H. J., & Ostrove, N. (1975). Beautiful but dangerous: Effects of offender attractiveness on juridic judgment. *Journal of Personality and Social Psychology, 31,* 410–414.

Silver, E. (1995). Punishment or treatment? Comparing the lengths of confinement of successful and unsuccessful insanity defendants. *Law and Human Behavior, 19*(4), 389–406.

Silver, E., Cirincione, C., & Steadman, H. J. (1994). Demythologizing inaccurate perceptions of the insanity defense. *Law and Human Behavior, 18,* 63–70.

Simon, R. J. (1966, May–June). Murder, juries, and the press. *Trans-Action,* 64–65.

Simon, R. J. (1967). *The jury and the defense of insanity.* Boston: Little, Brown.

Simon, R. J. (1975). *The jury system in America.* Beverly Hills, CA: Sage.

Simon, R. J., & Eimermann, T. (1971). The jury finds not guilty: Another look at media influence of jury. *Journalism Quarterly, 48,* 343–344.

Simon, R. J., & Mahan, L. (1971). Quantifying burdens of proof: A view from the bench, the jury, and the classroom. *Law and Society Review, 5,* 319–330.

Skinner, L., & Berry, K. B. (1993). Anatomically detailed dolls and evaluation of child sexual abuse allegations: Psychometric considerations. *Law and Human Behavior, 17*(4), 399–422.

Skolnick, J. L. (1993). *Above the law: Police and the use of excessive force.* New York: Free Press.

Skolnick, P., & Shaw, J. L. (1994). Is defendant status a liability or a shield? Crime severity and professional relatedness. *Journal of Applied Social Psychology, 24,* 1827–1836.

Slade, S. (1995, June). The defendant as victim. *APA Monitor,* p. 27.

Sleek, S. (1993a, December). Community policing approach suggested. *APA Monitor,* p. 33.

Sleek, S. (1993b, December). Guns' ubiquity a symbol of rising danger for cops. *APA Monitor,* p. 32.

Sleek, S. (1993c, December). Less harsh management urged for police agencies. *APA Monitor,* p. 31.

Sleek, S. (1993d, December). Stress of critical events affects officers. *APA Monitor,* p. 29.

Slovic, P., & Monahan, J. (1995). Probability, danger, and coercion: A study of risk perception and decision making in mental health law. *Law and Human Behavior, 19*(1), 49–66.

Smith, B. C., Penrod, S. D., Otto, A. L., & Park, R. C. (1966). Jurors' use of probabilistic evidence. *Law and Human Behavior, 20*(1), 49–82.

Smith, V. L. (1990). The feasibility and utility of pretrial instruction in the substantive law: A survey of judges. *Law and Human Behavior, 14*(3), 235–248.

Smith, V. L. (1991a). Impact of pretrial instruction on jurors' information processing and decision making. *Journal of Applied Psychology, 76*(2), 220–228.

Smith, V. L. (1991b). Prototypes in the courtroom: Lay representations of legal concepts. *Journal of Personality and Social Psychology, 61,* 857–865.

Smith, V. L. (1993). When prior knowledge and law collide: Helping jurors to use the law. *Law and Human Behavior, 17,* 507–536.

Smith, V. L., & Kassin, S. (1993). Effects of the dynamite charge on the deliberations of deadlocked mock juries. *Law and Human Behavior, 17*(6), 625–644.

Smith, V. L., Kassin, S. M., & Ellsworth, P. C. (1989). Eyewitness accuracy and confidence: Within versus between-subject correlations. *Journal of Applied Psychology, 74,* 356–359.

Sommer, K., Bourgeois, M., & Horowitz, I. A. (1997). *When perceptions of outcome fairness bias individual and group decision making.* Unpublished manuscript, Case Western Reserve University.

Spanos, N. P., Dubreuil, S. C., & Gwynn, M. I. (1991). The effects of expert testimony concerning rape on verdicts and beliefs of mock jurors. *Imagination, Cognition, & Personality, 11,* 37–52.

Spanos, N. P., Gwynn, M. I., Comer, S. L., Baltuweit, W. J., & de Groh, M. (1989). Are hypnotically induced pseudomemories resistant to cross-examination? *Law and Human Behavior, 13,* 271–289.

Sperlich, P. (1980). Social science evidence and the courts. *Judicature, 65,* 394–395.

Spohn, C. (1990). The sentencing decisions of black and white judges: Expected and unexpected similarities. *Law and Society Review, 24,* 1197–1216.

Spohn, C., Gruhl, J., & Welch, S. (1982). The effect of race on sentencing: A reexamination of an unsettled question. *Law and Society Review, 16,* 71–88.

Sporer, S. L. (1994). Decision times and eyewitness identification accuracy in simultaneous and sequential lineups. In D. F. Ross, J. D. Read, & M. P. Toglia (Eds.), *Adult eyewitness testimony* (pp. 300–327). New York: Cambridge University Press.

Sporer, S. L., Penrod, S. D., Read, J. D., & Cutler, B. L. (1995). Choosing, confidence, and accuracy: A meta-analysis of the confidence-accuracy relation in eyewitness identification studies. *Psychological Bulletin, 118,* 315–327.

Staib, M. E. (1994, April). Survey of prospective jurors. *Litigation News,* pp. 4, 6.

Stalans, L. J., & Diamond, S. S. (1990). Formation and change in lay evaluations of criminal sentencing: Misperceptions and discontent. *Law and Human Behavior, 14*(3), 199–214.

Stapp, J. (1996, January/February). An unusual career in psychology: Trial consultant. *Psychological Science Agenda,* p. 12.

Stasser, G., Kerr, N. L., & Davis, J. H. (1989). Influence processes and consensus models in decision making groups. In P. Paulus (Ed.), *Psychology of group influence* (2nd ed., pp. 279–326). Hillsdale, NJ: Erlbaum.

Steadman, H. J., & Braff, J. (1983). Defendants not guilty by reason of insanity. In J. Monahan & H. J. Steadman (Eds.), *Mentally disordered offenders: Perspectives from law and social science* (pp. 109–129). New York: Plenum Press.

Steadman, H., Monahan, J., Appelbaum, P., Mulvey, T., Roth, L., Robbins, P., & Klassen, D. (1994). Designing a new generation of risk assessment research. In J. Monahan & H. Steadman (Eds.). *Violence and mental disorder: Developments in risk assessment* (pp. 297–318). Chicago: University of Chicago Press.

Steblay, N. M. (1992). A meta-analytic review of the weapon focus effect. *Law and Human Behavior, 16,* 413–424.

Steblay, N. M., & Bothwell, R. K. (1994). Evidence for hypnotically refreshed testimony: The view from the laboratory. *Law and Human Behavior, 18*(6), 635–652.

Stienstra, D. (1985). *Unpublished dispositions: Problems of access and use in the courts of appeals.* Washington, DC: Federal Judicial Center.

Stienstra, D., & Willging, T. E. (1995). *Alternatives to litigation: Why they do and why they do not have a place in the federal trial courts.* Washington, DC: Federal Judicial Center.

Stinson, V., Davenport, J. L., Cutler, B. L., & Kravitz, D. A. (1996). How effective is the presence of counsel safeguard? Attorney perceptions of suggestiveness, fairness, and correctability of biased lineup procedures. *Journal of Applied Psychology, 81*(1), 64–75.

Strawn, D. J., & Buchanan, R. W. (1976). Jury confusion: A threat to justice. *Judicature, 59,* 478–483.

Strier, F. (1994). *Reconstructing justice: An agenda for trial reform.* Westport, CT: Quorum Books.

Sue, S., Smith, R. E., & Caldwell, C. (1973). Effects of inadmissible evidence on the decisions of simulated jurors: A moral dilemma. *Journal of Applied Social Psychology, 3,* 345–353.

Swann, W. B., Jr., Hixon, J. G., & de La Ronde, C. (1992). Embracing the bitter truth: Negative self concepts and marital commitment. *Psychological Science 3*(2), 118–121.

Tanford, J. A. (1986). An introduction to trial law. *Missouri Law Review, 51*(3), 624–710.

Tanford, J. A. (1990). The limits of scientific jurisprudence: The Supreme Court and psychology. *Indiana Law Journal, 66*(1), 137–174.

Tanford, J. A. (1991a). The law and psychology of jury instructions. *Nebraska Law Review, 69,* 71–111.

Tanford, J. A. (1991b). Law reform by courts, legislatures, and commissions following empirical research on jury instructions. *Law and Society Review, 25,* 158–175.

Tanford, J. A., & Tanford, S. (1988). Better trials through science: A defense of psychologist-lawyer collaboration. *North Carolina Law Review, 66*(4), 742–780.

Tanford, S., & Cox, M. (1988). The effect of impeachment evidence and limiting instructions on individual and group decision making. *Law and Human Behavior, 12,* 477–498.

Tanford, S., & Penrod, S. D. (1986). Jury deliberations: Content and influence processing in decision making. *Journal of Applied Social Psychology, 16*(4), 322–347.

Tans, M., & Chaffee, S. (1966). Pretrial publicity and juror prejudice. *Journalism Quarterly, 43,* 647–654.

Tapp, J. L. (1976). Psychology and the law: An overture. In M. L. Rozenzweig & L. W. Porter (Eds.), *Annual review of psychology, 27,* 176–194.

Tapp, J. L., & Levine, F. J. (Eds.). (1974). *Law, justice, and the individual in society: Psychological and legal issues.* New York: Holt, Rinehart and Winston.

Taylor, S., Jr. (1987, June 16). Challenging the police verbally wins backing. *New York Times,* p. 15.

Taylor, S., Jr. (1995, September 18). Why so many lawyer jokes ring true. *Legal Times,* p. 21.

Taylor, S. E. (1989). *Positive illusions: Creative self-deception and the healthy mind.* New York: Basic Books.

Teplin, L. A. (1983). The criminalization of the mentally ill: Speculation in search of data. *Psychological Bulletin, 94,* 54–67.

Teplin, L. A. (1984). Criminalizing mental disorder: The comparative arrest rate of the mentally ill. *American Psychologist, 39,* 794–803.

Teplin, L. A. (1985). The criminality of the mentally ill: A dangerous misconception. *American Journal of Psychiatry, 142,* 593–599.

Teplin, L. A. (1990a). Detecting disorder: The treatment of mental illness among jail detainees. *Journal of Consulting and Clinical Psychology, 58,* 233–236.

Teplin, L. A. (1990b). The prevalence of severe mental disorder among male urban jail detainees: Comparison with the Epidemiologic Catchment Area program. *American Journal of Public Health, 80,* 663–669.

Terr, L. (1994). *Unchained memories: True stories of traumatic memories, lost and found.* New York: Basic Books.

Thibaut, J., & Walker, L. (1975). *Procedural justice: A psychological analysis.* Hillsdale, NJ: Erlbaum.

Thompson, W. C. (1989a). Are juries competent to evaluate statistical evidence? *Law and Contemporary Problems, 52,* 9–41.

Thompson, W. C. (1989b). Death qualification after *Wainwright v. Witt* and *Lockhart v. McCree. Law and Human Behavior, 13*(2), 185–215.

Thompson, W. C., Cowan, C. L., Ellsworth, P. C., & Harrington, J. C. (1984). Death penalty attitudes and conviction proneness: The translation of attitudes into verdicts. *Law and Human Behavior, 8,* 95–113.

Thompson, W. C., & Schumann, E. L. (1987). Interpretation of statistical evidence in criminal trials: The prosecutor's fallacy and the defense attorney's fallacies. *Law and Human Behavior, 11,* 167–172.

Thornton, H. (1995). *Hung jury: The diary of a Menendez juror.* Philadelphia: Temple University Press.

Tomkins, A. (1995). Introduction to behavioral science evidence in the wake of Daubert. *Behavioral Sciences and the Law, 13*(3), 127–130.

Tonry, M. (1995). *Sentencing matters.* New York: Oxford University Press.

Toobin, J. (1996, April). Humility and justice. *The New Yorker,* 6.

Too many lawyers and too much litigation. (1992, April 13). *Business Week,* 61.

Touhy, A. P., Wrennal, M. J., McQueen, R. A., Stradling, S. G. (1993). Effect of socialization factors on decisions to prosecute. *Law and Human Behavior, 17*(2), 167–182.

Treaster, J. B. (1995, June 18). Lawyers on trial. *New York Times,* p. 10.

Tribe, L. H. (1971). Trial by mathematics: Precision and ritual in the legal process. *Harvard Law Review, 84*(6), 1329–1393.

Tulving, E. (1981). Similarity relations in recognition. *Journal of Verbal Learning and Verbal Behavior, 20,* 479–496.

Turtle, J. W., & Yuille, J. C. (1994). Lost but not forgotten details: Repeated eyewitness recall leads to reminiscence but not hypermnesia. *Journal of Applied Psychology, 79,* 260–271.

Tversky, A., & Kahneman, D. (1986). Judgment under uncertainty: Heuristics and biases. In H. R. Arkes & K. R. Hammond (Eds.), *Judgment and decision making: An interdisciplinary reader* (pp. 38–55). Cambridge, England: Cambridge University Press.

Tversky, B., & Tuchin, M. (1989). A reconciliation of the evidence on eyewitness testimony: Comments on McCloskey and Zaragoza. *Journal of Experimental Psychology: General, 118,* 86–91.

Twain, M. (1903). *Roughing it.* Hartford, CT: American Publishing Co. (Original work published 1871.)

Tyler, T. R., (1989). The psychology of procedural justice: A test of the group value model. *Journal of Personality and Social Psychology, 57*(5), 830–838.

Tyler, T. R. (1990). *Why people obey the law.* New Haven, CT: Yale University Press.

Tyler, T. R., Casper, J. D., & Fisher, B. (1989). Maintaining allegiance toward political authorities: The role of prior attitudes and the use of fair procedures. *American Journal of Political Science, 33*(3), 629–652.

Tyler, T. R., & DeGoey, P. (1995). Collective restraint in social dilemmas: Procedural justice and identification effects on support of authority. *Journal of Social and Personality Psychology, 69*(3), 482–497.

Tyler, T. R., & DeGoey, P. (1996). Trust in organizational authorities: The influence of motive attributions on willingness to accept decisions. In R. Kramer & T. R. Tyler (Eds.), *Trust in organizations* (pp. 331–356). Thousand Oaks, CA: Sage.

Tyler, T. R., DeGoey, P., & Smith, H. (1996). Understanding why the justice of group procedures matters: A test of the psychological dynamics of the group-value model. *Journal of Personality and Social Psychology, 70*(5), 913–930.

Tyler, T. R., & Lind, E. A. (1992). A relational model of authority in groups. In M. Zanna (Ed.), *Advances in experimental social psychology, 25,* 115–192. New York: Academic Press.

Tyson settles civil suit by rape victim. (1995, June 22). *Washington Post,* p. D7.

Umbreit, M. S. (1989). Crime victims seeking fairness, not revenge. *Federal Probation, 53,* 52–57.

United States Sentencing Commission. (1994). *Guidelines manual* (with Amendments through Nov. 1, 1993). St. Paul, MN: West.

Van Dyck, J. (1970). The jury as a political institution. *Catholic University Law Review, 16,* 224–270.

Verhovek, S. H. (1995, February 22). Across the U.S., executions are neither swift nor cheap. *New York Times,* p. A1.

Vidmar, N. (1979). The other issues in jury simulation research: A commentary with particular reference to defendant character studies. *Law and Human Behavior, 3,* 95–106.

Vidmar, N. (1992). *Medical malpractice litigation: The role of the jury.* Paper presented at the biennial meeting of the American Psychology and Law Society, San Diego.

Vidmar, N. (1993). Empirical evidence on the deep pockets hypothesis: Jury awards for pain and suffering in medical malpractice cases. *Duke Law Journal, 43,* 217–266.

Vidmar, N. (1994). Making inferences about jury behavior from jury verdict statistics: Cautions about the Lorelei's lied. *Law and Human Behavior, 18*(3), 599–618.

Vidmar, N. (1996). *Medical malpractice and the American jury.* Ann Arbor: University of Michigan Press.

Vidmar, N., & Judson, J. (1981). The use of social sciences in a change of venue application. *Canadian Bar Review, 59,* 76–102.

Vidmar, N., & Rice, J. J. (1991). Jury determined settlements and summary jury trials: Observations about alternative dispute resolution in an adversary culture. *Florida State Law Review, 19*(1), 89–103.

Vidmar, N., & Rice, J. J. (1993). Assessments of noneconomic damage awards in medical malpractice negligence: A comparison of jurors with legal professionals. *Iowa Law Review, 78*(4), 883–909.

Vincent, B. (1996, January 1). Prosecutors shun death penalty expert. *Legal Times,* pp. 8–10.

Visher, C. A. (1987). Juror decision making: The importance of evidence. *Law and Human Behavior, 11*(1), 1–17.

Vurpillot, E. (1968). The development of scanning strategies and their relation to visual differentiation. *Journal of Experimental Child Psychology, 6,* 632–650.

Walker, L., & Monahan, J. (1987). Social frameworks: A new use of social science in law. *Virginia Law Review, 73*(3), 559–598.

Walker, L., & Monahan, J. (1988). Social facts: Scientific methodology as legal precedent. *California Law Review, 76*(4), 877–896.

Walker, L. E. (1984). *The battered woman syndrome.* New York: Springer.

Walker, L. E. (1990). *Terrified love: Why battered women kill and how society responds.* New York: Harper & Row.

Wall, J. A., Jr., & Rude, D. E. (1991). The judge as mediator. *Journal of Applied Psychology, 76,* 54–59.

Warren, A., Hulse-Trotter, K., & Tubbs, E. C. (1991). Inducing suggestibility in children. *Law and Human Behavior, 15*(3), 273–286.

Washington Post Staff. (1993, April 1). Trial set in suit against Hinckley. *Washington Post,* p. D3.

Webster, T. M., King, H. N., & Kassin, S. M. (1991). Voices from an empty chair: The missing witness and the jury. *Law and Human Behavior, 15*(1), 31–42.

Wegner, D. M. (1989). *White bears and unwanted thoughts.* New York: Viking/Penguin.

Weinberg, A. (1975). *Attorney for the damned.* New York: Simon & Schuster.

Weinberg, H. I., & Baron, R. S. (1982). The discredible witness. *Personality and Social Psychology Bulletin, 8,* 60–67.

Welch, S., Combs, M., & Gruhl, J. (1988). Do black judges make a difference? *American Journal of Political Science, 32,* 126.

Weld, H. B., & Danzig, E. R. (1940). A study of the way a verdict is reached by a jury. *American Journal of Psychology, 53,* 518–536.

Wells, G. L. (1978). Applied eyewitness research: System variables and estimator variables. *Journal of Personality and Social Psychology, 36,* 1546–1557.

Wells, G. L. (1984a). How adequate is human intuition for judging eyewitness testimony? In G. L. Wells & E. F. Loftus (Eds.), *Eyewitness testimony: Psychological perspectives* (pp. 256–272). New York: Cambridge University Press.

Wells, G. L. (1984b). The psychology eyewitness identifications. *Journal of Applied Social Psychology, 14,* 89–103.

Wells, G. L. (1986). Expert psychological testimony: Empirical and conceptual analyses of effects. *Law and Human Behavior, 10,* 83–95.

Wells, G. L. (1992). Naked statistical evidence of liability: Is subjective probability enough? *Journal of Personality and Social Psychology, 63,* 739–752.

Wells, G. L. (1993). What do we know about eyewitness identification? *American Psychologist, 48,* 553–571.

Wells, G. L. (1995). Scientific study of witness memory: Implications for public and legal policy. *Psychology, Law, and Public Policy 1*(4), 726–731.

Wells, G. L., Ferguson, T. J., & Lindsay, R. C. L. (1981). The tractability of eyewitness confidence and its implications for triers of fact. *Journal of Applied Psychology, 66,* 688–696.

Wells, G. L., & Leippe, M. R. (1981). How do triers of fact infer the accuracy of eyewitness identifications? Using memory for peripheral detail can be misleading. *Journal of Applied Psychology, 66,* 682–687.

Wells, G. L., & Lindsay, R. C. L. (1985). Methodological notes on the accuracy-confidence relation in eyewitness identifications. *Journal of Applied Psychology, 70,* 413–419.

Wells, G. L., Lindsay, R. C. L., & Ferguson, T. J. (1979). Accuracy, confidence, and juror perceptions in eyewitness identification. *Journal of Applied Psychology, 64,* 440–448.

Wells, G. L., Lindsay, R. C. L., & Tousignant, J. P. (1980). Effects of expert psychological advice on human performance in judging the validity of eyewitness testimony. *Law and Human Behavior, 4,* 275–285.

Wells, G. L., & Loftus, E. F. (Eds.). (1984). *Eyewitness testimony: Psychological perspectives.* New York: Cambridge University Press.

Wells, G. L., & Luus, C. A. E. (1990). Police lineups as experiments: Social methodology as a framework for properly conducted lineups. *Personality and Social Psychology Bulletin, 16,* 106–117.

Wells, G. L., Rydell, S. M., & Seelau, E. P. (1993). On the selection of distractors for eyewitness lineups. *Journal of Applied Psychology, 78,* 835–844.

Wells, G. L., & Seelau, E. P. (1995) Eyewitness identification: Psychological research and legal policy on lineups. *Psychology, Law, & Public Policy, 1*(4), 765–791.

Wells, G. L., Wrightsman, L. S., & Miene, P. K. (1985). The timing of the defense opening statement: Don't wait until the evidence is in. *Journal of Applied Social Psychology, 15,* 758–772.

Werner, C., Strube, M. J., Cole, A. M., & Kagehiro, D. K. (1985). The impact of case characteristics and prior experience on jury verdicts. *Journal of Applied Psychology, 15*(5), 409–427.

Werner, C. M., Kagehiro, D. K., & Strube, M. J. (1982). Conviction proneness and the authoritarian juror: Inability to disregard information or attitudinal bias? *Journal of Applied Psychology, 67,* 629–636.

Wiener, R. L. (1990). A psycholegal and empirical approach to the medical standard of care. *Nebraska Law Review, 69,* 112–157.

Wiener, R. L., Gaborit, M., Pritchard, C. C., McDonough, E. M., Staebler, C. R., Wiley, D. C., & Habert, K. S. (1992, March). *Assessing liability in negligence law: The role of counterfactual thinking.* Paper presented at American Psychology-Law Society biennial meeting, San Diego.

Wiener, R. L., Habert, K., Shkodriani, G. & Staebler, C. (1991). The social psychology of jury nullification: Predicting when jurors disobey the law. *Journal of Applied Social Psychology, 21,* 1379–1401.

Wiener, R. L., Pritchard, C. C., & Weston, M. (1995). Comprehensibility of approved instructions in capital murder cases. *Journal of Applied Psychology, 80*(4,) 455–467.

Wiggins, E. C., & Breckler, S. (1987, August). *A framework for studying jury functioning in complex litigation.* Presented at the 95th annual meeting of the American Psychological Association.

Wigmore, H. H. (1909). Professor Munsterberg and the psychology of evidence. *Illinois Law Review, 3,* 339–343.

Willging, T. E. (1989). *Use of Rule 12(b)(6) in two federal district courts.* Washington, DC: Federal Judicial Center.

Williams, K. D., Bourgeois, M. J., & Croyle, R. T. (1993). The effects of stealing thunder in criminal and civil trials. *Law and Human Behavior, 17*(6), 597–610.

Williams, K. D., Loftus, E. F., & Deffenbacher, K. A. (1992). Eyewitness evidence and testimony. In D. K. Kagehiro & W. S. Laufer (Eds.), *Handbook of psychology and law.* New York: Springer-Verlag.

Willick, D. H., Gehlkor, C., & Watts, A. M. (1975). Social class as a factor affecting judicial disposition. *Criminology, 13,* 57–77.

Wilson, M. G., Northcraft, G. B., & Neale, M. A. (1989). Information competition and vividness effects in on-line judgments. *Organizational Behavior and Human Decision Processes, 44,* 132–139.

Winick, B. (1982). Prosecutorial peremptory challenge practices in capital cases: An empirical study and a constitutional analysis. *Michigan Law Review, 81,* 1–98.

Winick, B. (1995). The side effects of incompetency labeling and the implications for mental health law. *Psychology, Public Policy, and Law, 1*(2), 6–42.

Wissler, R. L., & Saks, M. J. (1985). On the inefficacy of limiting instructions. *Law and Human Behavior, 9*(1), 37–48.

Wolf, S., & Montgomery, D. A. (1977). Effects of inadmissible evidence and level of judicial admonishment to disregard on the judgments of mock jurors. *Journal of Applied Social Psychology, 7,* 205–219.

Wood, W., Lundgen, L., Ouellette, P. D., Busceme, W. E., & Blackstone, T. (1994). Minority influence: A meta-analytic review of social influences processes. *Psychological Bulletin, 115*(3), 323–345.

Woolard, J. L., Reppucci, N. D., & Redding, R. E. (1996). Theoretical and methodological issues in studying children's capacities in legal contexts. *Law and Human Behavior, 20*(3), 219–228.

Worden, R. E., & Pollitz, A. (1984). Police arrests in domestic disturbances: A further look. *Law and Society Review, 18,* 105–119.

Wortley, R. K., & Homel, R. J. (1995). Police prejudice as a function of training and outgroup contact: A longitudinal investigation. *Law and Human Behavior, 19*(3), 305–318.

Wright, J. C., & Vlietstra, A. G. (1975). The development of selective attention: From perceptual exploration to logical search. In H. W. Reese (Ed.), *Advances in child development and behavior* (Vol. 10, pp. 196–239). New York: Academic Press.

Wrightsman, L. S. (1987). *Psychology and the legal system.* Pacific Grove, CA: Brooks/Cole.

Yarmey, A. D. (1979). *The psychology of eyewitness testimony.* New York: Free Press.

Yarmey, A. D. (1995). Earwitness speaker identification. *Psychology, Law, & Public Policy, 1*(4), 792–816.

Yarmey, A. D., Yarmey, M. J., & Yarmey, A. L. (1996). Accuracy of eyewitness identificatiion in showups and lineups. *Law and Human Behavior, 20*(4), 459–478.

Youngstrom, N. (1991, November). Stockholm syndrome. *APA Monitor,* p. 31.

Youngstrom, N. (1992, September). New views of the rapists' personality. *APA Monitor,* p. 18.

Yuille, J. C., & Cutshall, J. L. (1986). A case study of eyewitness memory of a crime. *Journal of Applied Psychology, 71,* 291–301.

Zabel, S. (1993). A mathematician comments on models of juror decision making. In R. Hastie (Ed.), *Inside the juror.* New York: Cambridge University Press.

Zebrowitz, L. A., & McDonald, S. M. (1991). The impact of litigants' babyfacedness and attractiveness on adjudications in small claims court. *Law and Human Behavior, 15,* 603–623.

Zebrowitz, L. A., Olson, K., & Hoffman, K. (1993). Stability of babyfaceness and attractiveness across the life span. *Journal of Personality and Social Psychology, 64*(3), 453–466.

Zeisel, H., & Diamond, S. S. (1976). The jury selection in the Mitchill-Stans conspiracy trial. *American Bar Foundation Research Journal, 87,* 151–174.

Zimbardo, P. (1967, August). *The psychology of police interrogations.* Paper presented at the annual meeting of the American Psychological Association, New York City.

Zimring, F. E. (1991). Firearms, violence, and public policy. *Scientific American, 265*(5), 48–57.

TABLE OF CASES

INDEX OF NAMES AND CASES

INDEX OF SUBJECTS